Without Trimmings

Without Trimmings

The Legal, Moral, and Political Philosophy of Matthew Kramer

Edited by

MARK MCBRIDE AND VISA AJ KURKI

OXFORD
UNIVERSITY PRESS

OXFORD
UNIVERSITY PRESS

Great Clarendon Street, Oxford, OX2 6DP,
United Kingdom

Oxford University Press is a department of the University of Oxford.
It furthers the University's objective of excellence in research, scholarship,
and education by publishing worldwide. Oxford is a registered trade mark of
Oxford University Press in the UK and in certain other countries

First Edition published in 2022
Impression: 1

Published in the United States of America by Oxford University Press
198 Madison Avenue, New York, NY 10016, United States of America

British Library Cataloguing in Publication Data
Data available

Library of Congress Control Number: 2021951804

ISBN 978–0–19–886886–6

DOI: 10.1093/oso/9780198868866.001.0001

Printed and bound by
CPI Group (UK) Ltd, Croydon, CR0 4YY

Without Trimmings—Editors' Introduction

This volume is a celebration of Professor Matthew Kramer. The work started in 2018, as we editors realized that his sixtieth birthday on June 9, 2019 was fast approaching. We quickly got together many eager contributors who wished to honor him in this peculiar academic way: by subjecting his work to critical scrutiny. In July 2019, the majority of the contributors gathered at Cambridge for an intensive, three-day Workshop in Honour of Matthew Kramer—a name which the honoree found "pretentious." Fewer trimmings might have been appropriate.

Matthew Kramer was born on June 9, 1959, in Massachusetts, US. He has two older brothers who are both lawyers in the federal government, a twin brother who is a specialist in Cold War studies, and a younger brother who is a specialist in contemporary Russian and Ukrainian politics. Matthew's path to philosophy can almost be said to be predestined: he remembers discussing philosophical matters with his mother—who had majored in Philosophy—at the age of seven. His first encounter with the work of H.L.A. Hart was at the age of eleven, when his older brother brought home from college an anthology containing some of Hart's writings. It was around this time that Kramer became familiar with Stoicism, which would deeply influence both his intellectual outlook and his lifestyle. (He also began long-distance running around this time.) He went to college at Cornell University, where he majored in Philosophy, Government (Political Theory), and History (Intellectual History), graduating in 1981 with high honors. He went on to Harvard Law School—in his own words, "to learn more political philosophy." During his years at Harvard, he worked as a research assistant and volunteered as a clinical worker at the Jamaica Plain Legal Institute. It was also during this time that he started his daily pastime of systematically studying the Bible. This project has grown into a commentary spanning thousands of pages.

Kramer would receive his final degrees at the University of Cambridge: a PhD in 1989, and an LLD—a higher doctorate—in 2004. Apart from three years as a Research Fellow at the University of Wisconsin (1991–94), Kramer has worked at Cambridge ever since. He was appointed as a University Lecturer and a Fellow of Churchill College in 1994; as Reader in 1999; and as Professor of Legal and Political Philosophy in 2002. In 2014, he was elected a Fellow of the British Academy.

Merely the thought of producing an exhaustive list of Kramer's contributions and achievements is exhausting. In fact, given his prolificacy, even this sprawling volume does not completely succeed in covering all aspects of Kramer's work. One should start with Kramer's very first book: *Legal Theory, Political Theory, and Deconstruction: Against Rhadamanthus* (Indiana University Press, 1991). This book—which, unfortunately, is not addressed by any of the contributions—is interesting not only in its own right, but also when juxtaposed with Kramer's later oeuvre. *Against Rhadamanthus* combines analytic philosophy with Critical Legal Studies and the method of deconstruction. The same orientation is apparent in his second book, *Critical Legal Theory and the Challenge of Feminism: A Philosophical Reconception* (Rowman & Littlefield, 1995). However, the turn toward a predominantly analytic approach—which would characterize the majority of Kramer's subsequent work—is apparent in his third book, *John Locke and the Origins of Private Property* (Cambridge University Press, 1997). After this early phase, many of Kramer's books have articulated comprehensive accounts or theories of specific topics or concepts. Even though his interests have always been multifarious, one can here discern certain—partially mutually overlapping—phases. First, the "legal philosophy phase" comprises treatments of legal rights (*A Debate over Rights*, with Nigel Simmonds and Hillel Steiner, Oxford University Press, 1998), legal positivism (*In Defense of Legal Positivism*, Oxford University Press, 1999, and *Where Law and Morality Meet*, Oxford University Press, 2004), and legal objectivity (*Objectivity and the Rule of Law*, Cambridge University Press, 2007). Beginning with *The Quality of Freedom* (Oxford University Press, 2003), Kramer then turned his attention to ethics and political philosophy, investigating not only freedom but also moral realism (*Moral Realism as a Moral Doctrine*, Wiley-Blackwell, 2009), capital punishment (*The Ethics of Capital Punishment*, Oxford University Press, 2011), torture (*Torture and Moral Integrity: A Philosophical Enquiry*, Oxford University Press, 2014), liberalism (*Liberalism with Excellence*, Oxford University Press, 2017), and freedom of expression (*Freedom of Expression as Self-Restraint*, Oxford University Press, 2021). Finally, a turn back to legal philosophy may be discerned, beginning with Kramer's treatment of H.L.A. Hart's legal positivism (*H.L.A. Hart: The Nature of Law*, Polity Press, 2018) and continued in his forthcoming account of rights and right-holding.

The contributions to this volume are primarily from people who have had the privilege of knowing Kramer, in various capacities: as students, mentees, colleagues, or interlocutors. However, Kramer is well known for his interest in good ideas and arguments, regardless of their pedigree: we know he has occasionally invited undergraduates to present at his seminars. And we followed this philosophy by announcing an open Call for Abstracts, directed at junior scholars working on Kramer's ideas. Two chapters resulting from that call appear in this volume.

The volume is divided into six parts. The chapters therein are united by their rootedness in, and directedness at, aspects of Kramer's vast and stimulating oeuvre.

The first part, *Rights and Right-holding*, contains five essays, by Laura Donohue, Joseph Bowen, Rowan Cruft, Visa Kurki, and Mark McBride. The essays address Kramer's work in right-holding—from his groundbreaking work on Hohfeldian analysis to his development, and typically staunch defense, of his interest theory of claim-right holding. More specifically, Donohue drills into applications of what she calls the "Hohfeld-Kramer framework" to public law, and constitutional law in particular. The next four essays hang together in being trained, albeit in different ways, on Kramer's interest theory. Bowen patrols the boundaries of the interest theory, focusing ultimately on the issue of whether the dead and future people are right-holders. Cruft and Kurki, meanwhile, share a starting point of descrying tensions between Kramer's interest theory and his legal positivism. Cruft moves on to explore how Kramer's interest theory fares as an account of so-called "morally justified rights." Kurki drills further into the foregoing tensions to test for whether they ultimately disclose a troubling incompatibility between Kramer's theory of right-holding and his stance in general jurisprudence. Finally, McBride uses Kramer's (and Steiner's) renowned counter-example against hybrid theories of rights as a springboard to defending his own—tracking—hybrid theory of rights.

The second part, *General Jurisprudence*, contains four essays, by Brian Bix, Wilfrid J. Waluchow, Pierluigi Chiassoni, and Gerald Postema. The essays address Kramer's work in general jurisprudence—from the compatibility of positivism with universal legal error, to his robust defense of inclusive legal positivism, concluding with reflections on his writings on the rule of law. More specifically, Bix, using Kramer's work as a stimulus, enters the debate over whether legal positivism's focus on the conventional nature of law and legal norms forecloses the possibility that all legal officials could be mistaken regarding some matter of law. The next two contributions, from Waluchow and Chiassoni respectively, may be considered to form a pair, in terms of their focus on Kramer's defense of inclusive legal positivism in particular. Inclusive positivism, taken to be the view according to which morality can be incorporated into law by the legal system itself, is given a state-of-the-art overview by one of its progenitors, Waluchow. And that sympathetic overview devotes especial attention to some of Kramer's lines of defense of inclusivism, as Waluchow seeks to provide a novel positive defense thereof. Chiassoni, meanwhile, though joining Waluchow in training his focus on Kramer's inclusivism, does so from a slightly more critical perspective. Finally, Postema rounds off the general jurisprudential enquiry, by focusing on Kramer's work on the rule of law, and arguing that Kramer's (and Fuller's) understanding focuses too narrowly on formal *legality*, giving insufficient attention to the necessary element of *fidelity*.

The third part, *General Matters of Ethics*, contains two essays, by Christine Tiefensee and Lubomira Radoilska. The essays address Kramer's metaethical work on moral realism as a moral doctrine, and may be considered to form a pair. Tiefensee asks (and tentatively answers yes to) the question: Is there a metasemantic account of moral vocabulary available which is both compatible with Kramer's moral approach to moral objectivity and distinct from the metasemantic positions of metaphysical moral realism and quasi-realism? Radoilska, meanwhile, drills into Kramer's distinction between value-neutrality and value-independence, and argues for some upshots for moral epistemology.

The fourth part, *Freedom*, also contains two essays, by Michael Garnett, and Ian Carter and Hillel Steiner. The essays address Kramer's groundbreaking work in political philosophy on (giving an account of) negative freedom, and may again be considered to form a pair. Garnett argues for two distinct negative concepts of liberty: freedom as non-prevention (following Kramer), and (departing from Kramer) freedom as non-coercion. Carter and Steiner, meanwhile, vigorously critique Kramer's ability-based, trivalent account of freedom in favor of a bivalent approach.

The penultimate fifth part, *Liberalism*, continues to attend to Kramer's work in political philosophy, and likewise contains two essays, by Mark Reiff and Collis Tahzib. The essays address Kramer's more recently articulated aspirational-perfectionist liberal stance. Reiff's focus is on Kramer's arguments for how excellence may enter into liberalism, despite liberalism's strong commitment to neutrality, and he attempts to chart a different path to a similar endpoint. Tahzib, meanwhile, focuses on Kramer's attacks on mainstream so-called "edificatory" perfectionist philosophies.

The final sixth part, *Applied Ethics*, contains two essays, by R.A. Duff and Chris Kutz. The essays address Kramer's more applied work in normative ethics. Duff engages with Kramer's so-called "purgative rationale" for capital punishment, suggests distinguishing between first-, second-, and third-person perspectives can bolster the case for the rationale, but ultimately rejects it. Kutz, meanwhile, engages with Kramer's very recent work on freedom of expression, and uses incitement as a case-study to interrogate Kramer's distinction between distinctively communicative wrongdoing (that ought not to be the object of punishment) and communication-independent wrongdoing (that can be properly punishable).

The collection is rounded off by a staggeringly deep set of reflections on, and replies to, the contributions by Kramer himself. As the title of those reflections indicates, Kramer is looking ahead as much as he is looking back.

It remains to thank some institutions and people, without whom this project could not have been completed. First, thanks to the Cambridge Forum for Legal and Political Philosophy and to Churchill College for financial assistance. We extend special thanks to the non-academic staff at Churchill College for their adept support of the Workshop in numerous ways. Second, thanks also to our research assistants, Enna Hakala and Pinja Lindvall, for their careful handling of the manuscripts. Third, thanks to the Oxford University Press for their diligent handling of the book as a whole. In particular, we are grateful to Jamie Berezin, Alex Flach, Brianne Bellio, Kathryn Plunkett, and the anonymous readers for the press. Finally, thanks to Hillel Steiner, Ian Carter, Wilfrid J. Waluchow, and Brian Bix for some supererogatory outreach.

All told, we hope that the collection—in the chapters and in Kramer's replies—serves both as an adequate tribute to Kramer's oeuvre and as a stimulus to further philosophical enquiry on these topics.

Mark McBride and Visa Kurki

Contents

IV. FREEDOM

V. LIBERALISM

List of Contributors

Brian H. Bix, Frederick W. Thomas Professor of Law and Philosophy, University of Minnesota, Minneapolis, MN, US

Joseph Bowen, Postdoctoral Researcher, Stockholm Centre for the Ethics of War and Peace, Department of Philosophy, Stockholm University, Stockholm, Sweden

Ian Carter, Professor of Political Philosophy, Department of Political and Social Sciences, University of Pavia, Pavia, Italy

Pierluigi Chiassoni, Professor of Legal Philosophy, Department of Law, University of Genoa, Genoa, Italy

Rowan Cruft, Professor of Philosophy, University of Stirling, Stirling, UK

Laura K. Donohue, Professor of Law, Georgetown University, Washington DC, US

R.A. Duff, Professor Emeritus of Philosophy, University of Stirling, Stirling, UK

Michael Garnett, Senior Lecturer, Department of Philosophy, Birkbeck College, University of London, London, UK

Matthew H. Kramer, Professor of Legal & Political Philosophy, Faculty of Law, Cambridge University, Cambridge, UK

Visa A.J. Kurki, Associate Professor of Jurisprudence, Faculty of Law, University of Helsinki, Finland

Christopher Kutz, C. William Maxeiner Distinguished Professor of Law, Jurisprudence & Social Policy Program, School of Law, University of California at Berkeley, CA, US

Mark McBride, Assistant Professor, Faculty of Law, National University of Singapore, Singapore

Gerald J. Postema, Professor Emeritus, Department of Philosophy, University of North Carolina at Chapel Hill, Chapel Hill, NC, US

Lubomira Radoilska, Department of Philosophy, University of Kent, UK; African Centre for Epistemology and Philosophy of Science, University of Johannesburg, South Africa

Mark R. Reiff, Research Associate, Department of Philosophy, University of California at Davis, Davis, CA, US

Hillel Steiner, Emeritus Professor of Political Philosophy, Manchester Centre for Political Theory, University of Manchester, Manchester, UK

Collis Tahzib, Assistant Professor of Philosophy, School of Philosophy, University of Southern California, Los Angeles, CA, US

Christine Tiefensee, Associate Professor of Philosophy, Department of Philosophy & Law, Frankfurt School of Finance & Management, Frankfurt am Main, Germany

Wilfrid J. Waluchow, Emeritus Professor & Senator William McMaster Chair in Constitutional Studies, Department of Philosophy, McMaster University, Hamilton, ON, Canada

List of Abbreviations

AQAP	al-Qa'ida in the Arab Peninsula
BLM	Black Lives Matter
CCPA	California Consumer Privacy Act
CIA	Central Intelligence Agency
DOJ	Department of Justice
ELP	Exclusive Legal Positivism
EMs	evaluative multipliers
FBI	Federal Bureau of Investigation
FISA	Foreign Intelligence Surveillance Act
ILP	Inclusive Legal Positivism
JSOC	Joint Special Operations Command
UDHR	Universal Declaration of Human Rights

PART I
RIGHTS AND RIGHT-HOLDING

1

Correlation and Constitutional Rights

*Laura K. Donohue**

Over the past four decades, North American jurisprudence has shied away from Hohfeldian analytic jurisprudence in favor of natural law or positivist approaches bereft of the dominant analytic methodology.[1] Neither Professor John Finnis's embrace of natural law nor Professor Ernest Weinrib's revival of Landellian formalism draws on the analytic distinctions.[2] Professors Ronald Dworkin and Michael Moore eschew the same, even as Jeremy Waldron's scholarship is punctuated by outright hostility.[3] Yet there is much to be gained from analytic jurisprudence. In his seminal article setting out jural relations, Hohfeld observes that how you view entitlements partly shapes constitutional and statutory decision-making.[4] The problem is that as an analytical matter, the terms wielded in the course of those debates often lack precision. "Property," for instance, could mean "things" or "land"; or, when coupled with possession, a right to use, enjoy, or dispose of it.[5] To resolve such ambiguities, Hohfeld defines entitlements in terms of their relationship to certain obligations or conditions.[6]

One of Professor Matthew Kramer's enduring contributions is clarifying and deepening the meaning of the resulting juridical framing and using it as a tool to advance inclusive legal positivism.[7] In the process, he expands the framework's potential

* Anne Fleming Research Professor and Professor of Law, Georgetown Law. Thanks are owed to Jeremy McCabe, at Georgetown Law Library, for locating many of the works on which I draw for this chapter. David Luban, Mark Hanin, Visa Kurki, Mark McBride, John Mikhail, and Robin West provided thoughtful remarks on the text. I am further indebted to Matthew Kramer, whose tutelage and work has been foundational for my scholarship.

1 See Postema, "Analytic Jurisprudence Confronted," 547–75.

2 See Finnis, *Natural Law and Natural Rights* (advancing classic natural law theory); Weinrib, "Why Legal Formalism," 341 ("[I]nasmuch as [legal forms] are immanent to the juridical relationship they inform, they shed light on the traditional claim of natural law theory that law is an ordering of reason.")

3 Dworkin, "Law as Interpretation," 179–200 (critiquing contemporary positivist jurisprudence as inadequate for ascertaining the meaning of legal propositions); Moore, "A Natural Law Theory of Interpretation," 277–398 (arguing for a moral-realist understanding of law); Waldron, *Law and Disagreement*, 9 ("If one asks what analytic jurisprudence has offered ... to the judge, lawyer, or law professor interested in legislation, the answer is embarrassing. Even when they construct theories of interpretation, analytic legal philosophers have almost nothing to say about the structural features of legislation that distinguish the interpretation of a statute from the interpretation of a principle or a poem.").

4 See Hohfeld, "Some Fundamental Legal Conceptions as Applied in Judicial Reasoning," 18–20 (hereafter Hohfeld, FLC I).

5 Hohfeld, FLC I, 22–3.

6 See Hohfeld, 19–20.

7 See, e.g., Kramer, *The Ethics of Capital Punishment: A Philosophical Investigation of Evil and Its Consequences*, 46 n. 12 (referring to the "notion of a legal power ... in a standard Hohfeldian sense"); Kramer, *Objectivity and the Rule of Law*, 27 ("The term 'liability' is used here in the sense assigned to that term by the American jurist Wesley Hohfeld. That is, it designates a susceptibility to a change in one's legal position."); Kramer, *Where Law and Morality Meet*, 127, 212 (applying a Hohfeldian analysis to the Supreme Court's exercise of a legal power and addressing Simmonds's account of Hohfeldian claim-rights); Kramer,

Laura K. Donohue, *Correlation and Constitutional Rights* In: *Without Trimmings*. Edited by: Mark McBride and Visa AJ Kurki, Oxford University Press. © Mark McBride and Visa AJ Kurki 2022. DOI: 10.1093/oso/9780198868866.003.0001

application. Hohfeld, borrowing from Savigny's analysis of Roman civil law,[8] focuses *similiter* on private law. Kramer goes further, making good on Hohfeld's claims of broader relevance, extending claim-right and liberty correlations to public law. His scholarship demands careful attention, particularly in terms of its implications for constitutional law. Yet precision proves elusive. Kramer argues that most of the entitlements in bills of rights function as immunities—i.e., constraints on what actions the legislature can take.[9] Elsewhere, he considers privacy[10] and procedural due process[11] to be claim-rights. Freedom of expression, in turn, he considers a liberty/privilege.[12] Simultaneously, he considers entitlements incorporated into the First Amendment of the US Constitution (amongst which we find freedom of expression) to be immunities.[13]

How ought we understand the jural relations in regard to the rules regulating government action (and the mechanisms of judicial review) which impact individual or collective entitlements? Are they unique to certain pairings of entitlement/obligation or are they duplicative across categories? To what extent (if at all) do Hohfeld's jural relations capture constitutional entitlements? There are similarities in how law functions in the private and public arenas, and rules in each sphere may reflect similar values.[14] Nevertheless, as this chapter argues, the law acts in a very different capacity in relation to constraining state power than when it regulates relations among members of society.

In the former context, the entitlements held are neither *in rem* nor *in personam*, but *in res publica*. Although they tend to be referred to as individual rights, they also are collective entitlements. The resulting structure protects and places an obligation of non-infringement on the entitlement-holder. The legal relation cannot be altered, binding current generations for future times. It sweeps non-entitlement holders within its protection. Constitutional rights further fall subject to complex collectives, which may lead to increased cases of genuine conflict. It may be nearly impossible to identify power-holders—a situation complicated by new and emerging technologies.

In the Realm of Legal and Moral Philosophy: Critical Encounters, 115 (noting that "rights and duties are mutually entailing," further referring to the Hohfeldian framing throughout the book); Kramer, "There's Nothing Quasi about Quasi-Realism: Moral Realism as a Moral Doctrine," 185, 193 (using Hohfeldian distinction to respond to the potential for an error theorist to argue "that an ascription of moral permissibility entails an ascription of not-to-be-preventedness and an ascription of not-to-be-punishedness"); Kramer, "Of Final Things: Morality as One of the Ultimate Determinants of Legal Validity," 78 (using "power" in the Hohfeldian sense to rebut an attack on Inclusivism).

[8] See von Savigny, *Jural Relations, or, the Roman Law of Persons as Subjects of Jural Relations: Being a Translation of the Second Book of Friedrich Karl von Savigny's System of Modern Roman Law*, sec. 60 ("Every Jural Relation consists in the relation of one person to another person.... [W]ho can be the Bearer or Subject of a Jural Relation? This question concerns the possible Possession of Rights or the Jural Capacity, not the possible Acquisition of such rights or the Capacity of action, which will be considered in a subsequent volume § 106)."); sec. 103 (examining how jural relations arise between and among people).

[9] Kramer, "Rights in Legal and Political Philosophy," 417 (hereafter Kramer, RLPP).

[10] Kramer, "Rights Without Trimmings," 43–4 (hereafter Kramer, RWT).

[11] Kramer, "Moral Rights and the Limits of the Ought-Implies-Can Principle: Why Impeccable Precautions Are No Excuse," 328–9.

[12] Kramer, RWT, 11.

[13] Kramer, RLPP, 417.

[14] See generally Oliver, *Common Values and the Public-Private Divide.*

	First-Order Relations		Second-Order Relations	
Jural Correlatives	Right Duty	Privilege/liberty No-right	Power Liability	Immunity Disability
Jural Opposites	Rights No-rights	Privilege Duty	Power Disability	Immunity Liability

Figure 1.1 Hohfeldian Analysis of Legal Positions

As a substantive matter, the Hohfeldian framing fails to capture a different type of entitlement, which I term "dignities": unwritten elements that exist prior to the state and act as a shield for claim-rights in much the same way that claim-rights act as a shield for liberties. Drawing on examples from First, Second, Fourth, Fifth, and Sixth Amendment jurisprudence, the chapter also identifies limits on "powers" and their application in the constitutional realm. The juridical relations are not concerned with how an entitlement comes to be recognized, acknowledged, or created. As a result, they miss the distinction between legislatively-created and judicially-created entitlements and the relationship among them, much less how the framing should apply to rights that are not yet recognized or even foreseen, but which are said to exist. The chapter concludes by proposing a new category of "purported rights" for situations in which the state can sidestep enforcement with impunity.

1. Clarifying and Deepening the Hohfeldian Framing

Hohfeld's terrain is well-trodden: he proposes four pairs of correlatives (i.e., two legal positions, each entailing the other) and four pairs of contradictories (i.e., two legal positions negating each other). See Figure 1.1. Constituting his first-order relations are right/duty and privilege/no-right, and his second-order relations power/liability and immunity/disability. The result is a schema that Kramer describes as "marvelously capacious and flexible."[15] Kramer proceeds to clarify and deepen the framing in important ways.

A Hohfeldian "right" is understood in relation to its correlative "duty," such that the invasion of a the former entails a violation of the latter.[16] A right is therefore interchangeable with a "claim"—i.e., a right secured by law.[17] The legal element *is* what makes a genuine right or claim enforceable.[18] Thus, any breach entails the risk of incurring a (legal) penalty. Whether a claim is actually enforced is a different question.

A "privilege," in contrast to a right, is essentially a "liberty" to do something, free from the right or claim of others.[19] In this sense, it is the opposite of a duty, where one

[15] Kramer, RWT, 35.

[16] Hohfeld, FLC I, 31–2; Hohfeld, "Fundamental Legal Conceptions as Applied in Judicial Reasoning," 717 (hereafter Hohfeld, FLC II).

[17] Hohfeld, FLC I, 31–2. See also Hohfeld, FLC II, 717 n. 16; Kramer, RWT, 9 ("A right or claim ... is the legal position created through the imposing of a duty on someone else.")

[18] Kramer, RWT, 9.

[19] Hohfeld, FLC I, 36. This chapter uses "privilege" and "liberty" interchangeably.

is under an obligation to act in a certain manner. Kramer explains, "To have a **liberty** to engage in a certain action is to be free from any duty to eschew the action; likewise, to have a liberty to abstain from a certain action is to be free from any duty to undertake the action."[20] More succinctly, "a legal liberty consists in the absence of a legal duty."[21] The absence of the an obligation, in other words, lies with the holder of the liberty—not with some other person in regard to a requirement to act, or to forbear from acting (as is the case with claim-rights).

A liberty (or privilege) correlates to the neologism "no-right": defined by Hohfeld as the absence of a right to interfere in the activity or state of affairs related to the liberty.[22] Kramer refines this understanding, arguing for a distinction between a "no-right" and "no right."[23] The former is understood as concerning or regarding the content of the liberty: i.e., "the correlate of X's liberty to enter [] land ... is Y's no-right concerning X's entering the land."[24] The analysis thereby centers on straightforward discussion of the content of the liberty in question. Even when an individual has a no-right to halt an activity, she may have a separate privilege of interfering.[25] But it is possible to have a privilege without a concomitant claim-right. The only implication is the no-right of third parties. While the law, therefore, may not provide an instrument, an individual may proceed via personal "devices (and within the confines of the liberty-holder's rights)."[26] If X has a right that Y should stay off of X's land (and Y the correlative duty to do so), X generally also has the privilege of entering the land such that Y has a no-right in relation to the liberty-privilege. There is no duty of non-interference. Instead, there is merely a freedom, which may be limited in practice.

As Kramer emphasizes, rights and liberties have a different nexus: rights are specified in relation to the duty-bearer (to act or to forbear from acting), whereas liberties are specified in relation to the privilege-holder.[27] The distinction between "rights" and "liberties" thereby partially addresses the problem of conflicting rights, with some entitlements considered rights with correlative duties and others as liberties. It is possible that X may have a liberty to φ, even as Y has a liberty of interfering with X's φ-ing (as long as such interference does not violate any of X's rights).

While the first-order pairings (right/duty; liberty/no-right) relate primarily to conduct, the second-order pairings (power/liability; immunity/disability) exist in relation to other legal positions—notably, those articulated in the first-order relations.[28]

A Hohfeldian "power" here means the ability or capacity to effect a change in legal relations. The facts creating the conditions for the exercise of the power may be within or beyond human control.[29] If X has a legal power, she can be understood as being

[20] Kramer, RWT, 10 (emphasis in original).

[21] Kramer, RLPP, 416.

[22] Hohfeld, FLC I, 32–3 ("[T]he correlative of [a liberty] is a 'no-right,' there being no single term available to express the latter conception. Thus, the correlative of X's right that Y shall not enter on the land is Y's duty not to enter; but the correlative of X's [liberty to enter the land] is manifestly Y's 'no-right' that X shall not enter.") Hohfeld, 33.

[23] Kramer, "On No-Rights and No Rights," 214–17 (hereinafter ONNR).

[24] Kramer, 217.

[25] Kramer, RWT, 10.

[26] Kramer, 10.

[27] Kramer, 13–14, 109; Kramer, RLPP, 415–16.

[28] Kramer, RLPP, 416.

[29] Hohfeld, FLC I, 44.

entitled to exercise volitional control in the context of a certain fact-situation, such that when it occurs, she can effect a change in legal relations.[30] The definition encapsulates relations between (or, in Kramer's account of collectives, among) persons, as well as the entitlements of the power-holder (i.e., the relationship of the power-holder to herself). The person "whose volitional control is paramount may be said to have the (legal) power to effect the particular change of legal relations that is involved."[31] The exercise of a legal power can generate a right-duty relationship.

A legal power is thus a legal ability, as opposed to a legal "inability" or "disability." The owner of digital data, for instance, has the power to alter her own legal interest through the totality of operative facts that is understood as a contract. Simultaneously and correlatively, she can create in others privileges and powers relating to the data. She can transfer her interest to others. If I give my call detail records to Verizon to service my mobile phone, I have created an interest in Verizon to access and to use the information. It is of little consequence if I further delegate this authority to my daughter, who may have a greater understanding of information that can be gleaned through, for instance, geolocational data generated by using my cellphone—*qui facit per alium facit per se*. Hohfeld explains, "The creation of an agency relation involves, *inter alia*, the grant of legal powers to the so-called agent, and the creation of correlative liabilities in the principal."[32]

Power constitutes the opposite of a legal disability, and the correlative of legal liability.[33] The latter exists where an individual is exposed to the potential exercise of a power. It can, of course, be either pleasant or unpleasant.[34] Kramer replies to Hohfeldian critics, who charge that not all liabilities correlate with powers, by noting that under the framework, "a liability is susceptibility to changes (in legal positions) *that are brought about by the exercise of a power*"—not general vulnerability to legal change.[35] He observes that the power to change a legal position, moreover, is not the same as a power to preserve legal positions.[36] This is an important distinction, as it recognizes that an alteration in legal positions can be brought about through no action of the power-holder, underscoring that Hohfeld makes no claim to exclusivity in regard to power.

An "immunity" in some sense parallels a privilege: it means freedom from legal power or control by others. It thereby contrasts with a power, which is some sort of affirmative control over a legal relation.[37] Kramer notes that an immunity represents the negation of a liability, essentially constituting an "insusceptibility to some change in one's entitlements."[38] In this manner, if X has an immunity, she cannot fall under the power of another in regard to entitlements that constitute the immunity. Y is therefore under a "disability" (the correlative of an immunity) in regard to the exercise of a

30 Bamforth, "Hohfeldian Rights and Public Law," 4.
31 Hohfeld, FLC I, 44.
32 Hohfeld, 46.
33 Hohfeld, 44.
34 Kramer, RWT, 20–1, citing Hohfeld, FLC I, 54 n. 90.
35 Kramer, RWT, 102 (italics in original).
36 Kramer, 103.
37 Hohfeld, FLC I, 55.
38 Kramer, RLPP, 416.

power as against the entitlement. In other words, an attempt to exercise such a power would lack legal effect.

Kramer argues that Hohfeld's Correlativity Axiom renders theoretical arguments regarding priority and precedence moot.[39] He writes, "Just as a slope's downward direction is not logically or existentially prior to its upward direction, a duty is not logically or existentially prior to the right with which it is correlated. The existence of each is a necessary and sufficient condition for the existence of the other."[40] The same lack of priority marks the other pairings. They are, simply, logical relations.[41]

The Hohfeld-Kramer exposition enables more precise analysis of legal entitlements.[42] It elucidates overbreadth. A putative claim-right without a duty, for instance, may be merely a liberty. *Pari passu*, discussion of an individual's entitlement to act routes us directly to liberty considerations, even when protected by one or more rights.[43] What might appear to be a right may in fact be a bundle of more specific entitlements that bear a complex relationship to each other. "The Correlativity Axiom," Kramer writes, "points to one-to-one correlations between rights and duties of the *same* degree of specificity. It does not point to such correlations between rights and duties of *differing* degrees of specificity. [] It insists that a right must have the same content and hence the same degree of specificity as the duty with which the right is correlated."[44] Thus, a general right to privacy correlates with a general duty to abstain from invading it—not specific duties vis-à-vis the right-holder.

From Kramer, we also gain a greater understanding of the relationship between and among entitlements. Some of the first-order entitlements apply directly to conduct and social interaction, without mediation of entitlements in the second-order category; however, all of the entitlements in the latter category apply directly to first-order relations and only indirectly to conduct and social interaction.[45] First-order opposites, moreover, constitute logical "duals," while second-order relations constitute logical contradictories—another important distinction.[46]

Kramer goes beyond Hohfeld in two further respects. First, he applies the framing to moral entitlements.[47] He is not the first to stake this ground: in 1924, Professor Arthur Corbin argued in the *Yale Law Journal* that Hohfeld's "distinctions between moral rights and legal rights are identical with those between moral duties and legal duties."[48] Other scholars have advanced this position.[49] But Kramer uses the scheme to battle claims to legal and moral dissimilitude. One of the most well-known attacks

[39] See MacCormick, "Rights in Legislation"; White, *Rights*; Waldron, *The Right to Private Property*; Kramer, RWT, 24. See also Kurki, ch. 4, this volume (expressing skepticism about the Correlativity Axiom).

[40] Kramer, RWT, 26.

[41] See Kramer, 35.

[42] See Kramer, 22–5 (attributing this to Hohfeld).

[43] Kramer, 29.

[44] Kramer, 42 (italics in original).

[45] Kramer, 20.

[46] Kramer, ONNR, 214.

[47] Kramer, RWT, 8–9 (noting the distinction between genuine and nominal entitlements and the potential for conflicts between duties as two exceptions).

[48] Corbin, "Rights and Duties," 505.

[49] See, e.g., Wellman, *Real Rights*; Thomson, *The Realm of Rights*; Sumner, *The Moral Foundations of Rights*. For critiques of this position, see Westen, "Poor Wesley Hohfeld," 449–67; Hurd and Moore, "Hohfeldian Analysis of Rights," 295–354; Kleinig, "Human Rights, Legal Rights, and Social Change," 36–47.

is mounted by H.L.A. Hart, who argues, *inter alia*, that a distinction between the two can be drawn in regard to strict liability, which finds no purchase in the moral realm. Where an individual lacks culpability, owing to an inability to act in accordance with the demands of morality, the breach of a moral requirement may be excused.[50]

Kramer makes three critical moves to counter Hart. First, he invokes Hohfeld to clarify moral rights and their correlative duties.[51] The framing distinguishes elements of the Remedy Principle (i.e., the necessary and sufficient conditions for coming under the sway of a remedial duty): "If and only if X holds vis-à-vis Y a moral right against Y's φ-ing, Y's φ-ing will place Y under a moral obligation to X to remedy the resultant situation in some way."[52] Kramer next proposes that a moral remedy both *acknowledges* the wrongness of the action, and *seeks to redress the result* of the breach. This has numerous implications. A duty-bearer, for instance, has a moral obligation in certain circumstances to seek a waiver of the duty in advance of failing to uphold it. The release constitutes an anticipatory remedy.[53] It is the duty-holder, moreover, that bears the burden of remedial action.[54] The critical step is the breach itself: "Y's doing or omitting to do something—his φ-ing—must be sufficient for the obligatoriness of a remedy if Y is to be classifiable as a duty-bearer."[55] Thus, even if someone else supplies the remedy, the need for one is created by Y's actions. Kramer adds a distinction between exoneration (or absolution) and "extenuation." The latter, he proposes, refers to "some feature of a person's behavior or circumstances that lessens the gravity of a wrong that the person has committed."[56] It does not mean that the act itself was not wrong (i.e., impermissible), but blameworthiness alters.

Professor Walter Sinnott-Armstrong's scenario of missing a lunch date to save someone's life (only to hear later that the restaurant where the meeting would otherwise have occurred was bombed), provides a colorful example of extenuation.[57] Under these circumstances, Kramer suggests, the morally-optimal decision to save a human life, together with the gratifying consequences of the breach, "do not completely absolve the promisor of any obligations to remedy his breach of duty, but they do very heavily extenuate that breach."[58] Kramer concludes that impeccable precautions cannot fully absolve an individual of moral responsibility, even in the face of extenuating circumstances.[59] He proposes an example from public law: where a defendant, tried under perfectly executed criminal procedures, is deemed guilty—and serves time—for a crime he never commits. When the error is discovered, and the individual released from prison, a moral remedy is still required. Owing to the blamelessness

[50] Hart, *The Concept of Law*, 168–76, 174. See also Hart, *Punishment and Responsibility: Essays in the Philosophy of Law*, 35–40 (arguing that strict liability does not apply to the moral realm); Kramer, "Moral Rights," 310 (discussing, citing, and arguing against Hart's exclusion of strict liability).

[51] Kramer, "Moral Rights," 312 ("X vis-à-vis Y holds a right to Y's φ-ing if and only if Y owes a duty to X to φ (where 'φ' represents any course of conduct by Y).")

[52] Kramer, 313. Similarly, where Y owes X a moral duty *not* to φ, then Y is under an obligation to remedy the situation.

[53] Kramer, 314.

[54] Kramer, 314–16.

[55] Kramer, 317.

[56] Kramer, 310.

[57] Sinnott-Armstrong, "Moral Dilemmas and Rights," 54–5; see also Kramer, "Moral Rights," 317–33.

[58] Kramer, "Moral Rights," 318–19.

[59] Kramer, 328.

of the systemic mechanisms, the remedy may consist only of a formal apology as an acknowledgment that a wrong has occurred. Nevertheless, a remedy has been supplied.[60] Thus, while "falling short may be heavily extenuated by one's having adopted all reasonable precautions or by one's having had to avert an even worse outcome, it remains a falling short."[61]

For Kramer, the moral obligation (and breach thereof) reflects the seriousness of the impact on the defendant's basic interests—in this case, liberty.[62] It is in virtue of the importance of these interests that Kramer affirms the existence of strict liability in morality, although such serious interests may not always be necessary for its existence.

Here we see the second way in which Kramer draws broader implications: he applies the framing to public law in a more deliberate fashion than Hohfeld, noting how the distinctions should be understood in relation to the rights discourse. This very application, however, raises significant questions about the extent to which parallels can be drawn between private law and the public realm.

2. Constitutional Entitlements *In Res Publica*

The kinds of entitlements captured in the constitutional realm are held not just *in personam* or *in rem*, but *in res publica*. What this means, in a democratic state, is that the entitlement-holder and the obligation-bearer at some level can be considered *the same entity*. This is very different than the Hohfeldian concept of a "right," which is understood in relation to a correlative duty on *others*. Nor does it correspond to a Hohfeldian "liberty" in that it entails a non-infringement obligation, for which the nexus is not on the right-holder, but on the collective state—which, under Kramer's account, may be explainable by the individual obligations of its constituent members but is not reducible to them. Unlike the other entitlements contemplated by Hohfeld, moreover, the breach of constitutional entitlements, as long as they exist, cannot be waived—either by the entitlement-holder or by the state as a collective.[63]

Hohfeld proposes that all four entitlements can be considered either paucital or multital. As a matter of first-order relations, "A paucital right, or claim, (right *in personam*) is either a unique right residing in a person (or group of persons) and availing against a single person (or single group of persons); or else it is one of a few fundamentally similar, yet separate, rights availing respectively against a few definite persons."[64] While the primary rights may be *in rem*, the vindication proceedings can be *in personam*.[65] Multital rights, in contrast, avail among three or more people.[66] Hohfeld considers them an amalgamation of the rights held by individual members of the

[60] Kramer, 328.
[61] Kramer, 329–30.
[62] Kramer, 331.
[63] But see Kurki, "Hohfeldian Infinities: Why Not to Worry," 137–46 (arguing that non-waivable entitlements do not present a concern within the Hohfeldian structure).
[64] Hohfeld, FLC II, 718.
[65] Hohfeld, 763. He adds, "While the word 'paucital' is suggested as the generic term to cover all rights *in personam*, the word 'unital' would be available to denote that particular kind of right *in personam* that is 'unique' and 'uncompanioned.'" Hohfeld, 718 n. 18.
[66] See generally Hohfeld, 718.

collective.[67] Accordingly, "[I]nstead of there being a single right with a single correlative duty resting on all the persons against whom the right avails, there are many separate and distinct rights, actual and potential, each one of which has a correlative duty resting upon some one person."[68] Hohfeld summarizes, "A right *in rem*, or a multital right, correctly understood, is simply one of a large number of fundamentally similar rights residing in one person; and any one of such rights has as its correlative one, and only one, of a large number of general, or common, duties—that is, fundamentally similar duties residing respectively in many different persons."[69] The same holds for a duty *in rem*.

From Hohfeld's exposition, it would seem that constitutional entitlements in the public law realm ought to be considered multital, in that they are held by members of a collective—in this case, citizens of the state, as against the government. Unlike types of relationships that Hohfeld contemplates, they are held neither *in personam* nor *in rem*, but *in res publica*. Accordingly, they tend to be couched in terms of "the People." The US Bill of Rights protects "the right of the people peaceably to assemble, and to petition the Government for a redress of grievances"[70]; "the right of the people to keep and bear Arms"[71]; "[t]he right of the people to be secure in their persons, houses, papers, and effects, against unreasonable searches and seizures"[72]; construal of constitutional rights in a manner that does not "deny or disparage others retained by the people"[73]; and reservation of "[t]he powers not delegated to the United States" for "the people."[74] While such entitlements can be asserted on behalf of an individual, as an expression of their own constitutional right as held against the government, they reflect the rights of the people as a whole.

Simultaneously, courts regularly recognize private collectives, which are themselves covered by the constitutional right held by "the People." In *NAACP v. Alabama*, a unanimous Supreme Court thus held that the right to free association exempted the group from being forced to turn its membership lists over to the state government.[75] Justice John M. Harlan wrote, "[I]mmunity from state scrutiny of petitioner's membership lists ... is here so related to the right of members to pursue their lawful private interests privately and to associate freely with others in doing so as to come within the protection of the Fourteenth Amendment."[76] While the right to free association could be explained by the rights of constituent members, the NAACP was entitled to protect its members' associational privacy.

These same entitlements are held, too, by the individuals who make up "the People"—namely, citizens. Should an Administration forbid me from engaging in

[67] Hohfeld, 718 ("A multital right, or claim, (right *in rem*) is always one of a large class of fundamentally similar yet separate rights, actual and potential, residing in a *single* person (or single groups of persons) but availing respectively against persons constituting a very large and indefinite class of people.").
[68] Hohfeld, 742.
[69] Hohfeld, 745.
[70] US Const. amend. I.
[71] US Const. amend. II.
[72] US Const. amend. IV.
[73] US Const. amend. IX.
[74] US Const. amend. X.
[75] See *NAACP v. Alabama*, 357 U.S. 449 (1958).
[76] *NAACP*, 357 U.S. at 466.

peaceful protest, my individual (constitutional) right to free expression would be violated as a consequence of the obligation placed on the government in the First Amendment to abstain from infringing on the (collective) free speech of "the People."

This carries significant implications. To the extent that democratic governance means that citizens also constitute the state, the entitlement-holder simultaneously acts as the one in whom the duty of non-interference resides. The collective right in question is constituted in part by the individual rights of the citizens, who also hold the organs of state power in their hands. They are thus under a duty to refrain from interference in (their own) rights. This is a very different legal relationship than the one contemplated by the Hohfeld-Kramer framing, wherein a right exists on the basis of a duty held by another.

It appears, then, that constitutional entitlements do not fit squarely within the right/duty axis. No more so do they fall within the liberty/no-right correlative. The latter speaks to a freedom or privilege, with the scope defined in terms of the liberty-holder. A constitutional entitlement, in contrast, carries with it an obligation of non-infringement to the entitlement-holder *and* to the state—which, under Kramer's account, as a collective, both incorporates and goes beyond its constituent parts.

Kramer agrees with Hohfeld insofar as jural relations extend to corporate entitlements.[77] A claim right (or duty) may be held by a particular person (or, in the context of constitutional rights, group of persons), against another person (or group of persons). Because of the potential for multiple rights (or duties), any claim-right (or duty) could, potentially, exist alongside other claim-rights (or duties) held by the same individual in the same context.[78] Kramer goes on to suggest that collectives are not *just* reducible to claims about the entitlement held by each member of the collective. Instead, they reflect a set of entitlements held by one or more people. In his words, "reducibility does not amount to straightforward homologousness."[79] Individuals have certain entitlements in the context of the group and not just as a manifestation of their own, individualized entitlement. He extrapolates, "Once we have grasped that a collectivity's legal positions are quite as real as an individual's legal positions, we can submit that any public duty is owed to a collectivity (the state, the nation, the community) which holds the correlative right."[80]

Kramer's insight is that Hohfeld confuses explicability with reducibility and fictitiousness. On the one hand, we can understand corporate entitlement by looking at the individual entitlements via which it operates; however, this doesn't strip away the meaning (or reality) of the corporate entitlement as a whole.[81] Statements about a network of individually-held rights do not necessarily imply the existence (or absence) of a collective right. Something more is needed. Accordingly, where a collective has a legal protection, it can be explained through individual entitlements and their relationship to correlative obligations/conditions, but it cannot be reduced to that.[82] Kramer writes, "An account focused purely on individuals' entitlements can

[77] Kramer, RWT, 53–4.
[78] Kramer, 9–10.
[79] Kramer, 51.
[80] Kramer, 59.
[81] Kramer, 51.
[82] Kramer, "Getting Rights Right," in *Rights, Wrongs and Responsibilities*, 46 (hereafter Kramer, GRR).

in principle expound fully the ways in which any corporate entitlements operate, but cannot per se fully expound the effects which the operations of the corporate entitlements bring about."[83] The interests of the collective are both independent of and reliant on the interests of its constituent members.[84]

One of the most consistent characteristics of the relationship entailed in constitutional rights is that the state, as an entity (like the citizens), also is under an obligation of non-infringement. This obligation, moreover, unlike the first-order relations discussed by Hohfeld, cannot be altered. In other words, the entire point of a *constitutional* right, (as opposed, for instance, to a private law claim-right), is that the right-holder cannot waive it against his duty-bound self. That I have a right to speech as held against the government's duty of non-interference means that I cannot, in my sovereign capacity, vote to restrict that right, either against myself or future generations.[85] Further, the constitution establishes entitlements for future generations. The holding of legal rights by people not yet born "consists in the owing of legal duties to them by present-day people."[86] Both the legal duty and the legal right are held in the present.[87]

One response to this argument might be to note that the constitution itself could be altered. This was one of the critical contributions of the document forged in 1787: that it allowed for its own amendment. But this assertion rather sidesteps the point, which is that as long as the jural relation exists, the entitlement operates, regardless of whether citizens or the state would prefer to see it set aside.

The Kramer-Hohfeldian framing also misses ways in which constitutional rights act as an umbrella over non-right-holders—a form of transferred entitlement. Nor does it capture the (associated) extended obligation *in res publica*. For Kramer, "A strict right-duty correlation … characterize[s] every public duty along with every private duty; the only difference is that each public duty correlates with a collective right only, whereas each private duty correlates with an individual right. The party wronged by a breach of a public duty is the political grouping that holds the correlative right."[88] Certain constitutional rights, however, may be extended beyond the constitutional right-holder, to protect others.

In 2018, for instance, the state of California enacted the California Consumer Privacy Act (CCPA).[89] This statute gives consumers greater control over their personal data, securing the right to know what is being collected (and how it is being employed and shared); the right to delete certain personal information; the right to opt-out of the sale of data; and the right to non-discrimination for deciding to exercise rights under the CCPA. The duty to abide by the statute's requirements is imposed on *all* entities who collect Californians' private data. In the process, the state has created claim-rights for all consumers who use those businesses, goods, and services. That collective right cannot be explained just as a function of the rights held by Californians—although that is the ground on which the duty is constructed. Non-Californians do

[83] Kramer, 46.
[84] Kramer, 46.
[85] Kramer, 54–5.
[86] Kramer, 54.
[87] Kramer, GRR, 54–5.
[88] Kramer, RWT, 59.
[89] California Consumer Privacy Act of 2018, 2018 Cal. Stat. 1807.

not constitute the collective. Nevertheless, they hold the rights by virtue of those entitlements secured for those living in the Golden State.

While the example is from private law, correlates can be found in the constitutional realm: the right of "the People" in the First and Fourth Amendments extends to non-citizens on US soil. Even those illegally in the country have the benefit of the rights so conveyed—despite not being a constitutive part of "the People" as established by the preamble of the constitution.

The point flows the other way too, in that a reduction in rights held by a particular set of individuals may bring with it a reduction in rights held by others, outside of the collective to which the rights relate. In 2008, for instance, Congress changed its foreign intelligence law to allow for the collection overseas of communications among entities reasonably believed to be non-US persons and outside the United States.[90] The problem is that by virtue of how the Internet functions, multi-communication transactions collected under the law included tens of thousands of entirely domestic communications as well.[91] The result was that the narrowing of the collective rights of non-US persons overseas also narrowed the collective rights of US persons on domestic soil. These types of legal relationships, however, are not captured by the Hohfeldian jural relations. The establishment of citizen-rights entails the establishment of non-citizens-rights, and a duplication of duty vis-à-vis non-citizens, just as the narrowing of non-citizen-rights entails the narrowing of citizen-rights, with the same corresponding obligation on the state. A secondary legal relation echoing the establishment of the original claim-right vis-à-vis citizens (or non-citizens) exists.

3. Complex Collectives

Not only do multiple collectives constitute society (which carries implications for entitlement-holders), but multiple collectives constitute the state, impacting the number and structure of those on whom an obligation may rest. It creates a situation ripe for genuine conflict. Complex collectives in a public law context are especially prominent in the realm of second-order relations: who holds a power may be very difficult to ascertain—a problem exacerbated by new and emerging technologies.

Recognition of multiple duty-holders for the protection of asserted claim-rights is an integral part of Anglo-American jurisprudence. In the seventeenth century, equity famously triumphed over common law in the clash between the Lord Chancellor (Thomas Edgerton, Lord Ellesmere) and the Chief Justice of the King's Bench, Sir Edward Coke.[92] Injunctions were being granted in Chancery that prevented common law judgments from going into effect. James I, through his attorneys general, came down on the side of Chancery. The systems provided two distinct sources of rights.[93]

[90] FISA Amendments Act of 2008, Pub. L. No. 110–261, 122 Stat. 2436.

[91] See Memorandum Opinion and Order, [REDACTED], No. [REDACTED], GID.C.00073, at 41 (FISA Ct. October 3, 2011) (Bates, J.), https://repository.library.georgetown.edu/handle/10822/1052732.

[92] Henry VIII rewarded Lord Audley for securing the trial and execution of Anne Boleyn by awarding him land in Cambridge. Magdalene College, which inherited the land, sold it, enabling the Earl of Oxford to later purchase it. Magdalen brought suit to regain the property. *Earl of Oxford* case (1615) 21 Eng. Rep. 485.

[93] Supreme Court of Judicature Act 1873, 36 & 37 Vict. c. 66n (consolidating the Court of Chancery, the Court of Queen's Bench, the Court of Common Pleas, the Court of Exchequer, the High Court of Admiralty,

Both were judicial in nature, and both generated claim-rights on behalf of British subjects and the Crown, as well as correlative duties to those rights.

Citizens in democratic regimes are subject to multiple executive and legislative collectives, with jural relations dictated by group membership, even within the same collective entity. The US Constitution, for instance, recognizes dual sovereignty: powers not assigned to the national government are retained by the states, with both the federal government and the states acting on the People.[94] This means that state executives and legislative bodies also act on citizens who have membership in the federal government.

The existence of two entities simultaneously serving in a sovereign capacity compounds the risk that entitlements and obligations clash. Kramer does recognize that, within the Hohfeldian universe, conflicting rights and duties are possible.[95] While it may appear that a contradiction exists between being duty-bound to do φ and being duty-bound to refrain from φ-ing, it is not in fact a contradiction.[96] Both things can be true. A genuine contradiction occurs only where a person has a duty to φ and, simultaneously, liberty-right to abstain from φ-ing.[97] Further, if Y has a duty to act, then Y does not have the privilege of not acting. Similarly, if Y has a duty *not* to interfere, Y does not have a liberty to interfere.[98] Kramer distinguishes between legal obligations in conflict but not in contradiction: "Though the fulfilment of either one must rule out the fulfilment of the other, the existence of either one does not in any way preclude the existence of the other. This non-contradictoriness is one main feature of jural logic (with its categories of 'permissibility', 'impermissibility', and 'obligatoriness') that prevents it from being collapsed into modal logic (with its categories of 'possibility', 'impossibility', and 'necessity')."[99]

As a matter of constitutional rights, priority or precedence is settled by appeal to the structure. The delineation in Article I, § 8 of categorical subject-matter priority, together with the Supremacy clause, go some way toward resolving matters where there is a genuine conflict. The duty to do φ (or not to φ) is specified in regard to jurisdiction. But the existence of enumerated powers does not settle all questions.

One of the strongest examples that can be brought to bear currently exists in relation to the bifurcated approach to drugs that currently marks the United States. As of the time of writing, thirty-three states and the District of Columbia have legalized

the Court of Probate, and the Court of Divorce and Matrimonial Causes into one High Court); Supreme Court of Judicature Act 1875, 38 & 39 Vict. c. 77.

94 *United States v. Lanza*, 260 U.S. 377, 382 (1922) ("We have here two sovereignties, deriving power from different sources, capable of dealing with the same subject-matter within the same territory.... Each government in determining what shall be an offense against its peace and dignity is exercising its own sovereignty, not that of the other."); *Gamble v. United States*, 139 S. Ct. 1960, 1965 (2019) ("[W]here there are two sovereigns, there are two laws, and two 'offences.'"). See also *Abbate v. United States*, 359 U.S. 187, 195 (1959); *Bartkus v. Illinois*, 359 U.S. 121, 138 (1959).

95 Kramer, RWT, 19–20.

96 Note, however, that if you add an "ought implies can" principle (i.e., Lon Fuller's fifth rule of law canon—that the law must be capable of being obeyed), a contradiction results: an individual cannot both φ and not-φ, and thus cannot have duties (oughts) to do both.

97 Kramer, 13.

98 Kramer, 13.

99 Kramer, 19.

medical marijuana.[100] Until 2018, however, it was illegal to possess, use, or buy cannabis anywhere in the United States.[101] In *Gonzales v. Raich*, the Supreme Court came down firmly on the side of the federal government, ruling its ability to regulate private consumption of marijuana as being within federal Commerce clause powers.[102] Not only did a number of states largely ignore the ruling, but in 2013 the Deputy Attorney General sent a memorandum to all US attorneys indicating that the US Department of Justice would not be enforcing the law in states that had legalized marijuana and implemented an effective regulatory system.[103]

Under the Hohfeldian analysis, for citizens, the conditions do not represent an instance of non-contradictoriness but, rather, possible contradiction. Oregonians are not under both a *duty* to consume 24 ounces of medical marijuana (the amount allowed by state law) and a *duty* not to consume any marijuana (under federal law). Instead, under state law, they are *permitted* to consume marijuana (whereas under federal law, they are not). State law enforcement, in turn, is under a duty of non-interference in the consumption of marijuana within the allowed amount. But they, also, are not subject to conflicting duties: because of dual sovereignty and as recognized by the Tenth Amendment, the federal government cannot commandeer state governments to order them to carry out federal measures.[104]

For federal prosecutors, however, a contradiction exists: they both have a *duty* to enforce the existing law (which forbids marijuana in all fifty states and imposes criminal penalties for its possession) and a *duty*, according to the Attorney General's memorandum, not to enforce the existing law. The reason they are in this position is, in part, because of the tension inherent in dual sovereignty: what one sovereign permits, the other forbids.

The problem of multiples in the public law context extends to second-order relations. Consider powers. Kramer posits that "the exercise of a genuine legal power always occurs through a volitional act or forbearance of some sort."[105] This claim falls rather short of explaining the relationship among power-holders (whose actions or forbearance alter claim-rights), as well as situations in which no cognitive act occurs. The change in a claim-right—particularly when held against the government in a public law context—often entails complex legal relations.

On September 30, 2011, for instance, a Central Intelligence Agency (CIA) drone strike in Yemen killed Shaykh Anwar Aulaqi, an American citizen.[106] The attack also

[100] See "Legal Medical Marijuana States and DC: Laws, Fees, and Possession Limits," ProCon.org, updated March 23, 2020, https://medicalmarijuana.procon.org/legal-medical-marijuana-states-and-dc/.

[101] Controlled Substances Act, 21 U.S.C. §§ 801–904.

[102] See *Gonzales v. Raich*, 545 U.S. 1 (2005).

[103] Memorandum from James M. Cole, Deputy Att'y Gen., to all US attorneys, Guidance Regarding Marijuana Enforcement (August 29, 2013), https://www.justice.gov/iso/opa/resources/3052013829132756857467.pdf.

[104] See *Printz v. United States*, 521 U.S. 898 (1997) (holding that Congress cannot compel state law enforcement officers to carry out a federal law requiring background checks prior to firearms purchases); *New York v. United States*, 504 U.S. 144 (1992) (holding that Congress cannot commandeer state legislative branches to force states to accept radioactive waste).

[105] Kramer, GRR, 58.

[106] *Al-Aulaqi v. Panetta*, 35 F. Supp. 3d 56, 58 (D.D.C. 2014). See also Letter from Eric H. Holder, Jr., Att'y Gen., to Patrick J. Leahy, Chairman, Comm. on the Judiciary 1–2 (May 22, 2013); Remarks at National Defense University, 2013 Daily Comp. Pres. Doc. 361, at 7–8 (May 23, 2013) (President Barak Obama admitting to the targeting and killing of Al-Aulaqi).

killed Samir Khan, another US citizen in the vehicle.[107] Two weeks later, a second drone strike on an open air restaurant killed Aulaqi's sixteen-year-old son, Abdulrahman, and six others.[108] Both prior and subsequent to these acts, Aulaqi, Khan, and others' claim-rights had been altered. Was a "power," in a Hohfeldian sense, exercised?

Let's first focus on Anwar Aulaqi. More than a year before he was killed, the US Department of the Treasury determined that he was a leader of al-Qa'ida in the Arab Peninsula (AQAP), and designated him as a Specially Designated Global Terrorist under Executive Order 13224.[109] The decision was based in significant measure on testimony provided by Umar Farouk Abdulmutallab, who had tried to light an explosive device while flying from Amsterdam to Detroit on Christmas Day, 2009.[110] In a separate action, US Joint Special Operations Command (JSOC) placed Aulaqi on a military kill list.[111] Leon Panetta, the Director of the CIA, and Admiral William H. McRaven, Commander of JSOC, allegedly played a central role in adding his name to the targeting list.[112] In yet another act, on February 19, 2010, the Department of Justice Office of Legal Counsel issued a memorandum laying out the legal justification for the use of lethal force against Aulaqi, concluding that a drone strike would violate neither Executive Order 12333, which prohibits assassination, "or any applicable constitutional limitations due to [his] United States citizenship."[113] Separately, upon hearing that his son had been placed on the kill list, Nasser Al-Aulaqi filed suit to enjoin the government from carrying out the attack unless his son presented an imminent threat to human life and there were no other options but lethal force to stop him.[114] The military moved to dismiss the complaint based on state secrets—an assertion supported by declarations made by the Director of National Intelligence, James Clapper; the Secretary of Defense, Robert Gates; and Panetta.[115] Judge John Bates dismissed the case based on Aulaqi's father's lack of standing to assert his son's constitutional rights.[116]

[107] *Al-Aulaqi*, 35 F. Supp. 3d at 58.

[108] *Al-Aulaqi*, 35 F. Supp. 3d at 58–9.

[109] Exec. Order No. 13,224, 3 C.F.R. 786, *reprinted as amended in* 50 U.S.C.S. § 1701 note (issued pursuant to the International Economic Powers Act, 50 U.S.C. §§ 1701–06); Designation of Anwar Al-Aulaqi Pursuant to Executive Order 13224 and Global Terrorism Sanctions Regulations, 75 Fed. Reg. 43,233 (July 23, 2010) (publicly announced July 12, 2010).

[110] *Al-Aulaqi*, 35 F. Supp. 3d 56. See also *United States v. Abdulmutallab*, 739 F.3d 891 (6th Cir. 2014).

[111] See Dana Priest, "U.S. Military Teams, Intelligence Deeply Involved in Aiding Yemen on Strikes," *Washington Post*, January 27, 2010, https://www.washingtonpost.com/wp-dyn/content/article/2010/01/26/AR2010012604239.html?sid=ST2010012700394.

[112] *Al-Aulaqi*, 35 F. Supp. 3d at 59.

[113] Memorandum from David J. Barron, Acting Assistant Att'y Gen., to the Attorney General, Re: Lethal Operation Against Shaykh Anwar Aulaqi (February 19, 2010), https://www.nytimes.com/interactive/2014/08/16/us/16firstolcawlakimemo.html. The document also claimed that the strike was consistent with international law.

[114] See Complaint for Declaratory and Injunctive Relief, *Al-Aulaqi v. Obama*, 727 F. Supp. 2d 1 (D.D.C. 2010) (No. 10-cv-01469), 2010 WL 3478666.

[115] *Al-Aulaqi*, 35 F. Supp. 3d at 60.

[116] *Al-Aulaqi v. Obama*, 727 F. Supp. 2d 1, 54 (D.D.C. 2010). After Aulaqi's killing, the US Department of Justice produced a White Paper laying out three conditions under which the targeting of a US citizen in a leadership capacity in al-Qa'ida, or an associated force, would be lawful: "(1) an informed, high-level official of the U.S. government has determined that the targeted individual poses an imminent threat of violent attack against the United States; (2) capture is infeasible, and the United States continues to monitor whether capture becomes feasible; and (3) the operation would be conducted in a manner consistent with applicable law of war principles." Dep't of Justice (DOJ), White Paper, Lawfulness of a Lethal Operation

Each of these events—the determination by the Treasury that Aulaqi was a member of AQAP; his placement on the military kill list; the dismissal of his father's suit; the unchallenged declarations made by political appointees; the President's personal decision to order the strike; and the CIA's actual carrying out of the order—essentially waived Aulaqi's Fifth Amendment due process rights, as well as his claim-right against bodily assault. Alternatively, if you accept the argument that Aulaqi was a commander in an enemy army, then the broader judicial doctrine matters. In the Second World War era case of *In re Territo*, the Ninth Circuit held that a US citizen who joined the Italian army does not have access to habeas proceedings. In *Johnson v. Eisentrager*, non-resident enemy aliens were captured and tried in China by a US military commission and subsequently transferred to Germany.[117] The Supreme Court held that during wartime, non-resident enemy aliens lack any right of access to US civilian courts.[118]

Which of the above elements ought to be considered necessary to erosion of the claim-rights? Which are sufficient? Which action amounts to an exercise of the relevant power: that of executive branch officials, Congress, or federal judges, or that of Aulaqi (like Territo) in intentionally putting himself into a situation in which no lawful process is due prior to targeting? Was it even an exercise of power in a Hohfeldian sense? Without the legal justification, the decision to fire the missile would not have been made. But that decision—the order to launch the attack—was also critical. So, too, was Judge Bates's decision in the suit to dismiss it on standing grounds. Had he come to a different conclusion, it is possible that the order would never have been made. Is the power to insist on maintaining a claim-right distinguishable from a power to alter it? If exercised, what happens when a competing power to alter it, such as through an exercise of the President's commander-in-chief power, trumps?

And what of Samir Khan's death, or that of Aulaqi's son? They had their claim-rights violated, as would, ostensibly, any number of individuals under the criteria laid out in the DOJ White Paper—both targets and those who happen to be in the proximity of targets or who associate with them. Who has the power to alter their due process or right to life claim-rights? Does it matter that the President, who orders the strike, is elected—or that the cabinet members who add US citizens' names to the kill list are not? The jural relations, adapted from a private law realm, fail to account for the specificity as well as the complexity of the legal relations at play in government decision-making—even when the most critical of citizens' interests are on the line.

H.L.A. Hart characterizes powers that may be exercised by government officials, ranging from legislative, regulatory, and adjudicatory decisions, to investigation, arrest, and appointment.[119] There is a distinction to be drawn here between the power to do something that has a direct impact on others, and the ability to bring about changes

Directed Against a U.S. Citizen Who Is a Senior Operational Leader of Al-Qa'ida or An Associated Force (November 8, 2011 draft), http://bit.ly/Wv7Cdh. While the aim of the document was to provide an after-the-fact justification, it exhibited poor reasoning and focused on the notion of imminence, which did not go to the core of the analysis in the Office of Legal Counsel (OLC) opinion. I thus only highlight the OLC opinion, which, in any event, is the regnant doctrine.

[117] *In Re Territo*, 156 F.2d 142 (9th Cir. 1946); *Johnson v. Eisentrager*, 339 U.S. 763 (1950).

[118] ibid. See also *Ex parte Quirin*, 317 U.S. 1 (1942).

[119] See Hart, *Essays on Bentham: Studies in Jurisprudence and Political Theory*, 194–8.

in legal relations.[120] But in the case of Aulaqi, these distinctions collapse: the decision to place him on the kill list is precisely what altered his due process protections. How we understand the exercise of the powers will depend on the underlying approach to what is meant by a power.[121]

Kramer's assertion that the exercise of a power entails an affirmative decision to act (or to forbear from acting) also is not consistent with the types of new and emerging technologies that are beginning to impact law in profound ways. Sophisticated algorithms, machine learning, and artificial intelligence are being used with legal effect. Criminal risk assessment algorithms, for example, are being employed to determine whether individuals are granted parole, altering their liberty rights.[122] Predictive policing and geospatial profiling rely on crime maps and artificial intelligence to establish patrol patterns and surveillance of certain neighborhoods, effectively diminishing residents' right to the types of privacy interests encapsulated in the Fourth Amendment.[123] In June 2012, members of Congress raised concerns with President Obama about the continued use of signature drone strikes, in which patterns of behavior suggesting involvement in terrorist activity were sufficient to establish the target for a missile strike.[124] Targeting decisions implicate the claim-right against assault—both for the target and for the person unlucky enough to get into a vehicle with them, or to attend an event where the individual is present, on the day of the attack.

If the feature of decisionmaking constitutes the "first feature of legal power," as Professor Andrew Halpin argues, then question arises as to whether any of the decisions above constitute powers.[125] In each case, a decision was made in relation to the individual whose rights were thereby altered. Hohfeld, though, considers an exercise of a legal power to occur only when "some superadded fact" is "under the volitional control of . . . [a] human being."[126] Yet artificial intelligence and machine learning are being used to ascertain the extent to which claim-rights exist. The determination that an individual is a legitimate target for a drone attack immediately deprives that person of due process rights.

One response that Kramer might offer is to say that the decision to use machine learning is itself the exercise of the power. But this does not seem accurate, as it is in no way individualized in terms of its impact on the individual's claim-rights. Even expanding the assertion to say that the decision implicates members of a particular group (such as prisoners, a particular neighborhood, or members of al-Qa'ida) somewhat begs the question of who falls into that group and thereby has their rights

[120] Halpin, "The Concept of a Legal Power," 131. See also Joseph Raz, "Legal Principles and the Limits of Law," 829 (distinguishing between discretionary power in a given case versus the power granted to the courts generally).

[121] Compare Raz, "Legal Principles"; MacCormick, *H.L.A. Hart*; and Halpin, "Concept of a Legal Power," to Visa A.J. Kurki, "Legal Competence and Legal Power," 31–47.

[122] See Stevenson, "Assessing Risk Assessment in Action," 303–84.

[123] See Meijer and Wessels, "Predictive Policing: Review of Benefits and Drawbacks," 1031–9; Hardyns and Rummens, "Predictive Policing as a New Tool for Law Enforcement? Recent Developments and Challenges," 201–18.

[124] Letter from 26 Members of Congress to Barack Obama, President of the United States (June 12, 2012), https://web.archive.org/web/20121111034038/http://kucinich.house.gov/uploadedfiles/combat_drones_061212.pdf.

[125] Halpin, "Concept of a Legal Power," 140.

[126] Hohfeld, FLC I, 50.

altered—a decision determined by the same entity who has the duty to that individual in the first place. Moving the analysis to the algorithm or the criteria employed does not deflect the critique.

Alternatively, Kramer might suggest that the decision by a human judge or police official based on the *results* of artificial intelligence is the exercise of the power at stake. A sentencing judge could, for instance, use a computer to call up a defendant's record, which the judge then peruses before deciding on the sentence. In the realm of automation, the judge is merely relying on whatever algorithms go into making the database function properly. Either way, the power itself is that of the judge passing the sentence.

The problem with this analysis, though, is that it substitutes machine rationality for that of a human being: it is a complicated and inaccessible algorithm that comes up with the probability of recidivism or public risk. So it is not really the judge using her own analysis. It is the judge relying on a machine to make critical determinations.

4. Dignities

An important weakness in the Hohfeld-Kramer framing is its failure to account for a type of constitutional entitlement that I will refer to as "dignities." Anglo-American law has long distinguished between "alienable" and "inalienable" rights. By alienable, we mean one of three possibilities: the right-holder can waive the right altogether (which suggests that the right-holder has an associated power to waive it); the right-holder can assign it to someone else; or the people (a collective) can waive it through constitutional amendment or statutory instrument (depending upon the "right" in question). Inalienable means the converse: it cannot be waived under any of those circumstances. Numerous political and legal philosophers posit that individuals cannot, under any circumstances, be divested of an inalienable right.[127] Not only can citizens not divest themselves of such an entitlement, but the existence of such rights does not depend on any written articulation. To the extent, therefore, that a country relies on a written constitution, amending it would not alter the underlying entitlement.

Perhaps the most famous articulation of the entitlements subsequently subsumed into the category of inalienable rights comes from John Locke's *Second Treatise*, where he enumerates the importance of life, liberty, pursuit of happiness, equality, consent as a basis for political legitimacy, and the right of revolution.[128] By the time of Blackstone, the natural law concepts had become incorporated into common understanding as "absolute rights". The right to life, for instance, could not legally, "be disposed of or destroyed by any individual, neither by the person himself, nor by any other of his fellow creatures, merely upon their own authority."[129] These rights form the core of what have come to be considered inalienable rights.[130]

[127] See, e.g., Brown, Jr., "Inalienable Rights," 192–211; Schiller, "Are There Any Inalienable Rights?," 312.

[128] See generally Locke, *Second Treatise of Civil Government and a Letter Concerning Toleration.*

[129] Blackstone, *Commentaries on the Laws of England in Four Books*, 1:133.

[130] See, e.g., George Mason draft of the Virginia Declaration of Rights (adopted by the Virginia Assembly, June 12, 1776 (referring to the right of revolution as inalienable); US Declaration of Independence ("We hold these truths to be self-evident, that all men are created equal, that they are endowed by their Creator with certain unalienable Rights, that among these are Life, Liberty and the pursuit of Happiness."); Frances Hutcheson, *Inquiry into the Original of Our Ideas of Beauty and Virtue* ("For wherever any Invasion is made

Inalienable rights, not as moral rights but as *legal* rights, are not properly considered within Hohfeld's first-order pairing. I am not speaking here of natural law, but of recognized entitlements that carry legal force. As a formal matter, they are not claim-rights backed by law, because no written law establishes them. In a common law system, such rights may be recognized by the courts. But even if the foundational documents were altered, they would still exist. Unlike the other jural relations, they are both temporally and logically prior to constitution of the state. They pre-date government. As a matter of logic, it is their prior existence that places an obligation on the government not to breach them. They do not depend upon ordered society or governmental structures to be called into being.

Such was the logic used to decimate the Privileges or Immunities clause in the US Constitution.[131] At the time the Fourteenth Amendment was adopted, "privileges" and "immunities" were interchangeable with "rights," "liberties," and "freedom"'—and had been since Blackstone.[132] In the *Slaughter-House Cases*, the Supreme Court famously established that the "privileges" and "immunities" protected by the Fourteenth Amendment are limited to those spelled out in the constitution. They are a function of federal (not state) citizenship.[133] Thus, while the right might pre-exist citizenship, it is only the codification of the right that gives it legal meaning.

Similarly, in the 1876 case of *United States v. Cruikshank*, the Court determined that the brutal murder of 160 black citizens outside a Louisiana court house did not violate their (First Amendment) right to peaceable assembly, as the right pre-dated codification in the Bill of Rights.[134] It was up to the state to make the determination. Nor was the right to bear arms *created* by the Second Amendment.[135] Because of its status as an inalienable right, it could not be enforced through the Fourteenth Amendment. In the decades following *Cruikshank*, the Court twice underscored that the Privileges or Immunities clause did not apply to the Second Amendment.[136] The Court in *Heller* later observed, "[I]t has always been widely understood that the Second Amendment, like the First and Fourth Amendments, codified a *pre-existing* right."[137] Once cemented into law, it could be held as against the federal government, but (post-*Slaughter-House*) not as a general duty held by states to refrain from interference in the entitlement.

These entitlements reflect the dignity of individuals *qua* human beings and exist prior to, and contemporaneous with, establishment of the government. And they have

upon unalienable Rights, there must arise either a perfect, or external Right to Resistance ... Unalienable Rights are essential Limitations in all Governments."); Preamble, Universal Declaration of Human Rights (UDHR) ("Whereas recognition of the inherent dignity and of the equal and inalienable rights of all members of the human family is the foundation of freedom, justice and peace in the world.").

131 US Const. amend. XIV ("No State ... shall abridge the privileges or immunities of citizens of the United States.").

132 *McDonald v. City of Chicago*, 561 U.S. 742, 813–14 (2010) (Thomas, J., concurring) (citing and quoting Blackstone, *Commentaries on the Laws of England in Four Books*, 1:129).

133 See *Slaughter-House Cases*, 83 U.S. (16 Wall.) 36 (1872).

134 See *United States v. Cruikshank*, 92 U.S. 542, 552 (1876).

135 *Cruikshank*, 92 U.S. at 553.

136 See *Presser v. Illinois*, 116 U.S. 252 (1886); *Miller v. Texas*, 153 U.S. 535 (1894).

137 *District of Columbia v. Heller*, 554 U.S. 570, 592 (2008) (italics in the original).

legal force. The strength of the natural law discourse means that inalienable rights give meaning to legal relations. Locke's legacy here is hard to deny: drafting the Virginia Declaration of Rights, George Mason asserted, "all men are by nature equally free and independent, and have certain inherent Rights, of which, when they enter into a state of society, they cannot, by any Compact, deprive or divest their posterity; namely, the Enjoyment of Life and Liberty, with the Means of acquiring and possessing property, and pursuing and obtaining Happiness and Safety."[138] Less than a month later, Thomas Jefferson echoed his words in the Declaration of Independence.[139] These documents essentially severed the relationship between Great Britain and the American colonies, with violation of the (inalienable) rights due to colonists serving as the legal grounds on which they were acting. The failure of the Crown to protect those rights (which, in a revisionist claim assumedly were grounded in Magna Carta and the English Bill of Rights) justified rebellion.

One potential response to the seeming lacuna in the Hohfeldian framing might be to suggest that dignities are (foundational) claim-rights. *Ubi ius, ibi remedium*, in a democratic society, the electoral process may serve as the only remedy. In extreme cases, recourse may only be had via rebellion. Thus, while inalienable rights, alone, may be unenforceable through a judicial process, the key to redress may nevertheless lay in the hands of the People, who have the attendant power to exercise, or to waive, enforcement. There is a distinction to be drawn between enforceability through the courts and enforceability as what gives a right meaning or existence. A dignity may not be enforceable through the courts; nevertheless, it exists.

Under this account, can dignities properly be said to be enforceable at all? Recall that one of the defining characteristics of a right is that it be enforceable. Kramer recognizes that the claim-holder does not have to be the one with the discretion to seek enforcement. He or she (or it, in a collective sense) *may* be in such a position, but so could a person or entity acting as a fiduciary on their behalf, the government, or others. The only requirement, as a definitional matter, is that the claim be enforceable.[140]

Kramer proposes in response to Professor White's challenge to the Correlativity Axiom (i.e., that it fails to take account of ineffectual statutes), that nominal and genuine rights (and their correlative duties) can be distinguished.[141] The dissimilarity turns precisely on the (un)enforceability of a breach of the correlative duties in question. He writes, "[A]n assertion that a statute imposes duties which are not backed up with effective remedies is equivalent to an assertion that the statute confers rights which are not effectively enforced. Such rights are merely nominal rights rather than genuine rights, but, equally, the duties are merely nominal duties rather than genuine duties."[142] Enforced rights are operative, while unenforced rights are inoperative.[143] To be an operative legal right, for Kramer, one of two conditions holds: either violations

[138] Va. Declaration of Rights, Art. 1 (June 12, 1776).

[139] Declaration of Independence, cl. 2 (July 4, 1776) ("We hold these truths to be self-evident, that all Men are created equal, that they are endowed by their Creator with certain unalienable Rights, that among these are Life, Liberty and the pursuit of Happiness.")

[140] Kramer, RWT, 9.

[141] Kramer, 33–4 (citing White, *Rights*, 72).

[142] Kramer, 34.

[143] Kramer, GRR, 65.

of the correlative legal duty are regularly punished or remedied; or violations *would* be regularly punished/remedied if they regularly occurred. In contrast, if noncompliance with a legal duty seldom (or never) triggers any punitive or rectificatory response, it is an inoperative right.[144]

Kramer identifies two broad categories of inoperative duties: (a) those that are not enforced because the power of waiving enforcement is invariably (or almost always) exercised, and (b) those that are unenforced because of a lack of power to demand their effectuation. In the first category, the right-holder, or someone else, has a power to activate punishment if the duty is not performed.[145] If the power-holder chooses not to exercise the power, she has exercised a legal power of waiver. An additional condition applies: the power-holder must take no action against violations that she can realistically discover.[146] A lack of knowledge that a breach has occurred is not the same as an inability (i.e., a lack of authority) to redress it. In the second category, neither the right-holder nor anyone else holds either the power to enforce the duty or to waive it.

Whether a right is operative centers on whether a duty exists, as well as on the (actual) imposition of punishment and/or a remedy.[147] The potential for nominal duties arises from the requirement that law must be articulated.[148] Kramer explains, "Because all or some of the law's demands are presented in written or spoken formulations, gaps can arise between the demands that are expressed and the demands for which legal remedies are available."[149] If legal remedies are not provided for, then the legal requirements are nominal.

Returning to dignities, it may be that the state routinely violates such entitlements, for which no remedy is supplied. History is replete with examples. This doesn't mean that the entitlement had been waived—indeed, one characteristic that distinguishes dignities is that such a power of waiver *does not exist*. It is outside either the entitlement-holder's hands or the power of the state. Kramer may be right that the *ubi ius* maxim "is too sweeping in application to legal rights."[150] Legal rights can be severed from a remedy.[151] But what happens when a core right is made nominal by its (un)enforceability? The Madisonian electoral check may not always operate, owing to control of state power by certain factions. Does it make any sense to speak of an inalienable right as a claim-right, if the only redress is for a dissolution of government and construction of a new one? This seems to be a very different sort of animal than a typical claim-right emblematic of Hohfeld's first category.

Perhaps, instead, dignities ought to be understood as liberties. A liberty (or privilege), as Kramer notes, says more about the holder of the entitlement and less about the corresponding obligation. Perhaps inalienable rights are more akin to the types of liberties held in a state of nature

[144] Kramer, 65.
[145] Kramer, 67.
[146] Kramer, 68.
[147] Kramer, 65–6.
[148] Kramer, "Moral Rights," 326.
[149] Kramer, 326.
[150] Kramer, 326
[151] Kramer, 326 ("[A]lthough legal rights are often thought to be indissolubly linked to remedies, and although moral rights are often thought to be disseverable from remedies, the truth is precisely the reverse.").

Consider due process—one of the oldest entitlements consistently extended in democratic states. In 1215, the Magna Carta established, "No free man shall be taken, imprisoned, disseised, outlawed, banished, or in any way destroyed, nor will We proceed against or prosecute him, except by the lawful judgment of his peers and by the law of the land."[152] English statutory law replaced "law of the land" with "due process."[153] For Blackstone, this clause protected a cluster of "absolute rights": namely, personal security, personal liberty, and private property.[154] Personal liberty, for Blackstone, rested on a negative construction: i.e., "the power of loco-motion, of changing situation, or removing one's person to whatsoever place one's own inclination may direct; without imprisonment or restraint, unless by due course of law."[155]

The concepts isolated by Blackstone have significant persuasive force in the American context. In 1886, the US Supreme Court used them in the case of *Boyd v. United States* to find a "right to privacy" embedded in the Fourth and Fifth Amendments—a right that nowhere appears in the text of the constitution. In doing so, the Court hearkened back to the principles laid down by Lord Camden in *Entick v. Carrington*, suggesting that they "affect the very essence of constitutional liberty and security."[156] These principles "reach further than the concrete form of the case then before the court ... they apply to all invasions on the part of the government and its employes of the sanctity of a man's home and the privacies of life."[157] The Court continued, "It is not the breaking of his doors, and the rummaging of his drawers, that constitutes the essence of the offense; but it is the invasion of his indefeasible right of personal security, personal liberty and private property, where that right has never been forfeited by his conviction of some public offense—it is the invasion of this sacred right which underlies and constitutes the essence of Lord Camden's judgment."[158]

It was *because of* the existence of the inalienable entitlement that the government was found to have breached its duty to protect Boyd's privacy. Kramer, as aforementioned, points out the shielding effect of claim-rights to liberties. Thus, a liberty to walk on a public thoroughfare without a violation of bodily integrity is protected by a right against being punched, a right against being sexually assaulted, a right against being shot, and the like. Kramer stops short, though, of suggesting the possibility of liberties as the impetus *for the creation of the right*: i.e., the existence of a liberty *is* what motivates the creation of a claim-right. In the case of inalienable liberties, which have no specific legal document as their source, a different type of relationship than those laid out by Hohfeld seems to be at play. That is, the claim-right's existence depends on the prior existence and articulation (or recognition) of the liberty.

152 Magna Carta, cl. 39 (1215), in Howard, *Magna Carta: Text and Commentary*, 45. In 1225, the Crown reissued the document with minor changes to the provision: "No freeman shall be taken, or imprisoned, or be disseised of his freehold, or liberties, or free customs, or be outlawed, or exiled, or any otherwise destroyed; nor will we not pass upon him, nor condemn him, but by lawful judgment of his peers, or by the law of the land." Edward Coke, *The Second Part of the Institutes of the Laws of England* (1797), 1:45.

153 28 Edw. 3, c. 3 (1354).

154 Blackstone, *Commentaries on the Laws*, 1:123, 125.

155 Blackstone, 1:125, 130.

156 *Boyd v. United States*, 116 U.S. 616, 630 (1886) (citing *Entick v. Carrington*, 19 How. St. Tr. 1029 (1765)).

157 *Boyd*, 116 U.S. at 630.

158 *Boyd*, 116 U.S. at 630.

How should we think about inalienable rights that the Court finds as operable, as against the state—even where they are *nowhere* mentioned in the text of the constitution? Is this type of entitlement any different than the "inalienable rights" considered to be prior to the Bill of Rights and not incorporated in them as against one or more of the sovereign powers? Certainly, there are some entitlements that pre-date the Bill of Rights, whose existence stands as bulwark against the violation of certain other entitlements. The language of the framing document may not call them out by name. They capture a collective legal relation between the People and the Government—even as they hold the power to bring a claim-right into being. It is not the entitlement holder that acts on the liberty (or is able to do so), but the entitlement itself (vis-à-vis the state) that *creates* the claim-right.

Hohfeld's jural framings also appear to be inadequate for understanding the power to alter the meaning of textual entitlements associated with (and animated by) dignities. In contrast to the unwritten concepts encapsulated in due process, for instance, the text of the US Constitution twice includes the clause "due process." The document thus explicitly incorporates Blackstone's "absolute rights" into the entitlements afforded the People. Related judicial doctrine has evolved in three ways: procedural due process, incorporation of the first eight clauses in the Bill of Rights (as against the states), and substantive due process.

On the procedural side, the Supreme Court initially rejected efforts to read incorporation of inalienable (procedural) rights into Fourteenth Amendment Due Process clause on the grounds that the rights in question were not sufficiently "fundamental."[159] But over time, that position changed. In 1937, the Court enunciated the due process theory that now incorporates many of the rights in the first eight amendments as against the states.[160] Justice Benjamin N. Cardozo explained that some of the guarantees are so fundamental that they are "of the very essence of the scheme of ordered liberty" and "neither liberty nor justice would exist if they were sacrificed."[161] Exactly what is foundational for due process has expanded.[162]

The Supreme Court, with some regularity, "discovers" fundamental rights in the same written text that previously (ostensibly) did not include them.[163] How does the Hohfeldian framing account for entitlements explicitly incorporated into the text of the constitution, and only later understood as housing further, articulable entitlements? As a matter of substantive due process, in *Lochner v. New York*, the Court unearthed a workers' "freedom of contract."[164] The Court later repudiated its holding, indicating that it would not in the future act with such abandon.[165] The promise proved

[159] See, e.g., *Hurtado v. California*, 110 U.S. 516 (1884) (grand jury indictment not considered within Due Process); *Maxwell v. Dow*, 176 U.S. 581 (1900) (twelve-person jury not considered within Due Process); *Twining v. New Jersey*, 211 U.S. 78 (1908) (Fifth Amendment right against self-incrimination not considered within Due Process).

[160] See *Palko v. Connecticut*, 302 U.S. 319 (1937).

[161] *Palko*, 302 U.S. at 325, 326.

[162] See, e.g., *Grannis v. Ordean*, 234 U.S. 385, 394–5 (1914); *Mullane v. Cent. Hanover Bank*, 339 U.S. 306, 314 (1950); *Benton v. Maryland*, 395 U.S. 784, 794–5 (1969).

[163] See e.g., *Gitlow v. New York*, 268 U.S. 652 (1925) (right to free speech); *Near v. Minnesota ex rel. Olson*, 283 U.S. 697 (1931) (right to free speech).

[164] See *Lochner v. New York*, 198 U.S. 45 (1905).

[165] See *West Coast Hotel Co. v. Parrish*, 300 U.S. 379 (1937).

short-lived. Broad readings of what constitutes fundamental rights has meant that the Court has used various textual hooks to protect entitlements nowhere mentioned in the constitution.[166] Accordingly, in *Mapp v. Ohio*, the Court determined that the Fourth Amendment encapsulated a "right to privacy."[167] In *Griswold v. Connecticut*, the Court found that a couple's right to using contraceptives stemmed from a penumbra emanating from the First, Third, Fourth, and Ninth Amendments.[168] The Court explained in relation to marital privacy, "We deal with a right ... older than the Bill of Rights—older than our political parties, older than our school system."[169] The "right to marry"[170] is considered a fundamental right, as is the "right to an abortion,"[171] and the "right to engage in same-sex intimacy."[172] Entitlements can thus be discovered—and dismissed—in interpretations of the text.

The grounds on which the entitlement is justified as coming within the constitutional remit change. Instead of relying on history and tradition (which, notably, reject these rights), for instance, the Court considers "liberty of the person both in its spatial and in its more transcendent dimensions."[173] Its rationale focuses on unwritten principles that underlie the Bill of Rights. As Justice Anthony Kennedy explains in *Obergefell*, "The nature of injustice is that we may not always see it in our own times. The generations that wrote and ratified the Bill of Rights and the Fourteenth Amendment did not presume to know the extent of freedom in all of its dimensions, and so they entrusted to future generations a charter protecting the right of all persons to enjoy liberty as we learn its meaning."[174] To find same-sex marriage constitutional, the Court reasoned, "the right to personal choice regarding marriage is inherent in the concept of individual autonomy.... Like choices concerning contraception, family relationships, procreation, and childrearing, all of which are protected by the Constitution, decisions concerning marriage are among the most intimate that an individual can make."[175]

What is the status of unknown entitlements, that, assumedly, exist, but need to be "discovered"? One of the virtues of Kramer's account is that it provides for dynamic rights: the alteration or coming-into-being of rights. But that very alteration, *particularly when framed as identifying pre-existing entitlements*—when tradition and history emphatically deny them—raises particular problems. The Court, for instance, has concluded that the right to commit suicide is not a fundamental right because tradition, history, and practice fails to support it.[176] Nevertheless, there is a "constitutionally

[166] See, e.g., *Lochner*, 198 U.S. 45; *Roe v. Wade*, 410 U.S. 113 (1973); *Lawrence v. Texas*, 539 U.S. 558 (2003).

[167] *Mapp v. Ohio*, 367 U.S. 643, 656–7 (1961).

[168] *Griswold v. Connecticut*, 381 U.S. 479, 484 (1965).

[169] *Griswold*, 381 U.S. at 486.

[170] See *Loving v. Virginia*, 388 U.S. 1, 12 (1967) (marriage is "one of the vital personal rights essential to the orderly pursuit of happiness by free men."); *Zablocki v. Redhail*, 434 U.S. 374 (1978) (right to marry burdened from law prohibiting fathers owing child support from marrying); *Obergefell v. Hodges*, 576 U.S. 644 (2015) (right of same-sex couples to marry). See also *M.L.V. v. S.L.J.*, 519 U.S. 102, 116 (1996) (noting that the right to marry is a fundamental right under the Due Process clause).

[171] See *Roe*, 410 U.S. 113.

[172] See *Lawrence v. Texas*, 539 U.S. 558 (2003) (overturning *Bowers v. Hardwick*, 478 U.S. 186 (1986)).

[173] *Lawrence*, 539 U.S. at 562.

[174] *Obergefell*, 576 U.S. at 664.

[175] *Obergefell*, 576 U.S. at 665–6.

[176] *Washington v. Glucksberg*, 521 U.S. 702, 723 (1997) ("We now inquire whether this asserted right has any place in our Nation's traditions. Here ... we are confronted with a consistent and almost universal tradition that has long rejected the asserted right.").

protected right to refuse lifesaving hydration and nutrition."[177] The intervention of a third party is not protected. It is a negative liberty—i.e., the right not to act, but not the right of oneself or others *to* act. But it was not until 1990 that this entitlement was established, as stemming from a dignity that encapsulates bodily integrity.

5. Shielding Effect of Dignities

H.L.A. Hart, looking to general duties, observes how rights may protect the exercise of freedoms.[178] If two people are walking along and see a coin in the road, each may have a liberty to pick it up, but how they exercise that liberty may be dictated by various duties. They could not, for instance, murder the other person to prevent them from picking up the money, as they would be under a duty to respect the right to bodily integrity.[179] Kramer, with a nod to Hart's example, emphasizes the shielding effect as one characteristic of the right/duty and liberty/no-right axis.[180] It may be that a liberty is coupled with a different right—such as the right to bodily integrity, in which case a physical attack, for instance, on a speaker by Y would violate a duty not to assault X. This leads Kramer to observe,

> [O]ne's actions or inactions grounded in liberties are effectively protected—to a considerable extent—by rights that do not pertain specifically to those actions or inactions. Indeed, in almost every situation outside the Hobbesian state of nature, conduct in accordance with a liberty will receive at least a modicum of protection through a person's basic rights.[181]

For Kramer, there is no necessary connection between rights (or duties) and liberties.[182] An individual can have a right to be free from interference without the underlying liberty to perform that act.[183] Kramer points to a factory that is dumping waste (which it is not at liberty to do). Should fishermen occlude the pipe, they would interfere with the factory's right to an unimpeded discharge of emissions.[184] The right to unimpeded flow through the pipes does not entail a liberty to act to send anything through it. Kramer clarifies Hohfeld's scheme by noting that a duty to φ does not imply a liberty to φ, but instead the absence of a liberty to abstain from φ.[185] Similarly, no breach of duty is necessarily implied in a limitation on the privilege.[186]

Nevertheless, the existence of a right gives practical effect to privileges. Kramer writes, "[E]very private actor whose freedom is not a sham must be possessed of legal

177 *Cruzan v. Director, Mo. Dept. of Health*, 497 U.S. 261, 279 (1990).
178 See Hart, "Are There Any Natural Rights?," 179.
179 Hart, 179.
180 Kramer, RWT, 12.
181 Kramer, 11–12.
182 Kramer, 14–15.
183 Kramer, 14; see Kramer, RLPP, 416.
184 Kramer, RWT, 15–16.
185 Kramer, 17–18 (replying to Sumner, *Moral Foundation of Rights*, 23, 33).
186 Kramer, RLPP, 416 ("Moreover, even if the immediate cause of his or her inability to do φ is somebody else's conduct, there may well have been no breach of a legal duty involved.").

rights: rights to the exclusion of others from his body and goods, and rights to be given all things that are his due. Now, each person's overall set of entitlements will typically include legal powers of enforcing or waiving many of his rights. Accordingly, each person who is possessed of meaningful freedom can elect to activate the force of the state."[187] Because the very concept of individual autonomy requires that legal rights protect against others interfering with that right, "we can be certain that many of the legal liberties of all or most people in any free-market society will be accompanied by such rights."[188] The collective force of the state ensures the right: "If people try to engage in conduct that violates the owner's rights against interference with the use of his property, then the state will intervene to prevent or punish the outlawed conduct."[189]

Dignities appear to act in a similar manner toward claim-rights. In *Obergefell*, Kennedy explained: "The nature of marriage is that, through its enduring bond, two persons together can find other freedoms, such as expression, intimacy, and spirituality."[190] The right to marry draws "meaning from related rights of childrearing, procreation, and education."[191] The fact that at no point has the legislature established a claim-right via statutory provision matters naught:

> The dynamic of our constitutional system is that individuals need not await legislative action before asserting a fundamental right. The Nation's courts are open to injured individuals who come to them to vindicate their own direct, personal stake in our basic charter. An individual can invoke a right to a constitutional protection when he or she is harmed, even if the broader public disagrees and even if the legislature refuses to act.[192]

Dissenting in *Obergefell*, Justice Clarence Thomas took the position that what was at stake was a liberty, not a right—a conclusion that carried significant implications. Thomas argued, "Liberty has long been understood as individual freedom *from* governmental action, not as a right *to* a particular governmental entitlement."[193] His objection turned on whether it was a right to governmental recognition of marriage and assignation of benefits thereto, or a freedom of the individual to make vows, hold religious ceremonies recognizing the vows, raise children, and otherwise live with one's partner without interference from the government.[194]

In Hohfeldian terms, Thomas appears to have understood the marriage entitlement (as freedom from government interference) to be a liberty/privilege, not a claim-right. In this sense, it was no different from other liberties enjoyed in a state of nature, described by Locke to consist of "perfect freedom to order their actions and dispose of their possessions and persons as they think fit, within the bounds of the law of nature, without asking leave, or depending upon the will of any other man."[195] That liberty

[187] Kramer, *In the Realm*, 113.
[188] Kramer, 115.
[189] Kramer, 113.
[190] *Obergefell*, 576 U.S. at 666.
[191] *Obergefell*, 576 U.S. at 667.
[192] *Obergefell*, 576 U.S. at 677.
[193] *Obergefell*, 576 U.S. at 726 (Thomas, J., dissenting) (italics in the original).
[194] *Obergefell*, 576 U.S. at 728–9.
[195] Locke, *Second Treatise of Civil Government and a Letter Concerning Toleration*, 4.

might also be created and recognized by state legislation. But there is no attendant duty on the state to refrain from interference in state measures.

If the right to marry is a liberty, which can be altered, then a second-order relation also is in effect: namely, a power to change the privilege.[196] Two points here deserve notice: first, if there is a power in effect, then the entitlement is alienable, and we are no longer speaking about inalienable rights. Second, in the realm of constitutional law, it is primarily (but not exclusively) the courts who hold the power. This is very different from pure criminal measures, where legislatures may hold the power to introduce new provisions to protect persons and property. Where constitutional rights are on the line, post-*Marbury*, the judiciary has the power to alter the liberty. The legislature *cannot* divest a citizen of a constitutional entitlement established by the judiciary. This is largely a function of judicial review. It holds the upper hand for "discovering" rights or adjudicating conflict between rights.

It would be wrong, however, to say that the People, or the executive, or the legislature are under a disability in regard to the power. In the United States, some state judges are elected. Federal ones are appointed. Even those constitutionally protected with life tenure can be removed by elected officials. The legislature has to approve appointments to the Supreme Court. Presidential elections have at times turned in significant measure on judicial appointments. Thus, unlike the private law realm, where the exercise of a power entails the absence of a disability on the power-holder's part and the presence of a liability on someone else's part, in the constitutional rights arena, disability is tempered with various structural checks.

Kramer might respond to the lack of clarity about who holds the power by narrowing the power in question. The power to expand liberties to include the right to marry individuals of the same gender might itself carry some sort of qualification on the exercise of that power, subject to structural constraints. But then the understanding of the power itself is being described not in terms of the entitlement, but by prior conditions—which Kramer rejects in the context of jural relations.

Kramer does consider an example provided by Professor David Lyons, in which a right translates into a power to do something, and not just a duty of non-interference held by others. Lyons writes,

> Suppose that Alvin is atop a soap box speaking to a crowd against United States military involvement in Vietnam. His act is perfectly lawful, but he is assaulted by some private citizens, driven from the box and silenced. Their behavior is unlawful and constitutes unwarranted and prohibited interference with the exercise of his legal rights. In saying this we may refer to his general right of free speech or to a specific right to stand there addressing the crowd. In either case the right might be construed as a right *to do* something.[197]

[196] An additional question could be raised here about whether the right to marry is itself a power. An argument frequently raised in support of same-sex marriage centers on the legal entitlements gained through marriage. It is used here in a different sense than the right itself to form a union that is recognized by the state.

[197] Kramer, RWT, 110–11 (citing and quoting David Lyons, "The Correlativity of Rights and Duties," 49) (italics in original).

Kramer responds by proposing that in the scenario, Alvin has a liberty, but not a right, to speak. The right in question is a right to be free from assaults—which acts as a shield for the privilege of free expression.[198] He writes,

> Had the citizens been able to silence Alvin without assaulting him or violating any of his other rights, they could have done so. The fact that his speech is "perfectly lawful" simply means that the government is not entitled to interfere with his discourse. Unless Alvin breaks the law, he (very likely) has a right against governmental interference and an immunity against being stripped of that right. However, such entitlements scarcely mean that private citizens must abstain from interfering with his discourse.[199]

In some sense, then, Kramer is driven back upon claim-rights as a shield for the assertion of liberties. He applies this framing to a range of questions, such as the right not to be tortured.[200] But to the extent that claim-rights provide shields, they function not as inalienable rights (prior to the duty of non-infringement placed on the government), but as entitlements established by law.

6. Entitlement Creation and the Limits of Powers

How should we understand shifting interpretation of entitlements captured in constitutional text? What jural relations are prior and consequent to such a determination? Are these relations any different than the powers that mark private law?

For more than 100 years after the invention of the telegraph, the Supreme Court did not recognize any constitutional restrictions on government collection of communications carried on wires. It was not until the 1967 case of *Katz v. United States* that the Court shifted its Fourth Amendment property-based approach to one centered on the reasonable expectations of both society and the individual engaged in conversation.[201] That case established the right held by individuals (at least within the United States) to protection against warrantless surveillance for criminal law purposes, and the duty of the government to refrain from infringing that right, outside of a proper warrant procedure (as laid out in the second part of the Fourth Amendment).

If we are to understand the right to make telephone calls without the government listening in to be an (alienable) entitlement, then what brought the claim-right into existence? The answer, as in the same-sex marriage context discussed earlier, is the Court's ruling. In *Katz*, it was not even the majority's decision that carried the day: Justice Harlan's concurrence became the *de facto* standard for ascertaining reasonableness under the Fourth Amendment.[202] Thus, while the majority shifted the focus of Fourth Amendment inquiry from "places" to "persons," ultimately *one justice*

[198] Kramer, RWT, 111.
[199] Kramer, 111.
[200] Kramer, GRR, 81–9.
[201] See *Katz v. United States*, 389 U.S. 347 (1967).
[202] *Katz*, 389 U.S. at 360–2 (Harlan, J., dissenting).

set the course for determining which rights subsequently followed. That one justice thereby exercised a *de facto* power—one, ostensibly, available *de jure* to all nine. What is the jural relation that gave him that entitlement? Is it the power he has by virtue of his exercise of the role of a justice, coupled with facts about the rule of recognition?

Or is it the practice of *stare decisis*, deference by subsequent courts, and acquiescence by the other branches? The concurrence in *Katz* parallels that of a host of other opinions, such as Justice Jackson's concurrence in *Youngstown v. Sawyer* setting out the tripartite framing for the President's exercise of Article II powers in the realm of foreign affairs.[203] But is also reflects ways in which tests established by the majority subsequently govern the weighing of constitutional rights. The exclusionary rule grew from the 1886 case of *Boyd v. United States*.[204] Justice Bradley grasped the import of the decision, explaining: "The principles laid down in this opinion affect the very essence of constitutional liberty and security. They reach farther than the concrete form of the case then before the court, with its adventitious circumstances; they apply to all invasions on the part of the government and its employees of the sanctity of a man's home and the privacies of life."[205] In *Miranda v. Arizona* the Court held that prior to interrogation, a person must be apprised of their Fifth and Sixth Amendment rights—specifically, "he must be warned that he has a right to remain silent, that any statement he does make may be used as evidence against him, and that he has a right to the presence of an attorney, either retained or appointed."[206] The language has been adopted almost verbatim as a routine warning to individuals prior to questioning.

The Hohfeldian framing does not capture these types of legal-juridical relationships. The Court (post-*Marbury*) has an entitlement of deference as held against the executive branch, the legislature, and future courts. It is not just the decision, but the *reasoning* (or test) articulated by the Court that becomes binding. This is not the same as a duty of non-interference. It is an obligation to act consistent with the principle established by the judiciary. For the most part, courts themselves follow it, as an exercise in *stare decisis*. Yet it is not strictly binding. Future justices are free to adopt, or to ignore, the reasoning.

Dissents, too, encapsulate power to bring entitlements—both rights and liberties—into existence. It is not the same as the type of power that Hohfeld identifies, but it is there nonetheless. Constitutional law is replete with examples. Justice John Marshall Harlan's dissent in *Plessy v. Ferguson*, rejecting segregation, states the "Constitution is color-blind, and neither knows nor tolerates classes among citizens. In respect of civil rights, all citizens are equal before the law."[207] A unanimous Court affirmed his position in *Brown v. Board of Education*.[208] Justice Louis Brandeis's famous dissent in *Olmstead v. United States* similarly became the grounds for the Court's position in *Katz*.[209] Justice Scalia's dissent in *Lawrence v. Texas* undergirded the Court's position in *Obergefell*,[210] and so on. The same is true in the United Kingdom: in *Liversidge*

[203] *Youngstown Sheet & Tube Company v. Sawyer*, 343 U.S. 579, 635 (1952).
[204] *Boyd v. United States*, 116 U.S. 616 (1886).
[205] 116 U.S. 630.
[206] *Miranda v. Arizona*, 384 U.S. 436, 444 (1966).
[207] *Plessy v. Ferguson*, 163 U.S. 537, 559 (1896).
[208] *Brown v. Bd. of Educ.*, 347 U.S. 483, 493–5 (1954).
[209] *Olmstead v. United States*, 277 U.S. 438, 471–85 (1928) (Brandeis, J., dissenting); see *Katz*, 389 U.S. 347.
[210] *Lawrence v. Texas*, 539 U.S. 558, 586–605 (2003) (Scalia, J., dissenting); see *Obergefell*, 576 U.S. 644.

v. Anderson, Lord Atkin gave a resounding dissent that underscored the power of judicial review over executive action curtailing liberty—a position adopted by the Supreme Court in *H.M. Treasury v. Ahmad*.[211]

The Hohfeld-Kramer analysis misses the dynamic aspect of law, which is inherent in common law, by which it is the subsequent uptake (the *Rezeptionsgeschichte*) of reasoning and holdings that retroactively turn a prior decision into an entitlement-generator. Instead, they provide only a thin account of legal relations, even as the real legal structure is far more complex. This point has been nicely drawn by Professor Gerald Postema and again by Professor David Luban in their critiques of analytic jurisprudence.[212]

Compounding the analysis, the Court is not the only actor. The legislature, too, can bring a claim-right into being. Throughout much the twentieth century, the government, citing the President's commander-in-chief powers, engaged in warrantless surveillance for national security purposes.[213] In 1972, the Supreme Court rejected the proposition that for matters of domestic security, the executive could unilaterally surveil Americans on U.S. soil.[214] While some sort of process was necessary, it fell to Congress to institute new rules. The 1978 Foreign Intelligence Surveillance Act (FISA) subsequently established a special Court to issue orders approving of electronic surveillance within the United States.[215] Over time, Congress expanded the law to cover the surveillance of U.S. citizens located overseas.[216] The law affirmatively protects Americans' expressive, associative, and religious rights, prohibiting collection premised on otherwise protected First Amendment activities. It also creates a procedure that must be followed by the government to engage in any domestic electronic surveillance, physical search, pen register/trap and trace, or collection of tangible goods for foreign intelligence purposes. Failure to abide by the law carries criminal penalties.

The legislature has power to bring entitlements into being. In this case, that entitlement appears to be a claim-right, as the government is under a duty of non-intervention, with criminal penalties available should the executive overreach and obtain information in violation of the statute. Is the legislature the equivalent of "the People," acting through elected representatives? Perhaps.

7. Purported Rights

The structure of constitutional public law is such that the duty-holder also has the responsibility of enforcement, a situation that is not well-reflected in the Hohfeldian framing and which quickly runs afoul of *nemo iudex in causa sua*. Under the statute

211 *Liversidge v. Anderson* [1942] AC 206 (HL); *HM Treasury v. Ahmed* [2010] UKSC 2 (appeal taken from England).

212 See Gerald J. Postema, "Jurisprudence, the Sociable Science," 101 Va. L. Rev. 869 (2015); David Luban, "Time-Mindedness and Jurisprudence," 101 Va. L. Rev. 903, 912–13 (2015).

213 See, e.g., *Intelligence Activities Senate Resolution 21: Hearings Before the S. Select Comm. to Study Gov't Operations with Respect to Intel. Activities*, 7 vols., 94th Cong. (1975) (Church Committee hearings).

214 See *United States v. U.S. District Court*, 407 U.S. 297 (1972).

215 See Foreign Intelligence Surveillance Act of 1978, Pub. L. No. 95–511, 92 Stat. 1783 (codified as amended at 50 U.S.C. §§ 1801–1885c).

216 See FISA Amendments Act of 2008, Pub. L. No. 110-261, 122 Stat. 2436.

discussed above, for instance (FISA), because of the classified nature of the proceedings and the collection of intelligence, it may *only* be the government that is aware of transgressions. Yet the government must be the one to prosecute (itself) for any violations. Does it make any sense to say that the duty-holder also has the power to waive the right? Or is this a different kind of jural relationship than one contemplated by Hohfeld? If a duty-bearer can simply waive his duties at will, is the duty-bearer really under a duty to perform (or to refrain from performing) a certain act?

The scenario is not far-fetched: it is precisely the state of affairs that erupted into the public domain in December 2019 with a report issued by the Inspector General of the US DOJ. Even though Congress had created a special Court to oversee the process of collecting intelligence, the executive had misrepresented information to the Court, with the result that the government had routinely broken the law. In his first report, the Inspector General found seventeen significant errors, inaccuracies, and omissions in applications related to Carter Page, a foreign policy advisor to the Trump Campaign during the 2016 presidential election.[217] Three months later, a second report focused on twenty-nine applications in which US persons were targeted found errors in every single application, with up to sixty-five in one case.[218]

The situation is hardly novel. Over the past two decades, the executive branch has repeatedly flouted the statutory language and the prohibitions governing foreign intelligence collection on domestic soil.[219] Despite the routine violation of FISA—even where the courts have later determined that the statutory violations have breached the Fourth Amendment constitutional rights of the People—the statutory criminal penalties have never been applied. Not a single government employee has ever been charged with violation. The DOJ, which is in charge of prosecution, also submits applications for surveillance to the Court.

Kramer appears to deny that such a situation could exist. He writes, "criminal behaviour—will hardly be to the liking of the officials who run the legal system wherein the criminal conduct occurs."[220] His claim, though, rests on three premises: first, that officials know about the conduct; second, that the officials who know about the conduct are not compromised in relation to those who undertook the bad conduct; and third, that rule of law matters. In the realm of national security law, each of these can be challenged. Classified environments are famous for being siloed, with very little information getting in or out—including to those in charge of agencies, much less to prosecutors, who are in parallel roles. Further, there is a conflict of interest inherent in expecting the DOJ, which is the entity (mis)representing information to the court (and the agency within which the Federal Bureau of Investigation (FBI) is housed), to then turn around and prosecute itself for doing so. Moreover, a common argument

[217] See Office of the Inspector General, U.S. Department of Justice, *Review of Four FISA Applications and Other Aspects of the FBI's Crossfire Hurricane Investigation*, 378.

[218] See Office of the Inspector General, U.S. Department of Justice, *Management Advisory Memorandum for the Director of the Federal Bureau of Investigation Regarding the Execution of Woods Procedures for Applications Filed with the Foreign Intelligence Surveillance Court Relating to U.S. Persons*, 7.

[219] See Donohue, *The Future of Foreign Intelligence: Privacy and Surveillance in a Digital Age*; Donohue, "Section 702 and the Collection of International Telephone and Internet Content," 117–265; Donohue, "Bulk Metadata Collection: Statutory and Constitutional Considerations," 757–900.

[220] Kramer, GRR, 58.

mounted to defend actions outside the law is that agencies responsible to public safety may have to flout legal restrictions to keep people safe—an approach that itself eschews the importance of the rule of law.

One response that Kramer might have is that the cluster of associated claim-rights are inoperative, unenforced rights. But it is far from clear how to understand the entitlements in terms of Hohfeld's framing. The power of waiving enforcement is held by the executive and the courts (an example of multiple collectives bearing an obligation). Both have routinely waived it. In a classified world, where a clear conflict of interests exists between the government prosecuting (itself) for violations of the statute, it could also be said that there is no power to demand effectuation. This is particularly troublesome in light of the government's claim that it can classify judicial decisions—so that that no one ever can even find out about the violations (or at least those that the Court discovers).

Whilst the power to divest exists as a concomitant to the claim-right (and is thus distinguishable from it), the holding of that power by the entity on whom the obligation rests (i.e., the duty-bearer), raises question about the nature of the first-order relation at play in the constitutional realm.

Perhaps what is needed here is a new category altogether: that of "purported rights," where the enforcement and waiver mechanisms are held by those against whom the entitlement-holder has the right. Underlying the inoperative, unenforced right is a different jural relation: where the duty-holder also has the power of waiver. Central to the Hohfeldian framing is the idea that either the right-holder or someone else *who is not the duty-holder* has the power of waiver. Nigel Simmonds and other Will Theorists critique Interest Theory on these grounds: i.e., allowing for a circumstance in which all powers of enforcement/waiver are held by the state and its officials.[221] Kramer acknowledges, "A state of affairs wherein public officials hold all legal powers of enforcement/waiver would grievously distress anyone who values individual latitude and initiative."[222] But his underlying concern is individual autonomy. In the constitutional public law context, outside of voting new officials into office, significant powers of enforcement are in the hands of the state.

The problem of the duty-holder also determining when a breach can be waived is at times an inescapable aspect of constitutional law. In *Bivens v. Six Unknown Named Agents*, the US Supreme Court held that a suit alleging violation of Fourth Amendment rights could be lodged against federal officers acting under color of law.[223] But the Court went on to carve out exceptions: the President of the United States, for instance, and federal officials engaged in adjudicating administrative disputes, are entitled to absolute immunity.[224] *Pari passu*, lower courts have ruled *Bivens* remedies unavailable in circumstances ranging from First Amendment retaliatory prosecution claims to unconstitutional rendition, detention, and torture.[225] In *Vance v. Rumsfeld*, the

[221] See Kramer, 60–1.

[222] Kramer, 54–5.

[223] See *Bivens v. Six Unknown Named Agents*, 403 U.S. 388 (1971).

[224] See *Nixon v. Fitzgerald*, 457 U.S. 731 (1982); *Butz v. Economou*, 438 U.S. 478 (1978).

[225] See, e.g., *Loumiet v. United States*, 948 F.3d 376 (D.C. Cir. 2020) (First Amendment); *Lebron v. Rumsfeld*, 670 F.3d 540 (4th Cir. 2012) (detention and treatment as an "enemy combatant"); *Arar v. Ashcroft*, 585 F.3d 559 (2d Cir. 2009) (*en banc*) (rendition to Syria); *Rasul v. Myers*, 563 F.3d 527 (D.C. Cir. 2009) (*per curiam*)

Seventh Circuit, sitting *en banc*, categorically denied any *Bivens* remedy for claims of abuse during interrogation by the military.[226] Assuming, *arguendo*, that non-federal remedies do not exist,[227] how should we think about constitutional entitlements in this context?

Kramer argues that, "Most (though not all) of the entitlements conferred by so-called bills of rights are in fact immunities."[228] The clauses in the First Amendment, for instance, protect certain legal liberties by disabling Congress from restricting or removing them.[229] Every person in the United States thereby has an immunity vis-à-vis Congress with respect to the free exercise of religion, freedom of speech, freedom of the press, the right of assembly, and the right to petition.[230] For Kramer, immunities stabilize other legal entitlements. It is "[o]nly because legal rights are almost always accompanied by immunities against most types of divestiture, do they provide solid legal protection against interference or uncooperativeness."[231] The right against bodily harm, for instance, is accompanied by an immunity against others removing this protection. Immunities thus serve as a negative acknowledgement that the right-holder is the one with the choice: the jural relation establishing the claim-right *cannot* be altered by a third party. Simmonds adds that the negative recognition may (or may not) be accompanied by positive recognition (e.g., a power to waive an immunity).[232] If there is no power to waive it, then the immunity is conjoined with a disability.[233]

How ought we to think about the constitutional rights discourse in this context? Criminal law procedural rights seem to present the clearest example of immunities. The Sixth Amendment right to trial by jury means that individuals are free from any power *wielded by others* to waive that right. The state is under a disability in regard to suspending it. Any attempt by a prosecutor to exercise such a power would lack legal effect. So, too, in regard to the rights to a speedy and public trial, confront adverse witnesses, and assistance of counsel. *Pari passu*, the government cannot erode Fifth Amendment protections against double jeopardy or self-incrimination.

The fact *that* they are held by the People, under the constitution, as against the *Government* deprives the Government of the possibility of altering its obligations against the will of the entitlement-holder. Nevertheless, immunity-holders may routinely do precisely that. In public law centered on constitutional rights, where properly assigned as a claim-right, the state (or one of its constituent parts) is *always* the actor with the correlative duty. Where the People hold an immunity, though, the state can

(detention in Guantánamo); *Doe v. Rumsfeld*, 683 F.3d 390 (D.C. Cir. 2012) (treatment by military contractors); *Vance v. Rumsfeld*, 701 F.3d 193 (7th Cir. 2012) (*en banc*) (military interrogation).

[226] See *Vance*, 701 F.3d 195.

[227] But see Vázquez and Vladeck, "State Law, the Westfall Act, and the Nature of the Bivens Question," 509–83.

[228] Kramer, RLPP, 417.

[229] Kramer, 417.

[230] US Const. amend. I ("Congress shall make no law respecting an establishment of religion, or prohibiting the free exercise thereof; or abridging the freedom of speech, or of the press; or the right of the people peaceably to assemble, and to petition the Government for a redress of grievances.")

[231] Kramer, RLPP, 417.

[232] Simmonds, "Rights at the Cutting Edge," 153.

[233] Simmonds, 153.

erode it *in other ways*. It can threaten to bring different charges or to go after family members. It nearly always has access to greater resources than defendants, and it can wield them with devastating affect: loss of liberty, loss of property, or loss of life may follow. To speak of immunities in the face of overwhelming government power falls short of capturing the relationship that is shaped by certain forms of power.

8. Concluding Remarks

Kramer's scholarship advances the analytical value of the Hohfeldian framework. He applies it to the moral realm and tackles its implications for public law. In the process, however, questions arise that challenge whether the pairings capture the essence of the types of jural relations that mark constitutional law. Rights held *in res publica* by the People, collectives, and citizens place a corresponding duty on the entitlement holder not to infringe them. They cannot be altered, as they bind society in respect to future generations. They also act as an umbrella over others. In addition, complex collectives constitute the state, increasing the potential for conflict and, in regard to second order relations, making it nearly impossible to identify the power-holder—a situation exacerbated by the advent of new and emerging technologies. Entirely missing from the juridical framing are "dignities," which are not written and prior to the constitution, but nevertheless binding. By only being enforceable via the electoral process or rebellion, though, they could be considered nominal rights. Nevertheless, they provide an impetus, and shield, for claim-rights. The attendant powers, particularly in relation to written constitutional rights, are complex—to say nothing of purported rights, wherein the state's control of enforcement gives rise to a conflict of interest which, when exercised, alter the meaning of a "duty". The ability to waive one's own obligation, at will, raises question about the extent to which the requirement has meaning and could properly be understood as falling, at all, within Hohfeld's first order relations.

2

Rights, Positivism, and the Vice of Self-Puffery

Why Kramer's Interest Theory is Nearly Right

*Rowan Cruft**

1. Introduction

What is a right? A good answer to this question will explain what distinguishes those duties or obligations whose violation *wrongs someone* from those whose violation simply *does wrong*, without wronging anyone in particular.[1] Fulfillment of the former duties—"directed" duties correlating with rights—can be demanded in a personal way, as "mine by right," by those to whom they are owed; their violation triggers "personal" resentment. By contrast, fulfillment of "undirected" duties that do not correlate with rights can only be demanded in an impersonal way, perhaps on behalf of "the moral community" but not on behalf of specific individuals; and their violation triggers impersonal indignation.[2] Given the contemporary prevalence of rights-based conceptions of normativity, it is important to get clear on what exactly distinguishes those who hold rights correlating with a given duty from those who do not. It is natural to think that when you punch me, you do not simply do wrong, but rather specifically wrong me, violating my rights and not the rights of my neighbor or my dog. But what

* I am really delighted to contribute to this book in Matthew Kramer's honor. When I was a PhD student in philosophy at Cambridge, I contacted Matthew—who was not my supervisor—with some initial work on rights. I was overwhelmed by the generosity and incisive robustness of his comments and support for the remainder of my PhD. Both through his huge body of published work, and through his interactions with others, Matthew offers tireless, meticulous intellectual and practical support for the community of academics working at all stages in legal and political philosophy.

[1] In Thompson's memorable example, if environmental legislation gives rare birds legal rights, then they are wrongable parties under the law; while if it simply gives us legal duties to treat the birds in certain ways, without giving them rights, then they are "raw materials for wrongdoing" (Thompson, "What is it to Wrong Someone? A Puzzle about Justice," 372).

[2] See my Cruft, *Human Rights, Ownership, and the Individual*, ch. 3. See also Bowen "Beyond Normative Control: Against the Will Theory of Rights," 427, on the distinctiveness of directed duties. See Darwall's distinction between the "individual" authority a right-holder has, to make demands and bear reactive attitudes on her own behalf, and the "impersonal" demands and reactive attitudes that we can all hold in relation to any duty, as a "representative" authority ("Bipolar Obligation," 32–4); compare Schaab, "Why it is Disrespectful to Violate Rights: Contractualism and the Kind-Desire Theory," and Gilbert, *Rights and Demands*. Note that I think one can be owed a directed duty without it fully qualifying as a "right," but I ignore this complication in the current essay (Cruft, *Human Rights, Ownership, and the Individual*, ch. 6). Note also that Kramer denies that there are any undirected duties—duties with no correlative rights (see, e.g., Kramer, "Rights Without Trimmings," 59); but even if this is correct, we still need Kramer's theory to identify to whom a duty is owed.

Rowan Cruft, *Rights, Positivism, and the Vice of Self-Puffery* In: *Without Trimmings*. Edited by: Mark McBride and Visa AJ Kurki, Oxford University Press. © Mark McBride and Visa AJ Kurki 2022. DOI: 10.1093/oso/9780198868866.003.0002

does this distinction mark? A theory of rights explains this, and Matthew Kramer's Interest Theory is in my view one of the strongest and most illuminating versions of such an explanation.

In section 2, I explain Kramer's Interest Theory of rights: for Kramer, what makes your duty not to punch me owed to me as my right, and not to my neighbor as hers, is that my interests are necessarily at stake here, in a way that my neighbor's are not. More precisely, for Kramer, someone holds a right when a duty's fulfillment necessarily places that person in a position in which it is typically in the interests of a person to be placed. In section 3, I show where this theory goes wrong: lawmakers can create rights wherever they want, independently of the location of any interests. This makes the satisfaction of Kramer's theory neither sufficient nor necessary for the existence of a right—not even, I will argue, the existence of a morally justified right. In section 4, I note that nonetheless Kramer's theory seems to come very close as a necessary condition on morally justified rights: it is extremely rare to encounter a morally justified right that fails to satisfy Kramer's theory. I explain why this is: rights that fail to satisfy Kramer's conditions will sometimes demand a vicious form of self-puffery from the right-holder. They will sometimes require the right-holder to demand right-fulfilling action in a way that draws attention to themselves (*qua* "right-holder") even though their own good is in no way served by the action demanded. This is self-puffery, and we have moral reasons to avoid requiring it. While these reasons can be overridden, they are important enough to explain why we rarely encounter a justified right that fails to satisfy Kramer's theory. In section 5, I add a further layer of explanation to that developed in the previous section. I suggest that pre-legal moral or natural rights must serve their holders' interests. And I argue that it is rare for there to be strong moral reasons to create legal rights unless they have some foundation in such pre-legal moral or natural rights. This, alongside the self-puffery point of section 4, explains why Kramer's theory is nearly accurate as a necessary condition on justified legal rights; but it is not universally accurate, and it remains unsuccessful as a sufficient condition. So by the end of the essay we will understand why Kramer gets rights nearly right—but not quite!

2. Kramer's Interest Theory of Rights

Kramer's theory of rights says the following:

> A's duty to do PHI is owed to B (as B's right) iff:
>
> A's PHI-ing would necessarily place B in a position that it would typically be in the interests of a party of B's type (human, animal, group) to be so placed.[3]

[3] See Kramer, "Rights Without Trimmings" and the useful refinement in Kramer, "Refining the Interest Theory of Rights"; compare the very similar positive formulation—which highlights also that B must be able to hold rights—in Kurki, "Rights, Harming and Wronging: A Restatement of the Interest Theory," 439. Note the rather similar theory in MacCormick, *Legal Right and Social Democracy: Essays in Legal and Political Philosophy*, 160.

There are two things to note about this reading of Kramer. First, the theory is here offered as an account of rights in general, where this includes legal rights and also pre-legal natural moral rights; and it includes morally justified and morally unjustified legal rights. My reasons for understanding the theory in this way are, on the one hand, because although Kramer presents his theory as primarily focused on legal rights, he notes how it could be readily extended to encompass pre-legal moral rights.[4] On the other hand, I also think that for theoretical reasons we should avoid drawing a sharp distinction between legal and moral rights: these are surely not two separate concepts in the way that there are two types of bank (river bank and financial institution). Reading Kramer's theory as an account of rights in general, encompassing pre-legal moral rights, turns out not to place an unfair burden on the theory: instead, we will see that it is legal rights in particular (Kramer's explicit focus) that cause the biggest trouble for the account.

Secondly, note how the theory as interpreted above offers both a necessary *and a sufficient* condition for the existence of a right. Kramer often presents his theory as offering only a necessary condition.[5] But his famous "Bentham's test"—his test for who qualifies as a right-holder correlating with a given duty—clearly constitutes both a necessary and a sufficient condition for something's being a right. The test, in its final formulation,[6] says:

> In order to determine whether someone holds a legal right under a contract or under any other legal norm, we need to ask what facts are minimally sufficient to constitute a breach of the contract or norm. If and only if at least one minimally sufficient set of facts includes the undergoing of a detriment by some person Q at the hands of some other person R who bears a duty under the contract or norm, Q holds a right—correlative to that duty—under the contract or norm.[7]

At note 9, Kramer adds:

> I have slightly sacrificed accuracy for the sake of readability in this formulation. The phrase "undergoing of a detriment" should really be "undergoing of some development that is typically detrimental for a human being."[8]

The technical concept of "minimal sufficiency" is explained thus:

> The criterion elaborated in the preceding two paragraphs is centred on the property of minimal sufficiency. That property is to be understood as follows. A set of facts is minimally sufficient to constitute a violation of a legal mandate if and only if (1) the set is sufficient to constitute such a violation, and (2) every element of the set is necessary for the set's sufficiency.[9]

[4] See, e.g., Kramer, "Rights Without Trimmings," 8–9.
[5] Ibid., 62.
[6] For the earlier formulation, see ibid., 81–2.
[7] Kramer, "Refining the Interest Theory of Rights," 36–7.
[8] Ibid., n. 9.
[9] Ibid., 37.

To put it roughly, what these passages do is ask us to look at all the ways of violating a given duty or norm. If one such way necessarily—if the duty really is to be violated—places a party in a position that would typically be detrimental for a human being, then that party holds a right correlative to that duty or norm. For example, one way for me to violate my legal *duty not to assault* is for me to assault you: if this really is to be a violation of the legal duty, then it must involve placing you in a position (namely, being assaulted) that is typically detrimental for a human being. Even if you are the rare kind of person who is not damaged by being assaulted on this occasion, you nonetheless hold a right correlating with this duty, because one way of violating it (namely, assaulting *you*) necessarily places you in a position that would *typically* be detrimental for a human. My initial formulation of Kramer's theory at the start of this section focuses on the positive serving of interests involved in non-violation, rather than the detriments generated by violation. My presentation is equivalent to Kramer's in the quotations above.[10]

Kramer's theory is easy to read as correct by appeal to a circular conception of interests. Some of our interests are created by or constituted by our having rights. In particular, when some action is required by a right of mine, I thereby necessarily have a status interest in that action's being performed. Suppose, for example, that we are both soldiers and you have a duty to salute when you see me. Suppose that the rules of our army's law make clear that this duty—to salute in the presence of officers—is owed to the monarch as her right, and not to the officers receiving the salute.[11] In this situation, I might or might not have an interest in being saluted depending on, for example, whether saluting would help me. Even the typical officer might have no interest in being saluted: it would all depend on how useful saluting was overall, including how useful it was to show respect to the monarch in this way. But now suppose the military rules changed so that the duty to salute became owed to the officer saluted, as her right.[12] This bare change would be sufficient, I contend, to make it the case that the officer now had an interest in being saluted. This is a circular interest, created by the duty's being owed to her: an interest in respect for one's status as a right-holder here—that is, an interest in receiving what is owed to one here *as one's right*.[13] Such status interests, along with any others similarly generated by—and hence downstream of—one's having a right obviously have to be excluded from those interests to which we can appeal in applying Kramer's theory of rights. Otherwise, the theory would be too easy to fulfill, allowing us to say that a particular duty qualifies as someone's right because it necessarily serves interests that have been created by its being their right.

Kramer's theory looks strong even when the point above is taken into account. Most rights seem to be such that their fulfillment necessarily places their holder in a position that would typically serve the *rights-independent* interests of anyone so placed. For example, Kramer's theory makes me a right-holder correlative to your promissory duty to deliver what we agreed, because delivery will necessarily place me in a position

[10] See again Kurki, "Rights, Harming and Wronging: A Restatement of the Interest Theory," 439.

[11] This is, I believe, the convention in the British army, where saluting acknowledges the officer's commission from the queen.

[12] The convention in the US army, I believe.

[13] Cruft, *Human Rights, Ownership, and the Individual*, 23–6.

(receipt of what we agreed on) that is typically in the interests of people so placed. For it seems to be necessarily the case, given that a person has signed up to an agreement, that it is *typically* in such a person's interests to receive what they agreed to, even if it is not *inevitably* in their interests—as when one thinks one wants something, but it turns out not to fulfill one's desires after all. Similarly, others keeping off some property which one is uniquely empowered to use is typically in one's interests. And not being assaulted necessarily places one in a position (that of not-being-assaulted) that is typically in the interests of a party so placed. Perhaps some of these claims are debatable;[14] but in thinking through canonical cases of rights, it seems fairly clear that Kramer's theory fits them well.

3. Positivism and Interest-Free Rights

The major problem for Kramer's theory is that lawmakers can create rights wherever they want, independently of the location of rights-independent interests. Let us consider a well-discussed example: the legal right parents hold, under the British welfare system, to receive "child benefit payments" from the state to help them care for their children.[15] It seems to me that it is entirely up to those who make and reform English and Scottish welfare law to decide whether this legal duty—the state's duty to make payments to parents—is owed to parents as their legal right, to children as theirs, to communities, or to nobody. But as Kramer himself notes, parents typically have an interest in caring for their children. And receiving child benefit payments therefore necessarily places parents in a position that is typically beneficial for them.[16] The state's breaching its duty by not paying one parent would necessarily place that parent in a position that was typically detrimental. So Kramer's theory seems to give lawmakers no choice: if they are to create the duty to make child benefit payments to parents, it seems that that duty *has to* correlate with a right for parents, whatever lawmakers might want to say. (Note that it seems the same legal duty also has to correlate with a right for children; for they are also typically benefited by such payments.)[17]

[14] E.g., Wenar argues that if a certain kind of Marxist position is correct, in which it turns out that respect for property rights is typically bad for owners, then Kramer will have to conclude that the legal duties not to trespass that constitute property do not really constitute legal *rights* for owners (Wenar, "The Nature of Claim-Rights," 205 n. 9). Kramer's response to this ("In Defence of the Interest Theory of Right-Holding: Rejoinders to Leif Wenar," 71) reveals that genuinely to challenge his theory, the relevant Marxist position would have to maintain that respect for one's own property rights is bad for one even in our current capitalist world: that one as an individual would do better with one's own property disrespected even if all owners around one had theirs respected. This seems very unlikely. Nonetheless I still doubt that the status of legal property as a right should turn on whether it is good for one in any such sense. The concern here is akin to that raised in my next section.

[15] See, e.g., Raz, "Rights and Individual Well-Being," 50; Wenar, "The Nature of Claim-Rights," 204.

[16] Kramer, "In Defence of the Interest Theory of Right-Holding: Rejoinders to Leif Wenar," 81.

[17] If one tries to resist this by narrowing the relevant interests to "legally recognized" interests, I think one is moving towards the circular conception of interests rejected in the previous section: I do not see how one can get the right results without making the relevant "legally recognized interest" simply a status interest created by a party's having a right. Any other conception of "legally recognized interests" will reopen the possibility that a particular legal duty will have to correlate with someone's right despite the fact that lawmakers intend it not to.

In my view, this is an unhappy result for Kramer. It seems inconsistent with the spirit, if not the letter, of his legal positivism.[18] It seems to me that lawmakers should have the power to determine which legal duties correlate with whose legal rights, untethered by the location of rights-independent interests. This seems most consonant with a legal positivism in which the shape of the law is fully up to us, within the constraints of logic. In particular, it seems to me that just as the creation of legal duties is up to us without being constrained by the location of interests, so such duties' status as rights should be similarly up to us. Kramer could reply that it is the constraint of logic—the nature of our concepts—that limits lawmakers in the latter case. This would be a respectable reply, one that Will Theorists and indeed any reductive analysis of rights could also make.[19] But should we really see the concept of a right as so limiting for lawmakers? Must we insist that, for example, legal systems that require the state to make payments to parents necessarily therefore give parents legal rights? Surely lawmakers could, if they wish, decide that these same legal duties *do not confer legal rights on parents*, but instead confer legal rights on the monarch alone, or on the family dog, or on couples without children (each of whom would thereby hold a right *that parents be given child benefit payments*). Kramer's theory makes it impossible for the relevant legal duty to avoid correlating with parents' rights, and thereby unduly limits the leeway lawmakers have to create rights wherever they want, correlating with or uncorrelating with any duty at their say-so.[20]

The example just examined challenges Kramer's theory as a *sufficient condition* on a duty's correlating with a right: it is a case where a duty (to make child benefit payments) fulfills Kramer's condition, but still need not thereby confer the right (on parents) that Kramer says it must. It is harder to find examples challenging Kramer's approach as a *necessary condition*. Or at least it is harder to find morally justified examples. When we look at morally unjustified legal or conventional rights, many relevant examples emerge: take, for instance, the "right" to "protection payments" held by a crime boss. In my moralized view of interests, receipt of such payments does *not* serve the interests of the crime boss even if it makes them wealthy. Of course one might question this conception of interests but I leave that debate for another occasion.[21]

It seems to me that the cases from which we can learn most about Kramer's theory as a necessary condition are *morally justified legal rights*. Given the leeway lawmakers have to create rights wherever they want, as outlined in the previous paragraphs, it is surprisingly hard to find examples of morally justified legal rights that

[18] For similar more detailed discussion, see Kurki, ch. 4 in this book. Note that my position is close to the positions that he calls "Rights Deference," though I would not say that *whenever* lawmakers think they are creating rights, they therefore must be doing so: deluded lawmakers who think they are creating rights by growing potatoes, say, are just deluded.

[19] For argument that we should avoid any such reductive analysis, see Cruft, *Human Rights, Ownership, and the Individual*, chs 2 and 3. I develop an alternative account of rights in ibid., ch. 4.

[20] The military example in the previous section reinforces my point in this paragraph: surely those who create the military rules can decide whether the action of *saluting officers* is owed to officers as their right, or is instead owed simply to the monarch. Kramer's theory takes this decision out of military lawmakers' hands, making it depend simply on the rights-independent interests of the parties involved.

[21] Cruft, *Human Rights, Ownership, and the Individual*, 22. Consider also Wenar on Marx on property again: if property is unjustified and does not serve owners' real interests even in our capitalist world, then Kramer seems compelled to deny that legal property really confers rights—see n. 14. For relevant discussion of what interests are, see also Bowen, ch. 3 in this book.

do not serve their holders' interests in Kramer's way. Even though his theory forces us to find rights where we should not (as in the child benefit case), it is hard to find cases where we clearly encounter justified rights even though they do not fit his theory. Consequentialist moral justifications open some possible cases. For example, consider again the military case from section 2. Suppose that military lawmakers decide to create an absurd duty requiring private soldiers to salute officers in the heat of battle when this impedes everyone's military progress. It is hard to see what rights-independent interests this saluting could serve for the typical officer. And yet it seems to me that if military lawmakers say that this duty constitutes a right for officers, then it will do so: an absurd right-to-be-saluted-in-the-heat-of-battle-when-this-impedes-one.[22] Furthermore, it seems to me that such a right could be morally justified if, for example, it was the only way to satisfy the whim of an eccentric billionaire who had made the creation of such absurd rights a condition on her supporting some other very worthy cause elsewhere. This would be a consequentialist moral justification for creating a legal right that Kramer's theory tells us cannot be created. (Of course, Kramer allows that military lawmakers could create the relevant legal *duty*—he just disallows that this could be officers' legal *rights*, in the absence of appropriately located rights-independent interests. And that is what I deny.)

The possibility of consequentialist "all things considered" justifications seems to open the door for many morally justified legal rights that fail Kramer's analysis. Strange circumstances might morally justify lawmakers in making the college cat hold rights correlating with all legal duties in the land.[23] Or they might justify lawmakers in creating a standing legal duty to whistle on Tuesday evenings, owed as their right to all people under the age of twenty. With sufficient goods at stake, almost anything like this could be morally justified. Why, then, do such cases seem so rare in practice? Why are most of the morally justified rights we encounter in actuality related to right-holders' independent interests in the way Kramer's account would suggest—even if his account also wrongly over-generates rights, as in the child benefit case? I answer this question in the next two sections. This will get us to the heart of the partial truth in Kramer's account.

4. Rights Without Interests and the Vice of Self-Puffery

To understand why most morally justified rights satisfy Kramer's theory, we need to start by observing that to hold a right correlative to a duty gives one a special status to demand that duty's fulfillment *in one's own name as right-holder*, and to personally resent its violation—if one is capable of such things.[24] Such personal demanding or resentment draws special attention to oneself as right-holder. Paradigmatically, it

[22] Compare MacCormick's (*Legal Right and Social Democracy: Essays in Legal and Political Philosophy*, 64) claim that we should be ready to find rights whenever the relevant legal system says they exist: "when the legislature confers a right *eo nomine* . . . , it is in effect left to the courts to effect a structure of duties and remedies sufficient to secure the right in question." See also n. 18.

[23] Compare Feinberg's "sovereign rights monopoly" ("The Nature and Value of Rights," 146).

[24] See Feinberg "The Nature and Value of Rights,"; compare Cruft, *Human Rights, Ownership, and the Individual*, ch. 3, Darwall, "Bipolar Obligation," and Gilbert, *Rights and Demands*.

involves demanding in the first person that the duty-bearer do what they must *for me* or *to me*. Personal resentment is distinguished from impersonal indignation by a similar first-personal focus on the action in question as *wronging me*, rather than simply *being wrong*. It is notable that these special actions that right-holders can perform—personal demanding or resentment—are not simply morally permitted when one is a right-holder, but are also sometimes morally called for. In some circumstances, failing to demand that one's rights be respected involves a morally vicious failure to stick up for oneself.[25]

Now we should consider how these distinctive actions that come with the status of "right-holder" appear when performed by those who hold morally justified rights that fail Kramer's analysis. Think of the military officer holding the absurd right of the previous section. As a right-holder, she is permitted and sometimes even required to demand respect for her right: a demand issued in the first person that the relevant saluting is to be done, as she should put it, "to me." But in this case, such a demand by hypothesis does nothing for her interests, nor even would such demanding serve the interests of a typical holder of the absurd right. Demanding fulfillment of the right in this case involves the right-holder drawing attention to herself—as owed the salute in her own name *qua* right-holder—even though such action does nothing for her or anyone in her position, and her interests form no part of the moral justification for the existence of the right. Demanding respect for the right in this case looks like a vicious form of self-puffery: it says "this action is about me" or "this action is for me" when the action does nothing for the demander's rights-independent interests, and its justification has nothing to do with these interests either.[26]

Let me say more about why such self-puffery is a vice. Demanding and resentment, along with forgiveness, waiver, and punishment, are attitudes and actions whose possibility is logically parasitic on the existence of prior duties. When the demanding, resentment, and so on is "personal," to be done behalf of someone specific, it is logically parasitic on the existence of prior duties owed to someone as their right. To be possible at all, demanding, resentment, forgiveness, and so on have to be appropriately related to the prior duty or right on which they are parasitic: this is why consequentialist justifications for punishing those who have not violated any duty fail to justify an action that can really be called "punishment"—even if they succeed in justifying something like it.[27] But even when we have created or found a duty or right that makes

[25] I am not denying the importance of "turning the other cheek" in appropriate circumstances; I just claim that in many other circumstances virtue requires one to claim one's due in one's own name.

[26] One might try to argue against the charge of self-puffery in this case by claiming that the right-holder's standing interest in the fulfillment of *any* morally justified duty means that even in this case the right-holder has an interest served by fulfillment: the rather abstract "interest in people doing their justified duty." But is this really an interest? Is my well-being really advanced by others respecting each other—even on the other side of the world independently of any impact on me? Even if this is in my interests, it is an interest that cannot be admitted into Kramer's framework, on pain of making any morally justified duty owed to everyone as everyone's right: for this is the kind of interest that everyone has in your not punching me, or in your saluting in the absurd way, or in any other action required by morally justified duty. Allowing this interest into Kramer's framework would therefore make any given morally justified duty correlate with rights held by everyone—a very problematic result which fails to give those who intuitively hold rights their special status.

[27] See Hart on the "definitional stop" response to utilitarian justifications of punishment (*Punishment and Responsibility*, 5).

demanding, resentment, forgiveness, punishment, and the other parasitic actions and attitudes logically possible, to perform these virtuously our demanding, resentment, and so on must be done for the right reason: it must appropriately reflect the moral reasons for creating the right or duty. Or in the case of pre-legal, natural rights and duties, our demanding, resentment, and so on must reflect these rights' and duties' grounds. Demanding that you not torture my neighbor because this will make me upset is a vice of the kind we are considering: my demand here should focus on and be grounded in concerns about how your action harms my neighbor, not in how it upsets me. Similarly, if we have strong consequentialist reason to create a law banning whistling—because it is dangerous for domestic cats, say—then my resenting your whistling because of its untunefulness is another example of this vice: my resentment should focus on the reasons that justify creating the law, namely, the cats' well-being.

The self-puffery evident in demands by right-holders for fulfillment of rights that fail to satisfy Kramer's analysis is an example of the same vice. As a demand for fulfillment of a *right*, the relevant action has to draw attention to the right-holder as having special status in relation to the duty in question: this is an unavoidable feature of its being a demand for fulfillment of a right. But by hypothesis the relevant right is not related to its holder's interests. That is why the case fails Kramer's analysis. The absurd military saluting right was one example. Its structure as a right permits, or even sometimes compels, actions of demanding focused on the right-holder—where this just has to be vicious: such a "right-holder focus" is the morally wrong kind of focus, inappropriate to the case, given that the right's fulfillment does not serve the holder's interests, nor even the interests of the typical holder of such a right.

For clarity, I should summarize: I have argued that it is possible to create rights that fail Kramer's analysis, like the absurd military one just mentioned. Lawmakers have leeway to create rights independently of the location of interests. Further, it is possible to demand the satisfaction of these rights on one's own behalf as right-holder: the existence of the rights makes such demanding logically possible. It is just that one would act *pro tanto* wrongly were one to demand one's rights in those instances: one would be engaging in self-puffery.

If demanding fulfillment of rights that fail Kramer's analysis is necessarily vicious, involving self-puffery on the part of the right-holder, and if (as section 2 argued) we can create rights wherever we want through lawmaking untethered to interests, we might wonder why we do not encounter such rights-generated vicious self-puffery more often. I suggest that three reasons working together explain this. First the viciousness of this kind of self-puffing demanding gives us reason against creating any legal rights that will license it. This reason can be overridden by countervailing considerations, but it still has notable weight: other things being equal, we should avoid setting up legal or conventional normative structures that permit, or even sometimes require, the self-puffery outlined.

Secondly, there are often very few strong countervailing reasons that specifically speak in favor of creating a given legal duty *as a right*. Often we have reasons to create some sort of legal duty, and whether it is a party's right makes little difference to our achievement of the ends that justify the creation of the law. For instance, if our aim is to secure efficient traffic management, we can do that by creating a set of legal duties about the rules of the road and parking. Whether these involve *rights* (e.g., that others stop at red lights, or respect spaces one has paid for), and who might hold such rights, are in my view issues that are not central to whether the aims of the system will be achieved. A system that involved the same legal *duties* (to stop on red, to respect paid-for spaces) but without these being anyone's rights,[28] or with all the rights being held by the state as a "sovereign right monopoly,"[29] could be just as effective—or nearly as effective—as one that involved individually-held rights. Everyone would still have to respect the duties in question, and such respect could be demanded from each duty-bearer in an "impersonal" way as required by their duty; violation of the duties could similarly be resented in an "impersonal" way on behalf of all. The only thing missing by not creating individual rights would be the possibility for "personal" demanding on behalf of a particular party, and "personal" resentment, forgiveness, waiver, etc. Because impersonal versions of these actions and attitudes would still be possible, the case for creating these legal duties *as rights* turns simply on any extra value inhering in such "personal" actions rather than their "impersonal" counterparts. If our aim is simply to affect people's action, then there will rarely be much value in shifting to the "personal" here. Perhaps people are a little extra motivated to police what they conceive to be "their rights," owed specifically to them. But such considerations are fairly weak, and in my view unlikely to outweigh the reasons in the other direction—reasons not to create rights that would license self-puffery.

And yet, a reader might think, the example I have just given frequently is conceived in rights terms: for example, when someone drives on the wrong side of the road it can indeed seem plausible to say that they violate the rights of other road users. But here there is no self-puffery. The explanation of this is our third reason which, together with the two above, explains why we rarely encounter justified rights that fail Kramer's analysis. This third reason is that the strongest case for making a legal duty *take the form of a right* is when this legal duty is founded on or operationalizes a prior moral or natural right. And pre-legal moral or natural rights serve their holder's interests. I explain pre-legal rights' link to interests in the next section. In the current section I simply note that because—as the second reason above tells us—there is comparatively little change to people's actions effected by creating duties that take the form of rights, as opposed to undirected duties or duties held as a "sovereign right monopoly," it turns out that our best reason for creating legal duties *as right*s is not because of the effects we can generate through this on action. Rather, our best reason for creating legal duties as rights is because of the understanding we can engender by giving legal duties a rights-type shape that reflects their underlying natural rights foundations. Legal duties that operationalize natural rights should take a rights-type form so that people truly understand that in their dealings with such duties they are dealing with pre-legal moral natural rights.[30] This is why the legal duty to drive on the correct side of the road should take such a form: when it is violated, the violator threatens pre-legal

[28] Note that Kramer would deny this possibility (Kramer, *A Debate Over Rights: Philosophical Enquiries*, 59).

[29] Feinberg, "The Nature and Value of Rights"; compare Ihara, "Are Individual Rights Necessary? A Confucian Perspective" for a similar point to that in the main text.

[30] For a fuller argument to this conclusion, see Cruft, *Human Rights, Ownership, and the Individual*, esp. ch. 9. For a complication—a further good moral ground for creating legal rights, other than their foundation in pre-legal natural rights—see n. 38 below.

natural moral rights of other road users, such as the natural right not to be killed. If such pre-legal rights were not at stake, the case for giving the legal duties a rights-type form would be significantly weakened.

In summary, there are three reasons which together explain why we rarely encounter morally justified rights that fail Kramer's theory: (1) such rights would license a vicious self-puffery that we have reason to oppose; (2) in the absence of underlying pre-legal natural moral rights, there are rarely strong reasons to create legal rights as opposed to mere undirected legal duties; (3) the best reason to create legal rights is to reflect underlying pre-legal natural moral rights—and we will see in the next section that such natural moral rights must serve their holders' interests. Together, these factors explain why we should rarely encounter morally justified rights (i.e., rights for which there are successful moral reasons) that are wholly separate from holders' interests. But this does not mean that such rights can never be encountered, as Kramer's theory requires. Nor does it mean that all duties that are related to interests in the way Kramer's theory requires must therefore be rights; as noted before, Kramer's theory fails as a sufficient condition even though it gets very close as necessary one.

5. Pre-Legal Moral Rights and Kramer's Theory

An "Interest Theory" of specifically *pre-legal moral or natural rights* seems to me extremely plausible. If we consider those rights most likely to exist independently of law, as natural rights, we find rights that very plausibly serve their holders' interests: for example, rights against torture and assault, rights to have a say in how one's community is run, rights to minimal freedom or autonomy, rights against discrimination and to equal treatment and concern.[31] For such pre-legal moral or natural rights, an approach based on Raz's version of the "Interest Theory" strikes me as especially attractive: a person A holds a natural moral right that someone B perform some action or inaction (not torture A, give A a say in how we should live together, etc.) if and only if A's interests are sufficiently important to constitute a major part of the moral grounds for B's natural moral duty to perform that action or inaction.[32] On this account, to refer to a person's pre-legal moral or natural rights is to refer to those duties borne by others that exist independently of our say-so, and which *owe their existence largely to the importance of that particular person's interests*—rather than, for example, to the importance of the aggregated interests of many, or to the importance of values distinct from human interests. The existence of pre-legal moral or natural rights, on this Razian account, is essential to what Rawls identifies as the moral "separateness of persons."[33] For on this Razian account of pre-legal moral or natural rights, the idea is

[31] Consider the rights on the 1948 Universal Declaration, or the European Convention, or the 1789 French Declaration, or earlier lists and declarations, etc.

[32] Raz, *The Morality of Freedom*, ch. 7. Important theorists who adopt the Razian account for pre-legal moral rights include, in my view, Brownlee, *Being Sure of Each Other* and Fabre, *Whose Body is it Anyway?*. For more on this "justificatory" Interest Theory—as opposed to Kramer's Interest Theory in which the right-holder's interests need not *ground* or *justify* the relevant duty—see Bowen, "Beyond Normative Control: Against the Will Theory of Rights," 430, and Kurki's contribution to this volume.

[33] Rawls, *A Theory of Justice*, 27.

that a particular person's interests work largely on their own to generate the existence of duties that serve it: this picture sees natural duties as generated primarily by the individual's good in some sense prior to consideration of her relation to others.[34] Such duties generated pre-legally by an individual's interests will be owed to the relevant individual as her moral or natural rights.

I recognize that I have not argued for the Razian conception of pre-legal moral or natural rights above, but have simply sketched it. For argument, I refer the reader to other work.[35] For now, we should note, first, that Raz's account struggles as a general account of all rights, because many legal rights owe their moral justification centrally to factors beyond the individual's interests: consider a business manager's morally justified legal right that her employees do as she say, for example; this is not morally grounded by the business manager's own interests, but by much wider considerations about the value of economic structures that include businesses that can confer authority on people. Raz's account is plausible only as a theory of pre-legal moral or natural rights. Secondly, we should note that Kramer's account, while faring better overall as an account of rights in general (both legal and moral), seems not quite as strong as Raz's *as a theory specifically of pre-legal moral or natural rights*. By requiring only that rights be necessarily related to their holders' interests, rather than that their holders' interests morally ground them, Kramer's account does not register the way that pre-legal moral or natural rights are the normative structures that make practical reason reflect the Rawlsian separateness of persons. For Kramer's account would seem to allow a pre-legal moral or natural duty to count as my right even if my interests play no part in grounding it—just so long as its fulfillment necessarily places me in a position that would typically serve them.[36]

It is notable that if the sketched Razian account of pre-legal moral or natural rights is correct, then any pre-legal moral or natural right will *also* satisfy Kramer's account: a duty *morally justified* in part by how the dutiful action serves a particular person's interests will also be such that its fulfillment *necessarily serves* that person's interests. Because of this, any pre-legal moral or natural right will satisfy Kramer's conditions.[37] This gives us a further explanation of why it is hard to find examples of morally justified legal rights that fail to fit Kramer's theory. This is because, as argued in section 4, the best reason to make a legal rule or duty take the form of a right is when the relevant legal rule or duty reflects or gives legal form to an underlying pre-legal natural moral right. As mentioned before, there is normally little gained in making a legal duty into someone's right if the moral justification for creating and sustaining that legal duty is largely unrelated to the recognition of prior natural moral rights. If

[34] See Cruft, *Human Rights, Ownership, and the Individual*, ch. 8 for detailed analysis of different degrees of natural duty-generation by an individual's good.

[35] Ibid., chs 7–8.

[36] In correspondence, Kramer has come closer to Raz's account in relation to pre-legal moral rights. Note that Kramer's account also requires us to draw a distinction between vicarious and non-vicarious interests in a way that Raz's avoids: otherwise, Kramer would make me hold rights correlating with duties owed to, e.g., family members for whom I am concerned (see, e.g., Kramer and Steiner, "Theories of Rights: Is there a Third Way?," 303). Raz avoids this by distinguishing as right-holder only the party whose interests morally ground the relevant duty.

[37] Of course this does not hold the other way round: not all rights satisfying Kramer's analysis must be pre-legal natural moral rights.

this is correct—if most often the moral justification for creating a legal duty *as a right* is that it is founded on a prior natural moral right—then because pre-legal natural moral rights will satisfy Kramer's conditions, we should expect most justified legal rights similarly to satisfy his conditions. Morally justified legal rights that fail Kramer's conditions and license self-puffery must be rare.

6. Conclusion

Kramer's theory has been shown unsuccessful as a sufficient condition on a duty's correlating with someone's right (section 3), but nearly correct as a necessary condition on a morally justified duty's correlating with someone's right (sections 4 and 5). This, I have argued, is because pre-legal natural moral rights must fulfill Kramer's condition (because they must also fulfill Raz's), and the majority of morally justified legal and socially created rights are likely to be based on such pre-legal natural moral rights.[38] But we need to leave open the possibility of rare consequentialist moral reasons that justify creating legal or conventional rights with no underlying pre-legal natural moral right. Such justified legal or conventional rights could readily fail Kramer's theory. Their morally justified existence will then license their right-holders in engaging in self-puffing demands for the fulfillment of their rights, and self-puffing resentment at violation. We should avoid licensing such self-puffery, where possible.[39]

[38] There is a complication I have ignored in this essay. As well as institutionalizing pre-legal natural moral rights, legal rights can also be regularly plausibly morally justified when they enable someone to perform her specific morally justified duties—even in the absence of specific pre-legal natural rights to do this. But such cases will again fit Kramer's theory, given our standing interest in doing what we have morally justified duty to do (see Cruft, *Human Rights, Ownership, and the Individual*, ch. 14). So the space for morally justified legal rights that fail Kramer's theory is still very limited.

[39] Thanks to Joe Bowen, Mark McBride, and Visa Kurki for written comments, and to the participants at a Cambridge workshop on Kramer for earlier points. Thanks of course also to Matthew Kramer himself—see opening note!

3

The Interest Theory of Rights at the Margins

Posthumous Rights

Joseph Bowen[*]

1. Introduction

Many think that the Will Theory of Rights is implausibly underinclusive.[1] Roughly, the Will Theory says that, necessary and sufficient for an individual's holding a right is that the individual has some measure of control over the duty that will be correlative with the right.[2] Because of the theory's focus on normative control being necessary and sufficient for a right's existence—as well as its direction, that is, to whom the correlative directed duty is owed—the Will Theory has trouble recognizing people with undeveloped, compromised, or damaged rational capacities (e.g., very young children, the severely mentally disabled, and some of those suffering from Alzheimer's disease), animals, the dead, and future people as right-holders.

In "Getting Rights Right," Matthew Kramer takes up whether some of these entities are potential legal right-holders on the Interest Theory of rights. This is an important question when assessing the extensional adequacy of the Interest Theory.[3] The potential pressure can come from two directions. First, if one thinks some entity is *not* a right-holder, and yet the Interest Theory is *committed* to them being a right-holder, one might object to the Interest Theory. For example, suppose we think that it is both implausible that trees hold rights and yet think that the Interest Theory is committed

[*] My thanks for helpful discussion to Karamvir Chadha, Colin McLean, and participants at the workshop in honor of Matthew Kramer. For helpful written comments, thanks to Rowan Cruft, Matthew Kramer, Visa Kurki, Mark McBride, and Theron Pummer. My thanks also to Cécile Fabre, under whose supervision work on an earlier version of this chapter began. Finally, thanks to those involved in a discussion following Larry Temkin's Moral Philosophy Seminar in 2015, where Temkin and I tried to argue that posthumous harm and benefit is not possible; as will be seen from the discussion in section 3.2, I now think Temkin and I were wrong. This work was supported by an AHRC Scottish Graduate School for the Arts and Humanities doctoral training partnership studentship (grant no. 1804818) and a Society for Applied Philosophy doctoral scholarship.

[1] See, e.g., MacCormick, "Rights in Legislation," 189–209; MacCormick, "Children's Rights: A Test-Case for Legal Rights," 154–66; Kramer, "Rights Without Trimmings," 7–112; Bowen, "Beyond Normative Control: Against the Will Theory of Rights."

[2] This chapter focuses on claim-rights. On the Hohfeldian framework, X holds a claim-right against Y that $Y\ \Phi$, iff Y is under a duty to Φ, owed to X. We can see debates over theories of rights as debates over *what it is* to owe a duty to another.

[3] Extensional adequacy should not be taken as sufficient for a theory's plausibility. Rather, it should be seen as analogous to general appeal to intuitions as part of wide reflective equilibrium, found elsewhere across analytic moral, legal, and political theory. For discussion of methodology in rights theory, see Van Duffel, "Adequacy Constraints for a Theory of Rights," 187–202; Kurki, "Rights, Harming and Wronging: A Restatement of the Interest Theory."

Joseph Bowen, *The Interest Theory of Rights at the Margins* In: *Without Trimmings*. Edited by: Mark McBride and Visa AJ Kurki, Oxford University Press. © Mark McBride and Visa AJ Kurki 2022. DOI: 10.1093/oso/9780198868866.003.0003

to seeing trees as right-holders. Then, the Interest Theory is in trouble. Second, if one thinks some entity *is* a right-holder, and yet the Interest Theory *cannot* recognize that entity as being a right-holder, one might object to the Interest Theory. For example, suppose we think that it is both plausible that the dead hold rights and yet that the Interest Theory cannot recognize the dead as right-holders. Then, the Interest Theory is in trouble.

This chapter takes up whether the dead are potential right-holders on the Interest Theory, as well as laying clear how we should approach the question of whether other entities are potential right-holders on the Interest Theory. I argue the dead are potential right-holders on the Interest Theory, but that Kramer's argument for this thesis is not very convincing. This is because Kramer's argument looks in the wrong place by focusing only on the ways in which the dead figure in the lives of the living. Instead, I argue we should focus on the nature of the interests of the dead themselves.

Section 2 begins by introducing several choice-points for the Interest Theory. Of most importance for whether the dead are potential right-holders is what interests consist of. If we find the dead do not have interests, they are not potential right-holders on the Interest Theory. Section 2.3 distinguishes three types of views of interests. I argue that we should go for a narrow conception of interests, as opposed to the capacious notion of interests offered by Kramer. Yet, I also argue that deciding which way to go here is ultimately a terminological matter. Section 3 turns directly to whether the dead are potential right-holders on the Interest Theory. Section 3.1 argues that Kramer's argument for the dead being potential right-holders is not very convincing for it fails to focus on the nature of the dead's interests themselves. Section 3.2 introduces a different argument—that the dead have interests (or that the dead's interests matter for rights) for much the same reason that the living have interests.

Before beginning, three preliminaries. First, suppose we find that the dead do not hold rights on the Interest Theory. This does not mean, if the Interest Theory is correct, that the dead cannot figure in our duties nor, even, that the duties cannot exist for the sake of those deceased.[4] Rather, it means only that we would not owe those duties to the dead, and that the dead would not hold correlative rights against us. Let us take a different example. For sake of illustration, suppose that animals are not potential right-holders. This does not mean that we do not have duties in which animals figure. For example, we may have directed duties, owed to other human beings, not to harm animals (e.g., duties correlating with contractual, promissory, or property rights). We may have directed duties owed to ourselves not to harm animals. Further, we may have undirected duties not to harm animals.[5] These undirected duties could be agent-centred (because our moral or legal theory dictates that *we* ought not treat other living things in these ways) or patient-centred (for the animal's own sake). The same could be true of the dead.

[4] See Kramer, "Getting Rights Right," 30–1.

[5] Kramer would not admit this, since he does recognize undirected duties: Kramer, "Rights Without Trimmings," 24. I find the correlativity axiom implausible when understood in this way. Instead, I think it should be understood as saying all claim-rights correlate with *directed* duties (hence how I have defined claim-rights in n. 3). Understood in this way, we can be agnostic at a conceptual level on whether undirected duties exist. See also Kurki, ch. 4 in this volume for further discussion of the correlativity axiom.

Second, this leads to another reason to inquire whether the dead are potential right-holders. Above, I said it matters whether the dead are potential right-holders as it enables us to assess the extensional adequacy of the Interest Theory. But if the Interest Theory is correct, it matters in its own right whether the dead are potential rights-holders: if the dead cannot hold rights, then, even if we are under duties in which the dead figure, those duties will not be owed to the dead. And whether those duties are owed to the dead triggers certain normative upshots. For example, infringement of directed duties owed to the dead would wrong them. It would make apt certain reactive attitudes, for example, blame and resentment (though, obviously enough, the dead could not hold these attitudes themselves—rather, we, the living, could feel resentment toward the duty-bearer *on the dead's behalf*).[6]

Finally, third, Kramer's Interest Theory has been put forward as a theory of legal rights. For the most part, it straightforwardly applies to moral rights, too. However, there are a few places where Kramer thinks the Interest Theory will differ when it comes to moral rights, as opposed to legal rights. I highlight this where relevant.

2. The Interest Theory

This section introduces the Interest Theory in sufficient detail for our discussion below of whether the dead are potential right-holders on the Interest Theory. Section 2.1 introduces Kramer's version of the Interest Theory. Section 2.2 compares the Nonjustificatory nature of Kramer's Interest Theory with Justificatory versions of the theory. And, section 2.3 introduces Kramer's notion of interests, comparing it to the more familiar notions found in the literature. I then suggest that this disagreement is only terminological.

2.1 Kramer's Interest Theory

Let us begin by looking at Kramer's definition of the Interest Theory:

(1a) Necessary but insufficient for the actual holding of a right by *X* is that the right, when actual, protects one or more of *X*'s interests.

(2a) The mere fact that *X* is competent and authorized to demand or waive the enforcement of a right will be neither sufficient nor necessary for *X*'s holding of that right.[7]

One might wonder why it is worth including (2a). (2a) is the negation of (Kramer's definition of) the Will Theory of Rights, so sets the Interest Theory in stark opposition to the Will Theory. This is a worthwhile inclusion. (1a) alone would be consistent with it also being necessary, for *X* to hold a right, that *X* has the power to waive or demand enforcement of the right. This view would say that, jointly necessary for the holding of

[6] For more on why it matters why some entity is a right-holder, see the beginning of Basl and Bowen, "The Rights of Artificial Intelligences."

[7] Kramer, "Getting Rights Right," 28.

a right is that the right protects one or more of *X*'s interests *and* that *X* has the power to waive or demand enforcement of the right. This view would be more demanding to satisfy than both the standard version of the Interest Theory and the standard version of the Will Theory.

Kramer has since revised his definition. He now thinks:

(1b) Necessary though insufficient for the holding of a legal right by *X* is that the duty correlative to the right, when actual, normatively protects some aspects of *X*'s situation that on balance is typically beneficial for a being like *X* (namely, a human individual or a collectivity or a nonhuman animal).[8]

There are at least four changes between the old (1a) and revised (1b) version of Kramer's Interest Theory.[9] It is worth working through these changes since it lays clear several choice-points for a defender of the Interest Theory.

First, there is an explicit move from the correlative duty protecting *specific* interests to rights protecting interests all-things-considered.[10] Suppose you promise to meet me at the bar. It might be better for me, all-things-considered, for you not to show up. For example, if you do not show up, I might leave the bar before even having one drink, let alone several, meaning I get a lot of work done the following day. However, it is plausible that your not showing up does set back *an* interest of mine: my interest that you keep your promises made to me.[11] So, this move from specific to all-things-considered interests (in isolation) has extensional implications.

Second, on (1b), we look to whether the correlative duty protects *X*'s interests *under normal circumstances*, as opposed to how things turn out (or are expected to turn out).[12] Take, again, your promise to meet me at the bar. Although on this specific occasion it may not be in my interest all-things-considered for you to show up, under normal circumstances it may well be in my interest all-things-considered that you show up. Perhaps I usually make sure I have an easy morning of work after meeting

[8] Kramer, "In Defence of the Interest Theory of Right-Holding: Rejoinders to Leif Wenar on Rights," 49. The wording is slightly different in Kramer, "Refining the Interest Theory of Rights."

[9] There is reason to think Kramer intended (1a) to be read in ways made explicit by the revised (1b). See, e.g., nn. 12 and 14. In addition to the upcoming four points in the text, Kramer also now sees his version of the Interest Theory as a theory of right-*holding*, "a criterion that enables us to identify the holder of a legal right that correlates with a particular legal duty": Kramer, "In Defence of the Interest Theory of Right-Holding: Rejoinders to Leif Wenar on Rights," 49. I assume this is as opposed to seeing the Interest Theory as a theory of rights-*simpliciter*, which would tell you when a right exists. Kramer does not think he is offering such an account since that would depend on when a correlative duty exists, and he (justifiably) wants to keep that question separate: Kramer, 54–5. Yet, because we are presupposing the existence of a duty (we are just determining to whom, if anyone, the duty is owed), we can read (1b) as a necessary and sufficient condition. See Cruft, "The Circularity of the Interest and Will Theories of Rights," 174 fn. 25; Cruft, *Human Rights, Ownership, and the Individual*, 21 fn. 32; Kurki, "Rights, Harming and Wronging," 438–9.

[10] Cf. those who opt for a *pro tanto* reading of the Interest Theory: Raz, "Rights and Individual Well-Being"; Cruft, "Rights: Beyond Interest Theory and Will Theory?"; May, "Desires, Interests and Claim-Rights."

[11] There are interesting and open questions on whether, first, this specific interest is dependent on the duty's existence and, second, whether we ought to include so-called normative interests in the mix. On the first question, see Cruft, "The Circularity of the Interest and Will Theories of Rights." On the second question, see Owens, *Shaping the Normative Landscape*; Tadros, *Wrongs and Crimes*, 201–22.

[12] Discussion in Kramer's earlier work implies that Kramer was always thinking along these lines. See Kramer, "Rights Without Trimmings," 93–6; Kramer, "Getting Rights Right," 78–89.

you at the pub, that we normally have a good laugh, and so on. So, this explicit move to normality (in isolation) has extensional implications.[13]

Third, on (1b), we do not focus on what would be in *X*'s interests in particular, but on what would be in the interest of "a human being."[14] I take it this focus on the interests of a human being means that we take some generic human, and see if the potential correlative duty's being respected would be in the interest of that generic human. Since the generic human's interest will likely come apart from particular individuals' interests, this explicit move to the generic human (in isolation) has extensional implications.[15]

Finally, fourth, (1b) takes a stand on which interest-bearers are potential right-holders: human beings, collectivities, and nonhuman animals. Kramer's earlier definition, (1a), is silent on this, though taken up at length in the first half of that paper. It is that discussion to which we turn below (section 2.3). So as not to beg any questions on this key issue, let us assume Kramer's earlier definition. When Kramer's revised (1b) has different implications, I make this explicit.

2.2 Justificatory versus Nonjustificatory Interest Theories

(1a) and (1b) are both what we can call *Nonjustificatory* versions of the Interest Theory. On Kramer's version of the Interest Theory, "the essence of a right consists in the normative *protection* of some aspect(s) of the right-holder's well-being."[16] We look only to whether the interest *serves* or *protects* the potential right-holder's interests. This is different from what we can call *Justificatory* versions of the Interest Theory. To see the difference, compare the following two generic statements of the Interest Theory. (I use two generic formulations since that allows us to have the two views differ only along the Justificatory/Nonjustificatory dimension, and not the other choice-points discusses in the previous section.)

> *Interest Theory (Justificatory).* For *X* to have a right against *Y* that *Y* Φ, *X*'s interests must be of sufficient weight to place *Y* under a duty to Φ.

> *Interest Theory (Nonjustificatory).* For *X* to have a right against *Y* that *Y* Φ, *X*'s interests must be served by *Y*'s duty to Φ.[17]

[13] For problems with how far making an appeal to normality will get us with cases of harmless wronging, like the example of harmless promise-breaking in the text, see Bowen, Joseph "Robust Rights and Harmless Wronging", in Mark Timmons (ed) *Oxford Studies in Normative Ethics* Volume 12 (Oxford University Press; 2022).

[14] See, again, n. 12.

[15] For discussion, see Kramer, "Getting Rights Right," 81–9; Kurki, "Rights, Harming and Wronging," 440–1; cf. Cruft, "Rights: Beyond Interest Theory and Will Theory?" 376. It is unclear to me why, once we move to a focus on generic individuals, directed duties should be owed to particular individuals and why rights-violations wrong particular individuals. Suppose we kept the theory tied to *X*'s interests. Then we can say, what makes it the case that some putative duty correlates with *X*'s holding a right is that the duty's performance would typically be beneficial *for X*. But that is not what we are saying on Kramer's view—rather, it is that the duty's performance would typically be beneficial for a being like *X*. But that does not have anything to do with *X* in particular, as opposed to all the other beings like *X*.

[16] Kramer, "Getting Rights Right," 28, emphasis added.

[17] I omit that *Y*'s duty must be owed to *X* since I think the Interest Theory should be seen as offering an account of what it is to owe another a duty to another.

An example. The Justificatory version of the Interest Theory says that, for Ann to have a right that Beth not hit her, Ann's interests in not being hit must be of sufficient weight to place Beth under a duty not to hit her—that is, her interests must *justify* the duty's existence (hence the name ...). The most famous defender of the Interest Theory (Justificatory) is Joseph Raz. On his view, " 'X has a right' if and only if X can have rights, and, other things being equal, an aspect of X's well-being (his interest) is a sufficient reason for holding some other person(s) to be under a duty."[18] The Nonjustificatory version of the Interest Theory is not quite so strong. It says that, for Ann to have a right that Beth not hit her, her interests in not being hit need only be served by Beth's not hitting her; the duty may be justified by a whole host of other reasons.

So, the Justificatory and Nonjustificatory versions of the Interest Theory are *intensionally* different with respect to how they ground right-holding. (It is worth pausing to note that one might think that only the Justificatory version of the Interest Theory offers an account of the *grounds* of right-holding, since only it cares about the grounds of the correlative duty. But it would be mistaken to think this. While the Nonjustificatory version of the Interest Theory does not offer an account of the grounds of the correlative duty, it does offer an account of the grounds of *right-holding*: it offers an account of the thing, in virtue of which one holds a right—namely, that one's interests are served by the performance of the correlative duty.) The Justificatory and Nonjustificatory versions of the Interest Theory are also likely going to be *extensionally* different. This is because an entity's interests may be *served* by some duty, and so satisfy the Interest Theory (Nonjustificatory), but not be the *grounds* of that duty, and so not satisfy the Interest Theory (Justificatory).[19]

2.3 Interest

In the previous two sections, we have considered a range of choice-points for the Interest Theorist, and noted the stances that Kramer has taken. Let us consider one last choice-point, and begin to move closer to the question of whether the dead are potential right-holders on the Interest Theory. This final choice-point concerns what interests consist of. Whether the Interest Theory can recognize the dead as potential right-holders is going to depend, at the least, on whether they are bearers of interests—only then, on the Interest Theory (Nonjustificatory), can their interests be protected by correlative duties; and only then, on the Interest Theory (Justificatory), can their interests be of sufficient weight to place others under duties. In this subsection, I introduce three competing views of interests. I then suggest that deciding between these views is mostly a terminological dispute when it comes to the substance of whether the dead are potential right-holders.

On what we can call

the Well-being View of Interests, *X*'s interests consist of *X*'s well-being.

[18] Raz, *The Morality of Freedom*, 166.

[19] It is possible that they will not be extensionally different, namely, *if* it just so happens that one's interests are only served by a duty when one's interests are the grounds of the duty. But I doubt this will ever just so happen to be the case.

The Well-being View has prominence in the literature. For example, on Raz's version of the Interest Theory, well-being takes center stage and interests are reduced to the parenthesis. Well-being concerns what makes one's life go well. How our lives go is of importance. So, it is natural that one might think rights have something to do with well-being.

On the Well-being View, to know what interests consist of, we need to know what well-being consists of. We can distinguish broadly between four types of theory of well-being.[20] On *Hedonistic Theories*, well-being consists only of pleasure. On *Desire Theories*, well-being consists only of the satisfaction of one's desires. On *Objective List Theories*, well-being consists only of the advancement of certain aspects of our lives, regardless of our attitudes toward those aspects. Finally, on *Hybrid Theories*, well-being consists of some combination of these theories (it could be disjunctive, e.g., "pleasure or desire satisfaction," or conjunctive, e.g., "desire satisfaction one takes pleasure in").

Some people think the Well-being View is false. Victor Tadros thinks that "[o]ur interests are much broader than the things that make a difference to how our lives go."[21] For example, we have an interest in not being paternalistically interfered with. Yet, inasmuch as paternalistic interference needs to be good for us in order for it to be paternalistic (i.e., it needs to promote our well-being), we might think interests come apart from well-being.[22]

There are many ways one could make interests come apart from well-being. On what we can call

> *the Stakes View of Interests*, *X*'s interests are those things that *X* cares about, and that she has reason to care about it.[23]

Kramer agrees with the Stakes View that interests come apart from well-being. However, he radically disagrees with the Stakes View as to the extent to which interests come apart from well-being. He thinks,

> to say that some interest(s) of *X* will be advanced through the occurrence of an event or the emergence of a state of affairs is to say that *X* will benefit in some way(s) from the specified event or state of affairs. That is, the event or state of affairs will improved *X*'s condition or will avert a deterioration therein.[24]

[20] Parfit, *Reasons and Persons*, 493–502.

[21] Tadros, *Wrongs and Crimes*, 182.

[22] For discussion, see Tadros, 203–4. I think there is more to be said on behalf of the Well-being View in reply to this problem, but will leave that for another day. The purpose of the quick argument in the text is only to motivate why one might be skeptical of the Well-being View.

[23] This view is loosely based on Feinberg, *Moral Limits of the Criminal Law*, 31–61. It is not exactly clear where well-being fits into the picture for Feinberg. For Feinberg, one's "welfare interests" are a subset of one's interests, and welfare is often taken to be synonymous with well-being. So, we can infer well-being is a subset of interests. The Stakes View is also different from Tadros's precise view of what interests consist of.

[24] Kramer, "Getting Rights Right," 92 fn. 3. Kramer does not say too much else about his view of interests. Recently, he has defended his view against narrower views of interests. Yet, this defense rests on narrower views not being neutral in the sense liberals care about. But that does not help us when it comes to which view is correct as a matter of moral theory. He also suggests others' views beg the question against his view. Yet, that does not amount to an argument *for* his capacious view. See Kramer, *Liberalism with Excellence*, 134–44. Kramer has also recently clarified that his view of interests, though largely objective, does allow that we have an interest in the satisfaction of our strongly held desires; and, that these desires are not constrained by, e.g., what is actually of value. See Kramer, "In Defence of the Interest Theory of Right-Holding: Rejoinders to Leif Wenar on Rights," 80.

The second sentence is key, here, since it is that which implies a capacious view of interests. It implies that as well as humans and animals having interests, plants and many inanimate entities have interests too, including buildings and paintings, since their condition can be improved or deteriorated.[25]

Since all of these entities are interest-bearers for Kramer, does this imply all of these entities are potential right-holders on his version of the Interest Theory? It does not. Rather, Kramer thinks we need additionally to compare the moral status of different classes of interest-bearers with what he takes to be the paradigm right-holders, "mentally competent human adults."[26] We do so by looking at "the similarities and differences between such beings and mentally competent human adults. We simultaneously have to inquire … about the moral significance of those similarities and differences." Only then can we determine which classes of interest-bearers are potential right-holders.[27]

So, we have three competing views of interests and two competing methodologies of how to determine which classes of entities are potential right-holders on the Interest Theory. The Well-being and Stakes Views define interests quite narrowly, and imply that all interest-bearers are potential right-holders. Kramer's view defines interests very capaciously, but adds that it is a separate question which sorts of interests get to make it the case that the interest-bearer is a potential right-holder. Which to prefer? As it turns out, the choice is largely terminological. To explain why, I first need to explain why (as I thought on first writing this chapter) one might prefer defining interests more narrowly, as with the Well-being or Stakes View.[28]

[25] Most in the literature on the metaphysics of harm think one is harmed only when one is made worse off than one otherwise would have been, where one is worse off just in case one's well-being is diminished (e.g., Tadros goes this way). Alternatively, one could think one is harmed when one's interests are set back (Feinberg goes this way). Kramer's second sentence is in keeping with this wider, interest-based currency of harm, where one is harmed or benefited just in case their interests are frustrated or promoted.

[26] Kramer, "Getting Rights Right," 33.

[27] Things are more complicated. In his earlier work, Kramer often implied that he endorsed the Well-being View of Interests. For example: "Because various aspects of the *well-being* of animals and dead people and mentally infirm people can receive essential protection from legal norms, the Interest Theory lets us classify those creatures as potential right-holders"; "As has been stated at the outset of this essay, the Interest Theory submits that legal rights generally are instances of legal protection for elements of the *well-being* of anyone who holds such rights." Kramer, 28, 30, 46, emphasis added. And, "For the Interest Theorists, the essence of a legal right consists in its tendency to safeguard some aspect of the well-being of its holder. " Kramer, "Refining the Interest Theory of Rights," 33. But, Kramer defines interests capaciously in those works, which implies he thought well-being was very capacious at that time. In private communication, Kramer has said this was a mistake, since he now thinks well-being is a "property only of conscious organisms," whereas he maintains his capacious view of interests.

[28] In addition to the two reasons in the text, let me also note that I think it is implausible that interests are so capacious: to my ear, the grass does not have an interest in being watered, nor does my computer have an interest in having its RAM upgraded, nor does my house have an interest in having its pointing touched up. I admit, it is somewhat natural for one to say, "It would be good for your house to get the pointing done," but there I think we are talking about what would help my house function as it is designed to function; but, being skeptical of functional accounts of well-being/interests, that is beside the point as to what is good for a thing. Kramer will likely suggest I am begging the question at this stage. It is because of this that, in the text, I am suggesting we move past these disputes of what interests consist of. However, let me quickly note, if I am *egregiously* begging the question when I say "It is counterintuitive to say trees have interests," then Kramer is begging the question (i) against the Will Theorist when he objects that it cannot recognize children's rights and (ii) against my view of interests when he says trees can have interests. One person's *modus ponens* is another person's *modus tolens*.

First, if we define interests capaciously, but then say it is only a subset of interests that matter for rights, we are not really defending the *Interest* Theory of Rights. Rather, we are defending the Interest* Theory, where the asterisk denotes the subset of morally relevant interests. If we define interests more narrowly, we do not need to make such accommodations—it is interests in general that are doing the work.

Second, Kramer's capacious Interest Theory offers an implausible account of the grounds of right-holding. (Recall my remarks from section 2.2 that, even if we go for the Interest Theory (Nonjustificatory), we *are* offering an account of grounds of right-holding—we are offering an account of that in virtue of which one is a potential right-holder.) If we endorse the Well-being View, we have an intuitively compelling account of the grounds of right-holding. This is because how our lives go for us—what our well-being consists of—is obvious of importance. When one's well-being is the grounds of some duty *or* when one's well-being is necessarily, typically served by some duty (depending on whether we endorse the Justificatory or Nonjustificatory version of the Interest Theory, respectively), it is plausible that the duty would resultantly be owed to one. The same is true to a similar extent of the Stakes View of Interests (on that view, recall, interests are those things we care about and that we have reason to care about—so rights are grounded in those things we care about and have reason to care about). But once we move to Kramer's capacious view, it is just not clear to me why advancing something's condition, such as a painting's condition, would result in the duty being owed to that thing. (Below I say more about why I think this is.)

At this stage, one might reply: but if we endorse Kramer's capacious view, we cannot conclude from one's interest being necessarily, typically served by some duty that this will result in the duty being owed to the interest-bearer. This is because, as Kramer makes clear, we then need to inquire as to the moral status of the interest-bearer.

But it is now that one can appreciate why it seems a terminological matter whether we define interest narrowly or go for Kramer's methodology of defining interests capaciously, and then inquiring about the moral status of the interest-bearer: the same features that go into delineating interests on the narrower conceptions can be the very same features that go into determining, on Kramer's methodology, whether the moral status of the interest-bearer is such that they ought to be a potential right-holder. Take an example. Let us begin with the defender of the Well-being or Stakes View. Suppose, for sake of illustration, one thinks only sentient beings can bear interests. One might say, "It is implausible that things can be good or bad for one, or that things can matter for one, unless there is a subject for whom those things can be good or bad, or for whom those things can matter." For example, Tadros says, "only a conscious being ... has a perspective of its own which we can imaginatively adopt, perhaps at most partially, in determining how well or badly its life is going for it."[29] Now suppose one is a defender of Kramer's methodology. One could agree that one of the salient features of the paradigm right-holder is that they are conscious, and so one will agree that it is only conscious interest-bearers that are potential right-holders. Further, one can agree about why consciousness matters. While the two methodologies disagree about

[29] Tadros, *Wrongs and Crimes*, 182–4; Taylor, "The Concept of a Person." I think it is these sorts of considerations that motivate Fabre's rejection of posthumous rights, considered below. But as my argument below suggests, this idea—or something like it—is consistent with posthumous well-being/interests.

what interests consist of, they agree both *that* non-conscious things are not potential right-holders and *why* non-conscious things are not right-holders. And that is where the debate is at. When asking whether the dead are potential right-holders, the debate is not really about whether it is best to define interests narrowly or capaciously.[30]

All of this is to say, if we want to discover whether some entity is a potential right-holder, it is unclear it matters whether we define interests narrowly or capaciously. What does matter is that we do not talk past each other. In section 3 we turn to whether, on the Well-being View or the Stakes View, the dead are bearers of interests or, on Kramer's capacious view, whether the moral status of the dead makes them potential right-holders. Before that, though, let me offer two quick pragmatic reasons for preferring defining interests more narrowly.

First, there is an extensive literature on well-being (including, e.g., whether the dead and other entities, such as non-sentient organisms, are bearers of well-being).[31] Being able to engage with this literature directly, in its own terms, will be more helpful than having to translate that literature into talk of the moral status of the interest-bearer (if we were to define interests capaciously).

Second, and relatedly, taking Kramer's indirect route of defining interests capaciously and then comparing paradigmatic right-holders with other potential classes of right-holders (such as the dead) is more likely to lead us to overestimate non-salient similarities, and downplay salient similarities. For example, during discussion of whether infants, those with deteriorated rational capacities, and those with severely limited rational capacities are potential right-holders, Kramer says that "most infants will develop into ordinary human adults, the paradigmatic right-holders. Thus, even if we leave aside the fact that infants and lunatics and senile people belong to a species of which the typical adult members are quintessentially right-holders, we can find ample grounds for ascribing legal rights to them."[32] But it is not obvious why, without further serious argument, the fact that most children will develop into adults with sufficiently complex rational capacities, or the fact that they belong to the same species as those adults, would make their interests of the sort, the protection of which, makes them potential right-holders at that time. Rather, to be true to the Interest Theory itself, we should focus on the nature of the interests themselves.[33]

3. Posthumous Rights

In the previous section, I introduced the Interest Theory. I then argued that it is mostly a terminological dispute whether we define interests narrowly or define interests capaciously, with a view to determining the moral status of the interest-bearer. This is because the same considerations that could go into determining how to properly delineate interests can be the same considerations that go into determining the moral status

[30] Thanks to Karamvir Chadha for discussion on this.

[31] For illuminating discussion of the well-being of non-sentient organisms (albeit, discussion that does not assume all well-being matters), see Basl, *The Death of the Ethic of Life*.

[32] Kramer, "Getting Rights Right," 47.

[33] In a footnote, Kramer offers two reasons for preferring his capacious view not discussed here: Kramer, 92–3 fn. 3. I discuss these reasons in an appendix on file with author, available on request.

of the interest-bearer (were we to define interests more capaciously). In this section, we turn to the putative interests of the dead. First, in section 3.1, we look at Kramer's argument for why the dead are potential right-holders on the Interest Theory. I suggest this argument goes wrong because it fails to focus on the nature of the interests of the dead themselves. Second, in section 3.2, I introduce and defend what I take to be a more plausible argument.

3.1 Kramer and Posthumous Rights

3.1.1 Looking in the Wrong Place

Kramer's methodology for determining whether the dead are potential right-holders compares the similarities and differences of the dead with what Kramer takes to be uncontroversial right-holders, "mentally competent human adults." And while Kramer notes there are some potentially significant differences between the dead and "mentally competent human adults" (particularly, that the dead are neither animate nor sentient), Kramer thinks the key move to recognizing the dead as potential right-holders on the Interest Theory is to "subsume the aftermath of each dead person's life within the overall course of his or her existence."[34]

I think the general thought behind including one's posthumous existence in the overall course of one's existence is along the right lines, and my argument in section 3.2 can be seen as one way to unpack this thought. The problem comes when Kramer explains how he thinks we can unpack it. He says we can include one's posthumous existence into the overall course of one's existence by:

> highlighting the [various] constituents of that aftermath—for example, the continuing influence of the dead person on other people and on the development of various events, the memories of him that reside in the minds of people who knew him or knew of him, and the array of possessions which he accumulated and then bequeathed or failed to bequeath ... [the dead endure] not typically as an intact being but as a multi-faceted presence in the lives of his contemporaries and successors.[35]

The idea is, inasmuch as the dead continue to figure in the lives of the living, the dead are potential right-holders on the Interest Theory. Given Kramer's methodology of comparing the similarities and differences of paradigmatic right-holders with putative potential right-holders, I take it we are to assume that this—the dead's figuring in the lives of the living—is the morally significant feature that the dead share with the living. Let us call this Kramer's Argument. If we prefer either the Well-being View or the Stakes View of Interests, where we are not just to assume the dead are bearers of interests, we can take Kramer's Argument as one that suggests why the dead are bearers of well-being or interests.

An initial limitation of Kramer's Argument is that it cannot be relied upon by a defender of the Justificatory version of the Interest Theory. This is because, on that

[34] Kramer, 49.
[35] Kramer, 49–50.

version of the view, for one to be owed a duty and hold a right correlative to that duty, one's interests need to be the grounds of that duty. And, although the fact that the dead figure in the lives of the living may well be the grounds of duties that we treat the dead in certain ways, those duties will not be grounded in the interests of the dead—rather, they will be grounded in the interests of the living, the people whose lives the dead figure in. On the Justificatory version of the Interest Theory, then, Kramer's argument is able only to justify the living holding rights whose content refers to the dead, rather than the being holders of rights *themselves*.

While Kramer is not offering a Justificatory version of the Interest Theory, it would nonetheless be preferable that we had an argument for the dead being potential right-holders that was open to defenders of either the Justificatory or Nonjustificatory version of the Interest Theory. The choice between those versions of the theory is a substantive choice. Even if Kramer's Argument succeeded in showing the dead are potential right-holders on the Nonjustificatory version of the Interest Theory (which, below I argue it does not), we ought nonetheless to prefer the argument extended in the following subsection since it can be relied upon by defenders of both versions of the Interest Theory.[36]

There is a second, related limitation of Kramer's Argument. In the introduction, I said Kramer thinks some details of the Interest Theory of *legal* rights will differ from the Interest Theory of *moral* rights. We have reason to think that one place they will differ is whether to endorse a Justificatory or Nonjustificatory version of the Interest Theory. When it comes to legal rights, Kramer thinks the holder's interests need not have anything to do with the grounds of the duty, provided the right-holder's interests stand in the appropriate relation to that duty specified by the theory's necessary and jointly sufficient conditions.[37] Now, however plausible we find this when it comes to legal rights, it is much less plausible that the Nonjustificatory version of the Interest Theory is the correct theory of *moral* rights. Let me explain why.

Consider the following example.[38] Some innocent victims are kidnapped. The kidnappers make the victims carry out some strenuous labor. They threaten that, if any of the able victims do not carry out the labor, all of the victims will be killed. It is plausible that, without any reasonable means of escape, each of the victims is under a moral duty to carry out the labor—and it is plausible that they owe this duty to the other victims.[39] However, Kramer's discussion of other cases implies that performing the action required by the duty will also necessarily be typically beneficial for the kidnappers. Since this is sufficient for the duty to be owed to the kidnappers on what would be Kramer's Nonjustificatory version of the Interest Theory of *moral* rights, this would

[36] Appeal to something like theoretical neutrality appears to be part of the reason Kramer goes for his methodology of defining interests capaciously, so it is not clear why theoretical neutrality on the question of Justificatory and Nonjustificatory versions of the theory would not also be a virtue.

[37] Kramer, "Rights Without Trimmings," 35–41; Kramer, *Liberalism with Excellence*, 141–4.

[38] This example was originally offered to me by Kramer in comments on an earlier version of my "Beyond Normative Control: Against the Will Theory of Rights" as a counterexample to the claim that, when one violates a duty owed to *X*, one wrongs *X*. But as we see, it is better seen as a counterexample to Nonjustificatory versions of the Interest Theory.

[39] We can disagree about how demanding the labor would need to be for carrying it out to be supererogatory, but presumably there is some cost at which one is under a duty to carry out the labor *for the sake of one's fellow victims.*

mean the victims owe their duty to carry out the labor to the kidnappers (in addition to the other victims), and that the kidnappers have rights against the victims that they carry out the labor (in addition to the other victims).[40] But this is very implausible.

There are at least two replies one could offer. First, one could continue to endorse the Nonjustificatory version of the Interest Theory for moral rights, but suggest that *justificatory* considerations come into the picture when it comes to moral wronging. The victims do owe their moral duties to the kidnappers, and the kidnappers do hold moral rights correlative to those duties, but the victims would not morally wrong the kidnappers since the kidnappers' interests play no role in the grounds of the duty. There are at least two limitations of this reply. First, we would need to explain why justificatory considerations do not matter when it comes to *legal* wrongs but do matter when it comes to *moral* wrongs. Second, as relates to posthumous rights, this means we could not *wrong* the dead given Kramer's Argument for the dead being potential right-holders—for, as I argued above, that the dead figure in the lives of the living makes the justification of the duties depend on the interests of the living. And, albeit my sample audience is only those around me, most have a stronger intuition that we can wrong the dead than that the dead are potential right-holders. But, this reply gets things the other way around—the dead would be potential right-holders, but not be the sort of entity one could wrong.

The second reply, which I think is preferable, is to suggest that, while the Nonjustificatory version of the Interest Theory is correct when it comes to legal rights, some form of the Justificatory version of the Interest Theory is correct for moral rights: minimally, a moral duty is owed to someone, and they hold a correlative right to that duty, only if their interests play *some* role in grounding the duty. It is a separate question the extent to which one's interests must play a justificatory role in grounding the duty.[41] Going this way, one need not conclude that the victims' duties are owed to the kidnappers, that the kidnappers hold rights correlative to those duties, nor that the victims would wrong the kidnappers if they infringed the duty.

So how does all of this relate to posthumous rights? Well, inasmuch as (i) Kramer's Argument fails to accommodate the dead being potential right-holders on Justificatory versions of the Interest Theory and (ii) we ought to prefer some form of the Justificatory version of the Interest Theory when it comes to moral rights, Kramer's Argument fails to accommodate the dead being potential moral right-holders. And, again, even if Kramer is offering only an argument for why the dead are potential right-holders on the Interest Theory of *legal* rights, when all else is equal, it would be better to have an argument that would help out when it comes to moral rights also.

The preceding two limitations do not necessarily impugn Kramer's Argument when it comes to Kramer's Nonjustificatory version of the Interest Theory of legal rights (other than making the argument dialectically less preferable). However, I am inclined to think the argument does not work even there. Kramer's methodology is to begin

[40] In support of my claim that one's duty being served in this way is sufficient for a duty to be owed to one on Kramer's theory, see n. 9.

[41] For discussion, see the taxonomy offered in Cruft, *Human Rights, Ownership, and the Individual*, 118–35, as well as his ch. 2 in this volume.

with what he takes to be paradigmatic right-holders, "mentally competent human adults," and then to look at the similarities and differences between such right-holders and the class of putative potential right-holders under examination. We then need to attend to the moral significance of these similarities and differences. And, it looks like Kramer thinks the salient similarities between the dead and the living is that the dead figure prominently in the lives of the living. But that just seems beside the point. Lots of things figures in the lives of the living. What we are looking for are similarities and differences that are morally significant enough to leave the dead as potential right-holders.

Let us take an example. The Maori people of New Zealand take the Whanganui River to be a spiritual entity, Te Awa Tupua.[42] Let us assume it figures prominently in the lives of the Maori people accordingly, as much so for sake of argument as the dead. For Kramer, the river is an interest-bearer, since its condition can be improved or deteriorated. Yet, *that* the river's figuring in the lives of the Maori people is surely not enough to make the river a potential right-holder. At this stage, one might reply that it is not only an entity figuring in the lives of the living that matters, but other factors. We turn to what those factors look like below in section 3.2; yet, I submit, those factors alone are sufficient to make the dead potential right-holders (they also do not come with the other problems with Kramer's Argument).

Now, things might be different if Kramer's approach was part of some constructivist project about rights (or some conceptual engineering project). Roughly put, constructivists about value think that things are valuable *because* we value them. Perhaps a constructivist might think, as well as what is of value being determined by our attitudes, so the underlying deontic structure is determined by our attitudes—and so, inasmuch as the dead figure in our lives, those duties whose content refers to the dead becomes owed to the dead. But Kramer is avowedly not offering such a view. For Kramer, whether some entity is a potential right-holder is an objective, mind-independent matter:

> Under my theory, the status of individuals ... as potential holders of legal rights is an objective ethical matter rather than something that depends on the justificatory beliefs of legal-government officials in any particular jurisdiction. Slaves and cattle are potential holders of legal rights in every jurisdiction, while stone formations are not potential holders of legal rights in any jurisdiction.[43]

In sum, it is just not clear why focusing on the various ways in which the dead figure in the lives of the living amounts to a morally relevant similarity to Kramer's paradigm right-holders. The problem with Kramer's argument is that, even if we endorse some Nonjustificatory version of the Interest Theory—and so even if we think that the right-holder's interests need not do any work grounding the correlative duty—the status of

[42] See the beginning of Kurki's ch. 4 in this volume, from which this example is taken.

[43] Kramer, "In Defence of the Interest Theory of Right-Holding: Rejoinders to Leif Wenar on Rights," 65. As relates to conceptual engineering, I am imagining a project where a theorist thinks through the effects that our concepts around rights have on the world, and how changing those concepts could be for the better. But since Kramer thinks what rights obtain is a mind-independent matter, we cannot change the concepts *themselves*.

the right-holder as a potential right-holder still has to be to do with features of *them*. On the Well-being and Stakes Views, it has to depend on whether the putative potential right-holder has any interests capable of serving. And on Kramer's capacious view of interests, on what their interests are like. But Kramer's Argument does not focus on the nature of the dead's interests themselves. And that is where Kramer's Argument goes wrong.

In section 3.2, I offer an argument that relies on the nature of the dead's interests. Before that, in section 3.1.2, I raise an additional problem with Kramer's Argument. As well as giving us additional reason to be skeptical of Kramer's Argument for the view that the dead are potential right-holders on the Interest Theory, the objection lends weight to my suggestion that Kramer's Argument goes wrong in failing to focus on the nature of the interests of the dead.

3.1.2 The Durability of Being a Potential Right-Holder

We have seen that Kramer's Argument for the dead being potential right-holders depends on their figuring in the lives of the living. Kramer thinks this argument also helps answer the question how long are the dead potential right-holders: it "hinges on the durability of the person's presence in other people's lives."[44] Yet, how much one figures in the lives of the living is going to depend on how influential one is. No matter how successful I could hope to be in my philosophical career, for example, it is very likely that Shakespeare will figure more in the lives of others than I. This means that Shakespeare will be a potential right-holder for far longer than I. But this might strike one as implausible. Suppose Shakespeare and I were to have been contemporaries—then, our status as potential right-holders should have been morally equal; yet, this equality breaks down after we die.

Things get worse for Kramer's Argument.[45] As Kramer notes, one may figure in the lives of the living through doing particularly heinous things. For example, a tyrant will figure in the lives of the living more than one's average Joe. But if the durability of the dead's being a potential right-holder depends on the extent to which they figure in the lives of the living, the tyrant will be a potential right-holder far longer than your average Joe.

Kramer offers an argument in the alternative to reply to this specific form of the objection. I think the argument succeeds in disarming the variant of the objection but highlights a more general problem. First, Kramer suggests we could "withdraw the designation of 'potential right-holder' from anyone whose strong posthumous presence in people's lives is due to his numerous wicked exploits."[46] If we want to go this way, we would need to offer some reasoning behind this suggestion to avoid the charge that it is ad hoc. Yet, it is not obvious this task is not doable. For example, through one's actions while living one can forfeit their rights to be shown certain forms of respect. Why not think the same of posthumous rights?

[44] Kramer, "Getting Rights Right," 50.

[45] Visa Kurki has raised some additional complications in private communication. Following Shakespeare's death, the living's picture of him could well have gradually shifted from what he was actually like. At the limiting case, someone could die and the living could have a completely false view of them.

[46] Kramer, 51.

Notwithstanding this, Kramer's second reply is to question why, if our tyrant was a potential legal right-holder while she was alive, she should not be a potential right-holder once she is deceased, so long as she figures in the lives of the living. This line of thinking is in keeping with my forfeiture suggestion from the previous paragraph—perhaps there are some rights one cannot forfeit while living, and so the analogous posthumous rights cannot be forfeited also. For example, though Sadam Hussein may have forfeited rights to be shown certain forms of respect while living, he may not have forfeited rights against *gratuitous* bodily intrusions. Similarly, perhaps he retains posthumous rights that his remains not be gratuitously defiled.

However, this is the point at which we reach the more general objection. The complaint ought not be, "Hussein gets to hold posthumous rights—how implausible!" but "Hussein gets to remain a potential right-holder far longer than those of us who figure less prominently in the lives of the living—*that* is what is implausible." And, suggesting that we think "Hussein held rights while living, so why not think he holds posthumous rights?" does not really help along this dimension. This problem can be taken to its extreme by considering someone who does not figure in the lives of the living at all. Suppose the recently deceased had no friends, no remaining family, and so on. On the face of it, Kramer's view implies that she is not a potential posthumous legal right-holder. But that is implausible—whether one is a potential right-holder should not vary with such factors as whether one figures in the lives of the living.[47]

3.2 Posthumous Interests

In the previous two sections, I argued that Kramer's view goes awry in focusing on the ways in which the dead figure in the lives of the living. It would be preferable to focus on the interests of the dead themselves. We turn to an argument like that now. (Because most of the arguments I am engaging with in this subsection are found in the literature on well-being, I assume the Well-being View of Interests. The arguments easily extend to the Stakes View of Interest, as considerations on which wants get to count as interests. The arguments can also fit Kramer's methodology, as highlighting similarities between the interests of the dead and the interests of Kramer's paradigm right-holders.)

Suppose one was a Hedonist about well-being: one thinks well-being consists only of pleasure. Now suppose one was also a Welfarist: one thinks that the only thing that matters, morally, is well-being. Then, presumably one must conclude the dead are not potential right-holders on the Interest Theory. The dead do not experience pleasure, so they are not bearers of well-being if Hedonism is correct.[48]

Many people move away from Hedonistic Theories of Well-being, as theories of well-being, *because* they think things can be good and bad for one without one

[47] Kramer might reply by emphasizing that, in his revised view (1b), we do not look at how some duty's performance might affect X in particular, but how the duty's performance might affect the generic human being. And, the generic human figures in the lives of the living. But whatever the plausibility of this, it would be preferably not to have to focus on the extent to which the generic dead figure in the lives of the living; and, if successful, the argument offered in the following section extends such an argument.

[48] I include the Welfarism so as to accommodate the Stakes View and Kramer's View of Interests.

experiencing those things as being good or bad for them. For example, Hedonism seemingly implies it would be better for me to plug into Nozick's experience machine, a machine "that would give you any experience you desired," even if my life plugged in would contain (or would be expected to contain) only a marginal amount of additional pleasure.[49] Similarly, Hedonism cannot accommodate that many think my life goes worse for me if my life's work collapses, even if I am unaware of this. It cannot accommodate that my life goes worse for me if the relationships I partake in are inauthentic. The Desire Theorist says, "Well, you have a desire that your life's work succeeds. You have a desire that you be part of authentic relationships. Whether these desires are satisfied depends on the state of the world—whether, in fact, your life's work succeeds and whether, in fact, you are part of authentic relationships. It does not depend on whether you *experience* your life's work going well or poorly or whether you *experience* those relationships as authentic or inauthentic." Objective List Theorists say something similar, though they will couch the value of my life's work in accomplishment of the work itself and the value of the relationships themselves.

Now, many of my desires may be satisfied after I die. Many of the potential accomplishments that are relevant for the Objective List can be affected after I die. (In fact, it is plausible that many of my most strongly held desires and most important accomplishments survive my death, e.g. how my loved ones fare.) Because of this, both Desire and Objective List Theories can say that things can be good or bad for us (can affect our well-being) after we die. If we endorsed the Well-being View of Interests, this means the dead are bearers of interests, and so potential right-holders on the Interest Theory. This is because our interests can be served or potentially ground duties after we die. Similar remarks can be said of the Stakes View of Interests. What if we went for Kramer's methodology? Well, since we have reason to think the dead are bearers of well-being on Desire and Objective List Theories, and since being a bearer of well-being is a morally salient similarity between the dead and Kramer's paradigm right-holders, we should conclude the dead are potential right-holders.

We can take the argument further, from one that accommodates the dead being bearers of well-being to one that puts pressure on denying that the dead are posthumous bearers of well-being.[50] Suppose we endorse the Desire Theory. What is fundamental on that view? Well, that one has a desire for some state of affairs, and that state of affairs obtain. But as Derek Parfit puts it: "It is irrelevant to my desire whether it is fulfilled before or after I am dead ... If we think it irrelevant that I never know about the non-fulfilment of my desires, we cannot defensibly claim that my death makes a difference." Similarly, Jeff McMahan writes, "it seems hard to believe that it makes a difference to the misfortune [one] suffers whether the collapse of [one's] life's work occurs shortly before [one] is killed or shortly afterward. Yet, according to the Existence Requirement [that things are only good or bad for one while one is alive],

[49] Nozick, *Anarchy, State and Utopia*, 42.

[50] This is especially important when it comes to something as contentious as posthumous well-being. As Sumner writes: "The issue of whether posthumously satisfied desires can benefit their erstwhile holders is a hotly debated one. Some people find it just obvious that the dead can be neither benefited nor harmed, while others find it equally obvious that lives are capable of retroactive prudential improvement." Sumner, *Welfare, Happiness, and Ethics*, 127.

this difference in timing makes all the difference."[51] Again, we could tell a similar story for Objective List Theories. And so, unless we can tell a compelling story for why this difference matters, we must conclude the dead are bearers of well-being if we are Desire Theorists or Objective List Theorists. And if the dead are bearers of well-being, they are potential right-holders on the Interest Theory.

Still, some are skeptical. They attempt to articulate a difference. For example, during discussion of the Desire Theory, Chris Heathwood says we should "count a desire satisfaction only if the subject is aware that the desire is satisfied."[52] We can see this as a *robust* experience requirement being introduced on the Desire Theory. Heathwood's reason for endorsing the requirement is that it rules out the satisfaction of remote desires making one's life go well. Here is an example of such a desire:

> Suppose that I meet a stranger who has what is believed to be a fatal disease. My sympathy is aroused, and I strongly want this stranger to be cured. We never meet again. Later, unknown to me, this stranger is cured. On the Unrestricted Desire-Fulfillment Theory, this event is good for me, and makes my life go better. This is not plausible. We should reject this theory.[53]

While we have reason not to want the satisfaction of remote desires to matter for one's well-being, I do not think introducing such a robust experience requirement is the way to go. (For one thing, we could move to the Objective List Theory; but let us suppose we like the Desire Theory.) On the one hand, there are potentially other ways to parse remote desires from the desires we want, intuitively, to count. On the other hand, the robust experience requirement leads to worse problems: first, it means that death is not bad for the one who dies; second, it invites the objections considered above to Hedonism. But I am a lot more confident that (a) my death tomorrow would be bad for me and (b) things can be good or bad for me without them affecting my experiences than I am confident that (c) the satisfaction of remote desires does not make one's life go well (as in the case of the stranger above).

We can see this argument as introducing two requirements that, other things being equal, one must satisfy if one is to argue that the dead are not potential right-holders on the Interest Theory. First, one's argument must explain why death is bad for the one who dies. Second, one's argument must explain why things can be good or bad for one without those things affecting one's experiences.[54] One can ignore either of these requirements but, to many, this would be throwing the baby out with the bathwater.

[51] Parfit, *Reasons and Persons*, 495; McMahan, "Death and the Value of Life," 38.

[52] Heathwood, "Desire Satisfactionism and Hedonism," 544.

[53] Parfit, *Reasons and Persons*, 494.

[54] Note, we can adhere to the first of these requirements without adhering to the second. E.g., Hedonists do not think things can be good or bad for one without those things affecting one's experiences. However, they can accommodate death being good or bad for one. Assuming one's life would contain more pleasure were one not to die at some time *t*, death is bad for one at *t* because one experiences less pleasure than one would have experienced were one not to have died at *t*. For defense of this view, see Feldman, "Some Puzzles About the Evil of Death," 205–27; Bradley, *Well-Being and Death*. For discussion of this putative asymmetry between death being bad or good for one, but posthumous events not being bad or good for one, see Luper, "Posthumous Harm," 63–72.

Cécile Fabre introduces a weaker experience requirement on interests than Heathwood, though one that nonetheless rules out the dead from being interest-bearers. But, she thinks her weaker experience requirement can satisfy our two requirements above. Fabre suggests that it is a necessary condition for one to be an interest-bearer that one's experiences can be positively or negatively affected at the time one's interest is satisfied or frustrated.[55] The principal reason that Fabre endorses this condition is the following. She compares slashing a painting and kicking a car with a human, Red, getting a beating: "The crucial difference between them—to point out the obvious—is that Red is, but the car is not, a subject of experiences. The reason in turn why Red, unlike the car, is harmed by the beating is precisely that the beating makes a difference (and an adverse one at that) to his experience."[56] From this Fabre concludes the dead are not interest-bearers, nor therefore can they hold rights given the Interest Theory, because they are not subjects of experience.

Unlike Heathwood's more robust experience requirement, Fabre's weaker experience requirement can potentially deal with death being bad for the one who dies. This is because Fabre suggests there are lots of ways one's experiences can be negatively affected. One way for one's experiences to be negatively affected is if one's experience is turned from a good to a negative experience, as when Red gets the beating above. Yet, Fabre suggests, another way that one's experiences can be negatively affected is if those experiences are prevented from coming about: "for what matters, when determining whether X by some event E [is harmed] at t, is not whether or not X is a subject of experience then but, rather, whether or not his experience is adversely affected by E at t. In so far as death destroys X's experience, [E] affects it."[57]

I am not sure how principled this suggestion is. Recall, Fabre's motivation for her weak experiential requirement: "the beating makes a difference (and an adverse one at that) to [Red's] experience." The way this is stated trades off that Red experiences something, and that experience is worse than one he would otherwise have had (namely, not being beaten). However, were Red to be killed by that beating, though he is denied the good experiences he would otherwise have had, he does not experience anything that is worse than that. Accordingly, death cannot be bad for one given

[55] She says, "the requirement that E should set back X's (fundamental) interests, though necessary is not sufficient for X to be harmed by E at t: in addition, or so I argue, it must be the case that E adversely affects X's experience at t." Fabre, "Posthumous Rights," 228. It is unclear whether Fabre thinks interests are synonymous with well-being. Her earlier work suggests not: Fabre, *Social Rights Under the Constitution: Government and the Decent Life*, 18–21.

[56] Additionally, Fabre thinks the dead do not have interests since there is no interest-bearer. Following Feinberg and Pitcher, Fabre suggests the most plausible candidate for a subject of posthumous interests would be the antemortem person—for it is her desires, the thwarting of which, constitutes a setback to her well-being: "However ... the antemortem person, in fact, is the person while she was alive, in short, the living under another name. The posthumous event does not affect any interest of a dead person." Fabre, "Posthumous Rights," 228; Pitcher, "The Misfortunes of the Dead," 183–8; Feinberg, *Moral Limits of the Criminal Law. Volume 1, Harm to Others*. Whether this undermines posthumous rights *proper*, this does not undermine it being possible that there are duties we owe to people who no longer concretely exist before us; and that is what we are really interested in when we are asking do the dead hold rights. The more pertinent question, I think, is not who is the subject of posthumous harm, but when are posthumous harms bad for the subject? This is largely the same question as, when is death bad for the one who dies. For an excellent overview of this question, see Johansson, "The Timing Problem," 255–73.

[57] Fabre, "Posthumous Rights," 236.

the *spirit* of Fabre's experience requirement. But since I think we have good reason to think death is bad for one, we ought not to endorse Fabre's experience requirement.[58]

Fabre also thinks she can explain why it is bad for me when my life's work collapses and when my relationships are inauthentic, despite her experience requirement. As well as one's experiences being negatively affected by being turned from good to bad, Fabre also thinks one's experiences can be negatively affected by being made nonveridical. Compare the following two examples:

> Suppose that Jill betrays Jack's trust during Jack's life-time, that Jack will never know about it, and that his life will not be affected by it (his other friends will not turn away from him, he will not lose his job, etc). Imagine, alternatively, that Jill betrays Jack's trust after Jack's death. In the first case, or so I submit, Jill harms Jack precisely in so far as she makes his experience of his life untrue to his life as it is; in the latter, she does not harm him, or so I submit, precisely because he no longer has experiences—and, therefore, no longer has experiences of which it makes sense to say that they are, or not, veridical.[59]

The distinction Fabre is making is neat. However, it does not get the cases right for me. There are two ways to stop one's perception of the world from being nonveridical: first, you can correct the world; second, you can correct the belief. But, when it comes to nonveridical relationships and nonveridical accomplishments, making one's experiences veridical by changing one's beliefs is very different from making the world fit one's beliefs. That was a little abstract. Consider the following example: suppose that Jack finds out that Jill has betrayed his trust. Jack may well feel that it is bad for him that he has been deceived. That he has been living a lie. But I think he will also feel bad that he has not been enjoying an authentic relationship with Jill. And that is not so much to do with his *experience* of the relationship—rather, it is to do with the nature of the relationship itself. Take the example of my life's work collapsing without my knowledge. It is weird to think what is primarily bad about that happening is that, I believe my work is well respected when it is not; rather, what is bad about that happening is that I have not accomplished anything.

What is the upshot of all of this? Whether one's experiences are negatively affected seems beside the point when it comes to some desires and some aspects of one's lives—for example, one's desires that they are in authentic relationships and that their life's work is successful. And, even Fabre's weaker experience requirement is not faithful to

[58] Fabre has another argument. She says, "between E—the act which results in X's death—and X's dying, there is a lapse of time, however infinitesimally short, during which X still exists" (Fabre, 237). Why not say death is bad for one then? We can call this view *Concurrentism*, since it says death's badness is concurrent with the moment of one's death. Now, it is not obvious to me that there needs to be this lapse of time between E and one's death. But, setting that aside, I do not think Concurrentism is very plausible in general. For one thing, it makes death strangely *sui generis*. Suppose you break my leg. When is that harmful for me? It is not just at the point at which you break my leg. On a Counterfactual Account of harm, which Fabre endorses, it is bad for me for as long as I am worse off than I otherwise would have been. But the same is not true for death if Concurrentism is correct. For more difficulties, see Bradley, *Well-Being and Death*, 86–7; Johansson, "The Timing Problem," 261.

[59] Fabre, "Posthumous Rights," 234.

this. This means we have good reason not to think there is an experience requirement of the sorts Heathwood and Fabre have introduced.

In this section, I have argued that the dead are potential right-holders on the Interest Theory. And, I have laid down two requirements for any argument to the contrary. First, the argument must nonetheless explain why death is bad for the one who dies. Second, the argument must explain why things can be good or bad for one without those things affecting one's experiences. As indicated above, one could jettison either of these requirements. But insofar as one finds these ideas plausible, one should conclude the dead are potential right-holders on the Interest Theory.

4. Conclusion

This chapter has considered whether the dead are potential right-holders on the Interest Theory. I have argued they are, given plausible views about well-being. Yet, my hope is my chapter has done more than just that. Hopefully, it has set out how we ought to go about determining whether some putative potential right-holder is a potential right-holder: we should ask, either, whether they are bearers of well-being or interests, or we should inquire as to the nature of their interests.

4
Are Legal Positivism and the Interest Theory of Rights Compatible?

*Visa A.J. Kurki**

1. Introduction

Matthew Kramer is a self-described "diehard jurisprudential positivist" who rejects all of the salient connections between law and morality that have been proposed in the literature.[1] As a positivist, Kramer claims that law and morality are "strictly separable." On the other hand, he subscribes to the interest theory of legal rights, according to which the right of some *X* entails, and is entailed by, a duty that protects some aspect of *X*'s situation that on balance is typically beneficial for someone like *X*.[2] Ascriptions of legal rights are thus intertwined with evaluative considerations, such as what is "beneficial."

It is not difficult to see why some might find a tension between the two views. Let us take a relatively topical example. The Maori people of New Zealand consider the Whanganui River a spiritual entity, Te Awa Tupua. Under recent New Zealand legislation, the river has been declared a legal person. The relevant statute includes the following provisions:

> 12 Te Awa Tupua recognition
> Te Awa Tupua is an indivisible and living whole, comprising the Whanganui River from the mountains to the sea, incorporating all its physical and metaphysical elements.
> . . .

* Many thanks to Mark McBride for excellent comments on this essay, as well as to the workshop participants in Helsinki and Cambridge for stimulating discussion. Special thanks go to Matthew Kramer, who supervised my doctoral dissertation at Cambridge. I encountered the name Wesley Newcomb Hohfeld when my Bachelor's thesis supervisor Markku Suksi suggested I might be interested in his work. I became increasingly fascinated by the Hohfeldian analysis, to the point where no-one in Finland could answer my questions about it anymore. In 2013, with an LLM degree in my pocket, I remember emailing Professor Matthew Kramer to pose some rather obscure questions about Hohfeld. Some twenty to thirty minutes later, he wrote back to me, suggesting that I come over to Cambridge for a cafeteria dinner at Churchill College, where I could ask the questions. Well, that's an offer you cannot refuse—and accepting the offer eventually led to my applying to Cambridge to do a PhD under Kramer's supervision.

[1] Matthew H. Kramer, *In Defense of Legal Positivism: Law Without Trimmings*, 204. See also Bix, Waluchow, Chiassoni, and Postema, chs 6, 7, 8 and 9 respectively, in this volume on Kramer's positivism.

[2] Kramer propounds the interest theory as a general theory of rights, but this chapter focuses on legal rights.

Visa A.J. Kurki, *Are Legal Positivism and the Interest Theory of Rights Compatible?* In: *Without Trimmings*.
Edited by: Mark McBride and Visa AJ Kurki, Oxford University Press. © Mark McBride and Visa AJ Kurki 2022.
DOI: 10.1093/oso/9780198868866.003.0004

> 14 Te Awa Tupua declared to be legal person
> (1) Te Awa Tupua is a legal person and has all the rights, powers, duties, and liabilities of a legal person.
> (2) The rights, powers, and duties of Te Awa Tupua must be exercised or performed, and responsibility for its liabilities must be taken, by Te Pou Tupua [the "human face" of Te Awa Tupua] on behalf of, and in the name of, Te Awa Tupua, ...[3]

The legislator of New Zealand has deemed Te Awa Tupua to be "an indivisible and living whole" and purported to endow it with legal rights. However, according to many interest theorists, the river does not in fact hold legal rights. In fact, people such as Kramer and Joseph Raz—both legal positivists as well as interest theorists—declare rivers ineligible to hold legal rights on *moral* grounds.[4] How can such a claim be reconciled with core idea of legal positivism: insistence on the separability of law and morality?

Legal philosophers have not written much on the compatibility of legal positivism and the interest theory—which I will label "the Compatibility Question." Some of the few exceptions include Nigel Simmonds and, more recently, David Frydrych.[5] However, I often encounter skepticism about their compatibility from students as well as from academics who are not specialists in rights theory. There is thus reason to address this question thoroughly. I will start by presenting legal positivism and the interest theory, as well as assessing their interactions. I will then present some doubts about their compatibility that have been voiced by Simmonds and Frydrych, and proceed to assess a view that I will label "Rights Deference." Finally, I will discuss whether the so-called Correlativity Axiom, endorsed by Kramer, is problematic from the point of view of the Compatibility Question.

2. Assessing Positivism and the Interest Theory

What exactly constitutes legal positivism is a contested question in itself. Thankfully, in the context of this essay, it is natural to proceed based on how Kramer understands legal positivism. He takes legal positivism to consist of a number of claims, ranging from the denial of the inherent morality of the rule of law to an insistence on the credible possibility that power-hungry officials might have strong prudential reasons to adhere to rule-of-law requirements to quite high levels.[6] Legal positivism, then,

[3] Te Awa Tupua (Whanganui River Claims Settlement) Act 2017, emphases removed.

[4] Raz's theory is presented in Raz, "On the Nature of Rights," 194. It bears noting that Raz is not as "die-hard" a positivist as Kramer is: for Raz, law and morality are not wholly separable. Thanks to Mark McBride for pressing me on this.

[5] I have also heard a presentation by Milda Baltrimienė voicing this worry. However, the subsequent article she has published on the topic, despite also having an English title, is in Lithuanian. Baltrimienė, "The Problem of the Nature of Individual Rights in Contemporary Theories of Legal Positivism." The issue is also broached by David J. Calverley, who writes that "[c]ertainly under some theories of law, such as positivism, it is logically possible to argue that to the extent law defines what a legal person is, law could simply define a legal person to be anything law chooses it to be." Calverley, "Imagining a Non-Biological Machine as a Legal Person," 527 (reference removed).

[6] See Kramer, *In Defense of Legal Positivism: Law Without Trimmings*.

encompasses multifarious strands. However, I will in this essay focus on Kramer's claim that "legal requirements and moral requirements always *can* diverge"—which I will call the Separability Thesis, even if Kramer shuns that phrase.[7] As an inclusive legal positivist and an incorporationist, Kramer thinks that some norm's consistency with morality can serve as both a necessary and a sufficient condition for the validity of that norm in some jurisdiction.[8] However, such conditions must have a social basis—a requirement usually termed the Social Thesis.[9]

Understood in the way just delineated, legal positivism is a thesis about the validity of legal norms. However, this description should be made more precise in a way that may strike some as surprising and others as painstakingly obvious: legal positivism is, first and foremost, a thesis concerning legal duties and powers.

At least since H.L.A. Hart's *Concept of Law*, law has been seen to comprise duty-imposing and power-conferring norms.[10] We should note that all but two of the other Hohfeldian incidents stand in clear logical relations to duties and powers: a liberty is a lack of duty, a liability is being subject to a power, and so on.[11] As Nigel Simmonds has observed,

> it is hard to imagine *any* plausible account of legal powers that would not portray them as correlative to liabilities; similarly, immunity seems to entail disability (and vice versa) not simply within some limited context, but without qualification and in virtue of the meaning of the words.[12]

Thus, the duty-imposing and power-conferring norms of a legal system, taken together, determine the overall constellation of Hohfeldian legal positions held by those subject to the norms of that system. There is an exception, however: the logical relation between duties and claims—which are correlatives in Hohfeld's scheme—is not as obvious as with the other positions. Under what conditions does the duty of *X* entail the (claim-)right of *Y*? Neither Hohfeldian exegesis nor legal positivism alone can provide the answer. Given that claims are rights according to Kramer, his interest theory can be seen as a complement to legal positivism, which can on its own account for the other Hohfeldian legal positions. Furthermore, given that no-rights obtain where rights could obtain but do not, the interest theory is also a theory of no-rights.[13]

[7] Ibid., 1–2, emphasis in original.

[8] The most thorough treatment of inclusivism and incorporationism by Kramer is Kramer, *Where Law and Morality Meet*.

[9] Raz writes that "[i]n the most general terms the positivist social thesis is that what is law and what is not is a matter of social fact (that is, the variety of social theses supported by positivists are various refinements and elaborations of this crude formulation)." Raz, *The Authority of Law*, 37. I am here employing the phrase "social thesis" in this broad sense. However, Raz goes on to use the phrase "social thesis" in a narrower sense, which he renames the "sources thesis."

[10] Hart, *The Concept of Law*.

[11] See Hohfeld, "Some Fundamental Legal Conceptions as Applied in Legal Reasoning," 16–59. For a good introduction to Hohfeld, see the beginning of Kramer, "Rights Without Trimmings," 7–112.

[12] N.E. Simmonds, "Rights at the Cutting Edge," 113–232, 143. See also Kramer, "Rights Without Trimmings," 91–3.

[13] In addition, given that first-order Hohfeldian relations always consist of either a duty–right or a liberty–no-right pair, and given that the higher-order relations always ultimately pertain to a first-order relation, a complete account of any individual Hohfeldian relation always requires a theory of claim-rights and no-rights.

A central constraint that legal positivism places on a theory of rights is what I will call the Contingent Norms Requirement. According to this requirement, a theory of legal rights must account for the fact that a legal system may contain duties and powers of almost any content. There are, however, certain conceptual boundaries[14] (e.g., duties cannot be borne by mathematical entities) as well as restrictions stemming from the principles of legality and the minimum content of natural law.[15] Thus, legal norms must for instance be general to some extent in order for the overall system of norms to qualify as legal, and the norms must in some way take into account the fact that human beings can harm and kill each other, lest the system descend into chaos. However, within these parameters, there is room for duties and powers with any content—which a theory of legal rights must account for in order to be compatible with legal positivism.

2.1 What is the Interest Theory?

The interest theory (or benefit theory) is, in fact, a family of theories that associate rights with the furtherance of interests. Again, in what follows, I will mostly focus on Kramer's interest theory.

We should note at the outset that theories of rights can take ascriptions of legal rights to be either *premises* or *conclusions* of legal reasoning. In the words of Charlie Webb, "[s]ometimes rights are taken to describe concrete, bottom-line entitlements, sometimes a kind of ground of such entitlements."[16] Will theorists take rights to be bottom-line entitlements more often than not, whereas many influential interest theorists have taken rights to be grounds. A bottom-line approach is characteristically based on the Hohfeldian analysis and takes rights to be correlative with some other legal positions. Typically, rights entail duties and (usually) vice versa. For instance, Hart took rights to be "conclusions of law."[17] Contrariwise, a theory that treats rights as grounds—such as the theories of Raz and Neil MacCormick—does not take rights to correlate with any legal positions. Rather, rights provide reasons, or justifications, for duties. Kramer's theory is an atypical interest theory in that it treats rights as bottom-line entitlements rather than as reasons. Furthermore, the rights entailed by a duty are determined based on the *content* of the duty rather than on, say, its purpose.

Kramer's theory is a theory of right-holding: it seeks to provide the necessary and sufficient criteria for when some *X* holds a legal right. Kramer has taken his theory to consist of the following two tenets:

[14] These conceptual boundaries have not received a lot of attention in the literature. Presumably, all sorts of conceptual truths (e.g., concerning causation) could preclude norms with certain content.

[15] As regards the principles of legality, see Fuller, *The Morality of Law* and Kramer, *Objectivity and the Rule of Law*, 101–86. On the minimum content of natural law, see Hart, *The Concept of Law*, 193–9.

[16] Webb, "Three Concepts of Rights, Two of Property," 246, doi:10.1093/ojls/gqy006 (abstract).

[17] "But again it is important to see that one who says that '*A* has a right' does not *state* the relevant rule of law; and that though, given certain facts, it is correct to say '*A* has a right,' one who says this does not state or describe those facts. He has done something different from either of these two things: he has drawn a conclusion from the relevant but unstated rule, and from the relevant but unstated facts of the case. '*A* has a right' like 'He is out' is therefore the tail-end of a simple legal calculation: it records a result and may well be called a conclusion of law." Hart, "Definition and Theory in Jurisprudence," 10 (emphasis in original).

(IT-1) Necessary though insufficient for the holding of a legal right by X is that the duty correlative to the right, when actual, normatively protects some aspect of X's situation that on balance is typically beneficial for a being like X (namely, a human individual, a collectivity or a non-human animal).

(IT-2) Neither necessary nor sufficient for the holding of some specified legal right by X is that X is competent and authorized to demand or waive the enforcement of the duty that is correlative to the right.[18]

Further to these basic tenets, Kramer has included a number of refinements to his theory. In particular, he has devised a solution to a problem of overinclusiveness. The problem is that duties can often benefit a whole range of parties who should regardless not be termed right-holders. Interestingly, both of the authors who have doubted the compatibility of the interest theory with legal positivism have focused on this problem, which is why I will address it later in detail. At any rate, I have argued elsewhere that the solution, "Bentham's test"—focusing on the conditions under which a duty can be breached—lies, in fact, at the heart of the interest theory.[19]

I hold that the following formulation captures Kramer's interest theory:

X holds a right correlative to currently existing duty *D* if and only if:

(i) *X* can hold rights and

(ii-a) a set of facts minimally sufficient to establish the contravention of duty *D* includes a fact that affects *X*'s situation in a way typically detrimental for beings such as *X* (*Formulation 1*).[20]

Prong (i) has to do with the position, held by many interest theorists, that only certain kinds of beings can hold rights and that this delimitation is done on moral grounds.

Prong (ii-a) is Bentham's test. It incorporates Kramer's insight that the problems of overinclusiveness that had afflicted many interest theories can be solved by focusing on the conditions under which a duty can be breached. Consider Anne's duty not to assault Bertha. If Anne were to contravene this duty by assaulting Bertha, she would also affect the situation of Bertha's husband Charles in a typically negative manner. Charles would likely be at least upset, if nothing else. However, not even the fact that Charles exists would figure in any set of facts minimally sufficient to establish that Anne has breached her duty toward Bertha. Therefore, Charles does not hold a right-that-Anne-not-assault-Bertha.

Prong (ii-a) of the formulation can also be replaced with another, "positive" formulation:

[18] Kramer, "In Defence of the Interest Theory of Right-Holding: Rejoinders to Leif Wenar on Rights," 49, 49. This is Kramer's latest account of his theory of right-holding. What is striking about it is that it does not provide sufficient conditions for right-holding. However, Kramer has in private communication specified that he will henceforth formulate the interest theory in a single tenet that states what is both sufficient and necessary for the holding of a right by *X*.

[19] Kurki, "Rights, Harming and Wronging: A Restatement of the Interest Theory." See also Mark McBride, "Preserving the Interest Theory of Rights," *Legal Theory*.

[20] Kurki, "Rights, Harming and Wronging: A Restatement of the Interest Theory," 438.

(ii-b) a set of facts minimally sufficient to establish the fulfilment or non-contravention of duty *D* includes a fact that affects *X*'s situation in a way typically beneficial for beings such as *X* (*Formulation 2*).[21]

Applying either formulation gives the same results.

Prongs (i) and (ii) do not include the requirement that rights be protected by sundry immunities in order for them not to be "hollowly nominal." Kramer writes:

> Moreover, immunities are also of crucial importance because of their role in stabilizing other legal entitlements. For instance, if John has a legal right against being punched in the face by Jim, and if he has no immunities against being divested of that right through countless elementary means (for example, through Jim's looking at him or through Jim's utterance of any word in his presence), then John's right is hollowly nominal rather than genuine.[22]

Kramer must think that hollowly nominal rights are nevertheless rights. Denying that hollowly nominal rights are rights might *ipso facto* mean abandoning the Correlativity Axiom, according to which rights and duties always correlate with each other. If hollowly nominal rights were not rights, Jim would bear the duty not to punch John, but John would not hold any correlative right.[23]

We should now train our focus on two important features of Kramer's interest theory.

First, the theory is *an explication*: it builds on our quotidian understanding of rights, but tries to make it more exact and better in line with desiderata such as fruitfulness (consilience) and simplicity.[24] Hence, it is of course meritorious for the interest theory to correspond with our everyday ascriptions of rights, but its divergence from such everyday ascriptions is not in itself a knockdown argument against the interest theory. In fact, the theory may be used to show that our everyday ascriptions might be inconsistent and hence in need of revision.

In addition, the theory is intended as *system-independent*. The interest theory is a tool of philosophical analysis, to be applied to any legal system—even a system whose officials and other participants lack the concept of a right. It is often claimed that Romans lacked the concept of what Continental jurists term "subjective rights"; rather, the cognate concept was that of "objective right" (*ius*), i.e., what is right or just in a given situation.[25] Kramer's theory is, regardless, applicable to Roman law: we can employ the theory to ascertain whether, say, women or slaves held rights under Roman

[21] Ibid., 439.

[22] Kramer, "Rights in Legal and Political Philosophy," 417. David Frydrych notes that Kramer uses the phrase "nominal right" in two somewhat different senses: on one hand of unenforceable legal rights, and on the other hand of rights unaccompanied by sundry immunities. Frydrych, "The Theories of Rights Debate," 570f.

[23] Kramer does, however, think that all legal duties are also owed to the state. I will return to this issue later in this essay.

[24] See Kurki, "Rights, Harming and Wronging: A Restatement of the Interest Theory," 433–5 and Van Duffel, "Adequacy Constraints for a Theory of Rights," 187.

[25] Tierney, *The Idea of Natural Rights: Studies on Natural Rights, Natural Law and Church Law 1150–1625*, 13ff.

law. This is in line with the task of general jurisprudence, which seeks to determine which communities live under a legal system regardless of whether those communities have the concept of law. In this regard, Neil MacCormick's description of Hart's views also applies to Kramer: " 'a right' is a term used in discourse *about* the law, used for making statements *about* individual's positions as seen in terms of the law, rather than a term used *in* the law itself."[26] Understood as an empirical claim, this view is obviously false, as the term "a right" is certainly used in statutes and court judgments. However, the quoted passage describes aptly the system-independent perspective of Kramer's interest theory.

2.2 Aspects of Neutrality

A useful starting point for our assessment of whether the interest theory and legal positivism are compatible is Kramer's own distinction between value-independence and value-neutrality.[27]

A "project of theoretical elaboration" is value-independent if "it is not grounded on any ethical values. Some values do of course underlie any such project, but they are theoretical-explanatory or logical/mathematical or aesthetic rather than ethical."[28] Value-neutrality, on the other hand, has to do with the actual theses, rather than merely the justifications, of some theory:

> If certain theses are value-neutral, then we can gauge the fulfillment or nonfulfillment of those theses in any number of circumstances without having to undertake any ethical judgments. In other words, the states of affairs recounted by those theses can be ascertained (as present or absent) without any ethical assessments.[29]

Now, Kramer—in line with legal positivists more generally—contends that his reasons for espousing his particular version of legal positivism are analytical rather than moral. This would render his theory value-independent.[30] Furthermore, the existence of a legal system can be ascertained without any ethical evaluation, rendering legal positivism in this regard value-neutral. On the other hand, some of the norms of legal systems that have incorporated moral norms are ascertainable only by resorting to ethical evaluation. Thus, Kramer's legal positivism is value-neutral as a theory of *law*, but not always as a theory of *the law*.

[26] MacCormick, "Rights in Legislation," 190 (paraphrasing the views of H.L.A. Hart propounded in an unpublished lecture). It bears mentioning that Hart later distanced himself from this view of rights.

[27] See also Radoilska, ch. 11 in this volume.

[28] Kramer, "Conceptual Analysis and Distributive Justice," 376.

[29] Ibid.

[30] "I have argued throughout this book on analytical grounds for a positivist conception of law. My positivist orientation is methodological as well as substantive. To be sure, a reliance on analytical grounds must involve judgments about the importance or unimportance of various aspects of the phenomena that are being pondered. Much the same is true of any theory about anything. But judgments of importance are not perforce moral judgments; the considerations that have guided my focus throughout this book are nonmoral considerations." Kramer, *In Defense of Legal Positivism: Law Without Trimmings*, 179.

Kramer's interest theory, on the other hand, is certainly not value-neutral, and perhaps not value-independent either. I will briefly consider value-independence first. It is debatable whether all of the justifications Kramer offers for the interest theory are purely analytical-explanatory. For instance, Kramer criticizes "hard" will theorists for their denial of children's rights, describing such a denial as "outlandish."[31] This criticism can be construed as merely having to do with the considerable departure from ordinary-language rights ascriptions, but it can also be construed as exhibiting a moral tenor. Be that as it may, the value-neutrality of the interest theory is of more importance here. Let us now look in detail at how rights ascriptions are dependent on evaluative considerations under the interest theory.

2.3 Evaluation and the Interest Theory

At the risk of stating the obvious, I will now briefly recapitulate how the interest theory and legal positivism operate together. As already mentioned, the interest theory is focused on rights as conclusions of law. It declares rights to be the correlatives of duties, and asks: when does duty *D* correlate with right *R*? Hence, in order to ascertain whether some legal system *LS* endows entity *X* with right *R*, we will need to know the content of the norms of *LS*. The content of those norms is determined by employing the rule of recognition to which the officials of *LS* adhere. One will need to establish the existence and content of relevant duty-imposing and power-conferring norms.

With regard to duty-imposing norms, one will need to look in particular at the conditions of how some duty *D* can be contravened or fulfilled. *X* holds right *R* correlative to duty *D* only if a set of facts minimally sufficient to establish the contravention of *D* includes a fact that affects *X*'s situation in a way typically detrimental for beings such as *X*.

Furthermore, in order to establish that *R* is not hollowly nominal, one will need to ascertain that numerous power-conferring norms do not exist. The holder of *R* must hold "immunities against being divested of [*R*] through countless elementary means."[32] Kramer is somewhat vague on the exact nature of these immunities, and I do not intend to explore that question here.

Now, there are three ways in which the ascertainment of rights under the interest theory can depend on moral considerations.

First, the determination of duty-imposing and power-conferring norms can involve moral reasoning. However, this is really a feature of Kramer's inclusive legal positivism rather than the interest theory. It is hard to see how it would bear on the Compatibility Question.

Second, the candidate right-holder must belong to the domain of right-holders—he, she, or it must be able to hold rights. The domain of right-holders is settled based on openly moral criteria.[33]

[31] Kramer, "Rights Without Trimmings," 69.
[32] Kramer, "Rights in Legal and Political Philosophy," 417.
[33] See Bowen, ch. 3 in this volume.

Finally, determining the beneficiaries of some particular duty is an evaluative enterprise as well. What is beneficial or detrimental, good or bad, for someone or something is obviously an evaluative question. Such an evaluation is not exclusively ethical—prudential interests comprise the most central category of interests here—but it is certainly partly ethical.

We can now see an important difference in the ways in which Kramer's legal positivism and the interest theory are *not* value-neutral. Under positivism, it is contingent on social facts whether the ascertainment of some legal norm depends on moral evaluation. Moral evaluation only comes into play if the legal system has incorporated moral norms (as necessary or sufficient conditions of legal validity). On the other hand, under the interest theory, *no* token of right-holding is ascertainable without resorting to ethical evaluation. Regardless, this intertwinement will turn out to be surprisingly unproblematic as regards the Compatibility Question.

3. Compatibility Doubts

I will in this section start addressing doubts voiced about the compatibility of legal positivism and the interest theory. I will first briefly assess some remarks made by Nigel Simmonds in 1995—before Kramer had propounded his interest theory in "Rights without Trimmings"—and then focus on David Frydrych's more sustained attack. Though Frydrych's criticisms are generally unsuccessful, they do regardless provide interesting angles for assessing the Compatibility Question.

3.1 Simmonds's Doubts

Simmonds presents his compatibility doubts when addressing the so-called third-party beneficiary problem, a version of the overinclusiveness problem mentioned above. The third-party beneficiary problem obtains in a situation where *A* promises *B* to perform some action that benefits *C*. Does *B*, *C*, or both obtain rights as a result? Let us assume that we would like to ascribe a right to the promisee but not to the beneficiary, as the English law of 1995 would only give powers of enforcement to the promisee. Simmonds suggests that in order to solve the problem, "the [interest] theory would simply need to claim that right-holders are not all those who in fact benefit from the duty, but only those whose interests provide the reason for the existence of the duty."[34] Simmonds is here invoking an understanding of rights as interests that justify duties. He then suggests in a footnote that because the interest theory requires "us to ask questions about the rationale of, or justification for, particular legal rules," it might be incompatible with legal positivism—as well as liberal neutrality.[35] He goes on:

[34] Simmonds, "The Analytical Foundations of Justice," 316.
[35] Ibid., 316f.

> The choice theory, by contrast, allows us to ascertain the existence and content of legal rights simply by consulting the content of existing legal rules, without raising deeper questions of their rationale.... In fact, the choice theory's compatibility with liberal neutrality and legal positivism might at first be seen as a strong point in its favour, not only by legal positivists and liberal neutralists, but also by people who believe that we should seek an analysis of rights that does not prejudge wider issues of political philosophy and jurisprudence.[36]

Simmonds might of course be right in his doubts about the compatibility of legal positivism and reasons-based interest theories—though there is reason to doubt this, as the rationale of a legal rule can simply be understood as the *legal* rationale rather than, for example, moral justification.[37] For what it is worth, some nonpositivists have found the rights-as-reasons approach appealing. For instance, Pavlos Eleftheriadis claims that the positions in Hohfeldian legal relations are not rights; rather, "[l]egal rights work to ground clusters of legal relations in given circumstances, through a process of practical deliberation appropriate to each legal order."[38] Eleftheriadis's rejection of Hohfeldian positions as rights is intertwined with his rejection of legal positivism.[39] Furthermore, one of the positivists' archnemeses, Ronald Dworkin, takes rights to be reasons.[40]

However, as we are focused on Kramer's theory of rights, we need not worry whether an interest theory that treats rights as reasons or justifications is compatible with positivism. This is because Kramer's theory differs from that of Raz or MacCormick in a crucial respect: Kramer's theory does not require us to consider the justifications of legal norms. In fact, what Simmonds takes to be a strength of the will theory—that it "allows us to ascertain the existence and content of legal rights simply by consulting the content of existing legal rules"—applies equally well to the interest theory. Both identify rights by consulting legal norms and certain evaluative considerations.[41]

I will now move on to Frydrych's qualms, which are aimed specifically at Kramer's interest theory.

3.2 Frydrych's Criticism

Like Simmonds, Frydrych also presents his worries in the course of a discussion of the third-party beneficiary problem. I will begin by addressing his (unsuccessful)

[36] Ibid.

[37] However, George Rainbolt does see Raz's theory of legal rights as potentially creating problems for his legal positivism. Rainbolt, *The Concept of Rights*, 92–3.

[38] Eleftheriadis, *Legal Rights*, 168.

[39] Positivists generally deny that law must provide its subjects with any normative reasons for action; the law according to positivism is "normatively inert," to use John Gardner's phrasing. Given that Hohfeldian legal relations are simply conclusions of law, this denial applies to them as well. However, this conclusion is unsatisfactory for Eleftheriadis. Gardner, "Legal Positivism: 5 ½ Myths," 199, 202. See also Enoch, "Reason-Giving and the Law."

[40] See Dworkin, "Taking Rights Seriously," 223–48.

[41] Kramer argues that the will theory also needs to rely on evaluative considerations in Kramer, "Rights Without Trimmings," 92–3. However, one might very well argue that the will theory is less dependent on evaluative considerations when identifying rights.

criticisms of how Kramer's interest theory solves the problem, and will then move on to his compatibility doubts.

Frydrych first voices his doubts in the course of the following passage:

> Kramer's test is not a norm of a given legal system or set of such systems. So why give it any credence—especially if the Interest Theory's concern is with legal rights? It is also unclear how this can be squared with Kramer's legal positivist commitments. Should the meta-theoretical desideratum not be that it accurately identifies which parties in (certain? all?) legal systems actually have legal rights and which do not? If so, then the main reason to adopt or endorse the test is its identificatory power. If not, it is unclear why analytic legal theorists or others would adopt it.[42]

Frydrych does not really spell out here how the interest theory and legal positivism would be incompatible. The problem seems to be the interest theory's supposed inability to account for the fact that apposite rights ascriptions depend on contingent features of particular legal systems. This inability would violate the Contingent Norms Requirement. Frydrych then presents a number of examples supposed to be problematic for the interest theory. I will mention three of them. The first two have to do with third-party beneficiaries of contracts, where *A* and *B* enter a contract whereby *A* undertakes to perform some service to *C*.

> [T]he Minimum Sufficiency test [i.e., Bentham's test] cannot correctly delimit the set of rights when there is only one relevant action, e.g., where [*B* pays *A*] to fix *C*'s roof. Do *B* and *C* both have legal rights because the roof was not fixed? Once again, the answer is actually system contingent.
>
> So too regarding whether additional parties have rights because the roof was not fixed. For example, imagine that *D* rents a room in *C*'s house. *D*'s bedroom suffers leaks because of the unrepaired roof. Under Kramer's test, *D* (in addition to *C*) has a legal right based on the *A*-*B* contract to repair the roof: there is one minimally sufficient fact (an unrepaired roof), a breach of duty, and harm affecting *D*'s interests (a party bearing a "detriment" due to *B*'s failure to fulfill the contractual norm).[43]

These examples are intended to bring out certain unintended consequences of Bentham's test. Frydrych's ultimate aim is to show that whether the third parties (*C* in the first scenario, *C* and/or *D* in the second) hold legal rights is a system-contingent inquiry. However, the criticism is somewhat unclear.

Let us first note the phrasing of the following question: "Do *B* and *C* both have legal rights *because the roof was not fixed*?" (emphasis added). The emphasized part is surprising. *B* may very well incur remediary rights (or other legal positions) because the roof was not fixed, but it is not the case that *B*'s primary right-that-C's-room-be-fixed exists "because the roof was not fixed." Frydrych seems to suggest that the breach itself

[42] Frydrych, "Kramer's Delimiting Test for Legal Rights," 203, doi.10.1093/ajj/aux019.

[43] Ibid., 203–4. Frydrych actually writes "where *A* pays *B*" rather than "where *B* pays *A*," but he evidently intends *B* to be the commissioner and *A* the commissioned party.

entails the primary right. This is not so: it is the content of *A*'s duty that specifies both which rights the duty entails and how that duty can be breached.

At any rate, the test works exactly as intended. In the first scenario, *C* holds a legal right correlative to the duty, especially if *C* is specified as a beneficiary of the contract. Whether *C* holds enforcement powers or remediary rights pertaining to *B*'s duty is a different matter. It may of course be questioned whether deeming *C* a right-holder is a counterintuitive result; it is not, at any rate, a clear example of a misascription of rights. In the second scenario, *D* clearly does not hold a right correlative to *B*'s duty. There is no set of facts that both contains the fact that *D* exists and is minimally sufficient to establish breach of *B*'s duty. Without establishing that *D* exists, we cannot infer that he has suffered a typically detrimental development.

The same response applies to a scenario that Frydrych invokes, originally conceived of by Rudolf von Jhering:

> A domestic manufacturer, through political or financial pressure, or corruption, gains the government's favor. He convinces it to pass a law imposing tariffs on certain foreign goods that compete with his own. The domestic manufacturer has an interest in the new law being enforced (indeed, it was grounded in his interests), which also directly benefits him—and intentionally so, in a sense. Does he therefore have a right under that law? Is it a right correlative to other parties' duties to pay the tariff?[44]

Now, Frydrych claims that

> Kramer's test seems incapable of avoiding the attribution of a legal right to the domestic manufacturer: If a given party breaches the duty to pay the tariff—the minimal set of facts—that seems sufficient to entail that both the domestic manufacturer and the government have legal claim-rights.[45]

Frydrych does not specify why the duty-to-pay-the-tariff "seems sufficient" for the domestic manufacturer's holding of a right correlative to the duty.[46] Nor does such an entailment obtain: again, no minimally sufficient set of facts sufficient to establish the breach contains the fact that the domestic manufacturer exists.

3.3 Back to the Compatibility Question

Frydrych's criticisms are thus not very successful. However, he ends his attack with the following suggestion. The interest theory should only offer necessary rather than sufficient conditions for the existence of a right, and Bentham's test is unnecessary:

[44] Ibid., 204.

[45] Ibid.

[46] Again, Frydrych's formulation ("If a given party breaches the duty to pay the tariff . . . that seems sufficient to entail") suggests that it would be the breach itself that entails rights. This is not so: it is the content of the duty that specifies both which rights the duty entails and how it can be breached.

> For one thing, the test is unnecessary if a rights theorist is also committed to the Legal Positivist Sources Thesis. For on that view, determining which interests warrant legal recognition is a system-contingent inquiry; it is simply a matter of the law of a given jurisdiction. Just because 3PBs [i.e., third-party beneficiaries] (the roof-owner, the next-door neighbor, etc.) have an interest in a contract being fulfilled, it need not follow that the Interest Theory must attribute legal rights to them. It is not merely that the relevant types of interest[s] warranting legal rights status may be system contingent; it is also the case that, for Positivists, determining whether tokens of those types constitute bona fide rights is a matter for the Sources Thesis too. Even if, as a matter of normative theory, one believes that all 3PBs ought to have legal rights, it need not be true that they all do. A legal system may afford rights to some such parties and not others—for whatever meritorious or unmeritorious reasons its legal officials have so decided.[47]

Frydrych maintains that Bentham's test is unnecessary because rights-ascriptions can, in accordance with the Sources Thesis, be left to the lawmaker. (We should note that, as an inclusivist, Kramer does not subscribe to the Sources Thesis; however, this does not really make a difference.) Later, Frydrych concludes his article with the following suggestion:

> As he [Kramer] himself notes, his Interest Theory offers only the necessary, not the sufficient, conditions for a legal claim-right. Thus, instead of constructing delimitation tests, Kramer would be better off merely to note that determining the sufficient conditions for a legal right is a matter for a different kind of legal theory, e.g., Legal Positivism.[48]

Frydrych's claim can be unpacked in various ways. Let us examine two central statements from the longer extract above: (1) "the relevant types of interest[s] warranting legal rights status may be system contingent" and (2) "for Positivists, determining whether tokens of those types [of interests] constitute bona fide rights is a matter for the Sources Thesis too." Both statements can be given different interpretations.

In one sense of (1), it is obviously always up to the lawmaker to make a determination of whose interests warrant legal rights status. This is because rights are the correlatives of duties, and the lawmaker is free—in accordance with the Contingent Norms requirement—to enact whatever duties it likes, and this enactment is likely partly based on a determination of whose interests the legislator seeks to protect. Hence, which interests are protected by duties is obviously system-contingent.

However, Frydrych may in (1) perhaps also be propounding views that I will classify as falling under "Rights Deference." According to such a view the lawmaker is free to determine which types of entities can hold rights. The only explicit diehard endorsement of Rights Deference of which I am aware is by Michael Hartney. He writes:

[47] Frydrych, "Kramer's Delimiting Test for Legal Rights," 205. As was noted to me both by Kramer and McBride, Frydrych might be assuming the correctness of the will theory here: under the will theory, it is a system-contingent matter who has the power to waive some duty D, and therefore holds a right correlative to D.

[48] Ibid., 207.

> The ultimate touchstone . . . of all legal statements (and of the meaning of legal terms) is . . . the acts (and especially the utterances) of these legal authorities. . . . . No argument, philosophical or otherwise, can ever prevail against the pronouncement of the competent legal authority.
>
> This is especially true of the term "right". The utterance of a legal authority (legislature, official, court) that a right is being conferred is conclusive evidence that a legal right has been conferred. Whatever legal authorities say is a legal right, is a legal right, whether this agrees with what philosophers would say about moral rights. If a statute says that trees have rights, then trees have certain legal rights, whether we consider this to be morally defensible or even morally possible. The utterances of legal authorities constitute the raw data upon which our theory of legal rights must build. This theory must make room for all the rights and the kinds of rights which utterances of legal authorities say have been conferred.[49]

We can discern two versions of Rights Deference both in Frydrych's and Hartney's writings. First, the view that the legislator is free to endow any *X* with rights may be termed Domain Deference. Hartney writes: "If a statute says that trees have rights, then trees have certain legal rights, whether we consider this to be morally defensible or even morally possible." A somewhat less liberal version of Domain Deference is that the legislator can endow with rights any *X* that has interests. (We should note here that Kramer subscribes to a broad conception of interests that ascribes interests to buildings and paintings.)[50]

An even stronger version of Rights Deference is what I term "Conceptual Deference."[51] Hartney clearly subscribes to this position: "Whatever legal authorities say is a legal right, is a legal right." Frydrych's endorsement of this view is not quite as obvious. He contends that "for Positivists, determining whether tokens of those types [of interests] constitute bona fide rights is a matter for the Sources Thesis too." This passage lends itself to a number of interpretations. Frydrych could simply be reiterating the Contingent Norms Requirement, noting that officials can be inconsistent with regard to which interests they choose to protect with duties. However, he could also be claiming that what constitutes the criteria of ("bona fide") right-holding is a system-contingent question as well: a duty protecting an interest will only entail a right if deemed so by the criteria of right-holding adopted by that system.

[49] Hartney, "Some Confusions Concerning Collective Rights," 301–2. Hartney's position is very far-reaching, seeming to amount to "Deference Simpliciter," i.e., that legal authorities can determine the domain and intension of all legal concepts. Rowan Cruft seems to endorse Rights Deference as well: "Similarly again, Kramer's theory seems to compel us to see duties not to impede the prime minister's exercise of her power to declare war as owed to the prime minister, and duties to pay child benefits as owed to parents—for these parties are necessarily placed, by the duties' fulfilment, in a position that is typically beneficial in the relevant way. But it seems to me that we should not be compelled to accept this: the duties might or might not be owed to the parties in question, *and this depends simply on whether the systems creating the duties make the duties owed to the relevant parties*. They could do this, but they need not: a welfare system requiring child benefit payments to be made to parents could (as in the current British system) but need not confer on parents correlative rights." Cruft, *Human Rights, Ownership and the Individual*, 28, original emphases replaced with mine.

[50] Kramer, *Liberalism with Excellence*, 134–44.

[51] The same view could also be labelled "Rights Voluntarism," to reflect Pavlos Eleftheriadis's usage (in Eleftheriadis, *Legal Rights*, 173) or "Legal Omnipotence" as suggested by Miograd Jovanović (Jovanović, *Collective Rights. A Legal Theory*, 4–5).

Though I find especially Conceptual Deference bizarre for several reasons, I will here contend with appraising whether a commitment to legal positivism necessitates such an extreme stance.

3.4 Assessing Rights Deference

We should start with an important point: legal positivism is not a deferential doctrine with regard to duties or powers, under both Conceptual and Domain Deference. First, a legal positivist does not need to take the legislator's definition of "duty" or "power" as decisive. In fact, given that legal positivists strive to explain the essential features of all legal systems, adhering to the definitions endorsed by the lawmaker of some particular jurisdiction would be strange. And nor does a positivist need to subscribe to the notion that if the legislator purports to ascribe some legal duty or power to entity *E*, then *E* always bears that duty or holds that power. Rather, a positivist may very well hold that there are all sorts of conceptual limits at play here, such as limits regarding who or what can bear duties or hold powers.

Thus, if a statute of some country purports to impose upon a river the duty to phi, a positivist need not take this imposition at face value. The positivist can instead try to provide a meaningful account of who or what in fact bears the duty to phi. The actual duty-bearer might, for instance, be an appointed representative of the river. A classic example of a similar approach is the corporation. Suppose that a statute speaks of the duties of corporations. Now, a positivist can certainly maintain that only human individuals can in fact bear legal duties, and that any duties supposedly borne by corporations are in fact reducible to duties borne by individuals—regardless of statutory language.

Neither should legal positivists be deferential toward the non-positivist attitudes of a community or its officials. For instance, the officials of some legal system might think that their law is valid and in force in virtue of having been handed down by God. A legal positivist would have to dispute such a claim: the law of that legal system is valid and in force only because the officials treat it as such.

A theory of rights need not be deferential, either, in order to be compatible with legal positivism. The interest theory takes as "input" the duty-imposing and power-conferring norms of some legal system, and provides as "output" the rights of that legal system. This output partly depends on moral criteria. However, the theory does not prejudge what the input should be; it is therefore consistent with the Contingent Norms Requirement.

Regardless, a compatibility skeptic might be dissatisfied. Who is the interest theorist to tell the legislator that some beings can hold rights and others cannot? Here we should note that the interest theory is a not a theory of how the word "right," or cognate terms, should be interpreted when appearing in legal sources. Rather, the theory *presupposes* a theory of interpretation that can be used to ascertain the duty-imposing and power-conferring norms of some legal system. Recall the theory's system-independence: the interest theory is even applicable to legal systems that lack the concept of a right. Thus, if the New Zealand legislature purports to endow a river with rights, an interest theorist can simply ask what power-conferring and duty-imposing norms flow from such a legislative act, and then determine what rights ensue. I myself have argued that the right-holder here can be understood as the collectivity of human and nonhuman animals that depend on the river in one way or another.[52]

The same applies to Conceptual Deference as well. The legislator is free to define "a right" as it likes, but any such definitions only determine how the word is to be understood in statutory interpretation. The definition will likely have an impact on the duty-imposing and power-conferring norms of that legal system and, subsequently, to what rights are conferred by that legal system. Regardless, the statutory definition does not have any immediate bearing on the interest theory, which strives to be system-independent. (However, it bears mentioning that rights theorists must be sensitive to how the word "right" is actually used. If legislatures around the world started defining "right" in a way that is clearly at odds with the interest theory, or some other theory of rights, then this would weaken the credibility of that theory. To this extent, Hartney's claim that "[t]he utterances of legal authorities constitute the raw data upon which our theory of legal rights must build" is certainly correct.)[53]

4. A Final Doubt: Correlativity Axiom

I will finally address an issue that I take to be somewhat more problematic from the point of view of the Compatibility Question. Kramer is committed to the "Correlativity Axiom" that posits a mutual entailment between rights and duties: a right always entails a duty, and a duty always entails at least one right.[54]

As noted above, the interest theory takes the duty-imposing and power-conferring norms of some legal system as input and provides as output the ensuing rights. There is no compatibility issue because the interest theory does not prejudge what the input should be. However, the Correlativity Axiom may put this "input neutrality" to question.

In "Rights without Trimmings," Kramer insists that the axiom cannot be refuted by empirical counterexamples because it is a definitional stipulation:

> For Hohfeld, rights and duties—quite as much as the elements in each of the other three pairs of legal positions—were always correlative *by definition*. He did not draw his Correlativity Axiom as a contingent conclusion from empirical data. He posited the correlativity of rights and duties as a definitional fundament of his theory, by explicating the concepts of "right" and "duty" in such a way that each entails the other . . . .[55]

Insofar as Hohfeld provided definitions of "right" and "duty" at all, they were indeed defined in terms of each other. It is also true that a stipulative definition cannot be refuted by empirical counterexamples. On the other hand, Hohfeld was acutely aware of

[52] Kurki, *A Theory of Legal Personhood*, 147.

[53] Hartney, "Some Confusions Concerning Collective Rights," 302.

[54] In Hohfeld's original schema, a duty always entails *exactly* one right, whereas according to Kramer, a duty entails *at least* one right. This modification is of no substantive importance.

[55] Kramer, "Rights Without Trimmings," 24. See also Kramer, "Legal and Moral Obligation," in *The Blackwell Guide to the Philosophy of Law and Legal Theory*, 188–90.

the legal language used by his contemporaries and tried to label his conceptions such that they would correspond with actual legal usage. Thus, it may be that Hohfeld would have given up the Correlativity Axiom if provided with suitable counterexamples to it.[56] At any rate, defining duties in terms of rights means that non-directed duties will be excluded from the schema by definition. Such an exclusion is problematic.

Let us recall afresh the interest theory:

> *X* holds a right correlative to currently existing duty *D* if and only if:
> (i) *X* can hold rights and
> (ii-a) a set of facts minimally sufficient to establish the contravention of duty *D* includes a fact that affects *X*'s situation in a way typically detrimental for beings such as *X* (*Formulation 1*).[57]

Combined with the Correlativity Axiom, the formulation entails that for every legal duty, there must be some *X* that holds the correlative right. This *X* must be able to hold rights, and there must be a way of contravening the duty that necessarily affects *X*'s situation in a way typically detrimental for beings such as *X*. That every legal duty would meet these criteria is certainly subject to empirical refutation, or at least to conceivable counterexamples.

The most obvious examples of legal duties that might not entail rights are public-law and criminal-law duties, especially duties that are not owed to any individual. For instance, Section 10, Chapter 17 of the Finnish Criminal Code—a relic from a less liberal era—prohibits public blasphemy against God. Who holds the right correlative to the duty-not-to-engage-in-blasphemous-acts-publicly? Likely not God, given that non-existent beings cannot hold rights.[58] Kramer claims that public duties that are not borne toward individuals are rather owed to "a collectivity (the state, the nation, the community) which holds the correlative right."[59] In fact, Kramer thinks that all legal duties are owed to the state, in addition to any other private and public parties.[60] I have some doubts about whether this is true of all public duties. For instance, we could think of an anarchist party winning the majority in a parliamentary election and thereby enacting legislation aimed toward dismantling the state. Would the ensuing duties be correlated by the state's right-to-be-dismantled?

An example that I find particularly problematic is that of anencephalic infants. Such infants lack a brain cortex and can therefore never become sentient. This renders them unable to hold rights, as they are not of ultimate value. Anencephalic infants are, however, treated as natural persons by at least some Western legal systems.[61] Thus, causing

[56] See Perry, "Correlativity," 575.

[57] Kurki, "Rights, Harming and Wronging: A Restatement of the Interest Theory," 438.

[58] Kramer thinks that dead people can hold rights in virtue of "the continuing influence of the dead person on other people and on the development of various events, the memories of him that reside in the minds of people who knew him or knew of him." Could similar considerations justify the attribution of rights to non-existent beings? Kramer, "Do Animals and Dead People Have Legal Rights?," 47.

[59] Kramer, "Rights Without Trimmings," 59. For a defense of the correlativity axiom, see also Barker, "Private Law, Analytical Philosophy and the Modern Value of Wesley Newcomb Hohfeld: A Centennial Appraisal," 599–601.

[60] Kramer has made this clear in private correspondence.

[61] See, e.g., Berg, "Of Elephants and Embryos: A Proposed Framework for Legal Personhood" and Neuner, "Zur Rechtsfähigkeit Des Anencephalus."

bodily harm to such an infant may engender a tort-law duty to compensate. However, toward whom is such a duty borne? The infant cannot hold any rights. Are such rights, then, held by the state? Kramer would likely provide such a response, given that he thinks that all legal duties are also owed to the state.

It is beside the point to address thoroughly the issues just raised. What I wish to convey is that the question whether all duties entail rights is certainly substantive rather than something that should be settled axiomatically. It is certainly *conceivable* that there might be duties uncorrelated by rights. As Nigel Simmonds puts it,

> Unless one is prepared to drain the notion of "interest" of all content, treating it as an entirely formal notion that bears the name "interest" only as an arbitrary label, one must concede that duties without corresponding interests are logically conceivable. One may argue that certain contingent features of the real world dictate that it is impossible for duties to exist wholly disconnected from interests: legal duties are bound up with the interest in securing obedience to law, for example; and perhaps moral duties connect with interests by virtue of some constraint on the type of duty that can plausibly be regarded as moral in character. But here the existence of relevant interests is entailed by something other than the bare notion of duty: the involvement of duties with interests is deduced from the notion of law, or morality. Even for the Interest Theorist, therefore, the connection between duty and claim-right, as a jural relation obtaining between two persons, is not a necessary feature of the concept of duty.[62]

If the interest theory accepts as "input" only duty-imposing norms that entail correlative rights, it is at least potentially in tension with the Contingent Norms requirement. A more relaxed version of the Correlativity Axiom that only treats rights as necessarily entailing duties would be less problematic from the point of view of that requirement.

5. Conclusion

This essay has analyzed the compatibility of legal positivism with the interest theory of rights. Even though the interest theory relies on moral criteria to settle the question of who or what can hold rights, it is regardless not in conflict with legal positivism. This is because it takes as a given the "input" that legal positivism provides, and then provides an interpretation of that input. It thereby meets the Contingent Norms Requirement. However, the Correlativity Axiom could potentially be problematic with regard to the Contingent Norms Requirement—though the problem is averted if Kramer is correct in his claim that all legal duties are owed to the state.

Not accepting that the Whanganui River can hold rights—despite the explicit conferral of rights to the river by the New Zealand legislator—is therefore not a problem for a legal positivist. This is not to say that the refusal to consider rivers as right-holders might not be problematic for some other reason. Perhaps delimiting the scope

[62] Simmonds, "Rights at the Cutting Edge", 222–3.

of right-holders based on a Western materialist view of the world as well as secular ethics—and thereby not accommodating the beliefs of the Maori—renders the interest theory "colonialist" or arrogant. Be that as it may, legal positivism is no less a "relativist" doctrine. Positivists need not take a deferential approach to putative conferrals of duties or powers by the legislator any more than they need to take such an approach to non-positivist theses about the validity of law.

5
Tracking the Resilience of Hybridity

Mark McBride

Matthew Kramer is the preeminent contemporary proponent of the *interest theory* of rights—according to which rights function to protect the right-holder's interests. It is not an overstatement to say that his groundbreaking essay, "Rights Without Trimmings," in the exemplary book, *A Debate Over Rights*, set the agenda for current rights theorizing.[1] And thereafter, in a series of meticulously crafted papers, Kramer has continued the process of articulating and refining his interest theory, in the face of objections.[2]

One strand of that process of articulation and refinement has involved countering alternative theories—in particular, most recently, *third-way* alternatives to both interest *and will* theories. And one may divide Kramer's responses into two kinds. First, as exemplified by his response to Leif Wenar's putative third way, Kramer has denied certain of these alternatives are genuinely novel theories. Wenar's third way, for example, according to Kramer, resolves into an expansive version of the interest theory.[3] Second, Kramer has accepted certain of these alternatives are genuinely novel theories, and then sought to demonstrate their shortcomings. Gopal Sreenivasan's *hybrid* theory of (claim-)rights is an example of this second kind, and Kramer has delineated a putative counterexample against it, and indeed against hybrid theories *in general*.[4] My aim in this chapter is to counter the counterexample on behalf of hybridity in general—I am a hybrid theorist, but of a different stripe from Sreenivasan.[5] And it's my contention that grappling with the counterexample serves as a useful expository aid to deeper articulation of hybridity. Hybridity's resilience emerges therefrom.

More specifically, I shall do the following. In section 1, I set out hybridity in general. It is only by first getting a grip on hybridity as a *genus*, zooming out from Sreenivasan's *species* of hybridity, that we can both get a feel for the distinctive strengths of hybridity

[1] Kramer, "Rights Without Trimmings."

[2] See, perhaps most notably, Kramer "Rights Without Trimmings"; Kramer, "Theories of Rights: Is There a Third Way?"; Kramer, "Refining the Interest Theory of Rights"; Kramer, "Some Doubts about Alternatives to the Interest Theory of Rights"; Kramer, "In Defense of the Interest Theory of Right-Holding: Rejoinders to Leif Wenar on Rights."

[3] See Wenar "The Nature of Rights"; Wenar, "The Analysis of Rights"; Wenar, "The Nature of Claim-Rights"; Kramer and Steiner, "Theories of Rights: Is There a Third Way?"; Kramer, "Refining the Interest Theory of Rights"; Kramer, "In Defense of the Interest Theory of Right-Holding: Rejoinders to Leif Wenar on Rights."

[4] See Sreenivasan, "A Hybrid Theory of Claim-Rights"; Sreenivasan, "Duties and their Direction"; Kramer and Steiner, "Theories of Rights: Is There a Third Way?"; Kramer, "Some Doubts about Alternatives to the Interest Theory of Rights."

[5] Elsewhere ("The Tracking Theory of Rights"), I have confronted Kramer's counterexample, in the course of articulating my own hybrid theory, the Tracking Theory (hence this chapter's title); but the confrontation here, while piggy-backing on certain elements from the previous confrontation, is utterly fresh.

Mark McBride, *Tracking the Resilience of Hybridity* In: *Without Trimmings*. Edited by: Mark McBride and Visa AJ Kurki, Oxford University Press. © Mark McBride and Visa AJ Kurki 2022. DOI: 10.1093/oso/9780198868866.003.0005

and gain a true understanding of the nature of Kramer's counterexample thereto. In section 2, I set out Kramer's counterexample in its entirety, and delineate, with some criticisms, Sreenivasan's, to my mind, overly terse response thereto. Finally, in the most important section, section 3, I outline what I take to be a better response to Kramer's counterexample on behalf of hybridity. This section, after setting out the central elements of my own hybrid theory of rights, goes on to describe a taxonomy of ways to interpret Kramer's counterexample. Like any example in philosophy, Kramer's case is underdescribed, in the sense of being amenable to, and requiring, being filled in in different ways. I then chart Sreenivasan's varying responses to Kramer's case *when operating under my taxonomy*, before coming to my own responses. So Sreenivasan's responses will be contrasted with mine, and, naturally, I take mine to be better.

In the course of this last section three important conceptual distinctions central to elucidation of hybridity will be introduced in detail and explored. These distinctions are, by turn, as follows. First, the distinction between, on the one hand, a *binary* notion of control over a duty (i.e., on/off) and, on the other hand, a *scalar* notion, admitting of degrees of control. Second, the distinction between, on the one hand (wholly) *vicarious/parasitic* interests, and, on the other hand *non-vicarious/non-parasitic* interests. Finally, third, the distinction between *subjective* and *objective* justification with which the relevant authority acts in conferring control or otherwise over the relevant duty.

Kramer's groundbreaking essay, "Rights Without Trimmings," in some senses was one of the works that set me on my path to becoming a jurisprudent. It was hot off the press while I was taking the undergraduate Jurisprudence course at Cambridge, and was a core element of the rights component of that course. It is nice, thus, to be able to pay tribute to Kramer's interest theory—first articulated at full length in this groundbreaking essay of his—in the best philosophical way possible, namely, to criticize it. More specifically, I plan on showing here that hybrid theories of rights—theories which are viable and (more) nuanced genuine alternatives to the interest theory—are still standing in the advent of Kramer's counterexample. In fact, as noted, grappling with the counterexample, serves as a useful expository aid to deeper articulation of hybridity's unique strengths.

1. Hybridity in General[6]

Here, then, is Sreenivasan's (2005: 271; 2010: 488) last-pass formulation of his hybrid theory, called the *Complex Hybrid*:

> (CH) Suppose X is duty-bound to ϕ. Y has a claim-right[7] against X that X ϕ just in case: Y's measure (and, if Y has a surrogate Z, Z's measure) of control over a duty of X's to ϕ matches (by design) the measure of control that advances Y's interests on balance.

[6] This section draws heavily on material from my "The Tracking Theory of Claim-Rights."

[7] My note: I largely omit the "claim-" qualifier in what follows. Sreenivasan's is a not theory of rights *simpliciter*, but rather of *claim*-rights. We can note that Sreenivasan has not articulated a theory of other types of right, such that there be.

Now at the most general level we have a hybrid theory, in the sense that the account of right-holding combines elements of the interest theory and will theory. The will theory, at its most fundamental level, according to which rights are aligned with (the degree of) *control* over—in the sense of power to demand/waive—a duty, is clearly referenced. Moreover, the interest theory, likewise, according to which rights function to protect the interests of the right-holder, is also clearly referenced.

All quite true. But I have in mind a thicker sense of hybrid theories of rights as a genus, of which Sreenivasan's and my hybrid theory are species. Examples will be useful here, in the course of which we can see hybrid theories' distinctiveness. I have in multiple places elsewhere charted and assessed the differing verdicts of hybrid theories versus *interest* theories over right-holding in classic so-called *third party beneficiary* cases.[8] But that literature has developed a complex life of its own. And partly as a result of this complexity, beyond noting that differing verdicts by hybrid and *interest* theorists as to right-holding *are given* in such scenarios, we do well to side-step its details here. So let me simply assert the following. In a core such case, with X and Y contracting for X to provide something for Z, the interest theory wants to ascribe rights to both Y *and* Z. They both stand to benefit *in the right way* for the interest theorist.[9] For the hybrid theorist, meanwhile, Y, *but not* Z, is a right-holder: while Y's control, as promisee, matches (by design)[10] his interests on balance, Z's (*ex hypothesi*) lack of control does not match his interests on balance.

We can begin, though, to much more tractably get at the core of hybrid theories by considering some classic cases where they contrast, in determinations of right-holding, with the *will* theory. Hybrid theories are more inclusive than the will theory in the following way. As is well known, the will theory, in its most general formulation, makes the holding of a power to demand/waive enforcement of—this control over—the duty in question necessary and sufficient for the holding of a right. As is equally well known, such a thesis (on account of its necessity precept) precludes the will theory from ascribing rights in the case of duties which are unwaivable, and also in the case of incompetent adults and children. In the foregoing cases, such powers are not in play, thus the will theory, counterintuitively, cannot ascribe rights. By contrast, hybrid theories *can* ascribe rights in such cases: in the case of unwaivable duties, a right is in play *provided* the candidate right-holder's *lack* of a power of waiver matches (by design) his interests on balance. And, plausibly, in many such cases—for example, unwaivable duties not to torture or enslave another—this can be the case. For hybrid theories, then, I (and you) can have a right not to be tortured or enslaved: my (and your) interests can be, arguably, advanced on balance by lacking a power (having a

[8] See my "The Tracking Theory of Rights," "Preserving the Interest Theory of Rights," and "The Unavoidability of Evaluation for Interest Theories of Rights."

[9] For the authoritative statement of details on this *right way*, see Kramer, "Refining the Interest Theory of Rights," and his articulation of Bentham's test. It must be noted that, while this is the leading explicit test, adopted by a prominent contemporary version of the interest theory, other versions of the interest theory exist, most notably Raz's *The Morality of Freedom*, which do not use this test.

[10] These notions can just be utilized intuitively for now, particularly as we, here, are simply rolling out hybrid theories as a genus. So "matches" means "is equaled by," etc.; and "by design" means "deliberately," "on purpose," etc. The "by design" notion in particular will get filled in with much more detail as we proceed. In my "The Tracking Theory of Claim-Rights," drawing upon epistemological literature, I expound in detail on the central *anti-luck* dimension to "by design."

disability) to waive such duties. Likewise, *mutatis mutandis*, in the case of incompetent adults and children (setting aside, for another time, detailed investigation of *surrogacy* considerations).

Armed with this set of examples, and contrasts with the interest and will theories, we are in a position to do better in specifying the *thicker* sense of hybrid theories of rights as a genus, of which Sreenivasan's and my hybrid theory are species; better that is, than merely asserting that a hybrid theory combines elements of the interest theory and will theory. So on my thicker set of criteria for the genus hybrid theory, there are four severally necessary and jointly sufficient conditions for hybridity:

(i) A *match* condition: one's interests on balance (or lack thereof) in control over a duty must *be equaled by* one's degree of control (or lack thereof).
(ii) A *design* condition: (i) must obtain *deliberately*, or *on purpose*.
(iii) The possibility of right-holding in *no control* cases: for example, unwaivable duties, incompetent adults, children.
(iv) Two routes to right-holding: the *control* (e.g., a promisee under a contract, or a property-holder), and the *no control* (e.g., (iii)), routes.

Let's close this consideration of hybridity in general, before getting to Kramer's counterexample, by introducing one last telling example. The example picks up on all four of these conditions for hybridity, but I want to put it to particular use to highlight a point about the design condition (ii).

A hybrid theorist's treatment of criminal law is particularly nuanced—more so, to my mind, than either the interest or will theory. Suppose powers to demand/waive criminal law duties are held, not by citizens, but rather by the public prosecution service. Suppose further that in some circumstances, and for some citizens, that is in these citizens' interests on balance.[11] Hybrid theories allow whether such citizens have corresponding rights or not to depend on the *justificatory reasons* of the relevant authority for giving such citizens no measure of control over such duties, and vesting such control, instead, in the public prosecution service.[12] In a nutshell, if the operative *reasons* are trained on *the interests of the citizen*, that citizen will have a right (in a *no control* case, à la criteria (iii) and (iv) above); if not, and if they are instead trained, for example, on *the smooth administration of justice* (i.e., *efficiency*), that citizen will not have a right. Hence the comparative nuance: by contrast, the interest theory will *categorically ascribe* a right to this citizen (on account of the duty's *ex hypothesi* protection of the citizen's interests); and the will theory will *categorically deny* a right to this citizen (on account of the citizen's lack of control over the duty).

[11] The "some" qualifiers indicate another nuance in hybrid theories: for any particular criminal law duty, it could confer rights on some citizens, but not on others, depending on their interests in control. I see this as a virtue; or, at any rate, certainly not a vice. I think there's a clear parallel here with the thought that, e.g., for any particular criminal law, it could instantiate Razian authority vis-à-vis some citizens, but not others, depending on their knowledge of right reason.

[12] Of course, it is a further question whether the public prosecution service (additionally) holds such rights. Moreover, the possibility of the public prosecution service *additionally* holding such rights raises the specter of overdetermination cases—the relevant authority acting for two (or more) reasons. This is an interesting question, but I bracket such cases for present purposes.

2. Kramer's Counterexample to Hybridity, and Sreenivasan's (Overly) Terse Reply

Here, then, with the necessary orientation to hybrid theories in general, by way of preliminaries, completed, is Kramer's counterexample thereto (2013: 259):[13]

> Suppose that Mark is legally obligated to pay Paul $20,000. A third party, Liam, does not have any legal power to waive Mark's duty. His not having any power of that sort is very much in his interests, since Paul (who is far stronger) would be violently furious if Liam were ever to exercise such a power. Objectively, the furtherance of Liam's interests in that fashion is a sufficient justification for his not being vested with the power to waive Mark's obligation. Now suppose that the judge or other legal official whose directive has placed Mark under a duty to pay Paul was focused on Liam's interests when determining whether Mark's duty should be waivable by Liam. We can presume that the official reasoned as follows: "I know that Paul is extravagantly selfish and that he will not waive Mark's duty even in circumstances where the fulfillment of it would render Mark destitute. Given that Liam is such a humane person, I'd like to endow him with a power to waive the duty. However, for his own good, I had better withhold any such power from Liam. If he were ever to exercise such a power—however wisely and justifiably—Paul would be irate and would vent his wrath by pummeling or even killing him. Thus, although it would be good for Mark and good for the general decency of this society if I were to equip Liam with a legal power to waive Mark's duty, I feel that I must concentrate instead on the interests of Liam. As a consequence, I will not confer any such power upon him." Accordingly, Liam's wholesale lack of any control over Mark's duty is justified subjectively as well as objectively by reference to Liam's own interests. His measure of control—no control at all—is precisely the measure that advances his interests on balance.

Kramer contends that hybrid theories, such as Sreenivasan's, lead to the conclusion that Mark's duty is owed, not only to Paul, *but also to Liam*. And the case is generalizable. Kramer contends, that is, that Liam's lack of a power of waiver matches (by design) his interests on balance. And he concludes (2013: 260) that this (and other like) counterintuitive conclusion(s) fells hybrid theories:

> In a situation where Liam is not involved in any way in Mark's bearing of a duty or performance of a duty to pay $20,000 to Paul—and where Liam has deliberately been kept uninvolved by the judge who imposed the duty—no tenable theory of rights will generate the verdict that Liam has a right to Paul's being paid $20,000 by Mark. Since Sreenivasan's [hybrid] theory does generate that verdict, his [hybrid] theory is unsustainable.

[13] A counterexample not materially different from this one first appeared in Kramer and Steiner, "Theories of Rights: Is There a Third Way?." And so we can take Sreenivasan's "Duties and their Direction" reply as a reply to this case.

We can usefully tie the case back to our four criteria for the genus hybrid theory. Kramer's case involves a match (criterion (i)) between Liam's interests on balance (not to have control) and his degree of control (none). Moreover (design criterion (ii), putatively), the match is *deliberate*. And (criteria (iii) and (iv)) we are in the realm of a *no control* case of right-holding.

The very category of right-holding—the no control category—which I earlier lauded as a virtuous nuance of hybrid theories, using the example of its treatment of criminal law right-holding, is a natural locus or source for an objector to target. It's similar to sporting or personal characteristics being lauded as strengths and weaknesses depending on contextual variables: her one-handed backhand wins her a lot of points, but loses her many too; his gregariousness makes him a joy to be with socially, but lands him in trouble in the seminar room. So too with hybrid theories: this openness to a *no control* route to right-holding is a likely spot for counterexamplers to seek traction.

In sum, according to Kramer, all the conditions for hybrid theory right-holding are met with respect to Liam, yet it is wildly implausible to accord him a right, as hybrid theories seem to. This, then, is the single, prominent generalizable *no control* counterexample to hybrid theories. It is pleasing then, for hybrid theorists, that, not only can it be deflected, but grappling with it can serve as an aid to exposition of hybridity. I return to this matter—my response and exposition of hybridity—in section 3. Now, though, let me chart Sreenivasan's response.

Sreenivasan—as the foremost hybrid theorist at the time, and against whom Kramer was posing the counterexample—has indeed replied. Sreenivasan replies (somewhat tersely) as follows (2010: n. 68):

> [W]hile [Liam] therefore satisfies the matching condition by coincidence, he fails the design condition. Hence, on (CH) [i.e., the hybrid theory], [Mark] does not owe his duty to [Liam]. [Liam] fails the design condition because the assignment of control over [Mark]'s duty does not track the assignment that advances [Liam]'s interests on balance. Indeed, as Kramer and Steiner tell the story, it seems there is no one whose interests on balance are tracked by that assignment.

Now Sreenivasan's *direct* reply to Kramer's case is indeed, as noted, somewhat brief. However, that reply should be read in conjunction with the surrounding main text (489–91), in which Sreenivasan gives more information on how to understand the design condition. In particular, Sreenivasan provides suggestive remarks on the aforementioned counterfactual dimension of hybridity: "the design condition requires that the matching condition remain satisfied over a range of relevant counterfactual scenarios" (490). Sreenivasan then cashes out some such scenarios, but in the context of a surrogacy scenario.[14]

[14] There are pros and cons to this. On the pro side, surrogacy issues, to my mind, are some of the most complex applications of right-holding. So Sreenivasan is to be congratulated on getting his hands dirty. But on the con side that very complexity potentially makes it a non-ideal context in which to *introduce* the counterfactual dimension to hybridity's design condition. I will be devoting extended treatment to hybridity and surrogacy in future work (ms: *The Tracking Theory of Rights (Hart)*). Notably, my ensuing statement of my own hybrid theory prescinds from detailed investigation of *surrogacy* considerations, and so can at this

Alongside some fascinating discussion of particular applications especial to surrogacy scenarios, Sreenivasan (490) notes:

> For example, [the design condition] requires that Z [the surrogate] would be vested with *less* than the full measure of control over X's duty, were Y's interests better advanced on balance by Z's having a lesser measure of control instead of the full measure. Similarly, it requires that *W* would be vested with control over X's duty and not Z, were Y's interests better advanced on balance by having W as a surrogate instead of Z. In this way, the design condition requires the actual assignment of control over X's duty (not to operate on Y) to *track* the assignment that advances Y's interests on balance, rather than simply to coincide with it.

Now, though this passage is trained on the surrogacy scenario, I think two morals of general application can be extracted therefrom. First, we get a general sense of the *kinds* of tracking questions that are germane to an enquiry into the design condition. Second, and this is relevant to a distinction already introduced, and to be picked up on later, we get a sense that the design condition must be appropriately sensitive to a *scalar* notion of control, admitting of degrees of control.

But this contextualization of Sreenivasan's very terse direct reply to Kramer, while helpful, still, to my mind leaves hybridity short of a full answer. Put differently, hybridity is here selling itself short. Hybridity has more resources to hand to provide a complete answer to the counterexample.

In sum, one could think of a chief purpose of mine in the remainder of this chapter is to flesh out this rather condensed reply of Sreenivasan's, on behalf of hybridity in general, and to show how Kramer's counterexample doesn't dent hybridity. In essence, the point will be that Kramer's and Steiner's case lacks the requisite—the right kind of—*counterfactual dimension*. And we can see that best by foregrounding the counterfactual dimension which, to my mind, is aptly at the heart of hybridity itself.

3. Doing Better: My Hybridity Formalized, and Responding to Kramer's Counterexample More Fully as an Expository Aid for Hybridity

I want to set up a natural taxonomy of ways of filling detail into Kramer's counterexample. More specifically, I want to carve things up into three (potentially exhaustive, but certainly not exclusive) ways of further specifying detail. In broad outline, and somewhat crudely, the carving up pertains to the *basis* or *method*—in essence, the *justificatory reasons*—on which the relevant authority is granting or withholding control over the relevant duty. We can, by turn, label these three bases as those with a significant *moral dimension*, those with a significant *prudential dimension*, and those with a *mixed* (i.e., moral and prudential) *dimension*. These are all permissible, and natural,

stage be said to be at most a theory of core or paradigmatic claim-rights. At the risk of special pleading, the complexity of surrogacy demands extended treatment—treatment which is only apt once we secure an analysis of core or paradigmatic claim-rights.

ways of filling in further detail to Kramer's counterexample, while maintaining fidelity throughout to Kramer's stipulation that the relevant authority is trained on *Liam's* interests. Utilizing this taxonomy (and formalization of my species of hybridity) will be especially useful in charting and interrogating the three distinctions central to an understanding of hybridity—namely, binary/scalar, vicarious/non-vicarious,[15] and subjective/objective—which were introduced in bare outline, in the opening paragraphs.

3.1 My Hybridity Formalized, and the Binary/Scalar Distinction

Before getting to all that, we need to introduce *my own* gloss on hybridity, and on its design condition in particular. We've just seen that Sreenivasan's reply to Kramer—even zooming out to fully contextualize it—is still much too telegraphic and terse to be fully satisfying. Quite independently, I have articulated my own theory of rights which is a species of the genus hybridity. It is a species of the genus hybridity on account of meeting criteria (i) through (iv), delineated in section 1. It differs from Sreenivasan's in that, beyond hybridity's matching condition (i), I attempt to explain its design condition (ii) *wholly* in terms of the obtaining of a set of modal relations between an agent's interests on balance in control over a duty and that agent's control over said duty. Indeed, *explanation itself* of the design condition—never mind my precise means of doing so—distinguishes my theory from Sreenivasan's. I lay bare, render explicit, a matter which is left implicit in Sreenivasan's theory. Now is not the time to *defend* my own hybrid theory, the Tracking Theory of (claim-)rights—I have done that elsewhere.[16] Now is simply the time to assert it and to extract from it the key *tracking* questions which must be asked by the lights of *any plausible hybrid theory of rights*.

Here, then, is my hybrid Tracking Theory of (claim-)rights formalized.

Y has a claim-right against X that X ϕ if and only if:

(A) (1) It is in Y's interests on balance to have control over X's duty to ϕ & Y has control over X's duty to ϕ ("matching condition"; remainder "design")
&

(2) If it were in Y's interests on balance to have control over X's duty to ϕ, then Y would have control over X's duty to ϕ (this read as a Nozickian subjunctive conditional).[17]
&

[15] Or, which comes to the same thing, parasitic/non-parasitic.

[16] See my "The Tracking Theory of Rights" and, especially, my "The Tracking Theory of Claim-Rights," in which I detail the Nozickian epistemological origins of the Tracking Theory, and claim its superiority over Sreenivasan's hybrid theory (which itself I take to be superior to rivaling theories of (claim-)rights). Book length articulation of the theory is to come (ms: *The Tracking Theory of Rights* (Hart)). In brief, the design conditions exactly mirror conditions at the heart of Nozick's theory of knowledge.

[17] In brief, Nozickian semantics invites us to consider whether the closest *band* of antecedent-situations are consequent-situations. I highlight this as I elsewhere ("The Tracking Theory of Rights," "The Tracking Theory of Claim-Rights") ponder utilizing non-Nozickian, Lewis-Stalnaker, semantics at certain junctures. But I omit this parenthetical qualifier in what follows.

(3) If it were not in Y's interests on balance to have control over X's duty to ϕ then Y would not have control over X's duty to ϕ this read as a Nozickian subjunctive conditional).

Or:

(B) (1*) It is not in Y's interests on balance to have control over X's duty to ϕ & Y has no control over X's duty to ϕ ("matching condition"; remainder "design")

&

(2*) If it were not in Y's interests on balance to have control over X's duty to ϕ, then Y would not have control over X's duty to ϕ this read as a Nozickian subjunctive conditional).

&

(3*) If it were in Y's interests on balance to have control over X's duty to ϕ, then Y would have control over X's duty to ϕ this read as a Nozickian subjunctive conditional).

Where, throughout, the *basis* on which the match occurs is held fixed across the counterfactuals.[18]

Sreenivasan, we've noted, asserts that "the design condition *requires* that the matching condition remain satisfied over a range of relevant counterfactual scenarios" (490, emphasis added). Of course, this leaves open that it requires more than this, for him.[19] For now I can simply maintain that the two counterfactual tests I've just set out—namely, (2) and (3) via (A), the *control* case disjunct; and (2*) and (3*) via (B), the *no control* case disjunct—are ones that Sreenivasan does (or, should) endorse as components of hybridity's design condition. They are fixed points for any hybrid theory.[20] What of Kramer? While it is unfair to castigate Kramer for not being attentive to counterfactual tests for hybridity not explicitly articulated at the time he formulated his counterexample, I hope he can now see the natural sense in which the tests that I've just delineated are central to the genus hybridity. Examples will help here.

Applying them at a highly general level using a core *control* case of a promisee under a contract[21] will enable us to shed light on the first distinction mentioned in the opening paragraphs central to elucidation of hybridity. This is the distinction between, on the one hand, a *binary* notion of control over a duty (i.e., on/off) and, on the other hand, a *scalar* notion, admitting of degrees of control. Sreenivasan's remarks, detailed

[18] Space here prevents vindicating this condition. Elsewhere ("The Tracking Theory of Rights," "The Tracking Theory of Claim-Rights"), by drawing on the close parallel with Nozick's (1981) epistemology, and the famous case of Nozick's *Granny* in particular, I vindicate this constraint on hybrid right-holding. It is not something I place significant emphasis on in grappling with Kramer's counterexample, however. But it can be noted that the contextually salient bases which I utilize here, and hold fixed in the required way, are those with moral, prudential, and mixed dimensions.

[19] Elsewhere ("The Tracking Theory of Rights," "The Tracking Theory of Claim-Rights") I investigate this matter further.

[20] And their cognates are fixed points in Nozick's theory of knowledge (cf. n. 16).

[21] Kramer's counterexample, involving Liam, as a *no control* case, is less explanatorily helpful in elucidating this first distinction. Our engagement with the counterexample is operationalized in elucidating distinctions two and three.

in section 2, on surrogacy, in the context of responding to Kramer, highlight something to which any account of hybridity must be attentive. This is the relevance of *degrees* of control over a duty matching with *degrees* of interest in control over said duty. In the context of a promisee under a contract, and drawing upon Steiner (1998: 240) (who was in turn drawing upon Hart (1982)), we can mention demanding/waiving *compliance*, *proceedings* for enforcement, and *enforcement* itself, of the duty in question; and Steiner deftly explains certain logical relationships between the powers, which we'll advert to presently. Though there is much more to be said here,[22] that numbers six powers, and we can imagine a scale on which a promisee has (differing interests in) differing degrees of control over the duty in question. Hybridity's design condition must capture, and be appropriately sensitive, to this.

As we are in a *control* case here, disjunct (A) is operationalized. In turn, in the realm of hybridity's design condition (the match condition (1) is straightforwardly met), it means the following two conditions are operationalized:

(2) If it were in Y's interests on balance to have control over X's duty to ϕ, then Y would have control over X's duty to.
&
(3) If it were not in Y's interests on balance to have control over X's duty to ϕ, then Y would not have control over X's duty to ϕ

Now, I take it that (2) and (3) are straightforwardly met in quotidian cases of a promisee under a contract. So long as ((2)) it *continues to be* in Y's interests on balance, *qua* promisee, to have control, Y *continues to be* granted control. And in the closest situations in which ((3)) it *ceases to be* in Y's interests on balance to have control, Y *ceases to be* granted control. A paradigm case of the foregoing cessation is when Y ceases to be a promisee, on account of there no longer being an operative promise. And classic instantiations of this paradigm case—three standard routes to this—would be waiver by Y, fulfillment of the terms of the contract by X, or breach of the terms of the contract by X.[23] Y, *qua* promisee, is straightforwardly a hybrid theory (claim-) right-holder.

But, though it is independently useful simply to play out my species of hybridity in a core *control* case, this is not the principal use to which I wish to put this case here. Instead I want to say that, while the design conditions themselves ((2) and (3)) are enunciated at the *binary* level (control or otherwise over a duty), they are perfectly compatible with *degrees* of control over a duty. Moreover, the binary design conditions *being satisfied* may plausibly be taken to *fix* or *anchor* (sufficient) matching at the *scalar* level of degrees of control. And, in like manner, evidence at the ground level

[22] Kramer ("Some Doubts about Alternatives to the Interest Theory of Rights"), e.g., has perceptively noted that the aptness of classification of some of these positions as "powers" is a contingent matter, resting on the existence of certain background default rules in the normative system in question. Finally, I should note that I consider it something of a cheap shot against will theorists to pillory them in the event that they say the will theory simply requires a *sufficient* number of these powers to be vested in the right-holder. Maybe inherent vagueness is apt here (cf. Wenar "The Nature of Claim-Rights," 222); moreover, so too may be any context-dependency of "sufficient" here, depending on whether we are in the realm of public or private law right-holding.

[23] Of course, this is much too brief. In a moment I color some details in to show complexities.

concerning what exactly is going on in the particular contract under assessment will, of course, serve to determine whether or not the binary design conditions are satisfied. Back and forth between the binary and scalar is perfectly permissible;[24] indeed the levels can be mutually reinforcing.

So, to use our example, if we are in a quotidian cases of a promisee under a contract, and so if conditions (2) and (3) are met, we can imagine, within the band of situations encompassed in evaluating (2), a sliding scale of shifting and diminishing interests in control of the promisee, reaching (3) in the limit case where no interest on balance in control subsists (i.e., as a paradigm case, when Y ceases to be a promisee), and no control is granted. And if all this is so, it is highly likely that the shifting and diminishing interests in control of the promisee in the band of situations encompassed in evaluating (2) are *sufficiently matched* by the degrees of control granted to, and possessed by, the promisee.

That is to roll things out in the *binary to scalar direction*, so to speak. We can—and should—flip things and roll things out in the opposite, *scalar to binary direction*. Doing so will provide necessary further details. Above, following Steiner (who followed Hart), I set out three stages of importance to rights theorists concerning this contract (and indeed in general): what I labeled the compliance, proceedings, and enforcement stages. Moreover, I mentioned three central performances of interest here: waiver by Y, fulfillment of the terms of the contract by X, and breach of the terms of the contract by X.

Now the fulfillment of the terms of the contract by X isn't especially interesting for our purposes here: there is compliance, and Y's control vanishes, matching his interests. What interest can one have in controlling nothing? To see the scalar dimension in action, we should ponder waiver by Y/breach by X. In the event of waiver by Y at the (pre)compliance stage, again Y's control vanishes, matching his interests. Again, what interest can one have in controlling nothing? But in the event of breach by X, we advance to the proceedings stage. Here, Y's live powers pertain to the proceedings themselves, and certain background powers in their enforcement should that next stage be reached. Again, we have a match between interests in control and control itself. If Y waives proceedings, (standardly)[25] Y's control vanishes, matching his interests. No proceedings, no enforcement. Finally, should Y demand proceedings, his remaining powers at the enforcement stage match his interests.

Now this is all somewhat rough-and-ready. But that is exactly how it should be: while hybridity's design condition(s) should be attentive and responsive to, and its satisfaction should ensure, a sufficient level of matching at the *scalar level*, it should not be enslaved thereby. The binary level design conditions (2) and (3) provide an appropriate set of *fixed points* or *anchors* so as for their satisfaction to sufficiently engender matching at the scalar level. Any effort to specify design conditions more fine-grainedly would be unwise, and fraught with difficulties.[26] As a matter of

[24] And so it is not at all the case that there is any causal relation in play here. In like manner, see my "The Tracking Theory of Claim-Rights" for discussion, tracing Nozick's epistemology, of why the relationship between *interests* in control and *control* itself is not best construed as causal either.

[25] It could, I suppose, be that another party demands proceedings, and that Y subsequently acquires control at the enforcement stage. But this would be non-standard.

[26] Pursuing the close connection with Nozick's epistemology (cf. n. 16), Nozick's theory of knowledge requires *coarse-grained beliefs* to track truth, perfectly compatibly with which there can be *fine-grained degrees*

point-scoring with Sreenivasan, I have a worry that his elucidation of the design condition (pondered previously in section 2 in the context of surrogacy) veers toward just this misstep.

3.2 Kramer's Counterexample and Our Remaining Distinctions

We can now confront directly Kramer's counterexample—set out in section 2. In the course of this confrontation distinctions two and three—namely, vicarious/non-vicarious, and subjective/objective—central to elucidation of hybridity, will get fleshed out. As we are in a *no control* case here, disjunct (B) is operationalized. In turn, in the realm of hybridity's design condition (the match condition (1) is, again, straightforwardly met), it means the following two conditions are operationalized:

(2*) If it were not in Y's interests on balance to have control over X's duty to ϕ, then Y would not have control over X's duty to ϕ
&
(3*) If it were in Y's interests on balance to have control over X's duty to ϕ, then Y would have control over X's duty to ϕ

Now, piggy-backing on the reasoning of the judge in Kramer's case, we can set out our taxonomy of ways of filling detail into the case. Let us, as foreshadowed, divide interpretations of Kramer's case into those emphasizing a significant *moral dimension* to the judge's reasoning, those contrastingly emphasizing a significant *prudential dimension* to the judge's reasoning, and finally (and perhaps most faithfully to the example itself) those of a *mixed* (i.e., moral and prudential) nature. As previously noted, this is a permissible and natural taxonomy. Moreover, crucially, in a dialectical sense this is a neutral taxonomy.

I will presently fill these in in more detail, by turn. But, most generally, for now, I can make three quick points. First, these dimensions are connected to the judge's *justificatory reasons* for granting, or not, control to Liam over the duty in question. Second, *qua dimensions*, they should not, in any of the divisions, amount to the *sole animating reasons* of the judge; the division is rather effected to highlight, or draw attention to, issues which might arise when one of the foregoing dimensions is a, or the, *significant animating feature* of the judge's decision. Third, and most specifically, and following Kramer's case, in all the divisions, the judge is throughout taken to be trained on *Liam's interests*; these divisions simply help us tease out *different dimensions* of Liam's interests. Now let me effect the division.

Moral dimension. So, assuming our match on balance between Liam's *lack* of overall interest in control and *lack* of control, there is clearly *a* moral dimension to the judge's reasoning. Liam is, Kramer posits (2013: 259), "a humane person" with an interest in *(seeing) justice being done*; here, specifically, by ensuring Mark doesn't become

of belief or *credences*; and tracking at the coarse-grained level, may in a like manner to the rights domain, in some sense *fix* or *anchor* tracking at a finer-grained level. Moreover, like in the rights domain, any effort to further precisify matching at the finer-grained level could lead to a host of (further, unwanted) difficulties (e.g., the notion of *degrees of truth* would need to be confronted).

destitute. And the judge is evidently sensitive to this in his decision-making. The judge is sensitive, that is, in his decision not to allocate a power of waiver to Liam, not only to *Liam's* interests in not being pummeled (prudential dimensions, to which we shall come shortly), but also to Liam's interests *in Mark's interests* in not becoming destitute (moral dimensions). And insofar as this moral dimension is a significant animating feature of the judge's reasoning, according to (satisfaction of) (2*), in the band of close situations where it *continues to be* defeated by other considerations, no control is granted; and according to (satisfaction of) (3*), when it *ceases to be* so defeated, control *is* granted.

How might a situation, like that envisaged in contemplating satisfaction of (3*), in particular, in the moral dimension scenario, appear concretely? Plausibly, in a situation where the moral interests of Liam point on balance in favor of control over Mark's duty, this would be a scenario in which Liam's interests in (seeing) justice being done defeat all other countervailing considerations.

Now, as noted, we shall conclude our division of Kramer's case by considering the *mixed* interpretation—where both moral and prudential dimensions are (significantly) operative. And that interpretation may well be most faithful to the case itself. At that point I say more about the operation of hybridity's design conditions (2*) and (3*). For now we are effecting this division to see problems with specific dimensions of the judge's reasoning; and insofar as these specific dimensions form a component of the mixed interpretation, problems highlighted at the specific level will (to some degree) infect the mixed level.

So what is the chief problem here? A chief problem for Kramer—and this leads us to our second important distinction—is that this moral dimension to the judge's reasoning appears to involve the judge basing his attribution of control over a duty, a key element of right-holding for hybridity, on "wholly vicarious" interests. But such interests are *not* "interest[s] of the requisite sort" which could form "the bases for attributions of rights," according to Kramer (2007: 303). Kramer *precludes* invocation of such interests in determinations of right-holding.

This is all to say, the relevant *moral* dimension here of *Liam's* interests is an interest in *Mark's* interests in not becoming destitute. For Kramer (2007: 303), a wholly vicarious interest is an interest "resid[ing] wholly in the furtherance of somebody else's interests." I recognize that Kramer makes clear here that an interest can be benevolently other-directed and nonetheless not wholly vicarious. But, if Kramer is to argue that the moral dimension of Liam's interest in (not) being assigned the power to waive Mark's legal duty (here, say, for *the sake of justice*) is *not* wholly vicarious, we need to hear more as to why this is so (cf. Sreenivasan 2005: 263–4; 2017: 140–2).[27]

Now there is an issue here as to the extent to which this is merely an *ad hominem* reply to Kramer. Consistently with *Kramer* being prevented from mounting this counterexample, what would stop *another* philosopher of rights not encumbered by

[27] Insofar as, as is the case under the *mixed* view which I consider last, this moral dimension is not the *sole* operative dimension in the judge's reasoning, surely, even if this moral dimension to Liam's interests *is wholly vicarious*, the interests considered by the judge wouldn't be *wholly* vicarious, on account of their having *other* dimensions? True. But insofar as the wholly vicarious moral dimension is still a *significant animating feature* of the judge's decision in the mixed case, its exclusion would be a critical blow to the sustainability of Kramer's counterexample.

the preclusion on vicarious interests from the right-holding enquiry from wielding it? Moreover, Kramer has recently indicated that, though he thinks the vicarious/non-vicarious distinction is an ethically important and significant one, he no longer wishes to place much reliance on it as a component of his account of right-holding.[28] But I have recently (2020b) sustainedly denied that Kramer *can* disavow reliance on this evaluatively laden distinction in his account of right-holding. So this way out *for Kramer* is not open.

Be all this as it may, my point here is simply to raise serious concerns about a significant moral dimension of the foregoing sort housed within Kramer's counterexample—a concern of especial weight for, if not exclusive to, Kramer himself. I shall return to the moral dimension in my concluding consideration of the *mixed* dimension, where it will become clear that no *hybrid* theorist should foreclose *a priori* Liam's interests in Mark's interests in not becoming destitute from the right-holding enquiry—either in this case, or in general. Put differently, the hybrid theorist has nothing to fear from the inclusion of such interests in the setup of Kramer's case, or in general. Indeed, albeit indirectly, I shall start on the path to vindicating these claims right now.

Thus, relatedly, and before leaving this dimension, I want to add Sreenivasan—my hybrid comrade—to the mix. Sreenivasan (2005: 263–4) himself (earlier) introduced the same distinction, but by use of different terms, namely, the *parasitic/non-parasitic* interests distinction. Moreover, though he is not *explicit* in print, he can be read as endorsing the position, à la (2007)-Kramer, that wholly parasitic/vicarious interests should *not* count in the determination of whether someone is a (hybrid theory) right-holder. And Sreenivasan has recently indicated that he is open to a reading ascribing this position to him.[29]

Now, on the one hand, such a position would readily dispense with Kramer's counterexample, insofar as that case relies on a *parasitic* moral dimension to the relevant interests of Liam's, of the foregoing kind. Such a position would, in essence, *short-circuit* Kramer's counterexample. But, on the other—and more important—hand, I counsel against any hybrid theorist incorporating this evaluatively laden distinction into their account of right-holding.

The most pressing type of case for the interest theory, in terms of forcing its proponents to invoke the *parasitic/non-parasitic*[30] distinction in its account of right-holding, simply has no purchase when it comes to hybridity. That case (Sreenivasan's (2017: 139, reprising 2005 sec. 3)) involves, at its most basic level, a simple contract according to which the chief beneficiary thereof has a grandmother with natural interests in her grandchild receiving benefits (here, under the contract). The issue for the interest theorist was to distinguish the grandmother from the grandchild and the promisee:[31] they *all* have (sturdy)[32] interests in the performance of the contract, yet the grandmother is surely not a right-holder. And (2007)-Kramer invoked the parasitic/non-parasitic distinction to cut off the grandmother as a right-holder (putatively without

28 Kramer, personal correspondence.

29 Sreenivasan, personal correspondence.

30 Or, which comes to the same thing recall, the vicarious/non-vicarious distinction.

31 Assuming the promisee is a different agent from the grandchild. If not, let it be grandchild/promisee.

32 Cf. n. 9.

thereby cutting off the other relevant parties). Moreover, as noted, in my (2020b) I've argued this invocation is unavoidable for Kramer.

But it is clear that the *hybrid* theorist can cut off the grandmother straightforwardly as a right-holder (without thereby cutting off the other relevant parties), without need of this distinction.[33] There is no *match* between the grandmother's interest in control over the duty (a not insignificant one) and her control (*ex hypothesi*, none). Without more,[34] no hybrid theory right-holder. So I find any motivation of Sreenivasan's for incorporating the distinction between *parasitic/non-parasitic* interests into his hybrid account of right-holding (i.e., precluding the former from the right-holding enquiry) highly dubious. Moreover, Kramer's counterexample can be readily handled by the hybrid theorist without invoking this distinction. So let us move on, to another natural dimension of the judge's reasoning in Kramer's case.

Prudential dimension. Now it is important to stress a certain limitedness of what I've just done.[35] I've essentially simply posed a problem for Kramer's incorporation of a significant moral dimension of the foregoing kind into the judge's reasoning in Liam's case.[36] Moreover, I've yet to fully roll out and operationalize my own relevant design conditions—namely, (2*) and (3*)—to directly answer Kramer's case. That punchline will come in the third dimension, when confronting the *mixed* interpretation—the one I take to be most faithful to Kramer's case, and to inherit (to some degree) the defects of the moral and prudential dimensions.

Let us now focus on a, or the, prudential dimension of the judge's reasoning. Now, to flip things, Kramer tells us that the judge is sensitive, in his decision not to allocate a power of waiver to Liam, not only to Liam's interests in Mark's interests in not becoming destitute (moral dimensions), but also, critically, to *Liam's interests in not being pummeled* (prudential dimensions).[37] Again, we can take things a step further, by applying our design conditions. Insofar as this prudential dimension is a significant animating feature of the judge's reasoning, according to (satisfaction of) (2*), in the close band of situations where it *continues to* defeat (or play a role in defeating) other considerations, no control is granted; and according to (satisfaction of) (3*), when it *comes to be* defeated by other (prudential) considerations, control *is* granted.

As before, how might a situation, like that envisaged in contemplating satisfaction of (3*), in particular, in the prudential dimension scenario, appear concretely?[38] Plausibly, in a situation where prudential interests of Liam point on balance in favor of control over Mark's duty, this would be a scenario in which Liam has some personal,

[33] Indeed, a selling point of my own hybrid Tracking Theory, is its (near) *value-neutrality*: the justificatory status of right-holding is explained in terms of the holding of certain counterfactuals. So it is not just *this* value-laden distinction of which my Tracking Theory has no need; it is *any* such distinction.

[34] That is, in particular, without needing to invoke the design condition(s).

[35] In philosophy, small gains are a cause for celebration, however.

[36] Alongside this, I've argued hybridity, contrastingly, isn't, or shouldn't be, encumbered by the addition of an evaluatively laden distinction such as the parasitic/non-parasitic into its account of right-holding.

[37] Of course, morally, it matters that Liam isn't pummeled, but *Liam's interests* in not being pummeled (of chief relevance here) is aptly classed as prudential.

[38] As we are in the prudential dimension scenario, I consider *other prudential (and not moral) reasons* defeating this non-pummeling prudential reason. An advantage of this is that it clearly holds fixed the basis for occurrence of the match (cf. n. 18). In the coming *mixed* case, I perhaps more naturally, consider the moral reasons defeating this non-pummeling prudential reason.

likely pecuniary, interest in being able to waive the duty in question. Maybe Liam is likely to get the money himself in that case.[39]

For now, I want to postpone the consequences, in terms of the right-holding enquiry, of a situation in which Liam gets granted control over Mark's duty on the basis of a pecuniary interest in being able to waive the duty. For now, let us simply say that it is an odd case, to say the least. I will return to that shortly. For present purposes, it's worth noting that, in sketching out this prudential dimension, it could be argued that we have strayed quite far from the judge's reasoning. That is to say, though the judge in Kramer's case is attentive to Liam's prudential interests in not getting pummeled, we don't have a clear reason to think that the judge would come to grant control to Liam over Mark's duty when Liam's prudential interest in getting the money points in favor of control. Less still, that the judge would grant control to Liam *on that basis*. All just to say, by isolating the prudential dimension, we can be argued to have strayed some distance from Kramer's case. But putting on a prudential lens in this manner will prove salutary.

Now I will return to the prudential dimension in my concluding treatment of the mixed interpretation of Kramer's case—an interpretation where both moral and prudential dimensions are operative in a significant way. Before that, I want to reintroduce my hybrid comrade, Sreenivasan, to the mix. Kramer was at pains, in his presentation of the case, to set it up such that *subjective* and *objective* justification—subjective/objective being our third key distinction—was aligned. The judge was subjectively *motivated* by the objectively *right* reasons, in his decisions over allocation(s) of control over the relevant duty. Sreenivasan has recently indicated *his* hybrid theorist response to any interpretation of Kramer's case which puts significant weight on its prudential dimension, such as that just outlined.[40] In essence, Sreenivasan points out that any such interpretation of Kramer's case *prises apart* subjective and objective justification—the judge is *ex hypothesi* subjectively trained on objectively incorrect matters—and Kramer's counterexample promises to be *short-circuited* again. Kramer set up his case intending to *align* subjective and objective justification.

Some notes of caution, however. As noted, *isolation* of a prudential dimension to the judge's reasoning does, arguably, take us some distance from Kramer's case as presented. Second, a hybrid theorist should *welcome*, as an expository aid, cases where subjective and objective justification come apart. So this is to contrast myself with Sreenivasan (2010: 490 n. 66), who "do[es] not have anything particular to say about the special case(s) when objective and subjective justifications come apart." Pretty clearly, these two senses *can* come apart from one another: the objectively correct basis may not motivate the relevant authority, and—the flip side of the same coin—the relevant authority may be motivated by objectively incorrect bases. In both scenarios, tracking can obtain. The former scenario or perspective provides the germ of (one kind of) moral, but not legal, rights; while the latter (arguably, in a more basic or fundamental sense) provides the germ of (one kind of) legal, but not moral, rights.

[39] Recall: this is to *isolate* the prudential dimension. In so doing, we *risk* departure from Kramer's case. But this is done to highlight problems along the prudential dimension (alongside ensuring a fixed basis for occurrence of the match), and any fidelity concerns can be assuaged in the concluding *mixed* interpretation.

[40] Sreenivasan, personal correspondence.

Further exploration of this distinction is something to be welcomed, not dodged, by hybrid theorists. Indeed, confronting cases where they come apart is non-negotiable.

Mixed. Now, as noted, I used, and *isolated,* the previous two dimensions to the judge's reasoning *not* to attempt to capture, by turn, *exactly* what is going on in Kramer's case. The truth is, I think, more complex and involves a mixture of the foregoing dimensions. Alongside helping to elucidate some important distinctions, and setting up some contrasts between myself and Sreenivasan, the foregoing dimensions were isolated for two reasons. First, to pinpoint a clear problem with the highlighted significant moral dimension to the judge's reasoning, at any rate for Kramer. And second, to pinpoint an oddity with the highlighted significant prudential dimension to the judge's reasoning. And, naturally, I think, the problem and oddity will (to a degree) infect any mixed interpretation of Kramer's case. Let me vindicate this claim.

We need to recall our operative hybrid design conditions:

(2*) If it were not in Y's interests on balance to have control over X's duty to ϕ, then Y would not have control over X's duty to ϕ

&

(3*) If it were in Y's interests on balance to have control over X's duty to ϕ, then Y would have control over X's duty to ϕ

Recall, Liam, the *total outsider* to the contract, is meant to satisfy hybrid right-holding conditions, on account of lacking interests on balance in control and not being granted control (match); and the relevant authority is trained, at least in part, on Liam's interests when making such a decision (putatively, design). And, in the realm of this mixed interpretation, which I take to be most faithful to Kramer's case, both moral and prudential dimensions (of Liam's interests) are operative in the judge's reasoning. Yet, it is, according to Kramer, highly counterintuitive to accord Liam a right.

As before, how might a situation, like that envisaged in contemplating satisfaction of (3*), in particular, in the mixed dimension scenario, appear concretely? Plausibly, in a situation where the mixed interests of Liam point on balance in favor of control over Mark's duty, this would be a scenario in which Liam's moral interests in seeing justice being done defeat his prudential interest in not being pummeled. Either or both of the following *change-ups* could obtain to reach such a result: the *intensification* of these moral interests, and the *abatement* of his risk of being pummeled.

Here, then, I will pose my challenge(s) to Kramer: First, can you overcome the problems posed in the foregoing *moral* and *prudential dimensions* divisions? Second, now that you have seen the stringent conditions posed by disjunct (B) of the (best hybrid) Tracking Theory for right-holding, are all those conditions met in your case? Are the stringent conditions (2*) and, particularly, (3*) *really* met in Liam's case?[41] If not, Liam has no right. If so, I am prepared to say Liam has a right.

This is assuredly *not* bullet-biting, as the conditions are so stringent that no explosion of right-holding would ensue. In our foregoing work in the *moral, prudential,* and *mixed dimensions* divisions, we have gestured at what it would look like for conditions (2*) and (3*) to *really* be met in Liam's case. In (2*) we would need there to *continue to*

[41] Additionally, on the assumption there is a match in Liam's case, what, for you, is the *basis* for that match, and is it held *fixed* counterfactually? (cf. n. 18).

be a match between Liam's lack of interests on balance in control over Mark's duty, and lack of control itself over the duty, up till the point Liam comes to, on balance, *have* an interest in control over the duty. This leads us to (3*) and considering situations in which Liam comes to have an interest on balance in control over Mark's duty.

Quite plausibly, no control would be granted to Liam in such scenarios, and, on account of the failure of condition (3*), no hybrid theory right would follow. But, if, almost *per impossibile*, we are countenancing a judge trained resolutely on either or both of the following dimensions, and delivering satisfaction of condition (3*), we would have the following scenarios. First, insofar as, amongst the mixed reasons, Liam's *moral* interests are *dominant*, we have a judge coming to confer control over a duty in a contract which seems *constitutively designed* to serve Liam's interest in *(seeing) justice being done*. By contrast, second, insofar as, amongst the mixed reasons, Liam's *prudential* interests are *dominant*, we have a judge coming to confer control over a duty in a contract which seems *constitutively designed* to serve Liam's interest in *financial gain*. On either limb, we have a very odd situation, and no longer one in which it should count as bullet-biting to ascribe right-holding status to Liam. So this is to reprise our isolation of the moral and prudential dimensions, as dominant dimensions within this mixed enquiry, and to, by turn, confirm the extreme nature of what we are *really* countenancing in contemplating design condition (3*) *truly* being met.

Finally, on the *resolutely mixed* interpretation—a situation where the mixed interests of Liam point on balance in favor of control over Mark's duty, with neither the moral nor the prudential holding dominance—this would be a situation in which Liam's moral interests in (seeing) justice being done defeat his prudential interest in not being pummeled. Insofar as the judge grants control to Liam in such situations, again, we have an extremely odd situation where Liam's (mixed) interests seem almost *constitutive* of the design of the original contractual set up. It is no bullet for hybridity to bite to grant a right to Liam in such outre circumstances.

It is thus very hard to see how Kramer's case *truly* generalizes to create any kind of *rights explosion* issue for the hybrid (Tracking) theorist. Cases in which Liam truly satisfies conditions (2*) and, especially, (3*) in order for the match to be by design, if we take the satisfaction of these conditions sufficiently seriously, are so outre as to be unconcerning for hybridity.

4. Conclusion

Matthew Kramer has advanced our understanding of right-holding in many ways. To come full circle, and speaking as a hybrid theorist, he has here advanced our understanding of hybridity in a way he would not have wanted. His example doesn't, I've hoped to show, ultimately work. But it demanded a detailed answer, and grappling with it has forced me to articulate hybridity—my Tracking Theory—in a clearer way. So, though he may not want my thanks for *this*, I am grateful.[42]

[42] Thanks, though, to Matthew Kramer in innumerable other ways—including for setting me (and many others) on the path to becoming a legal philosopher. Thanks also to Joe Bowen, Andrew Halpin, and Visa Kurki for stimulating discussion.

PART II
GENERAL JURISPRUDENCE

6
Objectivity, Conventions, and the Possibility of Universal Error

Brian H. Bix[*]

1. Introduction

There was at one time—in the 1980s, and continuing through the early years of the new millennium—a vibrant literature among legal scholars about legal indeterminacy and the objectivity of law. This debate has largely faded, though I do not think that it is because one position in the debates clearly prevailed or that the many issues of those discussions were resolved to the satisfaction of all readers. It is just one of those mysteries within the sociology of knowledge, regarding why some issues and some schools of thought rise in salience, and later fade, for reasons seemingly unrelated to the underlying merits. However, the fact that these debates are no longer "fashionable" would never deter either Matthew Kramer or I—it is evident that neither of us are slaves to fashion of any kind; we are both happy to revisit these topics, however "uncool" or out of touch it might make us seem.

Back in 2008, Kramer published an article, "Is Law's Conventionality Consistent with Law's Objectivity?," which discussed the connection between legal positivism and objectivity. In the context of those discussions, Kramer considered whether legal positivism's focus on the conventional nature of law and legal norms forecloses the possibility that all legal officials could be mistaken regarding some legal matter. This work will revisit the question of "universal legal error," considering not only Kramer's views, but also those of a number of other prominent commentators, as well as reconsidering my own prior work on the topic.

In what follows, section 2 introduces some basic notions relating to objectivity and the possibility of error, explaining those ideas through their application to a number of areas of discourse, and then introducing their possible application to law. Section 3 summarizes Kramer's views from his 2008 article, regarding objectivity, legal positivism, and the possibility of universal error, and comparing his views to those of Andrei Marmor, Connie Rosati, and Brian Leiter, among others. Section 4 considers the way that the present debate exemplifies the varying aspects of law, and views how focusing on those different aspects may help to explain certain paradoxes in the discussion. Section 5 then revisits arguments from my earlier publication on universal error, prior to concluding (section 6).

[*] Frederick W. Thomas Professor of Law and Philosophy, University of Minnesota.

Brian H. Bix, *Objectivity, Conventions, and the Possibility of Universal Error* In: *Without Trimmings*. Edited by: Mark McBride and Visa AJ Kurki, Oxford University Press. © Mark McBride and Visa AJ Kurki 2022. DOI: 10.1093/oso/9780198868866.003.0006

2. Objectivity and Right Answers

One finds confusion and misunderstanding throughout the literature on the objectivity of law, in large part because there are various types of objectivity—though some might argue that they are only different (mis)understandings of a single concept. It is not my purpose here to try to bring order to that conversation.[1] In the present work, my focus will not be on objectivity, as such, but on a related (some might say, peripheral) aspect of the debate: the possibility of universal legal error.

The possibility of error, and universal error, is often put forward, either as part of the definition of objectivity (relative to an area of discourse), or at least as an important sign of the presence of objectivity. The possibility of error can also be thought of as the flip side of the claim that certain truths are independent of human judgment. Consider the range of possibilities regarding truth in some area of discourse. At one extreme, if an individual's view defines truth on some question (e.g., that person's favorite kind of ice cream), then the individual cannot be mistaken (in this case, about his or her favorite flavor) when making a sincere declaration. If there is a matter defined by the *collective* judgment of some group (think of fashion, which is generally defined by some designated "elite" group in society), then when the relevant group makes a claim about that matter (e.g., the fashionable length of skirt or width of tie for this year), they will, by definition, be correct. There are, however, many areas of discourse where we do not treat the views of individuals, or groups of individuals, as defining what is true. This is certainly the usual understanding of physical sciences (describing laws of nature, etc.) and the usual approach to morality.[2]

It is important to note that one can ground the possibility of error even without asserting independence from human judgments. This can occur if truth in an area of discourse is grounded not in *actual* judgments, but in judgments made *under ideal conditions*.[3] For example, Hilary Putnam at one point equated "being true with being warrantedly assertible under ideal conditions."[4] However, since (almost by definition) we are rarely if ever in ideal conditions, there is no conceptual barrier to asserting that others were mistaken—mistaken about what they *would* have believed in those (counter-factual) ideal conditions. Reference to ideal conditions is relevant to the present discussion, because some theories about the nature of law make legal truth depend on what judges (or other legal observers) would conclude under ideal conditions.[5]

[1] For different (and conflicting) efforts to do just that, see, e.g., Kramer, *Objectivity and the Rule of Law*, 14–100; Rosati, "Some Puzzles About the Objectivity of Law"; the contributors to Leiter, "Objectivity, Morality, and Adjudication"; and Coleman and Leiter, "Determinacy, Objectivity, and Authority."

[2] For morality, there are certain unconventional approaches, e.g., expressivism, which claim ties between individual or collective beliefs, on one hand, and moral truth, on the other hand. E.g., van Roojen, "Moral Cognitivism vs. Non-Cognitivism." See also Tiefensee, ch. 10 in this volume.

[3] E.g., Rosati, "Some Puzzles About the Objectivity of Law," 313–22. In that same discussion, Rosati points out some important difficulties and drawbacks to an analysis of legal truth in terms of what a judge would decide under "ideal conditions." These problems include difficulties in unpacking notions like "all relevant information," "full information," and "maximally empathetic and imaginative."

[4] Putnam, "Comments on Russell Goodman," 220.

[5] E.g., Rosati, "Some Puzzles About the Objectivity of Law," 313–17.

Returning to the issue about error, the question on which I wish to focus is whether it make sense to say that *everyone* (in a particular community, at a particular time) is wrong about something? It is certainly possible regarding (say) facts about the natural world. Everyone can be wrong about the speed of light or the molecular structure of rubber. What about other areas of discourse? We have already mentioned fashion as an area where one might reasonably doubt the possibility of universal error among the group that sets what counts as fashion for its community. A more common focus for discussing the possibility of universal error, especially given possible parallels to law, is language. The argument is that language, like law, is grounded on conventions. How to use words—singly, or in combination within phrases or propositions—is clearly rule-governed. Young children and others learning a language for the first time are taught right and wrong usage; mistakes are pointed out and corrected. But would it make sense to say that *everyone* in the language community was mistaken about some question of meaning or usage?

At first glance, it seems clear that a truly *universal* error would not be possible: if *every* user of the language believes that a given term refers to a certain object or color or emotion, on what basis could an external observer state that they were all mistaken?[6] However, matters are not as straightforward as they might at first appear. The first complication is that of reference: natural kinds analysis teaches that where a term picks out a group or category of (natural) objects, the way the world is, rather than the belief of language users, determines the range of reference.[7] So it may be that all language users were once mistaken if they believed that "gold" includes pyrite ("fool's gold").

The second complication in thinking about truth in language arises when one moves from universal views to near-universal views, and takes note of the presence of purported authorities about meaning and usage. From prestigious dictionaries, national committees to guard "correct usage" (like the Académie Française, for French), and certain other purportedly authoritative works, we are told that certain usages are "wrong," even if extremely common. This struggle about "proper usage" seems to have its own dynamic, and will not be discussed further here, though the tension between "what everyone does" or "what everyone believes," on one hand, and "what is [allegedly] right," on the other hand, will find a parallel in the discussions about universal error in law.

What about law? Does it make sense to speak about universal error here? Andrei Marmor famously argued that universal error is not possible. He wrote:

> Realism applied to a given type of discourse entails the possibility of attributing comprehensive mistakes (that is, when a whole community of speakers can err) about the truth of any given proposition with the realm one is realist about. For any concept one is a realist about, it should be possible to envisage a *whole community of speakers* misidentifying its real reference, or extension. With respect to concepts constituted by

[6] Of course, how "everyone" uses a word can change over time. E.g., "sentimental" has changed meaning in significant ways over the course of centuries, going from being a term of praise to a term of criticism. E.g., Levinson, "Law as Literature," 376.

[7] See, e.g., Putnam, "The Meaning of 'Meaning'"; see generally Bird and Tobin, "Natural Kinds."

> conventional practices, however, such comprehensive mistakes about their reference is implausible. If a given concept is constituted by social conventions, it is impossible for the pertinent community to misidentify its reference.[8]

The basic argument is that with a practice made up by conventions—as with language and, as argued, with law—the truth is simply a function of collective opinion. Many theorists have argued that law is conventional—in the sense that it is grounded on rules that could have been otherwise, that participants (at least legal officials) follow the rules in part because other participants do, and that, for participants, it is more important that there be agreement than that there be agreement *on these terms* (these rules) rather than alternative terms (rules).[9] With conventions, those who agree to the terms of the convention collectively determine what is right and wrong (acceptable and unacceptable). And if law is whatever officials collectively say it is, as a matter of convention, how could these officials, at the same time, collectively be mistaken?[10]

Another, perhaps implicit, supporting argument for the view that officials could not all be wrong about the law is that law is meant to guide behavior, and this central (and perhaps essential[11]) function constrains what law is and how we understand it. In other contexts, law's guidance function has been an argument for exclusive legal positivism against inclusive legal positivism[12] (while noting that Kramer is a prominent advocate for the contrary position, *inclusive* legal positivism,[13] I will leave *that* debate for another day). Here, it is sufficient to note that given the importance of guidance, a legal system regarding whose content all legal officials were mistaken would be as useless and paradoxical as its equivalent, a legal system where all the norms were kept secret from both officials and citizens.[14] Brian Leiter observes: "For any essentially normative concept, an adequate account of the concept must explain how the concept could discharge its normative [i.e., guidance] role. Any account of a concept that makes its satisfaction (or applicability) potentially undetectable violates this constraint. . . ."[15]

[8] Marmor, *Positive Law and Objective Values*, 138; see also Marmor, *Interpretation and Legal Theory*, 73–4.

[9] On conventions, generally, see Lewis, *Convention: A Philosophical Study*, Rescorla, "Convention"; on the conventional nature of law, see, e.g., Postema, "Coordination and Convention at the Foundations of Law," Marmor, "The Conventional Foundations of Law." Marmor distinguishes between coordinating conventions and constitutive conventions, Marmor, "The Conventional Foundations of Law," 152–4, but that difference does not seem to affect the present analysis.

[10] Consider an analogous example: if morality is, as divine command theorists claim (see, e.g., Murphy, "Theological Voluntarism"), whatever God commands, then God cannot command an action that is immoral, because divine commands *constitute* what counts as moral.

[11] For the argument that certain attributes can be *important* to understanding a concept without being "essential" to that concept, see, e.g., Schauer "Necessity, Importance, and the Nature of Law." (Schauer's focus in that work is on the connection between coercion and the concept of law.)

[12] In that context, the claim is sometimes called "the practical difference thesis." Jules Coleman summarizes the thesis as follows: "in order to be law, authoritative pronouncements must in principle be capable of making a practical difference." Coleman, "Incorporationism, Conventionality, and the Practical Difference Thesis," 383; see also Shapiro, "On Hart's Way Out." Law's guidance function is, of course, also central to Lon Fuller's procedural natural law theory. Fuller, *The Morality of Law*.

[13] E.g., Kramer, *Where Law and Morality Meet*; see also Waluchow, ch. 7 in this volume.

[14] Consider morality, another normative system that has guidance of behavior at its center. As Joseph Raz has argued, it makes no sense to speak of moral truths that are not accessible to us. Raz, *Engaging Reason*, 161–81.

[15] Leiter, "Objectivity and the Problems of Jurisprudence," 298. Rosati offers a more cautious response: "I'm not insisting, of course, that one couldn't say that people just never discovered what the law

However, Connie Rosati thinks that this critique is too strong, or at least too quick (using the examples of morality, and knowledge of the natural world). She writes: "A real problem would arise only if the facts were inaccessible in such a way that we could never hope even to approximate to them."[16] Thus, perhaps the more useful analogy is not a regime of entirely secret rules, but rather normative standards that are sufficiently unclear to require deciphering, and thus can lead to mistake, and long-term and pervasive disagreement. Biblical exegesis—for believers—could serve as an example. Difficult-to-discern standards, on one hand, can still guide, and, on the other hand, can also lead to situations of universal error.

The universal error question runs parallel to a different concern about convention-based approaches to legal truth: that such approaches have difficulty grounding any radical critique of existing practices. If the rule of recognition derives from (tracks) official practices,[17] or (what is perhaps the same view put in different terms) legal truth is a function of standards established by an "interpretive community," combined with or subject to the view of the highest appellate court,[18] it becomes difficult to ground an argument that the practices are significantly mistaken. To use Sanford Levinson's example, if conservative judges dominate the United States Supreme Court for long enough, one not only has conservative outcomes in cases, but also conservative-leaning decisions regarding what counts as appropriate approaches to statutory interpretation, constitutional interpretation, and legal reasoning generally. On what basis could a liberal commentator claim that the Supreme Court was getting things wrong, when it is that (conservative) court that largely sets the criteria for *what counts as wrong*?[19] Of course, one should not overstate the determinacy of conventions (which is what Dworkin arguably did, when he argued that significant disagreements in legal practice refute legal positivism[20]), but neither should one underestimate the difficulty of constructing a radical critique from within a conventional system.

What do our practices say about universal error? Two incisive observers come to different conclusions. On one side, Leiter writes: "My armchair sociology—as an academic and a lawyer—tells me that the idea of answers that are correct independent of what all lawyers and judges believe is not part of existing legal consciousness."[21] On the other side, Rosati writes: "our practices allow … that even an entire community can be mistaken about legal facts …."[22] As will be discussed below, Rosati likely has the better view, at least in regards to American legal practices. First, though, I would like to review Kramer's analysis of the topic.

really is, but one risks ending up with a conception of legal facts on which they can cease to be normative." Rosati, "Some Puzzles About the Objectivity of Law," 293 (footnote omitted).

[16] Rosati, "Some Puzzles About the Objectivity of Law," 312.

[17] Hart, *The Concept of Law*, 94–110.

[18] Levinson, "Law as Literature," 392–402.

[19] Levinson, "Law as Literature," 392–402. As Audre Lorde famously wrote, it is hard to dismantle the Master's house with the Master's tools. Lorde, *The Master's Tools Will Never Dismantle the Master's House*.

[20] See Dworkin, *Law's Empire*, 37–43. For responses to Dworkin, see, e.g., Kramer, *In Defense of Legal Positivism*, 146–51; Patterson, "Theoretical Disagreement, Legal Positivism, and Legal Interpretation."

[21] Leiter, "Objectivity and the Problems of Jurisprudence," 206.

[22] Rosati, "Some Puzzles About the Objectivity of Law," 314. In the ellipses, the original quote states "contrary to judicial majoritarianism."

3. Kramer's Argument

In his 2008 article, "Is Law's Conventionality Consistent with Law's Objectivity?," Kramer disagreed with Marmor's view that the whole community could not be mistaken about the meaning or reference of a legal concept. Kramer argued that the community could "collectively be in error about the substance and implications" of their shared beliefs and attitudes regarding some point of law, and could "therefore collectively be in error about the nature of some legal norm which those beliefs and attitudes sustain."[23]

Kramer offered the following argument: what if judges on some court concluded that the court's decision from some earlier period was mistaken?[24] (To make the example as sharp as it can be, it is to be assumed that both the earlier and later official views were unanimous.) This creates a paradox: there could now be a universally-held view that the prior, *also universally-held* view, was in error. Universally-held views could not thereby be infallible, because one of these two views must be wrong.[25]

Kramer acknowledged the point mentioned earlier, that (especially in legal systems, like that of the United States, where precedent is important) universal errors can *become* legal truths with the passage of time: "incorrect decisions" transform into "settled law."[26] He also noted that Marmor, in the work Kramer analyzed, initially took a less extreme position, not that universal error was impossible, but that it was "implausible."[27] And this position, Kramer suggests, is reasonable: that, after all, we have better reason to be confident in our collective judgments about the product of human conventions than we do about (say) our collective judgments regarding matters entirely independent of human judgment, like physical reality.[28]

One might try to resuscitate Marmor's (stronger) view about universal error by distinguishing types or levels of views. Perhaps, it could be argued, the collective could not be universally mistaken about the object of the discourse (law, legal norms), but they became fallible when speaking one level up, regarding (say) *propositions about legal norms*. Elsewhere in his article, Kramer himself makes use of a distinction "between the lower-order beliefs that underpin the existence and fix the content of legal norms, and the higher-order beliefs about the . . . implication of those lower-order beliefs."[29] However, this recourse would not be sufficient to salvage an argument about the impossibility of universal error. Whether the consensus views at time T_1 and T_2 are about "lower-order beliefs" *or* "the implications of those lower-order beliefs," the

[23] Kramer, "Is Law's Conventionality Consistent with Law's Objectivity?," 247.

[24] Kramer, "Is Law's Conventionality Consistent with Law's Objectivity?," 247. And for this example, the assumption is that the later court is not just concluding that the law has changed (perhaps due to a change of social norms); the later court is expressly stating—as courts sometimes do—that the law *has always been* the other way, and (thus) the earlier court was mistaken.

[25] Kramer, "Is Law's Conventionality Consistent with Law's Objectivity?," 247.

[26] Kramer, "Is Law's Conventionality Consistent with Law's Objectivity?," 247–8.

[27] Kramer, "Is Law's Conventionality Consistent with Law's Objectivity?," 248.

[28] Kramer, "Is Law's Conventionality Consistent with Law's Objectivity?," 248–9. Kramer offers an analysis in terms of the differences between existential and observational mind-independence, and between strong and weak versions of each, ibid., 242–52, but the present work will not discuss these distinctions.

[29] Kramer, "Is Law's Conventionality Consistent with Law's Objectivity?," 251.

same paradox would emerge. The difference in levels of discourse would not avoid the problem. In either circumstance, the Marmor position would seem to be that the consensus should guarantee truth, but, by hypothesis, the consensus view at T_2 in fact *contradicts* the consensus view at T_1.

Finally, Kramer argues that whatever conclusions about universal error followed from the conventional nature of law would not vary based on whether one was a legal positivist or a natural law theorist.[30] As Kramer pointed out, what distinguishes legal positivism and natural law theory is not the assertion or denial that law is primarily conventional: that is common ground among nearly all legal theorists. The difference is whether law should be understood as *exclusively* conventional.[31] Thus, whatever followed from the (primarily) conventional nature of law for the objectivity of law or the possibility of universal error, would do so regardless of whether one otherwise favored the legal positivist or natural law approach.

4. Different Aspects of Law

In examining universal error in law, it might be helpful to construct a distinction in terms of internal or external perspectives, or (in Robert Alexy's terms[32]) between participants and observers.[33] Under Alexy's analysis, a participant can offer a view of what the law requires (in her country) that is contrary to a recent decision of a high appellate court, while an observer cannot.[34] Alexy argues that a participant, when asked about what the law is, must also consider what the law ought to be, while this is not the case for an observer.[35] I do not think that this is entirely correct, but this general approach does touch on an important point.

To think more clearly about universal error, let me offer an example from American constitutional law. There are scholars who believe that the United States Supreme Court was badly wrong in its earlier interpretations of certain provisions of the federal Constitution, including the Eleventh Amendment (which has been read to create

[30] Or, one might add, *what kind* of legal positivist one was, inclusive or exclusive.

[31] Kramer, "Is Law's Conventionality Consistent with Law's Objectivity?," 249–52. Kramer suggested that Ronald Dworkin, in one of his works, came close to denying that law was predominantly conventional, but that even if one accepted the approach there proffered, Kramer asserted, the conclusions regarding universal error would not alter. Kramer, "Is Law's Conventionality Consistent with Law's Objectivity?," 249 n. 6, discussing Dworkin, *Law's Empire*, 136–9.

[32] See, e.g., Alexy, *The Argument from Injustice: A Reply to Legal Positivism.*

[33] "The participant's context is defined by the question 'What is the correct legal answer?', the observer's by the question 'How are legal decisions actually made?'" Alexy, "An Answer to Joseph Raz," 46. Also, according to Alexy, the observer's concept of law contains only social sources, ibid., 47, while the participant has a "non-positivistic concept of law that includes morality," ibid., 48. I am not adopting or endorsing Alexy's view in its entirety for this work, but I do believe that the distinction, roughly understood, captures something that is useful for the present analysis.

[34] Alexy, "An Answer to Joseph Raz," 45–46.

[35] Alexy, "An Answer to Joseph Raz," 48. There are other, but still relevant ways to think about the multiple aspects of law. John Finnis writes of the dual nature ("double life") of law, in terms of law as historical decision, as against law as a form of practical reasoning. Finnis, "On the Incoherence of Legal Positivism," 1602–3. Another alternative: Rosati argues the law is in part predictive (necessarily connected with official action), and in part critical (courts can be wrong). Rosati, "Some Puzzles About the Objectivity of Law," 290.

a broad sovereign immunity protecting states from liability[36]) and the "Privileges or Immunities Clause" of the Fourteenth Amendment (which had been narrowly read to have minimal significance[37]). These errors, if errors they be, were originally committed over a century ago, but the Court has consistently abided by those interpretations.

Certainly, a lawyer advising a client today about the law under the Eleventh and Fourteenth Amendments would be committing legal malpractice were that lawyer to state that the law was *anything other* than the interpretation the Supreme Court has consistently given. A law student who claimed on an exam that the law was anything other than that consistent answer would be marked as wrong. And a lower court that held the law to be anything else would be reversed for an error of law. Still, an advocate arguing before the Supreme Court today could (consistent with the norms of advocacy) urge the Court to overturn the century of contrary precedent, and hold that those constitutional provisions mean (*and always have meant*) something different from what the Court has held for the last century. And the Court itself *could* so hold. Of course, it is *unlikely* that the Court would do so (and it has in fact "declined the invitation" to do so on a number of occasions[38]). Still, one must keep in mind that the Supreme Court *has* reversed itself regarding other precedent, some long-established and seemingly settled. Such reversals have occurred, for example, in cases involving racial segregation, requiring schoolchildren to salute the flag, and the criminalization of homosexual sexual acts,[39] just to name some of the best-known examples. The differences between, on the one hand, the lawyer advising the client, the law student answering the exam question, and the lower court deciding a case, and, on the other hand, the advocate arguing before the Supreme Court and the Supreme Court re-visiting an issue, display an important aspect of legal practice and how we need to understand law.

There is a quite-recent example of a US Supreme Court Justice complaining about just the sort of reversal of long-established law considered here. This is from Justice Scalia's dissent in *Obergefell v. Hodges*, the case in which the Court concluded that same-sex couples have a right under the United States Constitution not to be excluded from state marriage laws:

> The five Justices who compose today's majority are entirely comfortable concluding that every State violated the Constitution for all of the 135 years between the Fourteenth Amendment's ratification and Massachusetts' permitting of same-sex marriages in 2003. They have discovered in the Fourteenth Amendment a "fundamental right" overlooked by every person alive at the time of ratification, and almost everyone else in the time since. They see what lesser legal minds—minds like Thomas

[36] See *Hans v. Louisiana*, 134 U.S. 1 (1890); for expansive later treatment, see, e.g., *Seminole Tribe of Florida v. Florida*, 517 U.S. 44 (1996). For an overview of the debate, see, e.g., Chemerinsky 2011: 191–7.

[37] See *Slaughter-House Cases*, 83 U.S. (16 Wall.) 36 (1873). On the history of the Privileges or Immunities Clause and its subsequent treatment by the Supreme Court, see, e.g., Barnett and Bernick, "The Privileges or Immunities Clause Abridged: A Critique of Kurt Lash on the Fourteenth Amendment."

[38] See, e.g., Barnett and Bernick, "The Privileges or Immunities Clause Abridged: A Critique of Kurt Lash on the Fourteenth Amendment."

[39] See *Brown v. Board of Education*, 347 U.S. 483 (1954) (racial segregation); *West Virginia v. Barnette*, 319 U.S. 624 (1943) (flag salute); *Lawrence v. Texas*, 539 U.S. 558 (2003) (homosexual sex).

> Cooley, John Marshall Harlan, Oliver Wendell Holmes, Jr., Learned Hand, Louis Brandeis, William Howard Taft, Benjamin Cardozo, Hugo Black, Felix Frankfurter, Robert Jackson, and Henry Friendly— could not.[40]

Justice Scalia is arguing that the majority in *Obergefell* had espoused an especially unpersuasive claim of past universal error: that under the majority's analysis, nearly every lawyer and judge—including some of the most famous, most respected, and most influential judges and commentators—had been wrong about the meaning of the Fourteenth Amendment (as applied to marriage law), only to be corrected by five (not quite so eminent or influential) judges in our time. This and other examples reflect the basic point mentioned in connection with Kramer's critique of Marmor: that in a system that is grounded on both convention and authority, erroneous judgments can become true (and vice versa) with some combination of the passage of time and the judgment (others would say, fiat) of a sufficiently high authority.

It may be helpful to think about a moment after a purportedly erroneous decision has been made, but before it *becomes settled*. Consider a decision that everyone now says was mistaken, the 1896 case of *Plessy v. Ferguson*, where the Supreme Court concluded that "separate but equal" treatment of different racial groups by the government (racial segregation) was consistent with the federal Constitution.[41] At the time, just after the decision was made, there is a sense, as Rosati states, in which the law both was, and was not, as stated in *Plessy*.[42] The case was wrong in its understanding of the federal Constitution, but it was the decision of the highest court. Law as a form of reasoning (based on authoritative texts) can conflict with law as guidance through hierarchy and settlement.

And let us take the analysis one step further. One can then imagine an alternative version of American legal history, one where *Plessy v. Ferguson* was never overruled by *Brown v. Board of Education*,[43] or any other case. Relating to that alternative legal history, Rosati comments: "it seems decidedly odd to say that people never discovered what the law really is, that they didn't know and never will know that the law is not *Plessy*."[44] The implied question is whether it would eventually be the case, with a sufficient passage of time, that the law truly, undoubtedly, and "once and for all" *became Plessy*. Of course, one can never be certain of the future; one can never be sure that some future court will not reverse the decision. To connect with an earlier discussion, it is always *possible* that a future Supreme Court will overrule the decades of contrary precedent regarding the Eleventh Amendment or the Privileges or Immunities clause.

The above discussion, touching on *Plessy* and how to describe judicial error (in the short term and the long term), is connected to the American legal realist argument H.L.A. Hart was responding to when he put forward the analysis in terms of a game of "scorer's discretion." Oliver Wendell Holmes had famously equated law with "the prophecies of what the courts will do in fact."[45] There is obviously *some truth* to

[40] *Obergefell v. Hodges*, 135 S.Ct. 2584, 2629 (2015) (Scalia, J., dissenting) (footnote omitted).
[41] *Plessy v. Ferguson*, 163 U.S. 537 (1896).
[42] Rosati, "Some Puzzles About the Objectivity of Law," 291.
[43] *Brown v. Board of Education*, 347 US 483 (1954).
[44] Rosati, "Some Puzzles About the Objectivity of Law," 292.
[45] Holmes, "The Path of the Law," 461.

the idea that the law is whatever the courts say it is, but, as Hart noted, it also misses something basic. And this is illustrated by Hart's imagined game of scorer's discretion, where a team scores whenever the referee says that a score has occurred, but—and this is the point—in this imagined game, neither the players nor the referee are given any further guidance as to what counts as "scoring."[46] Therefore, the matter is, indeed, entirely at the discretion (in Dworkin's "strong sense" of discretion[47]) of the referee.

While there is a sense that law is whatever the court says it is, it is also the case that courts *purport to be applying legal norms*, a standard separate from present and past court decisions. Because the court (like a football referee) purports to be applying this independent standard, one can sensibly say that the court (or the referee) "got it wrong," in a way that this statement would not make sense in a game of "scorer's discretion." Thus, the above observation from Rosati, that in the United States at one point, *Plessy v. Ferguson* both was and was not the law.

The problem of settled and erroneous law might also be seen as raising a different issue, relating to the complications inherent in theorizing about an ongoing social practice. Let us return to the Marmor claim that a universal consensus among legal officials regarding some legal point could not be mistaken. For present purposes, let us assume that this is correct: that it is simply nonsense, a category mistake, to claim that some universal official view was wrong. Now imagine some universally-held view in a particular jurisdiction. After some extended period of time has passed, the high court in the same jurisdiction declares that the officials at the earlier time period were wrong—despite their allegedly erroneous view having been unanimous at the time. It may be a nonsensical claim, it may be a category mistake,[48] but if made by the highest court, it is also the law. What I am getting at here is *not* the already-discussed paradox point Kramer made in his article, but rather one about theorizing about a social practice, when the social practice might later change in a way that seems to challenge the theory. This is not merely the banal point that theories should account for facts, but the more subtle point that with theories of social practices, one can never account for all the facts, for the future may provide examples that diverge sharply from anything that has happened before.

Keeping all the above points in mind, I now want to revisit my own earlier article on the topic of universal legal error.

5. Revisiting and Revising

In "Global Error and Legal Truth,"[49] I argued, first (agreeing with Marmor), that generally speaking universal error would not be possible (would not be sensible) in a conventional practice like law. I wrote:

[46] Hart, *The Concept of Law*, 142–5.
[47] Dworkin, *Taking Rights Seriously*, 31–9.
[48] And, as discussed earlier, it seems to involve a kind of paradox: consensus constitutes truth, but the consensus here is that an earlier consensus was false.
[49] Bix, "Global Error and Legal Truth."

> The reason why there might be difficulty with global error in this context is that legal discourse purports to describe a practice and a product that is, by most accounts, a social fact that has little or no existence outside the actions and intentions of its participants. In this, legal discourse can be contrasted with mathematics, physics, or even, to some extent, history. Legal practitioners do not merely describe some reality separate from themselves; their actions (unlike the actions of historians, physicists, and even legal theorists) *help to constitute* the subject.[50]

At the same time, in the article I carefully noted that there would be possible exceptions—circumstances where one *could* claim universal error about some past legal decision—where law incorporates a term (e.g., a moral term, like "reasonable," "fair," or "equal") from another discourse or where it is interpreting an authoritative text.[51] Even outside of those exceptional areas, the article should have followed Kramer in distinguishing shared collective beliefs and the implications of those shared beliefs. Also, while the article's focus, ultimately, was on "long-term global error,"[52] there should have been more focus on the transition period. This is the transformation emphasized by both Kramer and Rosati (discussed in sections 3 and 4), regarding how erroneous decision *become* settled law, and the difficulties in description during that transition period.

The article might, finally, have profitably pointed out that the exceptions noted in the piece threaten to swallow the rule. "Authoritative texts" seem to cover not only courts interpreting and applying constitutional provisions, but also decisions that turn on statutes and administrative regulations, and perhaps the interpretation of wills, trusts, and contracts as well. And "terms from other discourses" will also cover a large number of cases: for example, whenever courts are applying express or implied requirements of reasonableness and good faith. Finally, even for those cases that do not fall clearly into the exceptions, it would have been useful to think about the possibility of later actions, however "erroneous" or contrary to conventional understandings, that go beyond the boundaries of existing theory.

6. Conclusion

Does it make sense to say that every person or every legal official was wrong about some legal issue? Yes and no, but mostly yes. As Kramer pointed out, officials can agree about the foundational rules or basic observations, but (all) get the applications or implications wrong. Everyone might previously have misunderstood the original intentions of the constitutional or legislative drafters, or the real meaning of "equality" or "due process." However, the topic of universal error remains complex, because truth in law is complicated, for (at least) two reasons. First, law is not an area of clear

[50] Bix, "Global Error and Legal Truth," 538 (emphasis in original).
[51] Bix, "Global Error and Legal Truth," 541–3.
[52] E.g., Bix, "Global Error and Legal Truth," 540.

bivalence; we can sensibly say that, at a given point, "*Plessy* both is and is not the law." And second, as H.L.A. Hart once argued, there is a sense in which law is importantly defeasible: what is considered right and settled can become unsettled, and in ways that today's officials and theorists cannot fully predict.[53]

[53] Hart, "The Ascription of Responsibility and Rights." I am not here endorsing all aspects of Hart's analysis in that article. See Bix, "Defeasibility and Open Texture," 197–9. For a good overview of defeasibility in law, see Beltrán and Ratti, *The Logic of Legal Requirements: Essays on Defeasibility*.

7

Kramer and Inclusive Legal Positivism

Dancing on the Head of a Pin?

Wilfrid J. Waluchow

1. Inclusive Legal Positivism

Over the course of a distinguished thirty+ year career, Matthew Kramer has forged a well-deserved reputation as one of the world's leading moral, political, and legal philosophers. His corpus is both brimming with insight and enormous. It's also incredibly diverse, ranging from his early work on deconstruction, critical legal studies, and feminism to his later work on rights, freedom, property, moral realism, the ethics of capital punishment and torture, and the objectivity of moral and legal judgments. Among his most influential and valuable contributions is, undoubtedly, his defense of legal positivism, and in particular a type of legal positivism inspired and influenced by H.L.A Hart, a philosopher deeply admired by Kramer and widely regarded as the father of modern, analytic legal philosophy.[1] Throughout his writings on the nature of law, but most notably in his splendid book *Where Law and Morality Meet*, Kramer set out to defend a form of Hartian legal positivism that came to be known as *Incorporationism*, *Soft Positivism*, or *Inclusive Legal Positivism*.[2] General consensus eventually settled on the latter term, *Inclusive Legal Positivism* (henceforth *ILP*), if only because it contrasts nicely with the term *Exclusive Legal Positivism* (henceforth *ELP*), which designates the theory espoused by Joseph Raz and his followers, including Les Green, Andrei Marmor, and John Gardner. *ELP* essentially denies what *ILP* deems conceptually possible, namely, that the moral validity or worth of a norm might serve as a necessary, and quite possibly sufficient, condition of its legal validity.[3] What allowed defenders of *ILP* to remain within the positivist camp, they maintained, was their steadfast conviction that whatever role morality plays in establishing legal validity depends, not on the very nature of law, but on contingent legal practice—that is, on whether the legal system countenances such dependence in its accepted rule of recognition. And

[1] For Kramer's most developed thoughts on the significance of Hart's legal theory, see his *H.L.A. Hart*.

[2] Kramer, *Where Law and Morality Meet*, henceforth *WLMM*.

[3] In his own work, Kramer restricted the term *ILP* to theories that claim that moral validity might serve as a necessary condition of legal validity, reserving the term *Incorporationism* for theories, such as his own, that also countenance the arguably stronger claim that it might be a sufficient condition as well. Normally, and unless my discussion demands otherwise, I will depart from Kramer's usage and use *ILP* as an umbrella term designating any theory that asserts the possibility (but not the necessity) that moral validity might serve as some kind of condition of legal validity. When context renders it necessary to differentiate between necessity and sufficiency versions of *ILP*, I will follow Kramer's lead and use *ILP* to designate theories that countenance necessity conditions only and *Incorporationism* for those that countenance sufficiency conditions as well.

Wilfrid J. Waluchow, *Kramer and Inclusive Legal Positivism* In: *Without Trimmings*. Edited by: Mark McBride and Visa AJ Kurki,
Oxford University Press. © Mark McBride and Visa AJ Kurki 2022. DOI: 10.1093/oso/9780198868866.003.0007

it might not. Insisting on the contingency of these connections between moral and legal validity allowed defenders of *ILP* to separate themselves from natural lawyers and from Ronald Dworkin for whom, arguably, some such connections are conceptually necessitated by the very nature of law. According to *ILP*, legal and moral validity are not necessarily connected with one another, though they possibly could be.[4]

Among Kramer's distinctive contributions to the vigorous debates that took place among defenders of these competing theories was his robust defense of a version of *ILP* that limited the role morality could play in establishing a sufficient condition of legal validity. On this theory, which Kramer referred to as *moderate or mild Incorporationism*, the moral validity of a norm can serve as a sufficient criterion of its legal validity only in hard cases—that is, only in controversial cases where the law for some reason fails to provide an answer to the relevant legal question on which reasonable, well-informed lawyers and judges can all agree. In so doing he staked out a position that differed, not only from *ELP*, but also from the less restrictive Incorporationist theories of Jules Coleman, David Lyons, and Philip Soper, who did not limit the sufficiency condition to hard cases.[5] In their view, which Kramer dubbed *extreme Incorporationism*, the moral validity of a norm can serve as a sufficient condition of its legal validity in all cases, both hard and easy. Indeed, according to Coleman and Soper, it is conceptually possible that a rule of recognition in some conceivable legal system might specify moral validity as the sole criterion of legal validity. The rule of recognition in such a system might specify that "the only laws are incorporated moral principles" (*WLMM*, 6). Kramer's view was that such extreme Incorporationist theories allow for the possibility of a rule of recognition that will very likely "bring about its own quick displacement [by another rule of recognition that included other criteria of validity], or—if it somehow persists—it will very likely fail to provide the degree of regularity that is prerequisite to the functionality of a legal system. Though it might conceivably structure a legal system that is woefully inefficient, it will much more probably structure nothing at all that can qualify as the rule of law" (*WLMM*, 34). By restricting the moral sufficiency condition to hard cases where, by definition, significant disagreement exists, Kramer's moderate theory avoids what extreme Incorporationism seems to countenance: "the specter of cripplingly pervasive disagreements among officials in the process of ascertaining the law" (*WLMM*, 35).[6]

Vigorous debates among defenders of these competing theories of law, took place over a span of some thirty+ years, and Kramer was among its most active and creative

[4] Henceforth I will use the term *moral validity* to refer broadly to any moral condition that requires moral worthiness, truth, justifiability, etc.

[5] Coleman's view is defended in a number of places, most notably *The Practice of Principle: In Defence of a Pragmatist Approach to Legal Theory*. Lyons's view was outlined in "Principles, Positivism and Legal Theory," 415 and Soper's in "Legal Theory and the Obligation of a Judge: The Hart/Dworkin Dispute," 473.

[6] I once argued that *ILP* could, theoretically, sanction a rule of recognition that specified, as its sole criterion of legal validity, that a norm (or decision) follow from Hercules's soundest theory of the law. Hercules is Dworkin's ideal judge whose theory best explains and justifies the settled law—and establishes what counts as binding law within Hercules' jurisdiction. See "Herculean Positivism," 187–210. Professor Kramer's arguments against extreme Incorporationism have led me to think that my conclusion in that paper may have been too broad—and that perhaps I should have restricted its reach to hard cases in all but fanciful, imaginary societies where moral agreement is far more prevalent than we find in modern, pluralistic societies.

participants. Dworkin's article "The Model of Rules" got the ball rolling by making three key assertions: (1) that principles such as "No man may profit from his own wrong" often serve as recognized grounds for legal decisions in hard cases; (2) that these principles are considered legitimate grounds because of their moral validity, not their pedigree or the manner of their authoritative adoption; and (3) that legal positivism necessarily restricts the class of norms upon which judges may legitimately draw in deciding legal cases to rules that are valid in virtue of their pedigree, not their moral validity.[7] From this Dworkin was prepared to conclude (4) that positivism must be rejected as inconsistent with the familiar role morality plays in legal practice—as a source of norms establishing legal duties, rights, and so on.[8] *ILP* arose largely as a defense against Dworkin's critique of positivism. If, as defenders of *ILP* maintained, (3) is false, and there is nothing in the theoretical commitments of positivism that precludes the possibility that moral validity might sometimes serve as a condition of legal validity, then there is nothing to prevent a positivist from accepting Dworkin's claims about the role moral principles seem to serve in legal practice—and going on to thank Dworkin for bringing to light possible connections between moral and legal validity that had hitherto been underappreciated by positivists.[9]

Some positivists rejected *ILP*'s response to Dworkin. In order to be faithful to the positivist tradition, they said, one had to deny not only a *necessary* connection between legal and moral validity but their *possible* connection as well. Chief among those who took this line of argument was Joseph Raz, who argued that allowing moral validity to serve as a condition of legal validity would entail a highly unlikely result: deep incoherence in law's self-understanding, a self-understanding exemplified by its claim to possess supreme, legitimate authority over a population. For this essential claim of law to be anything more than nonsensical, Raz argued, law's valid norms must be identifiable independently of any and all moral considerations. That is, moral validity can be neither a necessary nor a sufficient condition of legal validity. In staking out this view of the theoretical commitments of positivism, Raz became associated with *ELP*, the form of positivism that denies the connections *ILP* accepts as possible.

So defenders of *ILP* found themselves in a precarious position. Not only were they required to answer to Dworkin and natural lawyers. They also had to come to terms

[7] Dworkin's essay included many other important claims, but for our purposes these are the crucial ones.

[8] Dworkin also went on to argue for a theory of law, *law as integrity* (*LI*), according to which it is not merely true that law and on the contrary, it is necessarily true that the two are connected insofar as law, by its very nature, furnishes grounds for the moral justification of state coercion. . According to *LI*, law, by its very nature, furnishes grounds for the justification of state coercion. It follows from this that legal validity is necessarily, not merely contingently, connected to moral validity as *ILP* maintains. Defenders of *ILP* were unwilling to push their view this far. In their view, all that was necessary to defeat Dworkin's critique was the claim that law and morality *could* be connected, though not necessarily so. For them, the connection between legal and moral validity is not necessary as Dworkin maintained, but dependent on contingent social practice.

[9] This is not to suggest that the connections brought to light were never acknowledged in previous positivist writings. Even though the distinction between *ILP* and *ELP* had yet to be clearly drawn, Hart, for instance, included an extensive discussion of the myriad ways in which law and morality are or could be connected with one another. And at one point, he said this: "In some systems, as in the United States, the ultimate criteria of validity explicitly incorporate principles of justice or substantive moral values ... The further ways in which law mirrors morality are myriad, and still insufficiently studied" (*Concept of Law*, 203–4). Among the benefits of Dworkin's initial critique of positivism was that these and other ways in which law can be connected to morality were anything but insufficiently studied!

with objections raised on their other flank, by their *ELP* cousins. These multi-frontal debates raged on for many years, with each argument met by counter-argument and further refinement of the theory being advanced. The most vigorous debates were between defenders of *ILP* and *ELP*. And arguably the most important move in this debate was an appeal, by *ELP*'s defenders, to what Raz termed *directed powers*. For each type of situation in which it *appears* as though moral validity is being used to establish legal validity or to determine existing legal rights and duties, the directed powers account had an alternative narrative. Moral validity is, in fact, serving as a condition for the exercise, by the relevant court, of its directed power to *change* the law so as to bring about compliance with the relevant moral norm. A prime illustration of these different narratives can be found in the constitutional provisions to which Hart made reference in *The Concept of Law*. Some constitutional rights provisions seem to make the legal validity of norms and official actions dependent on their conformity with moral rights or values like free expression and equality. That is, it appears as if, in countries such as the United States, "the ultimate criteria of validity explicitly incorporate principles of justice or substantive moral values." It appears, in other words, that the US Constitution embraces the possibility *ILP* endorses—a dependence of legal validity on moral validity. This is a dependence contingent, of course, on the fact that the relevant constitutional provisions were duly adopted by those with the requisite authority to create them, i.e., the founders or authors of the constitution, and on the fact that the US rule of recognition sanctions the US Constitution as superior law creating conditions of legal validity. But looks are deceiving, according to defenders of *ELP*. What might appear to be ultimate criteria of validity are in actual fact directives aimed at judges instructing them to change the law so as to avoid the conflict between the specified moral principle or value and the offending norm (e.g., a statute) or action (e.g., an executive order). The US Constitution empowers—and directs—judges to resolve the conflict by striking down or invalidating the legally valid norm or official action in light of its conflict with the relevant moral norm. It's important to be clear that, on this *ELP* account, legal validity itself depends on nothing remotely like a moral condition. Whether, for example, a statute is valid always depends on non-moral, pure pedigree conditions such as whether it has been duly passed by Congress and, importantly in the cases under consideration, whether it has also been struck down or invalidated by the act of a court in furtherance of its directed power to do so. And whether some such act of invalidation has occurred is a matter of pure social fact.

So both *ILP* and *ELP* had accounts of the role morality seems to play in establishing legal validity, rights, duties, and so on. Eventually these theories evolved to the point where it became reasonable to ask whether there was anything to distinguish between them beyond mere terminological preference or stipulation. Kramer himself was well aware of the danger inherent in this situation, cautioning that "[c]onsiderable circumspection is advisable here. An effort to choose between an Exclusivist theory and a mild Incorporationist theory is always prone to degenerate into an exercise in arid terminological stipulations" (*WLMM*, 38). One important legal theorist took an even dimmer view of the resultant state of play. In *Legal Philosophy in the Twentieth Century: The Common Law World*, Gerald Postema had this to say, particularly about the argumentative strategy pursued by defenders of *ILP*:

> The inclusive positivist approach arose directly in response to Dworkin's challenge to Hart's revision of positivism. From the outset, inclusivism looks for ways that philosophers, committed to positivism, could keep their positivist faith while acknowledging the force of Dworkin's most persuasive arguments. Exclusive positivism, on the other hand, took a harder line in response to Dworkin—Hart called it "hard positivism" —offering arguments against the incorporation thesis. Thus, inclusivists, finding the incorporation thesis plausible, found themselves on the defensive concerning their positivist credentials. From its birth in the early 1980s, up to the flurry of writing at the turn of the millennium, this entirely defensive posture has dictated not only the inclusive positivist strategy, but also determined the content of its doctrines. It has been defined exclusively by its opposition to positions on its theoretical flanks. It offered little by way of a positive case for positivism as a theory of the nature of law, but rather assumes a plateau of commitment to positivism relying largely on Hart's defense of a much more robust positivism. And it offered no positive case for its own endorsement of the truth of the incorporation thesis as an interpretation of the practice in familiar legal systems, relying largely on the persuasive power of Dworkin's original arguments.[10]

Postema took his critique one step further. Not only were defenses of *ILP* essentially reactionary and defensive; advocates of the view had strayed from the principal mission of offering a theory of law: deepening our understanding of law and the important role(s) it serves in our lives:

> Inclusivist theories, attempting with increasing desperation to find some way of reconciling recalcitrant phenomena of legal practice with core dogmas of positivism, have departed further and further from the task of deepening our understanding of the nature of law wherever we find it....[11]

This indictment was not, however, limited to *ILP*. *ELP*, was equally guilty of myopia, Postema went on to suggest:

> Although the phenomena of legal practice—the prevalence of appeals to principles of political morality on their merits in judicial argument—are widely acknowledged by contemporary analytic legal philosophers, their explanations of these phenomena are sharply opposed. However, the arguments offered in favor of competing explanations are in most cases unsatisfying. What is worse, in the course of the dialectic, we have seemed to have lost contact with the original phenomena, problems, and the theoretical and practical motivations that gave them life.[12]

[10] Postema, *Legal Philosophy in the Twentieth Century: The Common Law World*, 466–7, footnotes omitted.

[11] Ibid., 482.

[12] Ibid. For similar indictments of debates between defenders of *ILP* and *ELP*, see Bix, "Patrolling the Boundaries: Inclusive Legal Positivism and the Nature of Jurisprudential Debate." See also Schauer's "Positivism Through Thick and Thin." According to Schauer, the debate between defenders of *ILP* and *ELP* are "likely to confirm the worst fears of a large number of contemporary American law professors, the fear that analytical jurisprudence in general, and the debates about legal positivism in particular, are the largely

So what are we to make of Postema's indictment of a debate that occupied legal philosophers such as Kramer and his fellow positivists for close to thirty years? Is there really nothing of theoretical or practical interest in trying to determine whether, for example, *ILP* or *ELP* provides a more compelling or enlightening account of the nature of law? Is it true that *ILP* offers nothing that enhances our understanding of law and its role in our lives, and that the valiant efforts of Kramer and his *ILP* colleagues amount to nothing of much significance—of no more significance than, say, attempting to determine how many angels can dance on the head of a pin? It is my aim, in the remainder of this chapter, to blunt the force of Postema's indictment of the view Professor Kramer and his *ILP* allies spent so much effort developing and defending. I shall do so by arguing that *ILP* does indeed provide a better, more enlightening account of the nature of law than *ELP* does—that there are in fact good, positive reasons to prefer *ILP* to *ELP*. In what follows I will argue that (1) *ILP* better accounts for the conventional nature of law; (2) *ILP* offers a conceptual map of legal practice that is more consonant than *ELP* with the self-understanding expressed in the norms and practices of many legal systems; and (3) *ILP* better accounts for the variety of ways in which law is capable of structuring our practical reasoning and, as a result, serving our moral interests.[13] If I am right, then I will have provided what Postema finds missing—good reasons for thinking that Kramer's subtle and insightful jurisprudential theory was not, in the end, pretty much a waste of time.

2. An Array of Defensive Arguments

Let's begin by agreeing that there is some truth in Postema's assertion that the argumentative strategy pursued by defenders of *ILP* was largely defensive in orientation. Let's also agree that there is something unsatisfying about a theory that remains largely reactionary in orientation. But I hope that we might also agree on the following: it is quite understandable that defenders of *ILP* pursued the defensive strategies they did. When confronted with the repeated claim that one's theoretical commitments require one to accept a view one might otherwise wish to reject, the most obvious response is to deny the inference, or to show how the critics' claim rests on a misunderstanding of one's theoretical commitments. Generally speaking, when faced with the claim that one's acceptance of *A* requires commitment to (unpalatable) implication *B*, how else would one begin except by arguing that A, properly understood, does not in fact entail *B*—and that the interlocutor has simply misunderstood what was being claimed? So it was quite natural for positivists who saw merit in Dworkin's observations concerning the role moral principles sometimes play in legal practice, but who wished to remain true to the positivist tradition, to argue that that theory, properly understood, does not in fact entail what Dworkin claimed it did. Understood correctly, it does not entail that legal validity can never, under any circumstances, depend on moral validity.

irrelevant preoccupation of a small group of socially unaware but philosophically obsessed pedants, many of whom are English and most of whom are dead" (at 69).

[13] Arguments (1) and (2) already exist in the literature. Argument (3), so far as I am aware, is largely new.

Anyone (such as Dworkin) who thought otherwise had confused two crucially different claims: (a) that legal validity can never, under any circumstances, depend on moral validity; and (b) that legal validity need not depend on moral validity in all legal cases and in all legal systems. According to (a), legal and moral validity are necessarily separate. According to (b) they are only separable. Furthermore, according to (b) whether legal validity is in some instance dependent on moral validity rests on contingent facts of social practice—on whether, for example, the rule of recognition accepted and practiced by the officials of the legal system, includes criteria that make reference to "principles of justice or substantive moral values." Under the right social conditions, the existence of law can indeed be one thing and its merit or demerit something else entirely. Under different social conditions, this might not be so. In sum, it was quite natural to argue that there is nothing in the theoretical commitments of Hartian positivism, a view that sees law as essentially resting on fundamental social practices of recognition, that requires endorsement of the *separation thesis*, that legal validity and moral validity are *necessarily separate* from one another. All that is required is endorsement of the *separability thesis*, the claim that legal and moral validity are *separable* by contingent social practice. And to say that they are separable is consistent with saying that they could be brought together, the one being a condition of the other. Once again, it all depends on contingent social practice.

So defenders of *ILP* quite understandably pursued a defensive argument in response to Dworkin's critique. They did so by arguing that Dworkin had misconstrued their theory, ascribing to them the separation thesis when all that is necessary to count as a positivist—and answer Dworkin's critique—is endorsement of the separability thesis. *ILP*'s many critics were quick to counter this defensive move by constructing an array of arguments each purporting to show that the separability thesis is really not enough—that positivism actually demands the separation, not mere separability, of law and morals. And defenders of *ILP* were obliged to answer each one of these arguments. What follows is a brief survey of some of the more important ones.

2.1 Dworkin's Argument from Function

Let's begin with Dworkin himself, who argued that *ILP* is inconsistent with positivist views concerning the very function of law. On that view, Dworkin argued, the very point of law is to facilitate consensus on what ought to be done in the face of significant disagreement on important social and moral issues in respect of which consensus is highly desirable, if not practically necessary, in modern societies. Were a society ever to accept that legal validity depends in some way on moral validity, it would reintroduce the very dissensus law is intended to overcome. Responses to this argument revolved around a number of claims. For instance, I argued that it exaggerates the extent to which positivists are or need be concerned to stress the law's capacity to resolve moral and social issues in a clear, determinate manner. Hart, after all, had argued persuasively that it is sometimes advisable deliberately to fashion legal rules using open-textured terms that result in an increased possibility of dissensus as to their application in concrete cases. In Hart's view, there are often good moral and strategic reasons to pursue this option. Another counterargument was that Dworkin's argument presupposed too stark a contrast between pedigree and moral criteria of validity in respect of the disagreement each might generate. Sometimes satisfaction of the former can be more contentious than satisfaction of the latter. In addition, it was pointed out that Dworkin's argument failed adequately to distinguish between what is desirable in a legal system, on the one hand, and what is necessary for its very existence, on the other. Moral criteria for validity might well introduce an undesirable degree of dissensus into cases in which questions of legal validity arise. It fails to follow that they would result in nothing that could properly be called law.[14] And finally, not all defenders of *ILP* sanctioned the extreme form according to which P's status as a moral principle could be, in some putative legal system, a sufficient condition of its legal validity. In Kramer's view, any system which attempted to implement such a condition would have crossed the line between an undesirable legal system and a failed attempt to establish a legal system at all. Recall that it was Kramer's desire to rule out such a scenario that seemed largely to motivate his endorsement of mild Incorporationism. On this theory, "moral worthiness is a sufficient condition for the status of norms as legal norms [only] in *hard cases* that cannot be resolved by reference to legal norms from other sources" (*WLMM*, 28, emphasis added). In Kramer's view, extreme Incorporationism is indeed inconsistent with law's functions. It fails to follow that this is true of less extreme forms of *ILP*.

2.2 Shapiro's Practical Difference Thesis

A similar line of argument, appealing once again to law's supposed function according to the positivist tradition, was marshalled by Scott Shapiro who maintained that *ILP* robs law of one of its essential features: its ability to guide conduct by way of valid legal rules. If a rule's legal validity were dependent on its moral validity, it could not guide us in the way rules, *qua* rules, are intended to guide us. It could not make the "practical difference" rules are meant to make.[15] It could not provide reasons that excluded or pre-empted any and all moral reasons for action upon which we might otherwise act. *ILP*'s defenders responded in a number of ways to this argument. Coleman, for example, countered with the assertion that there is a difference between a legal system's success in serving its guidance function and the same being true of each and every law valid under that system's criteria of validity. All that is necessary for law is the former. And the former is consistent with the validity of some laws depending on their satisfaction of a moral condition.[16] Kramer's responses were subtle and multi-faceted. For instance, he pointed out that for a rule to make the practical difference it need not exclude or pre-empt *all* otherwise relevant moral considerations. This allows for the possibility that the moral condition included in the relevant rule of recognition might make reference to a moral consideration that lies outside the exclusionary scope of the rule whose legal validity is in question.[17] And

[14] These arguments were all put forward in my *Inclusive Legal Positivism*, 184–90.

[15] For responses to Shapiro's argument, see Waluchow, "Authority and the Practical Difference Thesis: A Defense of Inclusive Legal Positivism," 45; Coleman, "Incorporationism, Conventionality and the Practical Difference Thesis," 381; and Kramer, *WLMM* 61–4.

[16] I offered a similar argument. See "Herculean Positivism," n. 6, 205–6.

[17] For Kramer's responses to Shapiro, see *WLMM*, 17–35.

indeed this is often the case. The fact that a particular abortion law results in unequal access to lawful abortion procedures, and hence violates some women's constitutionally recognized right to equality, can be a moral reason that warrants a declaration of its invalidity. And yet such a reason is in all likelihood not among the moral reasons an abortion law is intended to pre-empt or exclude.

2.3 Dissensus and the Rule of Recognition

A third line of argument against *ILP* maintained that a rule of recognition containing moral criteria of legal validity could not conceivably be what Hart and his fellow positivists claimed it to be—a *social* rule whose existence depends on general agreement concerning its requirements, an agreement displaying itself in patterns of behavior conducted in accordance with what is widely, if not universally, believed to be the rule's requirements. If people—in particular judges—generally disagree about the demands of morality, they will generally disagree about whether the incorporated moral criteria of validity have been met, a fact that would be revealed in their variable conduct (and decisions in the case of judges) under the so-called rule. Under these conditions of dissensus, no pattern of behavior or decision could possibly emerge and be sustained in the way required for the existence of a social rule. There could, in short, be no rule of recognition, and hence no domain of legally valid standards settling questions concerning what we ought to do.

Coleman countered this argument by drawing two distinctions: first, the distinction between an *epistemic* and a *semantic* function of a rule of recognition. The critics' argument works only if we mistakenly assume that the role of a rule of recognition is to inform us reliably on what counts as valid law—an epistemic function. The argument does not work, however, if instead we assume (correctly, in Coleman's view) that it serves, at least in respect of judges and other officials of the legal system, the semantic role of specifying the truth conditions for propositions of law, for example, the proposition, P, that statute R is legally valid. The following somewhat fanciful example might help to explain why. Imagine a legal system in which most judges and officials disagree about the conditions specified in their rule of recognition, and hence the truth conditions of propositions of law like P. Some think that "R is valid law" is true only if R satisfies validity condition C, while others believe R must satisfy condition D. In this instance, there would be dissensus regarding the truth conditions for propositions of law like P. This would not, Coleman argued, necessarily lead to a breakdown in the pattern of behavior required to sustain the rule of recognition, and hence the legal system in which it serves such a vital role. Imagine further, and no doubt counterfactually, that the system is fortunate enough to have a member of its highest court, Serena, whose knowledge, skill, and acumen is such that she is almost invariably able to identify true propositions of law. And suppose that all the other judges and officials are aware of her ability to do so. So they know that if Serena endorses P as true, then almost certainly P is in fact true and R is indeed legally valid. This they will know even though they themselves cannot be sure *why* P is true. Given this scenario, it would be sensible for the other judges and officials always to defer to Serena and her ability to zero in on true propositions of law. As a result, they would all converge on compliance with the rule of recognition, thus avoiding the dissensus that threatens its existence and hence the legal system of which it serves such an integral role.

Coleman's second distinction—one noted by Kramer as well—was between disagreement about the content of the relevant criteria of validity, on the one hand, and disagreement about whether instance X satisfies them, on the other. "Manifold divergences among officials concerning the *ex*tension of such a criterion are compatible with a general consensus among them on the criterion's *in*tension" (*WLMM*, 65). In other words, it is possible to have manifold "disagreement over application" without having significant "disagreements over content" (*WLMM*, 66). It is only the latter that threatens the status of the rule of recognition as a social rule. But it is disagreement over the former on which critics base their argument.

2.4 The Argument from Authority

Perhaps the most influential rejoinder to *ILP* (and to both *NLT* and Dworkin's *LI*) was Joseph Raz's argument that allowing moral validity to serve as a possible condition of legal validity is inconsistent with law's self-image or conception, most notably its claim to supreme, legitimate authority. It is, according to Raz, in the essential nature of a legal system that it necessarily claims justified practical authority over a population—it necessarily claims the right to issue binding directives on which (it claims) members of that population have a moral duty to act. As an avowed defender of positivism, Raz denies, of course, that law necessarily possesses the justified practical authority it necessarily claims for itself. But law, in order to be law, has to *make* this claim. And, importantly, if its claim is to be at all intelligible and coherent, the law must at the very least be the *kind* of thing that is *capable* of possessing the practical authority it claims for itself. But, Raz claims, if it were possible for a legal system to be designed as *ILP* suggests it could be—legal validity in some way depending on moral validity—it could not be that kind of thing. Here's why.[18]

Each of us is constantly faced with the question: What should I do? In answering this question, we often appeal to reasons for doing one thing rather than another. Raz calls these *first-order reasons for action*. First-order reasons bear directly on the merits of doing or not doing X. In many situations in which we are faced with a choice about whether to do X, we weigh the applicable first-order reasons against one another and act on what we take to be the correct or right balance of reasons. But sometimes reason suggests that we pursue a different strategy. In some scenarios, right reason dictates that we act in accordance with a *second-order reason* that reflects someone else's judgment about the relevant first-order reasons that apply to us. Often the relevant second-order reason will be a directive to act in a particular way issued by a legal authority, A. On Raz's account, S is normally justified in accepting and acting on A's directives as authoritative when S is more likely to act in accordance with right reason by following

[18] Raz's authority argument is complex and subtle. And what is provided here is but a thumbnail sketch that conveys, it is hoped, its essential elements. For fuller accounts of the argument, and the theory of authority on which it relies, see Raz, *The Authority of Law*; "Authority and Justification," 3–29; "Authority, Law and Morality," 295–324.

A's directives than by attempting herself to act directly on the balance of first-order reasons.[19] This claim Raz calls *The Normal Justification Thesis* (NJT). Authority provides a kind of second-order *exclusionary reason* that not only purports to give us reason to act in a particular way, it purports to exclude, and replace, (at least some of) the relevant first-order reasons upon which we would otherwise be justified in acting. When the conditions of the NJT are met, right reason suggests that we should act on the authoritative directive rather than on (what we take to be) the balance of first-order reasons. According to the NJT, it is the normal role of a practical authority to provide this service.[20]

If authoritative legal directives are to be capable of serving their role in guiding us on the path to right reason, their identification and interpretation cannot, Raz further maintains, depend on our having to consider the first-order reasons they were meant to exclude and replace. But this is precisely what happens, Raz thinks, if we accept *ILP*. Consider a statute, L. As a second-order, authoritative directive, L is meant to exclude and replace whatever reasons of prudence, morality, and so on, apply to us in the situations over which the statute governs. But if L's identity as a valid legal directive depends on its conformity with a moral principle like fairness—a moral norm or reason that is often relevant in many situations governed by laws—then its identity as an authoritative directive may well depend on the very reasons, fairness included, it was meant to exclude and replace. We will therefore have to deliberate on at least some of those first-order reasons in determining whether L is valid and therefore authoritative. But if so, then we might just as well have dispensed with L altogether and instead acted directly on the relevant first-order reasons, including the relevant reasons of fairness. Hence, Raz concludes, *ILP* is incompatible with the law's claim to authority.

There were many *ILP* responses to Raz's argument. Among the most common was to reiterate a point noted above, that the moral considerations on which legal validity might depend are not necessarily members of the set of moral reasons excluded by the authoritative directive. Recall the abortion law considered earlier. Or consider a valid law prohibiting murder. Whatever moral reasons are excluded by this law have nothing to do with fairness. Yet basic fairness is what the American due process clause is usually understood as requiring. So requiring, for the legal validity of a rule dealing with murder, that it not violate due process does not require that we appeal to any excluded reasons. The law maintains its authoritative status, despite the moral condition of its legal validity.[21]

[19] A further condition of justified authority is that it is more important that one act in accordance with right reason than that one choose freely how to act. This condition Raz calls the *Independence Condition*, and for purposes of this very brief exposition, we can safely it set it aside. On the Independence Condition, see Raz, *The Morality of Freedom*, 154–5; Raz, *Ethics in the Public Domain*, 119; Raz, "The Problem of Authority: Revisiting the Service Conception," 1013–14.

[20] Once again, I have set aside the Independence Condition.

[21] Responses to Raz's authority argument were numerous and varied and extended well beyond the ones just considered. And they were not limited to defenders of *ILP*. One of Dworkin's defenders, Stephen Perry, argued against the claim that authoritative directives need be exclusionary. See Perry, "Judicial Obligation, Precedent and the Common Law," 221. For further responses by defenders of *ILP*, see my *Inclusive Legal Positivism*, 123–40 and Coleman, *The Practice of Principle*, 121–32.

2.5 The Argument from Foreign Law

A further argument for rejecting *ILP* draws on the ways in which judges are sometimes legally required to apply norms arising from other jurisdictions, and sees, in this, the basis for an analogy with the ways in which moral norms are treated. What we will call *the argument from foreign law* (AFL) runs as follows. No legal theorist denies that moral norms are sometimes used by judges in deciding legal cases. For instance, all legal positivists are happy to agree that such norms are sometimes used when judges exercise their law-making discretionary powers in hard cases. As Hart observed, it might even be true that, in some legal systems, judges are legally required to settle such cases by making the decision they think morally best. As we have also seen, no contemporary legal positivist denies that moral norms can sometimes be relevant *even when deciding issues surrounding legal validity*. They only divide on how best to understand or interpret this phenomenon. Defenders of *ILP* have their story of what this means: legal validity can sometimes depend on moral validity, while defenders of *ELP* have their tale to tell: courts can be required to exercise their directed power to invalidate legally valid norms when the latter conflict with certain moral norms. Validity never depends on moral conditions, on this alternative reading, but invalidation can.

ELP's defenders took their reluctance to sanction moral conditions of legal validity one step further by insisting that the moral norms that a legal system's courts are directed to apply remain outside that legal system. They are not, as defenders of *ILP* maintained, incorporated into the legal system as valid legal norms. And this is because a legal system "is an open system" insofar as "it contains norms the purpose of which is to give binding force within the system to norms *which do not belong to it*."[22] That a legal system sometimes requires courts to apply norms that originate outside of its boundaries means that we must distinguish "between standards that the courts have to apply and those that are the law of the land."[23] That courts are sometimes required to enforce the norms of a foreign legal system, in no way entails that the norms of the latter become the law of the land. And the same is true, Raz contends, when it comes to the moral norms courts are sometimes legally required to apply in deciding legal cases. *ILP*'s defenders have mistakenly assumed that the employment of a moral norm to answer a question surrounding validity entails its incorporation into law. But this ignores the fact that moral norms, though sometimes "standards that the courts have to apply" are not "those that are the law of the land." These moral norms are no more the law of the land than the rules of Polish contract law become part of British law when and if British judges are legally required to apply them to settle a contractual dispute in a British courtroom. In short, *ILP* rests on a simple confusion between norms the courts are required to apply and norms that are part of the legal system in which the obligation to apply arises. Once this confusion is cleared up, we can see straight away that the norms of morality on which the case for *ILP* depends are no more part of the legal system than foreign laws are. The two—moral norms and foreign laws—are in this respect on a par with each other. Neither is incorporated into the legal system.

[22] *Practical Reason and Norms*, 152–3. Emphasis added.
[23] Raz, *Between Authority and Interpretation*, 199.

Kramer fashioned the most sophisticated and powerful response to this line of argument. The key, as he saw it, was to show that morality and foreign law are actually not, in the relevant respect, analogous to one another at all. To do this he had to find some feature of moral norms that "pertinently distinguishes them from the rules of clubs and sporting associations and the laws of foreign jurisdictions" (*WLMM*, 38–9). He needed to find some feature that would explain our reluctance to view the latter norms as belonging to the legal system despite the fact that courts do sometimes treat them as legally binding. The relevant feature, Kramer maintained, is that they are all subject to the authoritative control of outside institutions and the persons who occupy official roles within them. "Exactly because the foreign laws and the rules of the clubs and associations are subject to the authoritative control of people outside [legal system] L, the occasional application of those rules and laws within L should not be regarded as the incorporation of them into L's matrix of legal norms" (*WLMM*, 39). "[T]he application of them is a way of showing due respect for the norms that have been chosen and formulated in systems of authority that exist alongside L. As a means of showing such respect, the effectuation of those norms within L tends to highlight their separateness from L's own norms" (*WLMM*, 39). When we turn to the norms of morality, however, no such outside authority is to be found. Moral norms are not subject to anyone's control, let alone the control of persons who operate within other authoritative institutions, such as league offices and foreign parliaments. On the contrary, they are, like customary legal norms, "not really within anyone's effective control" (*WLMM*, 40). "[W]hen they receive formal recognition within L as binding legal norms, they are not some borrowings from another system in which they have an authoritatively established status. Until that point of formal recognition, they are free-floating—that is, free of any institutional affiliation which has been authoritatively set. They are consequently available for incorporation into L" (*WLMM*, 40–1). Insofar as they are free-floating, then, moral norms are like customary norms, but unlike the norms of foreign legal systems, and clubs and sporting associations. So what is true of the latter—incorporation does not necessarily follow compulsory use in deciding cases—is not necessarily true of the former. Kramer took this argument against AFL one step further, by noting that defenders of *ELP* are happy to accept that free-floating customary norms can be and often are incorporated into "L's assemblage of legal norms" (*WLMM*, 40). If so, he reasoned, sheer consistency demands that *ELP*'s advocates be equally happy to view the moral norms that courts are legally bound to apply in some cases as "available for incorporation into L's laws" as well (*WLMM*, 41).

So by showing a relevant distinction between the norms of foreign law (subject to outside authoritative control) and the norms of morality (free-floating), Kramer was able to answer AFL and its *ELP* advocates. The reason we do not consider foreign law incorporated (respect for authority) does not apply to moral norms. Hence, AFL offers no reason not to consider moral norms incorporated. But this conclusion was apparently not enough for Kramer, who seemed to take his argument one step further—and in a way that brings us back to Postema's claim that *ILP*'s defenders fail to provide *positive* reasons to prefer their theory to *ELP*. "Unlike Exclusive Legal Positivism ... the position advocated [in *WLMM*] can distinguish pertinently between the status of customary norms and the status of sporting associations' rules (and of foreign laws) when those norms and rules are given effect within any particular legal system" (*WLMM*,

43). So far so good. AFL has successfully been answered. The next step is where the trouble begins. The fact that the one set of norms is subject to outside authoritative control while the other is free-floating also shows how the latter is "*available* for incorporation." Furthermore, "[t]the basis for such a distinction leads to the conclusion that the moral principles drawn upon by mildly Incorporationist judges in hard cases *are* sometimes laws of the system in which they are invoked and applied. In insisting on that very point, a mild version of Incorporationism is *superior* to Exclusive Legal Positivism" (*WLMM*, 43, emphases added).

Are these much stronger conclusions warranted? I'm not so sure. It is one thing to show an important difference between foreign law and moral norms, and that the reason that explains our reluctance to consider the former incorporated—respect for outside authority—does not apply to the latter. But this does not seem, in the end, to establish that moral norms really are available for incorporation. And this is because we have yet to rule out the possibility of some *other* reason that prohibits us from viewing them this way. Of course, *ELP*'s defenders thought there were plenty such reasons—reasons outlined above, and which were, arguably, successfully addressed by *ILP*'s advocates. But even if this is so, the possibility remains that there are further reasons or arguments, yet to be addressed, that rule out the incorporation of moral norms. And if this is so, then moral norms might not in fact be available for incorporation after all. So Kramer's insightful response to AFL doesn't seem to warrant the conclusion that moral norms are available for incorporation into legal systems. And finally, it seems a mistake to infer from Kramer's response to AFL that existing legal systems actually do incorporate moral norms. We cannot infer that they do if only because: (1) a possibility does not, in itself, entail an actuality; and, once again, (2) we have yet to rule out the possibility or some further reason or argument for why they can't be incorporated.

So we need, I think, to distinguish clearly among three very different possible conclusions to Kramer's counter-argument to AFL:

A. AFL offers no valid reason to exclude moral norms as candidates for incorporation into L;
B. There is no (further) reason to exclude moral norms from the possibility of being incorporated into L—i.e., moral norms are "available for incorporation" into a legal system, L; and
C. Moral norms are in fact incorporated into some actual legal systems (most notably those referenced by Dworkin in his initial critique of positivism).

Kramer's counterargument clearly supports conclusion A. But it's not so clear that it supports B and C. As a result, it no more supports the superiority of *ILP* over *ELP* than the *ILP* responses to the other arguments against *ILP* considered above. Each of those arguments was intended to show that *ILP* violated some cardinal tenet of legal positivism. The response of *ILP*'s defenders was to show that this is not so, that there are ways to view positivism's theoretical commitments that render *ILP* consistent with them. *ILP* does not, for example, conflict with what positivists supposedly say about the functions of law, about its ability to guide conduct, about its authoritative status, and so on. In so doing, *ILP*'s counterarguments were, as Postema rightly pointed out, all defensive in orientation. And the same seems true of Kramer's counterargument to AFL. It does not, despite Kramer's claim, provide reasons for thinking that *ILP* is the better theory. It does not show that *ILP* "is superior to Exclusive Legal Positivism" (*WLMM*, 43). At best, the counterargument does what each of the counterarguments considered above was able to do: support a *tie judgment*; that on the relevant measures—ability to account for law's claimed authority, its ability to deal with issues surrounding the possible incorporation of external norms into law, etc.—*ILP*'s story is at least as plausible as *ELP*'s. At the very least, *ILP* has a coherent story to tell.

So Kramer may have overstated his case against AFL: at best, it supported the tie judgment. But this is of little consequence if there are non-defensive, positive arguments that enable us to break the tie in favor of *ILP*—that show that *ILP* truly is the superior theory that Kramer believes it to be. In what follows I will briefly consider three such arguments. The first two—*the conventionality argument* and *the argument from descriptive adequacy*—can be found in the existing literature. The third, so far as I am aware, is largely new—though its seeds can be found, surprisingly enough, in Raz's views on the role law characteristically plays in our practical reasoning. It is my hope that these three arguments will be enough to answer Postema's charge that *ILP* fails as a theory that "deepen[s] our understanding of the nature of law wherever we find it."

3. Three Positive Arguments

3.1 The Conventionality Argument

According to legal positivism, law is fundamentally a matter of social practice.[24] As Ken Himma nicely puts it, "The most fundamental of positivism's core commitments is the idea that law is, in essence, a social creation or artifact."[25] Furthermore, it is a social creation that rests on conventional foundations. It "is the emphasis on law's *conventionality* that distinguishes positivism from other conceptual theories of law . . . ."[26] In Hart's theory, the conventional social practice most essential to establishing a legal system's existence is, of course, acceptance, by its officials, of a rule of recognition setting out the system's criteria of legal validity. As Coleman put it, "The rule of recognition must be a social rule; it expresses or represents a convention of a certain kind."[27] Coleman not only stressed this core commitment of positivism, he drew attention to an important implication of that commitment for debates between defenders and critics of *ILP*. "The key move for the Incorporationist is the claim that positivism imposes no constraint on the criterial of validity. Whether a particular rule of recognition does so depends on the practice of officials."[28] "The rule of recognition expresses a social practice among officials to treat certain standards as criteria of legal validity.

[24] Sections 3.1 and 3.2 draw on my "The Origins of Inclusive Legal Positivism" in *Cambridge Companion to Legal Positivism* (Cambridge University Press, 2021).

[25] Himma, "Substance and Method in Conceptual Jurisprudence and Theory," 1152.

[26] Himma, "Law's Claim of Legitimate Authority", 286.

[27] Coleman, "Incorporationism, Conventionality, and the Practical Difference Thesis," 407. What kind of convention a rule of recognition is—whether it is, e.g., a coordinating convention, or what Andrei Marmor calls a *constituent convention*—is a matter of some dispute. But all positivists seem agreed that it represents a convention of some kind. See Marmor, *Positive Law and Objective Values*, ch. 1; and Postema, "Coordination and Convention at the Foundations of Law," 165.

[28] Coleman, "Incorporationism, Conventionality, and the Practical Difference Thesis," 407.

There is nothing in this conception of it that imposes any constraints on the conditions of validity... For the Incorporationist, what matters in the rule recognition is not the criteria of validity set forth, but its existence conditions."[29]

So according to positivism, law essentially rests on a conventional social practice of recognition according to agreed criteria of validity. And there is nothing in this conception of law's foundations that mandates or entails constraints, over and above agreement, on what can count as a criterion of validity. Hart was, of course, well aware of this aspect of positivism. In *The Concept of Law*, he maintained that the criteria of validity agreed on and accepted by officials can vary enormously. One can imagine a system in which the only relevant criterion is: "Whatever Rex decrees as law is legally valid." One can equally imagine a system in which the relevant criteria might be as complicated and contentious as something like: "A norm, L, is legally valid if L has been duly passed by the legislature, does not conflict with superior law, and does not violate constitutionally guaranteed rights to equality, freedom of expression, due process, and so on." Now if, as positivism maintains, (1) the key to understanding law is its conventional nature; and if, as positivism further maintains, (2) the conventional nature of law rests ultimately on a social practice of recognition according to agreed criteria of validity; and (3) the concepts of convention and agreed criteria of validity in and of themselves neither entail nor require any substantive constraints on the nature of the criteria of legal validity upon which officials might agree; then (4) any theory, such as *ELP*, that dictates further, substantive constraints—beyond agreement and shared practice—on eligible criteria of validity, obscures the fundamental conventional nature of law.[30] At the very least, (5) such a theory shoulders the burden of showing precisely why we must restrict criteria of validity to the type it specifies: i.e., pure pedigree criteria in the case of *ELP*. By way of contrast, this is not a burden of proof with which defenders of *ILP* need be concerned. And this is because, once again, *ILP* imposes no substantial constraints on eligible conditions of validity.[31]

[29] Ibid., emphasis added. For more recent discussion on these and related matters, see McBride, "The Inner Logic of Exclusivism (and Inclusivism): Raz's Foreshadowing,' 81; and "The Inner Logic of Exclusivism(and Inclusivism): Shapiro's Shadowing," 363. In these insightful articles, McBride refers to *ILP* as the "anything goes" version of positivism and attempts to determine the crucial differences between *ILP* and *ELP*. He does so by formulating a series of key conditionals which defenders of the two views either reject or endorse. Though the two theories are, in McBride's judgment, conceptually separable they are not, in virtue of their agreement on many of the conditionals he lists, as far apart as many imagine them to be.

[30] The same can presumably be said in respect of Dworkin's *LI* and of versions of NLT, such as that of Aquinas, that place substantive moral constraints on what can count as valid law.

[31] Professor Kramer does posit at least one further constraint, other than agreement and shared practice. A criterion of validity that, e.g., validated norms selected through a process of throwing dice would not be acceptable. But this would be for reasons tied directly to the conventionality of law. Settling cases in accordance with such a criterion would result in "a bewildering higgledy-piggledy welter of conflicting signals." And "[u]nless legal positivists are comfortable with designating such a regime as a legal system, they ought to insist that that there are in fact some constraints on the sorts of criteria that can form a Rule of Recognition. No such rule can consist solely of criteria that fail to secure the minimum of regularity which is prerequisite to the existence of a legal system" (*WLMM*, 26). It is because a robust Incorporationist rule of recognition would, in real world societies with their characteristic moral pluralism and disagreement, lead to a "bewildering higgledy-piggledy welter of conflicting signals" that Kramer opts for his modest Incorporationism. Recall that that theory countenances two things: (1) moral validity can serve as a necessary condition of legal validity for norms that pass all other, non-moral relevant tests of validity, e.g., being duly passed by the legislature; and (2) moral validity might serve as a sufficient condition in hard cases where deep disagreement already exists and where, therefore, the admission of moral criteria would introduce no further irregularity.

As Coleman observed, "The Incorporationist sees no reason for assuming that these conditions cannot in principle include criteria making moral value or merit a condition of legality, at least for some norms."[32] It is up to the legal system itself to define its own agreed limits, to decide which criteria of validity for membership it wishes to adopt and practice. This is a point, ironically enough, seemingly noted by Raz: " 'Law regulates its own creation', said Kelsen. The law itself determines which facts create laws and which abrogate them."[33]

So the fact that it respects, highlights, and emphasizes the fundamentally conventional nature of law constitutes one, powerful reason for thinking *ILP* superior to *ELP* (and, by extension, LI and NLT). Absent a valid reason to restrict criteria of validity to pure pedigree criteria, *ELP* has no case for disputing the superiority of *ILP*. Of course, defenders of *ELP* do think they have valid reasons for their restriction on criteria of validity—reasons highlighted in the various arguments canvassed in section 2. But as we have seen, *ILP*'s defenders have persuasive counterarguments to each one of them. And barring any further reason for restricting criteria of validity in the way *ELP* demands, we have a very good reason for considering *ILP* the better theory of law. Unlike *ELP*, it highlights, and puts front and center, the fact that law ultimately rests on conventional practices of recognition. In this respect, it is unlike *ELP* (and by extension LI and NLT) in rejecting any further substantive constraints on validity save those required to sustain a conventional practice of recognition.

3.2 The Argument from Descriptive Adequacy

A second positive argument for *ILP* rests on its descriptive accuracy, more specifically on the fact that it better and more easily accounts for the ways in which moral and legal validity seem to interact with each other in modern constitutional democracies. More specifically, it accords better with legal practice within these jurisdictions and with the conceptual understandings inherent in that practice and seemingly shared by its participants. Let's focus on that aspect of the practice to which Hart drew attention in *The Concept of Law*—situations where legal validity is thought to depend on conformity with "principles of justice or other moral values." Recall the main idea behind *ELP*'s directed powers account of such cases. Constitutional rights provisions do not, on this theory, establish fundamental legal rights the violation of which by a government measure renders it legally invalid. Rather, they establish moral conditions under which courts are instructed to invalidate any such measure, a measure which is (and will remain) legally valid till such time as it is invalidated by the court. And should no court exercise its power to invalidate, the measure remains legally valid. All this despite the fact that the conflicting norm violates the relevant constitutionally recognized right. The *Argument from Descriptive Adequacy* (ADA) points out how discordant this account of constitutional rights cases is with how constitutional rights are typically conceived and framed in modern constitutional democracies. Consider the following provisions of Canada's Constitutional Charter of Rights and Freedoms.

[32] Coleman, "Incorporationism, Conventionality, and the Practical Difference Thesis," 407.
[33] *The Authority of Law*, 151–2.

> 1. The *Canadian Charter of Rights and Freedoms* guarantees the rights and freedoms set out in it subject only to such reasonable limits prescribed by law as can be demonstrably justified in a free and democratic society.
>
> 15. (1) Every individual is equal before and under the law and has the right to the equal protection and equal benefit of the law without discrimination and, in particular, without discrimination based on race, national or ethnic origin, colour, religion, sex, age or mental or physical disability.
>
> 52. (1) The Constitution of Canada is the supreme law of Canada, and any law that is inconsistent with the provisions of the Constitution is, to the extent of the inconsistency, of no force or effect.

Sections 1 and 15 guarantee citizens a (reasonably limited) moral right to equality. And section 52(1) makes explicit the result should a conflict arise between that right and an enactment or decision on the part of the government that unreasonably limits it. It does not say that the law is vulnerable or liable to invalidation by a court. Nor does it instruct judges to undertake this procedure. Rather, it says quite explicitly that the law *is of no force or effect*. The most natural reading of section 52, one we should accept absent a very good reason to prefer an alternative interpretation, is that the offending measure or decision is *already* invalid owing to its unreasonable infringement of the moral right to equality specified in section 15—and that, as a consequence of their duty to enforce superior law, judges are duty-bound to recognize it as such. Put simply, judges are not duty-bound to *make* the offending measure invalid. They are duty-bound to *recognize* that it already is invalid and to decide accordingly.

This Canadian understanding of constitutional rights seems shared by many other jurisdictions. The US Supreme Court once said in *Norton v Shelby* (1886) that "An unconstitutional act is not a law; it confers no rights; it imposes no duties; it affords no protection; it creates no office; it is, in legal contemplation, *as inoperative as though it had never been passed*."[34] In other words, an act of government that stands in conflict with a constitutional right is, in virtue of that fact, void or invalid. It is important to stress, once again, that a constitutional conflict of this kind exists independently of a court's ruling that it does. In other words, a judicial decision that an act is unconstitutional does not *create* the conflict and hence *create* the condition of invalidity. On the contrary, the judicial decision *recognizes* a pre-existing conflict and the resultant absence of validity. In short, legal validity is conceived as depending on moral validity, not on acts of invalidation by judges.

So an unfortunate implication of the *ELP*, directed powers account is that it is inconsistent with how constitutional rights appear to be conceived in at least some jurisdictions. A second, related implication is its inconsistency with further, key aspects of common legal practice. Consider a case where a citizen, A, is ruled to have acted at time t(1) in violation of a criminal statute, C, that is later, at time t(2), found to be unconstitutional by a Constitutional Court. Let's suppose further that the court accepts A's claim that C does indeed violate A's constitutional rights. How should the conduct that prompted A's prosecution be viewed on the directed powers account? The short

[34] *Norton v. Shelby County*, 118 U.S. 425 (1886). Emphasis added.

answer, it would seem, is that A's conduct should be viewed as having been illegal. After all, the statute was valid at t(1) and only *became invalid* after the fact, at t(2) when the court exercised its power to invalidate. In other words, given that A acted, at t(1), in violation of criminal law C that had yet to be invalidated, A's act *was* illegal at t(1). And this remains true even when the court later invalidates C at t(2); and even though any similar acts performed by A (or anyone else, for that matter) following the court's decision at t(2) would be perfectly legal.

But this is not how courts typically treat a defendant's actions in this kind of case. Most courts will routinely treat A as having done nothing legally wrong at t(1). In other words, A will typically be exonerated on the ground that the statute under which his actions were deemed illegal both is and was at the time he acted legally invalid, and that A did not, therefore, act contrary to valid law. In short, he did nothing wrong. The consequence is that his conviction will invariably be deemed void, as will any subsequent attempt at prosecution under the impugned statute.

So courts routinely treat those who acted in defiance of laws later found to have been invalid as having done nothing illegal. Some even go so far as to order that the aggrieved party be compensated for the illegal thwarting on his constitutional rights. The Canadian Constitution explicitly authorizes this step by providing that:

> 24. (1) Anyone whose rights or freedoms, as guaranteed by this Charter, have been infringed or denied may apply to a court of competent jurisdiction to obtain such remedy as the court considers appropriate and just in the circumstances.

But would such compensation be warranted if, as the *ELP* directed powers account suggests, A did in fact act illegally when he acted contrary to valid law at t(1)? Could it be because his act, though illegal, was in defiance of a measure that violated his moral right(s)? Generally speaking, the law is not in the business of excusing illegal conduct whenever citizens object to its directives on moral grounds. And it is certainly not in the business of offering compensation for illegal acts—even when it recognizes the soundness of the citizen's moral claim. Why should these cases be any different? It counts in favor of *ILP* that no such uncomfortable questions arise if we accept that theory. On the contrary, it is quite easy to understand the case for compensation: S did nothing illegal at t(1). Not only did S suffer the effects of a constitutional rights infringement, his suffering was the product of enforcing an invalid, unconstitutional government measure generated through what amounts to an abuse or misuse of government power to create laws within limits set by the constitution. The case for compensation seems crystal clear.

3.3 Law and Practical Reason

What role does the existence of law play in our practical reasoning? Raz has an answer to this fundamental jurisprudential question. And he thinks it rules out any theory, *ILP* included, that permits the legal validity of a norm to depend in any way on moral validity. The role of law, according to Raz, is to facilitate our practical reasoning by "providing publicly ascertainable ways of guiding behaviour and regulating aspects of social life."[35] In other words, "Law is a public measure by which one can measure one's own as well as other people's behaviour. It helps to secure social co-operation not only through its sanctions providing motivation for conformity but also through designating in an accessible way the patterns of behaviour required for such co-operation."[36] This fact, Raz goes on to observe, "has been emphasized by many a natural lawyer for it forms part of the justification of the need for positive law. Locke is a prominent and well-known example. Hart more than anybody else emphasized the point among legal positivists."[37] So far so good. Raz's story is one with which virtually all legal philosophers, from Plato and Aquinas to Hart and Dworkin, can stand in ready agreement. It is certainly one that in no ways marks an important point of difference between defenders of *ILP* and advocates of *ELP*. It is with Raz's next step that we begin to see crucial differences emerge. Raz writes:

> [M]arking a rule as legally binding [valid] is marking it as an authoritative ruling. This marking-off of authoritative rulings indicates the existence ... of an institution or organization claiming authority over members of the society that is holding them bound to conform to certain standards just because they were singled out by that purported authority regardless of whether or not they are justifiable standards on other grounds. Since it is in the very essence of the alleged authority that it issues rulings which are binding [valid] regardless of any other justification, it follows that it must be possible to identify those rulings without engaging in a justificatory argument, i.e., as issuing from certain activities and interpreted in the light of publicly ascertainable standards not involving moral argument ... In making this a test for the identification of law, [*ELP*] identifies it as an example of a kind of human institution which is of decisive importance to the regulation of social life."[38]

In short, *ELP* "captures and highlights a fundamental insight into the function of law."[39]

In this passage Raz is of course relying on his service conception of authority and on the argument from authority that emerges from it. If law is to be the kind of thing it claims to be—an institution with justified practical authority over us—then it must be possible to identify its directives without appealing to moral argument of any kind. We have already seen how defenders of *ILP* replied to this argument. And it is by no means my intention to rehearse those arguments here. Instead, I want to pick up on why, in Raz's view, we create institutions that claim the right to affect our practical reasoning in this manner. Why do we create an institution that purports to issue authoritative directives that are binding on us in light of their origin, and independently of whether they are otherwise justified? We do so, according to Raz, in order to facilitate, indirectly via our conformity with these authoritative directives, our conformity with right reason. It is the very purpose of law to provide us with this service, and it

[35] *The Authority of Law*, 51.
[36] Ibid.
[37] Ibid.
[38] Ibid., 51–2.
[39] Ibid., 50.

is justified to the extent that it succeeds in doing so. In short, we create law and give it the right to meddle in our practical reasoning in order to comply better with the demands of right reason. So how does law meddle, according to Raz? It meddles, as we have seen, by providing second-order exclusionary reasons that pre-empt and replace whatever reasons on which we would be justified in acting absent the law and its directive. And it meddles justifiably only when its directives are such that, by acting on them instead of our own judgments of right and wrong, we are more likely to act as right reason demands. So the function of law, on this Razian picture, is to facilitate conformity with right reason. And the only way law can fulfill its function, according to Raz, is if the identity and validity of its directives are immune from the effects of any and all moral conditions. Of course, as an avowed positivist, Raz does not believe that law necessarily fulfills its function. Sometimes the law fails and we are better off relying on our own best judgments. But if, and to the extent that, this is not the case, i.e., that we are, in fact, more likely to do the right thing if we follow the law's directives, then the law will have served its fundamental purpose and hence be justified.

The questions I would now like to address is this. If (1) we view law as Raz proposes—as a social institution we design and create so as to facilitate action in accordance with right reason; and if (2) an institution can be imagined that (a) serves that function reasonably well; (b) shares with the Razian legal system all the usual features, for example, it is comprehensive in its reach, has norm applying institutions, etc.; and yet (c) recognizes certain, specific moral limits on its right to meddle in our practical reasoning; then (3) why would we want to view this institution as anything but law? And (4) why would we insist on an alternative understanding of this institution's apparent moral limits, one according to which these are not, in actual fact, limits we place on the right to meddle but rather moral grounds on which courts are directed to correct an unjustified meddling by exercising its power to repair it? And, finally, and perhaps most importantly, (5) why would we insist on this when there are plainly all kinds of other ways in which an institution could meddle in our practical reasoning, and potentially render it more likely that we will reach our goal of complying with right reason, without taking the rather drastic step of excluding all otherwise relevant reasons?

Given what we have seen thus far, it is pretty clear that we have absolutely no reason at all to insist on these things. We have no reason to rule out other, less dramatic ways in which law might help facilitate conformity with right reason. Instead of excluding all otherwise relevant reasons, the law might exclude all moral reasons save for those specified in something like a charter of rights. Or the law might exclude all moral reasons, except when those moral reasons are particularly weighty. For example, a rule of recognition might specify that legal directives that satisfy all other relevant tests of validity fail to be valid if they bring about grave injustice, the implication being that lesser degrees of injustice are insufficient. Many constitutions seem to contemplate just this possibility. They include proportionality tests that envision a test of validity that neither excludes all reference to competing moral reasons, nor requires a simple balancing of one reason against the next. The *Oakes Test*, constructed by the Canadian Supreme Court as a means of dealing with section 1's "reasonable limitations" clause, provides an instructive example. It mandates, among other things, that a measure that infringes a Charter right must nevertheless be considered valid if the government is able to demonstrate that the measure's objective is of sufficiently compelling importance to warrant overriding the right in question. Three observations are worth making here. First, often a government's objective will have a decidedly moral flavor, for example, protection of life, or of some economically or socially vulnerable segment of the population. Second, a burden of proof—in this instance, establishing the reasonability of the limit on the balance of probabilities—is placed on the government. And third, there is much more contemplated here than the mere balancing of one reason against another, a simple balancing of the government's objective against the interests of the party whose right has been infringed. In specifying that the government's objective must be of sufficient importance to warrant the overriding of a right, the Oakes Test seems to establish that only a reason of some significant weight will be enough to override a Charter right. Moral reasons not of the required weight are, in effect, excluded.

A further example of how the law might meddle without excluding moral reasons entirely can be found in the practice of precedent. Precedents established in higher courts are usually treated as binding on lower courts—a practice that accords well with the exclusionary view. But a precedent is often not held to be binding on the court that establishes it if there is a particularly strong and compelling reason to depart from it, the implication being that right reason's claim that another rule is better than the one established in the precedent is not enough. A further implication, of course, is that not all moral reasons are excluded by the "binding" precedent in all circumstances. *Stare decisis* recognizes more than one possibility.

In both of these cases, constitutional law and the law of precedent, our practical reasoning is significantly affected by the presence of law. But the effect is not always the outright exclusion of all otherwise relevant reasons. Rather, the effect is to incline the balance of reasons toward certain moral interests as compared with others, or to create burdens of proof that would otherwise neither exist nor be appropriate. And, importantly for our purposes, it is most certainly not the elimination of anything that might reasonably be thought of as law.

So what does all this have to do with the question of whether *ILP* provides a superior theory of law as compared with *ELP*? The answer is, by now I hope, rather obvious. In my view, *ILP* is the superior theory of law because it does not rule out these and other ways in which law might facilitate conformity with right reason. It does not unduly restrict the myriad of ways in which a social institution like law might (in many instances, justifiably) meddle in our practical reasoning to good effect. Raz may well be correct that it is (often) in our moral interests to create laws or legal institutions that bar us completely from acting directly on the balance of first-order reasons. Sometimes right reason suggests we pursue less direct routes and avail ourselves of the services of a legal system with both the capacity and the right to meddle in our practical reasoning. But he seems wrong in demanding that the only means of meddling at law's disposal is the employment of exclusionary directives that pre-empt and replace all otherwise relevant reasons in all cases. There are plainly other options. And modern constitutional democracies have seen the value in pursuing some of them. For instance, recognizing that, in certain common scenarios, governments are prone to issue directives that fail to provide us with the service we seek—for example, they are prone to issue directives conformity with which might actually lead to the violation of certain crucial moral rights of minority groups—many democratic communities have created institutions incorporating limits on the government's right to meddle in their practical reasoning. And many of these limits translate into moral limits on the legal validity of the government's directives, directives that are *supposed* to lead us toward compliance with right reason but will predictably fail to do so in some scenarios. To be sure, *ILP* does not mandate the inclusion of any such moral conditions on legal validity. But it does not err in the opposite direction either, mandating their exclusion, which of course is precisely what Raz and his fellow *ELP* advocates have done. Whether to include or exclude moral criteria, whether to rig the balance of reasons in favor of one party over another, whether to place a heavy burden of proof on one party as opposed to another, these are all, according to *ILP*, matters not of what law *must* be but what it *ought to be* if law is to serve useful purposes. These are all questions of political morality that extend well beyond what *ILP* maintains. And *ELP* mistakenly crosses this line.

That it recognizes the wealth of options available to societies that wish to create and be regulated by legal institutions, other than the exclusion of any and all moral reasons, is a powerful reason for viewing *ILP* as the superior theory of law. It's also a strong reason for rejecting Postema's indictment of *ILP* as providing little insight into the nature of law and the crucial role(s) it can play in our lives. *ILP* highlights a number of key features of law: (a) that law has the inherent capacity to facilitate our practical reasoning; (b) that there are a multitude of different ways in which it can do so; (c) that some of these find room for moral validity to play a role in establishing legal validity; and (d) that some of these latter options do so without excluding moral reasons entirely or (e) without fully collapsing legal validity into moral validity and robbing law entirely of its capacity to facilitate conformity with right reason. If we bear in mind the point that one of law's central features is its capacity to facilitate action in accordance with the demands of right reason, *ILP* also allows us to see clearly that we often have very good moral reason for insisting on tests of validity that limit law's authority over us. In other words, we often have reason to actualize some of the possibilities *ILP* permits us to pursue and to avoid others. Among the most important possibilities are ones that subject legal validity to some kinds of moral condition, for example, the rigging of balances, assignments of burdens of proof, and so on. None of these is necessitated by the nature of law, of course, but then none is ruled out either. In much the same way that the conventional nature of law places no limits on the kinds of criteria of validity a system might accept into its rule recognition—moral criteria are therefore possible—the nature of law as a potentially beneficial meddler in our practical reasoning places no limits on how moral criteria might operate should a society choose to incorporate them.

4. Conclusion

So what, in the end, has all this established? What it establishes, quite clearly, is that *ILP* is not only faithful to the positivist tradition inherited by Hart and his followers; it is also superior to *ELP* in a number of ways, including: (a) the fact that it highlights and fully respects law's conventional nature; (b) that it provides the basis for a better account of certain common legal practices and how these are conceived by their participants; and (c) that it highlights and respects the variety of ways in which law can realize its potential to facilitate action in accordance with right reason. Furthermore, it demonstrates that those who set out to develop and defend *ILP* did not, contra Postema, "depart from the task of deepening our understanding of the nature of law wherever we find it." Nor did they lose "contact with the original phenomena, problems, and the theoretical and practical motivations that gave them life." So no, Professor Kramer's efforts to develop a plausible version of *ILP* and defend it against its many adversaries were not a complete waste of time. In elaborating and defending a subtle, powerful, and insightful version of *ILP*, Professor Kramer achieved something of great theoretical significance—certainly something of much more significance than counting dancing angels.[40]

[40] I wish to thank Matt Grellette for his comments on an earlier version of this paper and to the editors of this volume, Mark McBride and Visa Kurki, for their insightful suggestions for improvement. I am also indebted to the many outstanding philosophers who participated in a conference, held in July 2019 at Churchill College, Cambridge, dedicated to the work and career—thus far! —of Professor Kramer. I wish also to thank Mark and Visa for their invitation to contribute both to the conference and to this volume of essays. And finally, I wish to thank Matt Kramer for his support and friendship over the years—and for his many, many outstanding contributions to scholarship.

8

Kramer's Theory of Legal Positivism

Merits and Demerits

Pierluigi Chiassoni[*]

1. Introduction

In several essays, from *In Defence of Legal Positivism. Law without Trimmings*,[1] to *Where Law and Morality Meet*,[2] to the recent *H.L.A. Hart. The Nature of Law*,[3] Matthew Kramer poses as a staunch and philosophically sophisticated partisan of legal positivism.

As a tribute to Kramer's pro positivism efforts, I purport to provide a (hopefully fair) account and a critical examination of Kramer's theory. The gist of my critique can be recounted as follows.

1. Like every common law theory of positivism of Hartian descent, Kramer's theory understands "the separation thesis" as a signpost for a set of multiple and heterogeneous claims, encompassing both meta-theoretical and theoretical separation theses.[4]
2. Among the meta-theoretical separation theses, the epistemological separation thesis concerns the philosophically and scientifically proper way of making inquiries on the law as a complex social and political normative phenomenon.[5] It urges avoiding any confusion between "the law as it is," on the one side, and "the law as it ought to be" from some moral standpoint, on the other. It outlaws the smuggling of value-laden, ethically committed ingredients into descriptive accounts of law. It prescribes endorsing a rigorous divide between expository (descriptive) and censorial (justificatory, normative) jurisprudence.
3. Among the theoretical separation theses, the limits of the law thesis purports to provide viable criteria enabling us to discern, for any positive legal system whatsoever, existing law ("the law as it is") from the law yet to be made ("the law that ought to be"). Herbert Hart, for instance, defends a variety of limits of the law thesis according to which, at any moment in the life of a legal system, existing law is tantamount to the set of valid explicit and definite legal rules.[6]

[*] University of Genoa—Tarello Institute for Legal Philosophy (pierluigi.chiassoni@unige.it.).

[1] Kramer, *In Defense of Legal Positivism. Law without Trimmings.*

[2] Kramer, *Where Law and Morality Meet.*

[3] Kramer, *H. L. A. Hart. The Nature of Law.*

[4] See, e.g., Hart, *Positivism and the Separation of Law and Morals*, 57 n. 25; Hart, *The Concept of Law*, 302; Hart, *Legal Positivism*, 237–9; Hart, *El nuevo desafío al positivismo jurídico*, section I; Hart, *Answers to Eight Questions*, 281–7; Hart, *Postscript*, 272–6.

[5] Hart, *Postscript*, 239.

[6] Hart, *Answers to Eight Questions*, 281–7.

Pierluigi Chiassoni, *Kramer's Theory of Legal Positivism* In: *Without Trimmings.* Edited by: Mark McBride and Visa AJ Kurki, Oxford University Press. © Mark McBride and Visa AJ Kurki 2022. DOI: 10.1093/oso/9780198868866.003.0008

4. Unfortunately, the limits of the law thesis is at odds with the epistemological separation thesis. It represents a trespass censorial jurisprudence makes into the province of expository jurisprudence; indeed, the limits of the law are not something for a general and descriptive legal theory to establish once and for all, being contrariwise an issue that fatally belongs to the realm of legal scholarship, doctrines, ideologies and values. Accordingly, any positivist theory that encompasses at once the two theses is flawed by an internal inconsistency.
5. Insofar as Kramer's theory of legal positivism holds, as it does hold, as we shall see in a moment, both the epistemological separation thesis and a variety (different from Hart's own) of the limits of the law thesis, it is likewise flawed. Consistency would require letting down either the one or the other.

One terminological precision is needed before proceeding. Throughout the chapter I will use the phrase "theory of legal positivism" —and cognate expressions like "conception of legal positivism," "view about legal positivism," "account of legal positivism," etc. —to refer to any jurisprudential discourse, usually handed-down in paper or book form, which purports to identify, clarify, and argue for or against the set of theses that would constitute (the core of) a positivistic account of positive law in general. A theory of legal positivism can be, therefore, of a positivist, but also of a non-positivist, anti-positivist, or post-positivist cast. When it is of a positivist cast, we face a self-reflective positivist theory of positive law: one that shows a built-in preoccupation for developing a theory of positive law in tune with what the theorist regards as the veritable tenets of legal positivism.

2. Kramer's Theory of Positivism: An Overview

Kramer conceives a positivist account of law to be philosophically valuable if, and only if, it successfully manages to carry out at once a critical ("negative") and a constructive ("affirmative") task. The critical task should see to the charitable recognition and punctual refutation of the most relevant (and perilous) critiques to legal positivism. The constructive task should consist, contrariwise, in strengthening developing and extending the reach of legal positivism as a comprehensive philosophy of positive law of analytic allegiance.[7]

The output of such combined effort is a positivist theory of law that presents three major components.

The first component encompasses a sophisticated analysis of the separation ("separability") thesis together with a defense of the outcoming theory against friends (fellow positivists assuming a discrediting, trivializing, or even skeptical stance) and foes (natural lawyers and anti-positivists in general) alike.[8]

The second component argues for an inclusive and moderate incorporationist variety of legal positivism, as the sole theoretically sound view about the law in general,

[7] Kramer, *In Defense of Legal Positivism. Law Without Trimmings*, 14, 16.

[8] Kramer, *In Defense of Legal Positivism. Law Without Trimmings*; Kramer, *Where Law and Morality Meet*, part II; Kramer, *H. L. A. Hart. The Nature of Law*, ch. 5.

against extreme ("comprehensive," "thorough") incorporationism, on the one side, and exclusive legal positivism, on the other side.[9]

The third component, finally, is devoted to providing theoretically (more) refined re-definitions ("conceptual re-elaborations," "conceptual re-explications") of such "fundamental jural concepts" as legal normativity, legal authority, legal obligation, legal allegiance, and formal justice.[10]

The present account and critical assessment will focus on the first two components only.

3. The Separability Thesis Disentangled

Kramer's theory of legal positivism gives pride of place to the law and morality puzzle, i.e., to the preoccupation for working out a theoretically sound account of the relations between law and morals.[11] In his view, legal positivism is the jurisprudential outlook the "cardinal thesis" of which is to be seen in the claim that "law and morality are not necessarily conjoined," that "legality and morality are of course combinable" though "they are likewise disjoinable," that "propositions about law are [not] necessarily linked to propositions about morality," that there is, in sum, *no* "intrinsically moral import of law."[12] For the sake of avoiding any misunderstanding, this pivotal thesis he prefers to refer to, not by the potentially misleading label "separation thesis," but, rather, by the phrase "separability thesis" ("law and morality are strictly separable").[13]

Kramer's analysis of the separability thesis is characterized by two noteworthy features. To begin with, it underscores that a variety ("multiplicity") of different though related theses fare under the singular "separability thesis" label.[14] Furthermore, following in Hart's archetypical slogan-like formulation ("there is no necessary connection between law and morals or law as it is and law as it ought to be"[15]), it conceives the separability theses as a set of *negative* claims about law. The separability theses cast light on what the law is, by telling us what the law is *not*. Therefore, if we want to get a full grasp of them, we must consider what, in Kramer's perspective, the several separability theses severally *deny*.

As to the key notion of his argument, *morality*, Kramer opts for an antonymic definitory strategy that considers in turn four sets of opposites. First, *morality* is defined as the realm of morally "permissible," "legitimate," "right," "commendable," "salutary," "virtuous" human attitudes and behaviors, and also of morally "correct"

[9] Kramer, *Where Law and Morality Meet*, part I, and part II, ch. 7.

[10] Kramer, *In Defense of Legal Positivism. Law Without Trimmings*, part II.

[11] See Kramer, *In Defense of Legal Positivism. Law Without Trimmings*; Kramer, *Where Law and Morality Meet*.

[12] Kramer, *In Defense of Legal Positivism. Law Without Trimmings*, 1, 13; Kramer, *Where Law and Morality Meet*, ch. 7.

[13] Kramer, *In Defense of Legal Positivism. Law Without Trimmings*, 1; Kramer, *Where Law and Morality Meet*, 223; Kramer, *H. L. A. Hart. The Nature of Law*, 148–9.

[14] Kramer, *In Defense of Legal Positivism. Law Without Trimmings*, ch. 1; Kramer, *Where Law and Morality Meet*, ch. 7; Kramer, *H. L. A. Hart. The Nature of Law*, 149–64.

[15] See Hart, *Positivism and the Separation of Law and Morals*, 57 n. 25; Hart, *The Concept of Law*, 185–6 ("it is in no sense a necessary truth that laws reproduce or satisfy certain demands of morality, though in fact they have often done so"), 302; Hart, *Legal Positivism*, 237–9; Hart, *El nuevo desafío al positivismo jurídico*, section I.

standards (norms, rules, principles) of conduct and social institutions, as opposed to the realm of *immorality* or *wickedness* where, contrariwise, morally wicked attitudes, behaviors, norms, and social institutions dwell. Second, *morality* is defined as the realm of behaviors, norms, and reasons for action informed by an "essential," "exclusive," or "primary" concern for other people's interests or well-being, as opposed to the realm of *prudence* where, contrariwise, norms and behaviors are exclusively or primarily self-interested.[16] Third, *morality* is defined as the realm of moral matters, moral facts, moral discourse, and moral reasoning, as opposed to the realm of *factuality*, which is the realm of empirical matters, empirical facts, descriptive discourse, and purely empirical, logical, or mathematical reasoning. Fourth, and finally, *morality* is defined as the realm of the entities apt for moral assessment, evaluation, and criticism (basically, human attitudes, behaviors, norms, and institutions), as opposed to the realm of *non-moral* entities, i.e., of the entities that are not apt for moral assessment, evaluation, and criticism.[17]

Kramer regards the first three oppositions—between the moral and the immoral, the moral and the prudential, the moral and the factual—to be paramount for a truly clarifying analysis of the separability theses, together with a critical survey of the pretended connections between law and morality that would obtain from the standpoint of the procedural dimension of positive legal systems, the status of individual legal decisions, the overall function(s) of a legal system, and the beliefs and attitudes of legal officials.[18]

Anti-positivists claim that there *are* necessary ("intrinsic") connections between law and morality. In what I purport to propose as a fair reconstruction of his thought, Kramer's analysis of anti-positivist jurisprudence looks like picking out (not fewer than) six (pretended) necessary connections: six juncture points where law and morality would necessarily meet.[19] These juncture points represent the targets of as many positivist separability theses. In accounting for the anti-positivist and positivist theses identified in Kramer's analysis, I will use a terminology partly of my own coining, so as to present each of them in a (hopefully) clearer form and bring to the fore their theoretical virtues.

The first anti-positivist connection thesis points to a *necessary metaphysical* or *ontological*, and therefore *theoretical* and *conceptual*, *connection* between positive law and morality (as the opposite of immorality).[20] It claims that, due to the very nature or

[16] Kramer, *In Defense of Legal Positivism. Law Without Trimmings*, 3, 7–10, 25–6, 64–5; Kramer, *Where Law and Morality Meet*; Kramer, *H. L. A. Hart. The Nature of Law*, 159–62.

[17] Kramer, *In Defense of Legal Positivism. Law Without Trimmings*, 2–5; Kramer, *Where Law and Morality Meet*, 232–6; Kramer, *H. L. A. Hart. The Nature of Law*, 154–64.

[18] Kramer, *In Defense of Legal Positivism. Law Without Trimmings*, 7–10, and the several chapters devoted to defusing one or more of the pretended necessary connection between law and morality, through formal justice (ch. 2), the formal features of (the rule of) law (ch. 3, and Kramer, *Where Law and Morality Meet*, ch. 6), legal duty and obligation (ch. 4), officials' attitudes (ch. 5), legal principles and hard cases (ch. 6), and the ordering function of legal systems (ch. 9). As to irrelevance of the moral/non-moral opposition to a fruitful analysis of the separability theses Kramer is pithy: "no legal positivist has ever contended that law is non-moral" (Kramer, *H. L. A. Hart. The Nature of Law*, 156).

[19] Kramer, *In Defense of Legal Positivism. Law Without Trimmings*, 2–10; Kramer, *H. L. A. Hart. The Nature of Law*, 156–63.

[20] In anti-positivists' view, the conceptual connection, to be established from a genuine theoretical standpoint, is supposed to mirror, and record, a necessary metaphysical or ontological connection between the phenomena at stake.

essence of legal norms and legal systems, necessarily no social norm, no social normative system, no ongoing political regime that is morally wicked can count, from the standpoint of sound theory and concept, as *law*, or *law proper*, or *law* in something more than a *debased*, *weak*, or *formal way*. The first positivist separability thesis, the *metaphysical* or *ontological*, and therefore *theoretical* and *conceptual*, *separability* thesis, holds, by contrast, that wicked social norms and normative systems *can* count as law (morally wicked laws are still laws); that no reference to moral properties is needed in sound legal theory and law concept.[21]

The second anti-positivist connection thesis points to a *necessary epistemic connection* between positive law and morality (as the opposite of factuality). It holds that, necessarily, law ascertainment (also) depends on moral argument ("moral judgment"); that it is not the case that finding out for sure what is the law on any issue at hand can depend on factual enquiries *only*. By contrast, the second positivist separability thesis, the *epistemic separability thesis*, maintains that law ascertainment *can*, but *does not need* to, depend on moral argument; that such an eventuality occurs if, and only if, a legal system obligates or empowers "its officials to apply certain moral tests when identifying the law."[22]

The third anti-positivist connection thesis points to a *necessary psychological connection* between positive law and morality (as the opposite of prudence). It maintains that, necessarily, officials' coping with the social norms we are used to consider as legal norms is not merely a matter of prudence (self-interest ridden attitudes and behaviors), but also a matter of moral allegiance to the system and moral concern for other peoples' interests and well-being. In particular, anti-positivists argue, the "attitudes and commitments" of officials toward the norms of their legal system, other officials, ordinary citizens, specific decisions, and the general functioning of their regime necessarily (by way of an empirical, psychological necessity) involve *moral* attitudes and commitments. By contrast, the third positivist separability thesis, the *psychological separability thesis*, holds that officials *can*, but *need not* to, entertain moral attitudes and commitments toward the legal norms they produce and apply, their fellow officials, ordinary citizens, specific decisions, and the functioning of their regime; that they *can* carry out their job also out of sheer prudential, self-concerning attitudes and considerations.[23]

[21] Kramer, *In Defense of Legal Positivism. Law Without Trimmings*, 2, 3–5. Kramer emphasizes the "methodological" option behind the metaphysical-theoretical-conceptual separability thesis, basically appealing to Hart's *epistemological principle of no confusion* ("no blurring") between the law as it is and the law as it ought to be (Hart, *Positivism and the Separation of Law and Morals*, 55: "the utilitarian separation of law and morals ... something that enables lawyers to attain a new clarity"; Hart, *The Concept of Law*, 209–10) and Hart's *theoretical thesis of conceptual separation* of "law" and "morals" (no reference to morality is needed in, must enter into, a *theoretically adequate* elucidation of the concept of law or legal system: Hart, *The Concept of Law*, 209–10; Hart *Law, Liberty and Morality*, 2–4; Hart, *Answers to Eight Questions*, 284). He writes: "While this book calls for the term 'law' to be used broadly in jurisprudential discussions, it does so not as a sheer stipulation but in furtherance of analytical clarification and explanatory power; such a pattern of usage tends to serve the theoretical objective of ferreting out the full implications of various regimes' adherence to the rule of law" (Kramer, *In Defense of Legal Positivism. Law Without Trimmings*, 5; see also ch. 6). See also Kramer, *H. L. A. Hart. The Nature of Law*, 156–9.

[22] Kramer, *In Defense of Legal Positivism. Law Without Trimmings*, 3.

[23] Kramer, *In Defense of Legal Positivism. Law Without Trimmings*, 3, 6–10.

The fourth anti-positivist connection thesis points to a *necessary operational connection* between law and morality (here again, as the opposite of immorality). It claims that law is necessarily (intrinsically) connected to morality, because where there is law, there are necessarily *processes* and *operations* that are morally-laden, being (objectively) committed to formal legality values like treating like people alike, fair notice, formal justice, and integrity, which bolster "the autonomy of the ruled, who are shielded against the arbitrariness and personal grudges of officials."[24] By contrast, the fourth positivist separability thesis, the *operational separability thesis*, holds that legal systems' commitment to formal legality is not necessarily tantamount to a commitment to promoting and realizing moral values to the benefit of their citizenry (or sectors thereof): neither from the standpoint of their actual objective effects (*a parte obiecti*), nor from the subjective psychological standpoint of officials' attitudes (*a parte subiecti*).[25]

The fifth anti-positivist connection thesis points to a *necessary holistic connection* between concrete legal decisions and morality (as the opposite of prudential guidelines). It holds that isolated legal decisions, though they can in themselves be immoral ("wicked"), are nonetheless necessarily connected to—they necessarily imply and presuppose—a normative background made of moral norms from which they draw their value and credibility.[26] The fifth positivist separability thesis, the *holistic separability thesis*, holds by contrast that individual legal decisions can, but need not, be part of an overall morality-driven legal system, provided a legal system can happen to be morally wicked through and through.[27]

Finally, the sixth anti-positivist connection thesis points to a *necessary functional connection* between law and morality (here again, as the opposite of immorality). It holds that the very existence of legal systems shows their necessary connection to morality, since their overall functioning promotes morally valuable outcomes like order, peace, tranquility, security, etc., and is remedy against the evident moral evil of anarchy. Contrariwise, the sixth positivist separability thesis, the *functional separability thesis*, claims that the functioning of legal systems *can*, but need not, promote morally valuable outcomes: orderliness, tranquility, and security *per se* are not necessarily morally worth states of affairs.[28]

If we compare Kramer's account of the separability theses with Hart's view of the separation thesis, we are apparently led to pronounce a nuanced verdict.

1. Hart had already entertained a sophisticated view about "the separation thesis," pointing, at a fair reconstruction, to a set of four basic separation theses, plus a few theses of detail. From a bird's-eye view, the four Hartian basic separation theses encompass:

[24] Kramer, *In Defense of Legal Positivism. Law Without Trimmings*, 6.

[25] Kramer, *In Defense of Legal Positivism. Law Without Trimmings*, 5–6, 11, chs. 2 and 3; Kramer, *Where Law and Morality* Meet, ch. 6, 173; Kramer, *H. L. A. Hart. The Nature of Law*, 159.

[26] Kramer, *In Defense of Legal Positivism. Law Without Trimmings*, 6.

[27] Kramer, *In Defense of Legal Positivism. Law Without Trimmings*, 3.

[28] Kramer, *In Defense of Legal Positivism. Law Without Trimmings*, 7 and chs. 7 and 9, 307; Kramer, *H. L. A. Hart. The Nature of Law*, 158.

(a) the *epistemological principle of no confusion* between the law as it is and the law as it ought to be (there are good theoretical reasons, i.e., in view of furthering the exact and objective knowledge of law, for keeping the two entities separate);
(b) the *prudential principle of no confusion* between the law as it is and the law as it ought to be (there are good practical reasons, i.e., from the standpoint of moral assessment of legal systems, for keeping the two entities separate);
(c) the *theoretical thesis of conceptual separation* of "law" and "morals" (there are good theoretical reasons for adopting a morally-neutral elucidation of the concept of law);
(d) the *limits of the law thesis* (at any moment in the working of a legal system, existing law coincides with definite explicit law).[29]

Among the Hartian separation theses of detail fare those claiming that no reference to morality is needed in view of a theoretically adequate elucidation of basic legal concepts like "legal right," "legal duty," "legal validity," and "legal authority."[30]

Taking stock of the Hartian heritage, at the same time as the inspiring methodological model and the theoretical frontier to be pushed forward toward deeper and finer understanding, Kramer complements the Hartian insights with a meticulous and more exact coping with adverse claims and arguments, some of which Hart did not consider. We should think, in particular, of Kramer's epistemic, psychological, holistic, and functional separability theses.

There is, besides, one issue where Kramer's analysis purports to correct Hart's, though along the same path and taking the lead from an essay of David Lyons.[31] In *The Concept of Law*, Hart conceded that about legality and formal justice anti-positivists may be right: that resort to general norms by legal systems goes along with legality principles that seem to possess the mark of moral valuableness. Hart conceded *that*. But, at the same time, he emphasized how such a "necessary connection" between law and morals, if one likes to see it in that way, can go along with morally outrageous regimes.[32] Kramer takes a different path. He dedicates chapters to redress Hart's original concession to anti-positivists, arguing that it is theoretically unwarranted. That legality and the connected formal rule of law features of existing legal systems are, *per se*, morally indifferent: that, in complex, large, developed municipal legal systems, they prove to be necessary (i.e., complacent serviceable tools) to *any* purpose whatsoever the rulers may wish to pursue, morally good or morally wicked alike. In so arguing, he scores a major demystification achievement as regards to

[29] Coleman (*Legal Positivism: Anglo-American Legal Positivism since H. L. A. Hart*, 240) sums up Hart's position in the following terms: "The scope of judicial duty is fixed by meaning or practice. Where either meaning or practice runs out, judicial discretion . . . enters."

[30] See Hart, *Positivism and the Separation of Law and Morals*, 56–62; Hart, *The Concept of Law*, 167–80, 202–3, 207–12; Hart, *Legal and Moral Obligation*, 82–107; Hart, *Legal Duty and Obligation*, 147–61; Hart, *Answers to Eight Questions*, 281–4; Hart, *Commands and Authoritative Legal Reasons*, 262–8.

[31] Lyons, "On Formal Justice"; Kramer *In Defense of Legal Positivism. Law Without Trimmings*, ch. 2; Kramer, *H. L. A. Hart. The Nature of Law*, 159.

[32] Hart, *The Concept of Law*, 207; but see Hart, *Introduction*, 18, quoted by Kramer, *H. L. A. Hart. The Nature of Law*, 159.

legal philosophers too prone to take the supposedly intrinsic moral virtue of a purely formal rule of law for granted.[33]

2. There are two issues on which Kramer's separability theses are apparently silent, wherein Hart's separation theses speak in a clear voice. First, they do not account for the meta-theoretical epistemological or prudential import of "the separation of law and morals," while Hart's analysis addresses it by means of the epistemological and prudential principles of no confusion between theoretical description and practical evaluation of positive legal systems (theses (a) and (b) above). Second, they do not cope with the issue of the limits of law, while Hart's analysis sees to it by arguing for the theoretical coincidence between existing law and definite explicit law. Apparently, Kramer copes with the limits of law issue while taking part in the inclusive/exclusive positivism contest. It is time to have a look at it.

4. The Case for an Inclusive and Moderately Incorporationist Variety of Legal Positivism

As a contribution to an improved understanding of the tangled debate between inclusive and exclusive positivism, but also in view of favoring a sound theoretical taking side, Kramer adopts the analytical strategy of picking out, and wording in the clearest possible way, the elementary components of the several views at stake.[34] He assumes accordingly that the gist of the dispute between inclusivists and exclusivists can be captured by a careful characterization of three positions: "inclusivism," "incorporationism," and "exclusivism."[35]

In the following I will try to articulate a (hopefully) fair account of Kramer's analysis. I will also set forth a few exegetical queries and comment upon a few points I find troublesome.

4.1 Inclusivism

Kramer characterizes *inclusivism* as upholding one thesis concerning the legality ("lawness") of single norms in relation to an existing positive legal system ("jurisdiction").

[33] It may be worthwhile noting that the same skeptical attitude about the intrinsic moral worth of "legality" is assumed, as we know, from the standpoint of a subjectivist and non-cognitivist theory of justice and morality, by Hans Kelsen (see *General Theory of Law and State*, 13–14, 14, 47–9).

[34] On inclusive and exclusive positivism, see, e.g., Coleman, *Negative and Positive Positivism*, 28–48; Coleman, *Incorporationism, Conventionality, and the Practical Difference Thesis*, 99–147; Moreso, *In Defense of Inclusive Legal Positivism*, 37–62; Bayón, *El contenido mínimo del positivismo jurídico*; Himma, *Inclusive Legal Positivism*; Bulygin, *Il positivismo giuridico*; Coleman, *Legal Positivism: Anglo-American Legal Positivism since H. L. A. Hart*; Shapiro, *The "Hart-Dworkin" Debate: A Short Guide for the Perplexed*; Raz, *The Institutional Nature of Law*, 103–21; Raz, *Legal Positivism and the Sources of Law*, 37–52; Raz, *A Postscript to Legal Principles and the Limits of the Law*, 81–6; Raz, *Authority, Law and Morality*, 210–37; Raz, *The Problem of Authority: Revisiting the Service Conception*, 126ff.

[35] Kramer, *Where Law and Morality Meet*, 2–9, chs. 1–4; Kramer, *H. L. A. Hart. The Nature of Law*, 114–17, 157–8, 173–80.

In different books and different passages of the same book, he provides several different formulations, which are apparently meant to be formulations of that one and the same inclusivist legality thesis.[36]

However, if for clarity's sake we pause to consider the several formulations by Kramer at their face value, paying attention to their linguistic meaning, they turn out as being potentially expressive of different inclusivist legality theses; they come to suggest that inclusivism, as a thesis concerning the legality of single norms whatsoever, is really not one, but many. How many? Arguably, not fewer than five different varieties come to the mind. I shall call them *neutral inclusivism*, *pluralistic inclusivism*, *monistic inclusivism*, *relativistic inclusivism*, and *objectivist inclusivism*.

Neutral inclusivism. The first variety of inclusivism characterizes as a neutral uncompromised stance about the controversial issues concerning the ontological status and plurality of moral principles and moral systems.

The legality thesis of neutral inclusivism holds that the *consistency* or *compatibility* of a norm (e.g., N_i) with *some moral principle can*, but *need not*, *be* a *necessary condition* for the status of norm N_i as a *legal* norm.[37]

The point neutral inclusivism purports to emphasize is that the binding legality (validity) criteria ("the rule of recognition") of any positive legal system whatsoever can contingently make the legality of a norm to be conditioned by its morality. Notice, by contrast, that neutral inclusivism abstains from taking sides about whether the relevant moral principles (should) belong to positive or critical morality, whether they (should) belong to a homogeneous system, or, rather, are (can be) drawn from different moral outlooks, whether the relevant moral principles are objective entities (as ethical objectivists claim), or, rather, subjective entities (as ethical subjectivists claim), whether they are reducible to one basic encompassing principle (as ethical monists claim), or, rather, they make up an irreducibly plural set (as ethical pluralism claim), whether they are apt for genuine knowledge (as ethical cognitivists claim), or, rather, depend on ethical stipulations and practical argument (as ethical non-cognitivists claim). By generically conditioning the legality of a norm to its conformity to "some moral principle," neutral inclusivism leaves all those issues open: stands for an inclusivist thesis theoretically capable of embracing whatever of the several alternatives just mentioned may happen to be contingently selected by positive legal systems.

Monistic and pluralistic inclusivism. The second and third varieties of inclusivism emerge as the output of an analysis of an inclusivist legality thesis reading as follows: the *consistency* or *compatibility* of a norm (e.g., N_i) with *some* or *all of the requirements of morality can*, but *need not*, *be* a *necessary condition* for the status of norm N_i as a *legal* norm.[38]

The thesis raises an interpretive problem. How should we understand the key phrase "some or all of the requirements of morality"? Three alternative readings report for consideration.

[36] See, e.g., Kramer, *Where Law and Morality Meet*, 2, 17; Kramer, *H. L. A. Hart. The Nature of Law*, 114, 157, 173.

[37] Kramer, *Where Law and Morality Meet*, 17, Kramer, *H. L. A. Hart. The Nature of Law*, 114, 173.

[38] Kramer, *Where Law and Morality Meet*, 2, Kramer, *H. L. A. Hart. The Nature of Law*, 173.

The first reading takes the phrase to refer to the *whole bunch* of the requirements of all of the several moral systems afoot, to the whole bunch of the *moral requirements* as opposed to the whole bunch of *immoral ones*, be they of positive or critical morality alike. Accordingly, the thesis comes to hold that the *consistency* or *compatibility* of a norm (e.g., N_i) with *some* or *all of the requirements of each of the several critical or positive moralities afoot can*, but *need not*, *be* a *necessary condition* for the status of norm N_i as a *legal* norm. On this reading, it must be noted, the thesis points to a legality criterion that, if adopted by a legal system, appears to be doomed to unviability, if not to utter preposterousness.[39]

The second reading takes the phrase "some or all of the requirements of morality" to refer to *one* definite moral system: i.e., to *the unique and exclusive* (*system of*) *morality* to which the binding legality criteria of a legal system happen to have recourse to. This reading makes the legality thesis at stake point to a *prima facie* viable legality criterion. It does so, however, by turning it into the thesis of a *morally monistic variety* of *inclusivism*, according to which: the *consistency* or *compatibility* of a norm (e.g., N_i) with *some* or *all of the requirements of the relevant unique and exclusive morality* M_j *can*, but *need not*, *be* a *necessary condition* for the status of norm N_i as a *legal* norm (where "M_j" stands for any definite system of positive or critical morality a legal system may happen to refer to).

The third reading takes the phrase "some or all of the requirements of morality" in a liberal way, so to speak, as pointing to the possibility that a legal system may contingently condition the legality of norms *either* in the way captured by the first reading, *or* in the way captured by the second one. Accordingly, the legality thesis would read as follows: the *consistency* or *compatibility* of a norm (e.g., N_i) with *some* or *all of the requirements of each of the several critical or positive moralities afoot, or* with *some* or *all of the requirements of the relevant unique and exclusive morality* M_j, *can*, but *need not*, *be* a *necessary condition* for the status of norm N_i as a *legal* norm. This third reading is nothing more than a specification of the neutral inclusivism legality thesis.

Relativistic and objectivist inclusivism. The last two varieties of inclusivism—relativistic and objectivist inclusivism—come to the fore as soon as we pause to reflect on a further formulation of the inclusivist legality thesis Kramer provides. The formulation runs as follows: the *consistency* or *compatibility* of a norm (e.g., N_i) with *correct principles of morality can*, but *need not*, *be* a *necessary condition* for the status of norm N_i as a *legal* norm.[40]

Again, we face an interpretive problem. How should we understand the key phrase "correct principles of morality"? Three alternative readings show up for scrutiny.

The first reading takes the phrase "correct principles of morality" to refer to the set of moral principles that, in the relevant legal system, *are considered correct* (true, worthwhile, right, appropriate, reasonable, etc.) *as the own and proper moral principles of a given society* by (most of the) jurists, legislators, judges, lawyers, and people at large. In so doing, the reading turns the inclusive legality thesis into a *morally relativistic legality thesis*, presupposing a *relativistic conception* of morality (moral right

[39] A legal system corresponding to this sweeping variety of inclusivist legality thesis would make the identification of its legal norms by officials (and people at large) extremely time-consuming, uncertain, and open to continuous challenge.

[40] Kramer, *H. L. A. Hart. The Nature of Law*, 157.

and moral wrong are relative to spatio-temporally determined social and cultural contexts), according to which: the *consistency* or *compatibility* of a norm (e.g., N_i) with the *relatively correct principles of morality* M_s (i.e., with the principles of morality that a given society at any time considers correct) *can*, but *need not, be* a *necessary condition* for the status of norm N_i as a *legal* norm.

The second reading, contrariwise, takes the phrase "correct principles of morality" to refer to the set of moral principles that *are objectively correct* (true, worthwhile, right, etc.), whatever any society—i.e., (most of) the jurists, legislators, judges, lawyers, and people at large—may happen to think. In so doing, the reading turns the inclusive legality thesis into a *morally objectivist legality thesis*, presupposing an *objectivist conception* of morality, according to which: the *consistency* or *compatibility* of a norm (e.g., N_i) with the *objectively correct principles of morality* M_o (i.e., with the true principles of morality that have always existed and will always exist as strongly human mind-independent entities) *can*, but *need not, be* a *necessary condition* for the status of norm N_i as a *legal* norm.

The third reading, finally, takes the phrase "correct principles of morality" in a liberal way, as pointing to the possibility that a legal system may contingently condition the legality of norms *either* in the way captured by the first reading, *or* in the way captured by the second one. Accordingly, the legality thesis would come to read as follows: the *consistency* or *compatibility* of a norm (e.g., N_i) either with the *relatively correct principles of morality* M_s or with the *objectively correct principles of morality* M_o *can*, but *need not, be* a *necessary condition* for the status of norm N_i as a *legal* norm. This third reading, as in the case of the pluralistic/monistic alternative, is nothing more than a specification of the legality thesis of neutral inclusivism.

The above analysis has been a willful exercise in un-charitableness. My point, however, was to highlight the fact that very delicate items like the formulations of cardinal theoretical claims need precision and constancy, even at the cost of weariness. Theories can have recourse to catchphrases and terse sentences; but the price thereof is to be carefully estimated. Along this path, two further exegetical questions arise. I will just mention them. First, nowhere do the key words "consistency" and "compatibility" get defined. What do they mean? Which "consistency," which "compatibility," is at stake? Second, inclusivism is about morality as a "necessary condition" or "precondition" of the legality of norms. Which sort of norms? Apparently, the norms at stake are *derivative* norms, i.e., norms that do not stay at the top of the legal system. Think, for instance, of norms that are produced by way of legislation or judicial precedent. These are source-based *explicit* derivative norms: in such a case, the idea of morality as a necessary (but not sufficient) condition of legality applies pretty well. A further question comes to mind, however. What about derivative *implicit* norms? What about, for instance, a norm of conduct N_j, never previously endowed with any legislative or judicial formulation, that a jurist, in a doctrinal essay, claims to belong to the legal system because of its consistency to some moral principle? Is N_j a legal norm by the inclusivist criterion? If the answer is in the affirmative, morality would be not (only) a necessary, but (also) a sufficient condition of N_j's legality.[41] In such a case, however, inclusivism would seem to slide into incorporationism.

[41] See Kramer, "There's Nothing Quasi about Quasi-Realism: Moral Realism as a Moral Doctrine," 208–9.

Taking a more charitable view, which of the five varieties of inclusivism considered above correspond to Kramer's authorial intent? Apparently, he regards the formulations of the inclusivism legality thesis in terms of "compatibility with correct moral principles" as theoretically preferable. Furthermore, he stands for an objectivist conception of moral correctness, though he also allows for the possibility that a legal system adopt some *moderate* relativistic conception, i.e., one that falls short of "extreme subjectivism".[42]

The last point elicits a query. Is Kramer's view about the proper way of understanding the legality thesis of inclusivism theoretically proper? If we look at it from the standpoint of the twin Hartian principles of no confusion between law's description and law's practical evaluation, Kramer's view looks, to say the least, suspect. Why should a thesis purporting to account for the possible content of the legality criteria of actual legal systems rule out extreme subjectivist morality conditions? No theoretical reason appears to support that position. Considerations of ("true") moral legitimacy or practical viability seem contrariwise to be afoot, preventing the setting forth of a dispassionate and genuinely theoretical claim.

4.2 Incorporationism

Unlike inclusivism, Kramer characterizes *incorporationism* as upholding *one* thesis about the legality of correct moral principles, which he always formulates in roughly the same wording. The incorporationist legality thesis claims, in particular, that it can be the case, though it need not be the case, that a *norm's correctness as a moral principle* is a *sufficient condition* for its status as a legal norm in this or that jurisdiction. That is to say, it may be the case that, according to the binding legality (validity) criteria of a legal system (its "rule of recognition"), that system considers correct moral principles, *qua* correct moral principles, as legal norms belonging to it. It may be the case, in other words, that a legal system *incorporates* correct moral principles simply because of their moral correctness.[43]

What should count as a correct moral principle is, supposedly, something for each legal system (and each legal culture) to determine. It may be the case then that a legal system endorses a relativistic variety of incorporationism (but, in Kramer's view, as we have just seen, it *cannot* be an extremely subjectivist one), or, alternatively an objectivist variety, so that the incorporationist thesis should read, more precisely, as follows: a *norm's objective or relative correctness as a moral principle* can, but need not be, a *sufficient condition* for its status as a legal norm in this or that jurisdiction. Kramer, however, does not cast any light on the issue. Contrariwise, he thinks it theoretically necessary to pick out two sorts of incorporationism, namely: "extreme," "robust," or "thoroughgoing" incorporationism, on the one side, and "mild" or "moderate" incorporationism, on the other.

[42] See Kramer, *Where Law and Morality Meet*, 73 n. 18; Kramer "There's Nothing Quasi about Quasi-Realism: Moral Realism as a Moral Doctrine," 208–9.

[43] Kramer, *Where Law and Morality Meet*, 2–3, 17, Kramer, *H. L. A. Hart. The Nature of Law*, 174.

Extreme incorporationism holds that it can, but need not, be the case that a legal system's norms of conduct are only and entirely made of correct moral principles: in Kramer's words, that "*moral worthiness*" is "the *lone sufficient condition* for" the status of any norm as a legal norm.[44]

In Kramer's view, however, robust incorporationism is to be rejected as a theoretically invaluable, and indeed obnoxious, variety of incorporationism. Kramer, it must be emphasized, does not charge robust incorporationism with advancing a *false* legality thesis about positive legal systems.[45] Rather, he thinks robust incorporationism is wrong because, by envisaging the possibility of legal systems encompassing incorporated moral principles only, it provides a "not credible," "profoundly misleading," "prodigiously unlikely" picture of law;[46] it leaves open the misleading "unilluminating" possibility of sizable legal systems that actually betray the law's conduct-guiding function. Indeed, in a system where only incorporated moral principles are the standards to be applied by officials in settling disputes, it is highly probable that "extensive divergences among people's moral outlooks" will prevent the legal system from passing "the threshold of regularity," "uniformity," or "consistency" that "must obtain *if a legal system is to exist as a legal system*."[47]

Taking stock of this, Kramer thinks necessary to conceive a variety of incorporationism that is not likewise flawed. This is why *moderate* or *mild incorporationism* arises. Kramer characterizes it as the combination of a negative and an affirmative thesis:

(a) it cannot be the case of a (sizable) legal system proper the laws of which only are (made of) incorporated moral principles;
(b) it can be the case, in a (sizable) legal system proper, that the laws dealing with hard cases are (made of) incorporated moral principles.[48]

Concerning hard cases, Kramer further picks out those having "a uniquely correct moral solution" (let's call them: easy-hard cases), from those having "no uniquely correct moral solution" (let's call them: hard-hard cases). As Kramer makes clear, in any easy-hard case, officials have the duty to give voice to the uniquely correct solution; in any hard-hard case, by contrast, they have the duty to decide according to moral principles and in view of legal outcomes "within the range of acceptable principles and outcomes."[49]

Kramer's conception of incorporationism is deserving of a few critical comments.

1. Kramer's rejection of robust incorporationism is theoretically suspect. Kramer, as we have seen, charges it with being a misleading and unilluminating general jurisprudential position, because in the context of "any credible society more sizeable than a handful of families," a robustly incorporationist rule of recognition will not secure

[44] Kramer, *Where Law and Morality Meet*, 6, 25, emphasis added.
[45] Kramer, *Where Law and Morality Meet*, p. 54.
[46] Kramer, *Where Law and Morality Meet*, pp. 24–36, 54–8.
[47] Kramer, *Where Law and Morality Meet*, 28, 43, emphasis added.
[48] Kramer, *Where Law and Morality Meet*, 6, 28, 34, 35, 35–6, 53, 60 61, 73, Kramer, *Where Law and Morality Meet*, 36, 37.
[49] Kramer, *Where Law and Morality Meet*, 37.

the degree of regularity uniformity or consistency that is required "for a legal system to exist as a legal system."[50]

However, if we cast a dispassionate glance on the issue, what robust incorporationism claims is the *possibility* that any legal system (i.e. any normative set having, *qua* legal system, a dynamic and coercive character[51]) be grounded in fact on a robustly incorporationist rule of recognition. Claiming such a possibility goes together with, and does not rule out, the possibility for legal systems to adopt more moderate versions of the rule of recognition, and even strictly exclusivist ones keeping moral principles completely outside of positive law. What robust incorporationism points to, therefore, is a spectrum of possible forms of legal systems: from one extreme of those adopting a robust incorporationist rule of recognition, to the other extreme of those adopting a strictly exclusivist one. This way of proceeding seems perfectly in tune with the requirements of a genuinely general and descriptive jurisprudence.

The same cannot be said, contrariwise, of Kramer's argument against robust incorporationism.

To begin with, Kramer's sponsoring of a narrow notion of "existing legal system" (only normative social orders endowed with an adequate degree of regularity uniformity or consistency are existing legal systems) is open to the same form of criticism Hart waged against natural-lawyers' recourse to a narrow concept of law.[52] From the standpoint of dispassionate legal knowledge, there seems to be nothing wrong (and much to commend) in saying something like: "This is a legal system, but the degree of regularity uniformity or consistency in the decisions of its officials is so low that it fares pretty badly as a conduct-coordinating device."

Secondly, from an austere Benthamite perspective, Kramer's opposition to robust incorporationism appears to be laden with preoccupations that belong to the criticism of law, even though it is a rational criticism, or from the standpoint of instrumental, means-to-end, reason. Indeed, as Kramer avows, he adjusts the concept of "existing legal system" to the need of limiting «the range of possible law-ascertaining criteria» to what is «necessary to ensure the functionality of a legal system."[53]

2. Kramer's moderate incorporationism is theoretically ill conceived. On closer inspection, moderate incorporationism makes four claims, two of which I have just mentioned. First, incorporated moral principles are to be resorted to in the decision of hard cases *only*, i.e., in deciding those cases for which authoritative legal sources (legislation, precedent) do not provide a unique, definite, and hence correct solution. Second, incorporated moral principles sometimes do provide a uniquely correct solution to hard cases (easy-hard cases), and sometimes do not provide it (hard-hard cases). Third, the ascertainment of the uniquely correct solution in easy cases is a matter of empirical investigation about the existence and definite content of authoritative legal sources (that is why the cases are "easy"). Fourth, the ascertainment of the uniquely correct solution for a hard case is, contrariwise, a matter of moral argument,

[50] Kramer, *Where Law and Morality Meet*, 43.

[51] As appears from the presence both of *judges* authorized to settle disputes according to moral principles, and of *executive officials* endowed with the coercive power necessary to carry out judicial decisions.

[52] Hart, *The Concept of Law*, 206ff.

[53] Kramer, *Where Law and Morality Meet*, 43.

and this implies that "the unique correctness" of the solution "is *indemonstrable.*"[54] Kramer does not see any inconvenience in the indemonstrability of uniquely correct solutions for hard cases. However, it deals a fatal blow to his view. If there is *no demonstrable way* to tell whether incorporated moral principles do, or do not, provide a uniquely correct solution to a hard case at hand, the distinction between easy-hard cases and hard-hard cases falls apart. But mild incorporationism stands on that distinction. Therefore, mild incorporationism falls apart too.

3. Kramer's moderate incorporationism presupposes a thesis about the limits of the law that is theoretically ill conceived. The four claims of moderate incorporationism I have just recalled point to a thesis about the limits of the law. The thesis appears to run as follows: at any moment in the life of a legal system, existing law is tantamount to the sum of definite explicit laws (providing uniquely correct solutions to easy cases) plus the uniquely correct solutions provided by incorporated moral principles to easy-hard cases. We have seen, however, that there is no way of demonstrating that incorporated moral principles do provide a uniquely correct solution to a hard case at hand, that the distinction between easy-hard cases and hard-hard cases is theoretically unviable. This unviability fatally undermines Kramer's limits of the law thesis. If we cannot know whether incorporated moral principles do, or do not, provide a uniquely correct solution to a hard case at hand, we cannot know, by Kramer's own standard, whether in a hard case there is law to be applied by judges, or, rather, judges must make new law on the basis of acceptable moral principles.

4. Kramer's moderate incorporationism presupposes a thesis about the limits of the law that lies outside of the province of general and descriptive jurisprudence. I have argued that Kramer's limits of the law thesis is theoretically ill conceived insofar as its notion of existing law for hard cases is considered. However, along with this "post-Hartian" incorporationist component, the thesis also encompasses the "Hartian" component of the coincidence, so far as easy cases are considered, between existing law and definite explicit law. What I wish to suggest now, is not that Kramer's or Hart's limits of the law theses are theoretically ill conceived. Rather, I wish to suggest that it is doubtful that such theses are in tune with the tenets of general and descriptive jurisprudence. Let's consider Hart's limits of the law thesis (partially endorsed by Kramer). As we have seen, it affirms the coincidence between existing law and definite explicit law, and it does so in order to make the distinction between the law as it is and the law as it ought to be depend on solid empirical ground. Yet, one cannot help noticing the uncertain status of the thesis. To which branch of legal study does it belong? On the one hand, Hart regards it as a very important component of a general and descriptive positivist jurisprudence: as a genuinely *theoretical* thesis. On the other hand, from a Dworkinian standpoint, the thesis, and in general any thesis whatsoever purporting to draw the limits of law, looks like a piece of *interpretive* (and, in Hart's terminology, *normative* and *justificatory*) jurisprudence. To be sure, Hart's limits of the law thesis is theoretical in spirit and by design. Nonetheless, it is also likely to have a momentous

[54] Kramer, *Where Law and Morality Meet*, 37, emphasis added. See also Kramer, *In Defense of Legal Positivism. Law Without Trimmings*, 154–7; Kramer "There's Nothing Quasi about Quasi-Realism: Moral Realism as a Moral Doctrine," 208–9.

practical bearing (of which Hart, by the way, is apparently aware[55]). It can also be used to practical purposes in the practice-of-law game, which jurists, judges, and lawyers daily play out of professional privilege and duty. Which practical purposes may the Hartian thesis serve? Consider the following example. Suppose you are a jurist favoring a "passive" judicial attitude in constitutional interpretation. In such an event, you will find the Hartian limits of the law thesis quite congenial to your (normative and justificatory) view. In fact, it supports you, with all the authoritative weight of a seemingly *theoretical* claim, in arguing that the constitution reaches up to the point of the determinate linguistic or intentional meaning of its provisions, or, in any case, up to the point of their collectively determinate judicial meaning.[56] In so doing, you will be able to criticize as instances of *unconstitutional* judicial "activism" any reading of the constitution that departs, either from the determinate linguistic or intentional meaning of its provisions, if any, or from the determinate collective judicial meaning, once it has been established. In so doing, you will be able to claim that every judicial interpretation of a constitutional provision departing from the meanings above is *legally wrong*: it is a piece of contrary-to-law interpretation, or, in the terminology of medieval jurists, an instance of *interpretatio contra legem*, or, more precisely, *contra constitutionem*.

If the previous argument is sound, the Hartian thesis of the limits of the law turns out to be dubious as a genuinely theoretical thesis. Is there room for any limits of the law thesis within a genuinely general and descriptive positivist account of law? Is any limits of the law thesis conceivable, which, unlike the Hartian (or Kramerian) thesis, cannot be put to practical use? It is conceivable. But, unlike the Hartian (or Kramerian) thesis, it must avoid taking sides on the existing law/definite explicit law/implicit law issue. That issue should be regarded—and presented—as one that wholly belongs to the province of legal practice and juristic value-laden controversies. No legal theory, *qua* theory, can claim to be competent to provide a solution. Accordingly, from a genuinely theoretical point of view, the only limits of the law thesis that looks viable is a second-order, meta-doctrinal, descriptive thesis. To wit, a thesis that accounts for the juristic positions that are or can be argued for in "our" legal systems as to the existing law/definite explicit law/implicit law issue, and brings to the fore their respective ideological backgrounds and the practical consequences likely to follow from their adoption.

4.3 Exclusivism

Let's come, finally, to *exclusivism*. Kramer's presentation suggests conceiving it as the combination of three theses:

> *Anti-inclusivism*: By the very nature of positive law, moral principles can never work as criteria for the validation of laws of any positive legal system.

> *Anti-incorporationism*: By the very nature of positive law, moral principles can never work as laws of any positive legal system.

[55] Hart, *Answers to Eight Questions*, 286.
[56] Hart, *Answers to Eight Questions*, 286.

Externality of moral principles: By the very nature of positive law, the moral principles that are invoked, and should often be invoked, in the adjudicative and administrative activities are, and remain, extra-legal standards.[57]

Kramer deploys an articulate argumentative strategy both to rebut exclusivism's critiques to inclusivism and (mild) incorporationism, and show it to be, in itself, wrong.[58] On this latter path, the main argument Kramer works out against exclusivism is meant to show that the exclusivist anti-incorporationist and externality of moral principles theses are theoretically unsound.

How does Kramer argue to that effect? He conceives an analogical argument, purporting to suggest that exclusivism's theses are flawed by theoretical unreasonableness. The analogical argument runs as follows. Exclusivists deny the very possibility for moral principles to belong to positive legal systems. Exclusivists, by contrast, admit that customary laws belong to positive legal systems. Customary laws and moral principles, however, are essentially similar sorts of norms. Both can be regarded as "free-floating" norms, i.e., not amenable to any definite law-making agency, as opposed to the laws of foreign jurisdictions, or the rules of private associations and sporting clubs, that contrariwise are amenable to external law-making agencies. Provided customary laws and moral principles are essentially similar, Kramer concludes, exclusivists' negative attitude as regards to moral principles appears to be theoretically unjustified.[59]

Kramer's argument is ingenious. However, from the standpoint of general and descriptive jurisprudence, a stronger argument seems to be available against exclusivism. Exclusivism claims to derive the no-incorporation thesis and the externality of moral principles thesis, as Kramer emphasizes, from "the very nature of law." Such a derivation, unfortunately, looks like a piece of natural-law theory, in its "nature of things" variety. From the standpoint of a genuinely positivist jurisprudence, the issue about whether certain sorts of norms (say, moral principles or customary norms) do, or do not, belong to a legal system is not a matter for legal theory to settle by way of a general thesis, nor by appealing to intrinsic properties of the norms at stake, since it depends, rather, on each legal system's contingent *meta-norms* about membership and applicability.

5. Concluding Remarks

Which is, to conclude, the moral of the story (if there is any)?

Jeremy Bentham built his theory of jurisprudence on the divide between expository and censorial tasks. He thought both tasks were paramount for any rational coping with the phenomenon of law. He also thought it extremely important, though, that the two tasks, so far as possible, be carried out separately.

[57] See Kramer, *Where Law and Morality Meet*, 3 Kramer, *H. L. A. Hart. The Nature of Law*, 174–5.

[58] Kramer, *In Defense of Legal Positivism. Law without Trimmings*, ch. 4; Kramer, *Where Law and Morality Meet*, part I and ch. 7.

[59] Kramer, *Where Law and Morality Meet*, 38–43.

Contemporary common law positivists have taken Bentham's view seriously. Considering the problem of how a positivist theory of law in general, *qua* theory, should be, they have put themselves on the path of expository jurisprudence. Hart's idea of a general and descriptive jurisprudence is nothing but an updated version of Bentham's expository prototype, centered on the epistemological separation thesis.

It must be noted, however, that contemporary common law positivists sometimes seem to fall short of keeping their purportedly descriptive (explanatory, clarifying) claims free from the influence of practical preoccupations mirroring the needs of a rationalist censorial jurisprudence.

The limits of the law thesis, in the Hartian and Kramerian versions I have considered, looks as an answer to the rational need of encapsulating into "our" elucidated concept of law the idea of law as a normative social order with an *effective* conduct-guiding function. Similarly, Kramer's notion of an "existing legal system" and his rejection of robust incorporationism appear, again, to be as many trespasses into the province of practical needs and rationalist evaluation of positive legal systems.

The outcome in sum are theories of law that, all things considered, and somewhat paradoxically, have not entirely succeeded in providing accounts of positive legal systems that satisfy the requirements of being purely descriptive, value-neutral, and indifferent to practical consequences.

9

From Law's Existence to Law's Rule

Reflections on Kramer's Understanding of the Rule of Law

Gerald J. Postema[*]

With keen analytic skill and rigorous argument, Matthew Kramer has made invaluable contributions across a wide range of topics in legal, political, and moral philosophy. I leave to others in this volume to convey a fair sense of this vast terrain. I propose to look briefly at just one chapter of Kramer's important book *Objectivity and the Rule of Law*.[1] This chapter displays in microcosm the notable virtues of Kramer's entire philosophical corpus. I will not undertake here to challenge, except perhaps in passing, his analysis or arguments. In this chapter, he set understandable limits for his exploration, but seems open at certain points to exploration beyond those limits. My aim in this chapter is to consider how we might extend his analysis into richer, if more controversial, territory. Although my suggestions are offered in the spirit of a friendly amendment, I do not expect him to accept them without challenge or amendment of his own. Matthew understands and appreciates, as do I, the philosophical enterprise and the respect manifest in an argument sympathetically reviewed and generously assessed.

1. Kramer's Understanding of the Rule of Law in Outline

The key ideas of the rule-of-law ideal, if not the term itself, have been the focus of the attention of political philosophers and legal, especially constitutional, theorists for millennia. Anglo-American legal philosophers came to see the significance of the ideal for jurisprudence in the middle of the twentieth century when controversy arose over Lon Fuller's discussion of "eight ways to fail to make law."[2] Contemporary analytic jurisprudence, rarely in agreement about much, widely agrees that Fuller's eight canons—generality, perspicuity, prospectivity, public ascertainability, consistency, compliability, stability, and congruence—constitute the indispensable core of the idea of the rule of law. Controversy focused not on these core standards, but on Fuller's claim that they constitute a *morality* that is *internal* to law itself. Critics argued that, although they stand as conditions of the existence of a legal system, and hence *internal* to law, they are morally neutral. In his 2007 book, Kramer analyzes in careful detail the plausibility and provenance of each of Fuller's eight standards of lawgiving and sheds fresh and irenic light on the controversy regarding their status.

* Professor of Philosophy Emeritus, University of North Carolina at Chapel Hill.

1 Kramer, *Objectivity and the Rule of Law*. All subsequent references in the text will be to this work.

2 Fuller, *The Morality of Law*.

Gerald J. Postema, *From Law's Existence to Law's Rule* In: *Without Trimmings*. Edited by: Mark McBride and Visa AJ Kurki, Oxford University Press. © Mark McBride and Visa AJ Kurki 2022. DOI: 10.1093/oso/9780198868866.003.0009

The eight standards, he argues, *are* internal to law, to its very existence, *and*, taken together, constitute (a core part of) a "morally cherishable" ideal; but, he argues *pace* Fuller, the respect in which the standards are internal to law is not the respect in which they speak the language of moral ideals. Kramer is not the first to distinguish a moral-political conception of the rule of law from a purely jurisprudential conception of it, of course. Kramer's fresh claim is that these distinct conceptions share the same core ideas. The two conceptions offer different and separable ways of articulating the significance of Fuller's eight standards. One articulates conditions of the existence of a fully functioning legal system, the other expresses a constituent of the liberal-democratic ideal of good governance and a just society. These distinct accounts, Kramer argues, pivot on the shared assumption that individual legal subjects are rational, self-directing agents. Lawgivers acknowledge and assume for their purposes, that legal subjects are rational, self-directing agents, because law's fundamental function is to guide behavior through addressing rules and norms to them. Yet, from the liberal-democratic moral point of view, this feature of legal subjects is not merely a condition of law's effectiveness, but a fact of fundamental moral importance, demanding our respect. Human beings are responsible moral agents, capable of ordering their lives in light of chosen ends and goals and directing their conduct in light of norms that purport to guide them. This capacity of individuals grounds a morally fundamental kind of dignity demanding proper respect from other moral agents and from those who exercise authority over them. Because these conceptions rest on distinct understandings of the practical significance of respecting the agency of individuals, the scope and normative force of Fuller's standards turn out to be rather different from the different perspectives. Viewed as moral demands, they tend to have greater practical force and are more resistant to compromise with competing concerns than when viewed as conditions of effective functioning of the legal system.

2. Rule-of-Law Standards as Conditions of Law and Governance

Later in this chapter, we will consider Kramer's understanding of the rule of law as a moral-political ideal in its own right, but first let us consider some features of Kramer's jurisprudential conception, and his view that the two conceptions are sharply separable.

Kramer maintains that satisfaction of each of Fuller's standards is necessary, and satisfaction above a relatively high threshold is sufficient, for the existence of a functional legal regime (142–3). Fully one-half of his chapter is devoted to careful demonstration of this thesis with respect to each of the eight standards. He launches his arguments from the assumption that the law's primary ("cardinal," "paramount") function is to guide the conduct of rational agents by means of addressing norms to them (132), and argues that Fuller's standards mark out distinct conditions for effective execution of this function (or, as I prefer, law's *modus operandi*). Following Fuller, Kramer recognizes that law—or rather, governing according to the discipline of law—is just one mode of governance amongst others (104). But at several points in his chapter he makes the stronger claim that compliance (not necessarily perfect but at least above a relatively high threshold) with Fuller's standards is a necessary condition of any tenable functioning form of governance (111, 113, 127, 132, 136). Let us look first at the claim that Fuller's standards mark necessary conditions of effective governance, before considering whether they also identify conditions satisfaction of which are sufficient for the existence of a functioning legal system.

Why think satisfaction of Fuller's standards is necessary for the existence of *any* government? The argument appears to rest on the following thoughts. Every government seeks order, stability, and effective control and to achieve this it must attain a substantial degree of regularity, uniformity and predictability of its directives so that citizens can form reliable expectations concerning the conduct of government officials and other citizens. Fuller's standards are useful, even essential, guides to achieving uniformity and predictability of government control. Thus, although those who exercise ruling power may not be committed in principle to governing according to the discipline of law (or as I will put it, inelegantly, "ruling lawishly"), they will find it useful and even (up to a point) essential to deploy it, or at least to be perceived to be committed to deploying it.

This argument is not persuasive. Fuller spent much of his time distinguishing governing according to the discipline of law from what he called "managerial direction,"[3] and we can observe other modes of governance are in history and in our own times. Rule by repression, for example, regrettably, is not uncommon. Unpredictability of government intrusion into the lives of citizens can serve the purposes of some rulers. Being known to act entirely upon whim can force people subject to arbitrary will to curtail their own freedom of action, and, especially their willingness to express opposition to those who exercise ruling power over them. Stephen Holmes observes that

> Keeping things fluid can be an especially appealing strategy for a certain type of ruler.... Injecting uncertainty into social situations is a well-known mechanism of control. If a subject population never knows what is going to happen to it, it is unlikely to present a serious challenge.[4]

It is a matter of political calculation whether to govern by predictability or by unpredictability, and these calculations can change depending on the ruler's goals, resources, and perceived enemies. The ability to facilitate social coordination may be important for a healthy society, but coordinated opposition can represent a serious threat to a regime, and the regime may try to secure its political survival by dividing people, engendering distrust among them. As Holmes points out, Machiavelli argued that this strategy is counter-productive,[5] but whether the strategy succeeds depends on circumstances that can change over time. Surely, regimes of the kind Holmes described have existed and exist even today. Rule by repression is not a good form of governance, but the question at hand concerns existence not moral excellence. It is difficult to deny that such regimes exist and can survive for a long time.

[3] Fuller, *Morality of Law*, 204–8.
[4] Holmes, "Lineages of the Rule of Law," 21.
[5] Holmes, "Lineages," 20.

Similarly, examples of Fuller's model of managerial direction can be observed in the world around us. Mao Zedong instituted rule by Party in China. Every Party meeting and resolution is law, he declared.[6] Similarly, rulers in Myanmar, observers report, seek social order through particularistic directives applied through administrative agencies rather than judicial institutions. Myanmar officials act on specific instructions from their superiors, intervening directly in people's lives, rather than on general norms meeting Fuller's standards. The ultimate aim of Myanmar authorities, Simon Cheesman maintains, is "quietude"—"a condition of supervision, instruction, prescription, and notification"—maintained through "a superordinate-subordinate political relationship."[7] Typically, rules do not proceed entirely without use of general norms, but its dominant mode is bureaucratic, depending on personal allegiance, rather than protection of and respect for formal law that visibly transcends personal relationships. In this mode, Myanmar rulers may not completely ignore Fuller's standards, but neither are they richly satisfied; and yet order of a kind is kept and a mode of governance is sustained.

Another mode of governance that arguably falls short of governing lawishly we can call "governance by law manqué" or "legality at convenience." Laws exist in this even more common form of governance; governing regimes recognize the value of laws, but they are equally aware of their inconvenience. They are inclined to deploy them just to the extent that they promise to be politically useful. Turkmenistan has laws, James Crawford observed, but "the taps of that law may be turned on and off at will by Turkmenbashi."[8] Ernest Fraenkel described a thoroughly institutionalized form of governance by law at convenience in what he called the "dual state." His paradigm was the Nazi regime in Germany.[9] The "normative state"—the state ostensibly ruling with and itself governed by formally recognized law—was the public face of the regime, but lurking in its shadows was the "prerogative state," consisting of officials enjoying powers to set aside or ignore the norms of the normative states at their convenience. Formal laws existed, but a functioning legal regime did not; not because there was widespread social and political disorder, but because the laws were not functioning as laws. They were not functioning as laws because rulers exercised governing power, and effectively kept order, *despite* the laws, and despite the fact that Fuller's canons were not satisfied. (Among the most egregiously violated, it appears, was the standard that requires that official actions be congruent with announced laws.)

When people realize that the apparent laws govern only when convenient to those who, in the Chinese phrase, "use law to rule the country,"[10] laws tend to lose their ability to guide as norms. A general perception that those in power comply with Fuller's standards may be useful to them, in the right circumstances, but their compliance is a mode of presentation, not a principled rule-of-law mode of governance.

Thus, compliance with Fuller's standards is not necessary for every mode of governance to function. Governing according to the discipline of law is, as Kramer

[6] Weifang, *In the Name of Justice*, xxxvii.
[7] Cheesman, *Opposing the Rule of Law*, 25–9, 34–5.
[8] Crawford, "International Law and the Rule of Law," 4–5.
[9] Fraenkel, *The Dual State: A Contribution to the Theory of Dictatorship*.
[10] Weifang, *In the Name of Justice*, xxxvii.

acknowledged, only one mode of governance among others; and, we must concede, that the rule-of-law mode is not essential to governance. Nevertheless, we must ask, is Kramer right that compliance up to a relatively high threshold is necessary for a properly functioning legal regime to exist? To answer this question, we need to look more closely at Kramer's definition of law's cardinal function.

Kramer accepts Fuller's animating assumption that law's cardinal function or *modus operandi* is to guide behavior of rational, self-directing subjects of law by addressing rules and norms to them, rules that they can grasp and apply to their own practical circumstances. At the heart of this notion is the claim that law functions *as law* when it is in force in a political community and plays a key role in the deliberative economy of its members (or, at least, a substantial number of them).[11] It is not enough that the conduct of most members is in fact coincident with the requirements the law lays down for them, for that coincidence might be largely (if remarkably) accidental. Consider, for example, a community where most members are ignorant of the laws or have chosen to orient their conduct to some other source of norms. More to the point, consider those whom Hart calls law's "victims."[12] They, like Holmes's "bad man," view dictates of would-be lawmakers from a point of view "external" to law conceived as norms and from the norm-addressing intentions of those who exercise power over them. The difference between the "victim" and the "bad man" is that, on Hart's account, victims have no practical choice in the matter. Not only do victims have no reason voluntarily to comply with the dictates,[13] but more, as I have argued elsewhere, if the "victims have even the vaguest sense of the realities they face, they will find it extraordinarily difficult to regard the forces arrayed against them as anything other than utterly and irredeemably arbitrary."[14] The dictates will appear to them, not as someone else's norms, but as "other people's power."[15] Thus, for the laws to function *as laws* in the way Fuller and Kramer understand this notion, they must function in members' practical deliberation *as norms*; and to function as norms they must function as guides for conduct, not merely as reliable indicators of potential interference by officials in members' lives.

This mode of functioning requires that putative laws themselves be able to guide, but it requires more. If laws are to guide as norms, those whom law addresses must

[11] For an argument along these lines, see Postema, "Conformity, Custom, and Congruence: Rethinking the Efficacy of Law," 49–56. Note that Hart might resist this claim. In *The Concept of Law*, 144–7, Hart held that a functioning legal system exists even when only law-applying officials and the legal elite take the internal point of view on legal norms. In that case, the mass of those subject to the law may take an alienated view of the law game played on them by the legal elite. However, Kramer cannot take this view consistent with his argument in *Objectivity and the Rule of Law*. For, on his view, law cannot function as law, cannot effectively operate in its jurisdiction according to its distinctive mode, unless those addressed by law are able and willing to take up the dictates *as norms*. That is to say, Kramer can deny that legal norms must be able to play a key role in the deliberative economy of legal subjects only by abandoning the key claim of his rule-of-law argument. That claim is that the assumption of rational agency of legal subjects is the grounding premise of both the jurisprudential conception and the moral conception of the rule of law.

[12] Hart, *The Concept of Law*, 201–2; for a general discussion see, Postema, *Legal Philosophy in the Twentieth Century: The Common Law*, 7.4.2 and 7.7.3.

[13] Hart, *Concept of Law*, 193.

[14] Postema, "Jurisprudence as Practical Philosophy," 340.

[15] William Twining wrote that Holmes's "bad man" is "an enduring symbol of a positivist view of law seen as other people's power." Twining, *Globalization and Legal Theory*, 111.

take them up as norms. Uptake is crucial for normative guidance. Law fails to guide, if it fails to engage those whom it addresses. Law's guidance depends on communication. The signals that laws send must have a form that is receivable by those to whom they addressed, and, equally, the latter must have receivers tuned to the law's wavelength and be willing to use them. However, cultural or social circumstances in which law seeks to guide may obstruct reception or cause guidance-preventing static. Law may be disengaged from the lives of legal subjects due to various causes. The culture may be generally anomic or even antinomian; even the pretense of governing with law may engender opposition and rejection. Or members of the community may be alienated from it, seeing no point in complying, let alone allowing laws to figure as norms in their practical deliberation. This may be due to the fact that they see that it offers them no benefit, because they are powerless and they cannot use law to safeguard their interests. Or laws may fail to engage members of the community in their quotidian circumstances. It might just be practically irrelevant. Or, again, it may be due to the fact that extra-legal norms are more compelling. One example of this might be law in the South of the United States during the Jim Crow era. In that era, criminal laws protecting the lives of members of the Black community simply did not count in the white community.[16] This was the case in example might be societies in which more than one system of norms purports to govern the same community. Law may fail to guide in social conditions of anomy, anti-nomy, or polynomy. Thus, among the conditions necessary for law to function as law will be cultural and social conditions in which those addressed must live and interact. Especially important among these, I have argued elsewhere, is an ethos of *fidelity*.[17] I will return to this point presently.

We can pursue this notion of law's functioning *as law* a bit further. For, it is reasonable to consider the way law functions not only in the deliberative economy of legal subjects, but also in the deliberative economy of those who seek to rule with law. We have already wondered whether we should regard a case of rulers governing by law manqué as a functioning legal system. Let us look more closely at this matter.

It is clear that it does not meet minimal conditions of the rule of law as a moral-political ideal because it lacks entirely what we might call the dimension of *reflexivity*. Those who rule use law, law applies to and governs legal subjects, but the law does not rule those who rule with it. Is this, nevertheless, a functioning legal system? Is a principled submission to law's constraints by those who exercise ruling power a necessary condition of laws functioning *as law*? Of course, laws exist—or some things that purport to be laws exist—in these political situations, but can they function as laws proper? Kramer argued that retroactive directives *purporting* to be laws, or a set of norms purporting to be a legal system but riven by contradictions, cannot function as laws (119–22, 125–30). In the same spirit, we can ask, does guidance of rational, self-directing agents by announced norms require self-constraint of officials by that law as well?

[16] I have argued that this is the case in Postema, "Law's Ethos: Reflections on a Public Practice of Illegality," 1849–51.

[17] Postema, "Law's Rule: Reflexivity, Mutual Accountability, and the Rule of Law," in *Bentham's Theory of Law and Public Opinion*, 7–10, 18–21; and "Fidelity in Law's Commonwealth," 20–4.

Fuller thought so. He argued that the ability effectively to address and thereby guide other rational, self-directing agents depends on the willingness of those addressed to take the norms as norms, which in turn depends on their recognition of the lawgiver's commitment to being constrained by that same law. Governing lawishly, he argued, depends on a kind of reciprocity.[18] Rulers can fake such a public commitment, of course, but the commitment must be widely credible to those who are governed. Thus, governance by law manqué can function *as law* only where the rulers' actual commitments are not widely known and yet the public generally has reason to take as credible public expressions of their commitment to rule lawishly. However, it will be difficult to maintain that credibility, if people generally know that the ruler is legally and substantially free to alter legal constraints.[19] Thus, rulers must either make a sincere, principled, and public commitment to submit to law's constraints, *or* act entirely credibly *as if* they have undertaken such a commitment,[20] and make good on that commitment by putting in place institutions that hold them to it. But this looks very much like the basic infrastructure of reflexivity demanded by the moral-political ideal of the rule of law, the only difference being that we were led to this point by thinking of nothing more than what is necessary for law's functioning properly as law.

Of course, Fuller's argument turns on the premise that for law to function as law, legal subjects must take up the law willingly. They may not do so; and, possibly shortsightedly, rulers may not care whether they do. However, the question before us it not whether governance requires taking up purported legal directives as norms, but whether such governance counts as governing lawishly. So the question is whether willing uptake is necessary for law to guide. While it is not inconceivable that some legal subjects may use law as norms in their deliberation, despite their unwillingness to do so, it is not unreasonable to think that such cases must be rare. More fundamentally, one might argue that it is not necessary for law to function as law that legal subjects take up the law as norms. But that would amount to a challenge to the entire frame of Kramer's argument for the necessity of Fuller's standards to the existence of a functioning legal regime. So, if this is correct, then it follows from Kramer's premises that satisfaction of Fuller's standards alone is not sufficient for the existence of a functioning legal system; also necessary are conditions for uptake on the part of legal subjects and rulers' principled commitment to govern lawishly.

3. Kramer's Separation Thesis

If the above argument is sound, then the jurisprudential conception of the rule of law—the understanding of that ideal tied to law's distinctive *modus operandi*—may be more robust than Kramer and Fuller suggest. And one might ask whether the two understandings of the rule-of-law ideal are closer than Kramer's separation thesis seems to allow. I want to explore this question a little further.

[18] Fuller, *Morality of Law*, 219.

[19] See Tushnet, "Authoritarian Constitutionalism," 422–31.

[20] Stephen Holmes traces this argument to Machiavelli, "Lineages of the Rule of Law," 19–20, but the structure of this argument is familiar in Hobbes's reply to the Foole (Thomas Hobbes, *Leviathan*, 101–2) and Hume's reply to the sensible knave (David Hume, *Enquiry Concerning the Principles of Morals*, 81–2).

As Kramer presents it, the jurisprudential conception seems limited to rule by law alone—an ideal of law for subjects but not for rulers. On this view, law is regarded strictly as a *technique* of governing. As such, it imposes no discipline on the ruler, for if it is nothing more than a technique, it issues no prescriptions for its use. It is practically, and not only morally, inert. It gets its practical force only when and to the extent that there are reasons independent of law to deploy the technique. Nothing in the understanding of the rule of law internal to law counsels choosing this mode or submitting to its discipline; and nothing internal to the technique normatively holds rulers to their choice to use it.

But, then, it is misleading to speak of the rule of law in this context, for the rule of law is, if anything, a specific mode of governance, a discipline that imposes constraints on the exercise of power. Fuller's eight standards can be viewed narrowly as *technē*, but that does not yet engage a plausible understanding of the rule of law, jurisprudential or moral. Kramer's arguments for the necessity of compliance with Fuller's standards for the existence of a functioning legal system give us an account of the conditions of the existence of laws, but the rule of law as a mode of governance demands more than that laws exist. The law must rule. And it cannot rule without exerting some normative force on those who seek to rule by law. Thus, we can only keep separate the understanding of Fuller's standards as *technē* and a moral understanding of the rule of law by separating Fuller's standards as *technē* from any plausible notion of the rule of law.

However, our reflections in the previous section already led us to think that concerns internal to law's proper functioning call for more than Fuller's standards viewed strictly as *technē*. Compliance with Fuller's standards are not yet sufficient for a functioning legal regime. Those who exercise political power must act credibly as if they submit in a principled way to constraint by the law with which they rule, and endorse mechanisms that seek to hold them to that commitment. This approximates, at least, a credible notion of the rule of law, of a discipline of recognizing and respecting law's rule, that is, on Kramer's own terms, *internal* to law. Thus, we are here within the province of the rule-of-law ideal, although we have traveled here by way of reflection on what is necessary for a legal regime to function as law. This movement does not by itself enable us to bridge the gap between the jurisprudential and moral-political conceptions of the rule of law, but it is prepares a way for doing so.

Kristen Rundle's careful and faithful reconstruction of Fuller's jurisprudence may help us here. Fuller maintained that the self-constraining discipline of governing lawishly has significant moral value. For rulers "to opt into the distinctive enterprise of lawgiving," she argues, "is to take on an obligation to respect the legal subject as an agent, regardless of their motivation for choosing law."[21] That is, to undertake the distinctive enterprise of lawgiving entails: (a) submitting to the discipline of Fuller's standards, (b) taking as a focal concern the rational agency of law subjects, and (c) submitting to the moral obligation to respect legal subjects as a responsible moral agents. Kramer explicitly accepts (b) and I have argued that we have reason to accept (a) on the grounds Kramer offers for (b); however, he draws the line between (a)+(b), on the one hand and (c), on the other. The value served by rulers who submit to the discipline

[21] Rundle, *Forms Liberate: Reclaiming the Jurisprudence of Lon Fuller*, 117.

of Fuller's standards, and thereby take the rational, self-directing agent as a focal concern, is effective lawgiving, and, more generally, efficacious governing. Yet, this value is morally neutral. Such governing is of moral value only when its goals are morally valuable. On the other hand, the value served by the obligation to respect legal subjects is morally charged—it is, as we will see presently, the value of respecting human dignity. These two values, Kramer argues, represent distinct routes to the same range of behaviors mandated by the same set of standards.

However, this analysis is not quite right. Efficacious governance cannot be the reason for choosing to govern lawishly, for the discipline is practically necessary only *given* that rulers have already chosen governing lawishly as their preferred mode of governance. Efficacy of government, in contrast, has some (albeit clearly limited) currency as a reason for undertaking to rule lawishly and so for submitting to the discipline of the rule of law, but this value is not internal to law. We may use law for this purpose, but it is just one use among others. Efficacy of government is a value on the same level as justice, equality, and democracy—except that it is morally thinner, as it were. It is misleading, then, to think that we have in view one practice happily serving two distinct values, one internal to law and one not, one morally neutral and one morally charged.

Yet, Kramer may be right to pause before endorsing the claim that in choosing to govern lawishly rulers *thereby* undertake an obligation to respect citizens' dignity; for to say that, is to suggest that rulers choose this mode of exercising their power in order to secure proper respect for individual dignity. Surely, that is to expect too much.

Perhaps a weaker claim is true. Undertaking to govern lawishly (and thus accepting law's rule on a principled basis) is not only to adopt a technique, but also to establish an environment that has the hallmarks of a dignity-respecting relationship, one that individual citizens may experience as dignity-respecting. The effect of establishing this environment, regardless of motivations for doing so, is to put rulers and legal subjects into a morally inflected relationship in which certain reciprocal obligations are embedded. It is the nature of the relationship that is established, not the reasons for establishing it, that generates the obligations. If this claim can be sustained, it holds promise to bridge the gap between the two conceptions of the rule of law that Kramer sought sharply to distinguish. It is an interesting question whether the bridge can be built; however, I will leave that question unanswered in order to take up consideration of Kramer's discussion of the rule of law as a moral ideal in its own right.

4. The Rule of Law as a Moral Ideal: The Scope of the Ideal

David Lyons insisted that the law does not get respect free; it has to earn it.[22] Kramer disagrees. By complying with Fuller's eight standards to a satisfactory extent, he maintains, law serves an important value just by virtue of what it *is* (143). Fuller's standards supply the core of a morally cherishable moral-political ideal that stands alongside justice, liberty, democracy, and respect for human rights. It is clear that Fuller's standards

[22] Lyons, *The Moral Aspects of Legal Theory*, ix.

function as standards, as discrete but related components of an ideal; the task is to explain the morally recognizable value that this ideal serves. We will consider Kramer's explanation presently, but first it will be helpful for us to look at the nature and scope of this ideal.

Contemporary discussions typically assume that the rule of law is a modern ideal, the product of the emergence of liberal-democratic ideas and institutions in the West. While it is true that the English phrase, "the rule of law," is of relatively recent coining, the ideas, concerns, and ambitions that it comprises arose and flourished among thinkers in ancient and medieval political communities, long before distinctively liberal-democratic ideals and the modern nation-state took hold. Viewed from this wider historical perspective, the ideal of the rule of law looks remarkably bold. Johannes Althusius, at the turn of the seventeenth century, gave voice to this bold idea. He wrote, "What God is in the world, the navigator in a ship, the driver in a chariot, the director in a chorus, the commander in an army, so *lex* is in the city.... It is superior above all."[23] Put simply, *law rules*. The claim is not merely that it is good that law exists, or that it is good that people are ruled by law;[24] the bold claim is that law must be sovereign in the political community. The political community that realizes the rule of law is a *nomocracy*.

Law, on this bolder view, is not the instrument of power, but rather power's bridle, as Bracton put it.[25] It is likewise a bulwark protecting the powerless from those who wield power, whether in government or outside it; it seeks to constitute as well as constrain power over people wherever it is exercised. In addition, according to this long tradition, law provides a bond—"a standing rule to live by, common to every one of [a] society"[26]—the infrastructure of robust and healthy relations in the political community.

On this view, the rule of law recommends not only a valuable mode of governance, but also a mode of association, a mode of ordering social relations expressive of a valued kind of community. This ideal is cognate with other fundamental political values like justice, equality, and democracy, but it is not reducible to them. It represents a distinct ideal worthy of our allegiance.

Compared with this understanding, Kramer's rendering of the moral ideal of the rule of law is, in several respects, rather modest. First, it takes a narrow view of law's *modus operandi*. Following Fuller, Kramer focuses exclusively on the lawgiver. This encourages us to view law's distinctive *modus operandi* strictly in terms of its *directive* and *transitive* dimension, addressing directives directly to individuals, expecting them to take them up as norms by which to guide their conduct. However, law's guidance encompasses much more. Edward Rubin argued that much of the law is addressed not to citizens but to administrative agencies of the state, which guides citizens only indirectly and which guides those agencies by offering broad standards and goals and by intentionally granting wide discretion to work out how they are best

[23] Althusius, *Politica* Frederick S. Carney, ed & tr, 82.

[24] Marmor, "The Rule of Law and Its Limits," 2.

[25] "The law makes the king," Bracton wrote in the thirteenth century. "Let him, therefore, temper his power by law, which is the bridle of power, that he may live according to the laws." Bracton, *On the Laws and Customs of England*, 305.

[26] Locke, *Second Treatise of Government*, sec. 22.

to be served.[27] Also, as I have argued elsewhere, law characteristically offers *constitutive*, in addition to directive, guidance.[28] It is characteristic of law to seek to give texture, stability, and order to a wide range of social relations. Law constitutes positions, roles, and associated processes, bundled with complex combinations of rights, duties, powers, and responsibilities. While this dimension of law is familiar as (part of) the domain of constitutional law, it is equally evident in family law, employment law, property law, the law of trusts, and the like. The norms in these areas of the law sometimes offer direct normative guidance, but often they operate in a different way. They provide the infrastructure within which effective social interaction and meaningful social relations are possible. They define horizons that frame the practical reasoning of legal subjects. Similarly, laws guide by providing to legal subjects resources for evaluating and vindicating in public terms their own conduct and that of others in the community, thereby enabling members of the community to hold each other accountable for their conduct measured in public terms.

Second, Kramer's understanding of the moral-political rule-of-law ideal focuses exclusively on standards of formal *legality*, on standards for laws and officials administering them. However, another dimension of the ideal is a necessary complement of legality. I call it *fidelity*.[29] To appreciate this dimension we must start again with Fuller.

Fuller focused almost exclusively on the task of lawgiving. (Although his congruence standard promises to cast a wider net, neither he nor Kramer make good on this promise.) However, Fuller thought of his eight standards as defining the infrastructure of an *ethos*, a morally inflected relationship between the lawgiver and citizens, consisting of reciprocal responsibilities. On his view, the lawgiver's manifest commitment to exercise power within the limits of legality engenders confidence in legal subjects to respond with allegiance.[30] This thought, although salutary, is limited in two ways.

First, the relationship Fuller had in mind is not strictly speaking reciprocal. The requirement on the lawgiver to comply with the demands of legality is not conditional upon the compliance of citizens. These demands are made on the ruler independent of any reciprocation by legal subjects; and the demands remain in place even when legal subjects fail to do their part. The rule of law demands that authorities respect those who do not comply as well as those who do. Non-compliance does not put legal subjects beyond the scope of the rule of law's protections. On the contrary, the rule of law insists on procedural protections for them despite their non-compliance and constrains what the ruler may do to enforce compliance. Moreover, citizen allegiance is, on this picture, a response to action initiated by the lawgiver. It is reactive, not reciprocal. Of course, the lawgivers anticipate this response to some extent and cast directives in a form calculated to communicate its expectations to those who are addressed. Nevertheless, the relationship Fuller envisions is interactive but not reciprocal.

This is important to keep in mind in view of the moral ground of the rule-of-law ideal that Fuller and Kramer endorse. The imperative ground is respect for the moral responsible agency of individuals that is manifest in the attitudes and behavior of

[27] Rubin, "Law and Legislation in the Administrative State," 397–403.
[28] Postema, "Fidelity in Law's Commonwealth," 27–8.
[29] Postema, "Fidelity," 20–5.
[30] Fuller, *Morality of Law*, 219. See Rundle, *Forms Liberate*, 3, 130.

those exercising ruling power. However, citizens are not required to adopt this attitude of dignity-respect for government officials. Trust may be in order, perhaps, and willingness to do one's part is an appropriate response, but dignity-respect for officials goes too far. Thus, the demands of the rule-of-law relationship, on this view, are asymmetrical. Willing compliance is all that is required of citizens.

Second, Fuller's thought is limited in another way. The ethos of legality involves *compliance* with the law on the part of officials and legal subjects, but the rule of law demands more, if law is to rule. Adam Ferguson gives us a clue to what else is required. "The influence of laws," he wrote, depends on "the influence of men resolved to be free; of men, who, having adjusted in writing the terms on which they are to live with the state, and with their fellow-subjects, are determined, by their vigilance and spirit, to make these terms be observed."[31] Ferguson's suggestion is that, if law is to bridle ruling power, legality is not enough. Laws have no magical power; laws don't rule, only people rule insofar as they are "determined, by their vigilance and spirit, to make [the laws] be observed." The rule of law demands systematic accountability of those who exercise ruling power and that, in turn, requires an *ethos* of mutual accountability according to which all parties to the governance relationship take responsibility not only for their own compliance, but also for holding each other to their respective duties under the law.[32] The rule of law is realized in a political community to the extent that there is in that community a robust practice of members' generally taking responsibility for holding each other, and especially legal authorities, accountable with respect to the law.

I have called this ethos *fidelity*, but the faithfulness called into play has a specific normative content and direction. It requires taking responsibility not only for one's own conduct, but also for the conduct of others. This is a vital means of keeping sound and healthy a valued mode of association under common laws. Moreover, this faithfulness is owed not to government or to the law, but *to each other* as members of that association. Fuller may have understood fidelity only in terms of allegiance to law, but on this wider understanding of the rule-of-law ideal fidelity has a very different focus. If this is correct, then the rule-of-law ideal comprises two essential components: *legality*, concerning the formal, procedural, and other familiar institutional aspects of the ideal, and *fidelity*, the ethos necessary to sustain it.

With this in mind, we have reason to refocus our understanding of the moral ideal of the rule of law. We must turn our attention from the standards and institutions with which, in contemporary discussion, the rule of law is often equated to its underlying ambition and aim. In its general form, the ideal emerges from two orienting thoughts: that a polity is well ordered, and its members are accorded (at least in part) the dignity they can rightfully demand in the name of their co-membership in that polity, when they are secured against the arbitrary exercise of power; and that law, because of its distinctive features, is especially if not uniquely capable of providing such security. On this broader view, the rule of law is realized in a polity when and to the extent that law rules, and law rules in that polity when it provides protection and recourse against the arbitrary exercise of power. Framing the ideal in this way

[31] Ferguson, *An Essay on the History of Civil Society*, 249.
[32] I have argued for this thesis in "Law's Rule," 25–9 and "Fidelity in Law's Commonwealth," 30–6.

lays bare its normative structure. Its organizing or focal aim is control of the exercise of power over people. It seeks not to eliminate such power, but to temper it and especially protect against its arbitrary exercise.[33] Moreover, it does not hope to eradicate the arbitrary exercise of power, but to offer as much protection against it as is feasible and to provide recourse against it when it occurs. In terms Bentham preferred, the ideal seeks to provide "security against misrule,"[34] where misrule may have its source in governmental power or other forms of social power, within national boundaries or beyond. The rule of law sets its face against all forms of power over others insofar as they are susceptible to being arbitrarily exercised: the power of state against citizen, of employers against employees, of states against other states, of global non-state agencies, multinational business corporations, and global organizations that wield the enormous power of Big Data. Thus, the rule of law must have something significant to say about international and transnational, as well as domestic, relations of power.

Of course, what it has plausibly to say about these relations depends on what law is capable of doing. The demands of the rule of law are limited by the nature and limits of law. These limits to the scope of the rule of law take two forms. First, it is limited to tempering power by law's distinctive modalities and instrumentalities. Other means of tempering power may be available and may be more effective in some circumstances, but the rule of law attends exclusively to the means that law offers. Second, the rule of law is limited by the distinctive capabilities of this means of tempering power. These capabilities may, in turn, depend on social, cultural, and political circumstances in which law may be deployed. Thus, the rule of law's standards and the institutions needed to realize them must be determined not by definition or reflection on familiar models. Rather, we determine them by argument, keeping in mind the rule of law's guiding aim, the underlying values it seeks to serve, and salient features of law and their relative usefulness for this purpose in the circumstances in which we seek to deploy it. This broader framework, and the kinds of analysis and argument that it demands of its partisans, promises some protection against the cultural bias that has in recent decades undermined attempts to "promote" the rule of law around the world. Likewise, it enables us to think responsibly about the prospects of a globally relevant rule-of-law ideal, even though international law and its characteristic institutions depart in several ways from paradigmatic national legal systems.

Finally, the proposed broader manner of thinking about the rule of law invites attention to the question of the normative status and force of the ideal. While it is widely regarded as a very important moral-political ideal, it is only one value among others. It stands alongside, and at some points in competition with, other such values. Its requirements, then, may have to retreat when other values are more demanding in specific circumstances. It is also important to realize that the rule-of-law ideal is a middle-level principle or ideal. It underwrites more specific standards and institutions that are needed to implement them. It is able to do so because its normative force is grounded in, or serves, a yet more fundamental, moral-political value or principle, or integrated set of them. Understanding downstream standards and institutions—what we might regard as a *conception* of the rule of law appropriate for a particular political

[33] Martin Krygier, "Tempering Power."
[34] Bentham, *Securities against Misrule and Other Constitutional Writings for Tripoli and Greece.*

community—requires that we keep in mind three points of reference: the value(s) grounding the rule of law idea generally construed, the specific social, cultural, and political circumstances of the political community in view, and the distinctive modalities of law that may be deployed to realize the rule of law in that community. By triangulating among these components, we can survey the force and limits of the rule-of-law ideal. Thus, the underlying value of the ideal enables us to gain a deeper appreciation of the ideal and its demands. Kramer, to his credit, offers important insights into this value and the moral ideal it underwrites.

5. The Rule of Law as a Moral Ideal: The Moral Value Served

Kramer argues that compliance with rule-of-law standards beyond a relatively high threshold is morally valuable in a number of different ways. Discussing in careful detail each of Fuller's standards, he catalogues their contributions to good governance. He identifies a range of values from establishing and protecting public order and enabling social coordination to protecting and promoting individual liberty, from giving fair notice of government intrusion into the lives of citizens to enabling public scrutiny of laws, from respecting reasonable expectations to respecting the dignity and equality of citizens. This catalogue has no explicit structure, but with attention to Kramer's orienting frame we can detect plausible groupings of these values and priorities among them.

First, it is useful to distinguish values that are incidentally served or promoted by realization of the rule-of-law ideal and values more directly expressed or respected ("enshrined") in it. The former are extrinsic and hence incidental to the organizing aim of the rule of law. The latter are more directly implicated in that aim. Like Fuller, Kramer argues that laws, simply by virtue of what they are, serve or manifest respect for important moral values. Values intrinsic to the rule-of-law ideal are served by what law distinctively *is*, rather than what this or that set of laws seeks to *do* (or, more precisely, the policies and goals that governments seek to serve through the laws they enact). If we view the rule-of-law ideal, as suggested in the preceding section, as a middle-level moral-political ideal or principle, then it is reasonable to regard these intrinsic values, rather than incidental ones, as likely candidates for the moral ground of the rule of law, determining its normative force and scope.

Second, two features of Kramer's approach enable us to organize his catalogue of the values served by realization of the rule of law. First, Kramer's account of the ideal's moral value is built around the pivotal assumption that the moral conception shares with the jurisprudential conception, namely, that at the heart of the law is a special regard for the rational, self-directing agency of legal subjects. Second, he sets the moral ideal squarely in the constellation of familiar liberal-democratic values among which he includes liberty and autonomy of the individual, fundamental legal and political equality of persons, equality of opportunity, responsibility of government to protect the basic well-being of citizens, the importance of public deliberation, the value of opportunities for adult citizens to participate in elections, and the separation of powers (144). Kramer argues that the rule-of-law ideal works in partnership with this constellation of values.

With the above orientation in mind, we can safely place among incidental values served by realization of the rule of law, promotion of public order and social coordination and, building on them, economic efficiency and general prosperity. Serving these values, Kramer argues, is likely to be a consequence of a functioning legal regime (150, 154–5, 156–7, 171). The more robustly political values served by the rule of law also seem incidental to the ideal, as Kramer understands it. Two of Fuller's standards, promulgation and public ascertainability of laws, he argues, provide opportunities for public scrutiny of government policies and the legal means chosen to promote them. While important, these also seem incidental to the ideal. Likewise, we can reasonably take as incidental the fact that government compliance with several of Fuller's standards tends to give fair notice and promotes predictability of government intervention in individuals' lives, and consequently enhances and protects individual liberty of citizens. Yet, these values, unlike promoting economic prosperity, edge closer to concerns at the core of the rule-of-law ideal; for laws that conform to rule-of-law standards tend to respect the agency of citizens. The requirement of generality, he argues, directly serves fairness and the fundamental moral demand to treat like cases alike (148). However, the value underlying or promoted by each of the eight standards that stands out in Kramer's analysis is respect for persons as responsible moral agents (151, 154, 157, 158, 159, 162, 171, 176, 178). This value, in Kramer's articulation, takes two closely related forms: respect for the dignity of persons as moral agents, and respect for each citizen as an equal.

Given the prominence of respect for individual dignity and equality in Kramer's analysis, both as an intrinsic and an incidental value, it seems reasonable to treat it as his proposal for the ground of the rule of law as a moral ideal. He says as much at the outset of his chapter, writing that the rule of law "is a morally cherishable expression of commitments to the dignity and equality of individuals" (102). This ideal represents the formal dimension of the general commitment of liberal-democratic societies to respect for dignity and equality (144). Kramer concedes that the rule of law does not guarantee that the government otherwise respects dignity, and he recognizes that signal failures of the government to do so may undermine the efforts of the rule of law (175). Nevertheless, the realization of the rule of law is morally valuable in its own right, he argues, because the dignity and equality of individuals are respected in law's distinctive way, even if that value is to some degree contingent on background conditions in the political community.

Kramer is not unique among contemporary legal philosophers in understanding the ground value of the rule of law in this way. This value is arguably at the heart of Fuller's understanding of the rule of law.[35] More recently this view has been defended at length by Jeremy Waldron,[36] and there is at least a suggestion of the view in Joseph Raz's seminal essay on the rule of law.[37] Kramer's version of this view is complex and layered, modest (recognizing the limits of the rule of law to realize respect for human dignity), and decidedly individualist in its orientation. He has articulated for

[35] Rundle makes a compelling case for this reading of Fuller in *Forms Liberate*.

[36] E.g., in Waldron, "The Concept and the Rule of Law," 1–61; Waldron, "How Law Protects Dignity," 200–22.

[37] Raz, "The Rule of Law and its Virtue," 221.

liberal-democrats an attractive account of the rule-of-law ideal (or at least the formal part of that ideal) for contemporary liberal-democratic national communities.

Yet, the core ideas of the rule of law attracted partisans long before the emergence of the modern, largely capitalist, liberal-democratic nation-state, in political climates lacking its individualist focus. These ideas still reside in some form in the rule-of-law ideal to which we pledge allegiance today and continue to influence contemporary understandings of its ambitions. For example, the aim of containing the arbitrary exercise of power is plausibly linked historically to the republican ideal of non-domination.[38] But that ideal, in ancient and medieval times, envisioned communities and peoples as its beneficiaries at least as much as individuals, and individuals were regarded as beneficiaries *qua* members of their communities. We risk failing to do justice to the scope and force of the ideal by narrowly construing its normative base.

Similarly, we have seen that the ambitions at the heart of the ideal, in our contemporary circumstances, have encouraged a global reach for the ideal. Here, again, focusing the normative ground of the ideal on respect for the responsible agency, and dignity thus grounded, of individual persons leaves it with little to say in support of its transnational ambitions. The likely or intended beneficiaries of control of wielders of power in the transnational domain rarely include individual human beings, or do so only very indirectly.

The problem, in part, is that an explicitly liberal-democratic basis for the rule-of-law ideal merely confirms the charge of Western bias that many who are not antecedently committed to those values level against it. However, Kramer has resources to meet this charge, since he recognizes a range of values served by the rule of law as he understands it that are not plausibly construed as strictly liberal-democratic values. Public order, effective social coordination, promotion of economic prosperity, and control of corruption and self-dealing by government officials all are likely to appeal even to non-liberals. Constituencies whose rulers can act free of law and accountability risk being governed by cupidity, whim, anger, spite, bias, perversion, and stupidity.[39] In Kramer's framework, as I have construed it, these values are incidental, but regard for the rule-of-law ideal as a middle-level principle of political morality leaves room for alternative accounts of what is intrinsic and what incidental to the ideal.

The more serious concern, in my view, is that the exclusively individualist focus of Kramer's understanding of the ground of the rule-of-law ideal mutes its voice in the transnational domain, where there are enormous concentrations of power and where, arguably, law may play a role in containing and constituting this power and offering protection and recourse against its arbitrary exercise. We have reason, then, to consider other candidates for the moral ground of the rule-of-law ideal, candidates that might better appreciate the historical roots of its guiding ideas and enable it to speak with some authority to transnational as well as national domains. There is not room enough explore alternative candidates and defend any of them adequately, but I will here sketch the profile of one that may fill the bill.

We may begin by reflecting again on Fuller's understanding of the rule of law. Readers of *The Morality of Law* are often tempted to view Fuller's standards only as

[38] See Pettit, *Republicanism: A Theory of Freedom and Government* and Pettit, *On the People's Terms*.

[39] Tamanaha, "The Functions of the Rule of Law," Available at: https://ssrn.com/abstract=3113820, 5.

a set of tests for properly "legal" lawmaking. While this is not entirely mistaken, it mistakes the skeleton for the organism. Fuller understood the formal requirements of legality to give structure to something more substantial and robust. It provides, he thought, the infrastructure of a certain kind of relationship that obtains between lawgivers and legal subjects. It is this relationship, in his view, that bears moral value.

Some such relationships make possible a kind of dignity and equality of those who are parties to it. In such relationships, parties are recognized as occupying a valued place or status, we might even say a kind of dignity. This dignity is a relational property, the property of a party who occupies a position in relationship to others, and which carries with it responsibilities and rights. Public recognition of this valued place and its incumbent is expressed through the actions of others as they carry out their responsibilities in this relationship. Equality, in like manner, may be understood in terms of the position one person occupies relative to another: rather than a measure of what one has, relative to what others have, it concerns how one stands relative to, and in the eyes of, others.[40] Equality in this sense is understood as a matter of being treated *as an equal* or *peer*, publicly recognized as standing on the same level as others.

Dignity and equality understood in this way are internally-related cognate concepts that make sense only in a certain kind of association. Associations or relationships in which dignity and equality so understood can flourish are axiologically complex. The relationship is not merely a material condition of the value enjoyed by the members or reducible to that value. The relationship itself takes on value. This value is manifest in the attitudes and actions of members who not only care for and about other members, but also about their relationship and about other members' care for the relationship. Moreover, the care they take of each other is mediated and given shape by their understanding of each other as co-members. Yet, that value cannot be divorced from the dignity accorded to each of the members by the mutual responsibilities that define the relationship and the benefits that members enjoy in it.

We lack a convenient and familiar term for this value. *Community* comes to mind, but it is too broad. The value I have in mind is a specific kind of the value of community. I am inclined to call it *membership*, similar in grammatical form to *leadership* and especially *friendship*, which refer to kinds of value as well as to instantiations of that value. One might be tempted to follow Aristotle and call it *civic friendship*, but I find more apt St. Paul's suggestive image. "Speak every man truth with his neighbor," he wrote, "for we are members of one another."[41] This rich image implies inclusion—as numbers are members of a set—but also much more. For this image suggests that members are not merely parts of, and swallowed up by, a group or collectivity; rather, they were members *of each other*. This involves, as I read it, three further elements: *mutuality*—each has a place and responsibilities that fit together with those of other members; *peerhood*—as I am included in you, you are included in me, we stand face to face as peers; and *diversity*—neither you nor I lose our identities because *as members* we occupy the same status. Membership-inflected relationships need not be emotionally intimate and they need not presuppose a rich set of shared values. What

[40] See Anderson, "What is the Point of Equality?," 287–337; Scheffler, "What is Egalitarianism?," 5–39; Postema, "Covenant Membership as a Community of Equals."

[41] Ephesians 4.25, also Romans 12.5.

members share is a commitment to the set of mutual responsibilities that provide the infrastructure of the relationship. Membership relationships may be intimate and ideologically homogeneous, but they can also be emotionally thin and ideologically diverse.

Membership relationships, like many other kinds of relationships, are often the objects of deep attachment for their members. For them, the value of the relationships, their practical force, lies in part in this historically contingent attachment.[42] But the value of membership relationships is not exhausted by this agent-relative value. The relationships are objectively valuable in themselves. Membership relationships are worthy of respect and promotion by non-members as well as by those who find themselves participating in them. Membership understood in this way is a moral-political value that can stand alongside justice, peace, and promotion of human rights.

I suggest that we can understand the grounding value of the rule-of-law ideal to be membership so understood. It explains why it is morally important to constrain and contain power that can be exercised over others in a given community. Domination of some members of the community by other members is inconsistent with the standing of those dominated as co-members. Not all exercises of power over others pose this threat, but those which are potentially arbitrary and not subject to accountability surely do. The constraints of legality would seem to be important means to achieving this tempering of power, but so too is a robust ethos of fidelity, each member taking responsibility for holding themselves and others accountable to the law. In accord with this value, fidelity calls for mutual accountability as well as mutual compliance. Members of a community protected by the rule of law are accorded the dignity and equality appropriate for incumbents in a membership relationship. As subjects of a common body of laws, rather than being subject to the power or authority of others, as Rundle puts it,[43] their status as peers is recognized and protected; mutuality is given structure and direction in their common responsibilities of accountability-holding. The faithfulness required by fidelity is owed not to the community or the government as its agent, nor to the law as its instrument, but to each other as co-members of a community in which law rules.

Moreover, community relationships realizing to some approximation the model of membership, protected by the rule of law, need not be emotionally intense or rooted in a large set of shared values; they need not be associations of individual human beings. They may be relatively thin communities of communities, or of nations. Thus, this understanding of the value grounding the rule of law can do service in transnational domains as well as national communities. And it recognizes the communal-relational orientation of much of thinking about the rule of law in its pre-modern history, while clearly making room for a liberal-democratic version of the account along lines defended by Fuller, Kramer, and others.

It is this value, I suggest, that rule of law serves when it is robust in a political community. By virtue of its appeal and force, it imposes a demand upon and offers a target of aspiration for political communities where it is weak or lacking. It provides a point of orientation for our thinking of what the rule-of-law ideal calls for in the historical

[42] See Wallace, *The View from Here*, 25–9.
[43] Rundle, *Forms Liberate*, 134, 139.

conditions of specific political communities. This value, surely, calls for more than the rule of law, because the rule of law serves it only by establishing institutions and an ethos that makes possible the tempering of power through the distinctive modalities of the law. Moreover, while the rule of law, well-grounded in this value, is morally considerable, it is not sovereign over all other important moral-political values, even though it demands that law be sovereign over all persons, institutions, and wielders of power. It stands alongside other key moral-political concerns, working where it can in partnership with them, but also sometimes in competition with them. Moral concerns that are more urgent in the circumstances can defeat its demands, and its moral force can be rendered nugatory if social and political conditions make it pointless to seek to serve the guiding value of membership by its means.

This understanding of the value of the rule-of-law ideal, like the suggestions made earlier in this chapter to broaden the scope of the ideal, and the attempt to bring the jurisprudential and moral conceptions of the rule of law closer together, go well beyond the limits of Kramer's admirable account and his arguments for it. Yet, as he gave precision to and built upon Fuller's influential reflections on the rule of law, I have attempted to build upon and extend the analytical frame he deployed in his important chapter.

PART III
GENERAL MATTERS OF ETHICS

10
Metasemantics, Moral Realism, and Moral Doctrines

Christine Tiefensee

1. Introduction

When I first read Matthew Kramer's *Moral Realism as a Moral Doctrine* together with the works of kindred spirits, I was rather taken aback. Could it be that when I had been thinking about metaethical issues, such as the existence of moral facts, the possibility of moral knowledge, the action-guiding character of moral judgments and the meaning of moral concepts, I had really been thinking about *moral* questions all along? Kramer (2009: 5) certainly appeared to suggest as much when explaining that "there is no fundamental divide between the meta-ethical and the ethical. Meta-ethical theses are distinctive in the specific issues that they address, ... but we should not make the mistake of thinking that their distinctiveness places them outside the domain of substantive ethical principles."

After a second read, the overall picture looked rather different. This revealed that in declaring metaethical positions to be moral doctrines, Kramer (2009: 12) understood metaethics as pertaining predominantly to "morality *tout court*" which, in turn, refers "to the whole array of correct ethical/moral standards that truly determine the ethical/moral consequences of people's conduct, and to the diverse categories and properties associated with those standards." Understood as narrowly as this, I was certainly happy to agree with Kramer's moral interpretation of metaethics. Still, two observations puzzled me. First, it was obvious that "metaethics" had traditionally been given a much wider reading than one which would limit its remit to morality's objectivity, and thus to the existence, nature and knowability of moral truths and facts. Rather, investigations into the meaning and function of moral vocabulary, the mental states expressed by moral judgments and the link between these judgments and motivation, have also commonly been regarded as classic examples of metaethical enquiry. But if Kramer's moral interpretation of metaethics concerned only theses about morality's objectivity, which status were we to attribute to these further paradigmatically metaethical enquiries? Would Kramer intend that they too must be regarded as moral investigations, or was his moral interpretation of metaethics supposed to leave them untouched? The second observation registered what appeared to be a striking overlap between moral realism as a moral doctrine on the one hand and sophisticated expressivism on the other. After all, philosophers such as Simon Blackburn (1998) and Allan Gibbard (2003) have also long maintained that defending the existence of moral facts, their mind-independence and knowability amounts to putting forward moral

Christine Tiefensee, *Metasemantics, Moral Realism, and Moral Doctrines* In: *Without Trimmings*. Edited by: Mark McBride and Visa AJ Kurki, Oxford University Press. © Mark McBride and Visa AJ Kurki 2022. DOI: 10.1093/oso/9780198868866.003.0010

positions which, as *participants* of moral discourse, they are both happy to endorse. As they also never tire of stressing, though, none of this is supposed to stand in any conflict with their metaethical expressivism. But if Blackburn, Gibbard, and Kramer agree on the moral interpretation of theses about morality's objectivity, how (if at all) do their views differ?

A third read, this time featuring one of Kramer's later papers, shed light on both sources of puzzlement. In *There's Nothing Quasi About Quasi-Realism*, Kramer distinguishes more clearly between Blackburn's and Gibbard's expressivism, by which he (2017: 198) understands an account of the pragmatics of moral discourse, and what he calls their quasi-realism, which he takes to cover the moral defense of morality's objectivity. Expressivism, Kramer now clarifies, does *not* amount to a moral doctrine, but remains to be understood as a non-moral, philosophical position. More precisely:

> [I]f the field of meta-ethics is understood more expansively than I have construed it when I have proclaimed that all meta-ethical doctrines are substantive ethical doctrines [namely, as pertaining only to propositions about the existence, nature, and objectivity of moral principles and properties], and specifically if that field is understood to include endeavors such as Blackburnian expressivism, then those endeavors should continue as they have unfolded hitherto (Kramer 2017: 208).

In contrast, quasi-realism as Kramer understands it *just is* moral realism as a moral doctrine, or so he (2017: 204) asserts: "That is, it affirms the objectivity of morality in several different senses, and it does so entirely on moral grounds."[1] Accordingly, since quasi-realism is moral realism as a moral doctrine, and since quasi-realism is fully compatible with expressivism, expressivist endeavors "are entirely consistent with moral realism as a moral doctrine, and they complement it nicely" (Kramer 2017: 208).

Again, this changed the overall picture significantly. When first reading about moral realism as a moral doctrine I, like many others, had conceived of it as aiming to add a *new* position to the metaethical landscape that would offer an alternative *both* to metaphysically substantive moral realism *and* expressivism. After all, Kramer and like-minded philosophers appeared to spend considerable time opposing not only metaphysically substantive realist approaches to moral discourse, but also expressivism and its distinctive theses about moral judgment.[2] However, now I understood that moral realism as a moral doctrine did not even seek to address the same questions as expressivism. Far from standing in competition with it, then, moral realism as a moral doctrine was to be "complemented nicely" by expressivism.

But if so, what exactly *is* the relationship between moral realism as a moral doctrine and expressivism? And in which way, if any, does moral realism as a moral doctrine add *new* considerations to the metaethical debate, or any other debate for that

[1] For related thoughts on expressivism, realism, representationalism, and non-representationalism, see Tiefensee, "Saving which Differences?."

[2] For instance, see Kramer, *Moral Realism as a Moral Doctrine*, ch. 8; Dworkin, "Objectivity and Truth: You'd Better Believe it," *Justice for Hedgehogs* ch. 3, 108–12; Scanlon, *Being Realistic about Reasons*, ch. 3; and Parfit, *On What Matters: Volume Two*, ch. 28.

matter? Providing responses to both questions will be the objective of this chapter. To the first, I will reply that Kramer is right in stating that moral realism as a moral doctrine does not stand in conflict with expressivism. But I will also go further, by submitting that moral realism as a moral doctrine *must* be combined with theories such as expressivism. To the second question, I will respond that moral realism as a moral doctrine does indeed have new arguments to offer, but that these arguments neither pertain to substantive first-order ethics as traditionally pursued by consequentialists and Kantians, say, nor to metaethical debate as undertaken by expressivists and metaphysically substantive moral realists. Indeed, I will argue that *qua* advocates of moral realism as a moral doctrine, moral realists such as Kramer *cannot* participate in this metaethical debate *exactly because* of their specific take on moral realism. Were Kramer's understanding the only available interpretation of moral realism, then, moral realism would disappear from the field of metaethical enquiry altogether. Consequently, I will conclude that if you do not want to accept positions such as expressivism, you cannot defend moral realism as a moral doctrine. Similarly, if you want moral realism to be a metaethical competitor of expressivism, you cannot accept Kramer's take on moral realism either. Moral realism as a moral doctrine stands and falls with theories such as expressivism, or so I shall argue.

In what follows, I will concur with many of Kramer's points. With regard to others, I will confess to uncertainty about whether or not Kramer and I agree.[3] And concerning others, I will simply disagree. As such, I will start in section 2 by specifying how I understand expressivism and moral realism as a moral doctrine. While I will predominantly follow Kramer's description of the latter, I will disagree with him about the former's characterization by suggesting that expressivism should not be located within pragmatics, but metasemantics. The term "quasi-realism," in turn, I will abandon altogether. How moral realism as a moral doctrine relates to metasemantic projects and why it needs to be combined with theories such as expressivism will then be explained in section 3. Discussion of what follows from this result for the development and success of moral realism as a moral doctrine and the new insights it can offer rounds off this contribution in section 4.

Importantly, the conclusions I will draw are not limited to Kramer's specific take on moral realism as a moral doctrine. Rather, they apply to all forms of moral realism which defend a minimalist, discourse-internal approach to moral facts, truths, and properties.[4] To pay heed to this observation—and since "moral realism as a moral doctrine" is, after all, quite a bit of a mouthful—I will henceforth refer to this family of approaches as "minimalist moral realism."

[3] Matthew Kramer has since confirmed that he agrees with everything I say in this contribution. Nonetheless, throughout this chapter I will flag whenever agreement between Kramer and I seemed in doubt, given certain passages of Kramer's published work.

[4] As such, this includes the positions of Nagel, *The View from Nowhere*; Scanlon, *Being Realistic about Reasons*; Parfit, *On What Matters: Volume Two*; and Dworkin, "Objectivity and Truth: You'd Better Believe it," and *Justice for Hedgehogs*. For metaphysically substantive realism, see Brink, *Moral Realism and the Foundations of Ethics*; Shafer-Landau, *Moral Realism. A Defence*; Enoch, *Taking Morality Seriously*; and Wedgwood, *The Nature of Normativity*. What I will call "minimalist" moral realism also goes under the heading of relaxed realism, quietism, or even anti-realist cognitivism.

For most of this chapter, I will follow Matthew Kramer in his narrow focus on ideationalist expressivism as defended by Simon Blackburn and Allan Gibbard. At the same time, several of my conclusions concern metasemantic non-representationalism more widely, where this includes ideationalist expressivism, but also non-ideationalist approaches such as inferentialism. Whenever this difference between expressivism and non-representationalism becomes relevant, I will indicate as much in order to make explicit to what exactly minimalist moral realists are committed.

2. Minimalist Moral Realism and Expressivism

Let me begin, then, by explicating how I understand this essay's two protagonists, minimalist moral realism and expressivism. Since I believe that employment of the notions "minimalist moral realism" and "expressivism" enables us to express everything that we want to say in this debate, I will drop the expression "quasi-realism" altogether. The term "quasi" has been the source of many misunderstandings in the past; hence, there is no need to invite further unnecessary confusion by employing it here.

Minimalist moral realism will be understood as comprising two theses. The first we have already encountered earlier: Claims about morality's objectivity, minimalist moral realists maintain, are themselves moral. Let us call this the "morality thesis." The second thesis then concerns the affirmation of specific claims about moral objectivity by declaring that morality is indeed objective. Let us call this the "objectivity thesis." I look at these in turn.

Starting with the morality thesis, minimalist moral realists hold that questions pertaining to the objectivity of morality do not concern non-moral, discourse-external queries, but moral, discourse-internal matters. As such, they adamantly reject substantively metaphysical approaches to moral discourse which seek to examine the existence of moral truths and facts, their nature, and knowability by appealing to general, discourse-external metaphysical and epistemological criteria such as causal efficacy, explanatory potency, or deliberative indispensability, say. Rather, all propositions about morality's objectivity are moral themselves, or so minimalist moral realists submit: They do not amount to propositions which we bring forth from *outside* moral discourse *about* the moral domain, but are moral claims which are to be defended from *within* moral discourse on the basis of *moral* arguments.

As Kramer (2017) rightly indicates, adopting minimalist conceptions of truth, fact, representation, and property plays a crucial role in this moral interpretation of theses about morality's objectivity, and it is not hard to see why.[5] For, if facts are, as minimalists maintain, no more than true statements, and if assigning truth to a statement is conceptually equivalent to asserting this very statement, then holding there to be a moral fact that lying to the electorate is wrong, say, simply amounts to making the

[5] Things are not quite as simple as I make out here, as I explain in Tiefensee, "Relaxing about Moral Truths." Still, as far as I am aware, all minimalist moral realists adopt minimalism about truth in some shape or form. For instance, see Scanlon, *Being Realistic about Reasons*, 43; Parfit, *On What Matters: Volume Two*, 756 n. 295) and Kramer, *Moral Realism as a Moral Doctrine*, 261. Dworkin's (*Justice for Hedgehogs*, 173) position is somewhat less clear, although his take on truth might still be categorized as minimalist.

moral assertion that lying to the electorate is wrong. Similarly, if properties are the shadows of predicates, then all it takes for the moral property of wrongness to exist is that a moral claim featuring the predicate "wrong" is true. Finally, if all that is required for a statement purportedly to represent some moral fact is for it to have assertoric form and ascribe a moral predicate to some object, moral statements are clearly representational. As such, minimalism removes any metaphysical overtones from notions such as "truth" and "fact" by regarding them not as metaphysically heavyweight concepts, but as useful devices that we employ in language to do certain things that would not be possible without them. Consequently, applying these notions in moral contexts also enables us to do something in relation to moral statements *within* moral discourse, rather than leading us to metaphysically substantive spheres outside of it. Of course, all of this is music to minimalist moral realists' ears. Unsurprisingly then, minimalism about semantic notions is the natural bedfellow of minimalist moral realism.

However, minimalist moral realists do not stop at the moral interpretation of claims concerning the objectivity of morality. Rather, as part of their objectivity thesis they also endorse and defend *specific* propositions about moral objectivity. As such, they declare that there are indeed moral facts and properties, that these facts and properties are mind-independent, and that they are epistemically accessible. They maintain further that we do have at least some moral knowledge, that (most) moral questions receive determinately correct moral answers and that we can, of course, err about which moral answers are indeed correct. Hence, whereas minimalist moral realism's morality thesis concerns the moral categorization of propositions about moral objectivity, its objectivity thesis targets the actual vindication of moral objectivity from within moral discourse. As such, the former explains in which way Kramer and like-minded philosophers are *minimalist* moral realists; the latter explains why they are minimalist moral *realists*.

Note that given my understanding of this position, minimalist moral realism's defense of morality's objectivity concerns predominantly moral metaphysics and moral epistemology. Kramer (2017: 204), in turn, would also want to add semantics to this list. Without arguing this point here, let me merely register my disagreement: Whilst certain aspects of moral terms' semantics—as, for instance, fixing the specific extension of moral expressions such as "right" and "good," say—do indeed concern moral matters, others—including the truth-aptitude and purportedly representational character of moral sentences—do not.[6] Whenever I speak of morality's objectivity, I will, therefore, predominantly have moral metaphysics and moral epistemology in mind.

[6] To provide no more than the slightest of hints about the reasons for my disagreement, let me start with truth-aptitude, which Kramer locates within the moral domain. Indeed, he, "There's Nothing Quasi About Quasi-Realism: Moral Realism as a Moral Doctrine," 205, not only agrees with Dworkin that "the question whether moral judgments can be true or false is a substantive moral issue, not a distinct meta-ethical one," but also believes this position to be "uncontroversial" and that "Blackburn would certainly agree with [it]." I disagree and, I believe, so would Blackburn. First, the truth-aptitude of moral statements—together with their assertoric, representational, descriptive character—is to be explained by metasemantics, not by moral theorizing. That is, Blackburn's thoughts about the use and function of moral terms do not merely "[alert us] to the fact that the semantics of such discourse are (minimalistically) objective along the lines expounded by quasi-realism," as Kramer, "There's Nothing Quasi About Quasi-Realism: Moral Realism as a Moral Doctrine," 204 n. 16, puts it, but provide a metasemantic *explanation* of this descriptive, assertoric character of moral sentences. Accordingly, when asked how it comes about that moral sentences have assertoric form and can be ascribed truth-values, Blackburn would not provide a moral response; rather, he would explain

Which immediate conclusions follow from this characterization? Most importantly, we can see that minimalist moral realism is only *partly* a moral doctrine. More precisely, while its second, distinctly realist objectivity thesis about moral metaphysics and epistemology is indeed moral, its morality thesis concerning the moral interpretation of moral objectivity, is not. Rather, since the morality thesis is based on minimalism about semantic notions, and since minimalism is not a moral position but one that is to be defended within metasemantics and philosophical logic, minimalist moral realism's distinctive morality thesis crucially depends on non-moral considerations that are to be put forward and settled outside of moral discourse. Indeed, it is this theme of minimalist moral realism's non-moral commitments which will continue to occupy me for the remainder of this chapter.

However, before we can tackle these issues, we first need to clarify how to understand the position of expressivism. Here, three observations are particularly significant. The first concerns expressivism's general characterization, the second its connection to minimalist moral realism's morality thesis, and the third its relation to the latter's objectivity thesis. Much of what I will say in the context of these observations will be familiar to those who are well-acquainted with expressivism. Still, it will be helpful to repeat these insights here in order to achieve a better grasp on minimalist moral realism's relationship to expressivism.

Starting with expressivism's general characterization, I have already hinted that contrary to traditional understandings, Kramer (2017: 200) suggests that expressivism should not be interpreted as providing a semantics of moral sentences, but as presenting an account of the pragmatics of moral discourse:

> That is, instead of aiming to supply an exposition of what moral utterances mean, expressivism should be aiming to supply an exposition of what people do by engaging in such utterances and by articulating them in propositional forms. It should be endeavoring to chart what people achieve at practical levels by suffusing their interactions with moral judgments.

that moral sentences have this form because otherwise they could not realize their practical function. On the one hand, Kramer, "There's Nothing Quasi About Quasi-Realism: Moral Realism as a Moral Doctrine," 204 n. 16, appears to acknowledge as much when explaining that "[w]ere the semantics not objective in that fashion, moral discourse could not fulfill its central functions." On the other hand, I must admit that I struggle to square this acknowledgment with Kramer's moral interpretation of truth-aptitude. To offer a cautious diagnosis of this seeming mismatch, my hunch is that by locating expressivism within pragmatics, Kramer attributes to expressivism a more detached relationship with semantics than my metasemantic interpretation of expressivism would allow.

Just as theses about truth-aptitude do not fall into the moral domain, it also appears implausible to hold all components of semantics to be moral. To use a particularly clear example, take a quick look at the semantics of "ought." Here, we can see that spelling out the general truth-conditions of ought-claims along the lines of Kratzer-style (1981) deontic semantics is not a moral exercise. Quite the opposite: it is widely regarded to be a boon of this semantics that it provides the *same* general semantic formula for moral *and* non-moral uses of deontic operators alike. Importantly, this does not mean that moral considerations are irrelevant for this semantic project. However, they enter the scene only when determining the truth-value of specific moral ought-sentences, namely by examining which moral ordering source is to be plugged into the general Kratzer-style semantic formula. Determining the general semantic schema for deontic operators, though, remains a non-moral exercise. As a result, contrary to Kramer I will predominantly focus on moral metaphysics and epistemology when discussing moral objectivity.

I agree that expressivism should not be understood as a semantic theory. I also agree that considerations about the use of moral vocabulary play a key role in expressivist thinking. Still, despite its being a pragmat*ist* theory, I disagree that expressivism should be located within the field of pragmatics. After all, expressivism does not take the semantic meaning of moral assertoric sentences as given, to consider subsequently how these sentences are used within our practices. Rather, it examines the use of moral utterances in our practices because it takes meaning to be grounded in use.[7] In short, expressivism is best understood as a pragmatist *metasemantic* theory, which explains in virtue of what it is that moral sentences possess their specific meanings.[8] As such, it neither suspends judgment on what constitutes semantic meaning, as pragmatic theories would do, nor aims to attribute literal meanings to expressions, as semantic theories would do. Rather, it explains *why* expressions have these meanings, *why* names have their specific referents, and *why* predicates have their particular extensions.[9]

What makes expressivism distinctive, in turn, is how it sets out to answer these metasemantic questions. That is, in contrast to metasemantic representationalism, it does not seek to explain the meaning of moral expressions such as "good" or "ought" in terms of what these expressions represent in the world, say by specifying that "good" means GOOD because it stands in a representational relation to goodness, whereas "ought" means OUGHT because it represents some worldly ought-relation. Rather, expressivism pursues a distinctively *non*-representationalist approach, according to which these expressions have their specific meanings not because of what they *represent*, but because of how they are *used*. As such, ideationalist expressivists, such as Blackburn (1998) and Gibbard (2003), hold that moral sentences have their meanings in virtue of the mental states that these sentences are used to express, where these mental states are non-representational and play a specific role in motivation. In contrast, inferentialist

[7] Again, I am not entirely sure if Kramer would disagree with this characterization. On the one hand, some of Kramer's, "There's Nothing Quasi About Quasi-Realism: Moral Realism as a Moral Doctrine," 204 n. 16, explanations sound as if he comes at least close to acknowledging an interpretation of expressivism along these metasemantic lines. On the other hand, this metasemantic characterization entails consequences which Kramer seemingly wants to reject. First, these include implications for our understanding of moral sentences' truth-aptitude and purportedly representational character as explained in n. 6. Secondly and relatedly, they concern expressivism's quest for internal adequacy that will be explained below. Accordingly, I suspend judgment on whether or not Kramer would agree both with this metasemantic interpretation of expressivism and the thoughts on internal adequacy as will be spelt out shortly.

[8] This interpretation has gathered much support in recent years. As a small sample, see Chrisman, *The Meaning of "Ought," Beyond Descriptivism and Expressivism in Metaethics* and "Conceptual Role Accounts of Meaning in Metaethics"; Köhler, "Expressivism, Meaning, and All *That*"; Ridge, *Impassioned Belief*; Schroeter and Schroeter, "The Generalized Integration Challenge in Metaethics; and Tiefensee, "Saving which Differences?". For semantic interpretations of expressivism, see Rosen, "Blackburn's Essays in Quasi-Realism"; Schroeder, *Being For: Evaluating the Semantic Program of Expressivism)*; and Wedgwood, *The Nature of Normativity*.

[9] Although metasemantic accounts do not answer semantic questions, they have to explain what makes it the case that sentences can be modeled along the lines of a specific semantic theory. For instance, while we should not expect expressivists to assign specific semantic contents to "ought" claims, we should demand that they be able to explain in which way a Kratzer-style deontic semantics provides an adequate model for deontic expressions, given their expressivist metasemantics. *Pace* Kramer, "There's Nothing Quasi About Quasi-Realism: Moral Realism as a Moral Doctrine," 199–200, this also means that placing expressivism outside of semantics does not eschew problems associated with the Frege-Geach problem, but rather relocates them to another level. For both points, see Schroeter and Schroeter, "The Generalized Integration Challenge in Metaethics," 13.

non-representationalists, such as Brandom (1994) and Chrisman (2016), suggest (simplifying greatly) that moral sentences obtain their meanings by fulfilling a specific metaconceptual role within the game of giving and asking for reasons, which consists in making inferential relations explicit that would otherwise remain implicit. Although my alliances lie with the latter, which of these non-representationalist accounts we should adopt will not be important for my purposes. What will be important is, rather, that all expressivist accounts are forms of metasemantic non-representationalism, in that they eschew appeal to notions such as representation, truth, and reference when spelling out what constitutes moral terms' meaning.

Expressivism's non-representationalism also proves key for our second observation concerning its connection to minimalist moral realism's morality thesis. As I have remarked in the introduction, expressivists agree with minimalist moral realists that questions pertaining to morality's objectivity concern moral matters. Yet, besides endorsing the morality thesis, their non-representationalism also provides its theoretical foundation.

To see why, remember that I have just said that the morality thesis crucially relies on minimalist interpretations of notions such as "true," "fact," and "refers." But, we may ask, why should we accept minimalism in the first place? Non-representationalists provide an answer: Minimalism, they argue, should be accepted exactly because we cannot understand the meaning of notions such as "true" and "refers" on the basis of representationalist considerations about the property of truth or some metaphysically robust reference relation, but rather by considering what these concepts allow us to *do* within our language and practices. Put differently, minimalism is a non-representationalist theory about semantic notions, just as expressivism and inferentialism are non-representationalist accounts of moral notions. As such, non-representationalism weaves the golden thread linking expressivism, minimalism, and minimalist moral realism's morality thesis by embedding these positions within the wider metasemantic framework it provides.

The third and final observation concerns expressivism's relation to minimalist moral realism's objectivity thesis. I have already hinted that *qua* expressivists—and thus *qua* participants of *metasemantic* debate—philosophers such as Simon Blackburn and Allan Gibbard do not affirm morality's objectivity. This is not surprising: Since we have already specified in our discussion of the morality thesis that defending the existence of moral truths, their mind-independence, and knowability amounts to putting forward moral positions within moral discourse, endorsing the objectivity thesis cannot be part of metasemantic debate, but can only ever comprise adopting a specific stance in *moral* discourse. Still, even though Blackburn and Gibbard endorse moral objectivity not as expressivists, but as participants of moral practice, expressivism nonetheless aims to explain on a purely expressivist basis what is involved in defending this objectivity thesis within moral discourse. That is, as demanded by what has become known as the requirement of "internal adequacy" (Gibbard 2003: 186), in order to be successful expressivism must be able to account for what moral reasoners do when engaging in moral truth and fact talk, when defending moral properties' mind-independence and endorsing the existence of moral knowledge.

Given as much, expressivism neither entails nor endorses the claim that there are moral truths. Rather, it restricts itself to explaining that someone evaluating as true that lying to the electorate is morally wrong, expresses disapproval toward lying to the electorate. Similarly, expressivism neither entails nor endorses the mind-independence of moral properties. Instead, it goes no further than explaining that anybody defending the mind-independence of moral properties expresses disapproval of a certain dispositional setup and approval of an alternative. Nor does expressivism entail or endorse the possibility of moral knowledge. Rather, it seeks to explain (again simplifying greatly) that anybody attributing moral knowledge to someone else attributes a certain attitude to this person, whilst also endorsing this attitude herself. Accordingly, *qua* expressivists Blackburn and Gibbard do not seek to vindicate the objectivity thesis by defending the existence of moral truths and properties, their mind-independence, and knowability. Rather, they only ever aim to explain what is involved in defending this thesis by vindicating internal features of moral practice on a fully non-representationalist basis.[10]

Which immediate conclusions follow from these observations about expressivism's relationship with minimalist moral realism? On the one hand, we can see that whilst expressivism is compatible with minimalist moral realism, it does not entail it: Rather, expressivism is compatible with moral properties' mind-independence and knowability as defended by moral realists, just as it is compatible with their mind-dependence as championed by constructivists and epistemic inaccessibility as suggested by the skeptic. Accordingly, expressivists *can* but *need not* be minimalist moral realists. Whether or not they are is an open, distinct question that depends on which *moral* positions they seek to defend, not as expressivists but as participants of moral practice.

On the other hand, Kramer has already hinted in his more recent work that minimalist moral realists can be expressivists: expressivism, he states, complements minimalist moral realism nicely. We have already seen one aspect of this complementary relationship, in that non-representationalism, of which expressivism is one example, provides the theoretical underpinning for minimalist moral realists' morality thesis by supporting minimalist interpretations of semantic notions. However, it is not just the case that minimalist moral realists *can* be expressivists. Rather, as I will argue next, minimalist moral realists *must* accept some non-representationalist theory such as expressivism as the correct account of moral language if they want to preserve their minimalist take on moral realism. Before making my case, though, I first need to say a few more words about minimalist moral realism's general relationship to metasemantic enquiries into moral vocabulary.

3. Minimalist Moral Realism and Metasemantics

So far, I have distinguished between two separate kinds of endeavors: first, the *non-moral*, metasemantic project of accounting for the meaning of expressions including semantic notions and moral terms such that internal adequacy is achieved and, secondly, the *moral* project of establishing morality's objectivity. Minimalist moral

[10] For difference senses of vindication, see Tiefensee, *Expressivism, Minimalism and Moral Doctrines*, ch. 6.1.

realism is clearly involved in this second project. By suggesting that minimalist moral realists must accept some non-representationalist theory such as expressivism as the correct account of moral language, I presume that they must also take a stance on the first endeavor. But must they?

One might think that our answer should be negative. After all, what makes minimalist moral realism *minimalist* is its opposition to substantively metaphysical enquiries into moral discourse, holding instead that questions about morality's objectivity concern moral, and not non-moral matters. Accordingly, it might be argued that just as minimalist moral realists reject discourse-external meta*physical* investigations into moral discourse, they should also reject any discourse-external meta*semantic* studies about moral vocabulary. Hence, when asked how it comes about that moral words acquire their respective meanings, it could be suggested that minimalist moral realists should simply refuse to offer a response and declare instead that this is not a question that they, or anybody else for that matter, should seek to answer.

I find this suggestion utterly unconvincing. Whilst I am very sympathetic to the view that nothing metaphysically interesting can be said about morality's objectivity, there must be something informative that we can say about why "good" means GOOD, rather than RIGHT, TREE, or BIG, say. After all, neither are meanings simply brute facts, nor do moral notions receive their meanings "by magic," as Wedgwood (2007: 19) puts it. Accordingly, refusing to engage with metasemantic questions, denying their significance or adopting quietism about meaning, is not a convincing strategy for anybody to adopt. Rather, minimalist moral realists—as with anybody else—must be able to say *something* about the meaning of moral vocabulary. And this "something" must, of course, be such that it does not conflict with *anything else* minimalist moral realists would want to proclaim about moral metaphysics, moral epistemology, and the objectivity of morality.[11]

Kramer appears to agree. For instance, when discussing Wedgwood's (2007: 19) declaration that it would seem "incredible that it could be an absolutely unanalysable feature of a particular thought or statement that it is about one thing rather than another," Kramer (2017: 209–10) does not push back by denying that the metasemantic magic to which Wedgwood alludes would be incredible, but by pointing out that it would be wrong to assume that minimalist moral realism is committed to the unanalyzability of moral thought. Similarly, in response to Jamie Dreier's (2004: 35) challenge to fill in the blank in (G):

(E) Edith said that abortion is wrong.
(G) Its being the case that (E) consists of nothing more than ____,

Kramer (2017: 2010) declares:

> Dreier chidingly refers to "lazy theorists [who] might just try [to fill in the blank by] more or less repeating (E)." Filling in the blank by largely repeating E would of course

[11] Compare also Schroeter and Schroeter's, "The Generalized Integration Challenge in Metaethics," 194, related "generalized integration challenge" at this point, i.e., the "task of providing, for a given area, a simultaneously acceptable metaphysics, epistemology and metasemantics, and showing them to be so."

> be correct, but no proponent of moral realism as a moral doctrine has to rest content with that stark approach. Equally apt as a way of filling in the blank would be "Edith's having ascribed to the act-type of abortion the basic moral status that is conferred or would be conferred on that act-type by any moral principle that prohibits abortion." This latter way of filling in the blank is more controversial than the E-repeating approach—it would need to be defended (on moral grounds) against devotees of moral particularism, for example—but a proponent of moral realism as a moral doctrine can happily adopt it.

Again, Kramer thus appears to accept Dreier's challenge whilst rejecting the claim that minimalist moral realists have nothing informative to say about how to fill in the blank in (G). Still, whilst it should be clear that I fully support Kramer in picking up Dreier's gauntlet, I also believe that he provides the wrong kind of response to the challenge at hand.

To elaborate, the most plausible reading of Wedgwood's and Dreier's thoughts is, I believe, to interpret them as posing—you will have guessed it—a metasemantic challenge.[12] That is, just as Wedgwood asks us to explain *what makes it the case* that a particular thought is about one thing rather than another, Dreier asks us to explain *what makes it the case* that the sentence uttered by Edith means one thing rather than another. However, Kramer's response:

> (K) Its being the case that Edith said that abortion is wrong consists of nothing more than Edith's having ascribed to the act-type of abortion the basic moral status that is conferred or would be conferred on that act-type by any moral principle that prohibits abortion

does not address this question. First, noting that Edith ascribes the moral status of wrongness to abortion correctly describes Edith's statement, but does not tell us in virtue of what it is that the term "wrong" means WRONG and refers to wrongness. Secondly, explaining the meaning of "wrong" by appeal to other expressions, such as "being prohibited by a moral principle," might engage in the project of explicating the semantic meaning of "wrong," but again fails to provide a metasemantic explanation of how "wrong" obtains this meaning. To be absolutely clear, then, there is nothing wrong with (K) as such. Still, as a response to Dreier's challenge, it misses the point.

How, then, should Kramer and other minimalist moral realists respond instead? Here, two alternatives are conceivable. First, they could seek to develop a *novel*, distinctly minimalist-realist metasemantics of moral vocabulary and thus provide a response to Dreier's challenge which follows neither expressivists' non-representationalism nor the representationalism that metaphysically substantive moral realists will want to defend. In this case, minimalist moral realists would plant their own, new flag within the non-moral, metasemantic landscape and enter into genuine competition both with non-representationalism as defended by expressivists and representationalism as advanced by metaphysically substantive moral realists.

[12] For more on this interpretation, see Simpson, "Solving the Problem of Creeping Minimalism" and Dreier, "Metaethics and the Problem of Creeping Minimalism".

Secondly, they could fall back on *established* metasemantic responses that other metaethicists, such as expressivists and moral realists, have already developed. If so, minimalist moral realists would not add to the metasemantic debate, nor seek to compete with the metasemantics suggested by others. Instead, they would simply adopt whatever metasemantics is currently on offer that suits their moral defense of moral objectivity best. Which of these two alternatives is it going to be? I have already laid my cards on the table: I believe not only that minimalist moral realists *should* combine their account with an established metasemantic position, but also that they *cannot help* but do so. And this established account will inevitably be non-representationalism as defended—albeit not exclusively—by expressivists.

To see why, let us return to our distinction between the two metasemantic schools introduced above, representationalism and non-representationalism. Representationalists, we have said, explain the meaning of an expression on the basis of the relation that this expression bears to what it is about. For instance (and oversimplifying greatly), the term "tree" means TREE because our use of this term is causally regulated by trees; "bicycle" and "clock" have different meanings because they stand for different objects in the world; in order to find out what "good" means, we must discover to which property this term refers, etc. Non-representationalists, we have further said, reject this order of explanation. That is, rather than asking what a term stands for, they submit that we need to ask which role it plays in our language and practices in order to find out about its meaning. As such, "true" means what it does not because it refers to the property of truth, but because of its logical function in language; "good" obtains its meaning not because of its representation of goodness, but because it allows us to express certain motivational states, say; "tree" means TREE not because it stands in a metaphysically robust reference relation to trees, but because of what the use of "tree" commits and entitles us to infer within the game of giving and asking for reasons, where this includes, but is not exhausted by, considerations about our causal reactions to trees. Crucially, as these examples show, non-representationalism does *not* imply that all vocabularies fulfill the *same* function—far from it. Still, whichever role they play, it is this role which explains their meaning.

These two schools of representationalism and non-representationalism are generally taken to exhaust the metasemantic spectrum. Accordingly, minimalist moral realists must join one of them. Due to their own metaphysically lightweight commitments about moral properties, it is clear that this cannot be metasemantic representationalism.

To elaborate, note that by explaining meaning in terms of notions such as truth, reference, and representation, representationalism requires that these semantic notions shoulder explanatory weight within our account of meaning. Minimalist conceptions of these notions, though, cannot perform such an explanatory role. Since the minimalist truth-schema " 'S' is true iff S" presupposes that we know what "S" means, this schema cannot be used to explain the meaning of "S." Similarly, if properties are the shadows of predicates, we first need an understanding of the latter before we can make any judgments about the former. And if reference is not understood as a robust relation between words and the world, but is abstracted from meaning assignments so as to make sentences come out as true, reference assignments cannot precede meaning assignments, but must follow them.

In a nutshell, then, since representationalism requires semantic notions to feature in explanations of meaning, and since minimalist semantic notions cannot fulfil such an explanatory role, representationalism presupposes substantive conceptions of truth, reference, and properties. Yet, we said earlier that minimalist moral realists reject any such substantive interpretations by supporting minimalism about semantic properties. Accordingly, minimalist moral realists cannot be representationalists about moral vocabulary. Instead, they must join expressivists in being metasemantic non-representationalists.

Still, you might think that this does not quite settle the matter of minimalist moral realists' metasemantic position. After all, as I have indicated above, non-representationalists never tire of stressing that different vocabularies fulfill different functions, such that the notion "tree," for instance, plays a very different role within our language and practices than the term "true," say. Moreover, I have hinted that when spelling out the conceptual role of "tree," we must take into account our disposition to react to trees, whereas we need not include any such disposition to react to the property of truth when specifying the logical function of "true." Accordingly, could we not declare, *within* non-representationalism, that those vocabularies which work like "tree" fulfill a specifically *representational* function, whereas those which function more like "true" fulfill a *non*-representational role? Furthermore, could we not use this distinction to drive a wedge between minimalist moral realism and expressivism, in that minimalist moral realists could assimilate the function of moral terms such as "good" to that of "tree," whereas expressivists would declare that "good" functions more like "true"—and do all of this *within* the general metasemantics of non-representationalism?

The answer to the first question is "Yes"; however, that to the second is "No." More precisely, we can indeed introduce within the general approach of non-representationalism the distinction between representational and non-representational vocabularies as roughly suggested here. However, even if this is so, minimalist moral realists cannot assign moral vocabulary to the representational category. Again, it is their commitment to minimalism which explains why. To elaborate, note that all assertions qualify as being representational if "representational" is given a minimalist reading: Mathematical assertions truly or falsely represent what mathematical reality is like; aesthetic statements truly or falsely represent the aesthetic properties of our surroundings; empirical and moral assertions truly or falsely represent what the natural and moral worlds are like respectively, and so on. *Minimalist* representation, then, cannot sort assertoric sentences into those which fulfill a representational function and those whose function is non-representational. Hence, if having a representational function is to make it possible to distinguish between vocabularies that perform this function and those that do not, "representation" must be given a more substantive reading than minimalism about representation allows.[13]

[13] Compare Chrisman, *The Meaning of "Ought": Beyond Descriptivism and Expressivism in Metaethics*, 204 n. 1, on this point, who explains that "a sentence carries descriptive content just in case its use to make an assertion carries direct inferential consequences about the way reality is. (Roughly, it has to imply that reality is matched by its truth condition, whatever theses happen to be)," where this "matching" must be more substantive "than the deflationary way of a predicate being true of [an object]."

What exactly this substantive sense of representation involves need not concern us here.[14] Rather, it is sufficient to point out that by presupposing *some* substantive conception of representation, ascribing a representational function to moral vocabulary is incompatible with minimalist moral realism, given its rejection of any such substantive interpretation of moral representation. Accordingly, even if we introduce within non-representationalism the distinction between representational and non-representational vocabularies—as I believe we should—minimalist moral realists must join expressivists in ascribing a non-representational function to moral vocabulary.

Accordingly, we have now reached the point where we can see not only that expressivism *complements* minimalist moral realism, but also that minimalist moral realists *must* join expressivists in their defense of non-representationalism: Since they cannot withdraw to quietism about meaning due to quietism's general implausibility, and since they are barred from adopting metasemantic representationalism or ascribing a representational function to moral vocabulary due to their own minimalist commitments about moral discourse, minimalist moral realists have no choice but to team up with expressivists on the side of non-representationalism.[15]

4. Where Minimalist Moral Realism Shines

As a result, we now know that minimalist moral realists do not add a novel, distinctly minimalist-realist metasemantics of moral vocabulary to metasemantic debate, but rather must side with expressivists in their defense of non-representationalism. But even if so, could they, *qua* minimalist moral realists, still offer any new insights to these non-representationalist positions and metasemantic debate? Alternatively, could they offer any new insights to any other debate? I believe that our answer to the first question should be "No"; however, to the second we should respond with a "Yes."

Starting with the first question, let me begin by noting that even though we have now established that minimalist moral realists must be non-representationalists, this does not settle which kind of non-representationalism they should accept. As considered by Kramer, they may, of course, choose to adopt ideationalist expressivism as advocated by Blackburn (1998), Gibbard (2003), and Ridge (2014). Alternatively, they could opt for Brandom's (1994) and Chrisman's (2016) inferentialist non-representationalism, which seeks to explain meaning on the basis of inferential relations. There might also be further versions. Yet, although I lean toward combining minimalist moral realism with inferentialism, which variety of non-representationalism

[14] For instance, it might be fleshed out in terms of causal relations between us and what we describe (Brink, *Moral Realism and the Foundations of Ethics*); appeal to natural selection (Sinclair, "The Moral Belief Problem"); a substantive sense of property which constrains the conceptual role of corresponding predicates (Wedgwood, *The Nature of Normativity*); deliberative indispensability (Enoch, *Taking Morality Seriously*); specific explanations of success (Boyd, "How to be a Moral Realist"); language entry transitions (Tiefensee, "Inferentialism, Bifurcations and Ontological Commitment"), or some other substantive account of description and representation.

[15] Again, note that expressivism is not the only available form of non-representationalism: For instance, minimalist moral realism could also be combined with inferentialism (Tiefensee, "Metasemantics for the Relaxed"). I say more on this below.

minimalist moral realists should adopt shall not be my concern here. Instead, let me point out that no matter which of these versions they choose, minimalist moral realists will, of course, neither need to accept everything expressivists and inferentialists say about moral vocabulary, nor regard themselves as being barred from making new suggestions as to how these respective takes on moral vocabulary can be expanded and further improved—always making sure, of course, that whatever they suggest will achieve the best possible fit with their specific moral take on the objectivity of morality.[16] Still, when developing these suggestions, they will not, and cannot, do so *qua* moral realists and thus as defenders of moral objectivity. *Minimalist* moral properties, *minimalist* moral facts, and *minimalist* moral representation, I have argued earlier, cannot play any explanatory role within our account of meaning. Accordingly, if Kramer and his kindred spirits offered new suggestions within the realm of metasemantics, they would do so not as minimalist moral realists, but as non-moral metasemanticists whose aim it is to provide the best non-moral account of moral language that is compatible with their moral interpretation of claims about moral objectivity. *Qua* realists, minimalist moral realists simply have nothing to contribute to this metasemantic debate.

This, in turn, has two important implications. First, observing that the minimalist take on moral objectivity necessitates a non-representationalist metasemantics entails that the success of minimalist moral realism depends on the success of non-representationalism. More precisely, if non-representationalist theories such as expressivism *failed* to achieve internal adequacy—that is, if they could *not* successfully account for those propositions about moral objectivity that minimalist moral realists seek to defend within moral discourse—minimalist moral realists could no longer defend both the objectivity of morality and its minimalist interpretation, but would have to choose between them: Either, they could continue to defend morality's objectivity, but would now have to adopt representationalism and thus a substantive approach to moral facts and properties in order to account successfully for propositions about morality's objectivity. Or they could cling on to non-representationalism and minimalist interpretations of theses about moral truths and properties, but would now have to declare that these are not fully objective. Either way, if you believe that non-representationalist theories such as expressivism fail to be internally adequate, you cannot be a minimalist moral realist.

Secondly, finding that the minimalist take on moral objectivity requires a non-representationalist metasemantics shows that you cannot be a minimalist moral realist and yet hold moral realism to stand in conflict with theories such as expressivism. Rather, you once more face a choice: Either, you can hold that minimalist moral realists' view on moral objectivity is correct, but must now accept that moral realism cannot compete with non-representationalist theories such as expressivism. Or you believe that moral realism and expressivism do stand in conflict with one another, but must now abandon minimalist moral realism in favor of a representationalist account of moral vocabulary which presupposes substantive understandings of moral facts

[16] For instance, I (Tiefensee, "Metasemantics for the Relaxed") try to do so when presenting a new inferentialist account of evaluative moral notions that seeks to supplement inferentialists' focus on deontic operators such as "ought" with an inferentialist take on evaluative notions such as "good."

and properties.[17] Either way, holding moral realism to compete with theories such as expressivism is incompatible with being a minimalist moral realist.

But, we may ask, if *qua* moral realists, minimalist moral realists cannot contribute new insights to metasemantic debate, can they offer anything new to any *other* debate? Yes: they have a lot to offer to *moral* debate. Here, I do not have in mind paradigmatic first-order ethical debate as pursued by consequentialists and Kantians, say. Rather, minimalist moral realists can present novel and interesting arguments exactly about those *abstract* questions regarding moral objectivity which, as Kramer (2009: 11) repeatedly stresses, are still part of moral discourse. Accordingly, we should not expect minimalist moral realists to devise novel metasemantic accounts of meaning. Nor should we expect them to present answers to concrete moral questions, such as "Is it morally permissible not to treat patients with underlying health conditions?," "Are all equal resource distributions just?," or "Did Boris act morally recklessly?." Instead, we should expect minimalist moral realists to develop novel responses to abstract moral questions such as "Are there determinately correct answers to moral problems?," "Are moral truths mind-independent and if so, in which way?," and "Can our moral beliefs be false when we are in a state of ideal rational reflection?." Importantly, given their degree of abstraction, answering these questions requires very different arguments from providing responses to concrete moral queries. For instance, when asked about moral determinacy, we cannot simply respond that moral questions receive determinately true answers because it is true that breaking Emma's confidence is permissible, given that doing so will prevent great harm. Instead, we have to explain—*on moral grounds*—why it is true that claims such as "Either breaking Emma's confidence is permissible, or it is not permissible" hold.[18] Importantly, providing such moral answers to abstract moral questions is far from straightforward. Accordingly, it is with regard to the development of such abstract, moral arguments about moral objectivity that minimalist moral realism shines.

[17] While certain metaphysically substantive moral realists clearly opt for metasemantic representationalism (Brink, *Moral Realism and the Foundations of Ethics*; Boyd, "How to be a Moral Realist"), the assessment of other substantive realist accounts, such as Wedgwood's conceptual role account, is a little trickier, since Wedgwood combines his conceptual role account with a substantive theory of truth (Wedgwood, *The Nature of Normativity*). I ignore these complexities here.

[18] Compare Tiefensee, "Relaxing about Moral Truths," for further details on this example.

11

Distinguishing Value-Neutrality from Value-Independence

Toward a New Disentangling Strategy for Moral Epistemology

*Lubomira Radoilska**

1. Introduction

What are the prospects of conceptual analysis as a core methodology for normative theory? Could it respond to proponents of the so-called non-ideal theory highlighting such challenges as undue de-contextualization of ethical thought and unfair differentials of power within knowledge production and recognition? In this chapter, I consider the nature and scope of conceptual analysis in Kramer (2018)[1] as promising ground for a new, comprehensive disentangling strategy that can address these and related challenges in moral epistemology.

The discussion will proceed as follows. In section 2, I explore the distinction between value-neutrality and value-independence as two separate aspects of methodological austerity introduced by Kramer. The ambition is to show that this distinction is fundamental to understanding conceptual analysis in terms of dialogical inquiry advancing toward greater agreement. In section 3, I make a case for expanding on this understanding of conceptual analysis toward a comprehensive disentangling strategy that would apply to theoretical-explanatory values on a par with distinctly ethical values. In the final section 4, I focus on two major challenges in moral epistemology that arise from collapsing the fact/value dichotomy—globalized skepticism and debate fragmentation. I show that both challenges can be successfully addressed by a thorough disentangling strategy that encompasses both dimensions of conceptual analysis—value-neutrality vs. value non-neutrality and value-independence vs. value-dependence.

2. A Methodology for the Search of Justice

The distinction between value-independence and value-neutrality is introduced within the context of a wider methodological discussion aiming to establish the nature

* Department of Philosophy, University of Kent, UK and African Centre for Epistemology and Philosophy of Science, University of Johannesburg, South Africa.

[1] Kramer, "Conceptual Analysis and Distributive Justice."

Lubomira Radoilska, *Distinguishing Value-Neutrality from Value-Independence* In: *Without Trimmings*. Edited by: Mark McBride and Visa AJ Kurki, Oxford University Press. © Mark McBride and Visa AJ Kurki 2022.
DOI: 10.1093/oso/9780198868866.003.0011

and scope of conceptual analysis in contemporary political philosophy. Principal theories of distributive justice are considered as a case in point. By comparing and contrasting the underlying approaches in the works of philosophers such as John Rawls, Ronald Dworkin, and Joseph Raz, Matthew Kramer argues that conceptual analysis rarely fits the textbook picture of specification of necessary and sufficient conditions for the applicability of a concept.[2] Properly understood, it consists instead in a multi-level collaborative progression from a thin, high-level agreement to ever thicker levels of consequent theorizing that emerge as a result of philosophers taking divergent paths of moral reasoning rather than applying, more or less aptly, the same formal procedure.[3] The fact that conceptual analysis is multi-layered is significant on Kramer's view. For it allows us to employ the distinction between the overall concept of justice and the various competing conceptions, to which it gives rise, without assuming that they all stand, as it were, on the same plane. This bears on our ability to identify correctly the crux of the disagreements between different theories of justice. As Kramer points out with respect to Rawls's theory of justice as fairness: 'more than one level intervenes between that thin concept [of distributive justice] and ... his two lexically ordered principles that are applicable to the major legal-governmental institutions of any society.[4] Thus, at a higher level, there is thin agreement across liberal as well as illiberal theories of justice grounded in the exclusion of arbitrary distinctions as unjust that both sets of theories support. At a lower level, there is thicker agreement that obtains only across liberal theories in the broad sense. This agreement is rooted in the understanding of all persons as free and fundamentally equal that these theories have in common. And at a still lower level, only fully reasonable liberal theories would achieve an even thicker agreement, covering some basic rights and liberties that every citizen should have, over and above considerations of political morality. This substantive agreement would nevertheless leave room for a vast array of important disagreements demarcating versions of egalitarianism from one another but also from sufficientarian and prioritarian theories of justice.[5]

As this concise presentation shows, navigating different kinds of disagreements is an inherent part of conceptual analysis as a mainstream approach to theorizing about justice. This is because, at its best, this methodology does not take the form of a single-minded argument relentlessly unfolding from first premises but presupposes what we may term a diverse community of practice. This key feature becomes apparent in Kramer's interpretation of conceptual analysis as an essentially dialogical exercise generating distinctive philosophical views on justice in relation to rivals. In the Rawlsian frame, the collaborative core of the underlying dialectic is exemplified by the idea of wide reflective equilibrium where the balancing of high-level principles and pre-theoretical convictions is undertaken in the light of competing theories, in addition to one's own. In the Dworkinian frame, any meaningful argument about theories of justice rests on a substantive pre-theoretical agreement on paradigm cases among arguing theorists.

[2] Kramer, *Conceptual Analysis and Distributive Justice*, 368.
[3] Ibid., 376.
[4] Ibid., 370.
[5] Kramer, *Conceptual Analysis and Distributive Justice*, 371.

Against this background, the distinction between value-independence and value-neutrality comes to play a crucial role in separating out disagreements of different order that might be lumped, unhelpfully, together. Kramer defines these two contrasting features as follows:

> If a project of theoretical elaboration is value-independent in the sense specified here, it is not grounded on any ethical values. That is, the justifications for its theses do not consist in invocations of ethical values. Some values do of course underlie any such project, but they are theoretical-explanatory or logical/mathematical or aesthetic rather than ethical.
>
> Value-neutrality, in the sense specified here, is different. If certain theses are value-neutral, then we can gauge the fulfilment or non-fulfilment of those theses in any number of circumstances without having to undertake any ethical judgments. In other words, the states of affairs recounted by those theses can be ascertained (as present or absent) without any ethical assessments.[6]

The pair is further contrasted with two potential misnomers where neutrality is one of the reference terms: first, the neutrality of an abstract concept with respect to the various concrete cases instantiating it; and second, value-neutrality as a tenet of political liberalism contested by the proponents of liberal perfectionism. As Kramer demonstrates, neither kind of neutrality would qualify as value-neutral in the methodological sense he articulates.[7] For value-neutrality in this sense is a possible feature of philosophical discourse. It designates a distinct dimension of methodological austerity as opposed to methodological engagedness, that of purely factual descriptions of states of affairs as opposed to prescriptions commending the achievement of some states of affairs as just or appropriate in some other respect.[8] By contrast, value-independence, the other dimension of methodological austerity prioritizes analytic as opposed to synthetic, or formal as opposed to substantive argumentation. According to Kramer, while value-independence in the strict sense is inconsistent with a fruitful inquiry on the subject of distributive justice or any other core issue of political philosophy, value-neutrality has an important role to play.

As we shall see in the course of the present discussion, both the rejection of the former and the partial acceptance of the latter kind of methodological austerity have a common root, an underlying commitment to a version of the fact-value distinction. For instance, in Kramer, Hume's Law is formulated as follows: "There is no valid argument in which all of the premises are non-moral (and logically consistent) and in which the conclusion is a substantive moral proposition."[9] Returning to conceptual analysis as applied to distributive justice, the use of thin concepts would already commit theorists to some substantive moral views to the exclusion of others. This is a direct upshot of Hume's Law: extreme methodological austerity in terms of formal

[6] Kramer, *Conceptual Analysis and Distributive Justice*, 377. See Kurki, ch. 4 in this volume, for a related discussion on the distinction between value-independence and value-neutrality.

[7] Kramer, *Conceptual Analysis and Distributive Justice*, 377–9.

[8] Ibid., 378.

[9] Kramer, *Moral Realism as a Moral Doctrine*, 6.

argumentation about justice, either leads to trivial conclusions or conceals unacknowledged value commitments. Rawls's discussion of justification as an argumentative practice that goes beyond valid proof illustrates well this idea:

> Being designed to reconcile by reason, justification proceeds from what all parties to the discussion hold in common. Ideally, to justify a conception of justice to someone is to give him a proof of its principles from premises that we both accept, these principles having in turn consequences that match our considered judgements. Thus mere proof is not justification. A proof simply displays logical relations between propositions. But proofs become justification once the starting points have been mutually recognised, or the conclusions so comprehensive and compelling as to persuade us of the soundness of the conception expressed by their premises.[10]

So, by rejecting value-independence as a possible feature of meaningful theorizing about justice, we are better placed to acknowledge the significant background agreements which help focus relevant disagreements and enable the constructive exchange of competing interpretations. Hence, the key role of a community of practice we observed earlier: without the mutual recognition of participants as sharing some preexisting common ground, the conceptual analysis of justice cannot take off.

The partial acceptance of methodological value-neutrality also derives from the Humean version of the fact-value distinction that Kramer endorses. If pure descriptions of states of affairs cannot ground, on their own, any particular evaluative stance toward the states so described, then the occurrence of valued or disvalued states of affairs can be ascertained without any reference to their alleged value or disvalue. As a case in point, Kramer discusses the notion of measuring empirically the overall freedom individuals have in a society developed in Carter.[11] Such a measurement would not, in Kramer's terminology, be value-independent. For, to put it crudely, it presupposes valuing freedom. It would, however, be value-neutral since its extent can be ascertained without reference to any ethical considerations. Employing somewhat different terminology, Carter articulates a related distinction:

> The only basis we have for seeing comparisons of degrees of overall freedom as normatively significant lies in freedom's non-specific value. And in order to make room for freedom's non-specific value, we must understand degree-of-freedom judgements as having a purely empirical basis. We should not see such judgments as "value neutral"; for they are, after all, judgements in terms of freedom's non-specific value. But neither should we see them as referring to the value of specific freedoms in terms of the things those freedoms allow us to do.[12]

On one possible reading, we can equate Kramer's "value-independence" with Carter's "value neutrality." This reading is further supported by the existence of another term, "value freeness," which, considering Carter,[13] seems to match closely Kramer's notion

[10] Rawls, *A Theory of Justice*, 508.
[11] Carter, *A Measure of Freedom*.
[12] Carter, *A Measure of Freedom*, 289.
[13] Carter, *Value-Freeness*.

of value-neutrality. Yet, a further look at some of the earlier literature on how and why relevant facts should be established independently of value judgments in such areas of public policy as economics, might give us a pause for thought. For instance, in an extensive discussion of Putnam's *Collapse of the Fact/Value Dichotomy* Long stresses a particular sense in which some economists from the so-called Austrian School have advocated value-free economic analysis: "So long as economists can explain the effects of a particular policy without presupposing any evaluation of *that policy or its effects*, the fact that *other* evaluations must be presupposed need not perturb us."[14]

This sense of value freeness is consistent with a fact/value distinction. However, it does not unambiguously fit the scope of what Kramer terms "value-neutrality." Thus, on another possible reading, there is a drift between two competing ways in which conceptual analysis may go "value-neutral" with respect to moral and political concepts, such as distributive justice. A narrow-scope interpretation would see descriptions as value-neutral if they do not rely—either explicitly or implicitly—on taking a stance toward the specific value or values whose instantiation is ascertained. By contrast, a wide-scope interpretation would insist on descriptions that do not reference any moral values, not just the ones whose instantiation is at stake.

The discussion of value-neutrality in Kramer (2018) clearly supports the latter, more demanding interpretation. Having said that, it is important to bear in mind that value-neutrality with respect to empirical inquiry within the frame of a wider normative theory may not always be as thorough in disentangling facts from values. In such cases, the limited value-neutrality achieved could still fulfill an important methodological purpose, that of avoiding question-begging evaluations. As the next section will aim to show, distinguishing between wide- and narrow-scope value-neutrality is in fact crucial. For it enables methodological austerity to fulfill the role of a distinctive kind of disentangling strategy, in the context of acknowledged value-dependence.[15]

3. Revisiting the Fact/Value Distinction

In the discussion to follow, "disentanglement," viz. "disentangling" will be understood in the weak (and more interesting) sense explored in Blackburn.[16] Unlike disentanglement in the strong sense where the evaluative dimension of a concept can be easily detached from its descriptive dimension without any loss of meaning, disentanglement in the weak sense does not imply or aim at a similar endpoint where the "facts" are laid bare, with no trace of evaluation. According to Blackburn, undue focus on

[14] Long, *Review of Putnam*, 129–30.

[15] "Disentangling" is about the link between ethical evaluations and related descriptions of states of affairs. Philosophers committed to the fact/value dichotomy tend to interpret this procedure as complete only when the evaluative judgments under consideration have been fully separated out from the descriptive components that they have been—unhelpfully—entangled with. By contrast, authors who contest the fact/value dichotomy challenge the prospects of such a thorough disentangling. A major worry of theirs is that separating facts from values in this way leads to loss of meaning rather than greater clarity (J. McDowell, "Non-Cognitivism and Rule-Following"). The disentangling strategy that will be explored in the following section is distinctive in that it offers a promising middle ground—conceptual analysis in terms of a fact/value distinction with no commitment to either the fact/value dichotomy or its collapse.

[16] Blackburn, "Disentangling Disentangling."

disentanglement in the strong sense has obscured and undermined the key role disentanglement in the weak sense has to play in the analysis of the so-called thick concepts.[17] This focus imposes a false dilemma upon theorists working in such areas as normative ethics and political philosophy where most of the discussion is bound to employ thick concepts. The dilemma is as follows: either endorse disentanglement in the strong sense or, conversely, pronounce thick concepts as ultimately unanalyzable. The former would treat the evaluative dimension of such concepts as dispensable if not altogether parasitic on their descriptive dimension. The latter would insulate from critique objectionable attitudes that the use of thick concepts may propagate. On reflection, neither option is methodologically sound. The first blatantly disregards central features of ordinary moral language, where the extension of concepts, such as "steadfast," "determined," and "pig-headed" is partly determined by the different attitudes undertaken toward, by and large, overlapping representational content. The second option, by contrast, overstates the interdependence between attitudes and representation in a way that makes reasoned moral change unintelligible. If the evaluative and the factual dimensions of a thick concept cannot be disentangled at all without the loss of meaning, coming to appreciate as determined actions that one would previously qualify as pig-headed would amount to a "leap of faith" or a wholesale conversion to an alternative standpoint. Yet, both everyday conversations about ethical issues and ethical theorizing presuppose the idea that we can learn a lot from alternative thick conceptualizations by gradually thinning them out to expose the kinds of unspoken commitments that come with the use of this or that thick concept. As Blackburn puts it:

> The everyday metaphor of a loaded description makes salient the idea that a load is something that is put upon something else, and that can equally be taken off. Things can be said in derogatory ways, but rephrased to avoid the derogation ... But the issue is whether we should see the unitary, thick concept as fundamental, or the idea of a loaded way of describing things, where the load plays a role in determining which things are so described, but where the load can also in principle be shed.[18]

So understood, disentangling takes place whenever we get clearer and more reflective about our own moral stance. In some cases, this would involve revising, perhaps even abandoning practices we have previously followed without giving them a second thought. On such occasions, our distancing from a particular set of moral judgments and underlying attitudes would often come as a result of newly found appreciation for the less palatable sides of the loaded, entangled concepts we might be

[17] Evaluative concepts are divided into two categories: thick and thin. The distinction highlights the different roles that descriptive components might play in the use of such concepts. For instance, "good," "bad," "right," and "wrong" have minimal descriptive content. Being descriptively thin, they come as close as possible to pure evaluations. By contrast, such terms as "diligent," "nice," and "unfriendly" rely on thicker descriptive layers, in addition to some evaluative core. The resulting thick evaluations represent a person or an action as being good or bad in a particular way. The distinction between thick and thin ethical concepts was introduced in Williams, *Ethics and the Limits of Philosophy*. See Kirchin (2017) for an extensive discussion on interpreting thick concepts as more specific evaluations rather than separable fact/value composites.

[18] Blackburn, "Disentangling Disentangling," 123.

using unreflectively. Blackburn discusses the use of "cute" to compliment women as an example.[19] While the apparent intention when describing a woman as "cute" is to draw attention to a positive attribute of hers, the linguistic practice rests on some background presuppositions which portray women as decorative and subservient dependants at their best. A person might partake in this practice imagining it just a nice thing to say without ever considering what these presuppositions mean. When their offensiveness gets articulated, as a piece of everyday disentangling, they might be less inclined to use "cute" with reference to women or see it as a compliment at all.

Kramer's thesis, according to which conceptual analysis in political philosophy is inextricably value-dependent, introduces the theoretical counterpart to everyday disentangling in the sense specified earlier. When looking into substantive disagreements between different theories of justice, value-dependent conceptual analysis enables us to locate correctly the degree of thinness or thickness, at which these disagreements emerge. This is a first step toward the right kind of argumentative strategy that would speak to the relevant community of practice: theorists who have specific background assumptions in common they all may call upon. And, while theoretical disentangling, like its everyday analogue, is not expected to resolve every case of substantive disagreement among reasoners who engage in the process in good faith, it would always advance a more nuanced and reflective understanding of both one's own and competing interpretations amongst such participants.

Importantly, neither the everyday, nor the theoretical version of weak disentanglement comes with the untenable metaphysical commitments entailed by a strict fact/value dichotomy.[20] What's more, in each version, disentanglement is clearly consistent with a range of positions about the metaphysics of morals. This may lead us to believe that weak disentanglement is, quite simply, a sound, even perhaps uncontroversial, methodology that comes with no substantive commitments about the nature of values. Yet, on closer inspection, the extent of this methodology's engagedness, to follow Kramer's terminology, becomes clear. For the successful application of value-dependent conceptual analysis presupposes that disagreements about values are, overall, more difficult to settle than disagreements about facts. Since some of our beliefs and other attitudes are much more controversial than others, we can trade upon the largely uncontroversial ones to try to reach greater agreement on those that are more controversial. The discussion of weak disentanglement in Blackburn is explicit on this point:

> All that I hold is that in context, and for the purpose of enabling discussion and critique to go forward at any particular junction, the right methodological route is to distinguish as well as we may. We advance one step of fact at a time, distilling the

[19] Ibid., 124–5.

[20] Such commitments are only entailed by strong disentanglement as it posits the complete separability of evaluative and descriptive components within a thick concept. The thesis that ethical values cannot be part of the "fabric of the world" because of their peculiar metaphysical properties (Mackie, *Inventing Right and Wrong*) is an example. See also Streumer, *Unbelievable Errors: An Error Theory about All Normative Judgements* for a recent argument in support of the underlying error theory, according to which a closer look at the (impossible) metaphysics of values would lead us to see all ethical judgments as necessarily erroneous.

> residue of disagreements of value as far as we can, until if we are lucky (but only if) any that remain prove slight or tractable.[21]

Value-dependent conceptual analysis exhibits a similar structure. Although the distinction between formal and substantive components it aims to achieve within and across conceptions of distributive justice is not supposed to mirror a dichotomy between facts and values,[22] the process is expected to be straightforward with respect to the order in which layer after layer of conceptual thickness can be peeled off. Yet, as Kramer's own interpretation of the wrongful conviction of Tom Robinson in *To Kill A Mockingbird* indicates, there can be significant methodological disagreement in assessing how thick a specific concept is—even between closely related theories of justice, both of which qualify as liberal and fully reasonable in the Rawlsian sense. Thus, if we take, in agreement with Dworkin,[23] the conviction and punishment of a person known to be innocent of any crime to be a paradigm case of injustice, we should also think that the jurors in Tom Robinson's trial have no "grasp of the general concept of justice." For they knowingly convict a person who is innocent of the crime, of which he has been accused. By contrast, if we followed Rawls as Kramer suggests, we should instead grant these jurors grasp of the general concept of justice and appreciate that it can be, as it is on this occasion, combined with a "hideously illiberal understanding of what counts as an arbitrary distinction" (ibid.), excluding the difference in race between the accuser and the accused, on which their verdict is based.

Could this disagreement indicate that our methodological route has finally reached a point of intractable disagreement of ethical value, that of justice? Considering how close the two theories under consideration are in their understanding of justice, a more plausible suggestion seems to be that the methodological austerity should be extended to a further application. This application would target the entanglement of two kinds of values, ethical and theoretical-explanatory. Theoretical-explanatory values, whether explicitly endorsed or not, have direct implications for the ethics of inquiry since they help determine what counts as a "sound" methodological route and, as a result, which reasoners are to be treated as full participants in the community of practice. There is a growing literature on the notion of epistemic peers and its significance for differentiating intractable disagreements that ought to be taken seriously from those that can explained away or safely ignored.[24] In the next section, I will say more about this. For the purposes of the present discussion, suffice to say that different theoretical-explanatory values underpin different methodological choices which in turn have different substantive implications. Some of them would amount to what I propose to call "unjust theorizing." Examples include marginalizing epistemic peers or ignoring alternative conceptualizations as irrelevant or incompetent. By widening the scope of disentangling to include explicitly theoretical-explanatory values on a par with ethical values, we would give ourselves a better chance to keep in check potentially unjust theorizing. This commitment is of particular importance when we theorize about justice

[21] Blackburn, "Disentangling Disentangling," 135.
[22] Kramer, *Moral Realism as a Moral Doctrine*, 236–9.
[23] Dworkin, *Justice for Hedgehogs*.
[24] E.g., Christensen-Lackey, ed., *The Epistemology of Disagreement*.

since such theorizing has greater potential to replicate, obfuscate, and legitimize existing unjust institutions than theorizing on other subjects.[25]

To see how this might work, let us briefly consider an example from Dworkin,[26] the interpretation of the equal protection clause of the US Constitution in connection to racial discrimination. When this clause was adopted under the Fourteenth Amendment, it was deemed as compatible with the upkeep of racially segregated public schools. As Dworkin highlights:

> In fact the Fourteenth Amendment was proposed by lawmakers who thought they were not outlawing racially segregated education. The floor manager of the civil rights bill that preceded the amendment told the House that "civil rights do not mean that all children shall attend the same school", and the same Congress continued to segregate the schools of the District of Columbia after the Fourteenth Amendment had entered the Constitution.[27]

These schools remained segregated for some further ninety years, until segregation was ruled unconstitutional as inconsistent with the very same equal protection clause.

One possible explanation of why constitutional law scholars and judges took so long to appreciate such a glaring inconsistency as the above is to insist that it is not of a logical or theoretical-explanatory order. Instead, it reflects welcome changes in ethical consensus within wider society. Like value non-neutrality in political philosophy, legal interpretation rests on specific ethical commitments. When they change, the interpretation changes too.

Here is an alternative I would like to put forward. It expands on the idea that to fulfill its intended purpose disentangling should target specifically theoretical-explanatory values, in addition to ethical values. This presupposition is consistent with recent work on epistemic injustice, for example, Fricker,[28] Medina,[29] and Pohlhaus, Jr.[30] A central claim that emerges from various contributions is that individuals and groups are often wronged as inquirers and communicators in virtue of epistemic methods and habits conceived as independent from any value commitments by the mainstream. Moreover, such epistemic injustices are typically extremely difficult to identify because of their entanglement with epistemic norms seen as constitutive of otherwise worthwhile practices, such as democratic legislation or analytic philosophy. Medina suggests two complementary terms to designate the insidious mechanisms through which epistemic injustices tend to persist undetected: meta-ignorance and meta-insensitivity.[31] The first refers to the unshakable sense that there is "nothing to watch

[25] This is because the stakes we have in the outcomes of such theorizing are higher than in projects that look like a "disinterested search for the truth." At the very least, the conclusions we reach about justice are expected to be action-guiding. At times, the actions required might be extremely demanding. The discussion of rationalization in the following section will aim to shed further light on this.

[26] Dworkin, *Law's Empire*.

[27] Ibid., 360.

[28] Fricker, *Epistemic Injustice*.

[29] Medina, *The Epistemology of Resistance*.

[30] Pohlhaus, *Varieties of Epistemic Injustice*.

[31] Medina, *The Epistemology of Resistance* and Medina, "Epistemic Injustice and Epistemologies of Ignorance."

out for here" coming in the very "blind spots" that familiar unjust institutions cast over one's theorizing. The second precludes a community of practice from giving the benefit of the doubt to novel approaches. In so doing, it mimics bona fide concerns over unorthodox methods. Importantly, both mechanisms—meta-ignorance and meta-insensitivity—could support instances of unjust theorizing under the guise of sound methodology.

Let us now return to the case under consideration: how to explain the lawmakers' initial thought that the equal protection clause they championed is consistent with the racially segregated education they were accustomed to? In light of the preceding discussion, a more plausible explanation would point—in addition to the false belief that racial segregation is harmless—to insufficient scrutiny into the theoretical-explanatory commitments that might be at stake when considering such issues as relevance, salience, and comparability. At first blush, these issues could seem unrelated to concerns about justice or equality, as the idea of two separate categories of values—theoretic-explanatory on the one side, ethical on the other—might imply. Such understanding, however, could inadvertently lead to unjust theorizing.[32]

Keeping an eye on theoretical-explanatory values is of equal significance when we look at the other dimension of methodological austerity, that of partial value-neutrality. As shown in the previous section, partial value-neutrality may differ in scope. When it is narrow, the relevant factual descriptions are meant to exclude only evaluations based on the ethical values whose instantiation is currently ascertained. When, by contrast, it is wide, the relevant factual descriptions are expected to exclude all evaluations based on ethical values. Clearly, there will be some room for unjust theorizing as a result of this very difference in scope. When narrow-scope value-neutrality is treated as though wide in scope, disentangling might end too soon, keeping unexamined value commitments out of the spotlight. Some of these commitments might be as unappealing as complimenting grown-ups for being cute.

However, a more insidious form of halfway disentangling is encouraged by the notion that proper factual descriptions presuppose what Jane Heal calls a "disinterested search for truth."[33] According to Heal, the use of such metaphors as "the constitutive aim of belief is truth" tend to be confused and confusing. For they could prompt inquirers to think of truth as having its own intrinsic value, in abstraction of the inquiries, practices, and ways of life that make finding out the truth about specific matters significant to particular groups and individuals. Yet, were the search for truth fundamentally disinterested in this way, coming to believe as many truths as possible,

[32] The line of reasoning here is as follows. Defining the scope of principles and requirements of justice like the equal protection clause is the result of theoretical-explanatory choices. These choices should be scrutinized and disentangled applying a similar procedure to that we saw at work in the case of thick ethical concepts. This is because the content of such choices tends to appear as independent from ethical values. At the same time, however, it is in fact more likely to be entangled with expectations molded by familiar institutions in virtue of their familiarity and independently of how well they are justified. These expectations may not strike the reasoners involved as distinctly ethical. They could instead be convinced that the theoretical-explanatory choices they make are only constrained by sound disciplinary standards and, as a consequence, already value-independent in the required sense. In such cases, the disentangling strategy outlined earlier should also apply to the links between theoretical-explanatory values and ethical values, in addition to those between ethical evaluations and factual descriptions.

[33] Heal, *The Disinterested Search for Truth*.

no matter how trivial, random, or uninformative should be considered an epistemic achievement. This, however, does not even remotely look like a successful inquiry. So, a possible upshot of these common metaphors is often not the promotion of truly disinterested studies but lesser awareness of the interests that a particular search for truths would help realize or, conversely, obstruct.

Importantly, the correlation that Heal identifies can be acknowledged without at the same time rejecting that truth is the constitutive norm of beliefs. As I recently argued,[34] the metaphors conveying such a conception of truth do not always make clear how this constitutive norm is to be satisfied; however, this oversight can be remedied by a close contrast-and-compare strategy bringing together the norms of belief and the norms of action. As a result, it becomes possible to address the concerns raised by Heal, which are neither orthogonal, nor secondary to assessing the inquiry on its own, theoretical-explanatory terms. For they help track the background assumptions about such matters as relevance, scope, and method that are constitutive of the epistemic practice to which any particular inquiry belongs.

In a similar vein, by including theoretical-explanatory considerations when assessing the extent to which an investigation conducted under the auspices of an ethical or political theory is value-neutral, we can limit unjust theorizing. In this respect, it is safe to assume that any such investigation will be of narrow-scope neutrality with respect to theoretical-explanatory values even if its neutrality with respect to distinctly ethical values is wide in scope. It is beyond the limits of the present discussion to assess the prospects of a stronger claim, that theoretical-explanatory values are best understood as a semi-independent subclass of ethical values. The conclusions reached here are independent of this unduly strong claim: whether theoretical-explanatory and ethical values are different in kind or not, normative theorizing as a distinctive cluster of epistemic practices exhibits close interdependence between the two. The potential for inadvertently unjust theorizing derives from this interdependence. Hence, the need to employ a comprehensive disentangling strategy in the sense articulated here. Such a strategy would target theoretical-explanatory commitments on a par with ethical considerations along the complementary dimensions of presumed value independence and partial value-neutrality.

4. Implications for Moral Epistemology

I would like now to expand on the role that the comprehensive disentangling strategy inspired by Kramer (2018)[35] can play in moral epistemology. In particular, I will aim to show how this strategy can help address a couple of issues that have emerged in the aftermath of growing disenchantment with the fact/value dichotomy.

The first has to do with blanket responses to widespread disagreements in moral theory. While neither the existence nor the awareness of such disagreements are new, some ways of collapsing the fact/value dichotomy prompt generalized skepticism that ultimately undermines both value inquiries and the establishment of facts. In a

[34] Radoilska, *Aiming at the Truth and Aiming at Success*.
[35] Kramer, "Conceptual Analysis and Distributive Justice."

nutshell, the thought goes as follows. The most compelling reason for rejecting the fact/value dichotomy is epistemic rather than metaphysical: judgments of value are just as contestable as statements of facts. As a result, when we disagree about particular values, we should endorse a procedure similar to what we would deploy when we find ourselves disagreeing about states of affairs.[36] In such standard cases, the discovery of intractable disagreement with our epistemic peers should reduce confidence in our initial views leading to the suspension of any belief about matters contested in this way. Coming to appreciate the full extent of disagreements among respectable moral theories, many of them centuries-old, should have a similar effect. Yet, with respect to first-order morality, this effect would amount to corruption.[37] For it encourages lack of commitment and provides individuals with the means to spin ad hoc justifications for whatever they feel like doing, just by swapping moral theories around. This looks like a counterpart to what—according to the intersecting empirical and philosophical literatures on rationalization—is readily happening on the side of factual beliefs. Such beliefs are often, if not overwhelmingly, formed by adapting available evidence to fit subjective expectations. Once formed, rationalizing beliefs prove particularly resilient to emerging pieces of counterevidence which get discounted as irrelevant, unreliable, or inconclusive. Crucially, some of the underlying mechanisms operate outside of conscious awareness, for example, by priming or diverting attention. As Schwitzgebel and Ellis clarify:

> Rationalisation occurs when a person favours a particular conclusion as a result of some factor (such as self-interest) that is of little justificatory epistemic relevance. The thinker then seeks an adequate justification for that conclusion but the very factor responsible for her favouring it now biases how the research for justification unfolds. As a result of an epistemically illegitimate investigation, the person identifies and endorses a justification that makes no mention of the distorting factor that has helped guide her search.[38]

One possible outcome of rationalization is the further entrenchment of contrasting positions. Like failing commitment with respect to values, this kind of self-assurance would also hinder progress toward greater agreement. While in the former case, disagreement is taken as compelling evidence that no position is better than the others, in the latter case, disagreement is underplayed as peripheral to the assessment of evidence. Schwitzgebel and Ellis highlight this feature of rationalization: it not only "obstructs the critical evaluation of one's own reasoning"; in so doing, it also "impedes the productive exchange of reasons and ideas among well-meaning interlocutors."[39]

The disentangling strategy under consideration is particularly well-suited to counter the globalized skepticism that underlies such responses. As the earlier discussion showed, its two strands operate in tandem to help identify correctly what

[36] Cf. McGrath, *Moral Disagreement and Moral Expertise.*
[37] Cf. Setiya, *Does Moral Theory Corrupt Youth?.*
[38] Schwitzgebel-Ellis, *Rationalization in Moral and Philosophical Thought*, 170.
[39] Ibid., 171.

we disagree about and how deep that disagreement is. At times, we are able to step back a level to a thinner, shared understanding and then advance together to reach a thicker, still shared understanding that may, or not, match any of the initial views on the table. At others, disagreement will not be as fully overcome. Yet, even then, disentangling serves a constitutive role, building a diverse community of epistemic peers. In fact, following from the argument for explicit inclusion of theoretical-explanatory values on a par with ethical and political ones in the context of both analytic dimensions, value independence vs. value-dependence and value-neutrality vs. value non-neutrality, this constitutive role may just as often involve bringing deeper disagreements to the surface, as a first step to ending unjust theorizing. Importantly, the dialogical aspect of disentangling is as vital for value-neutral investigations, whether wide or narrow in scope, as for the conceptual analysis of thick evaluations. As outlined in our concise reconstruction of reasoning toward generalized skepticism, seemingly intractable disagreements of fact are a major motivating factor. By creating a community of practice that does not presuppose agreement but search as its common ground, the underlying disentangling strategy can effectively limit the scope for unchecked rationalizations.

The second issue in moral epistemology that this strategy can help us address is debate fragmentation. Like generalized skepticism, debate fragmentation responds to collapsing the fact/value dichotomy in a particular way. This time, the starting point is the realization that first-order moral disagreements are often treated as acceptable, seemingly in contrast to disagreements of fact. Deeply held convictions on the impermissibility of a particular conduct are rarely cast aside merely in virtue of learning that others have no qualms about it. At a theoretical level, there is related unease with respect to the moral knowledge acquired by testimony. Many would qualify it as "second-hand"[40] if knowledge at all. At first blush, the kind of asymmetry asserted here might look like a replay of the fact/value dichotomy. However, it does not have to be so. Returning to the literature on epistemic injustice, some of the most egregious cases identified are about the comprehensive obliteration of particular standpoints. Medina proposes the term "hermeneutical death" to capture the extreme nature of the epistemic harms involved when the experiences of oppressed groups and the social reality they point to are kept unintelligible.[41] The force of the charge derives precisely from collapsing fact/value dichotomy.[42] This charge also presupposes firm commitment to the idea that truth is of fundamental epistemic value. Otherwise, the harms under consideration cannot be acknowledged as distinctly epistemic rather than social or political. For they not only point to unfair inequalities across intersecting dimensions of individual and collective agency; crucially, they converge toward a comprehensive epistemology of ignorance whereby earnest inquirers are systematically obstructed in their search

[40] Jones, "Second-Hand Moral Knowledge."

[41] Medina, *Epistemic Injustice and Epistemologies of Ignorance.*

[42] The thought goes as follows: Marginalized groups are disvalued. This social fact explains why the theoretical tools needed to understand their experiences "from within" are not widely accessible, if developed at all. At the same time, however, the lack of appropriate theoretical tools feeds back into the underlying attitudes that keep marginalized experiences unrecognized or poorly understood, including by the people who live them.

for the truth and end up believing—unsuspectingly—falsehoods about significant areas of their own lives.

According to Medina, circumstances where the threat of such hermeneutical death becomes apparent, call for the epistemic equivalent of insurrection: withdrawal from projects instigated by the mainstream, including refusal to speak out when one's testimony is bound to be misheard or co-opted. As part of this process, underprivileged knowers should aim to come together and build their own alternative epistemic communities, in isolation from the mainstream.

While epistemic insurrection is a compelling approach to the extreme cases Medina discusses, such as the suppression of indigenous languages, it could also be counterproductive if extrapolated beyond the means of last resort it is supposed to be. For, once the idea of alternative epistemic communities laboring in isolation from one another settles in, epistemic achievements that challenge the status quo would become easier to ignore, fragmenting the notion of epistemic peers to identify only those whose standpoint one already shares. A disentangling strategy that pays particular attention to signs of unjust theorizing can offer a promising framework for epistemic peers in the making. In so doing, it would place the rational hope of collaborative inquiry on the horizon of epistemic insurrection as a distinctly epistemic engagement.

5. Conclusion

Reflecting on the nature and scope of conceptual analysis in Kramer (2018),[43] I outlined the contours of a new, comprehensive disentangling strategy for moral epistemology. This strategy builds on the fundamental distinction between value-neutrality and value-independence as two separate aspects of methodological austerity introduced by Kramer. The significance of this project for moral epistemology becomes apparent when we consider two major challenges that arise from collapsing the fact/value dichotomy—globalized skepticism and debate fragmentation. I showed that these challenges can be successfully addressed by a two-pronged disentangling strategy that encompasses both dimensions—value-neutrality vs. value non-neutrality and value independence vs. value-dependence. The success of this strategy rests on two factors. The first is broadening the scope of disentangling to include theoretical-explanatory values on a par with distinctly ethical values. The second is differentiating between wider and narrower conceptualizations of what value-neutrality requires with respect to contested matters. Both aim to pre-empt unjust theorizing, a distinctive form of epistemic injustice that derives from the exclusive methodological focus on ethical evaluations at the expense of epistemic ones. When these methodological conditions are fulfilled, opponents should gain the confidence to treat each other as fellow inquirers engaged in the same project, that of reducing the scope of unhelpful disagreements.

[43] Kramer, "Conceptual Analysis and Distributive Justice."

Acknowledgments

I would like to thank Matthew Kramer and the editors of this collection, Visa Kurki and Mark McBride, for their helpful comments on earlier drafts. I would also like to acknowledge the constructive feedback I received from audiences at the Universities of Cambridge, Kent, and Pavia. The research on this chapter was supported by a British Academy Newton Award, Ref.: NAFR1180082.

PART IV
FREEDOM

12
Prevention, Coercion, and Two Concepts of Negative Liberty

Michael Garnett

According to Thomas Hobbes, "Liberty, or FREEDOME signifieth (properly) the absence of... externall Impediments of motion."[1] On this pure, negative view, liberty requires only the absence of physical prevention. It's a conception that's been ingeniously defended and developed in recent years by philosophers such as Hillel Steiner, Ian Carter, and Matthew Kramer, all of whom argue for sophisticated versions of the view that one's degree of freedom is a function of the range of bodily movements that one is physically unprevented from performing.[2] We find the core of this traditional view succinctly expressed, for instance, in Kramer's *F Postulate*: "A person is free to φ if and only if he is unprevented from φ-ing."[3]

However, not every influential figure in the negative tradition chose to characterize freedom in terms of *nonprevention*. Others did so, instead or as well, in terms of *noncoercion*. Jeremy Bentham, for instance, tells us that "Liberty ... is neither more nor less than the absence of coercion."[4] Similarly, in his "Two Concepts of Liberty" Isaiah Berlin equates "the 'negative' conception of liberty in its classical form" with "non-interference, which is the opposite of coercion."[5] And in the opening pages of *The Constitution of Liberty*, F.A. Hayek defined "a state of liberty or freedom" as "that condition of men by which coercion of some by others is reduced as much as possible in society."[6]

How important is this difference? The distinction between freedom-as-nonprevention and freedom-as-noncoercion isn't one that's received much attention. This is probably for the following reason. On the one hand, it's common for nonprevention views of freedom to restrict the scope of freedom-limiting preventions to those *brought about by other people*, on the grounds that freedom (in the politically-relevant sense) is an inherently social concept.[7] On the other hand, accounts of coercion often take coercion necessarily to involve at least some physical restriction of

[1] *Leviathan*, 145.

[2] Steiner, "Individual Liberty," 33–50; Carter, *A Measure of Freedom*; Kramer, *The Quality of Freedom*.

[3] *The Quality of Freedom*, 3.

[4] UC: lxix.44. Quoted in Rosen, *Classical Utilitarianism from Hume to Mill*, 247. This view was also repeated almost *verbatim* by the eighteenth-century pamphleteer John Lind, according to whom liberty is "nothing more nor less than the absence of coercion" (*Three Letters to Dr Price*, 16).

[5] "Two Concepts of Liberty," 128.

[6] *The Constitution of Liberty*, 57. Note, too, that Hobbes himself admits a secondary sense of "liberty" understood as the absence of coercively enforced rules (i.e., "the Silence of the Law"): "In cases where the sovereign has prescribed no rule, there the Subject hath the Liberty to do, or forbear, according to his own discretion" (*Leviathan*, 152).

[7] See, e.g., Berlin, "Two Concepts of Liberty"; Miller, "Constraints on Freedom," 66–86; Kristjánsson, *Social Freedom: The Responsibility View*; Steiner, "Individual Liberty."

Michael Garnett, *Prevention, Coercion, and Two Concepts of Negative Liberty* In: *Without Trimmings*. Edited by: Mark McBride and Visa AJ Kurki, Oxford University Press. DOI: 10.1093/oso/9780198868866.003.0012

the victim's available options.[8] Putting these together, it's natural to think that both prevention (in the freedom-relevant sense) and coercion essentially involve being stopped from doing things by other people, and that the differences between them in this context are therefore negligible.

In this essay I argue that this obscures an important and useful distinction. Nonprevention and noncoercion are distinct goods. Although they often coincide, neither entirely suffices for the other. Moreover, negative theorists have reason to care about both of them. I therefore argue against the recent Hobbesian tendency to theorize negative freedom as nonprevention alone, arguing instead that a fully defensible negative account must draw on both of the tradition's core ideas: freedom-as-nonprevention and freedom-as-noncoercion.

1. Actions and Persons

1.1 A Distinction

I'm concerned with the distinction between prevention and coercion. In order to get it clearly in view, however, I need to begin with another. This is the distinction between the *freedom of a person* and the *freedom of an act*.

Sometimes we ascribe freedom and unfreedom to persons, or to groups of persons. We say that someone is or isn't a free person, or that they're more or less free now than they were before, or that they're free or unfree in certain respects or to do certain things. Other times, however, we ascribe freedom and unfreedom to actions or to choices. We say that someone acted freely or unfreely, or that they did or didn't make a free choice, or that they were or weren't free in performing some action.

Note that this distinction is different from that between *overall* and *specific* freedom. This latter distinction, frequently drawn in discussions of negative freedom, concerns the difference between judgments of the form "some person is free" (or "some person is freer than some other person"), on the one hand, and judgments of the form "some person is free to perform some action," on the other.[9] Both of these relate to the freedom of persons: in assessing the freedom of a person, one may assess their freedom *in toto*, or in specific domains, or with respect to certain actions. In each case, however, one is assessing the *person's* freedom to perform some action, and not the freedom of the *action* that they thereby perform. Hence the distinction between free persons and free actions precedes the distinction between overall and specific freedom.

To illustrate: suppose that a mugger threatens to stab me if I don't hand over my wallet. In this case, I'm free to hand over my wallet: it's a live option for me and nothing prevents me from doing it. Therefore, I have the specific freedom of handing over my wallet. When I do hand it over, however, I don't hand it over freely. I hand my wallet to the mugger under coercion. Hence the action I perform is an unfree action.

[8] Indeed, this was Bentham's view, inasmuch as he characterized liberty as the absence of coercion, and "the evil of coercion" as the evil of "restraint" (*An Introduction to the Principles of Morals and Legislation*, 175). See also Swanton, "Robert Stevens on Offers," 475; Zimmerman, "Coercive Wage Offers," 134; Wertheimer and Miller, "Payment for Research Participation: A Coercive Offer?," 390.

[9] Carter, *A Measure of Freedom*, 12–14; Kramer, *The Quality of Freedom*, 9.

Nevertheless, it's an unfree action that I was free to perform. If we want to assess my degree of personal freedom, then, we need to know what range of actions I'm free to perform, and so we need to know (*inter alia*) whether I'm free to perform the specific action of handing my wallet over to the mugger. If we want to assess the degree to which I'm acting freely, by contrast, we need to look at the circumstances of the action that I actually perform. Thus specific freedom is not freedom predicated of actions, but freedom predicated of persons with respect to their actions.

Judgments about the freedom of actions are often motivated by concerns about moral responsibility. For this reason, many accounts of free action are attempts to specify the conditions that must be met for an act to be morally attributable to an agent. However, our interest in free action isn't exhausted by concerns about moral responsibility. There's a distinctive good associated with acting freely, and some accounts of free action are attempts to elucidate that good in its own right. There may be intrinsic value, for instance, in acting creatively or with a free spirit; attempts to elucidate this value are attempts to provide an account of free action, but not one that's of any direct relevance to questions about moral responsibility.[10] Similarly, it may be valuable in itself to act in ways uninfluenced by coercion or the illegitimate interferences of others. One might think, for instance, that a person with severe mental illness who doesn't meet the competence threshold for moral accountability still loses something of value when their actions are coerced. In elucidating such a value, again, one will be giving an account of free action that isn't (or, at least, isn't yet) one that's directly relevant to questions about moral responsibility.

Indeed, it's worth noting that exactly parallel points about the detachability of our interests in freedom and responsibility apply with respect to the freedom of persons too. Just as one might be interested in what it is for an *action* to be one for which a person can be held morally responsible, one might also be interested in what it is for a *person* or *agent* to be the sort of thing that can be held morally responsible. To be a morally responsible agent is, most likely, to be a free agent in some morally important sense. But this isn't the sense of personal freedom that theories of socio-political freedom typically seek to understand. Such theories target a different form of personal freedom, one that's valuable independently of any role it may play in constituting one's status as a morally responsible being. In the same way, we may seek an account of what it is for a person to act freely in a socio-political sense without concerning ourselves directly with the question of what it is for a person to act with moral responsibility. Hence freedom may be predicated of both persons and actions, and it may be taken to pick out distinctively socio-political values in both cases.

1.2 Free Actions and Free Persons

Coercion is a property of actual actions or bodily movements: one cannot be coerced into doing something that one does not, in fact, do.[11] Yet with prevention the

[10] See, e.g., Gingerich, "Freedom's Spontaneity."

[11] Note the disjunct: if a police officer says "freeze or I'll shoot!" and you freeze, your freezing is an action—something you do, in the relevant sense—despite being an absence of bodily movement.

opposite is the case: one cannot do that which one has been prevented from doing. Hence to be coerced is to *act* unfreely, whereas to be prevented is not to act at all, but to *be* unfree. That is, coercion relates primarily to the freedom of actions, whereas prevention relates primarily to the freedom of persons. In order to understand the relationship between coercion and prevention, then, it's worth taking a step back and thinking about the general conceptual relationship between the freedom of a person and the freedom of their actions. What logical connections, if any, obtain between the two?

Some theories posit a very tight connection. Positive freedom theorists, for instance, typically take free action as basic and analyze personal freedom entirely in terms of it. That is, they begin with an account of what it is to act with true freedom—such as that to act freely is to act rationally, or from a correct understanding of the world, or authentically, or in accordance with one's essential nature—and then take a free person to be someone who succeeds in acting like that. On most positive views, that is, a free person *just is* someone who acts freely. Hence for the Stoics, the free person just is one who acts in accordance with reason (i.e., freely); for Spinoza, the free person just is one who acts on the basis of adequate ideas (i.e., freely); for Marx, one is truly emancipated only when one acts from consciousness of oneself as a species-being (i.e., freely); and so on.[12] Crucially, none of these theorists take the mere *capacity* or *opportunity* for free action to suffice for personal freedom: to be a free person, on their views, one must actually succeed in acting freely. Hence someone who had the option of acting from adequate ideas but somehow chose to act from inadequate ones instead would not, for Spinoza, qualify as a free person; someone who was able to act from their essential human nature but chose to engage in alienated activity instead would not, for Marx, qualify as a free person; and so on.

This is the point of Charles Taylor's famous comment that positive accounts treat freedom as an "exercise concept."[13] Negative accounts, by contrast, take freedom to be what he calls an "opportunity concept," which is to say that they *don't* analyze the freedom of persons entirely in terms of the freedom of their actions. On a Hobbesian view, for instance, a free person is one who is physically unprevented from performing (some sufficiently wide range of) possible actions. There is no entailment here to free action: such a person needn't act freely since, apart from anything else, such a person needn't act at all. Indeed, we might imagine someone confronted by a range of options so wide that they become paralyzed by indecision and fail to act; negative theorists will typically ascribe a high degree of freedom to such a person, regardless of the fact that they perform no actions and therefore no free actions.

One way to construe the fundamental difference between positive and negative accounts of freedom, then, is in terms of the contrary positions they take on the relationship between the freedom of persons and the freedom of their actions: negative views,

[12] See, e.g., Cooper, "Stoic Autonomy," 1–29; Kisner, *Spinoza on Human Freedom: Reason, Autonomy and the Good Life*; Wood, *Karl Marx*. Note, again, that such theorists don't take these to be requirements for moral responsibility; if they did, then their positions would entail that hardly anyone is ever morally responsible for anything.

[13] "What's Wrong with Negative Liberty."

unlike positive ones, allow the two to come apart. Moreover, since negative views allow them to come apart, it would seem that negative theorists owe separate accounts of them. And this, one might think, explains how the ideals of nonprevention and noncoercion might fit neatly together in a complete negative theory of freedom, with the former constituting the account of personal freedom and the latter the account of free action. In turn, this suggests that insofar as negative theorists like Steiner, Carter, and Kramer are concerned with analyzing the freedom of *persons* they may be right to focus exclusively on nonprevention. Unfortunately, however, the pieces of this conceptual puzzle don't fit together quite so cleanly.

That's because even negative accounts have reason to recognize some systematic connections between the freedom of persons and the freedom of their actions. Suppose, for instance, that an enslaved person is subject to pervasive coercion and hence acts unfreely much of the time. Any plausible negative account should make it possible to infer from this that such a person lacks a substantial degree of freedom. It would be an odd view of freedom—and, in particular, an odd interpretation of the idea of negative freedom—that allowed the idea of personal freedom to become so untethered from that of free action that such a person could qualify as a substantially free person. For this reason, negative accounts must, and typically do, accept that the freedom of persons necessarily correlates to some extent with (at least some aspects of) the freedom of their actions.

Moreover, recognizing such conceptual connections needn't undermine the negative theorist's principled opposition to "exercise"-based, positive accounts. This is for two reasons. First, taking personal freedom to require the absence of certain types of unfree action is different from taking it to require the presence of free action. Hence the negative theorist can continue to treat personal freedom (at a time) as consistent with inaction (at a time), and therefore as requiring no actual exercise of agency.

Second, in drawing some conceptual connections between the freedom of persons and the freedom of actions the negative theorist needn't accept the positive theorist's characterization of the latter. That is, the negative theorist needn't agree that to act freely in a socio-political sense is to act rationally, or virtuously, or authentically. They can instead conceive free action in purely negative terms, such that to act freely is merely to act in the absence of coercion or other illegitimate interference. Just as there are positive and negative conceptions of personal freedom, that is, there are positive and negative conceptions of free action—and in connecting one with the other, the negative theorist may adhere to negative versions of both.

Hence it's incumbent on a negative account of the freedom of persons to demonstrate that, insofar as people act unfreely in a relevant negative sense (for instance, under coercion), they thereby lack at least some degree of personal freedom. As I explain in the next section, this is something that contemporary negative freedom theorists have succeeded in demonstrating to a considerable extent; as I argue in the rest of the chapter, however, it's something that can never be achieved in full. The result is that nonprevention and noncoercion must be recognized as distinct components of a negative account of personal freedom: to be free one must not only be unprevented from acting but also uncoerced in acting, where these amount to different things.

1.3 Threats and Conjunctive Freedoms

Suppose that a mugger threatens to stab you unless you hand over your wallet, and that you hand over your wallet so as not to get stabbed. This is a paradigm case of coercion. As I've just been arguing, one would expect any plausible account of freedom—and, in particular, any plausible *negative* account of freedom—to yield the result that you suffer at least some loss of liberty here.

Not all negative accounts have done so, however. Hobbes, for example, denied that there is any loss of freedom-as-nonprevention (in his terms, "corporal liberty") in this kind of case. On his view, one loses such freedom only when one is physically prevented from doing something. Yet conditional threats don't appear to involve any form of physical prevention. Nothing physically prevents you from handing your wallet over to the mugger; more importantly, moreover, nothing physically prevents you from *not* handing your wallet over—yes, you'll get stabbed, but you'll still have your wallet. What prevents you from handing your wallet over is your *fear* of getting stabbed, and this fear isn't an external impediment of motion, but an internal one. Thus, Hobbes tells us, "Feare, and Liberty are consistent," and "all actions which men do in Commonwealths, for *feare* of the law, are actions, which the doers had *liberty* to omit."[14]

Modern negative theorists, by contrast, generally seek to avoid this result.[15] They accept that standard cases of conditional threats, like the mugging case, involve diminutions in personal freedom. Moreover, they seek to deliver this result without giving up the basic Hobbesian analysis of freedom as the absence of physical obstacles to possible bodily movements. Thus they argue that nonprevention views of freedom needn't be committed to counterintuitive results regarding coercion cases, and that Hobbes was, in effect, overly hasty in deriving his conclusions on this matter. Key to these modern arguments is the idea of *conjunctive freedoms*.

Suppose that I'm free to go to the park today, inasmuch as nothing prevents me from going. Suppose that I'm also free to go to the beach today, inasmuch as nothing prevents me from going. Am I free to go to the park *and* to the beach today? Well, that depends. If the park and the beach are in opposite directions and both far from my house, then it may be physically impossible for me to visit both in a day. This third freedom, the freedom to go to the park *and* to the beach today, is a conjunctive freedom, and its enjoyment isn't entailed by enjoyment of the two atomic freedoms that compose it. In assessing a person's overall freedom, then, we need to take account of their conjunctive freedoms, and this is what's missing from Hobbes's analysis of conditional threats. When the mugger threatens to stab you unless you hand your wallet over, you do indeed retain the specific freedom of keeping your wallet. However, you lose the conjunctive freedom of keeping your wallet *and not getting stabbed* (or, more precisely, of keeping your wallet and doing any of the many things that you wouldn't be able to do had you just been stabbed). So the threat does physically prevent you from doing something—in fact, a whole range of things—and physical nonprevention views of

[14] *Leviathan*, 146.

[15] An important exception is Steiner, who defends the austere Hobbesian view that "neither the making of threats nor that of offers constitutes a diminution of individual liberty" ("Individual Liberty," 43).

freedom are therefore able to deliver the intuitive conclusion that coercive conditional threats diminish freedom.

This is the line of argument adopted by J.P. Day, Carter, and Kramer, among others.[16] In this way, nonprevention views of freedom can be shown to yield plausible results concerning conditional threat cases. The impact of conditional threats on conjunctive freedoms means that, at least in a central range of cases, those who act under coercion have necessarily suffered some significant diminution in liberty. Nonprevention views therefore have the resources with which to establish plausible systematic connections between the freedom of persons and the freedom of their actions: it is no accident, on such views, that those who act unfreely (i.e., under coercion) are normally also to some extent unfree (i.e., prevented from acting in valuable ways).

Nevertheless, nonprevention views can't account for the freedom-limiting nature of coercion in its entirety. As I now argue, there are a number of cases in which prevention and coercion come apart, such that a person may be subject to active coercive control without being prevented from doing anything. These are cases of diminished personal freedom, and yet ones which nonprevention views struggle to handle. I focus on two such types of case: empty threats and preference manipulation. In each case I argue that there's a loss of negative freedom that can't be analyzed in terms of prevention alone, and that contemporary negative theorists must therefore move away from prevention-only views and toward a view that recognizes both prevention and coercion as distinct forms of personal unfreedom.

2. Coercion Without Prevention

2.1 Empty Threats

When someone issues a conditional threat, they normally make it *true* that the threat will come to pass if the victim fails to comply with their demands. Sometimes, however, they don't. This may be intentional, as when the threatener successfully bluffs, getting the victim to believe that the threat will be carried out when the threatener knows that it won't. It may also be unintentional. Consider:

> *Heart Chip: A* implants a chip in *B*'s heart that will kill *B* instantly if activated. *A* can activate the chip at any time by pressing a button on a remote control that *A* always carries. *A* uses this power to coerce *B* into serving *A*'s every whim. However, after five years the chip unexpectedly malfunctions and stops working. Nobody knows that this has happened. *A* and *B* continue as before, for a further five years.

[16] Day, "Threats, Offers, Law, Opinion and Liberty," 257–72; Carter, *A Measure of Freedom*, 224–32; Kramer, *The Quality of Freedom*, 194–210. As Kramer puts the point: "the following pair of particular freedoms cannot be exercised conjunctively by the recipient of a genuine threat: the freedom to adopt the mode of conduct which the threatener is trying to discourage, and the freedom to undertake any mode of conduct that will be stymied by the threatener's infliction of a penalty for non-compliance" (195).

In both of the two five-year periods *B* acts under credible threat of death. *A*'s effective coercive power over *B* is unaffected by the chip's invisible malfunction, and *B* continues to be subject to *A*'s will even after it stops working. Hence *B* acts unfreely for ten years: in stooping to shine *A*'s shoes in order to avoid instant death, that is, *B* isn't enjoying the good of free action, regardless of what's actually happening with the chip. Moreover, given that *B* acts unfreely throughout both periods, there would seem to be a clear sense in which *B*'s freedom is reduced throughout both periods. Someone whose every act is coerced is, to some extent, an unfree person. Yet prevention-only views of freedom must hold that whereas *B* is significantly unfree for the first five years, *B* is then fully liberated by the chip's malfunction.

This is for the following reason. In the first five years, *A* has successfully prevented *B* from performing a wide range of sets of compossible actions that *B* would otherwise have been free to perform: specifically, any such set predicated on *B*'s defying *A* without being instantly killed. In the subsequent five years, however, *A* no longer prevents *B* from doing anything. In this subsequent period *B* is free to defy *A* without being instantly killed or (let us stipulate) suffering any other ill effects as a result. *B* is unaware of having these freedoms, but has them nonetheless. On prevention-based views, therefore, *B* suffers no unfreedom at the hands of *A* after the first five years. But this, I submit, is implausible: there is at least one clear sense in which *B*'s freedom remains diminished in the subsequent five years, on account of the coercion to which *B* continues to be subject; moreover, this is a negative, socio-political form of unfreedom that a negative account may fairly be expected to capture.

In making this argument, I don't mean to deny the value of nonprevention. The chip's malfunction really does free *B* to do a whole raft of things that *B* couldn't previously do, and it matters what a person can do even if they aren't aware of it. Theories of freedom need to account for this, and nonprevention views succeed in doing so. At the same time, however, we omit something crucial if we stop our analysis here. *B* doesn't *act* any more freely as a result of the chip's malfunction; *B* continues to act under coercion. And it would seem perverse to insist, as the prevention-only theorist seemingly must, that a person so pervasively subject to coercion can nevertheless be perfectly free.

Must the prevention-only theorist really hold that *B* is fully liberated by the chip's malfunction? Perhaps *B*'s *ignorance* of the chip's malfunction prevents *B* from defying *A*, leaving *B* just as unfree as before. Modern prevention views do typically allow that ignorance can function as a freedom-limiting constraint in certain cases. As I now explain, however, prevention views can't coherently treat *B*'s ignorance as a freedom-limiting constraint in *this* type of case (and typically don't try to do so, for good reason).

Consider Kramer's characteristically sophisticated treatment of the relationship between ignorance and freedom. For him, not knowing *how* to do something can render one unfree to do it: if one doesn't know how to speak Italian,[17] for instance, or how to open a particular combination lock,[18] then one is unfree to do those things. Moreover, for Kramer the *extent* to which such ignorance reduces one's freedom depends upon the difficulty of overcoming it ("ignorance ... amounts to a freedom-curtailing

[17] *The Quality of Freedom*, 265.
[18] Ibid., 83.

condition in proportion to the difficulty of its being overcome"), where difficulty is understood in terms of probability of success ("the probabilistic qualification attached to any ascription of freedom will reflect the likelihood of the dissolution of a person's ignorance if the person were indeed to endeavour (without any blunders) to achieve such a dissolution").[19] To take Kramer's example, this means that if the correct code for a combination lock were hidden somewhere within one's cell, one's freedom to open the lock would depend, in part, on the probability of one's finding it were one to attempt to do so.[20]

However, none of this helps the prevention theorist get to the conclusion that *B* suffers reduced freedom in the second period of *Heart Chip*. *B* doesn't lack any relevant instrumental knowledge in that period: the problem isn't that *B* doesn't know *how* to defy *A*'s threats, but that *B* doesn't know that it's *possible* to defy *A*'s threats (without untoward consequences). Moreover, this ignorance is easy for *B* to overcome, in the relevant sense of "difficulty," since *B* can test the heart chip at any time by defying *A* and seeing what happens. Were *B* to endeavor to overcome their ignorance in this way there is a very high probability that both *A* and *B* would shortly discover that the chip had malfunctioned, and that *B* was free to defy *A* without consequence.[21] So *B*'s ignorance does not, on Kramer's analysis, render *B* unfree.

Indeed, *B*'s situation is relevantly similar to that of Kramer's *Kathy*:

> Suppose that Bob has abducted Kathy and has placed her in a shed. Inadvertently, he leaves the door to the shed unlocked. A simple turn of the knob by Kathy would open the door and would thus enable her to escape altogether with very little effort. Nonetheless, because Kathy wrongly believes that the door is firmly locked ... she does not even attempt to open the door, and consequently does not discover that she can readily escape. Her ignorance in this case does not deprive her of her freedom-to-leave-the-shed; instead, it simply leads her to fail to exercise that freedom.[22]

In the same way, *B*'s ignorance of the heart chip's malfunction doesn't deprive *B* of the conjunctive freedom of defying *A* and going on to act in ways that would be prevented by the activation of the chip; instead, it simply leads *B* to fail to exercise that freedom.

What's more, this is what any consistent prevention-based view of freedom *must* say about this kind of case. A unifying commitment of such views is their commitment to *preference neutrality*: the idea that facts about what a person is free to do are independent of facts about what that person wants to do. A supremely virtuous person, for instance, may have no desire whatsoever to act badly; indeed, the probability of their

[19] Ibid., 266.

[20] Ibid., 81.

[21] Is *B* not prevented, by the risk of death, from *trying to discover* whether the chip is still functioning? No: the objective probability of death from the chip in the second period is zero, so there is no risk of death. Given this, is *B* not prevented by the *false belief* that there is a substantial risk of death from trying to discover whether the chip is still functioning? No: this false belief is, again, one that could be overcome simply by trying to discover whether the chip is still functioning and seeing what happens. That is, the same considerations that apply to the question of whether *B* is prevented from defying *A* also apply, recursively, to the question of whether *B* is prevented from overcoming their ignorance as regards their preventedness with respect to defying *A*.

[22] *The Quality of Freedom*, 265–6.

acting badly may be close to nil. On a nonprevention view, however, they nevertheless remain *free* to act badly inasmuch as nothing prevents them from doing so. Motivations and preferences are not themselves constraints. In the same way, if the shed door is unlocked, then Kathy is free to leave, and she is free to leave regardless of whether or not she is motivated to leave. Although her belief that leaving is impossible defeats any motivation she may have had to try to leave, her motivations are irrelevant to her freedom. That is, her false belief prevents her from leaving only insofar as it defeats her motivation to leave, and lack of motivation to leave is no constraint on leaving. Tempting as it may be to think that a belief in the impossibility of your doing *x* prevents you from doing *x*, therefore, such a principle cannot, on reflection, be accepted.

In sum: nothing prevents *B* from defying *A* (and living to tell the tale) in the second five-year period of *Heart Chip*. That's an important kind of freedom for *B* to have, even if *B* is unaware of it. Yet *B* nevertheless continues to act under coercion, and hence unfreely. In this further sense, *B*'s freedom remains diminished. To account for this, we must recognize that freedom requires the absence of coercion as well as that of prevention.

Perhaps the prevention-only theorist will respond by insisting that, since *B* isn't prevented from doing anything in the second period of *Heart Chip*, *B* isn't coerced into doing anything either, on the grounds that coercion requires prevention. Such an insistence would, however, be little more than a Procrustean attempt to reshape the idea of coercion in line with the prevention theorist's prior commitments. The fundamental *normative* point about *Heart Chip* is that *B* is every bit as subject to *A*'s will in the second period as in the first period, and that there is therefore some significant sense in which *B* remains unfree in the second period. If the prevention theorist wishes to reserve talk of "coercion" for cases involving prevention, then we will simply need another term to pick out the distinctive bad that *B* suffers continuously throughout both periods, that of subordination to *A*'s foreign will. This will not affect the main claims of this section, which are that there are two distinct kinds of disvalue at work in the case—blocked opportunities and interpersonal subjection—and that both are relevant to judgments regarding *B*'s degree of socio-political freedom. Although I maintain that it's perfectly proper to call the second of these "coercion," this is not fundamentally a dispute about words.

2.2 Preference Manipulation

Not all forms of coercive interference involve threats. It's also possible to imagine cases in which behavior is controlled by other illegitimate means. Consider:

> *Brain Chip: A* secretly implants a chip in *B*'s brain that allows *A* to alter *B*'s motivational states. For example, if *B* faces an exclusive choice between *x* and *y* and favors *x*, *A* can get *B* to choose *y* instead by using the chip to induce a stronger motivation in favor of *y* (or to weaken the motivation in favor of *x*). *A* routinely uses the chip to get *B* to comply with *A*'s wishes.

When *B* acts under *A*'s control in this way, *B* doesn't act freely, and *B*'s freedom is diminished.

Despite the absence of any external form of physical prevention, most contemporary negative liberty theorists agree that preference manipulation of this type can diminish freedom. For Kristján Kristjánsson, for instance, "there is no morally relevant difference between preventing a man from entering a room by locking it up or by hypnotising him into staying away from it. In both cases, the victim is unfree to enter, on a correct negative view."[23] Benn, too, believes that preference manipulation, "for example by media exploitation, advertising techniques, or religious and political ritual practices," can diminish freedom, since with the person's "beliefs and preferences so managed, his actions can be controlled with no alteration to his objective choice conditions, effectively depriving him of the freedom to do what he nevertheless has the power or capacity to do."[24] Similarly, Carter holds that "forcible hypnosis and brainwashing can entail great reductions in freedom,"[25] a position also endorsed by Kramer.[26]

Yet prevention theorists aren't entitled to this view. As I now argue, there are decisive reasons to adopt an analysis of cases like *Brain Chip* on which *A* doesn't remove any of *B*'s options, and therefore doesn't prevent *B* from doing anything. If I'm right, this means that prevention-only views of personal freedom can't account for *B*'s loss of freedom; and it suggests, again, that such views require supplementation by an independent account of freedom-as-noncoercion.

It's not unnatural to think that, in manipulating someone into doing (or intending to do) something, the mind-controller thereby *prevents* that person from doing (or intending to do) anything else, at least within some salient domain and at some level of description. As Kramer puts it: "when the masters of [a person's] mind pre-decide her in favour of certain paths of conduct, they preclude her from opting for other such paths."[27] Applied to *Brain Chip*, the idea would be that in getting *B* to choose *y* by implanting a desire for *y* (and diminishing or eliminating *B*'s desire for *x*), *A* thereby prevents *B* from choosing *x*. The implanted desire for *y* thus functions as an obstacle, and constrains *B* just as surely as any external obstacle despite its internal location. However, while *some* forms of mind control may involve the creation of such internal obstacles, *preference manipulation* can't be understood in this way.

The problem is that one's own desires or motivations can't be treated as constraints on one's own possible actions.[28] Generally speaking, merely wanting to do something

[23] *Social Freedom*, 100.

[24] *A Theory of Freedom*, 154. Felix Oppenheim, similarly, holds that "to indoctrinate someone is to limit his freedom." *Dimensions of Freedom: An Analysis*, 125.

[25] *A Measure of Freedom*, 206.

[26] *The Quality of Freedom*, 255–60.

[27] Ibid., 257.

[28] This said, not all of one's desires and motivations may be "one's own" in the relevant sense; see Frankfurt, "Freedom of Will and the Concept of the Person," 5–20. In these cases, it may be possible to treat one's "alien" desires as constraints on oneself narrowly construed, i.e., as constraints on one's "true self." Since the negative theorist is unlikely to be enthusiastic about incorporating a theory of the "true self" into their analysis of socio-political freedom, however, I do not pursue this point here in any depth (though see my "Agency and Inner Freedom," 3–23). Nevertheless, it should be noted that not every illegitimately implanted desire must be alien in this sense, and we may therefore simply stipulate that, in *Brain Chip*, the alterations that *A* makes to *B*'s motivational states do not cause those states to violate the requirements for relevant ownership by *B*; see Watson, "Free Agency," 205–20; Frankfurt, "Three Concepts of Free Action," 47–57; Double, *The Non-Reality of Free Will*, 31–61.

doesn't prevent one from doing something else. If I prefer apples to oranges, I'm not thereby prevented from choosing oranges; and if I later come to prefer oranges to apples, I'm not thereby prevented from choosing apples. Neither motivations nor changes to one's motivations are, in themselves, forms of prevention—if they were, then we'd always be prevented from doing anything other than that which we actually do. So when *A* implants in *B* a preference for *y*, it doesn't look as though *A* introduces a *constraint*. This isn't because it's internal to *B*, but because desires and preferences, in general, aren't the sorts of things that can constrain.

Perhaps some mind controllers implant non-standard desires. We might imagine, for instance, that *A* implants in *B* a preference for *y* that *causally necessitates* *B*'s choosing *y*. Assuming that preferences don't normally determine choices in such a mechanistic way, this would constitute a special feature of the implanted preference. Moreover, it would be a relevantly special feature, for it would then be true of the implanted preference, but not of preferences in general, that it makes it physically impossible for *B* to choose *x*. In this case, therefore, it would be possible to hold that *A*'s interference prevents *B* from choosing (and therefore doing) *x* without having to hold, implausibly, that preferences are constraints in general.

However, manipulated preferences needn't causally necessitate choice in order to undermine freedom. As described, the chip generates in *B* a strong preference for *y* over *x* and this, presumably, raises the chances of *B*'s doing *y* considerably. Yet it needn't *deterministically* cause *B* to do *y*, just as an ordinary preference for *y* needn't deterministically cause *B* to do *y*. Hence suppose that, given *B*'s initial preferences, it's 99% probable that *B* will do *x*, but that the chip, once activated, makes it 99% probable that *B* will do *y*. If the chip is activated and indeed causes *B* to do *y*, then *B* is manipulated, and *B* acts unfreely. Freedom-undermining manipulation doesn't require deterministic causation.[29]

To flesh this out further: imagine, again, a person so supremely virtuous that the chances of their acting immorally in any given situation are at or close to nil. As previously noted, any nonprevention account of freedom must maintain that such a virtuous disposition is not itself a constraint on action, and that this person nevertheless remains *free* to act immorally absent other preventing conditions. Suppose, then, that *B*, who had previously been on course to choose *x*, is made (by activation of the brain chip) every bit as likely to avoid *x* as the supremely virtuous person is to avoid the immoral path. This is, clearly, an instance of freedom-undermining behavioral control. Moreover, its status as an instance of freedom-undermining behavioral control doesn't depend on any special assumptions about determinism or the nature of the implanted preferences. To the contrary, we may imagine that *A* inculcates in *B* an entirely normal motivational structure, one that is no more (nor less) effective in determining action

[29] This point is well established in the free will literature. As Bernard Berofsky puts it: "We are constrained to accept this conclusion on pain of conceding the possibility that no one has ever been manipulated, an absurd hypothesis. Although we can often feel supremely confident that a particular case of manipulation is also a case of determination, there is always at least a slight chance we are wrong. And should it turn out that a (prima facie) manipulated agent in situation *s* would respond under relevantly identical circumstances in the same way only 999 times out of 1000, would we really deny that he was manipulated in situation *s*?" ("Global Control and Freedom," 423). See also Mele, *Autonomous Agents: From Self-Control to Autonomy*, 139–43; Haji and Cuypers, *Moral Responsibility, Authenticity, and Education*, 10–11.

than the moral orientation of the supremely virtuous person. By parity of reasoning, a nonprevention account of freedom should yield the result that *B* is nevertheless free to do *x*.

Indeed, this just follows from preference neutrality. The extent of one's opportunity set at a time doesn't depend on which of its members one is disposed to select, and nor does one become more or less free to do something merely by desiring to do it more or less strongly. Hence neither *B*'s original preference for *x* over *y*, nor *B*'s subsequent preference for *y* over *x*, should have any bearing on *B*'s freedom to do *x*. In illegitimately switching *B* from one preference to the other, therefore, *A* is meddling in states of *B* that are strictly irrelevant to judgments concerning *B*'s degree of preventedness.

If the implanted preference doesn't constitute a constraint in virtue of its *nature*, however, perhaps it does so in virtue of its *source*. Many nonprevention views of freedom distinguish between constraints that arise naturally and constraints that are imposed by other people, holding that only the latter compromise freedom.[30] This might be thought to offer an explanation as to why *B*'s implanted preferences function as impediments whereas *B*'s other, "naturally arising" preferences don't. However, the distinction between natural and social constraints is of no help here, for two reasons. First, the point of the distinction is to restrict the domain of freedom-relevant constraints, not to define the concept of constraint itself. If a light breeze doesn't constrain you, then it doesn't matter whether it's caused by natural atmospheric changes or by a person with a fan; it has no impact on your freedom either way. Similarly, if preferences aren't constraints, then it doesn't matter how they come about. The problem here is that preferences don't seem to be constraints in the first place, and the thesis that only socially-imposed constraints restrict freedom doesn't help with this.

Second, there are many ways to bring about motivational changes in others, and not all of them compromise freedom. Suppose, for instance, that *A* gets *B* to desire *y* by providing *B* with new information about the relative merits of *x* and *y*, and by pointing out good reasons for preferring *y*. This doesn't seem to involve any detriment to *B*'s freedom. So even if it were possible to show that externally inculcated preferences somehow constrain merely in virtue of their social etiology, this would then prove too much, for it would also yield the implausible conclusion that rationally persuading someone to do something prevents them from doing otherwise.

Instead, the relevant difference between rational persuasion, on the one hand, and illegitimate modes of preference manipulation like that in *Brain Chip*, on the other, isn't that only one is a form of psychological *prevention*, but that only one is a form of *subjection to a foreign will*.[31] While nonprevention views are sensitive to the effects of interference on the opportunity sets of those interfered with, they're insensitive to the relation between wills constituted by such interference. To understand the loss of personal freedom in cases like *Brain Chip*, therefore, we need a way of thinking about coercion as a form of interpersonal subjection where this isn't just a special case of prevention.

[30] See, e.g., Berlin, "Two Concepts of Liberty"; Miller, "Constraints on Freedom"; Kristjánsson, *Social Freedom*; Steiner, "Individual Liberty."

[31] Elucidating this latter notion is obviously tricky. For attempts to do so in this context, see Yaffe, "Indoctrination, Coercion and Freedom of Will," 335–56; Garnett, "Freedom and Indoctrination," 93–108.

3. The Ideal of Noncoercion

I've been arguing that there are two overlapping concepts of negative freedom, each valuable in its own right. One is the idea of non-prevention. Descended ultimately from Hobbes, and developed in great detail by contemporary negative theorists, this is, fundamentally, a matter of unconstrained opportunities. The other is the idea of non-coercion. Although also a prominent theme in the negative tradition, it's rare for it to be explicitly distinguished from the idea of non-prevention. This is, fundamentally, a matter of non-subjection to foreign wills. I've argued that to be a free person in the negative sense one must *both* be unprevented from performing a wide range of actions *and* uncoerced insofar as one performs any of those actions.

In making this argument I've relied on a somewhat general understanding of coercion. Providing a more specific account of the relevant conception is a large undertaking—at least as large as that of providing a comprehensive account of the relevant idea of prevention, the subject of several book-length treatments.[32] Fortunately, however, this chapter's central claim—that nonprevention and noncoercion are distinct modes of negative freedom—can be made and defended without a fully comprehensive analysis of either. It requires only that we have a firm grasp on the normative *point* of the concepts of prevention and coercion, which is to pick out the distinctive bads of (respectively) blocked opportunities and interpersonal subjection.

Such talk of interpersonal subjection may seem to align the idea of coercion with that of *domination* as it figures in the republican tradition. Yet to equate the two would be to misunderstand both ideas. According to neo-republicans such as Quentin Skinner and Philip Pettit, freedom requires the absence of domination.[33] This relationship is "exemplified by the relationship of master to slave or master to servant":

> Such a relationship means, at the limit, that the dominating party can interfere on an arbitrary basis with the choices of the dominated: can interfere, in particular, on the basis of an interest or an opinion that need not be shared by the person affected. The dominating party can practise interference, then, at will and with impunity: they do not have to seek anyone's leave and they do not have to incur any scrutiny or penalty.[34]

As this passage makes clear, domination is not equivalent to interference: on Pettit's definition, domination is a *capacity* to interfere *on an arbitrary basis*.[35] Coercion, by contrast, is a mode of interference. Thus this chapter's central point isn't the republican one that negative theorists ought to be concerned with unactualized powers of interference. It's a point about which types of interference ought to matter for negative theorists. It's therefore an "in-house" dispute amongst negative theorists about how best to characterize the notion of freedom-relevant interference, one orthogonal

[32] For a partial attempt to provide a more detailed account of coercion, see my "Coercion: The Wrong and the Bad," 545–73.

[33] Skinner, "The Third Concept of Liberty," 237–68; Pettit, *Republicanism: A Theory of Freedom and Government*.

[34] *Republicanism*, 22.

[35] Ibid., 52.

to the central dispute between negative theorists and republicans. The claim is that both prevention and coercion ought to matter, and that they are both conceptually and evaluatively distinct: one, the evil of prevention, a matter of having obstacles put in one's way; the other, the evil of coercion, a matter of being forced to comply with another's will.

Hayek puts this point as follows:

> The question of how many courses of action are open to a person is, of course, very important. But it is a different question from that of how far in acting he can follow his own plans and intentions, to what extent the pattern of his conduct is of his own design, directed toward ends for which he has been persistently striving rather than toward necessities created by others in order to make him do what they want.[36]

Although coercion normally coincides with prevention, the two can sometimes come apart. An analysis of freedom that focuses only on the good of non-prevention will be incomplete insofar as it fails to capture the good of non-coercion, since a negatively free person is not only one who has unconstrained options, but also one who doesn't act under another's yoke.

[36] *The Constitution of Liberty*, 60–61.

13

Freedom Without Trimmings

The Perils of Trivalence

Ian Carter and Hillel Steiner[*]

By any reckoning, Matthew Kramer's *The Quality of Freedom* is a landmark in the analytical philosophy literature on the idea of freedom.[1] Its originality, its painstaking engagement in all the salient controversies surrounding that concept, and its probing challenges to other work in that field, distinguish it as essential reading for anyone seriously interested in this subject.

Its being a landmark makes the fact that it is dedicated to us a source of considerable gratification but, in the present context, also a source of not a little embarrassment. For, like any landmark work, its missteps are very nearly as illuminating as its many convincing arguments. As a result, excavating some of those missteps, as this chapter does, feels not only formidably challenging but also somewhat churlish. Our excuse for engaging in this exercise is the belief which so clearly informs all of Kramer's own work: namely, that such critical exchanges are indispensable for advancing our insight into the subject in question.

In particular, this chapter will focus on whether both the concept of negative freedom itself, and also its quantification, are better understood bivalently or trivalently. When we ask whether a person is *un*free to do x, should we take a negative answer to imply that she is free to do x? And when we ask *how free* that person is, are we implicitly asking a question about the *values* of the freedoms she has or lacks? Kramer's answer to the first of these questions is "No" and his answer to the second is "Yes." We disagree with both of those answers, and in both cases we raise concerns about the implications of trivalence.

More specifically, we argue, in section 1, that trivalent analyses of freedom are beset by serious conceptual difficulties. Section 2 responds to Kramer's criticism of the bivalent understanding of freedom, a criticism he formulates in the context of his trivalent insistence that a person's *ability* to do x-type actions is a necessary condition of her being free or unfree to do x. And finally, section 3 argues that, while Kramer's deployment of bivalent evaluation, in answering the "How free?" question, succeeds in overcoming the paradox generated by trivalently evaluative accounts of freedom measurement, it generates conceptual problems of its own.

[*] For helpful comments on an earlier draft of this chapter, we are grateful to Michael Garnett, Andrew Halpin, Andreas Schmidt, and Ronen Shnayderman, as well as audiences in London and Cambridge, and the editors of this volume, Visa Kurki and Mark McBride. We owe a special debt of gratitude to Matt Kramer who, as was perhaps to be expected, provided some very extensive feedback.

[1] Kramer, *The Quality of Freedom*, hereafter QF.

Ian Carter and Hillel Steiner, *Freedom Without Trimmings* In: *Without Trimmings*. Edited by: Mark McBride and Visa AJ Kurki, Oxford University Press. © Mark McBride and Visa AJ Kurki 2022. DOI: 10.1093/oso/9780198868866.003.0013

It is perhaps important to note—and Kramer would readily agree—that these bivalence-trivalence issues are not merely pedantic ones concerning minor technical points of disagreement. They are, rather, ones that have significant conceptual implications, not only for the relation between social freedom and ability, but also for how we are to understand judgments about overall freedom. And hence, they also have practical implications for those aiming to promote social freedom or distribute it more fairly.

1. Against Ability-based Trivalence

If freedom is *bivalent*, then for any conceivable action, I am either free or unfree to perform it.[2] *Tertium non datur.* If I am not free to leave my home, then I am unfree to leave it, and if I am not unfree to leave my home, then I am free to leave it. If freedom is *trivalent*, on the other hand, freedom and unfreedom are not contradictories, for there are some actions that I am neither free nor unfree to perform.

1.1 Bivalent versus Trivalent Specific Freedoms

The ordinary language of freedom does not tend to assume anything as sophisticated as a trivalent approach to freedom: for the most part, it is simply assumed that the negation of my freedom to do something entails my unfreedom to do it, and vice versa. Testimony to this fact can be found in non-Germanic languages, most of which contain no equivalent of the Germanic term "unfree." For example, the most natural way to translate "unfree" into Italian is by using the term "non libero," meaning "not free," and a neologism is therefore needed in order to make sense of the trivalent distinction between "unfree" and "not free." Translating a trivalent analysis of freedom into Italian is a somewhat laborious task.[3]

Because of this tendency in ordinary language, it has likewise been common for theorists of freedom to assume bivalence in their conceptual reconstructions. Perhaps the most straightforward way to define freedom bivalently is by saying that a person is free to do x if and only if she is able to do x, and is unfree to do x if and only if she is unable to do x. On this view, apparently (though not explicitly) endorsed by Philippe Van Parijs and Amartya Sen, freedom and unfreedom are contradictories because ability and inability are contradictories.[4] Let us call this conception "bivalent freedom-as-ability." The concepts of ability and inability no doubt serve many important purposes. As in the case of bivalent conceptions of freedom, moreover, the identification of unfreedom with inability has some support in ordinary language. However,

[2] We specify the relevant meaning of "conceivable" in section 2.1.

[3] To the best of our knowledge, the same is true at least of the following languages: French, Spanish, Portuguese, Romanian, Polish, Ukrainian, Russian, Turkish, Hebrew, Chinese. Ordinary language is of course not the last word in conceptual analysis, but "it *is* the *first* word" (Austin, "A Plea for Excuses," 185) (emphasis in the original).

[4] See, e.g., Van Parijs, *Real Freedom for All. What, If Anything, Can Justify Capitalism?*, section 1.7; Sen, *Inequality Reexamined*, chs. 1–5.

that identification fails to capture what political and social philosophers have in mind when they refer to unfreedom, explicitly or implicitly, as an *interpersonal relation*. If the phenomenon we are interested is *social* unfreedom—unfreedom as an empirical relation between persons—then we should say that a person is unfree to do x if x is prevented, actually or hypothetically, by the behavior of others.[5] More precisely, we should say the following: a person is socially unfree to do x if, and only if, there is some other action or set of actions, y, of another person or set of persons, where the occurrence of y implies the impossibility of the occurrence of x, and y either (i) does occur or (ii) would occur if x were attempted.[6]

It follows from this social conception of unfreedom that a person can be unable to do x without being unfree to do x. Inabilities that have natural causes or that are self-inflicted do not amount to cases of social unfreedom. Thus, on a social conception of unfreedom, I am *unable but not unfree* to leave my home if no one has prevented me from leaving but an avalanche has blocked the door from outside, or if no one has prevented me from leaving but I have locked the door from the inside and swallowed the key.

On a *bivalent* approach to social freedom, of the sort endorsed by Isaiah Berlin and Hillel Steiner, unfreedom is defined as the presence of such preventive actions on the part of others, and freedom is then defined simply as the *absence of unfreedom*.[7] This is perhaps the most plausible way of making sense of the idea that freedom is a "negative" concept. Thus, in the example just given, although I am *unable* to leave my home, I am nevertheless *free* to do so, simply because I am *not unfree* to do so. Let us call the negative conception emerging from this line of reasoning "bivalent social freedom." Our aim in this chapter is to defend the coherence of such a conception.

Even once we have distinguished clearly between social and non-social freedom, some people might still insist that it is counterintuitive to say that I can be free to do something I am unable to do. Freedom, they will say, must presuppose ability on the part of the agent.[8] Now, one can make this last claim without abandoning bivalence: as we have just seen, there is a consistent bivalent theory that identifies freedom with ability and unfreedom with inability. However, if one assumes bivalence, one cannot identify freedom with ability and also conceive of unfreedom as an interpersonal relation of prevention.

[5] On the concept of social freedom see, e.g., Berlin, *Four Essays on Liberty*, 122–3; Oppenheim, *Political Concepts*; Miller, "Constraints on Freedom," 66–75; Steiner, *An Essay on Rights*, hereafter ER; Kristjánsson, *Social Freedom. The Responsibility View*.

[6] This formulation paraphrases, with some amendments, the definition in Steiner, ER, 8. A further necessary specification is that the sufficiency of y (in rendering impossible x) not be triggered by an action, subsequent to y, of the person whose freedom is under consideration. Kramer implicitly rejects this further specification in ch. 4 of QF (see n. 23). We defend it in a separate paper tentatively entitled "A Causal Criterion for Interpersonal Unfreedom."

[7] Berlin, *Four Essays on Liberty*, 122; Steiner, ER, 14.

[8] Sometimes this claim is made for ideological reasons, in reaction to the claim of some right-libertarians to the effect that the poor are no less free than the rich, but are lacking only in certain abilities. It is a mistake, however, to think that poverty is essentially a set of inabilities rather than an indicator of sets of preventions by others. The difference between egalitarians and anti-egalitarians does not track that between advocates of freedom-as-ability and advocates of social freedom. See Cohen, *Self-Ownership, Freedom and Equality*, 58–9; Carter, *A Measure of Freedom*, hereafter AMF, 234–6.

One might then be tempted to say, "so much the worse for bivalence." This is the line taken by Matthew Kramer, according to whom the freedom to do x and the unfreedom to do x are two rather different kinds of thing: the former is *not* a social relation, whereas the latter *is*:

> A person is free to φ if and only if he is able to φ ... [whereas] [a] person is unfree to φ if and only if both of the following conditions obtain: (1) he would be able to φ in the absence of the second of these conditions; and (2) irrespective of whether he actually endeavours to φ, he is directly or indirectly prevented from φ-ing by some action(s) or some disposition(s)-to-perform-some-action(s) on the part of some other person(s).[9]

If we think of freedom and unfreedom in this more disjointed way, we can readily understand how there can be actions that one is *not free* to perform, because one is unable to perform them, but that one is also *not unfree* to perform, because the inabilities in question have natural causes or are self-inflicted.

Unlike bivalence, trivalence posits a condition that any action must satisfy in order to qualify as one that the agent is either free or unfree to perform. For Kramer, the relevant condition is that the agent be able to perform the action (in the absence of preventive actions of others). This stipulation implies what we shall call *ability-based* trivalence.[10] However, Kramer's is not the only candidate condition for a trivalent account of freedom. In the first edition of *Two Concepts of Liberty*, published in 1958, Isaiah Berlin implicitly defined "political liberty" as "the area within which a man can do what he wants," and added that I am unfree to the extent that I am "prevented by other persons from doing what I want."[11] He thereby implied that, if I do not want to do x, I am neither free nor unfree to do x. Call this account *desire-based* trivalence. Berlin corrected himself on this point in the 1969 edition of his essay, because he realized that his 1958 definition would allow one to claim, paradoxically, that a contented slave, who desires only to be a slave, suffers no unfreedoms at all.[12] Given the plausibility of this objection, desire-based trivalence is generally rejected by contemporary theorists of social freedom. The contemporary literature contains several other kinds of trivalence: one might claim, for example, that in order for a person to count as unfree to do x, x must not only be prevented but must be *wrongly* prevented,[13] or *arbitrarily* prevented.[14] But we need not investigate these alternative accounts here,

[9] Kramer QF, 15. For Kramer, φ can be either an action of the agent or a "becoming" (QF, 156–69). We here assume that freedom pertains only to actions. Kramer's rejection of this assumption is not relevant to the arguments presented in this chapter.

[10] Ability-based trivalence was also defended by J.P. Day. See his *Liberty and Justice*, 42–4.

[11] Berlin, *Two Concepts of Liberty*, 7. Similar definitions can be found in classic texts including those of Hobbes and Mill. For a discussion, see Day, *Liberty and Justice*, ch. 1.

[12] Berlin, *Four Essays on Liberty*, xxxviii–xl.

[13] This position is more or less explicitly adopted in several libertarian writings, including those of Robert Nozick, Murray Rothbard, and Bruno Leoni, who interpret the wrongful prevention in question as a violation of private property rights. For references, see Carter, AMF, 69 n. 2.

[14] On arbitrariness-based trivalence, see Pettit, "Keeping Republican Freedom Simple: On a Difference with Quentin Skinner," 346–8. Yet another trivalent account—which one might call "alternatives-based"—is defended in Oppenheim, in *Dimensions of Freedom. An Analysis*, 110–11, and criticized in Steiner, "Freedom and Bivalence."

since our argument will focus on Kramer's ability-based trivalence, comparing it first to desire-based trivalence and then to bivalence.

1.2 Combining Freedoms and Unfreedoms into a Single Measure of Overall Freedom

There is a general problem besetting the quantification of a person's overall freedom when the concept of freedom is itself understood trivalently. In ordinary usage, the answer to the question "How happy is person P?" normally takes into account both the extent of their happiness and the extent of their unhappiness. Similarly, in assessing the extent of their wealth, debts as well as assets are standardly entered into the computation. And illness has as much bearing as wellness in determining how healthy persons are. In short, when we quantify these various personal conditions—happiness, well-being, wealth, health—we integrate negatives with positives to arrive at a single quantity in our estimations of their overall extent. Moreover, negative and positive descriptions of these overall extents are normally understood as interchangeable: an increase in one's overall unhealthiness entails a decrease in one's overall health, and vice versa; a gain in one's overall unhappiness entails a decrease in one's overall happiness, and vice versa. And the same is true, analogously, when we seek to identify the extent of persons' overall freedom, but it is true only on condition that freedom is understood *bivalently*. On bivalent freedom, the answer to the question "How free is person P?" is arrived at by integrating freedoms with unfreedoms into a single quantified judgment, *where P's loss of a freedom logically entails P's acquisition of the corresponding unfreedom*, and *vice versa*.

We have already seen how the bivalent understanding of *specific* freedoms and unfreedoms is reflected in much of ordinary discourse about freedom. Similarly, the above understanding of *overall* freedom, whereby an *increase* in a person's freedom just is a *decrease* in her unfreedom, and vice versa, reflects much of ordinary discourse both about degrees of freedom and about its value: it is common to suppose that when a person or group or society has become more unfree, it has become less free, and vice versa; and to suppose that, if freedom is valuable to a certain extent, then unfreedom is disvaluable to that same extent, and vice versa.

But the same is *not* true of trivalent freedom. For in this case, the loss of P's freedom to do x, though it might be due simply to others' prevention of P's doing x (making P unfree to do x), might alternatively be due to the dissolution of whatever *additional condition* that trivalent conception imposes on P's being free or unfree to do x: whether that condition be x's desirability or rightfulness, or the arbitrariness of an act of prevention of x, or, as on Kramer's conception, P's ability to do x. In all these latter cases, x becomes an act which P is neither free nor unfree to do. Accordingly, P becomes less free, but not more unfree.

In order to clarify the problematic nature of the additional condition and its dissolution, we need first to recall how Steiner, Carter, and Kramer conceive of the measurement of overall freedom. All three authors suggest that overall freedom, understood as a quantitative attribute of an agent, consists in the ratio of that agent's freedoms to the set of her freedoms and unfreedoms combined. In other words, we take a list of actions that the agent is either free or unfree to perform, and we ask what *proportion* of that list the agent is free to perform. In the most straightforward version, originally put forward by Steiner, agent Red's measure of overall freedom is:

$$Fr / (Fr + Ur)$$

Where Fr and Ur are respectively the number of actions on the list that Red is free and unfree to perform.[15]

Steiner's formula has been revised by Carter, who suggests that Fr and Ur ought each to be understood as representing a set of spatio-temporally specific sets of compossible actions and, further, that the number representing each such set of compossible actions should be weighted by the probability of its being prevented/unprevented by others, as judged at the time of the freedom being measured.[16] Kramer accepts these revisions to Steiner's formula but adds two further qualifications of his own. The first is that the numerator of the fraction must be squared.[17] The second is that each act-combination should be multiplied by its value for the agent in pursuing certain general ends.[18] For the moment, we shall set aside both of these further qualifications. We shall return to Kramer's idea of squaring the numerator shortly, after having clarified the general problem, for trivalent theorists, of combining freedoms and unfreedoms into a single measure. We shall return to Kramer's "evaluative multipliers," on the other hand, in section 3 of this chapter. For the remainder of this section, we shall simplify matters by also setting aside Carter's revisions, although we endorse both of them and we will indeed return to the probabilistic dimension of overall freedom in section 2. Let us then proceed now on the basis of Steiner's simple formula set out above, which we shall call "the basic fraction."

One might ask why overall freedom should be conceived in terms of the above fraction rather than simply as the sum of the agent's specific freedoms (i.e., the numerator of the basic fraction). The focus on a ratio reflects the above-mentioned idea that overall freedom should take into account both freedoms *and unfreedoms*. It is also worth noting, however, that the difference between measuring overall freedom in terms of the fraction and measuring it in terms of the number of freedoms is much more dramatic in the case of trivalent freedom than in the case of bivalent freedom, for in the former case the denominator is typically subject to variation, both interpersonally and intrapersonally, as we shall see shortly by means of some examples. If the denominator is the same for every agent whose freedom we care to measure, as it is for bivalent freedom, then the difference between using Steiner's formula and counting the number of freedoms will be merely one of presentation.[19] This said, in section 2 we will introduce a more substantive reason, albeit a pragmatic one, for saying that bivalent freedom, no less than trivalent freedom, needs to be represented by means of a fraction.

[15] Steiner, "How Free: Computing Personal Liberty," 74–5.
[16] Carter, AMF, chs. 7 and 8.
[17] Kramer, QF, 368–79.
[18] Kramer, QF, 425–73.
[19] Interestingly, Steiner's original justification for using his fraction, as opposed to simply counting the number of freedoms, might seem to presuppose a form of trivalence, since it presupposes a variable denominator. See Steiner, "How Free," 75, and, relatedly, Steiner, ER, 43. However, these justifications might also be interpreted, with hindsight, in light of the analysis we provide in section 2.4.

1.3 A Problem in Kramer's Trivalent Approach

Consider now the following two examples:

> *Normal Citizen.* Blue is an average citizen of a stable liberal democratic state. There is a wide variety of things that she is able to do and that are neither punishable nor physically prevented by others (including, but not limited to, traveling, working, and going to concerts). Similarly, there is a wide variety of things that she is prevented by others from doing or would be punished by others for doing (including, but not limited to, driving her neighbor's Rolls Royce, walking in a military zone, and stealing from a bank).
>
> *Deluded Prisoner 1.* Red is confined to a prison for the foreseeable future. The prison guards are preventing him from doing most things (including traveling, working, and going to concerts), allowing only the very restricted options of eating, sleeping, attending to personal hygiene, reading the odd book, and moving around in the prison, all at certain allocated times. A friend of Red brings him a copy of the 1958 version of Berlin's *Two Concepts of Liberty*, together with a manual on stoic asceticism. Having read these books, Red decides to "liberate" himself by gradually learning not to desire to do any of the things that he is prevented from doing. After a few months, Red's sole ambition is to eat, sleep, attend to personal hygiene, read the odd book, and move around in the prison, all at the allocated times.

The case of *Deluded Prisoner 1* illustrates the absurdity of desire-based trivalence which, as we have seen, was later rejected by Berlin himself. We can formulate the objection to this version of trivalence in terms of the basic fraction representing Red's overall freedom: assuming desire-based trivalence, the relevant list of actions, with respect to which it makes sense to ask whether Red is free or unfree, is the list that Red *desires* to perform. For any action that Red has no desire to perform, he is neither free nor unfree to perform that action (the question of his freedom or unfreedom does not arise). This list of actions constitutes the *denominator* of the basic fraction representing Red's overall freedom. Red's coming to desire very little therefore has the effect of drastically reducing the size of the denominator of the fraction representing his overall freedom. Moreover, following Red's exercise in desire-removal, virtually all of the actions on the (now very short) list are actions he is unprevented from performing. Compare now Red's freedom to that of Blue. Only a thorough empirical investigation of Blue's situation will reveal whether and, if so, by how much, her freedoms outnumber her unfreedoms. However, if we assume desire-based trivalence together with normal desires on Blue's part, it cannot be doubted that Blue suffers a large number of unfreedoms. Let us assume by way of illustration that Blue's overall freedom is 5,000/10,000 = 0.5, and that Red's initial overall freedom is 20/10,000 = 0.002. After Red's exercise in desire removal, his overall freedom becomes 20/20 = 1. Red becomes much freer than Blue. Indeed, Red becomes maximally free.

Clearly the root of the problem revealed by the above examples is the fact that the denominator of the fraction can change and, in the extreme example of Red, is reduced to a very small number. As Steiner wrote in an early article: "it is absurd to suggest that the extent of one's liberty can be increased by increasing the number of instances in which the question whether one is free does not arise."[20] In *Deluded Prisoner 1*, moreover, those two increases are brought about by *the very agent whose freedom is under consideration*, while it is normally assumed that, because social freedom is a relation *between* agents, increases and decreases in one's freedom must depend directly on the actions and motivations of others, and not directly on one's own actions or motivations. On a relational conception of freedom, the term "self-liberation" should not be taken literally, as if one could liberate oneself unilaterally, but can at most refer to a course of action, violent or otherwise, that somehow motivates others to cease preventing one from doing certain things. One can affect one's own social freedom *indirectly*—by acting, intentionally or unintentionally, violently or non-violently, to change others' preventive dispositions—but one cannot affect it *directly*, simply by changing one's own dispositions.[21]

Despite widespread agreement on the above points, and the consequent rejection of *desire-based* trivalence on the part of contemporary theorists of freedom, an analogous implication in the case of *ability-based* trivalence seems to have gone largely unacknowledged. Consider the following example:

> *Deluded Prisoner 2*. White is in the same prison as Red and is subject to a similar set of preventions. A friend of White brings him a copy of Kramer's *The Quality of Freedom*, together with a special poison. Whoever drinks this poison will become paralyzed for life, save for the minimal bodily functions necessary for survival. Having read the first chapter of *The Quality of Freedom*, White laughs at Red for thinking he has made himself more free simply by desiring to do less. Convinced that he has discovered the true path to liberation, White then drinks the poison, as a result of which he spends the rest of his life staring into space and being spoon-fed by one of the guards.[22]

Deluded Prisoner 2 on the assumption of ability-based trivalence is analogous to *Deluded Prisoner 1* on the assumption of desire-based trivalence: White's action of drinking the poison removes the vast majority of his freedoms, but it also removes *all of his unfreedoms*, for that action makes it no longer the case that White would be able to do the relevant things in the absence of the preventive actions of others (see condition 1 in Kramer's definition of unfreedom cited above).[23] His degree of overall

[20] Steiner, "Individual Liberty," 34. Steiner did not, at the time, perceive the full implications of the quoted claim, for he implied on the same page that whereas desire-based trivalence is unacceptable, ability-based trivalence is not.

[21] On the distinction between a person's directly and indirectly affecting their own freedom, see Carter and Kramer, "How Changes in One's Preferences can Affect One's Freedom (and How They Cannot). A Reply to Dowding and van Hees," 81–96.

[22] Reading only the first chapter of QF gives White knowledge of Kramer's F and U postulates (which define freedom and unfreedom), but not of Kramer's analysis of the sources of unfreedom. See nn. 6 and 23).

[23] Our judgment that White removes all of his unfreedoms, on ability-based trivalence, depends on the view that any inability of agent A that has one of A's own actions as its proximate cause counts as a *self-inflicted* inability of A and therefore cannot qualify as a case of social unfreedom of A (see n. 6). In ch. 4 of QF, Kramer himself rejects this special status of the proximate cause. Kramer would say that White becomes *un*free to do all of the things that his poison-taking makes him unable to do, as long as the poison was made by another human being and he would not have taken it had he not read the first chapter of QF. This is because, according to ch. 4 of QF, an obstacle counts as self-inflicted *only* if its *entire* causal history contains

freedom has therefore increased, and his new position relative to Blue (assuming ability-based trivalence) is exactly the same as that of Red (assuming desire-based trivalence). He enjoys, let us suppose, an overall degree of freedom of 2/2 = 1.

As the freedom-rankings of Blue, Red, and White make clear, we do not necessarily overcome the absurd implications of desire-based trivalence merely by substituting it with another kind of trivalence. The problem goes deeper, and lies in trivalence itself, or at least in a certain family of trivalent conceptions including desire-based and ability-based conceptions. A conception of freedom that ranks either Red or White ahead of Blue in terms of overall freedom is more than slightly adrift from its ostensible anchoring in the concerns of social and political philosophy.

1.4 Squaring the Numerator?

In partial mitigation of the absurd implication of *Deluded Prisoner 2*, Kramer will appeal to his stipulation that a person's overall freedom is not represented by the basic fraction we have been working with up to now, but by the basic fraction with the numerator squared: Fr^2 / (Fr + Ur). Call the latter the "SN fraction." Kramer makes the move of squaring the numerator exactly in order to avoid various crazy measurements that would inevitably result from conjoining his ability-based trivalence with the measurement of overall freedom in terms of the basic fraction. His justification of this move is that squaring the numerator appropriately places "paramount emphasis" on abilities vis à vis social unfreedoms, "without obliterating" the importance of the distinction between social unfreedoms and mere inabilities.[24]

If we square the numerator in the above examples, it will indeed no longer be the case that Red or White overtake Blue in terms of their degrees of overall freedom: Blue's degree of freedom will be 25,000,000/10,000 = 25,000. By contrast, assuming desire-based trivalence, Red's freedom after removing most of her own desires will be 400/ 20 = 20, still a relatively low level of overall freedom; and assuming ability-based trivalence, White's freedom after drinking the poison will be 4/2 = 2, an even lower level. Because the numerator in Blue's basic fraction is so much larger than that of Red or White, her degree of overall freedom, as represented by the SN fraction, is bound to be much greater than that of Red or White (this, on either kind of trivalence and assuming an average set of desires on Blue's part). Similarly, while even *Blue's* degree of ability-based trivalent freedom, as represented by the basic fraction, would increase if she drank the poison (it would increase from 0.5 to 1), this will no longer be the case

no actions of other people. In our view, this interpretation of the sources of social unfreedom fails to track our common understanding of the category of self-inflicted inabilities, for it reduces that category almost to nothing. If I cut off my fingers with a carving knife, we do not conclude that the knife manufacturer is preventing me from playing the piano. Should any reader nevertheless prefer Kramer's interpretation of the causal sources of social unfreedom, we can accommodate their preference by assuming that White makes the poison himself from ingredients that occur naturally in his prison compound and that his choice to take the poison does not depend in the relevant way on the publication of *The Quality of Freedom* or on any other behavior of other agents. The same freedom-judgments will then follow.

[24] Kramer, QF, 368–71.

if her freedom is represented by the SN fraction. Instead, Blue's overall freedom will decrease drastically from 25,000 to 2.

Four points need to be made about Kramer's numerator-squaring move. The first is that it buys conformity to some commonsense comparisons of freedom only at the expense of contradicting other such comparisons. As a result of our squaring the numerator, the addition of particular freedoms will make marginally increasing contributions to a person's overall degree of freedom.[25] This is strongly counterintuitive. It entails, for example, that redistributing resources from the poor to the rich will generally increase the overall level of societal freedom. It is debatable whether specific freedoms make marginally diminishing contributions to overall freedom, but few would agree that they make marginally increasing contributions. Indeed, as we shall see in section 3, Kramer himself holds that the marginal contributions of qualitatively similar freedoms are *decreasing* ones. The intuition motivating this view is in tension with the more general assertion of marginally increasing contributions entailed by the numerator-squaring move.

The second point is that the numerator-squaring move only mitigates the absurdity of the outcome of *Deluded Prisoner 2* without eliminating it, for it leaves in place the judgment that White makes himself *freer* by drinking the poison. Kramer must therefore side with White in holding that, while Red's attempt to increase her own freedom is laughable, White's own attempt is successful. In intrapersonally relative terms, White indeed makes himself freer *fifty-fold*, increasing his own freedom from 400/10,000 = 0.04, to 4/2 = 2. Perhaps Kramer will be tempted at this point to bite the bullet and accept that White increases his own freedom, emphasizing the isolated nature of the case and the smallness of the increase when considered in *inter*personally relative terms. However, the idea that White can increase his freedom unilaterally through self-mutilation is more than just "mildly odd,"[26] and is generalizable beyond the examples just given. If White's self-disablement were less extreme and were to result in his basic fraction becoming 100/100 rather than 2/2, then his post-disablement level of overall freedom as reflected by his SN fraction would be 10,000/100 = 100. In this case, White's self-disablement would increase his overall freedom if his pre-disablement basic fraction was anything smaller than 316.2/1,000 = 0.3162 (quite a large fraction!), assuming a denominator of 1,000; or if it was anything smaller than 1,000/10,000 = 0.1, assuming a denominator of 10,000; and so on. Notice that the size of these pre-disablement basic fractions increases as the numbers of freedoms and unfreedoms become smaller. This is because the numerator of the basic fraction is the square root of the numerator of the SN fraction. At the very least, then, a great many of the world's most oppressed and least able people can increase their own Kramerian freedom through self-mutilation. Moreover, even *Normal Citizen* Blue can increase her freedom as measured by the SN fraction if she can limit her own hypothetical abilities in such a way as to remove only some of her unfreedoms without removing any of her freedoms, or if the number of unfreedoms she removes can exceed the number of freedoms she

[25] We are grateful to Andreas Schmidt for raising this objection. The only exception to this rule is where the agent has no unfreedoms at all.

[26] Kramer, QF, 376.

removes, to such an extent that the resultant reduction of the denominator is not compensated for by the squaring of the numerator.

The third point to be made about Kramer's numerator-squaring move follows from this last observation about the changing size of the basic fraction. The size of the numbers we are working with is partly the result of our *choice of unit size* in measuring physical extents of action. An example given by Carter is the fact that the activity of visiting a museum might count for seven alternative actions if the units of measurement are the "days" in a week on which one can visit "the museum," or might count for many more alternative actions if the units are the "hours" in which one can visit "this or that room" in the museum.[27] The smaller the units of space-time we can manage to work with, the more micro-preventions our measurements are likely to capture. But once we have captured all the micro-preventions that are of interest, choosing yet smaller units should make no difference to our measurements of people's degrees of freedom. This much is true on Kramer's proposed formula no less than on Steiner's or Carter's. However, as we can see from the above figures, Kramer's numerator-squaring move allows the choice of unit sizes to have arbitrary effects on substantive questions about how to increase or decrease a given person's freedom. In particular, the smaller the numbers we are working with in describing any given scenario, the larger the number of people in that scenario who will fall into the category of individuals who are in a position to increase their own freedom through self-disablement. Even if we assume the existence of such a category, it ought not to be the case that the substantive question of *whether or not* a specific person can increase her freedom though self-disablement depends on our *choice of unit size* in measuring the physical extents of her available actions. Yet this is exactly what will happen if we allow the *absolute size* of the numerator in the *basic* fraction to affect the *size of the fraction* representing a person's overall freedom.

The fourth point is methodological: the numerator-squaring move is of an ad hoc nature, and its limited efficacy is symptomatic of this fact. It is not unlike the ploy of an accountant who, in auditing a company whose financial health he would rather not question, decides to square the figure representing its assets, claiming that this gives "paramount emphasis" to assets vis à vis liabilities. Fortunately, squaring the numerator of our freedom-measuring fraction is unlikely to land us in jail, but it is similarly ad hoc inasmuch as it has no basis in an analysis of the concept of freedom, deriving instead from a disappointing degree of fit between the results of one such an analysis, on the one hand, and certain commonsense comparisons of degrees of freedom, on the other.

This is not to deny that we ought to test our analysis of the concept of freedom against commonsense comparisons, for this is the nearest thing we have, in the present context, to the test of isomorphism referred to by theorists of measurement.[28] Carter puts his own analysis to such a test: he points to the ways in which it achieves isomorphism with commonsense comparisons, and the ways in which it does not;[29]

[27] Carter, AMF, 186. Cf. Kramer, QF, 379–88.
[28] Carter, AMF, ch. 4.
[29] See, e.g., AMF, 204–11, 229–31.

he also defends his analysis by arguing that certain apparent failures in isomorphism are in fact illusory.[30] What he does not suggest is a tweaking of the formula so as to accommodate as many as possible of the remaining counterexamples, where such surface manipulation has no grounding in the analysis of freedom he has provided.

The ad hoc nature of Kramer's formula-tweaking is illustrated by the fact that he might just as well have favored cubing the numerator, or raising it to some yet greater power, or simply multiplying it by a constant. Each of these ad hoc adjustments will no doubt accommodate some further counterexamples and give rise to yet others (coming from the opposite direction in the sense of pointing to an underrepresentation of social unfreedoms). If we accept the validity of such adjustments, and yet are unable to judge between the various formula-tweaking alternatives in terms of their *overall* fit with commonsense comparisons, then the only features of our measurements of overall freedom that will continue to qualify as non-arbitrary will be those that are preserved across all formula-tweaking alternatives. Such features are likely to include the ordinal rankings of different agents in terms of their degrees of overall freedom. However, most theories of justice demand more of our powers of measurement than the mere power of ordinal ranking.[31]

A more radical theoretical response to the above counterexamples would be to admit that personal ability, on the one hand, and the relation of social unfreedom, on the other, are really two quite different quantitative attributes, and that ability-based trivalence does not really provide us with any sound reason to posit a single quantitative attribute, called "overall freedom," that somehow combines judgments about abilities, on the one hand, and social unfreedoms, on the other. Perhaps ability and social unfreedom are simply two rather different quantitative attributes. Unpalatable as it might be to abandon the unidimensional measurement of freedom in favor of the measurement of the two independent variables of freedom and unfreedom, this more radical response might be the most appropriate for those who insist on a trivalent approach to theorizing about specific freedoms and unfreedoms.

2. In Defense of Bivalent Social Freedom

If trivalent freedom-as-ability is to be rejected, what is the alternative? Does the simpler idea of bivalent social freedom provide us with a more plausible conception? To answer this question, we need first to take a closer look at the relation between specific social freedoms and specific abilities.

2.1 Freedoms and Abilities

One of Kramer's reasons for rejecting bivalent social freedom is the apparent indeterminacy of the very distinction between unfreedom and inability, as summed up in the following rhetorical question:

[30] See, e.g., AMF section 5.5, and Carter, "Social Power and Negative Freedom."

[31] Carter, AMF, ch. 3.

> If a man is unable to escape from the prison cell in which he has been detained, is the curtailment of his opportunities attributable to the actions of other people in jailing him or to his own natural strength which is insufficient for him to break down the wall and bars that confine him?[32]

In addressing this question, we need to pay careful attention to the different degrees of spatio-temporal specificity with which various action-types can be described.

On bivalent social freedom, I am free at time t to do x at t+1 if I am not unfree at t to do x at t+1. And I am *un*free at t to do x at t+1 if there is an action or set of actions of another person or group that is a sufficient condition for my non-performance of x at t+1. Now, in order to make sense of the idea of an action of another person being a sufficient condition at time t for my non-performance of x at t+1, we have to assume some set of abilities on my part, and the set of abilities that is relevant in judging the freedom I possess at t is clearly the set that I actually possess at t. My abilities at t *are* therefore relevant in determining what freedoms I enjoy at t—not in the sense that my abilities simply are my freedoms, but in the sense that they are a necessary part of what determines whether an action of another person *is a sufficient condition at t* for my *non-performance* of x at t+1. If the agent's abilities were not relevant in the latter sense, then no action would indeed ever qualify as preventing another.

One's abilities include the ability to affect one's own abilities, and these meta-abilities, appropriately specified in temporal terms, affect the preventive capacity of actions of others. For example, if Green locks Black in a cell at time t and leaves Black there indefinitely, and Black's arms are not muscular enough to prize apart the bars on the cell window, then Green renders Black unfree at t to leave the cell at t+1; but if Black is both free and able, at t, to start training to build up the necessary muscles to prize the bars apart, and if the necessary body-building would take her 10 units of time, then Green's action of locking Black in the cell at t fails to make Black unfree at t to leave the cell at t+11. If Black then omits to do any of the exercises between t and t+5, then Black is unfree at t+5 to leave the cell at t+11 as a result of Green's action at t.[33] (Although Black is causally responsible for her own lack of increased muscle power at t+5, Green's action at t is nevertheless a sufficient condition *at t+5* for Black's not leaving the cell at t+11.) This said, Black is then free at t+5 to exit the cell at t+16.

In clarifying the relation between social freedom and ability we need also to be attentive to the different *ways* in which a given act-type may be performed at a given time. As Steiner writes: "the freedom to fly business class to New York is not the same as the freedom to fly to New York *per se*. I can be unfree to do the former without being unfree to do the latter."[34] This is because "flying business class to New York" is one of many possible occurrences of the type "flying to New York," just as "flying business class to New York on Tuesday" is one of many possible occurrences of the type "flying business class to New York."

[32] Kramer, QF, 76 n. 75.

[33] The difference between actions and omissions is an important factor in determining our freedom-judgment in this example. Had Black already been able at t to prize the bars apart, but cut off her own arms at t+4 by operating a guillotine that happened to be present in her cell, Black would *not* thereby become socially *un*free at t+5 to leave the cell at t+11 by prizing the bars apart.

[34] Steiner, "Freedom and Bivalence," 64.

Thus, if Black has the ability at t to construct a pneumatic drill with which to break down the wall and leave the cell subsequent to Green's shutting her in at t, and none of the material resources necessary to construct and use the drill are withheld from Black by anyone (e.g., the required material objects and electricity supply are present in the cell at t and will remain so), and it would take Black five units of time to assemble the drill, then Green's action at t makes Black unfree at t to leave the cell through the window at t+6 by prizing the bars apart with her arms, but it does not make Black unfree at t to leave the cell through the wall at t+6 with the help of a drill.[35]

The measurement of *overall* bivalent freedom involves quantifying over all actions that are conceivable within the laws of physics, the test for inclusion being the question of whether we can speak meaningfully of the action in question being *physically prevented* by the action of another person. This is not to say, on the other hand, that every new act-description that passes this test is to be included in the list of all conceivable actions for the purposes of measuring overall freedom, for it is possible for the same action to be described in many different ways.[36] In order to avoid double-counting our specific freedoms and unfreedoms, then, the list should contain the set of conceivable actions *under descriptions pitched at the appropriate level of specificity* in terms of the spatio-temporally located physical components of which they make use. The appropriate level of specificity is determined by the size of the physical units of space, time, and matter appropriate to the kinds of comparisons of freedom we are interested in making.[37] Thus, if I am free to visit museum M on a Monday, on a Tuesday, and so on for each day of the week, then we can say that I have a total of seven freedoms. It would be a mistake at that point to take account, in addition, of the more abstract freedom-type to "visit museum M," as if this added an eighth freedom, let alone the even more abstract freedom-type of "visiting a museum," as if this added a ninth. Kramer explicitly accepts this point in his discussion of the choice of space-time units in gauging the physical extents of available actions.[38]

A final clarificatory point concerns science-fiction technology. As a case of "ability to acquire new abilities," future possible technological innovation represents something of a puzzle when it comes to measuring bivalent freedom. Although we rarely ask questions about specific freedoms of agents to do technologically impossible

[35] Despite Kramer's careful attention to the distinctions between more and less general act-types, one of his counterexamples to the bivalent conception of social freedom, an example referring to technological innovation, seems to involve slippage in this sense. Emily, he says, is unable to walk on a ledge of rock at the top of a hill because the hill is so shuddersomely steep that she cannot reach it, even though no one is preventing her from doing so. Kramer claims that, on bivalent social freedom, Emily is free to ascend the hill and walk on the ledge, *until* Elmer invents a contraption that enables a person to scale the hill, yet prevents Emily from using the contraption. According to Kramer, Steiner must take the view that, after Elmer's invention and withholding of the contraption, Emily is *unfree* to walk on the ledge, where before she was *free* to do so (QF, 221; see also Shnayderman, "Causal Tests in Subjunctive Judgements about Negative Freedom," 190). This unqualified freedom-judgment would certainly be counterintuitive, but it is not entailed by the bivalent conception of social freedom. Emily is free (albeit unable) to clamber up the shuddersomely steep slope with the sole aid of her own limbs both before *and after* Elmer's invention and withholding of his contraption, as long as no one else is preventing her from doing so. After Elmer's invention and withholding of the contraption, Emily becomes unfree to ascend the hill *using Elmer's contraption*.

[36] See Carter, AMF, 175–80.

[37] See section 1.4.

[38] Kramer, QF, 379–88.

things, it seems that science-fiction actions ought to be included in the list by reference to which overall bivalent freedom is measured, as long as they do not contradict the laws of physics; on the other hand, such actions are rarely, if ever, conceivable at the appropriate level of specificity, given that their descriptions fail to refer to the specific resources, mechanisms, and processes of energy-conversion involved in their performance. If we take bivalence seriously, it seems that we must include more general science-fiction act-types as proxies for sets of appropriately specified actions, assigning approximate weights to such act-types on the basis of the approximate number of appropriately specified occurrences over which they range. Such an inclusion will be warranted as long as we are able to make meaningful probability judgments about whether other agents control or withhold the underspecified physical components of such act-types. For example, if we compare the freedom of Bill Gates and the average citizen of the Democratic Republic of Congo to fly to Mars tomorrow, it is reasonable to say that the probability of other agents denying access to the underspecified physical components of such an action is much smaller for Gates than for the Congolese. We shall return to the question of technological feasibility in sections 2.3 and 2.4.

2.2 Infinite Freedom?

The potentially dizzying array of science-fiction freedoms (or unfreedoms) seems to be Kramer's principal motive for rejecting bivalence:

> Nobody is holding Mary back from flying around and around all the galaxies in the universe. She of course is unable to engage in such an escapade, but her inability is not due to anyone else's actions. It is instead a mere inability, an inability rooted in her natural finitude as a human being.[39]

Kramer takes this example to illustrate the fact that our inabilities are of an infinite number. If all inabilities were unfreedoms, as they must be on bivalent freedom-as-ability, then the set of our unfreedoms would be infinitely large.[40] Conversely, if mere inabilities were to count as freedoms, as they must on bivalent social freedom, then the set of our *freedoms* would be infinitely large. The level of each person's overall freedom would then be either minimal or maximal, depending on the relevant bivalent conception. Much better, then, to say that mere inabilities are neither freedoms nor unfreedoms.

Kramer's example of Mary's "flying around and around all the galaxies of the universe" is radically underspecified, invoking as it does forms of technology that we are unable to describe at anywhere near the appropriate level of specificity. It is important to remember that the measurement of bivalent freedom does not take account of magical actions that defy the laws of physics (such as Mary's simply making her body zoom up into the air and into outer space all on its own), and should therefore include

[39] Kramer, QF, 51.

[40] Recall that bivalent freedom-as-ability is a conception implicitly endorsed by writers such as Sen and Van Parijs (see section 1.1).

only actions involving the use of the relevant technological resources—in Mary's case, longevity-increasing resources as well as space-travel resources—access to which might be currently withheld by others. It is therefore difficult to assess the truth of Kramer's claim that "nobody is holding Mary back" from performing such actions. This said, the probability of its being true and of its being untrue must add up to one.

No less important is the distinction between the kind of infinity-problem Kramer is pointing to here, and three other reasons one might have for holding that the numbers of freedoms are infinitely, or at least indefinitely, large.[41] The latter three reasons arise irrespective of one's stance on the bivalence-trivalence issue. The first two reasons are that actions can be endlessly redescribed and that they can be endlessly subdivided in space and time. We have already seen how these problems can be overcome by focusing exclusively on the physical dimensions of actions understood as occupyings of equally-sized units of space-time by equally-sized physical objects under the agent's control (including parts of the agent herself). Kramer agrees with us on this point. The third reason is that some of the causal chains initiated by our bodily movements might continue indefinitely, uninterrupted by actions of other agents. The solution to this problem is to include in our calculations only the foreseeable consequences of our basic actions—as indeed we must if we are ever to assess anyone's degree of freedom. Again, Kramer agrees. But, as the example of Mary illustrates, Kramer thinks that there is a fourth problem besetting only bivalent conceptions of freedom: a problem of infinitely (or at least indefinitely) large sets of inabilities. In assessing this fourth problem, we need to keep it distinct from the other three. If we accept the solutions to the other three problems, the fourth problem derives entirely from the fact that the universe affords us unlimited space in which to move our bodies.

The fourth problem helps to explain why Kramer includes the agent's ability to do x (absent prevention by others) as a condition of her unfreedom to do x.[42] This condition is a major source of the worries discussed in section 1.3, and its deletion would preserve a form of trivalence while allowing Kramer to deny that White's drinking of the poison makes him more free. However, deleting that condition would also entail that White's imprisonment makes him unfree to fly around and around all the galaxies of the universe.

Regarding this fourth problem, our reply to Kramer is twofold, and is presented in the next two subsections. First, Kramer has a similar problem of indefinitely large sets of abilities (section 2.3). Second, trivalent and bivalent theorists alike need to establish criteria that sensibly limit the domain of relevant actions for the purposes of measuring overall freedom (section 2.4).

2.3 *Tu quoque*

Kramer thinks that the set of his actual abilities is finite. On closer examination, however, this understandably intuitive claim is false. As we have already seen,

[41] Carter, AMF, sections 7.2, 7.3, 7.4.

[42] See condition 1 in Kramer's definition of unfreedom, cited above in section 1.1.

Kramer's actual abilities include the ability to acquire further abilities. And we cannot rule out that these further abilities might include the ability to fly to Alpha Centauri. Kramer might answer this somewhat surprising claim by observing that, by the time humanity has developed the ability to fly to Alpha Centauri, he will certainly be dead. But the ability to extend our lifespans to that future time and beyond—more precisely, the ability to acquire that ability—is also among our current abilities.

To be sure, as things stand the probability of Kramer's ever acquiring the ability to fly to Alpha Centauri is shuddersomely low. It would depend on some agency much wealthier than Kramer investing massively in longevity research, on their making a major breakthrough, and on their subsequently making their longevity-extending technology available to him, and all within his currently expected lifetime (notice that the invention of that technology coupled with its being actively withheld from Kramer would convert his mere inability to live indefinitely into the unfreedom to do so). But the extremely low probability of Kramer's achieving an indefinitely long lifespan fails to confirm the claim that human abilities are finite. This, for two independently sufficient reasons.

First, the sum of an infinitely large set of freedoms, each weighted by a very low probability, is still infinity. Kramer himself suggests that freedoms with a *trivially* low probability, freedoms whose chance of realization is "shuddersomely minute," can be counted, for all intents and purposes, as inabilities.[43] But this suggestion looks implausible where the set of trivially-low-probability freedoms is infinitely large. If we progressively increase the size of a set of shuddersomely minute quantities of some substance or quality, there must be some point at which the size of that set becomes sufficiently large for the sum of those trivially small quantities to be nontrivial. And if there is *any* set that satisfies this sufficiency threshold, then an infinitely large one does. Notice, moreover, that the problem of indefinitely long lifespans is different from the third of the problems mentioned above—that of indefinitely long causal chains. While we might have no inkling of the causal consequences of a certain bodily movement carried out by Blue where those consequences are imagined to occur 300 years after that bodily movement, we have no difficulty characterizing at least some spatially specific bodily movements of Blue that she will be able to perform in 300 years' time if she lives long enough.

Second, the probability judgment appealed to in Kramer's hypothetical answer is in any case hostage to major empirical assumptions about rates of progress in medicine and space travel. That judgment might apply to Kramer himself, but it is much less obviously applicable to persons born in, say, 2103, one hundred years after the publication of *The Quality of Freedom*. Among the myriad possible subtitles for that book, Kramer's first choice would surely not have been "A Theory of Liberty for the Twenty-first Century Only." Genuine conceptual truths ought to enjoy a greater longevity, even if we do not.

[43] Kramer, QF, 84.

2.4 Overall Freedom Relative to a Domain

If the foregoing arguments are correct, the problem of infinities affects both bivalent social freedom and trivalent (or indeed bivalent) freedom-as-ability. Regardless of which of these approaches we adopt, then, we are in need of criteria that will sensibly limit the domain of relevant actions for the purpose of measuring overall freedom.

Despite the unlimited number of specific freedoms and unfreedoms, it is interesting from the point of view of political philosophy to be able to measure people's degrees of overall freedom relative to a given *spatio-temporal* domain.[44] As a spatial limitation, consider the domain of all jurisdictions existing at the time of the freedom being assessed. For present purposes we may define a jurisdiction as follows:

> *Jurisdiction*: a spatial area delimited by the set of physical components (space and matter) of actions by means of which an agency enforces conformity with a set of rules and directives, where such enforcement is carried out by that single agency either directly or by authorizing other agents to do so, and consists either in physical preventions of violations of the rules and directives or in the imposition of further preventions conditional upon such violations.

This definition refers to enforcement that actually takes place, or would take place if certain prohibited actions or omissions were performed. Thus, a declaration by the United States that it has jurisdiction over Jupiter is insufficient to extend the United States's jurisdiction as far as Jupiter. The definition also refers explicitly to the locations of the physical components of enforcement actions. In this way, jurisdiction is limited to those locations, even though certain punishable actions or omissions themselves might take place outside its borders.

Referring to the set of all jurisdictions allows us to avoid any complications arising from the undoubted existence of shared and physically overlapping jurisdictions, and instead implies focusing only on the outer perimeter of that set. Everything that happens within this outer perimeter is potentially of interest to political philosophers, for wherever jurisdiction is established there is a reason that has to do in some sense with human purposes, actual or hypothetical. Moreover, the set of all jurisdictions represents the widest possible domain of interest to political philosophers, and a focus on that set is therefore of particular interest if we adopt the view, endorsed by both Carter and Kramer, that freedom has "non-specific" or "content-independent" value. According to this view, "not only are many of *P*'s particular freedoms valuable for *P* because of their specific contents, but in addition her overall liberty is valuable for her independently of any of those specific contents."[45] Since the "content" of a freedom includes the spatial location of the action it is the freedom to perform, an evaluation of *P*'s situation that takes into account the content-independent value of freedom ought

[44] The need to limit the domain relative to which overall freedom is measured provides us with a strong reason, anticipated at the end of section 1.2, for measuring bivalent social freedom in terms of a fraction rather than simply in terms of the number of freedoms.

[45] Kramer, QF, 429. Carter uses the term "non-specific" (AMF, ch. 2), whereas Kramer uses the term "content-independent." Hereinafter we shall adopt Kramer's terminology.

to include an estimation of the extent of her freedom relative to the widest possible spatial domain.

There are other, more limited spatial domains relative to which it can be interesting for political philosophers to measure overall freedom. One such domain is that of a single jurisdiction. This is the domain that people have in mind when they compare the freedom of one country to another.[46] Such domains fail to capture the differences in freedom enjoyed by citizens of different countries when abroad (e.g., most British citizens are free to enter Saudi Arabia whereas most Israeli citizens are unfree to do so). Nevertheless, comparisons of this sort need not mislead as long as we make quite clear the relative domain and the kinds of freedoms and unfreedoms that it does and does not allow us to capture.

In light of Kramer's criticism of bivalent social freedom conjoined with our *tu quoque* argument, the domain relative to which we assess people's overall freedom must also be limited temporally. Those who are skeptical about the standard, commonsense view of personal identity over time might think it important to compare the degrees of freedom enjoyed by different agents over specific segments of their biological lives.[47] However, for most theorists of freedom—whether social or non-social—our very interest in the concept tends to presuppose agential continuity over a whole biological life. For these theorists, a temporal domain relative to which it is important to compare agents' degrees of freedom might be that of the maximal life expectancy of a human being as calculated by the best-placed epistemic authorities at the time of the freedom being measured.

Spatio-temporal boundaries are not the only criteria by reference to which one can limit the relevant domain. One might also measure overall freedom relative to the set of actions that are technologically feasible at the time of the freedom being measured. Or even, following Kramer, relative to the set of actions that the agent herself is actually able to perform absent prevention by others. As we have seen, however, these further criteria would need to be combined with a spatio-temporal criterion of the sort just canvassed.

The measurement of overall social freedom is always relative to a domain. But this fact does *not* entail that the concept of social freedom should itself be understood trivalently. The very plurality of possible domains suggests that it would be absurd to deny the status of actions lying outside a particular domain as ones that an agent can be socially free or unfree to perform. None of the above domains is constitutive in some way of the very concept of social freedom.[48] We have seen, moreover, that the possibility of an agent affecting the size of the relevant domain produces strongly counterintuitive results if that domain is interpreted as determining whether the question of an agent's freedom to perform a particular action arises. And while some domains, such as that proposed by Kramer, are particularly susceptible to being directly affected by actions of the agent whose freedom is under consideration, whereas others,

[46] As, e.g., in the annual reports produced by Freedom House: https://freedomhouse.org/reports.

[47] Carter, "Equality of Opportunity, Responsibility, and Personal Identity," 831.

[48] For this reason, it seems to us arbitrary to say, alternatively, that there are as many concepts of freedom as there are domains, and that each such concept is trivalent. A similar point applies to the idea that there are so many trivalent "conceptions of the concept" of freedom.

such as the set of all jurisdictions, are much less susceptible or only minimally susceptible in this respect, conceptually speaking none of the above-mentioned domain limitations are such that we can rule out all possibility of its size being directly affected by actions of the agent whose freedom is under consideration. *Pace* Kramer, neither social freedoms nor social unfreedoms can be directly affected by actions of the agent whose freedom or unfreedom is under consideration. But a particular domain relative to which we choose to measure overall social freedom might be so affected.

Our alternative conceptualization takes the sting out of the possibility of a domain being directly affected by the agent whose freedom is under consideration. We can and should be quite explicit about the fact that we are considering overall freedom relative to a domain that is more agent-affected or less agent-affected, and we need not therefore feel uncomfortable about admitting, for example, that an agent who inflicts certain disabilities on herself becomes more free *relative to the domain of her current abilities* even though she does *not* become more free relative to the jurisdiction she lives in or relative to the set of all jurisdictions; or that an agent who deliberately does things that shorten her own life expectancy might, under certain circumstances, become freer *relative to the temporal domain of her own individual life expectancy*, but *not* relative to the temporal domain of the maximal life-expectancy of a human being at the time of the freedom being measured. Some of these domains will of course be more interesting than others in the light of whatever freedom-based normative theory we are developing or applying.

The error of trivalent theorists is to confuse overall freedom per se with overall freedom relative to one (and only one) such domain. How much more sensible to say that social freedom is the absence of preventive actions on the part of others and that the measurement of overall social freedom is always relative to a particular domain!

3. Evaluation and Overall Freedom

There is another form of trivalence that rears its troublesome head in regard to estimating a person's degree of overall freedom. The magnitude of a person's overall freedom consists, *inter alia*, in the magnitudes of all the particular freedoms and unfreedoms they possess.[49] As we have seen, each particular freedom has physical dimensions: these consist in the sizes of the spatio-temporal locations and material objects involved in performing the action which that freedom is the freedom to perform. Thus, many will agree that the freedom to fly from London to New York is, at least *ceteris paribus*, of a lesser magnitude than the freedom to fly from London to Tokyo. But *ceteris* are not always *paribus* and, in particular, a freedom's physical dimensions are held by some philosophers to be an inadequate measure of its contribution to the overall amount of freedom its possessor enjoys. They claim that the *quality* or *significance* of a freedom, and not merely the quantity of action it is the freedom to perform, needs to be taken into account in estimating that contribution.

[49] Hereinafter, and to avoid cumbersome verbiage, we shall sometimes speak only of magnitudes of freedoms, and not of magnitudes of freedoms and unfreedoms. The magnitude of the freedom to do x is the same as the magnitude of the unfreedom to do x.

Now, on the face of it, this claim seems odd. It is certainly *not* true of most things and properties. If we identify a set of things as grains of sand, we can calculate how much sand that set amounts to without any reference at all to the value of each of those grains. And the same is true of physical properties. Take weight: if we know the weight of each person and thing in an elevator, we can know the total amount of weight borne by that elevator without having the slightest idea of those components' respective values. Even in the case of freedom itself, doctors, scientists, and engineers measure the freedom of diverse things—persons' limbs, non-human animals, clock pendulums—to move or remain stationary, without having recourse to its value.

And yet it must be acknowledged that our first reactions strongly incline us to the view that the significance of the actions which we are or are not free to do often does enter into our estimations of how free we are, and not just how valuable the freedom we have is. Thus, Joel Feinberg argues that

> [w]hen two or more properties or "respects" are subject to precise mathematical comparison, they will always have some quantitative element in common. The difficulty in striking resultant totals of "on balance freedom" derives from the fact that the relation among the various "areas" in which people are said to be free is not so much like the relation between the height, breadth and depth of a physical object as it is like the relation between the gasoline economy, styling, and comfort of an automobile .... What we more likely mean when we say that one subject is freer on balance than another is that his freedom is greater in the more valuable, important or significant dimensions, where the "value" of a dimension is determined by some independent standard.[50]

Similarly, Charles Taylor has famously attacked the "crude" and "tough-minded" negative conception of freedom on the grounds that "it has no place for the notion of significance" and "will allow only for purely quantitative judgments." He correctly identifies it as the same conception as the one which is also at work when scientists and engineers refer to the "freedom of some physical object, say a lever." It is said to license the "diabolical defence of [communist] Albania" against the charge of being a less free society than Britain, since the presence of severe restraints on religious practice in the former—and their absence in the latter—could thereby be forensically countered by invoking the considerably fewer traffic restrictions in Albania than in Britain. Surely, Taylor insists, the value or significance of the actions we are free (and unfree) to do must enter into our calculations of how free we are.[51]

3.1 The Paradox of Trivalent Evaluative Multipliers

On this suggestion, then, our assessment of the extent of a person's overall freedom must take into account not only its empirical or physical dimensions, but also its *value*. More precisely, our computation of the amount of freedom that each person has must

[50] Feinberg, *Social Philosophy*, 18–19.
[51] Taylor, "What's Wrong with Negative Liberty," 183.

reflect—by mathematically integrating—the amount of value attached to each of their particular freedoms and unfreedoms. These value weightings have been aptly designated by Kramer as *evaluative multipliers* (EMs).[52] An evaluative multiplier is applied to the physical dimensions of a particular freedom to determine *how much* freedom that freedom amounts to: the quality of that freedom has a direct determinative bearing on its quantitative contribution to a person's overall freedom.

How do we assess the value of a particular freedom? Taylor's suggestion straightforwardly implies that a freedom's EM is a function of the value of the action that it is the freedom to do. These actions themselves may be either intrinsically or instrumentally valuable (or both). So if acts of religious practice are more valuable than ones of relatively unrestricted driving, the freedoms to do them must have higher EMs.

But here we encounter a serious problem. Proposals that its valuational magnitude be integrated into the measurement of a freedom are typically underspecified. For it's evident that the actions which we're free or unfree to do not only vary in their value, but also that these variations must be negative as well as positive. Overall wealth measurements include debts as well as assets, and felicific calculi integrate pains along with pleasures. Similarly, if we believe that the freedom to save a person's life is highly valuable, we'd normally regard the freedom to take a person's life not merely as lower-valued but rather as *dis*valuable. That is, proposals to integrate values need to assign negative EMs as well as positive ones to freedoms, if those freedoms' magnitudes are to reflect not only their physical dimensions but also the values of the actions which they are the freedom to perform. Otherwise, a sufficiently large number of (unexcused) life-taking freedoms would, absurdly, have the same value as a life-saving freedom. In short, freedom valuations, like the values of the acts that they are the freedom to do, must be *trivalent*: a freedom's EM can be a number which is either (a) positive or (b) negative or (c) neutral, i.e., zero.

Now observe how trivalent EMs lead to very peculiar results. Suppose there are three actions, x, y, and z, which can also be taken to represent the physical dimensions of the respective freedoms to do them. And suppose that Blue is unprevented from doing—is free to do—x and y, and that the EMs used in measuring those two freedoms are 20 and 10, respectively. Blue is, however, prevented from doing z, but that's a *good* thing because the freedom to do z is not valuable at all: in fact, it's a disvaluable freedom whose EM is therefore negative, say -5. What then happens to Blue's overall freedom if/when Blue is liberated due to the prevention of her doing z being removed, that is, if she becomes free to do z? The strongly paradoxical implication of Taylor-like evaluative conceptions of overall freedom is that this liberation actually *reduces* Blue's overall freedom from 20x + 10y to 20x + 10y – 5z. Blue's acquisition of the added freedom to do z would entail a *decrease* in her overall freedom!

To avoid such contradictions, while still integrating valuational magnitudes into Taylor-like computations of overall freedom, it would therefore be necessary to exclude the use of negative numbers from valuational assessments of actions. But how can this be done? The answer is that it can't, at least not within the framework of a negative concept of freedom. To do it, one has to make a move which is indeed

[52] Kramer, QF, 387.

commonplace in many accounts of the so-called *positive* concept of freedom. That move is, simply and boldly, to delete all negatively valued actions from the set of actions which persons are describable as free or unfree to do. (Often these disqualified actions are denied the status of actions altogether and/or their performance is said to be an exercise of "license," not liberty.) For Blue, act z, being negatively valued, would thus be one which she cannot be said to be either free or unfree to do. The fact that she is prevented from doing it, or that that restraint gets lifted, would not affect her overall freedom. The resultant position amounts to a form of value-based or morality-based trivalence of the sort mentioned in section 1.1, a position that has been widely rejected by theorists of negative liberty for reasons that need not be repeated here.[53]

3.2 Bivalent Evaluative Multipliers as a Solution

It is, we think, very much to his credit that Kramer's own evaluative account of overall freedom acknowledges the problems involved in the above move, and commendably seeks to avoid them.[54] Like Steiner and Carter, Kramer advances a conception of freedom whereby questions of *whether* a person is free to do a specific act are to be construed as purely empirical questions about human prevention—ones to be answered on the basis of physical evidence alone. But, like Feinberg, Taylor, and others, he diverges from our view in contending that questions of *how much* freedom a person has must be answered by reference not only to physical magnitudes but also to evaluative ones.

> Whereas the existence of any particular freedom or unfreedom is strictly a matter of fact, the extent of anyone's overall liberty is a partly evaluative phenomenon .... [A] starkly non-evaluative approach to the measurement of freedom cannot suitably capture the distinctiveness of freedom as a socio-political desideratum.[55]

So while rejecting Steiner's and Carter's claim—that the purely physical dimensions, of the particular freedoms composing a set of freedoms, *alone* determine those freedoms' contributions to the overall amount of freedom in that set—he is nonetheless at pains to sustain the "primacy" of these physical dimensions by circumscribing the mathematical power of those freedoms' EMs. And he does this simply by stipulating that the EMs not be less than 1.

> The primacy of the purely physical dimensions of a person's overall freedom lies in the fact that the lowest value for any qualitatively-oriented multiplier is 1 .... Even when the possession of a particular freedom of some anomalous type is typically of disvalue for a human being, the qualitatively-oriented multiplier associated with any

[53] For references to works explaining the shortcomings of moralized conceptions of freedom, see Steiner, ER, 12 n. 11; Carter, AMF, 69 n. 1, 70 n. 5; Kramer, QF, 5 n. 3. For examples of other unsuccessful attempts to escape the incorporation of negative values, see Carter, AMF, section 5.3.

[54] Kramer, QF, 443.

[55] Kramer, QF, 9; see also 425ff.

> freedom of that type is not negative or zero .... If it does not make an augmentative difference to the weight of some particular freedom, then it makes no difference at all; it never makes a diminutional difference.[56]

Kramer thereby avoids the foregoing paradox by rejecting the trivalency of Taylor-like EMs, and instead advancing what can be described as a *bivalent* conception of them. He does not deny that the values of *actions themselves* can be negative or neutral. All he insists upon is that the value of the *freedom* to do any action, including negatively and neutrally valued ones, must be positive. So, whereas freedoms which, on both Taylor's and Kramer's schemes, are classified as being evaluatively positive and are correspondingly assigned varying positively numbered EMs, all of Taylor's negatively and neutrally valued freedoms are grouped together by Kramer and are each assigned a positive EM of 1. The bivalence of his evaluative multipliers thereby consists in their being only either (a) 1 or (b) greater than 1. Thus Kramer's analysis of the foregoing paradoxical example would treat the EM of the freedom to do z as 1, rather than −5, with the consequence that Blue's liberation from the imposed physical prevention of her doing z would indeed increase (rather than absurdly reduce) her overall freedom, but only slightly—from 20x + 10y to 20x + 10y + 1z.

3.3 Bivalent Evaluative Multipliers and Autonomy

Now, the question we need to ask ourselves at this point is whether this way of avoiding the perils of trivalent EMs makes any sense. Is that bivalent stipulation circumscribing the valency of evaluative multipliers really plausible? For whatever evaluative metric we might employ, one thing that common sense contrarily suggests is that—symmetrically with the EMs of freedoms to do valuable actions—the multipliers of freedoms to do disvaluable actions would also vary in their respective magnitudes, often considerably. If the freedom to do x can be twice as valuable as its counterpart for y, how can we make sense of the view that the freedom to do w (a mass murder) and the freedom to do z (a singleton murder) each carry a *positive* evaluative multiplier? And yet more puzzlingly, how can those two EMs both be the *same*—namely, 1?

Kramer's account addresses the first of these questions, but not the second. It begins by correctly maintaining that, since we can distinguish between the value of the *freedom* to do an action and the value of *doing* that action, it follows that we cannot infer that the former value is simply a function of the latter. As we have seen, Kramer endorses Carter's arguments to the effect "that freedom partakes of content-independent valuableness"—that a person's freedoms are valuable in virtue of their specific contents but that her liberty also has value "independently of any of those specific contents."[57]

The non-inferability of a freedom's value from the value of the action which it is the freedom to do, does indeed provide some conceptual space—albeit limited space—for the possibility that the former is positive even if the latter is negative: the clearly

[56] Kramer, QF, 428–9.
[57] Kramer, QF, 429.

negative value of doing z, let alone that of doing w, does not imply that their freedoms' respective EMs need themselves be negative.

> Even when the possession of a particular freedom of some anomalous type is typically of disvalue for a human being, the qualitatively-oriented multiplier associated with any freedom of that type is not negative or zero.[58]

This claim, that those anomalous freedoms' EMs are actually positive ones, evidently stands in need of justification. And that justification consists in Kramer's insistence that the freedom to do any action—even a negatively valued one—is positively valuable because it is "an integral constituent of something else that is intrinsically good."

> Specifically, it is a key ingredient of individual autonomy. An autonomous person gains and retains her status as such not only by arriving at most of her decisions in a reasonably reflective manner that bespeaks her self-determination, but also by having been free to behave in any number of ways that are contrary to the ways in which she actually behaves. In so far as the options open to a person have been tightly constricted, she has lacked the room necessary for achieving and exhibiting full-fledged autonomy.[59]

However, and even if all non-preventions—all freedoms—are autonomy-enhancing and thereby contribute a positive element to their EMs, that would still be insufficient to guarantee that no freedoms can have negative EMs. And this for one very salient reason:

> [T]he level of each person's overall freedom cannot be ascertained without any reliance on evaluative assumptions—specifically, assumptions concerning the content-dependent valuableness of each person's particular freedoms in connection with the fostering of certain ideals such as individual autonomy and development and well-being .... The purpose of our evaluations is to ascertain how much is qualitatively contributed by each particular liberty of some person *P* to her overall freedom. In other words, we are seeking to determine the bearing of each liberty on the appropriate answer to a 'how free' question about *P*.... We can now see that the matter of importance is gauged by recourse to desiderata—such as individual development and well-being and autonomy...[60]

Autonomy, then, is but one amongst several basic sources of a freedom's value. And some unprevented actions may be at once so tempting, *and* so damaging to a person's development and well-being, that their negative valuation would entirely outweigh the positiveness of their autonomy-enhancement, in determining the valency of the evaluative multipliers for the freedoms to do those actions: that is, they would make those multipliers *net* negative numbers.

[58] Kramer, QF, 428.
[59] Kramer, QF, 431.
[60] Kramer, QF, 9, 432ff.

This, for instance, seems to be just what happens in the case of Ulysses and the Sirens, where the freedom in question is that of steering his ship. Ulysses wants to be *rid* of that freedom: his valuation of it is undeniably negative. And so would be the evaluative multipliers generated by any evaluative metric based upon the "objective interests of typical human beings." More generally, this is exactly what is involved in those many common cases where persons choose to enter into *enforceable* agreements or contracts not to do certain actions which they would otherwise be unprevented from doing. In so choosing, they are clearly assigning negative values, not only to those actions themselves, but also to the *freedoms* to do those actions. Hence an evaluation metric's incorporation of an autonomy sub-metric which is always positive is insufficient to guarantee that metric's yielding only positive EMs. And as we've seen, if negative multipliers *were* to be employed in estimating particular freedoms' contributions to a person's overall freedom, we'd again incur the aforesaid paradoxical result: namely, that their retaining those negatively evaluated freedoms would actually make their overall freedom less than it would be if they were to lose them.

3.4 Bivalent Evaluative Multipliers and Option Diversity

Apart from its implausibility, Kramer's stipulation that no freedom's EM can be less than 1 also generates a consistency problem in his discussion of *option diversity*.[61] Responding to the belief that, *ceteris paribus*, a set of qualitatively diverse options contributes more freedom to overall freedom than does a set of similar options, he proposes that this belief can be reflected only in those freedoms' EMs. But, before considering this proposal, we should first sound a brief cautionary note about that belief itself.

For diversity, like beauty, is often in the eye of the beholder. Whether a set of objects, which might be used in exercising certain freedoms, *is* qualitatively more diverse than another such set, seems very much to depend upon functional judgments about those objects themselves: that is, judgments about what those objects are *for*. And those judgments, in turn, are ineluctably predicated on the particular purposes entertained by their various prospective users. To put the point somewhat archly, a paper-recycler might well find no great functional difference between a copy of *The Quality of Freedom* and a collection of *Batman* comic books: for him, an option set consisting of both of those items would be no more diverse than an option set consisting of two copies of that scholarly book. Any judgment that the former set represents more diversity than the latter in any objective sense—that is, in a sense that is not relative to the purposes of a user—would appear to embrace an implausibly teleological view of inanimate objects.[62]

[61] Kramer, QF, 463–71.

[62] Cf. Steiner, ER, 99. Relevant here is the acclaimed work of the mathematical economist, Kelvin Lancaster, in proposing a pathbreaking revision of standard microeconomic demand theory: "The chief technical novelty lies in breaking away from the traditional approach that goods are the direct objects of utility and, instead, supposing that it is the properties or characteristics of the goods from which utility is derived." "A New Approach to Consumer Theory," 133.

Thus warned, let us provisionally accept the belief that, *ceteris paribus*, qualitatively diverse options represent a greater amount of freedom—have higher EMs—than similar ones. Now, it is reasonably clear that the paradox besetting *trivalent* EMs renders them incapable of reflecting that belief: acquiring the freedom to commit one murder diminishes, rather than augments, one's overall freedom; and acquiring the freedom to commit a second, qualitatively similar, murder only diminishes it further, and presumably to the same extent. Can Kramer's conception of *bivalent* EMs fare better in reflecting that belief?

To do so, it must be consistent with two distinct claims: (a) that each additional option does indeed augment a person's overall freedom by at least that freedom's physical dimensions, and also (b) that each additional—but qualitatively similar—option augments that overall freedom by *less* than its similar predecessor. That is, the EM of the freedom to acquire a second copy of *The Quality of Freedom* is lower than its counterpart for the first copy, and the EM of the freedom to acquire a third copy is lower still. As Kramer confirms, to sustain the belief that option diversity increases overall freedom, one "has to explain the decreasing marginal weight of each new [similar] alternative."[63] And this, he says, cannot be done without recourse to evaluative multipliers.

> When we attach qualitatively-oriented multipliers to the numerical expressions of a person's particular freedoms, we can adjust their weights in light of the other freedoms which the person enjoys .... Thus, when *P* acquires the freedom-to-travel-to-the-swimming-pool-via-Route-2, theorists who measure her overall liberty should assign a considerably lower qualitatively-oriented weighting to that freedom than they have assigned to her freedom-to-travel-to-the-swimming-pool-via-Route-1. They should do so precisely because *P* is already endowed with the freedom-to-travel-via-Route-1 by the time she gains the freedom-to-travel-via-Route-2.[64]

In effect, Kramer is contending that the respective contributions to overall freedom, of successively similar options, obey a *law of diminishing marginal value*.[65] Now, the question we must ask ourselves is whether the aforementioned claims (a) and (b) can be plausibly sustained by bivalent EMs.

Let us safely suppose that the value of the freedom afforded by having copies of *The Quality of Freedom* is positive, that *P* is already endowed with a copy of it, and that the EM assigned to that freedom is 4. If she now acquires a second copy of it, claim (b) dictates that the assigned EM must be less than 4: say 3. And her third copy has an EM of, say, 2. What then happens when she acquires a fourth copy?

[63] Kramer, QF, 467.

[64] Kramer, QF, 471.

[65] Notice that, even if Kramer's EMs reflect the marginally diminishing value of additional qualitatively similar freedoms, the *marginal decreases* in the EMs might not be sufficient to offset the *marginal increases* in the purely physical contribution of new qualitatively similar freedoms to the person's overall freedom. Such marginal increases are entailed by Kramer's squaring of the numerator (see the first of the four critical points we listed in section 1.4). Only if Kramer abandons his numerator-squaring move can we guarantee that the introduction of EMs will allow us to capture the intuition that adding qualitatively similar freedoms *contributes to overall freedom* at a marginally decreasing rate.

Kramer's bivalent conception of evaluative multipliers stipulates that any valuable freedom must have an EM greater than 1. It must be greater than 1 because, otherwise, its contribution to overall freedom would reflect only that freedom's bare physical dimensions.[66] So the EM of that fourth copy must lie between 2 and 1. But the same is also true of the EMs of the fifth, sixth, seventh and . . . *n*th acquired copies: the freedom afforded by each successively acquired copy must be of less value than its predecessor, but none can have an EM as low as 1. Hence the amount by which each would be lower would itself continuously *diminish*: the difference in value between the fifth and sixth copies would be *less* than the difference in value between the fourth and fifth copies. Each successive valuable freedom is indeed less valuable than its similar predecessor but, due to Kramer's stipulation that its value must be greater than 1, the rate at which its value diminishes must itself diminish. Paradoxically, then, the *more* similar freedoms *P* acquires, the *less* dissimilar their values are: the diminution of their marginal value, we might say, is itself diminishing. To be sure, this makes sense in economists' indifference curves where the options are bundles with quantitatively varying combinations of two *different* positively valued goods. But it makes no sense where the options are simply different amounts of one and the same positively valued good. The economist assumes *a priori* that the goods in question are all positively valued, regardless of how much of them one has. Kramer's contrary (empirical) assumption is that, beyond a certain amount of the good, it has zero (specific) value. In short, bivalent evaluative multipliers are implausible theoretical instruments for capturing option diversity's alleged augmentative contribution to overall freedom.

4. Conclusion

The overall idea emerging from our critical examination of Kramer's concept of freedom is that political and social philosophers are better off working with a concept of freedom shorn of all the trimmings with which Kramer adorns his own. Those trimmings, consisting principally in the squared numerator of the fraction representing a person's degree of freedom, the inclusion of evaluative multipliers, and the artificial imposition of a kind of bivalence on those multipliers, all derive from the perils of trivalence: the trivalence of particular freedoms, whereby an agent is seen as either free, unfree, or neither free nor unfree to do a specific thing; and the trivalence of evaluations of particular freedoms, whereby those freedoms have value, disvalue, or neither value nor disvalue. Kramer *affirms* the first kind of trivalence, and this creates problems that lead him to adjust the formula for measuring people's overall freedom. We have argued that this adjustment only partially answers the charge of counterintuitivity and brings problems of its own. Kramer *rejects* the second kind of trivalence, but his insistence on evaluative multipliers again necessitates adjustments that bring problems of their own. In our view, none of these trimmings are really constitutive of the concept of freedom. Rather, they represent conceptually ungrounded

[66] And, if its EM were less than 1, its contribution would not reflect even those. It would thereby *dis*confirm the "primacy of the purely physical dimensions of a person's overall freedom" and contradict claim (a).

ad hoc adjustments aimed in the direction of isomorphism with commonsense comparisons of freedom.

We have defended, by way of an alternative, the simpler and more austere concept of bivalent social freedom. On the basis of this concept, we treat social freedom and social unfreedom as contradictories rather than as independent variables, and we do not ascribe to any agent the unilateral, and in this sense paradoxical, power to remove one or more of her own social freedoms. We recognize, as among a person's social freedoms and unfreedoms, all specific action-possibilities that can conceivably be physically removed by the action of another person, while allowing for the measurement of that person's overall social freedom relative to any finite domain of such action-possibilities. And we distinguish clearly not only between the *existence* of a person's freedom to do something and the *value* of their freedom to do that thing, but also between a person's enjoyment of a certain extent of freedom and the value of their enjoying that extent of freedom.

The complexity of the arguments we have had to muster in support of these conclusions is but further testimony, if any were needed, to the pathbreaking character of *The Quality of Freedom* in advancing our understanding of this most controversial of concepts in political philosophy.

PART V
LIBERALISM

14
Neutrality and Excellence

Mark R. Reiff[*]

It is customary, I suppose, to begin an essay for a festschrift with a story about the honoree. Mine is as follows. A few years after I had received my PhD under Matthew Kramer's supervision, I returned to Cambridge for a visit. I was in the Law Faculty building, in the huge atrium that I fear makes it look a little too much like the inside of a Hyatt Hotel, when two of his current PhD students came up to me asking for advice. "How were they to take Professor Kramer?" they wanted to know. "What insight could I impart on how to process the very extensive and detailed criticism he was providing on their work? How seriously should they take all that criticism, and how should they react to it?" I was somewhat surprised by the inquiry, because I simply assumed that it would be obvious that the level of feedback that Professor Kramer famously provided to his students, something that was unfortunately far less common than it should have been for students supervised by other people, was simply one of the special benefits of being supervised by him. In fairness, I think these two students saw that clearly, but were still a little unsure how to process all the feedback that Kramer was currently providing to them.

I hesitated for a minute, and then I delivered the following advice: "Just remember that Kramer is always right. Use that as a rule of thumb to process his comments and criticism. Not because he will resent it if you challenge his criticism (he won't). But because in my experience, he is indeed always right. Not necessarily about what you should do to correct whatever problems he sees in your work, for he is not inside your head, and therefore he cannot know what you were really thinking when something you have written seems incorrect or misleading or unclear. Because you may have expressed yourself imperfectly, he may have misunderstood what you were trying to do or say. His suggestions may accordingly miss the mark, although when his understanding is correct they are usually spot on. What he is always right about is that there is a problem with what you wrote. If he found something wrong or unclear or misleading, you need to do something about this, and you ignore this imperative at your peril."

I don't know whether those students took my advice, but it has always held me in good stead, and I do not intend to violate it here. I am therefore not going to criticize Kramer's work on how to justify bringing certain forms of excellence into liberalism without violating the principle of neutrality. Not only out of respect but also because I truly find nothing objectionable there. Instead, what I am going to do is try to show

[*] My thanks, as always, to Matthew Kramer for both his criticisms and inspiration. Thanks also to the editors of this volume, and to all those in Cambridge at the workshop presentation of this essay for their comments and suggestions.

Mark R. Reiff, *Neutrality and Excellence* In: *Without Trimmings*. Edited by: Mark McBride and Visa A.J Kurki, Oxford University Press. © Mark McBride and Visa AJ Kurki 2022. DOI: 10.1093/oso/9780198868866.003.0014

that there is another route to the place that Kramer has taken us. Nothing about what I am going to say suggests that Kramer's approach is wrong, or even that it has to be adjusted in some small way to accommodate the alternative I propose. My proposal simply takes us down a different path, one that travels through markedly different countryside and encounters different obstacles along the way, but arrives at the same point in the end. I believe that nothing in Kramer's work suggests that one cannot follow the path I will identify if one wants to do so, and nothing I will say suggests that one cannot follow the path he has already identified, as different as the two paths may be. In any event, that's my story and I will be sticking with it. For on this I will be invoking the privileges of age. Although I am his former student, I am also older by almost two years, something Kramer has always delighted in reminding me (I came to academia late in life whereas he came straight away). And having said that, since this also means I am running out of time slightly faster than Kramer is, I shall now get on with it.

1. Kramer's Aspirational Perfectionism

In *Liberalism with Excellence*,[1] Kramer makes an argument for how government support for the pursuit of excellence may enter into liberalism, despite liberalism's strong commitment to neutrality. Kramer seeks to challenge not only the uncompromising rejection of this position by liberal "neutralists" such a Jonathan Quong,[2] but also the so-called "blended" approach of "soft perfectionist" scholars such as Joseph Raz and George Sher,[3] whom Kramer labels "edificatory perfectionists." What Kramer advocates is what he calls "aspirational perfectionism:" the idea that government should promote certain kinds of excellence in order to heighten what he calls "warranted self-respect." In making this argument, Kramer draws heavily on the work of John Rawls, who lists "the social bases of self-respect" as well as wealth and income and rights and opportunities as being among what Rawls calls "primary goods;" that is, goods that play an important part in the pursuit of a wide range of others forms of good.[4] Although I am simplifying Kamer's argument in some important ways just to get its essence on the table, Kramer argues that because warranted self-respect is a primary good, its furtherance is not ruled out by liberalism's insistence on government neutrality, the idea that government should remain neutral as between controversial but nevertheless reasonable competing comprehensive conceptions of the good.[5] Indeed, promoting warranted self-respect is not only consistent with the principle of neutrality, properly understood, promoting it is effectively required given the important role warranted self-respect plays in creating a robust and resilient liberal society.[6]

[1] Kramer, *Liberalism with Excellence*.
[2] See Quong, *Liberalism without Perfection*.
[3] See, e.g., Sher, *Beyond Neutrality: Perfectionism and Politics*; Raz, *The Morality of Freedom*.
[4] See Kramer, *Liberalism with Excellence*, 325–8.
[5] See Kramer, *Liberalism with Excellence*, 342–3.
[6] See Kramer, *Liberalism with Excellence*, 341–2.

Kramer calls his view a form of perfectionism, by which he means a form of soft perfectionism, but his argument actually establishes that it is not, although most liberal neutralists would no doubt disagree. I would actually characterize Kramer's aspirational view as a form of liberalism: it does not make a perfectionist exception to the usual liberal requirement of government neutrality; it simply relies on a more nuanced and precise conception of how the principle of neutrality should be understood by liberals. Accordingly, I might have preferred that Kramer call his theory "aspirational liberalism," but this is merely a semantic quibble. The point is that Kramer makes clear he thinks that support for the arts and for culture—indeed support for many of the same things that edificatory perfectionists advocate, albeit for very different reasons, is entirely consistent with the underlying commitments of liberalism. One need not be perfectionist at all to advocate this; one simply needs to appreciate the relationship between certain kinds of excellence and warranted self-respect and the essential nature of such a good in the creation and maintenance of a liberal society.

2. A Thicker Conception of Liberalism and Perfectionism

I suppose this is the point where I should say a little more about what I have in mind when I use the terms "liberalism" and "perfectionism." I conceive of these terms as describing two great families of political theories, each of which has many members. What makes a particular political theory a member of one family rather than the other is that at a higher level of abstraction, the members of each family all share various fundamental presuppositions about political morality, presuppositions that members of the other family reject. In itself, the claim that all political theories can be placed in one family or another is not a controversial position, but identifying the relevant presuppositions is. Many theorists claim that the distinction between these two families boils down to a single question: whether the particular theory at issue recognizes the principle of neutrality. Others are a little more expansive, claiming that a society's commitment to toleration is also a key distinguishing feature. My conception, in contrast, includes a much greater number of fundamental presuppositions. These include an embrace of the principles of neutrality and toleration, of course, but also a commitment to the following views: respecting individual liberty and the rule of law is to be given priority over maintaining government authority and national security; informed public discourse and debate is to have an extensive role in directing government action; the individual and not the community is the fundamental social unit; empiricism and not ideology should be the basis of both pure and practical reasoning; religious and political authority should not be conflated; all members of the polity are entitled to be treated with equal concern and respect; and punishment should, in some meaningful sense, be proportional to the legal, social, or moral wrong at issue.[7] My conception of what makes a theory more like a member of one family rather than the other is accordingly much thicker than either liberals or perfectionists typically employ.

[7] See Reiff, *The Unbearable Resilience of Illiberalism*; Reiff, "Trump and the End of Liberalism,"; Reiff, "The Attack on Liberalism," 173–210.

The reason for using a much thicker description of what distinguishes liberalism from perfectionism here is that doing so is far more useful analytically than trying to distill this to a single presupposition or two. For one thing, it allows us to see how so many people who each think of themselves as liberals can differ so dramatically on what they think liberalism requires. They can do this because each of the fundamental presuppositions I have identified are general concepts rather than detailed conceptions. Each fundamental presupposition needs to be given further content before it can be implemented, and this can be and often is done in different ways.[8] Liberals can be for or against abortion, for or against greater redistribution of income, for or against greater government regulation of the market, for or against free trade with other nation-states, for or against stricter limits on immigration, and on either side of any number of other hotly contested social, domestic, and foreign policy issues of the day. Despite disagreeing about what liberalism requires in specific situations, however, each member of the liberal family draws their views from the same fundamental presuppositions; they just interpret these differently. There are of course limits to the range of interpretations that can still claim to be within each fundamental presupposition—the need for further specification does not make any of them meaningless. But there exists a wide range of interpretive possibilities nonetheless.

Because neutrality is the focus of the discussion that follows, I will not say much about the range of possible interpretations of the other fundamental presuppositions here. But the fact that the differences between liberalism and perfectionism do not depend on one's attitude toward neutrality alone is still important to recognize. For if we do use a thicker conception of the differences between liberalism and perfectionism, as I contend we should, the distinction between these two families of political thought becomes much more complex and variegated. To account for this, we must construct a *y* axis between liberalism and perfectionism that is as multi-factorial and nuanced as the *x* axis typically used to distinguish the range of views between left and right. To fully plot where some person, party, or policy falls on the political spectrum, one needs to do so on both axes, not just one. One can be on either the left or the right and anywhere in between and also be a liberal or a perfectionist or anything in between.[9]

Recognizing this is important, even when focusing on the principle of neutrality alone, because it is unlikely that we can otherwise appreciate what is at stake in the battle between liberalism and perfectionism, or fully understand the role the principle of neutrality plays in that battle. Some versions of perfectionism are relatively inoffensive, perhaps even attractive. But under my more general conception, excellence is in the mind of the beholder. The kind of Aristotelian virtues that many people think of when they think of kinds of excellence are of course virtues that many perfectionists embrace, at least many soft perfectionists. But other kinds of perfectionists identify starkly different characteristics as virtues and therefore embrace very different conceptions of excellence. Kramer's own conception is not Aristotelian, but Stoical,

[8] For further discussion of the difference between a concept and a conception, see Dworkin, *Law's Empire*, 70–2.

[9] See Reiff, *The Unbearable Resilience of Illiberalism*; Reiff, "Trump and the End of Liberalism;" and Reiff, "The Attack on Liberalism."

another form of soft perfectionism and therefore generally not discomfiting to those who embrace liberalism. But hard perfectionism is different.

Hard perfectionists generally interpret excellence along strict racial, gender, religious, ethnic, nationalistic, heterosexual, cultural, and/or class lines. Some hard perfectionists, for example, interpret excellence as constituting the elevation and promotion and protection of white, male, Christian, heterosexual culture of a specific national, ethnic, and even class background. This kind of perfectionism is probably not at all what Aristotle had in mind (although the matter is not free from doubt), but it is a form of perfectionism nonetheless. Other labels, such as populism, nationalism, fascism, totalitarianism, authoritarianism, and so on, are often used to describe these views, but each of these labels is misleading in important ways and in any event none of them (with the possible exception of populism) are commonly used to describe views that can range from the far left to the far right.[10] Populism, in turn, is misleading because populists are rarely popular (especially on the right) outside a particular hard perfectionist segment of the polity. Thus, even though my thick conception of perfectionism goes well beyond the form of perfectionism embraced by soft perfectionists—the form articulated by Aristotle, at least as it is understood today, and that of the Stoics that inspire Kramer—this is still the best term on offer to refer to what I have in mind.

What this means is that many forms of perfectionism are perverse by liberal lights. The fact that some are not, given that they allegedly violate only the principle of neutrality and embrace a relatively inoffensive conception of excellence according to liberal sensibilities, does not mean that in considering the relationship between liberalism and perfectionism we should ignore the fact that there are some very unattractive versions of perfectionism out there given the highly dubious forms of excellence they promote. Indeed, in the real world, most of the regimes that have held power throughout history fall into the hard perfectionist category. As Isaiah Berlin once reminded us, strength, success, wealth, and power may be unattractive moral values to liberals, or to put it in perfectionist terms, unattractive forms of excellence, but they are moral values nonetheless, and are expressly embraced as forms of excellence by various illiberal conceptions of morality.[11]

Using a thick conception also makes it much easier to see how being liberal or perfectionist need not be an either/or proposition: people, political theorists, governments, and political parties can be and usually are liberal or perfectionist in degrees. Indeed, this is an important part of the claim that the soft perfectionists are making, and Kramer does not fault them for this. But I do not intend to rely on the "one can be liberal or perfectionist in degrees" point to make my argument in this chapter. On the contrary, what I will argue is that if we employ a richer definition of liberalism, one that includes a more nuanced definition of neutrality, we can see that liberalism has all the resources that soft perfectionists think they need to borrow from perfectionism in order to get to where they want to go. It is not necessary to reject any liberal presuppositions and adopt any perfectionist ones to do this, although one can get to the same point via this latter routing too. But more importantly, it is largely because of the confusion created by the use of a very thin theory of the differences between liberalism

[10] See Reiff, *The Unbearable Resilience of Illiberalism.*
[11] See Isaiah Berlin, "The Originality of Machiavelli," 25–79.

and perfectionism that many people have come to the mistaken conclusion that one has to reject some parts of liberalism and accept some parts of perfectionism in order to justify government support for sport, culture and the arts, and certain other forms of excellence too.

Indeed, something like this might be behind Kramer's decision to label his view aspirational perfectionism rather than aspirational liberalism, although as I have already said, I do not think that this matters for any of the substantive points that Kramer makes. But I do think it is important that those of us who are basically liberals not concede that we must reach outside liberalism to justify our views. Because I do not disagree with Kramer's overall argument, however, and because I am not attacking it in any event, I will not spend time going over the detailed steps within it and explaining exactly how it works. I will also not attempt to defend it from edificatory perfectionist or liberal neutralist attacks. Kramer has done this already, and I see little that I could constructively add to the defenses Kramer has already provided. Instead, I shall propose a way of getting to the same place using a different route. Perhaps my argument will be less controversial than his, perhaps it will be more, but in either case it leads to the same conclusion: that government support for the kinds of excellence that both Kramer and the edificatory soft perfectionists promote does not violate the liberal commitment to neutrality. One need not be a perfectionist of any sort in order to argue for this. Exactly how this might work is what I shall spend the rest of this chapter discussing.

3. Neutrality and Justice, Rights, Aims, and Effects

The first distinction I want to make in our journey toward a resolution of the relationship between neutrality and excellence is one between commutative and distributive justice. Commutative justice, as I am using this term, is about the recognition of individual rights, their description, interpretation, protection, and enforcement. The principle of neutrality was never meant to require the government to be neutral with regard to either the establishment or enforcement of such rights. On the contrary, these rights are derived from whatever principles are thought to give us natural rights or human rights, or from the fundamental presuppositions (other than neutrality) that I already identified as underlying liberalism and from the constitutional and derivative rights promulgated pursuant thereto. I recognize that this is contrary to conventional wisdom, for it is often said that the principle of neutrality should and indeed does come into play with regard to the question of which rights should be recognized. For those who take this view, government should neither encourage or prohibit anyone from pursuing their particular conception of their good or chosen forms of excellence, and therefore should not recognize any right that would give a private person the ability to do so either.

Of course, it certainly is true that under liberalism, government should not recognize a right against something merely because a majority of the population disfavors the conception of the good it represents, even if the recognition of such a right might be in the common good. But the aspiration of neutrality is itself not a factor in determining what is or might be a right. Otherwise, it is difficult to see how there could be any rights at all. The refusal to provide service to black people at an establishment that is otherwise open to the public is a violation of right in a liberal society, for example, even though treating this as such is not neutral between racist and egalitarian ways of life. It is nevertheless a violation of right because racist ways of life offend one of the other fundamental presuppositions of liberalism, the idea that all people have equal moral worth. Simply put, the neutrality limitation does not come into play when we are deciding which rights liberalism can recognize, for it is not a restriction on what a liberal society can do in the name of commutative justice. The only issue in those cases is whether the fundamental moral presuppositions which provide the framework for resolving individual claims of right under liberalism have been properly interpreted and instantiated. If they have, the principle of neutrality cannot be used for denying that claim of right enforcement, even when enforcing that right would indeed express a preference for one conception of the good over another. That is simply not what the principle of neutrality was ever intended to do.

I recognize, of course, that there is alternative explanation for why the recognition of anti-discrimination rights is not a violation of the principle of neutrality. This is that the principle of neutrality requires only that government be neutral between *reasonable* conceptions of the good, and racism is not reasonable for the same reason that it is appropriate to ban discrimination on the basis of race in the first place. In this sense, I suppose, the principle of neutrality does come into play as a potential defense to enforcement of non-discrimination rights; that defense is simply unsuccessful because government need not be neutral between a reasonable conception of the good and an unreasonable one. But the fact that the principle of neutrality is not available as a defense to a claim of right does not mean it provides a basis for the recognition of the right itself. So I think that this way of thinking about the role of the principle of neutrality is a mistake. It involves a form of double counting or, more accurately in this case, a form of double *not*-counting. Whatever reason we have for doing so, if something has been identified as an individual right despite whatever controversial conception of the good this may reflect, then this also entails the view that the argument against this position is unreasonable. Thinking of neutrality as playing any sort of role here is simply adding an unnecessary layer of analysis. Whatever work the reasonable/unreasonable distinction is doing is being done because this distinction is also embedded in other fundamental presuppositions and their progeny, principles that provide the basis for recognition of individual rights. Any consideration of whether the principle of neutrality is satisfied or violated is superfluous. Of course, anyone in a liberal society can always argue that the society should revisit the question of whether the right at issue was properly recognized. But this is not the same as concluding that the principle of neutrality is to be applied as a filter through which all liberal rights must pass. In determining whether a liberal society has properly recognized the right at issue, satisfaction of the principle of neutrality is neither necessary nor relevant.

Note that there is another distinction that is often asked to carry a lot of weight when dealing with the application of the principle of neutrality. This is the distinction between neutrality in effect and neutrality in justification (what Rawls calls "neutrality of aim").[12] The liberal principle of neutrality is said to require the latter, but not the

[12] See Rawls, "The Priority of the Right and Ideas of the Good," 449–72, 457–65.

former.[13] Thus, the prohibition on murder is not a violation of the principle of neutrality even though it expresses disfavor for the conception of the good the murderer embraces, one might argue, because the pursuit of that conception also interferes with the pursuit of a wide variety of other conceptions of the good, a neutral reason.[14] But this raises the question of whether the principle of neutrality requires that the actual motivation be neutral in justification or only that there be some hypothetical neutral motivation available, because it seems pretty clear that the prohibition on murder is actually driven by condemnation of the murderer's conception of the good. Indeed, it seems aimed directly at it. This makes relying on this distinction to operationalize the principle of neutrality very unsatisfying, for it gives greater moral force to the presence of a neutral hypothetical justification than to the presence of overwhelming evidence of an actual, non-neutral one. It makes neutrality more of a technical, almost bureaucratic requirement than a moral one.

In some cases, of course, giving the hypothetical moral priority over the actual might give an argument more moral force, as it does with Rawls's argument for the difference principle.[15] But in this case, it is hard to see why it should be treated as having a similar effect. In his argument for the hypothetical decision situation that Rawls contends produces the difference principle, the move from the actual to the hypothetical gives us a way of seeing what people would do if they were not biased. In this case, in contrast, the same move would allow us to pander to our biases and pretend our actual decisions were not biased when they may very well have been. This is not a way of giving a hypothetical decision greater moral force, which we can then use to generate more just actual decisions. It is a way of disguising the problematic moral nature of an actual decision that has already been made.

As Kramer himself points out, even if we were to ignore this problem, there are situations in which even the presence of an actual neutral justification—say the maintenance of civil order—would sometimes lead to morally objectionable outcomes.[16] It could, for example, lead to the segregation or even the expulsion of minority populations on the grounds that this would be one way of eliminating the violence their presence is serving to provoke. In some situations, it might even be the most cost-effective way of doing this considering the cost of effectively suppressing violence, no matter how unjust that violence is. If a mere hypothetical neutral justification is enough, this could only serve to multiply the number of situations in which these problems arise. In contrast, we can avoid the need for such intellectual contortions if we simply recognize that while the neutrality in effect/justification distinction cannot do the work that is being required of it, it does not have to. For once we have decided that some form of conduct is a violation of right, the principle of neutrality simply does not come into play. The only relevant question is whether that right has been properly identified and described according to the other substantive and procedural moral principles we embrace.

[13] See Kymlicka, "Liberal Individualism and Liberal Neutrality," 883–905, 885–6; Arneson, "Liberal Neutrality on the Good: An Autopsy," 191–218.

[14] See Simmonds, *Central Issues in Jurisprudence*, 14–15. See also Rawls, *A Theory of Justice*, 354–5; Rawls, *Justice as Fairness: A Restatement*, 153 n. 27 and 28; Rawls, "The Priority of the Right and Ideas of the Good," 457–65.

[15] See Rawls, *A Theory of Justice*.

[16] See Kramer, *Liberalism with Excellence*, 16–18.

4. Neutrality and Liberty

While the principle of neutrality does not come into play when we are dealing with claims of right, one of the places where it does come into play is when we are trying to explain the liberal concept of liberty. People can mean very different things when they talk about liberty, and they often slide back and forth between one meaning and another without realizing it. This leads to some very garbled thinking about the role these various kinds of liberty actually play in regulating our social and political life. To help us think more clearly about liberty, political philosophers have accordingly identified three main kinds of liberty with which we might be concerned: negative liberty, positive liberty, and republican liberty. While there are other kinds of liberty that various academics refer to and ordinary people do as well—economic liberty and religious liberty being two prominent examples—these are in fact merely applied versions of one or more of the three main philosophical categories and the principle of neutrality. Indeed, while many people seem to think these various kinds of liberty can conflict, and many philosophers seem to think so too, this is not correct. And it is the principle of neutrality that explains why. It provides the lubricant through which these various kinds of liberty can co-exist and interact.

To see how, let us begin by describing the main forms of liberty that are on the table. Negative liberty is infringed whenever someone (including but not limited to the government) interferes with the ability of someone else to do something that people generally have the capacity to do. But this does not mean such interference is necessarily wrongful. There is no general right to negative liberty in a liberal society. Indeed, ordered social life would be impossible if government did not interfere with negative liberty in a massive number of ways every day. Under liberalism, negative liberty is merely an analytical theory—it helps us identify when a particular kind of interference by other human agents has occurred and therefore needs to be justified. But it does not tell us what counts as a justification or how strong that justification needs to be. Some other theory, a political theory, a theory that identifies and embraces ends and sets priorities between them is needed to do that.[17]

Positive liberty, in contrast, is such a theory. Conceptions of positive liberty are political in the sense they set forth detailed instructions about how to live a fully realized life. They accordingly do set forth specific ends and set priorities between them. But they (or at least components of them) are also often highly controversial. Under the principle of neutrality, these controversial components of conceptions of positive liberty are not eligible to provide justifications for an infringement of negative liberty, even if they are reasonable. For in a world that is characterized by the presence of many reasonable yet conflicting views about how to lead a fully realized life, government is not being neutral if it favors one over another. It is also not treating people who hold different reasonable conceptions with the requisite equal concern and respect. And there is even a consequentialist argument supporting neutrality here too, for in a society characterized by reasonable pluralism, non-neutrality by the government is a recipe for conflict and oppression. So under the principle of neutrality, we must

[17] See Reiff, *In the Name of Liberty*, 86–7.

not look to controversial components of conceptions of positive liberty to determine whether an interference with negative liberty in a liberal society is justified or not.

One place we might look, however, is to republican liberty. (Equality would be another, but since I am trying to explain how liberty and neutrality interact, I will not say much about the role of equality here.) Republican liberty conceives of freedom as freedom from domination by the arbitrary will of another. While it does have positive content, it is not controversial—at least it can be non-controversial if one employs a suitably thin conception of it.[18] I recognize, of course, that the current trend is to go in the opposite direction. That is, it is becoming popular to articulate ever thicker conceptions of republican liberty, so thick in fact that some purport to be able to serve as comprehensive theories of justice rather than mere theories of republican liberty. I am not suggesting that these more comprehensive theories are incoherent or indefensible or might not be useful for some purposes; I am merely suggesting that we do not need (and indeed could not use) a more comprehensive and therefore more controversial theory of republican liberty for determining whether an infringement of negative liberty is justified, for using a controversial theory would violate the principle of neutrality. Like Kramer's conception of warranted self-respect, a thin conception of republican liberty that decries arbitrariness but nothing else can be seen as part of what Rawls called "a thin theory of the good," that is, a theory of the good that is part of and indeed essential to the pursuit of a wide variety of more comprehensive reasonable theories of the good.[19] Consideration of elements of this thin theory of the good can therefore provide a justification for government interference with negative liberty without violating the principle of neutrality. I will say more about my view of what constitutes arbitrariness and therefore provide some further content to my thin conception of republican liberty at the end of this chapter, but I think I have said enough now to show that in its narrow form, republican liberty can indeed be used to justify interferences with negative liberty without violating the liberal principle of neutrality.

To see how these three concepts of liberty and the principle of neutrality all fit together and interact in practice, consider the current dispute about the scope of what is commonly called "religious" liberty. Some people claim that religious liberty is a right, and that this right prevents the government from forcing those who hold sincere religious objections to homosexuality to refrain from discriminating against LGBTQ people in various ways. But this represents a misunderstanding what religious liberty is and how it arises in a liberal society. Religious liberty is not a right in the Hohfeldian sense; it is, as its label suggests, a liberty.[20] It does not preclude interference. So while anti-discrimination rules do interfere with the negative liberty to discriminate, and some people may sincerely feel that their religion requires them to discriminate against LGBTQ people, prohibiting such discrimination, like any other infringement of negative liberty, may or may not be justified. This depends on what the justification for that interference is and how strong that justification may be.

[18] See Reiff, *In the Name of Liberty*, 88–94.

[19] See Rawls, *A Theory of Justice*, 347–50.

[20] For a comprehensive discussion of the Hohfeldian system of analyzing juridical relationships, see Kramer, "Rights without Trimmings," 7–60.

Where the principle of neutrality comes in, then, is that it provides guidance for determining what kinds of justifications are eligible for consideration when deciding the question of justification. For example, it tells us that controversial components of conceptions of positive liberty, the kinds of things that make up particular sets of religious beliefs, are ruled out as justifications. For if they were not, government could establish a state religion or at least favor one religion over another and even try to suppress some, for the infringements of negative liberty that would be required to do this would be justified. And if controversial components of conceptions of positive liberty cannot be used to justify infringements of negative liberty, they also cannot be used to justify non-compliance with rules that infringe negative liberty but are nevertheless justified on other, non-controversial grounds. Otherwise, the prohibition of the consideration of these controversial components as positive justifications for an interference with negative liberty would be meaningless, for it would lead to the creation of lots of rules and regulations that many people would then not be required to follow. So any claim that non-discrimination rules, even if those rules are otherwise justified, cannot be enforced against someone if compliance with that rule would violate that person's particular controversial religious conception of the good, must be rejected under the liberal principle of neutrality.[21]

Of course, so far, I have only established that a claim for a religious exemption from compliance is not justified. And this does not entail the conclusion that the infringement of negative liberty that these non-discrimination rules impose would itself be justified. Some other justification is needed to establish this. Again, reliance on controversial conceptions of positive liberty are ruled out by the principle of neutrality. But this is not the case when it comes to the narrow conception of republican liberty I have identified, for this would be part of the applicable thin theory of the good. And if we look to that conception of republican liberty, we can find the required guidance. For remember, republican liberty protects people against arbitrary treatment. Distinctions must be based on principles that are possible to defend based on considerations that are relevant to the decision at issue, and people who are similarly situated must be treated similarly. If we were to accept the idea that merchants could not be compelled to engage in what they considered "aiding and abetting" gay marriage given their religious beliefs, how could we decide what would constitute such aiding and abetting and what would not? The usual example given is that of a baker who does not want to provide a gay couple a wedding cake, as in the case the Supreme Court recently heard but ultimately failed to definitively decide.[22] But could a gas station attendant refuse to fill up the tanks of those on their way to the ceremony or the reception? Could the local bank refuse to process the couple's checks? Could the local motel refuse to rent accommodation to the couple's guests? Indeed, could local business owners deny service to *everyone* involved or only to the couple getting married? Could service be denied only in connection with the marriage ceremony itself, or could it be denied to *all* gay people at *all* times on the grounds that facilitating gay relationships would inevitably lead some gay people to get married? How could gay people conduct

[21] See Reiff, *In the Name of Liberty*; Reiff, "A Philosopher Argues Why No One Has the Right to Refuse Services to LGBT People."

[22] See *Masterpiece Cakeshop v. Colorado Civil Rights Commission*, 584 U.S. ___ (2018).

their lives if all the facilities of commerce were available to them only on a contingent basis, depending on a business owner's particular religious beliefs? It seems that there is no way to do any line drawing here without relying on what would be some pretty arbitrary distinctions.

But more importantly, the refusal of service to gay couples is itself an arbitrary act. It is an act of arbitrary domination—just like the refusal to provide service to black or Jewish people or inter-racial couples.[23] Nothing about who these people are is relevant to the question of whether they can pay, which is the only relevant criterion in a liberal society for the exchange being proposed in the bakery case. And nothing about the introduction of such irrelevant criteria here is trivial. For those who have any doubt about this, simply imagine what it was like to experience life as a black person under Jim Crow. One cannot imagine being subject to these kinds of restrictions and still thinking of oneself as fully free. The protection against such arbitrary treatment is central to almost every possible conception of the good and plan of life a freedom-loving person might select. Unlike enforcing some controversial comprehensive conception of positive liberty, enforcing republican liberty is not inconsistent with the idea that government should be neutral between controversial conceptions of the good. And this means that any interference with the negative liberty of those who would refuse service to LGBTQ people *is* justified, for this protects the republican liberty of LGBTQ people and does not infringe the republican liberty of anyone else.

It is true, of course, that we sometimes do grant exceptions to compliance with various regulations for those whose compliance would contradict their sincere religious convictions. Religious students, for example, do not have to attend school on their religion's holidays even if attendance on that day would otherwise be compulsory. But this is because granting an accommodation here, unlike permitting discrimination, does not interfere with anyone else's republican liberty. It does not even interfere with anyone's else negative liberty. Giving students who embrace minority religions a day off on their religious holidays is nevertheless required by equality, given that all students are given days off on the religious holidays of majority religions, and doing so for one group does not interfere with doing so for another. And as long as non-religious students have the option of taking the same number of days off too, neutrality is complied with as well. So unlike the situation in which we are adding a superfluous level of neutrality analysis when it comes to deciding whether something can be a right, when we are considering how the various relevant conceptions of liberty fit together, the principle of neutrality is doing some real work. And unlike treating what is going on here as a conflict of rights, we can do this without having to explain why one right should be given priority over another, or how both rights can be respected when the enforcement of one would undercut the other.

Kramer, of course, is one of the leading exponents of negative liberty theory.[24] But in *Liberalism with Excellence*, he is primarily interested in questions of distributive justice, and especially in what limits, if any, apply to government support of what seem

[23] See, e.g., Swenson, "Company's Ban Against Gay Weddings Is Akin to 'White Applicants Only' Sign, Judge Says,"; Stolberg, "The Faces of Intermarriage, 50 Years After Loving v. Virginia."

[24] See, e.g., Kramer, *The Quality of Freedom*. For one of the many discussions of Kramer's theory, see Carter and Steiner, ch. 13 in this volume.

to be reasonable but controversial conceptions of the good. He does not say much about how he thinks negative liberty, positive liberty, republican liberty, and neutrality all come together in analyzing particular exercises of government power. So I do not know whether he would think the approach I have described would be contrary to his views. But I suspect he would agree that my approach is not inconsistent with his views. He ultimately argues that the forms of excellence he thinks government should support are *not* controversial—that is, he argues that support for activities that boost warranted self-respect does not violate neutrality because such support is instrumentally useful or even absolutely necessary to a wide variety of other, reasonable comprehensive conceptions of the good, and therefore can properly be thought of as part a thin theory of the good. For Kramer, then, support for these forms of excellence is not prohibited by the principle of neutrality, which is what I have just argued as well. But this still leaves open the question of what happens with regard to reasonable forms of excellence that are controversial, and therefore cannot be brought within the relevant thin theory of the good. These would indeed seem to be covered by the principle of neutrality. What I intend to show is that even so, there are ways the principle of neutrality can be satisfied without denying these forms of excellence government support.

5. Neutrality and Proportionality

Within the academy, a great deal of the dispute between those who identify as liberal neutralists and those who identify as soft perfectionists has to do with support for excellence in sport, culture, and the arts. With respect to more fundamental matters, theorists often disagree on the appropriate route to take to get to where they want to go, but nevertheless ultimately arrive at the same place. While routing is important, for this often has ramifications beyond the particular matter at issue, the controversy over how neutrality and the pursuit of excellence interrelate in a liberal society mostly plays itself out with regard to whether government can support forms of self-improvement and artistic expression. To liberal neutralists, providing support to the various forms of excellence within these broader categories seems straightforwardly non-neutral, both in the sense of supporting any forms of excellence in a society where the question of what constitutes excellence is reasonably contested and, to the extent some forms of excellence are nevertheless supported, in the sense of favoring "elitist" forms of culture and disfavoring forms of excellence in "popular" culture. The last claim, of course, is an empirical claim, and while lots of people make it, empirical work that confirms or debunks it is decidedly lacking. But people on both sides seem to assume that it is true, and therefore focus their arguments on whether this can be justified. I will say more about this in a moment, but first I want to get some other important points on the table.

First, note that support of excellence in sport, culture, and the arts does not typically raise questions of commutative justice. Absent unusual circumstances, no one has an individual right to support from the government for their favored form of excellence, and it violates no one's individual right to provide it. The questions such support raise are accordingly purely distributive—that is, these questions are simply about how government should allocate the burdens and benefits of the collection and application of the various resources at its command within the scope of what commutative justice allows. And the neutralist argument, of course, is that these questions should be resolved in a way that does not suggest the government disfavors one permissible form of excellence, or favors one over another.

In a paper called "Proportionality, Winner-Take-All, and Distributive Justice,"[25] I argued that there were two moral theories required to resolve any distributive dispute: one that tells you what weights to assign to the various arguments made by the competing parties, and another, often unrecognized theory that tells you which method of distribution to use once you have made the required weighing up. For there are two methods of distribution one could employ in every case: one could give the entire disputed good to the party with the strongest claim, a method of distribution I called "winner-take-all." Alternatively, one could distribute the good proportionally, with each party receiving a share of the good equivalent to the relative moral strength of their argument for receiving it, a method of distribution I called "proportional division" or "strength-of-the-arguments." Because resolution of the question of the appropriate distributive method can have a huge effect on how the good at issue was ultimately distributed, choosing which method to apply in a particular case clearly presents a question of justice.

I know some people suggest that dividing the relevant burdens or benefits up like this cannot be done in every case, for whatever is to be distributed may not as a practical matter be divisible, and therefore the number of cases in which this latter question of justice is present is limited. But this is not correct. Everything is divisible either in kind, by value, by time, by adding something else into the mix to make the sum total of what is under consideration divisible and then dividing that, or by lottery, and often by more than one of these methods. In the paper, I give numerous examples to show what I mean by this, but I will not repeat them here, because what we are talking about dividing here is money, which clearly is divisible. So applying proportional division here would not be problematic.

Given divisibility, then, the question of the appropriate method of distribution is squarely presented. I describe the various kinds of arguments that could be raised in favor of one method of distribution or the other in the paper, and I also give three examples of how recognition of the question of the method of distribution would help explain three aspects of our moral practice that otherwise seem mysterious. One was how settlement rather than adjudication of almost all legal disputes could possibly be just, given that this means neither party's claimed rights are ever fully enforced. Another was how calling something a right could indeed do some real work and not simply lead to the same outcome that occurs when one is balancing competing interests, for balancing does indeed seem to occur in not only interest versus interest contests but in right versus interest contests and right versus right contests as well, where it takes place in the context of defining more precisely the scope of the right or rights involved. And the third was how to resolve the long-running problem of explaining how a moral theory can avoid being too demanding without failing to be demanding enough. In connection with that last argument, I noted as follows:

[25] *Politics, Philosophy, and Economics* 8 (2009): 5–42.

> There is precedent for this approach to moral reasoning in the allocative decisions of nation-states. How can a government justify spending some of its limited resources on the arts, or on national parks, or on foreign aid when there are people within its own borders in need of food, shelter, and the basic necessities of life? Clearly, the claims of these people have greater moral weight than the claims of those who would benefit from a subsidized national theatre, or government-maintained parks, or any of the innumerable other less pressing projects that often seek a share of the limited resources in society's coffers. But even though these claims are weaker, they nevertheless have some moral weight. To explain why we divide our resources among these various projects rather than apply all our resources to our most pressing needs, we simply have to focus on the question of distributive method. Indeed, if we characterize what we are doing as satisfying the requirements of the principle of proportionality when we use public money to fund less pressing claims, we can avoid the twin charges of elitism and paternalism that often attend attempts to defend such uses of public funds. Because we are not favoring the interests of the minority over the interests of the majority or giving the majority what we think they would want if they only knew better, but rather recognizing the actual percentage of support for these projects within the relevant population, funding these projects in proportionate amounts is neither elitist nor paternalistic. It is simply a reflection of the fact that it is proportional division, not winner take all, which enjoys the privileged position in our moral thinking about distributive justice.[26]

So how is supporting different forms of sport, culture, and the arts in proportion to their support within the relevant community consistent with the liberal commitment to neutrality? The reason, as I suggested above, is that we can look at how the government distributes its support to various reasonable activities and forms of excellence as presenting a question of distributive justice. People may reasonably disagree as to what is a form of excellence and which particular forms should receive government support, given their embrace of differing comprehensive conceptions of the good. But this does not mean that we must withhold support from all forms of excellence under the principle of neutrality. We don't need to weigh up any of the arguments in the sense of coming to an independent view of how strong each is either—that has already been done for us by the public as a whole in distributing their support over the various forms of excellence available. Accordingly, as long as funding is distributed to each individual form in proportion to the relative strength of its support within the community, the principle of neutrality is satisfied.

Note that by suggesting this, I am not simply assuming that consequentialist moral reasoning is the way to decide this question, or that rights and interests are treated no differently even if one rejects consequentialist forms of moral reasoning. For under my approach, if one of the claims on a government resource comes in the form of claim of right, winner-take-all applies. But even when claims of right are presented, balancing occurs. While balancing is the main event for those employing some form of consequentialist moral reasoning, those employing some form of deontological moral

[26] Reiff, "Proportionality, Winner-Take-All, and Distributive Justice," 5–42, 38.

reasoning have to do this too. They just do it in the context of more precisely defining the scope of the right or rights at issue, for only if what appears to be a conflict between one right and another or a right and a competing interest is an actual conflict, and not one that can be resolved by coming to a better understanding of the scope of the rights involved, would winner-take-all apply.[27] Indeed, if some sort of balancing was not part of the process of resolving borderline disputes about the scope of rights, it is unclear how these disputes could possibly be resolved. It is simply part of the process by which people think. So the kind of balancing or weighing up process that I am referring to here is always required. The distinction between consequentialist and deontological moral reasoning only matters with regard to where this occurs, not whether. The form of moral reasoning employed determines whether balancing *is* the decision procedure, or merely part of the process of determining what the precise conflict at issue is and therefore what is to be decided, after which the conflict is then resolved according to a much more straightforward decision procedure than balancing (rights are absolute and therefore cannot conflict and rights always prevail over competing interest).

In any event, it is hard to see here how a claim to exclude support for some or even all reasonable forms of excellence could be a claim of individual right. We cannot just assume that the principle of neutrality provides such a right, for this is the very question at issue. So unless such a right can be established on some independent grounds, the worry that employing a form of weighing up privileges consequentialist moral reasoning over deontological moral reasoning is not really relevant anyway. For even those who reject consequentialist moral reasoning agree that within the realm of the permissible, weighing up is an acceptable decision procedure. Which means that dividing up government support for various forms of excellence according to their respective support within the community is in no way inconsistent with recognizing a deontological justification for the principle of neutrality.

Is it true, however, that an individual right barring all support for controversial forms of excellence cannot be established on independent grounds? For that matter, is it true that such a right cannot be derived from the principle of neutrality itself without begging the question? Let us reconsider the claim that under the principle of neutrality, individuals have a right to demand that their tax payments not be used for projects whose goodness they can reasonably deny. The thinking here, I suppose, is that people can reasonably deny the good of even reasonable forms of excellence. And they can—this is in fact built into the idea of what being reasonable means in a world characterized by reasonable pluralism, which is the kind of world liberalism is supposed to address. Prohibiting government from supporting an activity whose goodness some people do or perhaps merely even could reasonably deny is, as the argument would then go, a violation of what neutrality requires. In support of this view, theorists point to the fact that liberalism requires that people be able to justify their actions about at least important matters using reasons that others could not reasonably reject. But this comes not from the principle of neutrality, but from liberalism's conception of the role of public discourse and debate. Most liberals call this "the idea of public reason" after Rawls's use of the term,[28] although unlike Rawls they often attach it to neutrality

[27] See Reiff, "Proportionality, Winner-Take-All, and Distributive Justice," 27–32.

[28] See, e.g., Rawls, "The Idea of Public Reason," 212–54; Rawls, "The Idea of Public Reason Revisited," 573–615.

rather than see it as I do as embodied in a separate principle.[29] In either case, however, "because God says so" would be an example of a reason that people could reasonably reject, for people can reasonably disagree that this is indeed what God says or even whether there is a God and even if there is, whether God's Word should be given any much less decisive political authority.

But embracing the idea of public reason is a long way from saying that the government cannot assist in the pursuit of forms of excellence, the good of which some people can reasonably deny. This is not what the requirement of public reason could possibly mean, whether it is seen as part of the principle of neutrality or free-standing. In a liberal society, which by definition is characterized by reasonable pluralism about the good, anything that has a reasonable justification will almost always also be subject to reasonable objections. If neutrality precluded government from acting in these cases, then government could do nothing, or hardly anything. The principle of neutrality would be paralytic. The only way to avoid this problem is to keep the idea of neutrality between conceptions of good and the idea of public reason separate and distinct. Public reason requires that only certain kinds of reasons should be offered in support of whatever issues to which it applies. Even if we assume that the requirement of public reason applies to everything and not just fundamental constitutional and political questions, as some theorists do, this does not mean that the requirement of public reason is unsatisfied if a reasonable objection is raised to the support of a particular form of excellence. Public reason is meant to require that unreasonable arguments not be offered in favor of a position in public discourse and debate—not that there be no reasonable arguments *against* that position. Not being able to reasonably reject an argument does not mean that one has to accept it or be unreasonable, for then reasonable pluralism could not exist. Indeed, this idea is built into Rawls's conception of the "burdens of judgment," or the reasons why people may reasonably disagree.[30] And if we understand the requirement of public reason in this light, we can see that both it and the principle of neutrality can be satisfied when we allocate government support between various reasonable conceptions of excellence according to their relative support in the community. The criteria used for allocation in this case *is* a public reason, and it results in government being neutral toward the competing conceptions of the good involved because it means that government is not substituting its judgment about the good for the judgment of the governed as a whole. And neither principle gives anyone a right to veto support for a conception of the good that is otherwise reasonable no matter how reasonable their objection to it might be.

Nevertheless, there are precedents for recognizing a veto in our actual practice. For example, such thinking is behind various practices of private dues-collecting organizations such as bar associations and unions that allow members the option of deducting a certain amount from their dues if they do not want to fund the organization's political activities, given that these activities can be controversial. Of course, the principle of neutrality is meant to apply only to the government, not to private organizations, so even in cases where the private organization is required to offer such a deduction by law, it is not clear why we should think of this as an example of the principle of

[29] See generally Quong, *Liberalism without Perfection*, 41–3.
[30] See Rawls, *Justice as Fairness*, 191; Rawls, *Political Liberalism*, 54.

neutrality in motion. But some theorists do think that the principle of neutrality applies to everything, usually by again relying on some misconception of the requirement of public reason and mistakenly conflating this with the principle of neutrality in the way I have already identified.[31] But let's ignore this mistake and consider whether the claim that affording everyone a veto over how their tax dollars can be used is a reasonable position. For it seems clear that government could not possibly function if it gave each individual taxpayer a veto over how their tax money is spent across innumerable permissible activities. What if I am a pacifist and therefore reasonably object to funding national defense? Or perhaps I believe the correctional system is hopelessly discriminatory (not an unreasonable view) and so object to any funding for that? Or perhaps I am a right libertarian and believe that it is not the job of government to regulate pollution, or employment practices, or even competition, as some right libertarians reasonably do, and therefore do not want my taxes to be used to fund this? And why would those who did not believe these things nevertheless not claim they did if it could provide them a way of reducing their own taxes? Those who hold views about how government should allocate its resources have an opportunity to express these views by participating in the political and electoral process. But if their views lose out, the principle of neutrality does not provide them with a way of snatching a personal victory from the jaws of their general defeat. The principle of neutrality is designed to regulate what liberal government can do within the set of reasonable options it could feasibly pursue, not to be a tool for making it so government cannot do anything to which anyone reasonably objects, for this would make it impossible for government to function in a pluralistic society. And while we could alleviate some of this concern by categorizing a significant number of goods as part of a thin theory of the good to which the principle of neutrality does not apply, which some liberal neutralists try to do, the more we do this the more it seems like our interpretation of the principle of neutrality is itself being driven by a comprehensive conception of the good instead of creating the groundwork for a society characterized by reasonable pluralism as to such comprehensive conceptions. Instead of making liberalism a social place where a wide variety of reasonable comprehensive conceptions can flourish, it would leave the space available to do this pretty limited. This alone supplies a reason to reject any such interpretation of the principle of neutrality.

The same thinking applies if we argue that such an individual veto somehow arises from the right of equal concern and respect. That principle was also designed to enable government to function justly in a pluralistic society. If we interpret this requirement in such a way as to make it impossible for government to function at all, the principle is self-defeating. If we address this problem by recognizing numerous exceptions to the principle, we seriously chip away at the idea that equality regulates what we can do rather than being simply an expression of our pre-existing biases and prejudices. There is an additional problem too: the principle of equality does not tell us whether to treat people well or badly. It merely tells us that however we treat people, we must treat everyone who is similarly situated the same. Which is what we would be doing if everyone's favored form of excellence received government support in proportion

[31] See the discussion in Kramer, *Liberalism with Excellence*, 29–30.

to its support within the community and no one had the right to a veto. And I do not see how a right to veto government support for forms of excellence whose goodness one could reasonably deny could be gotten out of some irreducibly minimal notion of what it means to be treated with respect either, except by stipulation. So I do not see how we could get a right to a veto out of the principle of equality either.

What if we do not focus on funding the essential practices of government, however, and instead just focus on support for sport, culture, and the arts? As Kramer notes, in an attempt to get to the same place as soft perfectionists, some liberal neutralists attempt to make this very distinction and segregate decisions with regard to "the fundamentals of constitutions and justice," to which they contend neutrality applies, from less important matters, to which they contend it does not.[32] I do not see how this approach is any more implementable if it entails a veto to only the most important decisions than if it entails a veto to everything, for by definition it still operates in the most important cases. But let us consider the opposite approach. What if we treat only less important decisions, those about self-improvement and expression, as covered by the principle of neutrality? I do not think anyone expressly admits to taking this view, but so much of the discussion about the principle of neutrality focuses on the extent to which, if any, government can support certain forms of sport, culture, and the arts, they might as well do.[33] When it comes to how these issues play out on the ground, this, as I said, is where the disagreement tends to lie.

In any event, if we do spin the common approach 180 degrees, the requirements of neutrality probably become implementable as a practical matter. But this does not make that approach reasonable. Why distinguish these forms of excellence from other aspects of our social life? The principle of neutrality was designed to require government to be neutral between reasonable but controversial conceptions of the good, and conceptions of the good regulate all aspects of our behavior, not just physical and mental self-improvement and expression. Besides, how would we describe the borderlines line here without relying on some pretty arbitrary distinctions? Is support for self-improvement and expression really different than support for more fundamental questions of social and political life? Cannot self-improvement and expression be political as well? Many liberal neutralists find the attempted distinction here untenable.[34] Moreover, the US Supreme Court has recently ruled that the compelled payment of any sum that could be used to promote even the most mundane bureaucratic functions of an organization that engages in any political activities whatsoever, or whose mere existence is politically controversial, is a form of compelled expression and therefore unconstitutional if the payor objects to these activities.[35] Whether one agrees with this decision or not, it demonstrates that drawing the relevant borderlines here between the more and less fundamental is no simple matter, whichever side of the border bears the constraint of neutrality. But more importantly, reducing the principle of neutrality to a principle solely regulating government support for self-improvement

[32] Kramer, *Liberalism with Excellence*, 25–7.

[33] For references to just some of the literature focusing on this issue, see Kramer, *Liberalism with Excellence*, 346, n. 2.

[34] See the various theorists referenced in Kramer, *Liberalism with Excellence*, 27.

[35] See *Janus v. AFSCME*, 585 U.S. ___ (2018). For a more extensive discussion of this ruling and the problems it raises, see Reiff, *In the Name of Liberty*, 230–8.

and expression, instead of a principle about how liberal government can accommodate the existence of reasonable pluralism about all aspects of the good, would turn it into a mere fashion accessory of liberalism rather than a fundamental presupposition. It would require us to treat certain aspects of the good differently than other aspects, which itself would violate neutrality, making this interpretation of the principle of neutrality self-contradictory.

But this does not mean the principle of neutrality has no application when it comes to decisions about how to fund particular forms of excellence. Even if neither the principle of equality nor the principle of neutrality nor the principle of public reason prohibits the government from supporting non-essential forms of excellence, if this is what the majority of the electorate wants the government to do, the government still needs to do so in a manner consistent with the principle of neutrality. This means that it cannot just distribute its support without regard to the extent these activities are supported in the community. It cannot just give vast sums to underwrite opera and other forms of "high art" and nothing to anything else. Nor can it provide support only for popular culture and give nothing to more elitist forms of excellence, even if this is what the majority of voters would approve. As I argued above, proportional division is the default position; winner-take-all is only used where there is some special reason requiring this. But circumstances in which one or more of these special reasons might apply are rare.[36] And I can see no reason here that would justify departing from the default position of proportional division that the principle of neutrality would allow us to consider. Which means that neutrality is preserved when government does not favor one form of excellence over another but simply supports various kinds of excellence in proportion to their support within the community. Proportional division is not the result of government embracing a particular reasonable but controversial moral theory and deciding on this basis that certain projects are worth supporting and others are not. It is the result of the determination that many different paths toward excellence are reasonable and a recognition that dividing the available resources between these does not involve the government substituting its judgment for that of the community. Proportional division is not a violation of neutrality, it is an application of it.

What do we do then with racists, religious fundamentalists, misogynists, homophobes, and so on who claim a share of government support for engaging in private activities or forms of excellence that express these attitudes but do not violate anyone's individual rights given the way the holders of these attitudes intend to pursue them? Must they be given some government support as well? No, because under any reasonable liberal moral theory, such views are unreasonable, not because they violate neutrality, but because they violate one or more of the other fundamental presuppositions of liberalism. Whether we think of this as meaning that no obligation to treat them neutrally could possibly arise, or as meaning that arguments in support of these unreasonable views are entitled to no weight at all in the balancing process, hardly matters. In either case, such activities are not entitled to government support even if some portion of the population supports them.

[36] I will not list these here because my space here is limited, but see Reiff, "Proportionality, Winner-Take-All, and Distributive Justice" for a full discussion.

But does the approach I am recommending not raise practical problems too? How are we to determine the degree of community support for any particular form of excellence? And what do we do about forms of excellence that are reasonable but only garner a trivial amount of public support? Must government provide each of these many, many types of activities a small amount of funds? Does this not pose an administrative nightmare that is almost as bad of giving everyone a veto? No, for as I argued in "Proportionality, Winner-Take-All, and Distributive Justice," claims for support that garner only trivial amounts of support can be justly disregarded. Too fine-grained an approach to compliance with a general principle often makes that principle self-defeating, and threatens to undermine the whole project of which that principle is part. Under liberalism, fidelity to principle does not require unwavering, absolute, full, and strict compliance. Indeed, this is one of the most important distinctions between liberalism and perfectionism. The principles of liberalism are aspirational; one is committed to them and works toward them, and the aspiration is for pretty good compliance. It is understood that perfect compliance is neither expected nor possible, even when it comes to respecting pluralism.

6. External and Personal Preferences

There is also another way of determining whether a preference is entitled to proportional support or no support at all that I want to mention. This is to rely on the work of Ronald Dworkin. Dworkin pointed out that in applying the principle of neutrality, external preferences should not be counted.[37] External preferences are preferences about what other people should be able to do or receive. Personal preferences, in contrast, are about what you yourself should be able to do or receive. Under this view, external preferences such as preferences that certain kinds of excellence be denied funding are excluded in the decision procedure that determines which forms of excellence get what amount of support, because this is what neutrality requires. Only personal preferences can be legitimately counted under the principle of neutrality in deciding the relative extent to which government should support the various forms of excellence that its citizens support. The personal preference must still be reasonable, of course, and it is the government that must decide this according to the moral framework in place in the particular liberal society—this is not open to popular vote. But the fact that certain members of society may despise a particular form of excellence cannot be used to deprive it of government support under the principle of neutrality, or so Dworkin contends. Dworkin does not explain what he thinks neutrality requires with regard to determining how much support each reasonable form of excellence should receive, but he says nothing that would indicate he might disagree with my claim that neutrality requires proportional division.

Of course, as Dworkin himself acknowledges, it is sometimes difficult to tell an external preference from a personal one. Preferences phrased in one manner can often be rephrased and expressed in the other, especially if the preference is associational.

[37] See Dworkin, "What Rights Do We Have?," 266–78, 275–6.

A white racist's external preference that black people be barred from living in his neighborhood, for example, can be rephrased as a personal preference that he live in a neighborhood where everyone is white. In most cases, however, this preference will be deemed unreasonable in whichever way it is phrased, so the difficulty in telling which phrasing is appropriate in the most problematic cases will never arise. This will only arise when dealing with reasonable preferences. And there is a more determinate way of telling whether a preference is personal or external here. We can think of a preference as external no matter how it is expressed if its effect is to deny certain forms of excellence support, in contrast to crediting one or more forms of excellence with support so that they get a share of whatever support is available. Preferences about the amount of support are irrelevant, for the government determines that by dividing up whatever amount of support is available according to their overall level of support within the community. If we use this as the test, we should not run into difficulties distinguishing the personal from the external as Dworkin suggests we should.

Indeed, this roughly approximates what we actually do in liberal societies. Opera, ballet, symphonies, fine art, and other forms of "high" culture do receive government support, but far less than professional sports or movie or TV production or other forms of excellence that might fairly be characterized as examples of popular culture, which receive support in the form of tax breaks and land giveaways that vastly exceed the value of what is given to the high arts. Forms of avant-garde art and performance receive some government support, but far less, which correlates roughly with the degree to which these forms of excellence are embraced by members of the relevant community. We can certainly argue about whether the proportions are right here, but the claim by those who prefer some forms of excellence and find others offensive, as well as the claims of those who find the support for any form of excellence offensive, are simply based on external preferences and therefore not something that must be taken into account for the government to remain neutral, even if these are reasonable. And if they are not, they are simply excluded outright under one or more of the other fundamental presuppositions of liberalism. Again, this is not a violation of the principle of neutrality, it is an example of it in motion.

7. Proportionality and Checkerboard Solutions

There is a more serious concern, however, that instead of being alleviated by Dworkin's work is actually intensified by it. This is the idea that that it is a violation of moral integrity to adopt what Dworkin calls "checkerboard solutions" to moral disputes.[38] For example, many people believe that women must have the right to control their own bodies, and therefore be given access to legal and safe abortion services when they need them. Others believe that abortion in almost all circumstances is the moral equivalent of murder. A checkerboard solution, one which is derived according to the support for each respective position within the population, which let us assume is 50-50, would allow abortions for women born on even numbered days but outlaw them for women born on odd numbers days or some equivalently probabilistic allocation.

[38] See Dworkin, *Law's Empire*, 176–84, 217–18.

But what I am advocating in the form of proportional division is not a checkerboard solution. In the abortion example, the even/odd day solution means that some women will have a right to abortion, and some women will not, as the result of a criterion that is entirely arbitrary. This is an infringement of moral integrity, according to Dworkin, because we are embracing two conflicting accounts of morality at one and the same time. Abortion cannot be morally permissible on even numbered days and morally prohibited on odd days under any moral theory that is entitled to our respect. In order to maintain its moral integrity, government simply needs to choose which moral argument it feels is correct and then support that on every day of the week. And doing otherwise is not only a violation of moral integrity; it is also an infringement of equality and of republican liberty, given the arbitrariness of the distinction that is doing all the work. Finally, depending on which moral view one takes, there is either a right to abortion or abortion is a violation of rights of the fetus, meaning the opposing moral view is unreasonable, and therefore not something toward which the principle of neutrality would even apply.

In contrast, when I am advocating support for certain forms of excellence according to their support within the community, I am not advocating that we embrace some sort of moral schizophrenia. Using the proportional division approach does not entail creating a checkerboard solution to competing moral claims of right. Proportional division does not require we maintain that something is morally worthy and morally condemnable at one and the same time. It merely instantiates the idea that to the extent these different views are reasonable, as determined by one or more of the other fundamental presuppositions of liberalism or the principles derived therefrom, it is not government's job to favor one view over the other, but to support each according to its support in the political community. In the abortion case, each side views the other's view as unreasonable and in fact a violation of individual right. Accordingly, choosing between these competing views does not implicate the principle of neutrality in any way. Rather, it implicates the interpretation of the other fundamental principles of liberalism, and implementing a checkerboard solution when these principles are determinative would indeed be a violation of moral integrity. When each of the competing claims are reasonable, however, supporting both is not a violation of individual right. And with regard to the amount of that support, neutrality requires proportional division, because that does not entail a moral commitment to one competing reasonable claim over others and therefore does not compromise integrity.

The one occasion on which an exception might arise to my claim that proportional division is what the principle of neutrality requires is when the competing forms of excellence involved are rivalrous. A form of excellence is rivalrous, in the sense I am using the term, when the pursuit of that form of excellence prevents others from pursuing reasonable forms of excellence that they support. Not in terms of depriving those forms of excellence of increased levels of funding, for we have already decided that the amount of funding provided must reflect the level of support in the community. But forms of excellence may be rivalrous if conditions are such that supporting one form, even proportionally, prevents other forms from being pursued. Designating certain land as a nature conservancy and thereby preventing those who would like to hunt on it from doing so might, for example, make the competing conceptions of the good involved here rivalrous. But these cases can usually be dealt with by simply designating some other piece of land for hunting if the entire parcel in dispute is to be protected against hunting, and thereby apply the proportional division approach on a larger scale. In other words, this problem can be dealt with by making whatever is rivalrous more readily divisible in some way and thereby making it non-rivalrous. People cannot be entirely prevented from pursuing a reasonable form of excellence or, if they prefer, no form of excellence at all, but cases in which this would be the result of supporting another reasonable form of excellence are likely to be rare.

8. The Reasonable and Unreasonable and the Fear of Paternalism

I will finish by saying a little more about how we can tell a reasonable conception of the good from an unreasonable one, and by talking a little about paternalism. One criterion for distinguishing the reasonable from the unreasonable can be derived from liberalism's commitment to reasonable pluralism. Any theory that rejects reasonable pluralism, that claims there is only one true way to live a moral life and that all other conceptions are unreasonable, that advocates intolerance of the tolerant and rejection of neutrality no matter what the circumstances, is unreasonable, and therefore need not be assigned moral weight or otherwise treated with equal concern and respect under the liberal commitment to neutrality. Conceptions which reject the burdens of judgment, Rawls tells us, are unreasonable as well.[39] Rawls also tells us that those who are not willing to propose and abide by fair terms of social cooperation with those who are willing to do the same are unreasonable.[40] This last statement, however, strikes me as rather unhelpful. What is "fair" is simply another word for what is reasonable, so without specifying some more content for that alternative descriptor, which Rawls fails to do, this criterion probably has no uncontroversial applications beyond telling us that we need not be neutral toward, and tolerant of, those who expressly to reject the "fair terms" principle, whatever it may mean.

Despite the limited extent to which these various attempts to give further content to the reasonable/unreasonable distinction can be operationalized, they do provide some guidance and, perhaps even more importantly, they are limits that are accepted by even the most committed liberal neutralists, and most soft perfectionists as well. We can give the line between the reasonable and the unreasonable more content, however, by relying again on our thin conception of republican liberty. After all, the principle of neutrality is primarily designed to protect liberty, at least in my conception of it, so it would make sense to give it content by using a principle of liberty to do so. Once again, under my thin conception, there has been an interference with republican liberty when and only when a decision is arbitrary. A decision is arbitrary, in turn, only when it is based on no criteria, or is made without relevant criteria being adequately considered, or is based in whole or in part on criteria that are unrelated to the performance of the task or role under consideration, or is based on performance-related

[39] See Rawls, *Justice as Fairness*; Rawls, *Political Liberalism*, 54.

[40] See, e.g., John Rawls, *Political Liberalism*, 49.

criteria but does not treat similarly situated people similarly.[41] Liberalism does not require neutrality toward conceptions of the good which are arbitrary in any of these ways. I realize that the edges of this definition of arbitrariness may be a little blurry—what does it mean for relevant criteria to be "adequately considered?" When are people "similarly situated?" And so on. But this is true whenever significant judgments must be made. The only way to make neutrality not blurry around the edges is to require neutrality toward either everything or nothing, and no liberal worth taking seriously advocates that.

Violations of rights that have been properly recognized would certainly be considered arbitrary in one of these ways. But there are many other actions or omissions that would also be considered arbitrary in one of these ways even though these actions or omissions do not constitute a violation of right. Refusing to hire people who are left-handed for a job in which handedness was irrelevant would be just one example out of countless possible others. Thus, this definition of what makes something unreasonable has greater scope than simply labeling all conduct which consists in a rights violation unreasonable. It will do some real work. To the extent this helps us determine the limits of the principle of neutrality, it is available for us to use. And it does not seem that the kind of government support for the arts and culture that both edificatory and aspirational perfectionists want to see is arbitrary—these claims are related to relevant goals and have at least some real moral weight. It is accordingly within the scope of the principle of neutrality for government to support them in some way. We need not stray into perfectionist territory to justify doing so.

Finally, I want to say something about paternalism, the substitution of one's own judgment for another's, and its relationship to the principle of neutrality. Surprisingly, despite being written about extensively, this relationship is not well-understood. Some theorists act as if paternalism is simply the opposite of neutrality—that is, they act as if paternalism and neutrality were simply different sides of the same coin. But this is not correct. The principle of neutrality is a principle of political morality; paternalism, or rather anti-paternalism, a principle of personal morality. The objective of the principle of neutrality is to create a certain kind of society, one which recognizes the existence and benefits of reasonable pluralism, and strives to ensure that government honors this by not expressing preferences between reasonable but conflicting conceptions of the good. Those who raise objections to paternalism, in contrast, are trying to protect a certain kind of personal autonomy—the ability to freely choose one's own conception of the good without interference by other people, whether this be the state, one's parents, one's school, or an officious busybody—on the grounds that showing the appropriate respect for persons entails allowing individuals to make these choices for themselves. And it is true that when a state is not being neutral in the required way, it is also being paternalistic, at least according to most theorists. But the principle of neutrality is worried about something way beyond mere personal autonomy. It is worried about creating the background circumstances in which a certain kind of social and political life can take place, one in which what we commonly call "society" can be cohesive despite the existence of reasonable pluralism with regard to the good.

[41] See Reiff, *In the Name of Liberty*, 89–93.

Operationalizing the different objectives behind the principle of neutrality and the paternalism objection does not and need not always lead to the same outcome.

For example, some theorists think it is not paternalistic for government to encourage certain activities but not require them, when this clearly would be a violation of neutrality if it were an activity to which the principle of neutrality applied. Incorporating the anti-paternalism objection into the principle of neutrality might accordingly pull us in two different directions and lead us analytically astray. But more importantly, mistakenly thinking that a concern for paternalism as at the center of the principle of neutrality and as therefore having some influence over its interpretation and application misses the significance that the principle of neutrality attributes to the attitudes and actions of the state. State paternalism is not simply a special case of paternalism. Thinking that it is fails to recognize that there are important social and political values at stake when we are trying to circumscribe the power of the state to conform to some overall vision of liberalism rather than simply express a rule of personal conduct. Whether Kramer's aspirational perfectionism or my version of liberal neutralism can be seen in some sense as paternalistic is accordingly irrelevant—if they cannot then the paternalism objection does not apply, and if they can, the paternalism objection is simply overcome by the more pressing need to ensure that this thing called liberalism can continue to exist.

15
Does Edificatory Perfectionism Express a Quidnunc Mentality?

*Collis Tahzib**

It is a central tenet of much contemporary liberal political philosophy that the state should be, in some sense, neutral among the competing reasonable conceptions of the good life that exist within society.[1] A neutral state, it is often said, is one that does not impose or promote any particular ethical, religious, or metaphysical doctrine and instead simply upholds a fair system of laws and institutions within which each individual can freely pursue his or her own conception of the good life. By contrast, perfectionists hold that an important function of the state is to encourage citizens to pursue virtuous, meaningful, or worthwhile ways of life and to discourage them from pursuing degrading or hollow ways of life. For perfectionists, then, liberal neutrality needlessly "cordon[s] off political morality from our best understanding of human flourishing."[2]

Over the years, a wide variety of objections and criticisms have been leveled against perfectionist politics. Some have argued that states should remain neutral because reasonable citizens disagree about what makes for a good life and so perfectionism would inevitably involve the promotion of ends that some citizens could reasonably reject.[3] Others have alleged that perfectionist public policy is paternalistic insofar as it is generally premised on the belief that citizens are weak-willed and cognitively biased and so would, if left to their own devices, squander their time and resources on worthless pursuits and allurements.[4] Still others have objected that perfectionist political action violates the Millian principle that each person is the best judge of his or her own interests,[5] that it is manipulative and invasive of autonomy,[6] that it is elitist,[7] that it is intolerant of pluralism and diversity,[8] that it contravenes the "endorsement

* For very helpful comments and discussions, I owe thanks to Raven Adams, Henrik Kugelberg, Visa Kurki, Mark McBride, Fergus Peace, Jonathan Quong, and Tom Sinclair, as well as to participants of the Workshop in Honour of Matthew Kramer at which I presented this paper in July 2019. I am especially grateful to Jeff McMahan and David Miller for invaluable feedback, as well as to Matthew Kramer for two rounds of detailed and highly perceptive written comments on earlier drafts of this paper.

[1] See, e.g., Larmore, *Patterns of Moral Complexity*; Rawls, *Political Liberalism*; Quong, *Liberalism Without Perfection*; Patten, "Liberal Neutrality: A Reinterpretation and Defense," 249–72; Schouten, *Liberalism, Neutrality, and the Gendered Division of Labor*.

[2] Wall, *Liberalism, Perfectionism and Restraint*, 123.

[3] Rawls, *Political Liberalism*; Quong, *Liberalism Without Perfection*.

[4] Quong, *Liberalism Without Perfection*, 73–107.

[5] See discussion in Caney, "Consequentialist Defences of Liberal Neutrality," 463–5.

[6] Quong, *Liberalism Without Perfection*, 45–72.

[7] See discussion in Wall, *Liberalism, Perfectionism and Restraint*, 15–17.

[8] Ibid., 17–19.

Collis Tahzib, *Does Edificatory Perfectionism Express a Quidnunc Mentality?* In: *Without Trimmings*. Edited by: Mark McBride and Visa AJ Kurki, Oxford University Press. © Mark McBride and Visa AJ Kurki 2022. DOI: 10.1093/oso/9780198868866.003.0015

constraint" according to which political measures cannot improve a citizen's life unless he or she positively affirms them "from the inside,"[9] and that it jeopardizes stable social cooperation and peace, and even risks the abuse of state power.[10]

Recently, Matthew Kramer has developed an intriguing, sophisticated, and highly original objection to perfectionism in its mainstream "edificatory" form—namely, that perfectionist regimes that seek the elevation and edification of the citizenry are guilty of a "quidnunc mentality" that is akin in important respects to the mentality of a busybody who distributes "boxes of delicious homemade fudge" to "inspire her fellow inhabitants to lead lives of propriety" and who in general meddles in matters that are "none of [her] business."[11] What makes the activities of a perfectionist state illegitimate, on this view, is that such activities emanate from, and are animated by, an objectionable mentality—one that is redolent of the mentality of a village busybody, a curtain-twitcher, or a Nosey Parker.

In this chapter, I first examine, in section 1, what Kramer means by the quidnunc mentality and why he considers such a mentality objectionable. I then argue, in section 2, that the quidnunc mentality objection fails because it begs the question against edificatory perfectionism by assuming precisely what needs to be shown, namely that the edification of the citizenry falls outside the proper bounds of government. I consider and reject, in sections 3 and 4, two potential responses available to Kramer. I conclude, in section 5, by commenting on a sense in which I think Kramer's quidnunc mentality objection, despite not succeeding in undermining edificatory perfectionism, nonetheless contains an underlying insight that opens up a fascinating and novel set of questions.

1. What is the Quidnunc Mentality and Why is it Wrongful?

Though this chapter will focus on the quidnunc mentality objection in particular, it is worth briefly situating that critique within Kramer's broader view. In *Liberalism with Excellence*, Kramer advocates a view that he classifies as perfectionist, and he defends perfectionism against a number of objections. However, Kramer's defense of perfectionism is decidedly "arm's-length" because he has little sympathy for virtually all contemporary perfectionist theories such as those of Joseph Raz and Steven Wall.[12] Distancing himself from these existing perfectionist theories—which he groups together under the label "edificatory perfectionism" and which he vigorously assails on a number of fronts, including most significantly their quidnunc mentality—Kramer argues instead for a view he refers to as "aspirational perfectionism." Though edificatory and aspirational perfectionism largely converge on the bottom line insofar as they both permit the promotion of excellence in a range of areas of human endeavor, they

[9] Dworkin, "Foundations of Liberal Equality," 264–73.

[10] See discussion in Sher, *Beyond Neutrality: Perfectionism and Politics*, 106–39.

[11] Kramer, *Liberalism with Excellence*, 282, 287. For a related thought, see Gaus, "On the Difficult Virtue of Minding One's Own Business: Towards the Political Rehabilitation of Ebenezer Scrooge," 24–8.

[12] Kramer, *Liberalism with Excellence*, 45.

differ in their underlying justificatory structure. For whereas edificatory perfectionists seek "to induce citizens to lead lives that are more wholesome or cultivated or worthily autonomous," an aspirational perfectionist eschews this "edificatory impulse" and instead promotes the attainment of excellence within society because this is "a necessary condition for the warrantedness of a robust sense of self-respect on the part of each individual who belongs to that society."[13] In what follows, I focus exclusively on edificatory perfectionism and so I will sometimes drop the qualification "edificatory" for the sake of readability.

One of the most interesting and distinctive features of Kramer's quidnunc mentality objection to edificatory perfectionism is that it involves "a change of perspective."[14] To date, critics of edificatory perfectionism have adopted what Kramer calls a "citizen-focused perspective" and have held that the illegitimacy of edificatory-perfectionist politics derives from the way in which it treats citizens (unfairly, unequally, disrespectfully, paternalistically, in ways that they could reasonably reject, and so on).[15] By contrast, Kramer adopts what he calls a "government-focused perspective," according to which the illegitimacy of edificatory-perfectionist politics derives from the mentality or outlook of an edificatory-perfectionist system of governance and its state officials.[16] In the course of his analysis, he uses a variety of richly suggestive terms to evoke aspects of this mentality: officious, overweening, prickly, heavy-handed, unaccommodating, overbearing, meddlesome, busybody, censorious, nosy, and, of course, its delightful official label "quidnunc."

This shift of perspective, says Kramer, is important for understanding what makes edificatory perfectionism "always and everywhere morally wrong" and parallels a similar shift in his earlier work on the ethics of torture.[17] There too he argues that any absolutist account of the wrongness of torture must refer not only to the interests, rights, and dignity of the victim but also to the perpetrators of torture, who, by stooping to this atrocious practice, tarnish their moral integrity as well as the moral integrity of the system of governance on whose behalf they act. The perpetrator-focused perspective is necessary for explaining the absolute wrongness of torture because if we consider matters solely from the perspective of the victim it is difficult to account for the wrongness of certain instances of torture, such as the torture of a victim who is physiologically incapable of experiencing pain or the torture of monstrous individuals guilty of enormous crimes who (at least on certain retributivist accounts of punishment) might deserve to suffer. Similarly, there can be cases in which edificatory perfectionism is

[13] Ibid., 279. A taxonomical quibble: in my view, Kramer's view is more aptly classified as a species of liberal neutrality than as a species of perfectionism, since its touchstone is the impeccably neutral value of warranted self-respect. The fact that Kramer believes that many policies standardly associated with perfectionism (such as state support for the arts) are necessary for citizens' warranted self-respect does not suffice to make his view perfectionist. After all, many neutralists readily concede that there can be arguments from neutral values to perfectionist policies. See, e.g., Dworkin, "Can a Liberal State Support Art?," 221–33; Reiff, ch. 14 in this volume. Nor does Kramer's rejection of public reason suffice to make his view perfectionist (see *Liberalism with Excellence*, 341–2). After all, comprehensive liberals uphold neutrality whilst rejecting the requirements of public reason. See, e.g., Dworkin, "Foundations of Liberal Equality"; Pallikkathayil, "Neither Perfectionism nor Political Liberalism," 171–96.

[14] Kramer, *Liberalism with Excellence*, 254.

[15] Ibid.

[16] Ibid.

[17] Ibid., 255. See also Kramer, *Torture and Moral Integrity: A Philosophical Enquiry*.

not disrespectful or otherwise problematic from the citizen's perspective, and so the government-focused perspective is necessary for capturing what makes the "drive for edification" always and everywhere wrong.[18]

But what, more precisely, *is* the quidnunc mentality and what makes it *wrongful*, as opposed to merely less than ideal? Here it is helpful to turn to the main analogy that Kramer uses to illustrate the quidnunc mentality, namely that of the village busybody. On Kramer's view, officials who uphold a perfectionist system of governance interact with their fellow citizens "in broadly the same fashion in which a busybody of some village interacts with her fellow villagers."[19] In seeking to promote the edification of citizens through elevating their tastes, refining their sensibilities, or perfecting their characters, the perfectionist state expresses the same cast of mind as that of a village busybody who "keeps track of how her fellow residents behave" and who "hectors or ostracizes anyone whom she believes to be falling significantly short" even though the relevant conduct of the residents "affect[s] her only through her own sentiments of offendedness and gratification."[20]

Kramer argues that the attitude of the village busybody is objectionable in two main ways, namely by being "a form of self-aggrandizement and a form of self-abasement."[21] Since so much of the (admittedly considerable) intuitive force of this objection is bound up with Kramer's vivid and inimitable depictions of the pathologies of the village busybody, it is difficult to resist quoting at some length here:

> At the level of an individual, the quidnunc mentality is quite evidently a failure of self-restraint. It is both a form of self-aggrandizement and a form of self-abasement. It is a meddlesome form of *self-aggrandizement* because it takes for granted that one's fellows can rightly be prevailed upon—through coercion or through vehement exhortation—to modify patterns of behavior that are not legitimately of concern to anybody except the individuals themselves who engage in those patterns of behavior. Yet the quidnunc mentality also consists in *self-abasement*, since it makes one's own sense of satisfaction partly dependent on the responsiveness of one's fellows to one's officious badgering about their private pursuits. Instead of abiding by a live-and-let-live ethos, a busybody partly ties the success of her own life to her effectiveness in not letting other people lead their lives as they see fit. That is, the success of her own life partly hinges on the willingness of other people to desist from conduct that offends her (even though the conduct does not otherwise harm her or anybody else). In precisely that respect, one's possession of a quidnunc mentality is a manifestation of weakness.[22]

Moving back to politics, Kramer contends that similar points apply to the mentality that characterizes edificatory-perfectionist governments:

[18] Kramer, *Liberalism with Excellence*, 264.
[19] Ibid., 276.
[20] Ibid.
[21] Ibid., 277.
[22] Ibid., emphases added.

> At the level of a system of governance, a quidnunc mentality that underlies various laws or policies is even more egregiously a failure of self-restraint. Again, it is both a form of self-aggrandizement and a form of self-abasement. It is a meddlesome form of *self-aggrandizement* because any laws or policies that emanate from it are aimed neither at preventing the infliction of harm by some people on others nor at fulfilling any of the further responsibilities [of government]. Rather, those laws or policies are aimed at prevailing upon people—coercively or enticingly—to abandon certain patterns of behavior that are not harmful to other people in any significant ways. Furthermore, the overweeningness of the quidnunc mentality in that regard is integrally linked to the sense in which such a mentality is also a self-abasing manifestation of weakness. It is an outlook of *self-abasingness* because it presumes that the success of a system of governance is partly dependent on the willingness of citizens to alter their private pursuits in response to inducements by the system's officials. Instead of remaining confined to the dispensation of information and the maintenance of fair conditions for informed decisions by citizens about the aforementioned pursuits, a system of governance with laws or policies that stem from a quidnunc mentality will have tied the success of its endeavors partly to its effectiveness in not letting citizens arrive at disfavored decisions about the ways in which they should lead their lives ... A scheme of governance should not be dependent for its success on its prodding of citizens about their preferred lifestyles when no requirements of justice are at stake; a scheme of governance should not resemble a busybody whose equanimity hinges on the effectiveness of the similarly officious prodding in which she engages.[23]

In acting on the basis of a mentality that renders it "both grandiosely presumptuous and demeaningly vulnerable," the edificatory-perfectionist state violates a "deontological ethic of self-restraint"—a wrong that "tarnishes its moral integrity," that "far-reachingly informs and taints" its relationship with the citizenry, and that "deprives [its edificatory-perfectionist laws] of moral legitimacy."[24]

Before proceeding, three important clarifications are in order. The first is that this objection is not meant to be an accusation of error. Kramer clarifies that although "most busybodies are indeed error-prone when they identify standards of propriety which they apply in their censorious judgments about the behavior of other people," the quidnunc mentality objection does not allege that the edificatory-perfectionist state will make mistakes about what ways of life are worthy or unworthy.[25] Even if we assume that the edificatory-perfectionist state will "always be correct" in its judgments about worthiness and unworthiness, its interactions with citizens will still be both self-aggrandizing and self-abasing.[26]

The second clarification is that this objection is not limited to the edificatory-perfectionist state's discouragement of the worthless through measures such as sin

[23] Ibid., 277–8, emphases added.

[24] Ibid., 253, 277, 278. Kramer's message to edificatory perfectionists is thus likely to echo James Fitzjames Stephen's remark, when discussing intrusive conceptions of fraternity: "Keep your love to yourself, and do not daub me or mine with it." See Stephen, *Liberty, Equality, and Fraternity*, 221.

[25] Kramer, *Liberalism with Excellence*, 279.

[26] Ibid.

taxes and legal prohibitions ("the stick"); it also applies to its encouragement of the worthy through measures such as subsidies, educational programs, incentives, and awards ("the carrot"):

> A busybody might berate or ostentatiously shun any of her fellow villagers who have not lived up to her standards of propriety, or she might instead regularly and conspicuously provide inducements—such as boxes of delicious homemade fudge—to her fellow villagers who have managed to live up to those standards. In either case, she is acting with the aim of influencing the lifestyles of other people beyond what is required of them as matters of justice and basic civility. She implements that aim in a more objectionably heavy-handed fashion when she pursues it through vilification and ostracism than when she pursues it through selective largesse, but her project is overweeningly officious in either case. It manifests her presumptuousness as she obtrudes her judgmental assessments upon the other residents of her village, and it likewise manifests her abject tendency to let her peace of mind depend on the choices of those residents concerning their pastimes and private ideals. Similarly, when an edificatory-perfectionist system of governance draws upon subventions and other affirmative means of encouragement to press citizens to improve their modes of living (beyond what is required of them as matters of justice), it partakes of the meddlesomeness of a busybody . . . The officials in an edificatory-perfectionist system of governance exhibit the mentality of a quidnunc as they nosily judge that, in the absence of subsidies or other stimuli, too many citizens will lead lives that are insufficiently refined or wholesome or autonomous. Those officials dispense subsidies or apply other stimuli accordingly, just as the busybody in the village distributes her boxes of fudge to inspire her fellow inhabitants to lead lives of propriety. Like the busybody, the edificatory-perfectionist functionaries reveal their own impertinence and condescension as they take it upon themselves to elevate the citizens of their country into finer specimens of urbaneness.[27]

Finally, the third clarification is that, in attributing to perfectionist governments a quidnunc mentality, Kramer is not seeking to advance an empirical hypothesis about the actual mental states and self-understandings of the officials and functionaries of a perfectionist government.[28] It is not an exercise in social science or in mind-reading: the "imputation of a quidnunc mentality to edificatory perfectionism is not an exercise in psychological speculation from one's armchair" but is instead "the distillation of an outlook from which the drive for edification makes most sense."[29] That is, the quidnunc mentality is meant to refer to a normative property that, "at a high level of generality," would "most credibly account for [the] decisions and behavior" of perfectionist state officials, whether or not they are conscious of it.[30] In this sense, Kramer's argument is in line with much jurisprudential literature on legal interpretation and legislative intent, according to which the attribution

[27] Ibid., 282.
[28] Ibid., 254, 269–70.
[29] Ibid., 254.
[30] Ibid., 270.

of an intention to a law or to a government involves not peering into the souls of legislators but rather trying, in light of a range of considerations, to make sense of a law and the objectives that most plausibly account for its having been adopted and sustained.[31] The relevant considerations will include the terms of the law itself, but also the various public statements made about the law by those officials responsible for its enactment or sustainment, and the general social context within which such statements are made.

2. How the Quidnunc Mentality Objection Begs the Question

As a preliminary to my principal critique, it is worth noting that there are at least five ways in which one might criticize the quidnunc mentality objection.[32] First, one can question whether being self-aggrandizing and self-abasing in the Kramerian sense (i.e., going beyond what is morally required of one, and making one's sense of success dependent on the responsiveness of others to one's efforts to alter their private pursuits, respectively) accurately captures what it means to be self-aggrandizing and self-abasing in the ordinary morally significant senses of those terms. For instance, does an individual who feels more successful when he manages to persuade his neighbor or his colleague to adopt a healthier, less calorific diet really thereby *abase* himself? If not, Kramer might be getting undue moral and rhetorical mileage out of evocative labels that do not fit the behavior to which they are applied.

Second, even if Kramer captures what it means to be self-aggrandizing and self-abasing in the ordinary morally significant sense, one might wonder how the attitudes of self-aggrandizement and self-abasement are relevant to permissibility as opposed to character evaluation.[33] Why not say that village busybodies act permissibly yet possess flawed characters—in the same way that if someone donates money to a famine-relief charity on the basis of a Mrs Jellyby mentality, or with an attitude of sanctimonious self-congratulation, then, while this shows that she has a flawed character, it does not clearly make her donation impermissible?

Third, even if self-aggrandizement and self-abasement are relevant to permissibility, it is unclear why these vices are *so* great—and why manifesting them is *so* wrong—that they could form the basis of a deontological prohibition of the particularly stringent kind Kramer seeks. Even if it is *ordinarily* impermissible to be self-aggrandizing and self-abasing, that is, these traits are presumably all-things-considered permissible when something more important is at stake. Yet might not the importance of village busybodies' objectives—namely, the improvement of other people's lives—exceed in stringency considerations of self-aggrandizement and self-abasement, thereby generally rendering their actions all-things-considered permissible?

[31] See ibid., 75–87.

[32] I thank Jeff McMahan for helping me to distinguish these five lines of criticism.

[33] For the view that individual intentions are irrelevant to permissibility (though relevant to blameworthiness and character assessment), see, e.g., Thomson, "Self-Defense," 283–310; Scanlon, *Moral Dimensions: Permissibility, Meaning, Blame.*

A fourth line of potential criticism concerns the extrapolation Kramer makes from individual vices to state vices. It is, after all, debatable whether the properties of self-aggrandizement and self-abasement can meaningfully be imputed to states through the kind of exercise in institutional interpretation and distillation that Kramer describes. Waldron, for instance, is skeptical of the possibility of our "being able to discern or attribute to [a legislature] any thoughts, intentions, motives, or beliefs" (and presumably mentalities too), and he argues that "beyond the meanings embodied conventionally in the text of the statute, there is no state or condition corresponding to 'the intention of the legislature' to which anything else—such as what particular individuals or groups of legislators said, wrote, or did—could possibly provide a clue."[34]

Fifth, even if states can, as a conceptual matter, be bearers of attitudes and mentalities, it is unclear that self-aggrandizement and self-abasement have the same moral status when understood as generalized supervenient properties imputed to a collective "self" as they do when understood as actual psychological character flaws of a village busybody.[35] Given that state attitudes are not at all like individual attitudes, is it really plausible to suppose that they are deeply morally significant in the way that individual attitudes and intentions are sometimes thought to be?

Though I have sympathy for some of these lines of argument, in this chapter I grant (i) that Kramer accurately captures the morally significant essence of self-aggrandizement and self-abasement; (ii) that these vices are relevant to permissibility; (iii) that they are of sufficient moral significance to ground a particularly stringent prohibition; (iv) that they can be applied meaningfully at the state level; and (v) that they still retain their stringent-prohibition-grounding moral significance when applied to the state. Still, I argue that the quidnunc mentality objection fails because it begs the question against edificatory perfectionism.

Edificatory perfectionism, recall, is supposedly *self-abasing* in the sense that "it presumes that the success of a system of governance is partly dependent on the willingness of citizens to alter their private pursuits in response to inducements by the system's officials."[36] As he elsewhere puts it, the edificatory-perfectionist state is self-abasing because it makes its success "dependent on choices that are none of its business"—choices that are private, choices about which it should not care, choices that should be beneath its notice.[37] Similarly, edificatory perfectionism is supposedly *self-aggrandizing* in the sense of being "aimed neither at preventing the infliction of harm by some people on others nor at fulfilling any of the further responsibilities" of government such as maintaining public order or the provision of public education.[38] As

[34] See Waldron, *Law and Disagreement*, 142.

[35] For the view that the case for the irrelevance of *state* intentions to legitimacy is even stronger than the case for the irrelevance of *individual* intentions to permissibility, see Enoch, "Intending, Foreseeing and the State," 69–99; Brinkmann, "Political Anti-Intentionalism," 159–79. As Enoch puts this point: "whatever reasons we have to be suspicious about [intention's] moral significance in general, we have *very* good reasons to believe it lacks intrinsic moral significance when applied to state action" (69).

[36] Kramer, *Liberalism with Excellence*, 277.

[37] Ibid., 289.

[38] Ibid., 277.

he elsewhere puts this point, the edificatory-perfectionist state is self-aggrandizing because edificatory-perfectionist "laws and policies are not necessary for the fulfilment of the elementary moral responsibilities that are incumbent on any system of governance."[39]

The problem with this argument, however, is that edificatory perfectionists can argue, and have extensively argued, that governments have duties of edification toward their citizens. Call this view *duty-based* edificatory perfectionism.[40] For duty-based edificatory perfectionists, social terms ought to be deeply shaped by perfectionist considerations and ought to be promotive of and conducive to excellent, edified, or flourishing ways of life. On this understanding, the choices that citizens make about how to live are not "private pursuits" but are instead a legitimate concern of the state. The state might, for instance, have duties to steer people away from wasting their time on mind-numbing videogames and toward more worthwhile and meaningful avenues. The charge of self-aggrandizement and self-abasement thus begs the question against duty-based edificatory perfectionists for whom the edification of the citizenry is a matter of public rather than "private" concern, is the proper "business" of the state, is one of the "further responsibilities" of government, and is an "elementary moral responsibility" incumbent on the state.[41] Another way of putting this point is as follows: when Kramer says that edificatory-perfectionist states stick their nose where it does not belong, he already assumes that states have no duties to promote the edification of the citizenry; but he cannot help himself to this assumption because whether the edificatory impulse falls within or outside the proper bounds of government is precisely what is at stake here.

[39] Ibid., 285.

[40] The distinction between duty-based and non-duty-based perfectionism is related to yet distinct from the distinction, drawn by Quong, between "perfectionist justice" and "non-justice-based perfectionism" (see Quong, *Liberalism Without Perfection*, 29–30, 85, 120–6). These distinctions diverge because not all moral duties are duties of justice. One could therefore endorse duty-based perfectionism without endorsing perfectionist justice. I discuss duty-based perfectionism in greater depth in Tahzib, "Perfectionist Duties" and in Tahzib, *A Perfectionist Theory of Justice*.

[41] In the course of a more wide-ranging critique of Kramer's views, Billingham and Taylor also make the point that if perfectionist duties exist then the quidnunc mentality objection has no force. (See Billingham and Taylor, "Liberal Perfectionism, Moral Integrity, and Self-Respect," 69.) But they think that it is possible to undermine perfectionist duties (and thereby to "salvage" the quidnunc mentality objection) by pointing out that any such duties would involve "reasonably rejectable claims" and the promotion of ways of life that "various reasonable conceptions of the good will not value" (at 71, 79). In the remainder of their paper, they try to show that taking this line of argument *also* undermines Kramer's positive views, thus leaving Kramer a choice between his quidnunc mentality objection and his positive views. It is not possible to assess this argument properly here: doing so would take us too far away from the quidnunc mentality objection and into a substantially different set of debates. But, in brief, I am doubtful that considerations of reasonable disagreement, prominent in the work of political liberals such as Rawls and Quong, undermine perfectionist duties. In particular, I deny the premise that perfectionist goods such as moral, intellectual, and artistic excellence are reasonably rejectable. On the view I favor, then, reasonableness is conditional not only on acceptance of certain liberal values such as freedom, equality, and fairness (as political liberals tend to say) but also on acceptance of certain perfectionist values such as moral, intellectual, and artistic excellence. (For a defense of this view, see Tahzib, "Perfectionism: Political not Metaphysical," 164–73.) So although I agree with Billingham and Taylor's observation that, as stated, the quidnunc mentality objection begs the question against duty-based perfectionism, my argument differs from theirs in that I am considerably less optimistic than they are about the prospects of salvaging the quidnunc mentality objection.

Raz and Wall—whom Kramer takes to be the foremost exemplars of edificatory perfectionism—are both duty-based edificatory perfectionists. Both, that is, defend the view that states have a responsibility to promote the edification of the citizenry. In *The Morality of Freedom*, Raz argues that "governments are subject to *autonomy-based duties* to provide the conditions of autonomy for people who lack them."[42] "The autonomy principle," he further explains, "permits and even *requires* governments to create morally valuable opportunities, and to eliminate repugnant ones."[43] As Raz elsewhere puts it, the state "*should* act with discrimination to encourage the good and the valuable and to discourage the worthless and the bad."[44] Similarly, in *Liberalism, Perfectionism and Restraint*, Wall argues that "political authorities *should* take an active role in creating and maintaining social conditions that best enable their subjects to lead valuable and worthwhile lives."[45] He argues that by steering people toward worthy ways of life and away from unworthy ways of life, "the government discharges its *duty* to promote and sustain social conditions that promote the flourishing of those subject to its authority."[46] In more recent work, Wall argues that edificatory-perfectionist duties are derivable from duties to promote welfare, from duties of fairness, and from duties to secure citizens' merited self-respect.[47]

If Raz's and Wall's substantive arguments are sound—if, in other words, it is true that one of the major responsibilities of government is to induce citizens to lead wholesome, cultivated, virtuous, or autonomous lives—then edificatory perfectionists do not stick their nose where it does not belong and do not meddle in matters that are none of their business. In such a case, an edificatory-perfectionist state is no more self-aggrandizing or self-abasing than a neutral state that pursues imperatives such as justice and security, because their edificatory-perfectionist policies are in fact "necessary for the fulfillment of the elementary moral responsibilities that are incumbent on any system of government."[48] So, if we must employ provincial analogies, duty-based edificatory perfectionists are likely to view governmental efforts to encourage the worthwhile and to discourage the worthless as more analogous to the activities of the local magistrate than the local busybody.[49]

[42] Raz, *The Morality of Freedom*, 415 (emphasis added).

[43] Ibid., 417 (emphasis added).

[44] Raz, "Liberalism, Skepticism, and Democracy," 785 (emphasis added).

[45] Wall, *Liberalism, Perfectionism and Restraint*, 8 (emphasis added).

[46] Ibid., 224 (emphasis added).

[47] For the arguments from welfare and fairness, see Wall, "Moral Environmentalism," 93–114; for the argument from merited self-resect, see Wall, "Enforcing Morality," 455–71.

[48] Kramer, *Liberalism with Excellence*, 285.

[49] Another reason why the local magistrate is, as far as it goes, a better analogy of the edificatory-perfectionist state than the local busybody (in addition, that is, to the fact that local magistrates generally act in pursuit of objectives that are morally required, and hence are not self-aggrandizing or self-abasing in Kramer's sense) is that busybodies are generally *self-appointed*, whereas magistrates and edificatory-perfectionist governments are generally not. That is to say, in addition to self-aggrandizement and self-abasement, a further feature (though not one that Kramer focuses on) that makes the village busybody an unappealing character is that she *takes it upon herself* to promote the edification of others. But an edificatory-perfectionist system of governance receives a democratic mandate to pursue edificatory objectives such as opera and art galleries, and so it is not self-appointed. So insofar as the magistrate analogy does not trade on this morally relevant feature, it is preferable to the busybody analogy. (I thank Rowan Cruft for discussion of this point.)

Here Kramer might want to say that the charge of begging the question can be hurled in either direction in this debate, and that assuming the existence of edificatory-perfectionist duties simply begs the question in the opposite direction, namely against the proponent of the quidnunc mentality objection.[50] But, as I see it, to say this would be to subtly misdiagnose the dialectical situation. After all, and as alluded to above, edificatory perfectionists such as Raz and Wall have already provided what is, by Kramer's own admission elsewhere, "elaborate" and "extensive argumentation" in favor of edificatory-perfectionist duties.[51] In referring to these arguments in response to the quidnunc mentality objection, the edificatory perfectionist is not *assuming* the existence of edificatory-perfectionist duties (which would indeed beg the question in the opposite direction). Rather, the edificatory perfectionist refers to these arguments as a way of *supporting* the existence of edificatory-perfectionist duties. The edificatory perfectionist accepts, of course, that these elaborate and extensive arguments in support of the existence of edificatory-perfectionist duties might ultimately fail.[52] But he simply maintains that the proponent of the quidnunc mentality objection must *demonstrate* how they fail. To demonstrate such failure, the proponent of the quidnunc mentality objection would need either to provide some specific reason to reject the arguments of Raz and Wall, or to provide some general reason to think that duties of edification do not exist, or ideally both. At this particular stage in the dialectic, then, it seems fair to say that, in the absence of supplementary arguments along these lines, the proponent of the quidnunc mentality objection looks especially vulnerable to the charge of begging the question.

The moral of the story is that, in order to successfully wield the quidnunc mentality objection, one cannot remain at this level of abstraction. It is one's prior view of the state's duties and its legitimate domain of activity (and, correspondingly, one's prior view of the public/private distinction) that does all the real moral work in determining whether a quidnunc mentality is present. So Kramer needs to engage the substantive question of whether states really have moral duties to promote the flourishing and edification of the citizenry—for *that* is where the action really is. One cannot, that is, critique edificatory-perfectionist policies on the grounds that they "exceed the confines of the roles of officials, whose responsibilities do not properly include the shepherding of sane adults" toward worthwhile ways of life, without offering some further, independent argument for why state officials have no such shepherding responsibility.[53]

[50] I thank Matthew Kramer for putting this point to me.

[51] See Kramer, *Liberalism with Excellence*, 62; and Kramer, "One Cheer for Autonomy-centered Perfectionism: An Arm's-length Defense of Joseph Raz's Perfectionism Against an Allegation of Internal Inconsistency," 92.

[52] Indeed, though I do endorse edificatory-perfectionist duties, I have my doubts about some of Wall's arguments in favor of them. See Tahzib, "Perfectionist Duties," 128–34.

[53] Kramer, *Liberalism with Excellence*, 288. Of course, this is not yet to say that edificatory-perfectionist policies are in the clear. Perhaps other arguments—for instance, political liberals' concern that perfectionist judgments are subject to reasonable disagreement and thus that perfectionist policies violate the public justification requirement—tell against edificatory-perfectionist policies. (See n. 41.) The point is just that such policies cannot be impugned on the specific grounds that they manifest the mentality of a village busybody, with its unattractive combination of self-aggrandizement and self-abasement.

3. A Substantive Argument Against Edificatory-Perfectionist Duties?

While Kramer does not engage in specific rebuttals of Raz's and Wall's arguments in favor of edificatory-perfectionist duties, he has indicated that some general reason to doubt the existence of edificatory-perfectionist duties is given in his discussion of the passages from Shakespeare:[54]

> I there maintain that, outside the sway of the harm principle (the genuine harm principle [rather than Raz's perfectionist reformulation of it—CT]) and the preservation of a societal infrastructure, the measure of the ethical strength of a system of governance is given by what it can safely ignore and does ignore. An ethical eagle can and does safely ignore the chirping of the little birds. Since the ethical strength of a system of governance is a key constituent of the political and social and economic conditions under which everyone can be warranted in harboring an ample sense of self-respect, edificatory-perfectionist duties would run athwart a system's responsibility for bringing about those conditions.[55]

This argument—that the conditions of citizens' warranted self-respect depend on the ethical strength of government, and that the ethical strength of government depends in turn on what it safely ignores—is developed too briefly in the relevant pages of *Liberalism with Excellence* to allow for a proper evaluation of its merits, and my understanding is that it will be explored in much greater depth in Kramer's book-in-progress *A Stoical Theory of Justice*. Nonetheless, let me comment specifically on the suggestion that this argument would rule out edificatory-perfectionist duties.

For this argument to rule out edificatory-perfectionist duties, it would have to be the case that those things that trouble edificatory perfectionists—such as individuals wasting endless hours playing mind-numbing videogames—can be safely ignored by the state. But the burning question that edificatory perfectionists will have at this point is this: why is it that citizens' failures to realize edification and flourishing can be safely ignored by the state, whereas citizens' failures to realize other values such as freedom and equality cannot be safely ignored by the state? Why, to use the Shakespearean idiom, does the former failure but not the latter failure count as the trifling and ignorable "chirping of little birds"? A lot here will hinge, I think, on what is meant by "safely ignore." In general, one is not just safe but safe *from* something. So a natural way of tackling the burning question alluded to above is to ask: *In what sense, and from what threat,* could states remain safe whilst ignoring the failure of some citizens to live edified and flourishing lives?[56]

[54] See ibid., 270–8.

[55] In written comments received on May 6, 2019.

[56] Perhaps safety is to be cashed out with reference to the conditions for warranted self-respect: thus states can safely ignore citizens' failures to live edified lives because the edification of the citizenry falls outside of the state's duty to promote the conditions of citizens' warranted self-respect. (I thank Matthew Kramer for putting this point to me.) But this looks circular. Why, we asked at the outset of this section, does the edification of the citizenry fall outside of the state's duty to promote the conditions of citizens' warranted self-respect? Because the edification of the citizenry can be safely ignored. And why, we now ask, can the

On the one hand, Kramer could hold that citizens' failures to live edified and flourishing lives could be safely ignored in the sense that they could be ignored *without thereby threatening the continued existence of society*. This seems clearly true, and edificatory perfectionists should readily agree that their concerns can be safely ignored in this sense. But this interpretation of safety would generate an overly demanding criterion of state action: it would rule out efforts to promote important neutral values such as freedom and equality because, as the political experience of many less liberal countries today demonstrates, states can ignore unfreedom and inequality without thereby threatening the collapse of society.

On the other hand, and in an attempt to rule in freedom and equality, Kramer could hold that citizens' failures to live edified and flourishing lives could be safely ignored in the sense that they could be ignored *without thereby threatening important values*. But then edificatory perfectionists are unlikely to agree that their concerns can be safely ignored, because they see edification and flourishing as important values—as comparable in importance to values such as freedom and equality.

In short, it is unclear how the notion of what can be safely ignored could justify the asymmetric treatment by the state of perfectionist goals (such as edification and flourishing) and of anti-perfectionist goals (such as freedom and equality). It is unclear, that is, how the distinction between what can and what cannot be safely ignored tracks the distinction between what falls inside and what falls outside the edificatory impulse.[57]

Perhaps, as a third possibility, the idea is that citizens' failures to live edified and flourishing lives could be safely ignored in the sense that they could be ignored *without thereby threatening harm to others*. Something along these lines does seem to be playing a role in Kramer's argument; although he does not provide a specification or defense of Mill's harm principle, Kramer does make a number of passing references to it.[58]

But it is unclear that hitching the quidnunc mentality objection to the wagon of Mill's harm principle will help Kramer here. To see why, it is worth noting that there are two main ways of conceptualizing harm: *moralized* accounts of harm and *non-moralized* accounts of harm. According to moralized accounts of harm, what is harmful is just a matter of what violates positive and negative duties. As Raz puts this point, "one causes harm if one fails in one's duty to a person."[59] He further explains:

edification of the citizenry be safely ignored? Because the edification of the citizenry falls outside of the state's duty to promote the conditions of citizens' warranted self-respect.

[57] See Chan's related discussion of Nagel's anti-perfectionist argument from practical necessity: Chan, "Legitimacy, Unanimity, and Perfectionism," 24ff.

[58] See especially Kramer, *Liberalism with Excellence*, 275–7. Elsewhere Kramer explains that edificatory-perfectionist policies "demean the system of governance by tying the success of its operations partly to matters that would be beneath its notice if it concerned itself not with citizens' *harmless foibles* but with its own foremost responsibility" (Kramer, "On Political Morality and the Conditions for Warranted Self-Respect," 339, emphasis added). Kramer discusses some features of the harm principle in greater depth in another article, but there too he does not offer a full specification and defense of the harm principle. See Kramer, "Legal Responses to Consensual Sexuality between Adults: Through and Beyond the Harm Principle," 109–28.

[59] Raz, *The Morality of Freedom*, 416. See also Wall, "Moral Environmentalism," 107.

> One can harm another by denying him what is due to him. This is obscured by the common misconception which confines harming a person to acting in a way the result of which is that that person is worse off after the action than he was before. While such actions do indeed harm, so do acts or omissions the result of which is that a person is worse off after them than he *should* then be. One harms another by failing in one's duty to him, even though this is a duty to improve his situation and the failure does not leave him worse off than he was before. Consider a disabled person who has a legal right to be employed by any employer to whom he applies and who has fewer than four per cent disabled employees in his work force. If such an employer turns him down he harms him though he does not worsen his situation.[60]

Mill himself appears to endorse a moralized account of harm.[61] He agrees that actions or omissions that violate positive or negative duties count as harms, and that the prevention of such duty-violations can justify state action compatibly with the harm principle:

> There are also many positive acts for the benefit of others which he may rightfully be compelled to perform, such as to give evidence in a court of justice, to bear his fair share in the common defence or in any other joint work necessary to the interest of the society of which he enjoys the protection, and to perform certain acts of individual beneficence, such as saving a fellow creature's life or interposing to protect the defenceless against ill usage—things which whenever it is obviously a man's duty to do he may rightfully be made responsible to society for not doing. A person may cause evil to others not only by his actions but by his inaction, and in either case he is justly accountable to them for the injury.[62]

This means that if edificatory-perfectionist duties exist, then a state that fails to promote the edification of the citizenry *harms* the citizenry and a citizen who fails to contribute (through paying taxes) toward programs aimed at the edification of her fellow citizens *harms* those other citizens.[63] Edificatory-perfectionist state action would then

[60] Raz, *The Morality of Freedom*, 416, emphasis added.

[61] Joel Feinberg, an influential defender of Mill's harm principle in recent times, also appears to endorse a moralized account of harm. Despite his slogan that harm is to be understood as a "setback to interests," Feinberg recognizes that harm (at least for the purposes of the harm principle) cannot be defined without any reference to rights and duties, since some setbacks to interests do not violate rights (e.g., a setback to interest that is consented to, or that is incurred in legitimate competition). Thus Feinberg ends up settling on a moralized conception of harm as a *wrongful* setback to interests. See Feinberg, *Harm to Others: The Moral Limits of the Criminal Law*. A common criticism of Feinberg on this score is that, while he provides detailed and careful analysis of the idea of a setback to interests, he offers little by way of a general and systematic moral theory that specifies the rights and duties of individuals and thus that could help us to determine in any given case whether a setback to interests is wrongful (and thus harmful). See, e.g., Thomson, "Feinberg on Harm, Offense, and the Criminal Law: A Review Essay," 381–95; Stewart, "Harms, Wrongs, and Set-Backs in Feinberg's *Moral Limits of the Criminal Law*," 47–67.

[62] Mill, *On Liberty*, 70. Mill relatedly says that when a person "violate[s] a distinct and assignable obligation to any other person or persons, the case is taken out of the self-regarding class and becomes amenable to moral disapprobation in the proper sense of the term" (148). He goes on to give the example of someone who is derelict in his duty to educate his children, saying that such a person can, compatibly with the harm principle, be forced to educate his children.

[63] In another paper, Kramer concedes the possibility of a perfectionist account of harm along these lines, on the assumption (which he there grants *arguendo*) that edificatory-perfectionist duties exist. See Kramer,

be compatible with the moralized harm principle. As Raz puts this point: "A person who fails to discharge his autonomy-based obligations towards others is harming them, even if those obligations are designed to promote the others' autonomy rather than to prevent its deterioration."[64] And again:

> The government has an obligation to create an environment providing individuals with an adequate range of options and the opportunities to choose them. The duty arises out of people's interest in having a valuable autonomous life. Its violation will harm those it is meant to benefit. Therefore its fulfillment is consistent with the harm principle.[65]

Again, Kramer would of course deny that any such edificatory-perfectionist duties exist, and so he would deny that edificatory-perfectionist policies are consistent with the harm principle. But, as the foregoing discussion illustrates, if we adopt a moralized account of harm, inconsistency with the harm principle is not an independent argument against edificatory-perfectionist duties. To say that edificatory-perfectionist policies are inconsistent with the harm principle, one must first have established that there are no edificatory-perfectionist duties. So, like the quidnunc mentality objection itself, the claim that citizens' failures to live edified lives could be safely ignored by the state without thereby harming others *already presupposes* the non-existence of edificatory-perfectionist duties—again, at least if we are working with a moralized account of harm. Hitching the quidnunc mentality objection to the wagon of the moralized harm principle thus does not help here because it fails to give us what we are looking for: an independently persuasive, morally substantive argument against edificatory-perfectionist duties.

It is important to note here that the passage from Raz quoted above does of course presuppose the *existence* of edificatory-perfectionist duties, and so it too cannot constitute an independently persuasive, morally substantive argument *for* edificatory-perfectionist duties. Those arguments are developed, extensively and elaborately, elsewhere in the work of edificatory perfectionists such as Raz and Wall. The important point for our purposes is simply about the inability of the moralized harm principle to do moral work here one way or the other: this harm principle cannot rescue the quidnunc mentality objection by helping us to determine whether or not edificatory-perfectionist duties exist, because on moralized accounts judgments about harm depend on prior judgments about what duties we owe to others. The moralized version of the harm principle, in other words, is conceptually downstream; it comes in later in the day, only once the deep and difficult questions about the existence or non-existence of edificatory-perfectionist duties have been figured out.

"One Cheer for Autonomy-centered Perfectionism: An Arm's-length Defense of Joseph Raz's Perfectionism Against an Allegation of Internal Inconsistency," 92.

[64] Raz, *The Morality of Freedom*, 417.

[65] Ibid., 417–18.

Perhaps, then, we should look for a *non-moralized* account of harm: an account that does not simply define harm in terms of pre-existing rights and duties. Prominent among these non-moralized accounts of harm is the counterfactual account. According to a straightforward version of this counterfactual account of harm, A's action harms B if and only if it makes B worse off than B would otherwise have been. It is natural to wonder whether a counterfactual account of harm along these lines could be plugged into the harm principle to yield an independently persuasive argument against edificatory-perfectionist duties.

However, counterfactual accounts of harm notoriously fail to accommodate many of our pre-theoretical intuitions about harm.[66] This can be shown by considering three kinds of cases.[67] The first kind of case involves *pre-emption*.[68] Suppose that A breaks one of V's legs, but that if A had not done this then B would have broken both of V's legs. The counterfactual account entails that A does not harm V. After all, A's action does not make V worse off than V would otherwise have been: if A had not broken V's leg, then both of V's legs would have been broken. Yet intuitively it seems clear that A harms V. The fact that V would have been harmed to an even greater extent were it not for A's action seems irrelevant to whether A's breaking of V's leg is harmful. The counterfactual account thus under-generates harm: it counts as harmless what seems clearly harmful. A second problem involves *failures to benefit*.[69] Suppose that C buys a coffee to give to D as a random act of kindness. Tempted by the smell of the coffee, though, C decides instead to drink it himself. The counterfactual account entails that C harms D by drinking the coffee. After all, D is worse off than he would have been if C had given D the coffee rather than drinking it himself. Yet intuitively it seems clear that C does not harm D. C merely fails to bestow a benefit on D, and merely failing to bestow a benefit on someone surely does not amount to harming that person. The counterfactual account thus over-generates harm: it counts as harmful what seems clearly harmless. A third problem involves *non-identity cases*.[70] Suppose that if E becomes pregnant now she will conceive a child, F, who will have a permanent and painful disease, and if E becomes pregnant in one month's time she will conceive a different child, G, who will not have this disease. Knowing this, E decides to become pregnant now. F comes into existence and has a life that, while still worth living, is full of pain and is thus significantly worse than the life that G would otherwise have had. The counterfactual account entails that E does not harm F by becoming pregnant now.

[66] Counterfactual accounts have also come under fire for failing to meet other desiderata beyond extensional adequacy. For instance, it is typically held that an account of harm should entail that harm has prudential and moral importance: it should entail, that is, that harm is the sort of thing that we should try to avoid for ourselves and others. For an argument that counterfactual accounts of harm do not meet this desideratum, see Carlson, "More Problems for the Counterfactual Comparative Account of Harm and Benefit," 795–807.

[67] For the remainder of this paragraph I closely follow Bradley: see Bradley, "Doing Away with Harm," 396–8; see also 405–9.

[68] For a rejection of various ingenious recent attempts by counterfactual theorists of harm to overcome this problem, see Johansson and Risberg, "The Preemption Problem," 351–65.

[69] For a recent attempt by a counterfactual theorist to overcome this problem by invoking the doing/allowing distinction, see Purves, "Harming as Making Worse Off," 2629–56. This argument is criticized in Johansson and Risberg, "Harming and Failing to Benefit: A Reply to Purves," 1539–48.

[70] See Parfit, *Reasons and Persons*, ch. 16. For a comprehensive recent discussion of the non-identity problem, see Boonin, *The Non-Identity Problem and the Ethics of Future People*.

After all, if E had not become pregnant now, F would never have been brought into existence, and F's existence, though marred by pain, is still better than non-existence. Yet it seems intuitive—even if the intuition is perhaps not as strong in this case as in the previous two cases—that E harms F by becoming pregnant now and knowingly bringing F into existence with a permanent and painful disease.

Moreover, even if there were an intuitively plausible non-moralized account of harm such as the counterfactual account, plugging this account into the harm principle would not yield an intuitively plausible principle of political morality.[71] The reason for this is that non-moralized accounts of harm allow for the possibility of non-wrongful harms (such as losses incurred in legitimate competition, and perhaps offense) and harmless wrongs (such as the destruction of the last member of a little-known species whose extinction will have no adverse impact on others). Harmless wrongs in particular pose problems for the harm principle because they are actions that do not harm others yet that still seemingly ought to be regulated by political authorities. Familiar examples, some of which are alluded to above in the passage from Mill, include voluntary self-enslavement, the failure to save a drowning child in a case of easy rescue, secretly recording the private actions of an individual who never discovers that this has occurred, and the exploitation of someone's misfortune through a mutually beneficial transaction such as charging a stranded backpacker an exorbitant price for a lift home.[72] None of these actions is harmful to others—at least in the non-moralized counterfactual sense that none of these actions leaves others worse off than they would have been in the absence of the action. Indeed, in some of these cases, such as that of exploitative price gouging, others are made better off than they would have been in the absence of the action. Yet it is difficult to believe that the state therefore cannot legitimately discourage or prohibit actions such as voluntary self-enslavement, Bad Samaritanism, unnoticed invasions of privacy, and price gouging. So once harm is conceptualized in non-moralized terms, the claim that harm to others is a necessary condition for the legitimacy of coercive state action is not a plausible principle of political morality.

In short, any attempt to supplement the quidnunc mentality objection with a harm-principle-based argument against edificatory-perfectionist duties would appear to face a dilemma: on the one hand, if the harm principle is construed in moralized terms, then it will struggle to provide non-redundant and independently persuasive grounds for doubting the existence of edificatory-perfectionist duties; on the other hand, if the harm principle is construed in non-moralized terms, then it will struggle to track our intuitions about both the nature of harm and the legitimate sphere of coercive state action. While I have not shown that it is *impossible* to overcome this dilemma, I hope to have indicated the formidable difficulties confronting anyone who wishes to do so.

[71] Further arguments to this effect are provided by Holtug, who canvasses a variety of non-moralized accounts of harm and concludes that none of them gives rise to a plausible version of the harm principle. See Holtug, "The Harm Principle," 364–77.

[72] For further examples of so-called "harmless wrongdoing," see, e.g., Woodward, "The Non-Identity Problem," 804–31, esp. 809–11; Feinberg, *Harmless Wrongdoing: The Moral Limits of the Criminal Law*; Gardner and Shute, "The Wrongness of Rape," 193–218; Ripstein, "Beyond the Harm Principle," 215–45; Tadros, *Wrongs and Crimes*, 102, 201–3, 216–22, 292–8.

4. Indistinguishability from Liberal Neutrality?

At one point, Kramer considers the possibility of a version of the duty-based edificatory perfectionism outlined in section 2.[73] He says that "autonomy-centered perfectionists," for whom "the nurturing of each individual's autonomy" is a "matter of justice," may argue that the quidnunc mentality objection simply begs the question by assuming that the promotion of autonomy is not a proper responsibility of government.[74] "A riposte of [this] kind," Kramer continues, "could most promisingly be advanced in a Rawlsian guise" whereby autonomy is viewed as a "primary natural good in Rawls's sense."[75]

But the main problem with presenting edificatory perfectionism as a doctrine of justice, argues Kramer, is that it would no longer be distinctively perfectionist:

> When the attainment of autonomy is taken to be a primary natural good ... and when opportunities to attain autonomy are taken to be distribuenda covered by the principles of justice that should apportion primary goods in any liberal-democratic society, the proponents of an autonomy-centered account of justice are not disagreeing with Rawlsians over the doctrine of liberal neutrality. Instead, at the very most, they are disagreeing with Rawlsians over the index of primary natural and social goods ... Hence [the view] would not itself be perfectionist. It would be concerned with modifying or clarifying Rawls's thin theory of the good rather than with affirming that a system of governance can legitimately aim to promote some thicker conception(s) of the good.[76]

Indeed, Kramer argues that, given that Rawls himself recognizes the value of autonomy, this approach may end up being not just similar but *identical* to Rawlsianism: "instead of turning autonomy-centered perfectionism into a *variant* of Rawls's theory of justice, the re-elaboration would turn it into Rawls's theory *simpliciter* or into something extremely close to Rawls's theory."[77] After all "when we ask what principles of justice can appropriately distribute opportunities for autonomy in order to foster the attainment of autonomy as a primary natural good, we could plausibly conclude that Rawls's principles (or principles very close to Rawls's) serve that purpose admirably."[78] Thus, "somebody developing an autonomy-centered account of justice might well fix upon Rawls's principles."[79]

However, there are two main problems with Kramer's worry about indistinguishability. First, it is not clear why duty-based edificatory perfectionists would need to present their view in terms of primary goods. Kramer's argumentation is curious here because he himself states that duty-based edificatory perfectionism "could most promisingly be advanced in a Rawlsian guise" before going

73 See Kramer, *Liberalism with Excellence*, 289–96.
74 Ibid., 289–90.
75 Ibid., 289.
76 Ibid., 292–3.
77 Ibid., 294 (emphasis added).
78 Ibid., 295.
79 Ibid.

on to critique such a view for being indistinguishable from Rawlsianism. But duty-based edificatory perfectionists such as Raz and Wall have not themselves gone about defending their views in Rawlsian terms. Behind Wall's endorsement of edificatory-perfectionist duties, for instance, is not a Rawlsian picture in which autonomy is a primary good to be distributed in accordance with some distributive principle but rather a fairly un-Rawlsian picture in which autonomy is a component of an objectively valuable and flourishing human life and the role of the state is to foster human flourishing:

> [Perfectionism] is the thesis that political authorities should take an active role in creating and maintaining social conditions that best enable their subjects to lead valuable and worthwhile lives. If autonomy is a central component of a fully good life, and if we ought to accept the general thesis of perfectionism, then it would follow that political authorities should take an active role in creating and maintaining social conditions that help their subjects realize this ideal.[80]

Once duty-based edificatory perfectionism is presented in this form, and not forced into a Rawlsian mold, it is difficult to see how this view has lost its distinctively perfectionist character just because it makes claims about what the state ought (as opposed to may) to do. Duty-based edificatory perfectionism, after all, asks a very different question from that asked by liberal neutralism (as well as by Kramer's own aspirational perfectionism). For good or for bad, it asks: What do people in general need to flourish, to live a life of meaning and worth? Which conditions generally conduce to, and which detract from, the moral, intellectual, cultural, and artistic excellence of the citizenry? How can an edifying social environment of this kind be established and maintained? What are the best things in life, and how can all citizens be encouraged and assisted to pursue them? What steps should the state take to elevate citizens' tastes, to refine their sensibilities, and to perfect their characters? These are full-bloodedly perfectionist questions and are very different from the questions that animate Rawlsian liberalism, namely: What are the fair terms of social cooperation between free and equal citizens who remain profoundly divided by comprehensive religious, philosophical, and moral doctrines? How in these circumstances are the benefits and burdens of cooperative social life to be fairly distributed? How can the state sustain a fair and impartial framework of rights, opportunities, and resources within which each citizen can pursue his or her own understanding of what constitutes a good life?

The second problem with Kramer's move here is that, even if (contra the preceding point) the best way to formally depict the difference between Rawlsians and duty-based edificatory perfectionists were in terms of a disagreement about

[80] Wall, *Liberalism, Perfectionism and Restraint*, 131. It is worth noting that Kramer does consider this passage from Wall but his only comment on it is that its "strongly perfectionist understanding of the role of government" is "redolent of the quidnunc mentality" (Kramer, *Liberalism with Excellence*, 293). But this takes us back to the argument in section 2. For what makes it quidnunc? It cannot be that Wall's conception of the role of government goes beyond the proper responsibilities of government because, again, whether or not the promotion of valuable and worthwhile lives is a proper responsibility of government is the question at issue here.

the index of primary natural and social goods, it would not follow that duty-based edificatory perfectionism is indistinguishable from Rawlsianism or that it endorses liberal neutrality. This becomes particularly clear when we consider what Wall calls "non-autonomy-based perfectionist political action"—that is, when we consider not just *autonomy-centered* duty-based edificatory perfectionism (the form of duty-based edificatory perfectionism on which Kramer focuses) but also other ideals, distinct from autonomy, that edificatory perfectionists have sought to promote.[81]

To see this, consider some autonomy-unrelated examples from Wall. Suppose that an edificatory-perfectionist state "grants public subsidies to artists" and museums in "an effort to promote and stimulate appreciation of high art."[82] Suppose next that an edificatory-perfectionist state "implements regulations and restrictions designed to discourage the consumption of a class of drugs" as a way of "taking steps to promote the well-being of its subjects."[83] Suppose, finally, that an edificatory-perfectionist state "adopts an immigration policy that favors those who are familiar with the national culture" as part of an effort to ensure "the preservation of its distinctive national culture."[84] The most natural way to understand Wall's point here, it seems to me, is that the role of the state is to promote human flourishing and thus that the state should promote these elements of the flourishing life (i.e., appreciation of high art, well-being, and a distinctive national culture). But even if, somewhat contrivedly, we read Wall as suggesting that appreciation of high art, well-being, and a distinctive national culture should be understood as primary goods, as "distribuenda covered by the principles of justice," it does not follow that Wall's view is indistinguishable from Rawlsianism or that it endorses liberal neutrality. After all, Rawlsians and defenders of liberal neutrality tend to eschew artistic and cultural judgments of this kind in politics. Rawlsians and liberal neutralists, that is, tend to hold that "the liberal state should not be in the business of deciding what constitutes a valuable or worthwhile life and trying to make sure that citizens live up to this ideal—that job should be left to citizens themselves."[85] A disagreement about the index of primary goods, then, is not just a minor intramural matter for Rawlsians: it can conceal deep substantive disagreements between Rawlsians and edificatory perfectionists.

5. Conclusion: In Search of New Mentalities?

I have argued that Kramer's quidnunc mentality objection begs the question against edificatory perfectionism by assuming that efforts to promote the edification of the citizenry are outside of the proper remit of government.

However, while I ultimately do not think that Kramer's quidnunc mentality objection succeeds, let me close by commenting on a sense in which I think Kramer's

[81] As Wall also puts it, "autonomy-based political action is one type of perfectionist political action. But it is not the only type." See Wall, *Liberalism, Perfectionism and Restraint*, 213.

[82] Ibid., 213.

[83] Ibid., 219.

[84] Ibid., 228.

[85] Quong, *Liberalism Without Perfection*, 1.

discussion nonetheless contains an underlying insight that opens up a fascinating and novel set of questions. The insight I have in mind is Kramer's "change of perspective"—his shift from evaluating the treatment of the citizen to evaluating the mentality of the state. After all, one might accept Kramer's general contention that the deeply objectionable feature of edificatory perfectionism resides in its mentality (or more precisely: in the mentality credibly ascribable to it), even while rejecting (as I have done) his particular contention that the quidnunc mentality with its attendant self-aggrandizement and self-abasement is the relevantly objectionable mentality that sets edificatory perfectionism apart from its rivals.

One interesting line of further inquiry, then, is to try to understand what other mentalities might be reasonably ascribable to states, perfectionist and otherwise. Of course, this search for new mentalities, as we might call it, need not be undertaken only with the aim of criticizing perfectionism and in fact it might end up providing grist for perfectionism's mill. For perhaps the mentality that at a high level of generality credibly accounts for edificatory perfectionism is not quidnunc meddlesomeness but rather an attractive form of solicitude and benevolence and a genuine desire to see other people flourish—an ethos perhaps most powerfully affirmed by Martin Luther King:

> We are tied together in a single garment of destiny, caught in an inescapable network of mutuality. And whatever affects one directly affects all indirectly. For some strange reason I can never be what I ought to be until you are what you ought to be. And you can never be what you ought to be until I am what I ought to be ... John Donne caught it years ago and placed it in graphic terms—"No man is an island entire of itself. Every man is a piece of the continent—a part of the main." And he goes on to say, "Any man's death diminishes me because I am involved in mankind. Therefore never send to know for whom the bell tolls; it tolls for thee".[86]

Similarly, I wonder whether the high-level mentality most plausibly imputable to liberal neutralism is not some admirable ethic of self-restraint but rather an unappealing and more Scrooge-like attitude of indifference, frostiness, alienation, and self-absorption. So where perfectionism embodies the ethos evoked by Martin Luther King, perhaps neutralist liberalism channels the spirit of Cain who asks, "Am I my brother's keeper?"[87]

Naturally, many difficult questions arise here, including that of how to adjudicate which of a range of potentially ascribable mentalities is predominant in any given system of governance. There is also the worry that the objection I have leveled above—namely, that facts about mentality are morally epiphenomenal and cannot be constitutive of moral legitimacy, because mentality-facts already presuppose a specific account of the state's duties and its legitimate domain of activity—will generalize to other mentality-based arguments.

[86] Martin Luther King Jr., "Remaining Awake Through a Great Revolution," 269–70. (I thank Mark Reiff for drawing my attention to this passage.)

[87] I thank Jeff McMahan for suggesting this reference.

But the point remains that the success of Kramer's "change of perspective" is in principle detachable from the success of his quidnunc mentality objection. The legacy of the quidnunc mentality objection could thus be to initiate a shift toward the identification and evaluation of the mentalities of perfectionist and neutral states—a shift that could produce new theories and new language and that could shed new light on what is deeply at stake in the neutrality-perfectionism debate.

PART VI
APPLIED ETHICS

16

Purgative Punishment and the Importance of Perspective

R.A. Duff

1. Introduction: Kramer's "Purgative Rationale for Capital Punishment"[1]

Amongst Matt Kramer's many intellectual virtues is his readiness to follow where reason, where the argument, leads him—even when it leads him to a position that will be unpopular with his fellows and expose him to hostile criticism (this is also, of course, a matter of moral virtue: to follow where the argument leads requires not only intellectual honesty, but courage). This virtue is prominently displayed in his argument that capital punishment can, in practice as well as in principle, be justified for a very small number of criminal offenders, through what he calls the "purgative rationale."[2]

In this tribute to Kramer (a tribute that, as is common among philosophers, consists in trying to persuade him that, and why, he is deeply mistaken), I will explore how far down Kramer's path towards the purgative justification of capital punishment we should follow him: further, I will argue, than his critics often allow, since the purgative rationale directs our attention to some aspects and implications of horrifically evil crimes that do not receive enough attention from penal theorists; but not, I will also argue, to the conclusion that he reaches, since the aspects of evil and of our responses to its implications on which he focuses do not compel the conclusion that "executions in some contexts are morally obligatory and morally permissible" (179).[3] Given the horrifying character of capital punishment, a justification succeeds only if it does *compel* that conclusion—it would not be enough to show merely that the conclusion is plausible. But, I will argue, once we attend to the differences between the perspectives (first-, second-, and third-personal) from which we can speak and act; and once we recognize that punishment should involve addressing the offender in the second person, and that what we can say or do to him from that perspective will not always

[1] The title of the key chapter of M. Kramer, *The Ethics of Capital Punishment: A Philosophical Investigation of Evil and its Consequences* (2011): bare page references in the text of this chapter will be to this book.

[2] The purgative rationale, as providing an in principle justification for capital punishment, is developed in ch. 6 of *The Ethics of Capital Punishment*. Ch. 7 then discusses the question of whether actual institutions of capital punishment can in practice ever be justified, given the familiar moral deficiencies that infect such institutions; it concludes that capital punishment *might* be justifiable in practice. (I will not discuss the earlier chapters of the book, which offer a thorough, detailed critique of other arguments for capital punishment.)

[3] Kramer needs, he recognizes, to establish both obligatoriness and permissibility, since he is alert to the fact that what is obligatory might also be impermissible (indeed, this is the focus of ch. 7).

R.A. Duff, *Purgative Punishment and the Importance of Perspective* In: *Without Trimmings*. Edited by: Mark McBride and Visa AJ Kurki, Oxford University Press. © Mark McBride and Visa AJ Kurki 2022. DOI: 10.1093/oso/9780198868866.003.0016

be the same as what he can say or do to himself from the first-person perspective: we will be able to see why a version of the purgative rationale might make sense of certain first-personal responses to one's own wrongdoing, but that it cannot compel us to the kind of second-personal response that capital punishment must involve.

This line of argument will be explained in section 4. Before that, however, I need to sketch the gist of Kramer's purgative rationale: I will first, in section 2, discuss his account of "extravagant evil" and its implications for the evil-doer; and then, in section 3, turn to his account of its implications for the political community to which the evil-doer belongs (or which is in some way responsible for him).[4] Finally, in section 4, I will explain why Kramer's insights into the implications (both moral and political) of extravagantly evil wrongdoing do not compel the conclusion that "executions in some contexts are morally obligatory and morally permissible" (179). I should confess to some unease about whether we should follow Kramer as far as I follow him in this chapter: sometimes I think that we should instead stop short and simply reject, on moral grounds, what he says about "extravagant evil" and its implications for the evil-doer's place in the world. However, it seems worth exploring the question of how far we can be led toward his conclusions if we accept some of his starting points.

2. Extravagant Evils and their Perpetrators

Suppose that someone commits a crime that is not just evil, but "extravagantly evil." What makes the evil extravagant is not just its material impact on the world or on other people, but the meaning of the evil-doer's actions as displaying an "utter contempt" not only for their particular victims, but for "humankind as a whole" (230), a "repudiation of humankind through monstrous behaviour" involving "profuse and horrendous acts of violence" (232). Such actions repudiate or display contempt for humankind because what should have dissuaded (but did not dissuade) the perpetrator from committing them were "features of the victims ... that are characteristic of human beings generally" (230–1). Kramer offers two "paradigmatic cases" of such extravagant evil (226–8): though the borderline between extravagant and non-extravagant evil is neither sharp or clear, we can, he argues, recognize clear cases on either side of that border; extravagantly evil wrongs are marked out (or constituted as extravagant) by, for instance, their "extreme gruesomeness and destructiveness, sadistic malice or heartlessness or grotesque recklessness" (226).

There is of course much more to be said—and Kramer says much more—both about evil and about what marks a kind of evil out as "extravagant," but I will not pursue that discussion here. I agree that we can identify cases (of which we must hope there are rather few) of horrific evil, of which we might in all seriousness say that they display an utter contempt for humanity; and that we can indeed identify some such

[4] A word about pronouns. I find the "she or he" style cumbersome, whilst the "they"/"them" style can be awkward. Normally, I alternate between masculine and feminine pronouns from one paragraph to another; but this seems less apt here, since the vast majority of those whom Kramer would count as perpetrators of "extravagant evil" are men. So, rather than trying to match the frequency of my use of each pronoun to the proportions of male and of female offenders, I will simply use masculine pronouns for such perpetrators.

cases with confidence—cases in which there is no real room for doubt not just about the impact of the agent's actions or the immediate intentions with which and beliefs in which they are committed, but about the attitudes that those actions manifest.[5] To be more precise, and more cautious, I agree that if our aim is to characterize certain kinds of evil, we can confidently identify some cases of what Kramer calls extravagant evil. When we turn our attention to the practical implications that Kramer draws from such identifications, however, that confidence should wane: the question now will not be whether we could in fact ever be confident enough to be justified in drawing and acting on those implications, but whether anything could or should in principle count as being confident enough to act on them.

It is important to Kramer's argument that the agent of such extravagantly evil acts can still be held responsible for his deeds: that he is "not insane (in a way that negates responsibility); he is defilingly evil" (245). We might be tempted to call him "psychopathic": but "a monstrously psychopathic state of mind does not amount to an insane outlook in any sense that precludes moral responsibility" (244). There is room for argument here about how we can understand the idea of "psychopathy," and about the proper criteria for responsibility-negating insanity. Kramer suggests that responsibility can be negated only by "fundamental mistakes about the harmfulness of one's own conduct," not by "fundamental mistakes about … moral principles": the former can be "lunatically mistaken," or involve "crazy blindness," in a way that negates responsibility; the latter, it seems, although they might amount to "gross misapprehensions of moral principles," cannot count as disordered in a way that negates responsibility (245). Now it could be argued that there are kinds of radical moral "blindness" that should be seen as responsibility-negating incapacities which place the unfortunate agent outside the bounds of our practices of responsibility-attribution;[6] in which case at least some of those whom Kramer would count as responsible perpetrators of extravagant evil might instead be better understood as horrendously harmed and harming victims of mental disorder. But I will not pursue that argument here: partly because it would take us too far from the main concerns of this chapter, but partly because I do not want to claim that *everyone* who commits extravagant evils is or must be "insane" in a way that negates responsibility. At least sometimes it makes sense to try to engage such perpetrators in a moral discussion of what they have done, to try to call them to account for their terrible wrongs: not because we can realistically hope that they will be persuaded to recognize and repent those wrongs, but because it at least makes sense to engage in that communicative effort—because we can or should still see and treat them as being within the realm, within the reach, of moral reason.[7]

The possibility (the conceivability) of repentance is important to Kramer's argument—though not quite in the way suggested above. For the implications of

[5] Bearing in mind that discerning those attitudes is not a matter of making inferences from overt conduct to hidden, "inner," feelings or emotions, but of discerning the meaning or significance of those actions themselves.

[6] I have argued this in Duff, "Psychopathy and Answerability," 198.

[7] A further question, which again I cannot pursue here, is whether we can or should do this because there is some factual basis for the effort—because the agent is in fact capable of responding; or because we owe it to him to act *as if* he could respond. For an illuminating discussion of some of the issues involved here, see Winch, "Eine Einstellung zur Seele."

extravagant evil-doing depend, he thinks, not just on the extravagant character of a single terrible action, or course of action, but on the agent's persistence in such evil-doing. Someone who commits a "[h]orrendous … act of mass murder," Kramer argues, could still "reinvest[] his life with positive value through genuine repentance," if "his perpetration of an appalling atrocity was confined to one occasion": he "might be able to redeem himself through genuine and perdurable repentance," which "could separate[] that atrocity from the rest of his life sufficiently to render the purgative rationale for capital punishment inapplicable" (240). We can begin to see the core idea behind the "purgative rationale for capital punishment" by asking what the key difference is between the single act of extravagant evil that still leaves room for redemption through "genuine repentance," and the more persistent or repeated commission of such acts that leaves no such room, and so makes capital punishment, in Kramer's view, both permissible and obligatory.

The first point to note is that Kramer does not rely on the "psychological claim" that it is extremely "unlikel[y] that anyone responsible for such acts will ever undergo durable feelings of contrition" (238), although he accepts that claim. He does, secondly, appeal to the "epistemic difficulties pertaining to the occurrence of genuine repentance," which are "huge" (239): but this raises an important question about the role of (possible, conceivable) repentance. Kramer seems to believe that only actual ("genuine and perdurable") repentance can render capital punishment unnecessary, in which case it would of course matter if it was (virtually) impossible for courts to determine whether the offender had truly repented; but it could instead be argued that what is crucial is the moral possibility of, the existence of a moral space for, repentance. Compare the role of the idea of a "*locus poenitentiae*" in the law of criminal attempts. One reason for defining the *actus reus* of attempts narrowly is that the law should leave would-be criminals a *locus poenitentiae*: a moral space within which they could repent their criminal enterprise and voluntarily withdraw from it.[8] The point here is not that many intending criminals might in fact avail themselves of this *locus poenitentiae*: it depends not on empirical probabilities, but on the conceptual point that to see another as a responsible agent is, *inter alia*, to see her as one who is within the reach of reasons, who could come to see the error of her ways for herself; and the related moral point that to treat her with the respect that is due to her as a responsible agent is, *inter alia*, to leave her free, as far as is reasonably possible, to determine her own actions in the light of her own grasp of reasons. We might also appeal to the idea that in sentencing offenders, even very serious offenders, courts should always leave them with some prospect, some hope, of redemption—understood in secular terms as a way back to full civic fellowship as a member of the polity: that as Lord Judge put it, an indeterminate sentence of "Imprisonment for Public Protection"

> does not require the abandonment of all hope for offenders on whom it is imposed. They are not consigned to penal oblivion. To the contrary, common humanity, if nothing else, must allow for the possibility of rehabilitation.[9]

[8] On the significance of the *locus poenitentiae*, see Duff, *Criminal Attempts*, 167–8, 387–8.

[9] R *(on the application of Wells) v. Parole Board for England and Wales* [2010] 1 AC 553, para. 105.

Again, this demand of "common humanity" does not depend on an empirical claim about the likelihood that such offenders will rehabilitate themselves: it is the demand that they must be treated, by their fellow citizens and by the criminal law, as responsible beings for whom redemption is always possible.[10]

Why then should we not argue, against Kramer, that the law should leave even the most serious offender, even the perpetrator of the most extravagant evils, a chance to repent: that this is due to him as a responsible agent—as a human being who is still "possessed of human dignity" (259, 262)? I don't know whether Kramer would agree that *if* "genuine repentance" were (conceptually, morally) possible for the perpetrator of extravagant evils, he should be given a chance to achieve it, and should therefore not be executed. But the question is moot, since Kramer's deeper objection to such an appeal to the possibility of repentance is that for someone who persists in the commission of extravagant evil there is no such possibility. For genuine repentance is a matter not just of how one comes to feel or think about what one has done, but of what one does about it by way of atonement: to repent one's wrongs is to seek some way to atone for them. But for the perpetrators of such extravagant evils, "there might well be nothing—short of unflinchingly abject submission to capital punishment—that would amount to a satisfactory form of atonement" (238); in some such cases

> [t]he very features of the crimes that bring them within the purgative rationale for capital punishment—their extravagant vileness and profuseness—also place them collectively beyond repentance. Only the voluntary undergoing of an execution would adequately give effect to genuine penitence (239).

There is an apparent paradox here: undergoing execution could "adequately give effect to genuine penitence"; but the crimes are still in some sense "beyond repentance." What this brings out, I think, is that there are two significantly different ways of understanding the meaning of a person's voluntary submission to execution for his extravagant crimes: this difference matters to how the person himself, and others, can understand and respond to his crimes.

It is difficult to imagine what it would be to come to a full understanding of the wrongs one committed in committing "extravagant evils": what it would be to grasp, in the first person, what I have done; and how a person who came to such an understanding could go on, what they could think or do in response to those wrongs. It is entirely conceivable that such a person would see death, whether by execution or by suicide, as the only possibility—not for selfish or prudential reasons to do with the unattractiveness of all the available modes of continued life, but as the only response that would do justice to what he has done. However, we need to distinguish two ways in which death might thus appear morally necessary (one of which would make the choice between suicide and execution inherently insignificant, whereas the other might make execution the more appropriate course).

First, the seeking or acceptance of death might be an expression of a kind of despair. I realize that my crimes make my continued life morally impossible: I cannot live with

[10] If redemption must *always* be possible, it is not enough that there is a time for possible repentance between the sentence and the execution (see 105–8; also at nn. 40–2).

myself (which is a moral rather than a psychological remark), because I can see no way in which my life can, given the extravagantly evil deeds that it now contains, make acceptable sense; I cannot live with other people, since those crimes irretrievably sundered the moral bonds (of humanity) between us, so that there is no way back. If that is my attitude, then the choice between suicide and execution is a contingent one: there is nothing inherently preferable about either mode of death. But, second, I might seek or accept death as an act not of despair, but of atonement: as the only way in which I can adequately express my recognition of what I have done, and communicate that recognition to others.[11] Seeking death is now a positive act, belonging in the same moral category as other acts of atonement for lesser wrongs. It might also, perhaps paradoxically, be a means of reconciling myself with other people, by showing my repentant recognition of the horror of my deeds, and my earnest desire to atone for them as best I can: I can make my peace with others through my death, which thus restores a kind of community with them even as I leave them—in and by my leaving them in this way (one manifestation of such reconciliation might be the way in which others think and talk of me after my death, and perhaps the way in which they deal with my body). Now if that is how and why I seek death, I might see execution (if my polity practices capital punishment) as the more appropriate mode of death: in pleading "Guilty" at my trial, and accepting the judicial execution that follows, I subject myself to the polity's (my polity's) law (to my law); I show that I am ready to answer for my crimes in the appropriate public forum, and subject myself to what the polity prescribes as the appropriate kind of atonement.

We have yet to see *why* death might seem necessary on either view, and the answer to that question might determine whether both views sketched in the previous paragraph are possible, in particular whether the second is tenable.[12] Kramer's explanation of why death is necessary seems to favor the former view: the perpetrator's crimes are "beyond repentance" because nothing, not even willingly accepted execution, could achieve the kind of reconciliation that repentance seeks. Given the perpetrator's horrendously extravagant crimes, Kramer argues, "his life is antithetical to," it is "an affront to," "the dignity of humanity" (236); his "continued existence" is, therefore, "defilingly abominable" (224). Relatedly (it seems) his life is "of negative value," so that "sparing [him] from execution is wrong" (186); although he "remains a human being and is thus possessed of human dignity," "the moral worth of [his] life is negative" (259). I am, I confess, unsure what to make of the claim that his life is of "negative [moral] value." We can say that he has made the world irreparably worse (materially and morally) by his deeds, which might also be to imply that the world would have been a (materially and morally) better place had he never existed—though we should be more cautious than philosophers often are in trying to make such judgments about how good or bad "the world" is. We (and he) might say that whatever future he had, whatever else he had done (or might yet do if allowed to live), the overall judgment

[11] See further Duff, *Punishment, Communication, and Community*, 152–5.

[12] But we should bear in mind that the question so far is why the offender's death could seem necessary to him from the first-person perspective, as a reason for action. We have yet to ask what could be said or done from a second- or third-person perspective, and part of my argument will be that we cannot directly infer answers to that latter question from our answer to the former.

on his life could not but be that it was a bad, atrociously bad, life (for if we can talk of a good life, we can surely also talk of a bad life). On the other hand, if Kramer allows (as he does) that even the perpetrator of such atrocities is still "a human being ... possessed of human dignity," is this not to say that his life has an ineradicable value? We might say that

> even such people are owed unconditional respect, meaning, not that they are deserving of esteem, but that they are owed a kind of respect which is not conditional upon what they have done and which cannot be forfeited. Some will say that even the most terrible evil-doers are owed this respect as human beings and that we owe it to them because we are human beings.[13]

This is to say, in part, that even such evil-doers must not (morally cannot, whilst recognizing their humanity) "be shot in the street like dogs," or "killed in the spirit of ridding the world of vermin":[14] which is not to say that they cannot justifiably (and justly) be killed, but that there are moral limits (limits set by their humanity) on the reasons for which, and the spirit in which, they can be killed. Kramer seems to insist on a cognate point when he argues that even the perpetrator of extravagant evils must be given a "fair trial," and be executed only if convicted through such a trial: for the fairness of a trial consists not just in the "epistemic reliability" of its procedures, but "principally in the respect shown to a defendant (even a vile defendant) as someone possessed of human dignity" (262). Kramer is not, I think, suggesting here that the actually guilty defendant is a lucky beneficiary of fair procedures that are properly owed only to those who are not guilty of such horrendous crimes: that he must be treated fairly because we do not yet know with enough certainty that he is guilty. He is owed such fairness, such respect, in his own right, even if he is guilty of the extravagant crimes of which he stands accused.[15]

Perhaps, however, we can understand Kramer's argument better if we focus not on the idea that the wrongdoer's life is of "negative [moral] value," which appears to invite us to evaluate his life in isolation, but on the claim that it is "an affront to the dignity of humankind" (236), and "defilingly abominable" (224): for this turns our attention to the relationship between such a wrongdoer and "humankind." In a range of contexts we can understand, and indeed draw practical implications from, the idea that a wrongdoer's continued membership of a community would be intolerable, given the way in which her wrongs have utterly and irrevocably repudiated the defining values of that community: that is the basis on which people may be expelled from a range of associations, or (as a particular form of expulsion) sacked from a variety of jobs; and although there is much to be discussed about the proper criteria for such expulsions, and about what kinds of (repeated, unrepented) wrongs can make expulsion permissible and even necessary, there are surely cases of justified expulsion. An

[13] Gaita, *Good and Evil: An Absolute Conception*, 2.

[14] ibid, 3.

[15] For a related argument about what is involved in, or presupposed by, putting those who are guilty of horrendous crimes on trial, rather than "disposing of them," see Duff, "Can We Punish the Perpetrators of Atrocities?," 79. However, that argument appeals to a conception of the criminal trial, as a communicative exercise in calling alleged wrongdoers to account, that Kramer might well not share.

academic who persistently flouts the defining values of the academic enterprise (she plagiarizes, she bullies or sexually harasses or ignores her students, ...) can in the end be dismissed, and rightly so (we need not here discuss how many times she should undergo less dramatic disciplinary measures short of dismissal): she is thus expelled from the academic community (at least from this branch of it), and it might be said that her continued membership would have been an "affront" to the community and its members, because her persistent conduct was so utterly "antithetical" to its values. We might say the same about doctors or lawyers who are struck off for persistent, serious professional misconduct; soldiers who are cashiered from the army; members of clubs, and other kinds of association, who are expelled; and, less dramatically and less formally, housemates who are told to leave because of their persistent misconduct. For a simple example, imagine a household of committed vegans, one of whom lapses into carnivorous habits, and insists on bringing animal products into the house: the others might reasonably come to see his continued tenancy as a serious "affront," and demand that he leave.[16]

Can we then say, in support of Kramer's argument, that if someone persists in committing extravagantly evil crimes "against humanity" (232), thus utterly repudiating the defining values of that community (of humankind), his continued membership would be a serious affront to that community? One question is whether we can talk of humanity, or humankind, as a community in this way: but it does seem plausible to think that although "humanity" does not constitute a political or legal community, it does constitute (at least in aspiration if not yet in established fact) a moral community. We talk naturally about what we owe to each other as fellow human beings, which is to portray ourselves as belonging to a community with all other human beings; we can also see "humanitarian" efforts of various kinds, including institution-building efforts, as attempts to give that community a more robust existence.[17] A more serious question concerns the radical (to put it very mildly) character of expulsion from the community of humanity. Someone who is expelled from a more specific, limited community might thereby suffer quite devastating harm: think of someone who is expelled from a monastery and excommunicated from the church; or someone who loses the career (as doctor, or lawyer, or scholar) to which she had devoted her life. But she can still find, rebuild, a life for herself—and she will probably also belong to other communities from which she is not expelled. "Expulsion" from humanity is very different: it is expulsion from life or any possibility of life, and we must therefore ask whether we can justify such "expulsion" in a way analogous to that in which we might justify the other, more limited, kinds of expulsion noted above. Kramer can reply that that is one reason why capital punishment is justifiable only in a very limited set of cases, those

[16] We should note that, as Kramer points out (225), to talk in these terms of "affront" is not to talk of, or to appeal to, the way others might in fact react to the wrongdoer: the claim that his continued membership is an affront is not the claim that others are or will in fact feel "affronted" by it—any more than the claim that a certain type of conduct is "offensive" is the claim that others are or will in fact be offended (feel offended) by it. The claim is one about what kinds of reaction would be appropriate—and why.

[17] I do not mean to be starry-eyed about this point: all kinds of sectional partiality, including nationalism in its various forms, hinder humanitarian endeavors, and there are questions to be asked about how far we should go down the cosmopolitan road. But it does make sense to talk (at least aspirationally) in such terms.

of determinately, undeniably extravagant evil:[18] but we must still ask whether such a radical exclusion can be justified even in these cases.

Here again the differences between first-, second-, and third-person perspectives matter. I have suggested that one who has perpetrated extravagant evil might come to believe that his continued life is morally impossible: he cannot continue to live with other people, as part of humanity or as a member of humankind, since his crimes have irretrievably sundered the moral bonds that tied him to his fellows, leaving no way back into community. Others should be able to understand such a response, and respect it as marking an authentic recognition of the moral significance of what he has done. However, that is not yet to say—as presumably Kramer would have us say—that this is the only kind of response that marks a proper comprehension of the implications of one's wrongdoing; that any attempt to find a way to atone for his crimes whilst staying alive, to devote the rest of his life to reparative and penitential activities, would be doomed to futility. Nor is it yet to say that others should believe that he was right to respond in this way—rather than, for instance, that he should (ideally) remain alive and try to find other ways to atone for his crimes, or that they lack the standing to make such a judgment. Nor is it yet to say that others should feel entitled to tell him that that is how he ought to respond, or to urge him to do so. Nor, *a fortiori*, is it yet to say that others should think themselves entitled to give coercive effect to that judgment, by killing the wrongdoer—either by lynching him, or by subjecting him to a judicial process of trial and execution. Others can and must respond to his wrongs, in a way that recognizes their horrendous character; but we have yet to determine what kind of response that must be.

This brings us to the second dimension of Kramer's purgative rationale: his account of why a political community that is responsible for a perpetrator of extravagant evils has an obligation to execute him (after a fair trial that respects his dignity).

3. The Responsibilities of a Political Community

We could, I have argued, understand and respect the decision of a perpetrator of extravagant evils to kill himself, on the grounds that he can have no continuing place in the community of humanity—that he must remove himself. Suppose that we also come to believe that that is what he ought to do: that his continued life, his continued membership of that community, is an affront, and that the world would be a better place if it did not include him—if he died. We might doubt, I have suggested, whether we are in a position to make such confident judgments: but for the sake of the argument I will accept that they can be legitimately made. However, this is still a long way from justifying capital punishment—from showing that we may, or must, give practical effect to such judgments by executing the perpetrator. So we must ask how Kramer can lead us to that conclusion.

More precisely, we must ask which of two possible conclusions he can, or should, justify in this way. One conclusion concerns what we may, or must, do about the

[18] Kramer insists that the purgative rationale justifies capital punishment only for wrongs that are "determinately," "straightforward[ly]," "unmistakeably" extravagant (227).

perpetrator: it portrays him simply as the object of our actions—someone about whom we can decide and act in the third person. The other conclusion concerns what is morally possible, or necessary, from the second-person perspective: what can or must we say to him by way of communication (bearing in mind, of course, that our actions can communicate as well as our words)? The difference between these two kinds of conclusion should become clearer in what follows: to put it crudely, and as yet too allusively, the key question for the latter kind of conclusion is whether capital punishment can be a way of addressing, of communicating with, the offender. If it cannot, and if punishment should generally be a communicative enterprise, then the purgative rationale might fail, because in that case the first kind of conclusion will be insufficient as a justification of capital *punishment*.[19] Or so I will argue in what follows.

What constitutes an intolerable affront to humanity, on Kramer's account, is the evil-doer's continued existence, his very survival (in section 4 I will offer a different account of this affront): but what gives any polity the right, let alone the obligation, to seek to remove such affronts through a practice of capital punishment? On one view of criminal law, the answer to this question is quite straightforward. The removal of such an affront will make the world a morally better place, and any polity's legislature therefore has good reason to institute the death penalty for those whose continued existence constitutes such an affront: for "the world is better if it is morally better, and to the extent legislators can achieve that moral betterment through law, they should do so."[20] On Moore's particular retributivist account, what makes the world "morally better" is that culpable wrongdoers receive the punitive suffering they deserve, and Kramer is not offering a retributivist rationale for capital punishment: but if the world would be morally better if it did not contain this perpetrator of extravagant evils, this would give Moorean legislators reason to institute a system of capital punishment to achieve that betterment. As to which particular polity ought to pursue, or might have an obligation to pursue, the execution of such a wrongdoer, the question becomes an essentially practical one: which polity is best placed to execute him, through a judicial process that respects the demands of justice. Among the various problems with such a view is that it does not take the issue of jurisdiction or standing seriously enough: it is one thing to show that a certain outcome would be good or would improve the world, but quite another to show that any particular person, or body, or polity, has the right or the standing to try to secure that outcome.[21] However, Kramer does take that issue seriously (see 249–52), and does not initially seem to take the Moorean route: what makes it obligatory for a polity to institute a system of capital punishment for perpetrators of extravagant evils is not simply the fact that their continued existence would be an affront to humanity. That fact (assuming for the moment that it is a moral fact) might give the wrongdoer reason to end his own life: but it is not clear that, or why, it could give a polity reason to mobilize its institutions of criminal law to execute him.

[19] On punishment as communication, see Duff, *Punishment, Communication, and Community*. The argument here also has some affinity with Nagel's classic (if obscure) claim that "whatever one does to another person intentionally must be aimed at him as a subject, with the intention that he receive it as a subject" ("War and Massacre," 136).

[20] Moore, "Four Reflections on Law and Morality," 1540.

[21] Compare J.G. Murphy, "Marxism and Retribution," 220; see further Duff, *The Realm of Criminal Law*, 73–5, and ch. 3.

As Kramer notes, the wrongdoer's deeds initially bear on his relationship to humanity (as well as to his particular victims): that is the relationship that they destroy. But what could give a polity reason (indeed, place it under an obligation) to make that relationship its business, and to give the destruction of that relationship material effect by executing the wrongdoer?

Kramer's answer appeals to the responsibilities of "the community in whose jurisdiction [the perpetrator] resides" (184). That community might not bear any retrospective responsibility for a perpetrator's evil-doing, nor can its failure to execute him somehow create such a retrospective responsibility: but such failure makes it retrospectively responsible for "the ancillary misdeed of declining to execute someone whose very survival calls into question the moral ties that hold the community together as such" (185). This failure, allowing the continued existence of an evil-doer whose life should have been ended, "besmirch[es]," "defile[s]," or "sull[ies]" the community; it is "a blot on the moral order" of the community, whose "moral integrity is lessened" by that failure (185–7). More precisely (or furthermore) that failure sullies the wrongdoer's community because it "taints the relationship between [that] community and the rest of humanity" (230); and it taints that relationship because it is a failure to remove from the world a wrongdoer whose continued existence is an affront to humanity.[22] Now not executing such a wrongdoer (i.e., not instituting a practice of capital punishment that will execute him) can constitute *failure*, and can thus taint the community and its relationship to humanity, only in virtue of a *prospective* responsibility that the community has in relation to the wrongdoer—only in virtue of its "collective responsibility for the continued existence" of the wrongdoer (228): that "collective responsibility" then becomes a retrospective responsibility for the wrongdoer's continued existence if the community fails to execute him; but this can only be because the community first has a prospective responsibility for his continued life—or death. On Kramer's view, it has just such a responsibility: through its "legal-governmental system," it becomes "collectively responsible for the subsequent handling of [his] case. His fate, including the very continuation of his existence, is now in the community's hands" (233).

What kind of relationship between an extravagant evil-doer and a political community could generate such a demanding prospective responsibility for the political community—could suffice to put an evil-doer's "fate, including the very continuation of his existence, ... in the community's hands"? What principles or criteria of jurisdiction are appropriate here? The simple case is one in which the evil-doer is a citizen of this polity, and commits his crimes within its territory (perhaps also committing them against other citizens of the polity): it seems obvious enough that a polity has a prospective responsibility not only to protect its citizens against such wrongdoings, but

[22] It seems at times that what taints the community, and its relationship to humanity, is the very existence of the wrongdoer—a taint that presumably operates from the very time of his evil-doing (in which case the community is tainted even during the time when it puts the evil-doer on trial and goes through the often lengthy process of appeals). I think the better reading, however, is that both taints (of the community itself, and of its relationship to humanity) flow only from the failure to bring the evil-doer to trial, to convict him (if adequate proof is available in a trial that respects the demands of due process), and to execute him; or at least that the taint flows not from the very fact of his wrongdoing, but from his unpunished wrongdoing (on the understanding that it is punished only if he is executed). But see further n. 28.

also to respond to them after the event, and to deal appropriately with the wrongdoer; even when the polity bears no retrospective responsibility for the commission of the crimes, it cannot now shrug its collective shoulders at such wrongs and say "Not our business." This does not yet show that it must deal with the wrongdoer by executing him (after a fair judicial process), but Kramer offers us a further argument toward that conclusion. The perpetrator's polity "plays a decisive role in continuing or discontinuing [his] life," by "determining whether resources are to be devoted to prolonging or terminating his existence" (233): assuming that, if he is not executed, he will have to be sentenced at the least to life imprisonment, which is a costly business, in keeping him alive the community will thus be directing substantial resources to "the persistence of a state of affairs that sullies its relationship with the rest of humanity" (234). Now Kramer makes clear (234) that it does not matter where those resources come from—the argument would still hold even if they came from a wealthy evil-doer himself, since the polity still determines how those resources will be used. Nor does it matter whether life imprisonment is more costly than execution: what is objectionable is, it seems, devoting any resources to keeping him alive.[23] This argument depends on a plausible assumption, that it is not open to the polity to do nothing; but two questions now arise. First, granted that the polity has the effective power to kill or to keep alive, does it have the authority to kill in this way (does it have the moral authority, should it claim the political authority)? Second, even if it does have such authority, is it clear that it must use it in this way?

As to the first question, Kramer is perhaps too quick in saying that the extravagant perpetrator's "fate, including the very continuation of his existence, is now in the community's hands," or that the polity "plays a decisive role in determining whether resources are to be devoted to prolonging or terminating his existence" (233). That is clearly, empirically, true: a polity has the power and the resources to terminate, as well as to prolong, any citizen's existence. In just the same sense, a doctor "plays a decisive role in determining whether resources are to be devoted to prolonging or terminating" the life of her curable patient; the patient's "fate, including the very continuation of his existence, is now in the [doctor's] hands." But it does not follow from this that the doctor has the right or the authority to decide whether to devote the medical resources to killing the patient (though of course she might have to decide not to devote them to continuing his life). Those who think that euthanasia might be justifiable must of course believe this, but one kind of opponent of euthanasia will insist that the doctor's responsibilities, and thus her authority, do not reach that far: it is not for her to decide that, or whether, the patient should die, even if she is confident that continued life is not for the patient's own good. My aim here is not to justify this attitude, but to note that it must be addressed by anyone who justifies (medical) euthanasia: similarly,

[23] Compare Kramer's striking claim that a victim of "horrific[] persecution" who could save her persecutor's life by donating a kidney not only has no obligation to do so, but "is under an ethical obligation to *decline* to sustain his life," since "she would debase herself" if she took such steps to prolong his life: "The Purgative Rationale for the Death Penalty: Replies to Steiker and Danaher," 387 (emphasis in original). Kramer is certainly right that some responses to those who have wronged me, including an over-ready forgiveness, can be criticized as self-demeaning (see Murphy, *Getting Even: Forgiveness and its Limits*): but I do not share his apparent confidence that it is impossible to help, even to save the life of, one who has seriously wronged me in a morally appropriate spirit that does not debase or demean me.

although a polity's responsibilities clearly include many matters of life and death, it is not yet clear that they should include the responsibility to decide whether to kill someone (other than, for instance, as a defensive necessity).

However, Kramer anyway cannot rely on the argument about allocating resources to reach the conclusion he wants: for whilst that argument can apply to the simple case of the perpetrator who commits his crimes within the territory of the polity of which he is a citizen, Kramer works with a much broader conception of jurisdiction than that, and would hold a polity responsible for perpetrators to whom the resources argument cannot apply. Jurisdiction, and the responsibilities it brings, extends to "any community that bears some special association with the offender or with his atrocities" (252): that relationship might be based on the Territoriality Principle, which gives a polity jurisdiction over wrongs committed within its territory (including those initiated within its territory but completed elsewhere, or completed in its territory though initiated elsewhere); or on a Nationality Principle that gives jurisdiction over wrongs committed by the polity's citizens anywhere in the world; or on a Passive Personality Principle that gives jurisdiction over wrongs committed against the polity's citizens anywhere in the world;[24] or on the fact that the wrongdoer fled to the polity's territory and is now detected there, although in this case there is likely to be a polity with a stronger claim to jurisdiction (the polity in which the crimes were committed, or of which the evil-doer is a citizen), and to which he should therefore be extradited. In at least some of these cases, a decision not to arrest, prosecute, and (if he is duly convicted) execute the evil-doer is not a decision to devote resources to keeping him alive: but the polity still, Kramer thinks, has an obligation to seek to execute him.

For instance, if the polity that seeks his extradition does not itself operate a legitimate, just system of capital punishment, the polity that now holds him ought to refuse to extradite him, and must instead put him on trial itself (251):[25] but to extradite him would not be to devote resources to keeping him alive; indeed, as far as this argument goes, a polity into which a perpetrator of extravagant evils seeks entry could simply refuse him entry, without going to the trouble and expense of arresting him and extraditing him. Similarly, if a perpetrator over whom a polity has jurisdiction, in virtue of its "association" with him, flees and is discovered elsewhere, the polity is then "under a moral obligation to take all reasonable steps to ensure that [he] is brought to justice" (251), as Israel was in relation to Eichmann.[26] But that obligation could have nothing to do with not devoting resources to keeping Eichmann alive, since if Israel had made no attempt to extradite him or otherwise ensure that he was brought to justice, it would not have devoted any resources to keeping him alive. (Furthermore, had Israel taken all reasonable steps to bring him to justice, but without success, its citizens would have been "tarnished by [his] continued existence ... , but not any more so than the members of communities which have no special association with

[24] On these principles of jurisdiction see generally Ryngaert, *Jurisdiction in International Law*. For Kramer, citizenship is not actually crucial: he extends the principles of nationality and of passive personality to cover non-citizens who normally reside in the polity (250).

[25] Compare the doctrine of "*aut dedere aut judicare*" (either extradite or prosecute) in international law: see Bassiouni and Wise, *Aut Dedere Aut Judicare: The Duty to Extradite or Prosecute in International Law*.

[26] Indeed, given Argentina's refusal to extradite Eichmann, Israel was, Kramer thinks, morally permitted, though not obligated, to kidnap him (252).

him or with his crimes" (252).) Kramer also argues that if there is no polity with an appropriate special relationship to the offender that is willing, able, and morally entitled to try him and to execute him, any polity that maintains a legitimate system of purgative capital punishment may, as a last resort, assert a universal jurisdiction and try to bring him to trial:[27] "[i]n some circumstances ... the importance of removing the moral taint produced by a defilingly evil offender is sufficient to outweigh the importance of the reasons for circumspection" in claiming such jurisdiction (252). Here again, however, a decision to assert and to seek to enforce universal jurisdiction is not a decision to allocate resources to executing the wrongdoer rather than to keeping him alive; for not seeking to prosecute him does not commit the polity to devoting resources to keeping him alive.

Perhaps, then, the real core of Kramer's argument is more Moorean that it initially seemed. The continued existence of a perpetrator of extravagant evils is an affront to humankind, which should therefore be eliminated (if that can be done in accordance with the demands of procedural justice): any human polity therefore has reason to maintain a system of capital punishment that can bring such perpetrators to lethal justice. How strong that reason is, however, depends on the relationship, if any, that the polity has with the perpetrator: the closer that relationship, the more stringent the polity's responsibility for the perpetrator; if that responsibility is stringent enough, it generates an obligation to bring the perpetrator to lethal justice. It is the failure to discharge that obligation that "besmirch[es]," "defile[s]," and "sull[ies]" the community, and constitutes "a blot on [its] moral order," because it "taints the relationship between [that] community and the rest of humanity."[28] What ultimately matters, what should matter to every polity, is that the moral taint of the wrongdoer's continued life, the affront to humanity that his continued life constitutes, be removed; whilst the responsibility to ensure that removal will normally fall to polities that have some special relationship with the perpetrator or his crimes, in the end it is one in which every polity shares.

For simplicity's sake, we can focus now on the simplest case in which a polity has a clearly close normative relationship to, and thus clearly has jurisdiction over, the perpetrator: the case in which he is a citizen of the polity, and committed his crimes within its territory. We can leave aside for now the question of how far beyond that simple case, and in what ways, jurisdictional responsibility and the obligations that it brings might extend; and whether polities should have some responsibility to seek or to help to bring any extravagant evil-doer to justice, even if it has no special relationship to him (a question that clearly bears on the issue of universal jurisdiction and on the moral foundations of the International Criminal Court).

There is (as is often true of Kramer's arguments) something right and important at the root of his argument. Polities have a range of prospective responsibilities for, in relation to, their citizens; these include responsibilities not just to take certain kinds

[27] See Reydams, *Universal Jurisdiction: International and Municipal Legal Perspectives*. We can leave aside here the possibility that polities could cooperate to institute an international criminal court to deal with such cases.

[28] See at n. 22. From Kramer's comments on Eichmann, as noted in the previous paragraph, it also seems that the members of all polities are "tainted" by the evil-doer's continued existence, even when they could have done nothing to bring him to justice, or did all that could have reasonably been expected of them.

of care of them (to provide the apparatus of a welfare state, for instance, and tax citizens in order to fund it), but also to deal with, to respond to, their wrongdoings—more precisely, those kinds of wrongdoing that properly count as "public" wrongs which are the polity's business.[29] We can therefore argue (although the full argument would be long) that a polity ought to maintain an institution of criminal law, through which such wrongs can be addressed; that it ought to criminalize, and thus bring within the reach of that institution, a range of serious public wrongs—a range that would certainly include the kinds of extravagant evil that concern Kramer; and that it ought to seek to bring those who commit such wrongs to a public accounting that consists in a fair trial and a just punishment. If it fails to do all of this, it fails in its responsibilities, and thus "sullies" its own character; it also impairs its relationship to those who have a proper interest in such wrongs. Both these points require further explanation—especially the latter.

As to sullying its own character, the point is quite simple. A polity purports to be committed to certain values, and the extravagant wrongdoer flouts those values—his wrongdoing displays an utter contempt for them. Now to be committed to certain values is, *inter alia*, to be committed to taking appropriate notice of violations of them: a claim to be committed to academic honesty, for instance, is undermined not only by my own acts of dishonesty, but also by a failure to respond to egregious acts of dishonesty by others; indeed, it is rebutted by such failures, unless they can be explained in a way consistent with that purported commitment. This is not to say that my reason for responding to others' dishonesty (and, of course, to my own) is to preserve my integrity, or to avoid "sullying" my life or character:[30] the damage to my character or integrity would be an implication of my failure to respond appropriately, but it would be a perversion of moral motivation to make that my reason for responding—and also futile; integrity is not preserved by attempting to preserve it.

As to impairing relationships, the point is most obvious in relation to the victims of crime. The polity has, of course, a prospective responsibility to protect its members against crime, and victims are sometimes victims not just of the wrongdoer himself, but of their polity's failure to protect them against such wrongs—in which case the polity acquires a responsibility to do what it can to make up for that failure. But given the many constraints, both material and moral, on what a polity may do by way of crime prevention, given the importance of leaving its citizens an extensive realm of freedom, and given too the radical imperfections of human nature, the best a polity can hope to do is to reduce crime to "tolerable" levels. However, an implication—or perhaps even an aspect—of its prospective protective responsibility is a prospective responsibility to respond to crimes that are committed: one responsibility that we collectively owe to each other, as fellow members of a normative community, is to recognize and respond to the wrongs that we suffer; and whilst such a response is in significant part appropriately victim-focused, it will also properly include an attempt

[29] For my own account of this matter (which I do not take Kramer to share, but which for present purposes takes us to a conclusion relevantly similar to his) see Duff, *The Realm of Criminal Law*.

[30] Compare Kramer, "The Purgative Rationale for the Death Penalty," 385: "In a system of capital punishment properly oriented toward the purgative rationale, executions are administered not deludedly in a bid for moral purity but clear-sightedly in a bid to remove some of the myriad ways in which any community falls short of such purity."

to hold the wrongdoer to account—which is precisely what the criminal process is supposed to do. Now on Kramer's account most—almost all—crimes implicate only the wrongdoer's relationship with his victims and with the political community to which he belongs, and can be adequately addressed by modes of punishment short of execution (which include "lifelong imprisonment-without-parole in conditions of solitary confinement" (236)): the polity can, that is, do justice to these wrongs without resorting to capital punishment—something less than that can constitute an adequate response. But extravagant evils also implicate the wrongdoer's relationship to humanity, and thus also implicate the polity's own relationship to humanity: its response must constitute an adequate response to the "utter contempt for," the "repudiation of," humankind that his wrongs displayed. To put the point crudely, since his crimes were "crimes against humanity," then the polity owes it to "humanity" to respond to them in an appropriate way;[31] a failure to respond appropriately will then undermine or damage the polity's relationship not just to the victims or to itself, but to humanity.

An obvious question is whether a polity has a relationship of this normative kind to "humanity." I noted above the question of whether humanity can be seen as a community at all, but the question here goes further: even if humanity can be seen as a community, is it a kind of community to which polities can have a relationship? Polities, as political entities, certainly have relationships with other political communities, and with the "international community,"[32] if we understand that as a community of nations: but even if humanity can be seen as a moral community, it is not a political community. Perhaps, however, a moral community is all we need in this context: the "humanitarian" goals and concerns by which polities can be motivated can be seen as concerns for (fellow) human beings, and thus for humanity, as such. Thus if the wrongdoer's extravagantly evil crimes, or his continued life after committing those crimes, are "an affront to humanity," it is an affront that properly concerns the wrongdoer's polity, which therefore owes it to humanity to respond appropriately—and which will therefore undermine its normative relationship to humanity if it fails to do so.

We can therefore be led at least some way down Kramer's path toward capital punishment. We can agree that if a polity does nothing to address such wrongs, makes no serious attempt to hold the wrongdoer to account, it will betray (or sully) itself, and seriously impair its relationship with those who have a stake in the matter—the wrongdoer's victims, his fellow citizens, and perhaps humanity as a whole; this will also be true if the polity's response fails to do justice to, fails to mark adequate recognition of, the wrong—for instance if the perpetrator was convicted, but then received the kind of punishment typically imposed on much more trivial crimes. It would be an affront to humanity if the perpetrator was able to continue his ordinary life without any attempt to hold him adequately to account, or after the mildest of punishments.[33] But this brings us back to the second question noted earlier in this section: why is

[31] There is of course much more to be said here, both about the sense of "against" in "crimes against humanity," and about the scope of such crimes: for an interesting discussion, which also argues for a much wider category of crimes against humanity than is usually recognized, see Renzo, "Responsibility and Answerability in the Criminal Law," 209.

[32] See *Rome Statute of the International Criminal Court*, Preamble, talking of "the most serious crimes of concern to the international community as a whole."

[33] And perhaps even if the responsible polity made all reasonable efforts to hold him to adequate account, but was unable to do so: see n. 28.

capital punishment the only adequate punishment for such crimes—the only way to remove the affront to humanity? Why should the polity's authority to deal with such a perpetrator include the authority to execute him; and why is it obligated to use that authority?

We have seen that Kramer's argument that it would be wrong for a polity to devote resources to keeping such a wrongdoer alive cannot provide a complete answer to this question, since it does not apply to some kinds of case in which, Kramer thinks, a polity ought still to assert jurisdiction over a perpetrator, and seek his execution. We are, therefore, brought back to the claim that the affront to humanity consists in the very fact of the perpetrator's continued existence; that, accordingly, it can be removed only by his death; and that the polity therefore has an obligation to seek to bring about his death. For, Kramer argues, the most plausible alternative sentence, of "lifelong imprisonment-without-parole in conditions of solitary confinement" would not be adequate, even if "the drabness of his confinement" was intensified (236). In the following section, I will suggest, first, that even if we agreed that a perpetrator's evil deeds could be so horrendous that they put him beyond repentance, and that his continued existence would then be an "affront to humanity," we should not give others, or the polity, the authority to make, and to give practical effect to, such a judgment on a perpetrator; second, that punishment, including capital punishment, should constitute an attempt to engage with the perpetrator in the second person—and that this makes the capital punishment of someone whom we might think is beyond repentance highly problematic; third, that we should not accept Kramer's account of what constitutes the affront to humanity, or of how it could be removed.

4. Affronting Humanity?

I agreed earlier that we could understand and respect the judgment of someone who came to see his extravagant evil-doing, in the first person, in the way that Kramer suggests it should be seen, as irretrievably rupturing his relationship with his fellow human beings, thus leaving him no way forward other than suicide or submission to state execution. Such an action marks a definitively final, unalterable, practical judgment on the person's life: we must ask whether this is a judgment that anyone other than the person himself has the right to make, and to enforce. The point here is not that we may be mistaken about some key fact to do with the person's guilt; or that we cannot be certain *enough* that his wrongs put him beyond repentance—as if there was some degree of human certainty that would suffice, if only we could attain it. The point is rather that we should recognize, as a matter of human modesty, that such judgments are not ours to make. Some would say that to make and act on such judgments would be to "play God," which it is not for humans to do; and we can make secular sense of that thought by suggesting that they are a kind of judgment that only a being who could claim the supreme power of life and death over his creatures would be in a position to make—a claim that we should not allow to a human polity.[34]

[34] Perhaps Kramer's argument about devoting resources to keeping such evil-doers alive would reappear here (see at nn. 23–7): in deciding not to execute the offender we are deciding to devote resources to keeping

This, it might be said, simply offers a counter-assertion to Kramer's account, rather than a counterargument. That counter-assertion is important, and worth explicating; but it can also find support in my second response, about just what kind of claim the polity would need to make in claiming the right to execute an evil-doer.[35] Is it enough to make that claim in the third person, as a claim about the evil-doer and about what may or must be done to him; or must it be a claim that we, the polity, can make in the second person, to the offender? A clue is provided by Kramer's insistence that however horrific his crimes, the perpetrator is still, and must therefore still be treated as, a human being who is "possessed of human dignity" (259, 262): what does this entail not just for the criminal process, but for his punishment?

Consider here what Kramer says about an evil-doer who has become "thoroughly insane" since his crimes or his conviction. He should not be executed because, Kramer first says, "he has permanently or temporarily ceased to exist as the person who carried out extravagantly evil atrocities" (247); that person does not now exist as an affront to humanity. That is unpersuasive, without a much fuller account of what it is to continue, or not to continue, to exist as a particular person, and Kramer later amends his explanation. The purgative rationale is still "applicable" to such a person—which implies that it still demands his execution; however, "his responsibility as a reflective agent at the time of his trial and at the time of his execution is a necessary condition for the legitimacy of any implementation of that rationale."[36] But why is it a necessary condition—and just what does it require? At first glance it seems not to bear on the implementation of the purgative rationale (unless we are to assume, which Kramer does not suggest, that the convicted perpetrator's insanity might prevent him from offering new evidence or arguments that would justify a successful appeal or reprieve): for what that rationale requires is simply the removal of the evil-doer from existence, and the only constraints on its implementation seem to be those generated first by the need for certainty that the person really is guilty of suitably extravagant evils, and second by the demand that his removal is not secured by cruel or inhuman means.

Kramer faces here a problem that faces many proponents of capital punishment. On the one hand, there is a widely shared sense, or intuition, even among supporters of the death penalty that it would be grotesquely wrong to execute someone who is now insane, even if he was fully sane at the time when he committed his horrendous crimes, and indeed at the time of his trial; and that sense reflects, I think, not some constraint on the administration of capital punishment external to the rationale for that punishment, but an understanding of the meaning of (capital) punishment—so that the execution of an insane person is a grotesque travesty of punishment. On the other hand, however, the familiar rationales for (capital) punishment—including Kramer's, as we have just seen—do not seem capable of explaining that sense.[37]

him alive. But if it is not for us to decide that he should die, then as a matter of "common humanity" we must devote resources to keeping him alive (as Kramer recognizes).

[35] See at n. 19.

[36] Kramer, "The Purgative Rationale for the Death Penalty," 392, responding to Danaher, "Kramer's Purgative Rationale for Capital Punishment: A Critique," 238.

[37] For further and more detailed discussion, see Duff, *Trials and Punishments*, 15–22.

We need to ask, of course, what kind of insanity, having what kind of impact on the person, should bar his execution—it is not enough to say that he must have become "thoroughly insane," or have "completely lost his mind" (247–8), or be "gripped by insanity."[38] Kramer's appeal to "his responsibility as a reflective agent" is suggestive: for it suggests that what matters is whether the wrongdoer retains, or has lost, his capacity for reflection—for reflection, presumably (if it is to be relevant to the legitimacy of his execution) on what is being done to him and why. Is he able, that is, to understand (is he capable of coming to understand) that he is being executed (not just killed), as a punishment for his horrendous crimes—which must include being able to (come to) understand those crimes as horrendous wrongs? But why should that matter: why should the fact not that he does not, but that he could not come to such an understanding bar his execution? Here is one answer: that punishment has an integral communicative dimension. In punishing someone, we do not just do something to her, or inflict or impose something on her: we speak to her—and the mode of her punishment gives a more specific meaning to that would-be communication.[39] (To say this does not commit us to a "communicative theory of punishment," according to which communication is *the* essential aim, or justifying purpose, of punishment: it says only that part of punishment's aim is to communicate; this distinguishes punishment from other materially similar burdens that states may impose.) Now communication seeks a response: unlike mere expression, it seeks the other person's understanding; whilst I can express myself even if the person to whom I express myself does not understand me, a would-be communication fails if it is not understood by its recipient. Communication also often seeks to persuade: this is certainly true when what we communicate is censure or criticism of another's conduct, since to censure you is to try *inter alia* to persuade you to recognize that you did wrong. This line of thought needs a fuller explanation: but it points to the suggestion that in punishing someone we must aim to communicate to him an appropriate understanding of the wrong for which he is being punished, and of his punishment as a justified response to that wrong.

In trying thus to communicate to, with, him we are engaged in an essentially second personal enterprise—which is why the difference between second- and third-person perspectives, as well as that between first person and the others, is important: we are not simply inflicting something on him, but trying to speak to him; and our aim must then be that he comes to accept, as well as to understand, our communication. We might well not expect, as a matter of empirical likelihood, that he will in fact attend or listen to the communication, or allow himself to be persuaded by it: but we must believe that such understanding and acceptance are available to him; and that is why any mental disorder that radically impairs his capacity for reflection must bar his execution (or indeed any form of punishment).

Now this kind of account can explain why we may not execute someone who has become, in a relevant way, "thoroughly insane" since he committed his crimes: but it might also seem to present no threat to Kramer's purgative rationale for the execution of extravagant evil-doers who are still sane and reflectively competent; for we

[38] Kramer, "The Purgative Rationale for the Death Penalty," 392.

[39] See Hoskins and Duff, "Legal Punishment," in the *Stanford Encyclopedia of Philosophy*; https://plato.stanford.edu/archives/win2019/entries/legal-punishment/) s. 5.

can surely intend and hope (even if that is a hope against hope) that the evil-doer will understand his execution for what it is, and will come to see it, and accept it, as the only morally adequate response to his crimes.[40] But what of the offender who is not thus persuaded by the time at which his execution is due: if his execution goes ahead, we have given up that hope of persuading him, and thus denied him the chance of redemption—of redeeming himself by accepting his execution. In ordinary punishments there is always room to hope that the offender will come in the end to accept his punishment as a justified response to his wrongdoing, even after his sentence is completed; but carrying out an execution removes any such hope. Is this something that we can properly do to a human being who retains his "dignity"? Much depends, of course, on what we build into the idea of dignity: but it is plausible to suggest that to treat a person with the dignity due to him must be, *inter alia*, to treat him as someone who is within the reach of reasons (including moral reasons);[41] to treat him as someone who is beyond the reach of reasons and of morality is precisely to deny his dignity as a responsible, "reflective" human being, and to give up both on him and on any hope that the punishment could succeed in its communicative aims.[42]

That might seem too quick: for suppose that the wrongdoer's trial, conviction, and sentence do persuade him of the horror of his deeds and of the Kramerian necessity of his execution; that he comes to see that "no mode of conduct other than the abject undergoing of an execution could satisfactorily atone" for his crimes or "adequately give effect to [his] genuine penitence" (239). It looks as if the argument that I sketched above, while disallowing the execution of an unrepentant evil-doer, would still allow—indeed would mandate—the execution of a repentant evil-doer. Is this paradoxical? I'm not sure that it is, but am equally not happy with a response that leaves me with a justification for the execution of those who come to agree that this is the only way to give adequate effect or expression to their penitence. Furthermore, Kramer might still want to insist that the necessity of removing the "affront" to humanity of the evil-doer's continued existence must set a limit to any continuing attempts to persuade him.

So I come to my third response, concerning that "affront" to humanity and how it is to be removed: is Kramer right to argue that the affront consists in the continued existence of the evil-doer, and thus that death is the only way to remove it? There is another possible answer: that the affront consists in the evil-doer continuing to live without being held properly to account for his wrongs—in his impunity. Thus one avowed aim

[40] Compare the bishop who, during the debates on the death penalty in England in the 1950s, argued in its favor on the grounds that the prospect of execution could itself induce death-cell repentances.

[41] This might go beyond Kramer's quite deflationary conception of human dignity (61), which includes only the rational capacity to "set[] and pursu[e] objectives in ways that are far more sophisticated" than other animals.

[42] If he is not to be executed, how can he be punished? Kramer suggests "lifelong imprisonment-without-parole in conditions of solitary confinement" (236). I do not suggest that this would be acceptable either: depending on the conditions of the confinement (think of an American "supermax" prison) it too might not be a mode of address to a responsible reflective agent. We should note, *contra* Kramer, that such confinement could create radical "normative distance" between the offender and his community, and indeed the rest of humanity (contrast Kramer's comment on banishment, at 234): for he is symbolically as well as materially pushed out from that community—and if his sentence is an LWOP (life without prospect of parole), that exclusion is guaranteed to be permanent. However, we cannot here discuss the question of whether an argument akin to Kramer's could justify such permanent exclusion from one's political community as an, or the only, appropriate response to certain types of crime.

of the creators of the International Criminal Court was "to put an end to impunity for the perpetrators" of crimes consisting in "unimaginable atrocities that deeply shock the conscience of humanity."[43] Now the drafters of the Rome Statute clearly assumed that ending impunity required subjecting those who perpetrated such crimes to punishment (following a fair trial):[44] but they clearly also assumed that this did not require the death penalty, even in the most horrendous cases, since the "applicable penalties" specified by Article 77 of the Rome Statute included imprisonment (which could be for life), forfeitures, and fines, but not death. To which Kramer might reasonably reply, first, that we should not accept as authoritative, or even as a manifestation of the real beliefs of all the parties, the penal provisions resulting from the complex political processes that created the International Criminal Court; and, second, that even if the state parties shared a belief that the death penalty was not necessary, they were wrong—that a proper accounting for the perpetrator's extravagant evils must involve his death, since nothing short of death can adequately mark their implications.[45] So we return to the question of why death is the only morally adequate response to such crimes.

The alternative that Kramer envisages involves making the wrongdoer's life as miserable, burdensome, and isolated as possible: "lifelong imprisonment-without-parole in conditions of solitary confinement," perhaps with an intensification of "the drabness of his confinement" (236). Perhaps, however, that is not the way to think. Suppose instead that the alternative consisted in a protracted, even endless, attempt to bring the wrongdoer to recognize the evil he perpetrated: an attempt that might include life imprisonment, perhaps even periods of solitary confinement, but not simply as ways of isolating him or making him suffer; they would instead be integral parts of a communicative endeavor to convey to him, to persuade him to grasp, the terrible implications of his crimes—an endeavor that of its very nature seeks a response from him. He would still exist in the world: but perhaps what affronts the world is not his existence as such, but an existence in which his wrongdoing is not addressed with adequate seriousness, in which he is allowed not to confront it; and that is not the existence he would have on this account. The point is not that such a communicative endeavor is likely to succeed—we might be empirically fairly confident that it will not: it is, rather, that we can in this way do justice to the seriousness of the offender's wrongdoing without thinking that we must end his life; and in doing so we treat him as someone who retains his dignity as a responsible, reflective human being. If that is right, it follows that a polity does not sully itself, or impair its relationship to humanity, if it refuses to operate a system of capital punishment for such wrongdoers: it would adequately discharge its responsibilities—to the wrongdoer's victims, to its citizens, to humanity, to the wrongdoer himself—if it responded in this kind of way to his crimes.

[43] *Rome Statute of the International Criminal Court* (1998), Preamble.

[44] Thus just before declaring the state parties' determination "to put an end to impunity," the Preamble affirmed their recognition "that the most serious crimes of concern to the international community as a whole must not go unpunished."

[45] Or perhaps they were right, even on Kramer's account: perhaps executions, in the particular context of the International Criminal Court, while still "morally obligatory" for the most extravagantly evil crimes against humanity, would also be "morally impermissible," given the impossibility of ensuring their justice (256–7).

Or suppose—to approach the same point from a different angle—I am inclined to think that a wrongdoer's deeds are so extravagantly terrible that nothing short of his death, or "unflinchingly abject submission to capital punishment" could constitute "a satisfactory form of atonement" for those crimes (238). But then I learn that he found a way to devote his life to reparative penitential activities—a way that I did not imagine: must I say—as I take it Kramer would have me say—that he is wrong, that his efforts are doomed to futility? Or should I instead recognize, first, that his very efforts (sincere, wholehearted, life-consuming) to find a way to make reparation for his crimes show that he is not beyond repentance; and, second, that we cannot say in advance what forms repentance might take?

This then must be my central argument (or claim) against Kramer. Although we should agree that a polity that fails to call such extravagant wrongdoers to appropriate public account commits a serious wrong (a wrong, perhaps, against "humanity"); and that such a wrongdoer's continued existence without being called to appropriate account is an "affront" (perhaps to "humanity"): we need not, and should not, agree that only execution constitutes an adequate accounting. Whether we imagine a repentant offender trying to find (with the help of the polity and of its correctional officials) a suitable way to live out his repentance; or an unrepentant offender whom the polity is still continuing to try to persuade to repentance: it does not seem to me that we are imagining a case in which the person's continued existence is an "affront" to humanity, or in which the polity is failing to treat the wrongdoing with the seriousness it deserves.

Kramer's argument for a "purgative rationale for capital punishment" forces us to think about the moral implications of the most terrible kinds of human wrongdoing, about what it would be to take those implications seriously, and about how political communities could respond to them in ways that treat both those wrongs and their perpetrators with appropriate seriousness; it offers us a way of thinking about these issues that is often illuminating. However, I have argued that it does not show us that capital punishment is "morally obligatory and morally permissible" (179) for those who commit such wrongs.[46]

[46] Thanks to the editors, and to Sandra Marshall, for helpful comments on an earlier draft.

17
Kramer's Razor and the Freedom of Expression

Christopher Kutz[*]

1. Kramer's Razor

Matthew Kramer's razor-sharp theory of freedom of expression offers clarity to what is often confused: the distinction between speech that ought not to be the object of punishment and behavior induced by speech that is properly punishable. Expression thus falls into the ever-expanding Kramer Conceptual Universe—a universe of sharply edged and coherent concepts, manipulable and combinable by intellectually agile philosophers.

Among the virtues of Kramer's work over his career has been its precision and his bracing willingness to defend a clear thesis into every possible corner of exception, across a remarkable range of subjects. But what if Kramer's signal clarity could sometimes be a vice as well as a virtue, because the world is irreducibly complex? What if we actively depend for our substantive political freedom on messy borders between protected speech and unprotected acts? Kramer's ambition is laudable, namely to ensure that all who venture to use speech in politics can be assured that, so long as they do not cross certain lines, their verbal autonomy is protected because of the constitutive relation of expression to equal warranted self-respect. Clarity about the bounds of speech protects individuals from opaque authority, and thus maximizes the self-respect that comes with being able to chart one's course through political shoals with precision. We can see this most clearly with respect to the absolutist defense of academic or political speech, which can assert any claim, or make any factual representation, without fear of reprisal. Such does not describe the current world of the university, where a mistake of respect can lead to a Kafka-esque process of apology and expulsion.

But matters become more complicated when speech turns in the direction authorities label "sedition" or "incitement" and that its speakers label "advocacy." Seditious speech is speech aimed at subverting legal authority, and perforce undermining law. The clear lines of speech endorsed by Kramer protect the rights of the authorities to police the speech that challenges them, by giving them a number of arguments according to which they can claim that though they target speech, they do not do so

[*] C. William Maxeiner Distinguished Professor of Law, Jurisprudence & Social Policy Program, School of Law, University of California at Berkeley. I am delighted to contribute to this collection honoring Matt, one of the most interesting scholars writing in contemporary moral, legal, and political philosophy. Although I have not had the pleasure of being Matt's student or colleague, I have admired his work for decades and enjoyed his hospitality. I hope I do not abuse that hospitality by offering, in the spirit of engagement, a sustained disagreement. I am grateful to the editors for helpful comments.

Christopher Kutz, *Kramer's Razor and the Freedom of Expression* In: *Without Trimmings*. Edited by: Mark McBride and Visa AJ Kurki, Oxford University Press. © Mark McBride and Visa AJ Kurki 2022. DOI: 10.1093/oso/9780198868866.003.0017

qua speech, but *qua* something else eminently restrictable. So long as the authorities can plausibly identify the object of their concern as not "inherently communicative," they are home free. And so here, I will argue, some unclarity is needed, to unsettle the authorities and reclaim the space of rebellious possibility for individual subjects. Put otherwise, the logical clarity of Kramer's principle is what renders it risky for liberal democratic service. Here I focus on the case of incitement, as a way of showing why Kramer might want to dull his razor if he wants to protect freedom. But my argument will involve examining a number of other cases where Kramer (and virtually all theorists) agree that speech may be limited.

2. Communicative-Independence and the Problem of Incitement

Kramer defends a very simple proposition: "the freedom of expression is perfectly consistent with legal prohibitions on various types of misdeeds that can be perpetrated through communicative conduct"[1] (I, 1). On its face, Kramer's claim about restriction is both obvious and surprising. It is obvious insofar as a great deal of conventional criminal activity occurs by way of communication—the highwayman's "your money or your life" or the kited check or the stock swindle all take place thanks to the words emitted by the criminal. But it is surprising insofar as Kramer also insists that he defends a position of "absolutism," suitably defined, about free speech (I, 3). So Kramer is an absolutist, someone who brooks no compromise or exception to a principle of freedom of expression, but who accepts that citizens are properly politically unfree to engage in large swathes of conduct through expression. The puzzle is not, of course, why a defender of free speech would make exceptions for speech-dependent criminality; but rather on what basis could such a view be labeled an absolutist in the first place? Resolving this essentially semantic puzzle set by Kramer will enable us to see some of the substantive concerns his proposal engenders.

Kramer considers himself an absolutist thanks to a distinction he elaborates in Chapter 3 between "communication-dependent" and "communication-independent" forms of conduct or wrongdoing. This distinction allows him to maintain what he calls an "unswayable" principle: that no system of governance "can ever legitimately prohibit or restrict forms of speech qua modes of communication." So long as the principle of freedom of expression is restricted to the domain of communication-dependent conduct, its sway can rest absolute, or so Kramer argues. This, of course, is to place a great deal of weight on a fine distinction. Can it bear that weight?

By "communication-independence," Kramer means to point to the wrong-making features of a situation or course of conduct, and whether they inhere in the speech itself, as it were, or in some set of (presumably physical) causes and effects that can be cleaved off from the speech. Kramer does not, in fact, offer an explicit definition of this key term, but instead adumbrates it by way of two examples (III, 66–7). The first is the old friend of the (mendacious) shout of "Fire!" in a crowded theatre. Such

[1] All parenthetical references are to Kramer *(Freedom of Expression as Self-Restraint)* by chapter and page number.

an utterance can be penalized because the target of the penalty is an intent to cause "a perilous public disturbance"; and the "wrong-making" feature of that intent can be characterized as independent from any objective of communicating thoughts about the incidence of fires in local theaters. The latter communication could not be penalized under the principle. Kramer acknowledges that the means of instigating the disturbance is obviously communicatively-dependent; what matters for the principle is whether it is possible to describe the concern animating the prohibition in a way that does not make reference to communication.

In his second exemplary definition, Kramer relies heavily on Mill's example of the firebrand orator in front of the grain dealer, raising a crowd to a passionate view that corn dealers are robbers of the poor. For Kramer, as for Mill, such speech is properly punishable as criminal incitement and subject to sanction. Although the wrongdoer's wrong comes about essentially through the communicative power of speech, what makes that speech wrong is that it has a tendency to cause others to commit physical acts of violence upon the grain dealer. As Kramer says, the wrong is the lynching, and lynchings are wrong whether done silently and spontaneously, or when done at the urging of a rabble-rouser. One might compare the orator to an opera singer who decides to shatter someone's crystal goblet maliciously by singing a high aria.[2] The fact that some specific words (or notes) rather than others were used to break the glass is irrelevant to the moral matter at hand: wanton destruction of fine glassware. We handle the highwayman similarly: although communication (perhaps even with a fictitious gun) is how he gets the purse, the wrong for which he is punished is the taking of the purse, not the words he uttered. He might well have uttered the same words in a play, or shouted them from a rooftop, and no wrong would have occurred, no conduct to be criminalized.

Or is this right? The highwayman and the firebrand seem to involve two rather different categories of conduct. The firebrand's words are like a physical push to the mob, transmitting its force ultimately to the grain dealer. As Kramer says, the speech just is the orator's way of physically participating in the lynching, and it is easy to imagine alternative pathways to the same criminal conduct. But the highwayman, especially one unarmed, might have no non-communicative way of getting the purse, assuming he cannot overwhelm his target without a firearm. Moreover, it seems a mistake to say that the wrong committed by the highwayman just is the taking of the purse, for there would be a criminal act even if the purse were empty or dropped in a drain before being handed over (in which case the crime would be an attempted robbery). If done by threat, the wrong seems to lie in the speech itself, and in the communication of a threat. Of course, what the law seeks to avoid is a consequence of that communication—the engendering of fear, or the coerced transmission of property. Kramer appeals to a distinction between communication as (mere) means, and communication as the target itself of the penalty. But if the target of the penalty just is the uptake of a threat, this is a hard distinction to maintain—and quite different from a consequent lynching or panicked exit. It would seem that even in Kramer's

[2] It's not clear whether an opera singer has ever successfully done so, without amplification, but the television show *Mythbusters* did find a rock singer who, with a suitably imperfect glass, was able to shatter it with his unamplified voice. https://youtu.be/aU2qSseA9N8. Just thought you should know.

own example, the reed of "communicative-independence" has bent very close to the ground.

Other examples explored by Kramer also seem hard to defend as anything other than exceptions to freedom of expression. Solicitation of a complex crime, not to be engaged in imminently, is clearly subject to prohibition in any legal system. And yet the solicitation itself is inherently communicative, operating by way of persuasion and cooperative planning, and so unlike the firebrand's working of emotional-causal levers. While some crimes solicited may involve physical acts or harms, others might involve yet more communication, such as soliciting a witness to give false testimony. For that matter, as Kramer notes, the criminalization of perjury itself seems to be an exception to the freedom of expression, since the crime itself is purely communicative. Ditto for civil liability for defamation: "Instead, the bestowal of protection by that principle upon some mode of expressive activity hinges on whether that mode of activity is constitutive of misconduct that is generally perpetrated through non-expressive endeavors as well as through expressive endeavors" (III, 74).

Kramer's response to such examples thus involves two possible moves. With respect to solicitation, he suggests that the communication is continuous with the crime or wrong, either as part of a physical chain of cause and effect, or as a matter of logic. Only if the expression is conceptually separable from the crime, not part of its explanation, will it be protected. "Because an act of solicitation is so much more concretely focused than is an act of mere advocacy, the former—unlike the latter—is *subsumed* [my emphasis] into the wrongdoing to which it designedly gives rise" (III, 67). When they are separable as general "advocacy"—for instance, someone posting pamphlets insisting that "property is theft"—they are subject to protection as free expression, Kramer insists. But when they are "definite" in their aims, such utterances can be charged as criminal solicitation.

I confess I am puzzled by this seemingly communication-dependent distinction between solicitation-speech that is part of a crime, and advocacy-speech that is not. As Kramer acknowledges, solicitation can be remote in time, and involve the independent judgment of the person solicited. If his distinction between utterances that are part of the crime and those that are not is to hold, the difference cannot therefore be temporal remoteness. Nor can it be generality, since such a distinction would be subject to abuse ("Will no one rid me of this turbulent priest?").

In such cases, context can supply particularity. It is open to Kramer to insist that the meaning of an utterance is supplied both by pragmatics and semantics. But such a response would seem to cross categories, since what is needed is a sharp distinction between utterances that are "subsumed" into an ensuing crime and utterances that are not. Here we might wonder whether there is a difference in principle to be found between the militant agitator who writes a pamphlet saying, "Will someone do justice to these greedy banks?" and the crime boss who lets the word go out that he would be pleased to see some banks knocked off.

The difference between protected advocacy and unprotected incitement or solicitation cannot be specificity of intent. Criminal law generally requires what Anglo-Americans call a "specific intent" for the crime of solicitation, in the sense that the solicitor must positively intend that a crime of a specific sort be committed. But people can be convicted of solicitation without knowing the concrete details of the person they are engaging or exactly what means they will use. Nor can the difference lie in criminality of purpose, since the activist may hope to instigate acts of law-breaking. When those acts take place, inspired by the anarchist's pamphlets, there will be as direct a causal chain running from utterance to theft as in the mob boss's indirection. Indeed, in one of the most notorious incitement cases in recent years, against the Rwandan RTLM radio station for propagating genocidal violence, the broadcasts involved no explicit open wishes at all, but merely inflammatory descriptions of fictitious anti-Hutu plots, and descriptions of Tutsis as cockroaches.[3] While there are disputes about the magnitude of the effect of these broadcasts on the ensuing violence, there is little question that despite their generality, the broadcasts supplied a piece in the causal chain, and that criminal liability for the defendants was generally appropriate. One might try to defend the RTLM broadcasters from liability on grounds of communicative generality, as indeed their lawyers did. But, assuming incitement to be a crime, the distinction cannot be made out on purely formal grounds.

The trouble is that Kramer's distinction between communication that is "subsumed" by the following crime and those independent is a conclusory distinction, not a logical or semantic one. A prosecutor will charge and a jury convict the crime boss on his utterance, not because it is somehow linked to a communicatively-independent crime, but because we understand the crime boss to be operating within a structure that gives his utterances the force of commands therein: it will (likely) be acted upon once uttered (or so presents a danger), because of the broader set of norms and roles inhabited by boss and underling. The judgment that the utterance is subsumed in the consequent crime just is the judgment that liability is appropriately pinned on the crime boss. We excuse—in a liberal society—the anarchist's pamphlet, not because resulting crimes are communicatively-dependent, nor because the anarchist's words are, or might be, suitably general. Rather, we protect the utterance because we understand it to be a general message conveyed not as command but potential persuasion, in a community of rational equals; and protecting their status (as audience members) entails protecting the speaker as well, even at some risk of incidental crime. Or we do not protect the anarchist, as many states have not, because we fear the effect of words upon their audience, and we (those in power) lack confidence in the conformity of the audience to the norms prescribed by the state.

The distinction, in other words, is a substantive political judgment, one sensitive to both the facticity of a polity's past and present, and either optimistic or pessimistic about its future. No work is done by a formal criterion. Contrary to Kramer, who apparently endorses the liability of RTLM, if RTLM's communications should be penalized, it will have to be because the risk posed by the speech (viewed *ex post*) to the civil liberties of Tutsis was too great, weighed against the low value of its content, and not because it is somehow itself "part of" the genocide (VI, 266–7). Otherwise there will be no way to protect those instances and types of speech that must be protected for the freedom of expression principle to have any content at all. For example, pro-Hutu speech in a political campaign might have had a similarly predictable causal long-term effect on Tutsi civil liberties, but restricting such speech would be tantamount to

[3] Nahimana et al. (Media case), International Criminal Tribunal for Rwanda (ICTR-99-52)(2007).

shutting down the political arena altogether. (I shall argue below that Kramer's overall, admirable framework of liberal theory can supply precisely the argument I have just offered, but on pain of acknowledging the weighing and value-balancing at stake.)

Or to take another example, as current as the writing of this chapter: an American President who urges a crowd of supporters to march on the legislature in order to be "strong," "show strength," and "fight like hell" to "stop" the certification of the election of his opponent, *might* be thought to be merely engaging in the usual political tropes of a rally, and so to be engaged in protected, "hot" speech. But when it is clear that the President knows the crowd includes many who are armed, whose prior communications have evinced a desire for violent action, who then engage in violent action while the President himself watches on television and refrains from coming to the aid of the legislature, then potential criminal liability for such speech would seem to be necessary to the survival of the state of law itself. An ambiguous message, with no evidence of violent intent, might have led to the same destruction; as might a more specific speech, delivered in prior, calmer times. If we decide to protect these latter forms of speech (as the *Brandenburg* test does), but not the actual speech delivered to the hot crowd, that is because we judge that the dangers posed by immediate exhortation outweigh the dangers of reduced scope for political rhetoric. Nothing metaphysical here.

3. Perjury, Libel, Advertising, and More Problems of Communicative Independence

So the first move, of distinguishing communications that are "part of" the prohibited conduct from those that are not part of it, but merely advocate it, fails for lack of a non-conclusory basis with which to make the mereological judgment. Kramer's second move, deployed in the case of perjury and elsewhere, is to distinguish between cases where the wrong can itself be committed in a way free of communication, and cases where it cannot. In the former cases, he argues, expression is only contingently related to the crime, and so the expression can be restricted. Of perjury, Kramer says "the misconduct constituted by the utterance of such statements is communication-independent and is therefore susceptible to being prohibited by a system of governance in compliance with that principle. A law that forbids any acts of perjury can be morally legitimate if and only if it is directed against such acts as endeavors to undermine the integrity of legal proceedings rather than as instances of communicative conduct" (III, 70).

Kramer's general test, recall, is to ask whether we can imagine producing the wrongful effect without communication; if so, then expression is not being targeted *qua* expression, but *qua* something else. So long, in other words, as the targeted "wrongdoing ... comprises communicative instances and non-communicative instances alike," it is irrelevant that in this particular instance, communicative means were chosen (III, 66–7). In the case of perjury, so long as we can imagine a trial corrupted through non-communicative means—for instance by someone releasing a hallucinogenic gas in the jury room, or a police-"thrown" gun introduced as evidence—we can see that the perjurer's testimony is being singled out as a token of a larger non-communicative type of epistemic corruption. Kramer adopts a similar strategy for libel: though libels are routinely committed through verbal expression, they can be committed in other ways, such as by displaying embarrassing photographs. If the non-verbal act-token would be punished as well, then Kramer believes that the law does not target expression *qua* expression, but expression *qua* something else. And so the principle of freedom of expression is untouched, insofar as the expressive character of the act is merely a collateral consequence of the legal protection of court testimony, reputation, etc. Of course there is reason in Kramer's point here. It might be possible, for instance, to commit a murder by shouting "Boo!" at someone standing at the edge of a subway track. But prosecuting the murder would be only incidentally related to the exclamation, and so consistent with Kramer's principle.

But does Kramer's principle actually explain how states can repress perjury and libel can be repressed, without their also being exceptions to free expression? I have my doubts, for two reasons. First, unlike a murder that can be executed with a verbal exhalation, perjury and libel rely on inherently expressive forms of conduct. Perjury is not only interference with a legal proceeding, but the intentional arousal of misplaced confidence in a witness's own statements. Indeed, as Kramer notes in criticism of Rubenfeld (III, 73–4), the intentional and malicious aspect of perjury is essential to its definition, and not merely the falsity of the statement. There really would appear to be no non-expressive way of engaging in precisely that conduct, and thus no non-expressive wrong of the same type. There is, to be sure, the closely related crime of fabricating or tampering with evidence, which implicates the same value of truth-seeking in trial, without being straightforwardly classified as an instance of communication.[4] Both perjury and evidence-tampering are instances of the genre of obstruction of justice. But it is notable that perjury is punished substantially more severely.[5] This is likely because the successful perjurer trades precisely on the testimonial good will extended to the explicit communications of a witness, and so perjury reflects a more intimate betrayal of that good will than, say, a bag of drugs. The extra severity of perjury's punishment, then, reflects its explicitly communicative character and the special harm done by willfully false expression in the juridical context. If that isn't punishment of expression *qua* expression, I'm not sure what is.

This leads to a more general concern about Kramer's "*qua*" strategy. As I have said above, Kramer's argument relies on showing that he can explain apparent exceptions to his rule as sanctions of something other than expression—for example, obstruction of justice, direct participation in crime. But the distinction between protected expression qua expression and unprotected expression qua illegal contribution to criminality remains obscure. If a government punishes the expression of an ethical or political belief, for instance "This government hates Black lives," or "Military induction violates

[4] On the other hand, the deliberate presentation of fabricated or misleading evidence does seem like a species of communication along Gricean or Searlean lines, since it involves the intentional presentation of some physical token, aimed at inducing a belief in the recipient, and—typically—with the reflexive intention that the presenter's intention be recognized by the recipient.

[5] In California, from where I write, fabricating evidence has a maximum sentence of three years, perjury four. In the United Kingdom, perjury is regarded as one of the most serious forms of perverting the course of justice, with a maximum sentence of seven years; it appears that evidence tampering, though susceptible to life imprisonment as a common law offense, is actually punished in the recommended range of between ten and thirty-six months.

the 13th Amendment," then it is clearly targeting expression *qua* expression. But it is also presumably targeting that expression because of anticipated causal, behavioral consequences, for example, disrespect shown to police forces, vandalism of government property, insubordination of active troops, or delegitimation of the government itself.

At fear of pointing out the obvious, states always target expression for either support or punishment because of non-expressive circumstances. If Kramer's principle is to serve as a critical standard for state practice, it should help us decide when support, neutrality, or punishment is appropriate. But, returning to the advocacy/incitement distinction, I cannot discern any difference in that respect between the (rightful) punishment of perjurious speech and the wrongful punishment of seditious or inflammatory speech. Any of those consequences can presumably be achieved through non-expressive means, and so it would seem appropriate, on Kramer's argument, that both types could be sanctioned. Troops could be stirred to insubordination by military defeats or debacles, resistance to police could be encouraged by provocateurs, and so forth. The fact that the object or likely effect of the communication could be separately targeted by law, or that the act can be subsumed into a joint communicative and non-communicative category, seems irrelevant to the question whether the expressive side of the grouping should be free from sanction. It is virtually always possible to show that the governmental objective is unrelated to speech. Therefore all the work has to be done on balancing the burden on speech against that interest. There is no categorical way to protect speech as such while acknowledging the state's power to pursue interests that incidentally affect communicative media.

Kramer's solution to the problem that a non-communicative objective may always be asserted seems to be that one can look to prosecutorial motive (II, 83ff.). In some specific cases he mentions, this strategy does show that the expressive conduct targeted by prosecution under a law of general application is indeed targeted because of its communicative import, as in the US prosecution of draft card burners (upheld, according to Kramer, on the mistaken grounds that there was a reasonable, non-communicative purpose involved in ensuring that all young men were in possession of their draft cards); or in the (also mistakenly sustained) prosecution of Bud Davis for displaying a wrecked truck in protest of police conduct, in defiance of a local ordinance requiring disposal of junked vehicles. Both acts were singled out because of their communicative character.[6] I agree with Kramer that both decisions seem mistaken—but not because we properly see the state instead as exclusively concerned with their communicative character. In the draft case, the state concern was the encouragement of non-compliance with the draft; and in the *Davis* case, it was presumably with concern that leaving the display would engender further disrespect for law enforcement, as well as the other purposes of the ordinance, including maintenance of property values and eliminating attractive nuisances dangerous to children. These are appropriate interests for the state to protect through its laws in many forms, such as mandating draft registration, protecting the integrity of the draft exemption process (not that the US government actually did police the exemption system carefully!), providing low-cost

[6] See *U.S. v. O'Brien* 391 U.S. 467 (1968) (upholding sanction for burning a draft card); and *Davis v. Norman*, 555 F.2nd 189 (1977) (sustaining prosecution under nuisance ordinance).

haul-away services for junk cars, imposing tort liability on individuals. And indeed the state would have been within its rights to proscribe certain forms of communication in relation to these interests, for example confiscating advertisements for fraudulent medical deferments, or for instructions for sabotaging city tow trucks.

Rather, what offends about the *O'Brien* and *Davis* cases is that the speech targeted by authorities specifically questions the legitimacy of those authorities themselves. While it is understandable that authorities should want to protect their own legitimacy, a liberal democracy constrained by the freedom of expression will dramatically restrict officials' ability to do so. State action in these cases was wrong, not because they targeted an inherently communicative object, but because they targeted a communicative means to a non-communicative object forbidden to state authorities. That forbidden object is discussion of the grounds of state legitimacy itself. It is often, and incorrectly, said that the liberal is the person who cannot take their own side in an argument. Liberals can defend freedom against unfreedom. They cannot, on pain of contradiction, limit discussion of the basis of state authority itself. The contradiction would consist in, on the one hand, accepting as foundational the principle that state authority is granted by, never demanded of, free individuals exercising their sovereign reason; and on the other hand restricting the deployment of reason by those same individuals.

I will return to how Kramer might properly defend a rougher-edged version of his principle below, but first let us look at his remaining example of a putative exception to the exceptionless principle: advertisement of illegalities. Kramer says:

> When for example somebody advertises the availability of children as prostitutes for the gratification of paedophiles, he or she is deliberately bringing about—or is seeking to bring about—the imminent occurrence of heinous crimes. Any advertisement of that kind is one of the initial stages in the occurrence of those crimes, and as such it can legitimately be subjected to sanctions by the prevailing system of governance. Someone who undergoes those appropriate sanctions is punished not for expressing odious ideas but instead for participating directly in the perpetration of wicked abuse. (III, 90)

This is a repeat of the first strategy, deployed initially against the firebrand or criminal solicitor: the communicative act somehow merges metaphysically into the resulting crime, and so the legitimacy of punishing the crime extends to the legitimacy of punishing the advertisement. In the case of the firebrand orator, whose words act like a spark to the tinder of prole excitement, there is some point to this claim—the orator is effectively the assailant, the mob his arms. The crime boss who "asks" a favor of an underling is, similarly, relying on a dependable causal mechanism to instigate the crime. If we look from a distance, there is little difference between pulling a physical trigger and triggering a hitman. But we have already noted problems with more distant, or less commandeering, forms of criminal inducement, and all the more so with the criminalization of attempted inducement. Criminal law's own metaphysics make Kramer's assimilation difficult. To take his example, the crime of child sexual abuse generally requires as conduct that the defendant engages in sexual touching of a minor. By contrast, the crime of child sex trafficking (18 U.S.C. §1591) requires (among other possibilities) the conduct of advertising a child for commercial sex work, in reckless disregard of the fact that the child has been coerced to perform such work. The advertisement is, of course, neither a necessary nor a sufficient condition for the criminal sexual activity to take place. While successful commission of the trafficking may lead to successful commission of sexual abuse, it is of course possible to complete the second crime without the first occurring (so that it is not even a matter of an attempted trafficking). There is no non-rhetorical way that advertisement can be thought conceptually or causally "subsumed" by sexual assault (or by coerced trafficking), since the elements of proof are wholly distinct.

Put more abstractly, the question is how to sort and individuate wrongs. At a certain level of description, all wrongs might be thought to blend together—for example, crimes against the state, or crimes against persons, or attacks on the public trust. And within each broad grouping, communicative and non-communicative instances might be found—in which case Kramer's principle will restrict no occasions of liability, since all might be deemed cases of communicative independence. Alternatively each instance of wrongdoing might be individuated by its specific characteristics—so verbal encouragement to another person to hire a child prostitute would a different type of act from tacit encouragement by way of presenting the child directly, in which case there could be liability only for the latter. The test itself can do nothing, since it rests on an necessarily under-specified theory of act-individuation—necessarily because the categories we sort various instances into will reflect a variety of heterogenous substantive concerns about maximizing freedom, preventing risky behaviors, and responding symbolically to harm.[7]

So the subsumption strategy fails. If any act is inherently communicative, it is advertisement. *Contra* Kramer, the advertiser may not be seeking to bring about the imminent occurrence of the heinous crime (though the person who pays the advertiser may be doing so). The advertiser can be fully pleased with the communicative performance itself, independent of any criminal outcome therefrom. Perhaps the advertiser views the advertisement as artwork, or commentary on a corrupt society, or hopes that anyone responding to the advertisement will in fact be arrested. It is a distinct wrong from the pedophilic crime itself. An unstinting commitment to freedom of expression would demand the freedom to express oneself thus. But such an unstinting commitment would have to accept the moral cost of supporting, even non-deliberately, a market for sexual abuse, and a form of moral complicity (if not quite criminal complicity) in the resulting acts.[8] Kramer is right to resist unrestrained freedom to advertise illegal services. Alas, doing so involves recognizing limits to the principle of freedom of expression.

The difficulty of Kramer's position is well shown by his treatment of a *counter*-counterexample: in his view, the illegitimacy of regulating cigarette advertisements (III, 40–1). It would seem that, per Kramer's logic, a government intent on reducing the physical incidence of smoking could justify restricting cigarette advertising

[7] I am grateful to Mark McBride for this suggestion.

[8] By hypothesis, a disinterested one-off advertiser lacks the specific intent that child sexual abuse take place. This distinguishes the advertiser from the solicitor, and locates them doctrinally with the mere "facilitator," who provides the copy machine or other technology for the illicit business.

on that same basis—just as it can restrict the sale of cigarettes to the young, or ban smoking altogether, or tax it heavily. Its object (smoking cessation or public health) is communication-independent. But Kramer rejects this argument, not on the grounds that advertising cannot be causally linked to smoking, but because the government has, thus far, not formally prohibited smoking as such: "Those restrictions [on advertising] have not been directed against the advertisements *qua* instances of communication-independent wrongdoing, since the advertisements are not constitutive of any such wrongdoing" (III, 92). But this is only because there is no legal wrong in which the advertisement can participate. We can conceptually separate the act that the restriction seeks to hinder from the advertisement as well as we can for the other restrictions Kramer endorses. The relevant criticism to apply to the state is that unless and until it has had the gumption to render smoking illegal, it should not be intruding on its subjects' capacities to weigh for themselves the pros and cons of smoking. That position, whether or not ultimately defensible, is, boringly, a matter of weighing the value of citizen autonomy against the public health and paternalistic concerns underlying the restriction, and in consideration of whether less speech-restrictive means might accomplish the same result.[9] Kramer may be right to think that the permissibility of the communicative restrictions depends on the legal status of the ultimate object of those restrictions, but not because it cleaves the restriction along the line of the inherently communicative versus communicatively independent.

4. Can Self-Respect be Represented by an Absolute Principle?

Let me propose a new start, this time focusing on the advocacy/incitement line. I believe that Kramer's overall warranted self-respect theory provides the material for defending extensive freedom of advocacy, even if his principle will not cleanly carve the two categories apart. We must reckon with the fact that there is an inevitably conclusory character to our determinations of what is protected by a principle of freedom of expression, in the sense that its particular applications (what is protected) will be a product of substantive political morality, not conceptual definition.

Kramer rests his principle of freedom of expression in what he says is:

> the paramount responsibility of any [system of governance] to bring about the political and social and economic conditions wherein a hearty sense of self-respect can be warranted for every member of the society over which the system presides. (IV, 144)

These are recognizable, compelling grounds for freedom of expression: they combine, as Kramer says, an individual ethical concern of self-perfection adumbrated in classical Stoicism, with the Kantian-egalitarian commitments of Rawlsian political philosophy. Kramer's argument, as I understand it, is: The moral status of the individual is placed before that of either state or social group; the state's function is enabling

[9] I argue for the contrary position below, in section 5.

individuals to live valuable lives by their own lights. Living a valuable life is a matter of having both the material and psychological resources that enable you to imagine and strive for goals and objectives that realize your full range of cognitive and affective capacities. A sense of (objectively warranted) self-respect is clearly central to individuals' willingness and capacity to form and act on such projects; people who doubt the worth of their own lives or interests are psychologically paralyzed, and motivated to tear down the aspirations of others.[10] If we understand "governance" to be a normative, functional condition, aiming at a defensible object, then governance directed at creating the conditions of warranted self-respect aims at a good that, in effect, justifies the project of governance itself. Hence it is a reasonable "paramount responsibility," one which can be understood to underlay a range of specific policies.

Warranted self-respect cannot itself, as Kramer says, be the direct object of government guarantee or voucher. But we have clear knowledge of the conditions that can foster self-respect, or undermine it. Lack of adequate nutrition, health care, housing, or income make self-respect nearly impossible to obtain. Given a further liberal constraint that governments treat all citizens as beings of equal value, they must thereby ensure that no individual is deprived of conditions in which warranted self-respect is possible. From this, says Kramer, the role of a system of free expression is straightforward, in particular the role of a principle of viewpoint neutrality. A policy of state censorship or distorted communication is one that degrades the capacity of individuals to judge for themselves among conflicting ethical claims, and thereby prevents what Kramer calls the citizens' development of their own liberal ethos of affirmation:

> Those laws or actions thus presumptuously supplant the judgments of individuals about the ideas and sentiments conveyed by communications that are not constitutive of any communication-independent wrongdoing, and they implicitly or explicitly rest on the premise that the society governed by the officials is not ethically strong enough to counteract any untoward effects that could ultimately be caused by those communications. (IV, 148)

In short, a decent system of governance is obliged to do two broad categories of things: it must create the material conditions that enable citizens to live valuable lives; and then it must back out of efforts to regulate those lives directly. Call this a strategy of two-level perfectionism. As Kramer wisely notes, most policies of censorship take root in a state's failure to protect the material level. Fearing revolt by the masses, it bans revolutionary pamphlets. Fearing racial or ethnic violence, it bans bigoted speech. Censorship is the politics of failure, says Kramer.

My concern with Kramer's overall approach lies not in its underlying values, but its attempt to finesse the tradeoffs that must inevitably occur. Governance in our fallen condition almost invariably takes place from a posture of recovery from previous policy failure, or at least inadequacy. The conditions of revolt, temptation to

[10] Of course, people with *un*warranted senses of self-respect may be very energetically motivated to pursue their projects, as perhaps is true of the 45th President of the United States (though a fear-reaction to a lack of self-respect is just as plausible). But fostering unwarranted self-respect cannot be the ground for state action or the redistributive policies that are needed.

criminality, and socially-condoned forms of racial oppression and discrimination are always present, each with terrible material effects. As I have elaborated above, the state is always in a credible position to assert that, regrettably, restrictions on certain expression must be enacted, because the communications present too great a danger to legitimate non-communicative objects of state concern. If this is so, then defining the principle of freedom of expression as applying only to the realm of the exclusively communicative is, effectively, to rule out its application to almost any significant cases of real or contemplated censorship, beyond either the (utterly technologically infeasible) program of anti-pornography activists, whose concern is sexual objectification as such (and not just rape-reduction), or Holocaust-denial statutes in states like Canada where, arguably, there is little risk of anti-Semitism motivating an actually dangerous political party.

Take a more contemporary example. The summer of 2020 has seen enormous protests around the world, but especially in the United States, under the Black Lives Matter (BLM) banner, focusing on the lethal dangers to, especially, Black people from racist policing. Among the chants and signs waved were many saying "Fuck the police" and "All Cops are Bastards." Physical attacks on police, while rare during the protests, did occur, against the backdrop of the killing of five Dallas police officers in 2016 and wounding of nine others by an anti-racist sniper. The goals of the BLM protestors, while varied, included a demand for profound structural change in American society, not just in the funding and deployment of police, but in eradicating various forms of structural racism within the American economy and government.

I take it as a fixed point of freedom of speech (as well as, in the United States, of First Amendment jurisprudence) that even the most pointed chants and signs of the protestors are absolutely protected, notwithstanding the real risk that these expressions, by their content, make anti-police violence more likely; and indirectly that they might contribute simultaneously to the under-policing of Black communities, and the violence that results therefrom The night-time curfews, often imposed with the defensible object of impeding opportunistic looting and violence, themselves stood on a knife-edge of legal and moral permissibility, insofar as they also had the effect of dissipating the energy of the protests.

On a Kramerian view, it would be wrong to prohibit such expression, because the capacity to form and articulate arguments about the proper limits on policing, and on the remediation of racism in American society, is a core attribute of warranted self-respect for citizens alert to the historical and current injustices of their society. A state that does not respect its citizens' capacity, as addressors and addressees alike, to determine the bounds of state authority demeans those citizens. But Kramer's conceptual razor cannot save the speech categorically from the state's legitimate objectives of protecting lives and property. The fact that the effects of the speech cannot be precisely known and predicted in advance doesn't loosen, as a metaphysical matter, the connection between the expression and its effects. As I have argued above, we cannot avoid evaluating the tradeoff, of a bedrock commitment to a principle of respecting political agency, against the risks of how that agency might manifest. Regardless of the state's sincerity in focusing on non-communicative objects, we must protect that political speech up to the—always vaguely foreseen—threshold of significant risk of imminent violence. Only at that point, and only when other defensive measures have been exhausted, can a protesting crowd be cleared. Sadly, the same is true with respect to the speech rights of legally but obtrusively armed zealots protesting "fascist" public health measures. Only when the speech veers into direct criminality, such as compassing the kidnapping and murder of a sitting state governor, can the speech be restricted, its speakers jailed.[11] Up until that point, speakers have a right to voice, and listeners to entertain, a range of views, even heatedly put, about the possible tradeoffs of health versus freedom of commerce.

Here is the point in positive form: We, as subjects and citizens, think of ourselves as individuals and as members of a polity. Our warranted basis of self-respect stems from our sense of ourselves as agents of our lives, both individual and collective. To be self-respecting members of a democratic polity, we must understand ourselves as participants in a project of collective will-formation, creation of a Rousseauean *moi commun*.[12] The conditions under which that is possible include various institutions for channeling and determining that collective will within state institutions, turning it into law, and institutions and avenues for criticizing and objecting to law that are external to the state. Democratic legitimacy and warranted (collective) self-respect thus go hand-in-hand: the conditions of legitimacy just are the conditions in which individuals can, as equals, understand themselves to be participants in shaping their own political world, albeit sometimes as winners, sometimes as losers.

Kramer's view of free expression is attractive in not resting solely on the shoulders of addressors nor of addressees (though it is perhaps appropriately tilted in favor of the latter). The conditions of self-respect for us as democratic agents indeed call upon us to play both roles. A democracy of few speakers and many listeners risks demagoguery; a democracy of many speakers and few listeners falls into *Life of Brian*-esque factionalism. We participate in the formation of a collective will when we speak, listen, deliberate, and then act. And thus, Kramer's principle countenances neither the silencing of the new firebrand on the scene, nor confiscation of the works of Hobbes, Mill, or Marx from the citizenry as a whole. Modern BLM marchers have a right both to the words of Malcolm X and Alicia Garza, even if only Garza is here to speak them herself. To restrict either of those sources of perspective, information, and passionate engagement is to subvert the capacity of citizens to reckon with the limits of what can be done to eradicate racism.

A further attractive feature of Kramer's free expression foundationalism is that, unlike a more strictly Meiklejohnian view, it protects both political and non-political expression. I have given, above, my brief Kramerian version of how freedom of expression secures the conditions of collective self-respect (or, rather, individual self-respect for those who also see themselves as members of a political collective). In the purely individual context, the forum of familiar Millian self-realization, the argument is even stronger. Becoming who we are is a complex interplay of mimicry, self-discovery, and self-definition. Becoming the selves we want to be, and acquiring the values we want to have, requires a range of possible models and exemplars, and conditions in which it becomes meaningful to say "I choose *this*!" We are both orator and audience;

[11] To be sure, there should be no restriction on laws prohibiting civilians going lethally armed into public disturbances, even if the point of going armed is itself communicative.

[12] Rousseau (1762): Bk. I, ch. 6.

self-respect demands freedom in both roles. This model of speech grounds a profound constraint on governmental restrictions of both fiction and fact, art and representation, restrictions whose effect would be to restrict the models and values we can make and emulate. *Contra* Meiklejohn, we do not need to read *Ulysses* to know how to vote; we need to read it (or have the right to read it) to know how to be.[13]

5. Kramerian Foundations for a Non-Absolute Principle

Thus far I have mainly paraphrased Kramer's foundations, and acknowledged their strengths. These are individualistic, deontological footings, and so not given to simple tradeoffs with other values, or grounded in empirical hand-waving about the likely effects of different kinds of institutions in relation to such abstractions as truth or welfare. A governmental restriction is either supportive of, neutral toward, or undermines the conditions under which individuals can rightly understand themselves to be the agents of their individual and collective lives. But have I therefore backed myself into Kramer's corner, in which I must either defend an absolutism that countenances no communicative restrictions whatsoever, or rely on a conceptual division that nominally preserves the absolutism at the principle, but at the cost of ad hocery? I think not.

Let us look first at the advocacy/incitement line at the core of these issues, always the hardest to draw for anyone concerned, on the one hand, with preserving a people's right to seriously contemplate revolution; and on the other hand, with preserving the lives and liberties of the bystanders or obstacles to said revolution. The *Brandenburg* test Kramer (and US constitutional law) endorses, which requires the government to show that incendiary speech is both intentionally aimed at producing imminent lawless action and likely to produce such action, represents a reasonable accommodation of the two goals. Those secured in their positions by the status quo are always, to some degree, at risk from changes in the political winds; and since those secured by the status quo can usually see their security in the specific forms of law, they could in principle object to any speech that makes violations of the law likely. But a speech standard that allowed its repression whenever legal interests might be threatened would be a speech standard inconsistent with any free process of political legitimation, which requires the possibility of revolution as its complement.[14] The restriction of repressible speech to speech that is intentionally and imminently directed towards specific criminal acts can thus provide space for revolutionary discourse while still allowing state authority to serve as a kind of circuit breaker before direct violence ensues.[15] The protection of the specific legal and personal interests the firebrand threatens is itself the object of the government's "fundamental responsibility," since people assaulted by a mob or whose businesses are torched are themselves left without the conditions of warranted self-respect. (This is part of the wrong of the racist under-policing of Black

[13] Meiklejohn, "The First Amendment as an Absolute": 263..

[14] For a theory focusing on the relation between free expression and democratic legitimation, see Post, *Democracy, Expertise and Academic Freedom*..

[15] Indeed, we need a qualifier to the *Brandenburg* test, restricting incitement only to serious breaches of the law—it would be absurd to charge someone encouraging acts of littering, for example. But such a qualifier is usually implicit in practice.

neighborhoods.) Where exactly that line falls—when advocacy becomes incitement—is a matter of judging a very specific tradeoff, not between values, but between different examples of the value of self-respect, and applying the difficult egalitarian calculus when individual interests oppose each other.[16]

Kramer's mistake, therefore, is not that his theory is without resources to define a proper limit to speech in such circumstances. His mistake lies in thinking that the line separating protected from unprotected speech can be defined by the formal characterization of some set of effects, as communicatively-dependent or independent. The state's object, whether protecting or restricting speech, is the same. Since protecting the conditions of self-respect is fundamentally a matter of protecting the conditions of free and reasoned communication, Kramer seems to me to step in the wrong direction when he defends restrictions on speech as applying only to the communication-independent genre.

We can make similar work of the problem of pernicious advertisements, whether of objects illegal or merely unhealthy. Kramer, recall, supports restricting the former but not the latter. His key criterion, that the state should only be able to restrict speech directed at encouraging those acts that are already proscribed as a matter of law, has the virtue of posing a practical threshold to state authorities, requiring them to put the full weight of the state on one side or the other of its citizens' freedoms (and so, perhaps, rendering issues more salient as a matter of political accountability). There would also be, perhaps, a kind of entrapment if the state were to permit advertising for goods or services whose consumption it then prosecuted. But it is hard to see a principled, non-pragmatic reason that coheres with the rest of Kramer's view for why the state cannot prohibit advertisements for legal goods. After all, Kramer's account of the incitement/advocacy line resists such consistency, since the interesting (and protected) cases of advocacy have as their object illegal communication-independent activities (strikes, draft resistance, revolution). At most, therefore, Kramer's criterion of consistency seems to generate a rule-of-thumb presumption against officials trying to have things both ways. But it is hard to see any greater force to the consideration.

To the contrary, the state's interest in maintaining the conditions of warranted self-respect in its citizenry includes an interest in maintaining their health, including their protection from heart and lung disease, obesity, and their sobriety. At the same time, concern for the conditions of self-respect entails permitting, on Millian grounds, a high degree of self-experimentation and autonomous decision-making. Information about the risks of smoking, sugary sodas, etc., whether pro ("consumed as part of a balanced diet, this is not so bad ... ") or con ("the ill effects are gradual but irreversible, and the stimulant characteristics of the product

[16] Although Kramer's idea of "warranted self-respect" seems capacious enough to include a number of subsidiary, yet more fundamental, interests, I have no quarrel with regarding the balancing as between different values, each defensible as a proper object of governance, instead of within a single value's register. A pluralist approach of the second kind, to which my argument is akin, is that more recently developed by T.M. Scanlon, in his (unpublished) "A Framework for Thinking About Free Speech." It is notable that Scanlon himself famously offered a single-criterion, absolutist "autonomy" principle of free speech, which he later came to find too crude to deal with the range of interests at stake. Scanlon, "A Theory of Freedom of Expression."

make it hard to self-regulate") enables those autonomous decisions, and must not be restricted. But "glamour ads" that do nothing other than juxtaposing an objectively risky product with attractive models do not contribute in any significant way to reasoned decision-making; if anything, they deform it. And so, it seems not an unreasonable accommodation, within the same value field, to permit individuals to consume a product while restricting uninformative forms of their promotion. This is true *a fortiori* when the target or susceptible audience of the advertisement is a youth population not fully capable of autonomous decision-making. To be sure, the balance could be justified on the side of freedom of commercial advertising; but not because the advertising is somehow more separable from the invited act when the latter is not criminal than when it is. By contrast, with respect to advertisements aimed at the clearly illegal, and assuming the acts themselves are properly repressed, there is no balance to be made, as the proscribed acts do not, by hypothesis, contribute to warranted self-respect.

A balancing approach, therefore, has many values, not least including intellectual consistency. And it is capable of handling an obstacle that Kramer thinks befalls alternative theories. Among Kramer's objections to consequentialist approaches is that he thinks they cannot explain why a partial restriction on speech might be more objectionable than a complete restriction, as when a city might permissibly decide to forbid any advertising on its buses, but may not permissibly allow only one form of advertising (IV, 153). I should say that I am unpersuaded of the merits of this concern, for it seems to me again reasonable for a city to restrict advertisements to those, for example, issued by public health authorities about the danger of smoking, and not permit advertisements encouraging smoking (even if such advertisements are elsewhere permitted). Moreover, it is certainly possible to imagine cases where a blanket restriction of a category of speech is far worse than a selective restriction, since a blanket restriction may effectively prevent an entire subject of concern from alighting in the public mind, while a selective presentation might at least spark a citizenry to inquire elsewhere about the subject. That said, Kramer is right, I believe, to perceive that there may be a special insult to a citizenry in permitting them to view only one side of a multi-faceted issue, for a selective presentation of information might be said to aim at perverting the faculty of autonomous judgment whose maintenance is central to warranted self-respect. Individuals who think they have reflectively considered a matter aright because of the influence of selective persuasion might have confidence in their capacity to decide for themselves; but insofar as they have not considered the counterarguments, such a feeling is unwarranted.

6. A Better Shave with a Duller Blade?

To sum up, Kramer has given us a powerfully expressed theory of expression, grounded in values that resonate with the range of social and political commitments of liberal democrats. And his theory does much to create a powerful presumption against any restriction on freedom of expression, on grounds no less fundamental than the object of governance itself, and so not easily set aside by hand-waving consequentialists.

But his attempt to render as absolute a principle whose exceptions he rightly acknowledges instead points to a limit to his methodological ambitions. Life, politics, and the grounds of warranted self-respect are irreducibly complex. A theory that acknowledges that complexity forgoes only a false precision. Sometimes a duller edge may be the right blade for the job.

REPLIES

18
Looking Back and Looking Ahead
Replies to the Contributors

Matthew H. Kramer

I wish to begin by warmly thanking quite a few people. First and foremost, I am extremely grateful to Visa Kurki and Mark McBride for their sedulous labors in putting together not only this collection of essays but also a festschrift conference at Churchill College (Cambridge) in July 2019. Their energy and perspicacity in those endeavors have been truly admirable. I am also much obliged to the other people who participated in that conference, several of whom are contributors to this volume. Hearty thanks are due as well to Jamie Berezin and Alex Flach and Brianne Bellio and Kate Plunkett and their colleagues at the Oxford University Press, which has long been my favorite publisher precisely because the processes of editing and production are handled so adeptly there. Finally, I am naturally very grateful to all the authors of the essays in this collection. Engaging with their incisive arguments, for the purpose of writing this set of replies, has been both highly agreeable and highly demanding. I am greatly indebted to them for the time and effort which they have devoted to this project.

My replies to some of the essays in this volume will be brief, because I agree with nearly everything in each of those contributions. My replies to the remaining essays will be lengthier, sometimes much lengthier—because each of those remaining essays contains a number of arguments and assertions which I feel obliged to contest. Hence, the terseness of some of my responses is certainly not intended as a slight to any of the chapters which I discuss only laconically; it does not bespeak a negative assessment of any of those chapters. Quite the contrary.

The contributions to this volume fall into discernible clusters (with some contributions that each belong to more than one of those clusters). In this set of replies, I address the essays batch by batch.

1. Reflections on Rights and Right-Holding

The essays by Kurki, McBride, Laura Donohue, Joseph Bowen, and Rowan Cruft are all focused principally on the nature of rights or right-holding (though the contributions by Kurki and Cruft are also focused on matters of general jurisprudence about the nature of law). These essays are particularly timely, for I have just embarked on a book that will redevelop the sundry reflections on rights and right-holding which I have propounded in an array of publications; that book will aim to systematize and refine and amplify those reflections. Hence, the chapters by the philosophers just

Matthew H. Kramer, *Looking Back and Looking Ahead* In: *Without Trimmings*. Edited by: Mark McBride and Visa AJ Kurki, Oxford University Press. © Mark McBride and Visa AJ Kurki 2022. DOI: 10.1093/oso/9780198868866.003.0018

mentioned are irresistibly enticing as points of entry for my encounters with the piquant challenges posed by the contributors to this collection.

1.1 Laura Donohue: Beyond the Hohfeldian Analysis but Not at Odds with It

I have known Donohue for more than a quarter of a century. She was my second PhD student at Cambridge University, and I have therefore felt a sense of fatherly pride while keeping an eye on her estimable career as a specialist in counter-terrorism law and in other matters of governmental surveillance. She packs a host of interesting and perceptive observations into her essay for this volume. I will not attempt here to grapple with all of her premises and conclusions (especially because some of them—such as her apparent assumption that the property of inalienability entails the property of unenforceability, or her assumption that the property of inalienability entails the property of not being established by law—strike me as baffling). However, I will take issue with a few of her most important lines of thought.

Donohue adduces a number of complicated situations which she believes to be indicative of limitations on the scope of the Hohfeldian analysis of legal positions.[1] Now, on the one hand, there is a clear sense in which she is correct to highlight the limits of Hohfeld's schema. As I have always readily affirmed, there are many aspects of legal relationships that are not addressed by Hohfeld's exposition of such relationships. For example, that exposition does not address any ethical questions concerning what the substance and the configuration of the legal relationships in any given society should be. Moreover, even on analytical matters, the Hohfeldian analysis leaves many questions open. Prominent among those questions are the points of contention in the debates between Interest Theorists and Will Theorists over the necessary and sufficient conditions for the holding of legal claim-rights.[2] Although both the Interest Theory and the Will Theory in their principal contemporary forms are consistent with Hohfeld's categorization of legal positions, the issues in dispute between them cannot be resolved solely through recourse to that categorization. Further considerations have to be invoked. Precisely for that reason, the controversies between the proponents of the Interest Theory and the proponents of the Will Theory have persisted even when those proponents all subscribe to the Hohfeldian analysis and agree on its contours and implications.

My mention here of the debates between Interest Theorists and Will Theorists is pertinent because some of the matters raised by Donohue have to be handled within those

[1] I shall here take for granted that readers have some familiarity with the Hohfeldian analysis. Donohue provides a sketch of it in the first half of her chapter. For a much longer treatment of it, see Kramer 1998: 7–60, 101–11.

[2] I take for granted here that readers have some familiarity with the disputes between Interest Theorists and Will Theorists, which are recounted to varying degrees by Bowen, Cruft, Kurki, and McBride in this collection. Nearly every one of my essays on rights has endeavored (at least partly) to vindicate the Interest Theory of right-holding. For my first main discussion with such an aim, see Kramer 1998: 60–101. For my three most recently published discussions, see Kramer 2010; 2013; and 2017a. In my forthcoming book on rights and right-holding, the controversies between Interest Theorists and Will Theorists will figure saliently and sustainedly—with many refinements of my previous ruminations on the matter.

debates rather than simply by reference to the Hohfeldian framework of legal relationships. The clearest example emerges in her comments on the 2008 FISA Amendments Act introduced by the US Congress (Donohue 2022: 14, footnotes omitted):

> In 2008, for instance, Congress changed its foreign intelligence law to allow for the collection overseas of communications among entities reasonably believed to be non-US persons and outside the United States. The problem is that by virtue of how the Internet functions, multi-communication transactions collected under the law included tens of thousands of entirely domestic communications as well. The result was that the narrowing of the collective rights of non-US Persons overseas also narrowed the collective rights of US persons on domestic soil .... The establishment of citizen-rights entails the establishment of non-citizens-rights, and a duplication of duty vis-à-vis non-citizens, just as the narrowing of non-citizen-rights entails the narrowing of citizen-rights, with the same corresponding obligation on the state.

As a proponent of the Interest Theory of right-holding, I concur with Donohue's characterization of the deontic upshot of the 2008 enactment. Given how communications over the Internet operate, the statute's curtailment of certain claim-rights of non-citizens against being placed under surveillance was inevitably also a curtailment of some homologous claim-rights theretofore held by American citizens. Such a conclusion follows from the Interest Theory's criterion for the identification of right-holders, in application to the situation brought about by the passage of the 2008 law. Prior to that enactment, at least one set of conditions minimally sufficient to constitute a breach of the prevailing law on surveillance by the American government included the fact that the communications of an American citizen had been monitored in ways that would subsequently be authorized by that enactment.[3] Since the passage of the 2008 statute, it is no longer the case that at least one set of conditions minimally sufficient to constitute a breach of the prevailing law on surveillance by the American government includes the fact that the communications of an American citizen have been monitored in the ways just mentioned. Because being placed under governmental surveillance is typically detrimental for the person who undergoes such a development, a proponent of the Interest Theory will conclude that the FISA Amendments Act deprived American citizens of certain claim-rights. Although the Hohfeldian schema alone does not generate such a conclusion, the Hohfeldian schema complemented by the Interest Theory of right-holding does indeed generate it.

On the other hand, notwithstanding that Donohue is correct in thinking that Hohfeld's categorization of legal positions would never suffice on its own to handle some of the complex questions which she poses, she errs in contending that the legal relationships to which those questions pertain are beyond the scope of that categorization. In the extract from her essay which I have quoted above, the ellipses signal the omission of the following sentence: "These types of legal relationships, however, are not captured by the Hohfeldian jural relations" (Donohue 2022: 14). Donohue here

[3] As is explained in Kramer 2010: 37, a set of conditions S is minimally sufficient for some effect E if and only if (1) S is sufficient for E and (2) S does not comprise any conditions that are unnecessary to make S sufficient for E.

goes astray, for the legal positions which she delineates are perfectly well captured within the Hohfeldian categorization. Indeed, as I have argued at length in some of my earlier writings on these matters, the Hohfeldian framework is comprehensive in that its categories encompass all types and instances of legal relationships. *A fortiori*, it encompasses the legal positions which Donohue sketches. To be sure, as has just been discussed, the Hohfeldian analysis cannot in itself answer the question whether American citizens have been deprived of claim-rights by the 2008 statute. However, once we have answered that question affirmatively by drawing upon the Interest Theory of right-holding and upon some facts about certain elementary features of any communications that are conducted through the Internet, we can then draw upon the Hohfeldian schema to chart the relevant legal relationships rigorously and precisely.

The comprehensiveness of the Hohfeldian analysis becomes further apparent when we examine Donohue's discussion of the killing of Anwar al-Awlaki by an American drone strike in 2011. As Donohue recounts, an anfractuous concatenation of decisions and actions by a wide array of officials in different agencies and branches of the American system of governance led to the extinguishing of al-Awlaki's legal claim-right against deliberate and violent attacks by the Central Intelligence Agency. She believes that Hohfeld's category of legal powers cannot meaningfully be brought to bear on that throng of decisions and actions (2022: 18): "Which of [those decisions and actions] were necessary to erosion of the claim-rights? Which were sufficient? Which action amounted to an exercise of the power? Was it even an exercise of power in a Hohfeldian sense?" Donohue here seriously underestimates the resourcefulness and the fine-grained subtlety of the Hohfeldian analysis. Her misstep in that regard is connected to another misstep which she commits at a couple of junctures in her essay. That is, she twice suggests that exercises of Hohfeldian powers bring about changes in first-order legal relationships only. In fact, exercises of Hohfeldian powers can bring about changes in any legal relationships. Powers and liabilities and immunities and disabilities can be altered by exertions of Hohfeldian powers, just as much as can claim-rights and duties and liberties and no-rights. This point is particularly important in the present context, because the changes in legal positions induced by most of the decisions and actions that led to the removal of al-Awlaki's claim-right against being deliberately killed were changes consisting in the creation of legal liabilities. Most of those sundry decisions and actions imposed on al-Awlaki certain liabilities to incur various other liabilities which ultimately eventuated in his incurring a liability to undergo the removal of his claim-right against being deliberately killed. The exercise of the legal power correlative to that final legal liability resulted in the extinguishing of his claim-right. Though such an upshot was produced through a highly complex succession of liabilities arising from the medley of actions and decisions which Donohue summarizes, the succession of liabilities culminated in the exercise of a power that extinguished al-Awlaki's claim-right. All the steps in that succession are precisely describable with Hohfeld's categories; Donohue's cataloguing of those tortuous steps does not tell at all against my insistence on the comprehensiveness of the Hohfeldian analysis.

In the penultimate portion of her essay with which I will wrestle here, Donohue proclaims that "Kramer's assertion that the exercise of a power entails an affirmative decision to act . . . also is not consistent with the types of new and emerging technologies that are beginning to impact law in profound ways. Sophisticated algorithms, machine learning, and artificial intelligence are being used with legal effect. Criminal risk assessment algorithms, for example, are being employed to determine whether individuals are granted parole, altering their liberty rights" (2022: 19). In my book *Moral Realism as a Moral Doctrine* (2009: 78–82), I discuss quasi-powers and quasi-liabilities. A quasi-power is the ability of some non-human entity or occurrence to bring about transformations in legal relationships. A quasi-liability is a position of susceptibility to the transformative effects of the workings of a quasi-power. Such a position of susceptibility can be occupied by everyone who is a potential occupant of any of the standard Hohfeldian legal positions.

In many cases, the workings of quasi-powers operate independently of the designs pursued by human beings. For example, in any ordinary situation where a cautious person is struck by lightning while she is walking or standing outdoors, the mishap is not something sought or arranged by anybody. Nor is it due to culpability—negligence or recklessness or malice—on the part of the victim or on the part of anyone else. In some other cases, by contrast, the existence of a quasi-power as such is due to the designs or the culpability of somebody. In a case of this latter kind, the creation of a quasi-power and the placing of some person or class of persons under a quasi-liability are the products of an exercise of a legal power. That exercise of a legal power has resulted not in the creation of any Hohfeldian legal positions but instead in the creation of the quasi-legal positions just mentioned (the quasi-power and the quasi-liability) which are parallel to some Hohfeldian positions.

As is evident, the quasi-powers recounted by Donohue in the sentences which I have quoted in the penultimate paragraph above—that is, the abilities of computerized machines to alter people's legal relationships by arriving at certain determinations—have been brought into existence deliberately by legal-governmental officials who (with the aid of technicians) have put into place the arrangements for their operations. Hence, the actions of those officials in settling the arrangements are exercises of legal powers that place each person in the relevant jurisdiction under quasi-liabilities to undergo changes in his or her legal relationships through the determinations of the computerized machines. Any changes brought about through those determinations are not directly engendered by exercises of Hohfeldian powers, but the quasi-powers which (when exerted) do directly engender such changes are themselves the products of certain exercises of Hohfeldian powers. When we correctly descry the location of the operative powers, we can see that Donohue errs in thinking that exercises of those powers do not involve choices and actions by human beings.

Now, Hohfeld himself did not discuss quasi-powers and quasi-liabilities at all. Should we conclude, then, that Donohue has exposed a gap in the comprehensiveness of the Hohfeldian framework? The answer to this question is negative, for the comprehensiveness of that framework pertains to the multifarious legal relationships that obtain among human beings.[4] Although some quasi-powers originate from exercises

[4] I am here using the phrase "human beings" as shorthand for "potential holders of legal claim-rights and other legal entitlements." Elsewhere (2001: 34–45), I have argued that quite a few non-human animals are within the class of potential holders of such entitlements. Since there is no basis for thinking that Hohfeld shared my position on that matter—a position that will be expanded and buttressed in my forthcoming book *Rights and Right-Holding*—the phrase "human beings" is apt as an encapsulation of his own view concerning the range of members in the class just mentioned.

of legal powers held by human beings, the quasi-powers themselves are not possessed by human beings; *ex hypothesi*, they are possessed by inanimate entities or forces. Accordingly, although a quasi-liability as the correlate of a quasi-power is borne by a human being, it is not borne vis-à-vis some other human being. Hence, unlike a power/liability relationship, a quasi-power/quasi-liability relationship does not obtain between human beings. Instead, it obtains between some human being(s) and some inanimate thing(s) or force(s). A quasi-power/quasi-liability relationship is therefore not among the countless relationships which Hohfeld sought to encompass within his schema.

Having said as much, I readily avow that Hohfeld's failure to discuss quasi-powers and quasi-liabilities is a lacuna in his overall theorizing about jural relationships. Given that many quasi-powers have arisen through actions that constitute exercises of legal powers, and given that exertions of quasi-powers induce changes in the legal relationships that obtain among human beings, a general theory of such relationships should take the roles of quasi-powers carefully into account. Still, my acceptance of that point is perfectly consistent with my affirmation that the comprehensiveness of Hohfeld's analytical framework is not impugned by Donohue's remarks on the operations of computerized machines in processes of governmental decision-making.

One further strand of Donohue's chapter can be addressed briefly here. Donohue appears to think that the divergences in the United States between federal law and the laws of many states on the use of marijuana are somehow problematic for the Hohfeldian account of legal positions. Her discussion of the matter is lacking in lucidity, but she appears to believe that there is a "possible contradiction" which consists in the fact that the use of marijuana is legally prohibited by the federal government while being legally permissible for medical purposes under the laws of quite a few states (Donohue 2022: 16). Yet there is no contradiction whatsoever in the fact that some mode of conduct banned under the law of one jurisdiction is permitted under the law of another jurisdiction—even when the jurisdictions are complexly overlapping in the manner of the relationship between each state government and the federal government in the United States. In regard to any matter over which the states and the national government have concurrent jurisdiction, there is the potential for incongruities between what is permitted under the laws of the national government and what is permitted under the laws of this or that state. Because every legal norm is jurisdiction-specific, the incongruities just mentioned do not amount to contradictions at all (any more than do the possible incongruities between what is permitted under the law of some jurisdiction and what is permitted under the correct principles of morality). What would be impossibly contradictory is a state of affairs in which the law of a single jurisdiction permits and simultaneously forbids a certain mode of conduct. If some laws in a given jurisdiction J purport to provide that a mode of conduct MC is permitted, and if some other laws in J simultaneously purport to provide that MC is forbidden, there is an ostensible contradiction. There is not a genuine contradiction—because one and only one of the two contradictory sets of laws can actually be in effect in a particular jurisdiction at any juncture[5]—but there is indeed

[5] On ostensible contradictions in the laws of a system of governance, see Kramer 2001: 73–8; 2007: 125–6.

an ostensible contradiction that has to be resolved implicitly if not explicitly by the legal-governmental officials in J. By contrast, if the laws which prohibit MC belong to another jurisdiction K while the laws which permit MC belong to J, there is not any ostensible contradiction that has to be resolved. In J's system of governance, the officials responsible for giving effect to the laws of J are legally obligated to treat MC as permissible; and, in K's system of governance, the officials responsible for giving effect to the laws of K are legally obligated to treat MC as forbidden. Far from being impossible or unintelligible, such a state of affairs is commonplace. Its straightforward possibility is unimpaired in a situation where some or all of the people whose conduct is regulated by the laws of J are the same as some or all of the people whose conduct is regulated by the laws of K.

Donohue proceeds to write: "For federal prosecutors, however, a contradiction exists: they both have a *duty* to enforce the existing law (which forbids marijuana in all fifty states and imposes criminal penalties for its possession) and a *duty*, according to the Attorney General's memorandum, not to enforce the existing law. The reason they are in this position is, in part, because of the tension inherent in dual sovereignty" (2022: 16, emphases in original). This passage is misguided in multiple respects. For one thing, the memorandum to which Donohue adverts—a 2013 memorandum in which the US Department of Justice advises against the enforcement of the federal prohibition on the use of marijuana, in states where the use of that narcotic is permitted and suitably regulated—expressly affirms that it is only providing guidance for the exercise of prosecutorial discretion and that it is not imposing any duties on federal prosecutors. Had the Attorney General purported to impose a duty of non-enforcement on federal prosecutors, he would probably have been acting unconstitutionally; the imposition of such a duty would have been tantamount to the partial repeal of a statute by an executive official. Moreover, even if the memorandum had had the effect of imposing a duty of non-enforcement on federal prosecutors alongside the already-existent duty of enforcement, the resultant situation would have been a deontic conflict rather than a contradiction. The stumble by Donohue on that point is particularly puzzling, given that it occurs shortly after she quotes from my writings on the difference between conflicts and contradictions. Furthermore, the best way of construing the upshot of the Attorney General's memorandum is the opposite of what she suggests. Instead of adding a duty of non-enforcement to a duty of enforcement, the memorandum partially removed the duty of enforcement. Hence, instead of being faced with a situation of conflicting duties, federal prosecutors are faced with a situation in which they are both legally at liberty to enforce the federal prohibition on the use of marijuana and legally at liberty (in some circumstances) to abstain from enforcing that prohibition. Finally, in the original draft of her chapter, Donohue used the unembellished noun "prosecutors" in the passage which I have quoted here. In the latest version of her chapter, she makes clear that she is in fact talking only about *federal* prosecutors. Such a clarification of the original draft is salutary, because the position of the state prosecutors is very different from that of the federal prosecutors. For state prosecutors in California or in any other American jurisdiction where the use of marijuana has been legalized, there is a straightforward legal obligation to abstain from the pursuit of legal proceedings against people who have used marijuana in compliance with any conditions specified by the prevailing laws. Donohue herself states this point in some sentences that were not in the original draft of her chapter: "State law enforcement ... is under a duty of non-interference in the consumption of marijuana within the allowed amount. But [state prosecutors] are not subject to conflicting duties: because of dual sovereignty and as recognized by the Tenth Amendment, the federal government cannot commandeer state governments to order them to carry out federal measures" (2022: 16, footnote omitted). Donohue's changes to her original draft are welcome, because differentiating clearly between the role of federal prosecutors and the role of state prosecutors is a key step in fathoming the points made by my last paragraph above.

1.2 Joseph Bowen on Dead People as Potential Holders of Legal Entitlements

Although Bowen agrees with me that dead people are among the potential holders of legal claim-rights and other legal entitlements—and although he relatedly agrees with me that dead people can be harmed or benefited posthumously—he believes that my justification for including dead people in the class of potential holders of legal entitlements is unsound. Its unsoundness is due, he maintains, to my focusing on inapposite considerations. In this reply, I will endeavor to rebut his main criticisms of me and to impeach his own justification for the inclusion of dead people in the class of potential holders of rights. Concentrating on those two tasks, I will not here take issue with some other doubtful assertions and arguments in Bowen's thought-provoking chapter.

In my 2001 essay "Getting Rights Right," which contains my principal discussion of the status of dead people as potential holders of legal claim-rights, I proceed on the premise that dead people have interests and that they can be harmed or benefited posthumously. That premise is a straightforward corollary of several strands in my accounts of right-holding: my expansive conception of interests; my assertions that the life of a dead person can be made better or worse by events that occur after his or her death; my contention that the harm incurred or benefit undergone by a person through any event at some time *t* that posthumously worsens or improves her life is incurred or undergone by her at *t* rather than while she was still alive; and my explanation that a no-longer-existent person can be harmed or benefited because the property of being harmed or benefited is a relational property that can be acquired posthumously by that person just as countless other relational properties can be.[6] Bowen takes aim at the first of these strands in my discussions (even while he agrees with me about the susceptibility of dead people to being harmed or benefited posthumously), and he relatedly and even more vigorously takes exception to my focus on the ways in which dead people influence the lives of people who survive them. Let us examine these objections.

[6] On this last point, about relational properties, see Kramer 2001: 54–5.

1.2.1 The Capacious Conception of Interests

Disagreeing with my capacious conception of interests—a conception sufficiently expansive to warrant the ascription of interests to various inanimate entities—Bowen resorts to some terminological intuitions. He writes as follows: "I think it is implausible that interests are so capacious: to my ear, the grass does not have an interest in being watered, nor does my computer have an interest in having its RAM upgraded, nor does my house have an interest in having its painting touched up" (2022: 58 n.28). Though the formulations in the quoted sentence are awkward, each of them can easily be reworded to eliminate the awkwardness while retaining the invocation of an interest: "It is in the interest of the grass that it be watered regularly; it is in the interest of your computer that its software be up-graded regularly; it is in the interest of your house that its paint be touched up." In any event, the objection pressed here by Bowen is a superficial matter of terminology. The Interest Theory of right-holding has sometimes been designated as the "Benefit Theory," and the attachment of that latter designation to my account of right-holding might be advisable—both because it would forestall the sort of cavil raised here by Bowen and because it would underscore the fact that my account of right-holding is markedly different from the account of rights propounded (under the name of the "Interest Theory") by Joseph Raz.[7] Were the language of "benefits" to be substituted for the language of "interests" in the observations about the grass and the computer and the house, Bowen's terminological misgivings would have no purchase at all. Entirely idiomatic are the following formulations: "The grass will benefit from being watered regularly; the computer and its operations will benefit from the regular upgrading of its software; the house will benefit from the touching up of its paint." I am concerned chiefly with the substance of my account of right-holding rather than with the labeling of it. If the reframing of my theory with the language of "benefits" in lieu of the language of "interests" would avert any terminological squeamishness on the part of Bowen or others, then I would be content with the reframing. Having said as much, I should add that I do not currently feel impelled to undertake such a change. My view at present is that the language of "interests" is sufficiently capacious to be amply serviceable for all the purposes for which I have wielded it.

In addition to expressing his terminological qualms, Bowen advances a couple of substantive objections to my expansive understanding of interests. He states the first of those substantive worries as follows (2022: 59, emphasis in original):

> [I]f we define interests capaciously, but then say it is only a subset of interests that matter for rights, we are not really defending the *Interest* Theory of Rights. Rather, we are defending the Interest* Theory, where the asterisk denotes the subset of morally relevant interests. If we define interests more narrowly, we do not need to make such accommodations—it is interests in general that are doing the work.

Far from exposing any insurmountable difficulties that confront my broad conception of interests, Bowen's argument on this point will prompt me to adduce one of the chief

[7] Bowen is aware of the differences between the Razian theory and mine, which he encapsulates in his distinction between justificatory versions and non-justificatory versions of the Interest Theory.

reasons for embracing that conception. Let us here recall the thesis with which I encapsulate the Interest Theory of right-holding:

> Necessary and sufficient for the holding of a legal claim-right by *X* is that the duty correlative to the claim-right deontically and inherently protects some aspect of *X*'s situation that on balance is typically beneficial for a being like *X* (namely, a human individual or a collectivity or a nonhuman animal).

As I have remarked elsewhere (2013: 246 n.5; 2017a, 49 n.1), the concluding portion of this thesis is consigned to parentheses in order to indicate that other proponents of the Interest Theory might wish to narrow or widen the phrasing of that portion. The parenthetical part of the thesis distills the extension of the category of potential right-holders as I believe it to be, but someone can take a different view of that extension while subscribing wholeheartedly to the Interest Theory as a correct account of right-holding. When this aspect of the Interest Theory is duly recognized, the futility of Bowen's first substantive objection to my capacious conception of interests should be apparent. Contrary to what is suggested in that objection, the advocates of the Interest Theory are not espousing distinct accounts of right-holding that have to be labeled separately when those advocates differ with one another over the range of beings whose interests are covered by the Interest Theory. Such divergences among those advocates pertain not to the correct exposition of right-holding—on which the advocates all agree—but instead to the specific conclusions derivable from the criterion which the Interest Theory provides for the identification of holders of claim-rights. The divergences concern the extension of that criterion rather than its intension.

By contrast, the approach to these matters which Bowen commends will run afoul of exactly the problem of equivocality which he incorrectly imputes to my approach. For Bowen, the class of beings with interests is equivalent to the class of potential holders of claim-rights. Accordingly, any disagreement about either of those classes is a disagreement about the other. Consequently, insofar as Bowen's approach is followed, there is no univocal Interest Theory of right-holding on which various philosophers converge while differing with one another over the breadth of the class of potential right-holders. Under Bowen's approach, controversies relating to the breadth of that class are controversies relating to the very nature of interests and vice versa. Thus, instead of sharing a single account of right-holding, Bowenite philosophers would be propounding incompatible accounts that should be separately designated as the Interest* Theory and the Interest** Theory and so forth.

One major reason for combining my capacious conception of interests with the Interest Theory of right-holding, then, is that such a combination renders the Interest Theory univocal while leaving ample room for proponents of the theory to quarrel at the extensional level about the ambit of the class of potential right-holders. Having raised the problem of equivocality, Bowen obviously and rightly attaches importance to the devising of a univocal theory of right-holding. He should therefore follow my approach to these matters—an approach consisting in the combination which I have just outlined—and should eschew his own approach.

A second substantive criticism raised by Bowen is wholly misdirected. He submits that, when combined with my capacious conception of interests, the Interest Theory "offers an implausible account of the grounds of right-holding." He elaborates (2022: 59, emphasis in original):

> [E]ven if we go for the Interest Theory (Nonjustificatory), we *are* offering an account of grounds of right-holding—we are offering an account of that in virtue of which one is a potential right-holder. If we endorse the Well-being View, we have an intuitively compelling account of the grounds of right-holding. This is because how our lives go for us—what our well-being consists of—is obviously of importance. When one's well-being is the grounds of some duty *or* when one's well-being is necessarily, typically served by some duty (depending on whether we endorse the Justificatory or Nonjustificatory version of the Interest Theory, respectively), it is plausible that the duty would resultantly be owed to one. The same is true to a similar extent of the Stakes View of Interests (on that view, recall, interests are those things we care about and that we have reason to care about—so rights are grounded in those things we care about and have reason to care about). But once we move to Kramer's capacious view, it is just not clear to me why advancing something's condition, such as a painting's condition, would result in the duty being owed to that thing.

What makes this passage so puzzlingly misguided is that it completely overlooks the main point of my ruminations in "Getting Rights Right" on the class of potential right-holders. As is argued there, the chief tenet of the Interest Theory shorn of its closing parenthetical portion is not sufficient to delimit the class of potential right-holders properly. Although different proponents of the Interest Theory can fill in the closing parenthetical portion differently, every credible version of the theory has to include some such portion—because nobody could plausibly maintain that everything susceptible to improvement or deterioration is a member of the class of potential right-holders. My 2001 essay has sought to underline the preposterousness of the notion that the class of potential right-holders is equivalent to the class of beings endowed with interests (where interests are understood in accordance with my capacious conception thereof). Yet Bowen proceeds in the quoted passage as if I had espoused that preposterous notion. Given that I in fact have sustainedly rejected it, his second substantive objection to my capacious conception of interests is badly misdirected.

Bowen himself straightaway acknowledges as much: "At this stage, one might reply: but if we endorse Kramer's capacious view, we cannot conclude from one's interest being necessarily, typically served by some duty that this will result in the duty being owed to the interest-bearer. This is because, as Kramer makes clear, we then need to inquire as to the moral status of the interest-bearer" (2022: 59). Having admitted that his second substantive criticism is misconceived, Bowen goes on to conclude that either my broad conception or a narrower conception of interests can be serviceable for the task of demarcating the range of potential holders of claim-rights. He asserts that "if we want to discover whether some entity is a potential right-holder, it is unclear it matters whether we define interests narrowly or capaciously" (2022: 60). Though I welcome the concessionary tenor of Bowen's discussion at this juncture, I am disinclined to be equally concessionary in return. As I have indicated in my riposte to his first substantive query, anyone who aspires to propound the Interest Theory of right-holding as a univocal theory should recognize that the choice between the capacious view and a narrower view of interests does matter.

In short, neither in his terminological quibbling nor in his substantive worries does Bowen expose any genuine shortcomings in my expansive conception of interests. Moreover, the first of his substantive criticisms has turned out to tell against his own understanding of interests, and it helps to reveal why my capacious understanding is superior. Like the quip by Tranio directed against Petruchio in Act V of Shakespeare's *The Taming of the Shrew*, the critique by Bowen directed against my position on the nature of interests "did glance away from me, [and] 'tis ten to one it maim'd [Bowen] outright."[8]

1.2.2 Infants as Members of the Community of Potential Right-Holders

Another query raised by Bowen against my expansive conception of interests is really targeting some of my reflections on the moral import of certain interests. He first quotes a passage from my "Getting Rights Right" in which I ponder the status of infants as potential holders of legal claim-rights. I there mention two considerations which undergird that status: the fact that most infants will develop into human adults of sound mind, who are the paradigmatic members of the class of potential right-holders; and the fact that all human infants belong to the species which includes those adults. Bowen retorts that "it is not obvious why, without further serious argument, the fact that most children will develop into adults with sufficiently complex rational capacities, or the fact that they belong to the same species as those adults, would make their interests of the sort, the protection of which, makes them potential right-holders at that time" (2022: 60). Now, on the one hand, Bowen is correct in submitting that further reasoning is needed in support of the considerations which I have invoked as my grounds for classifying infants as potential holders of rights. In "Getting Rights Right," I was not endeavoring to present full-scale arguments to vindicate my sundry contentions about the extension of the category of potential right-holders. Rather, I was seeking to delineate the sorts of factors on which some suitable arguments would elaborate. On the other hand, in a number of my more recent books I have advanced some arguments of political morality that can be adapted and extended to address the matter of the status of infants as potential holders of claim-rights.[9] Particularly relevant will be my forthcoming book *Rights and Right-Holding* and another book *Abortion and the Limits of Governance* which I will write immediately thereafter. For the moment, we should simply glance at the general orientation that will imbue the account of the status of infants as right-holders which I shall expound in those future writings.

Just after the sentence which I have quoted most recently above, Bowen declares: "[T]o be true to the Interest Theory itself, we should focus on the nature of the interests themselves" (2022: 60). On the contrary, the key to explaining satisfactorily why infants are potential holders of legal claim-rights is to concentrate primarily instead on the moral integrity of the beings—namely, sane human adults—who are the

[8] V.ii.61–2. For my quotations from Shakespeare's plays in these replies, I have used Shakespeare 1974.

[9] See especially Kramer 2011a; 2014; 2017b; 2021. For a distillation of some of the main ideas that connect those books, see Kramer 2017c.

paradigmatic potential holders of claim-rights. Questions about the inclusion of other beings in the category of potential right-holders are questions about the extent to which the paradigmatic members of that category are morally obligated to accept that other beings are also members. That matter in turn hinges on whether the exclusion of certain other beings would be consistent with the social and political and economic conditions under which every paradigmatic member can be warranted in harboring an ample sense of self-respect. Now, among the factors which bear on the question about warranted self-respect in this context are the two considerations which I have mentioned in the preceding paragraph: namely, the fact that most human infants become adults of sound mind, and the fact that all human infants belong to the species that comprises such adults. Those two considerations bear on the question about warranted self-respect in complex ways that are connected to the property of ultimate value with which any potential right-holder is endowed. I cannot delve further into this matter here without making this portion of my replies unmanageably lengthy, but I will treat of it fully in my books on rights and right-holding and on abortion.

In fairness to Bowen, I should note again that the relevant argumentation which I have just been adumbrating is not yet contained in any of my published writings. Although that argumentation will in many respects be an extrapolation from the recent books of mine which I have mentioned (and also from some bits of "Getting Rights Right"), and although some of the argumentation has been included during the past several years in my lectures on rights and right-holding for my Cambridge University course on Topics in Legal and Political Philosophy, I have not yet presented it in a published form. Thus, Bowen cannot be faulted for asserting that my position on this matter is in need of further reasoned support.

1.2.3 The Presence of Dead People in the Conduct and Outlooks of the Living

Bowen reserves his harshest criticism for my emphasis on the ways in which the conduct and outlooks of living people are affected by those who are dead. As is obvious in the passage which he quotes from me on this matter—and as he himself of course fully recognizes—I am not talking about occult influences or other such twaddle. Rather, I am referring to the memories of a dead person left in the minds of the living, and to the ways in which a person's past conduct can shape the unfolding of certain events after the person has died, and to any assets bequeathed by a dead person unto others, and so forth. As I maintain in "Getting Rights Right," such traces of a dead person in the lives of people who survive him or her are some key determinants of the length of time during which that person posthumously occupies the status of a potential holder of legal claim-rights. Those traces are such determinants because, as a moral matter, they render a dead person partly assimilable to the person who he or she was during his or her lifetime.

1.2.3.1 A first onslaught

Bowen begins his onslaughts with the following line of reasoning (2022: 62, emphasis in original):

> An initial limitation of Kramer's argument is that it cannot be relied upon by a defender of the Justificatory version of the Interest Theory. This is because, on that

> version of the view, for one to be owed a duty and hold a right correlative to that duty, one's interests need to be the grounds of that duty. And, though the fact that the dead figure in the lives of the living may well be the grounds of duties that we treat the dead in certain ways, those duties will not be grounded in the interests of the dead—rather, they will be grounded in the interests of the living, the people whose lives the dead figure in. On the Justificatory version of the Interest Theory, then, Kramer's argument is able only to justify the living holding rights whose content refers to the dead, rather than the dead being holders of rights *themselves*.

Bowen here goes astray in two interrelated ways. In the first place, there is no basis for his supposition that my focus on the presence of the dead in the conduct and outlooks of the living would somehow commit me to the thesis that all duties pertaining to the dead are grounded in the interests of the living. In my discussions of dead people as potential holders of claim-rights, the duties correlative to those claim-rights are typically promotive of the interests of dead people and are often burdensomely contrary to the interests of the living people who bear the duties. Admittedly, that fact alone does not suffice to establish that the duties are grounded at least partly on the interests of the dead people. Nonetheless, it warrants our inferring quite confidently that in many cases the grounds for the duties are indeed located in those interests. *Pace* Bowen, nothing in "Getting Rights Right" excludes such a grounding.

A second and connected shortcoming in the reasoning by Bowen is that he conflates two moral issues (or two sets of moral issues) which I take pains to distinguish in "Getting Rights Right." As has been stated in the penultimate paragraph above, the issue addressed when I contemplate the influence of the dead on the conduct and outlooks of the living is the length of time (if any) during which a dead person is a potential holder of claim-rights. During that span of time, whatever it may be, any legal protections conferred upon the interests of a dead person through the imposition of legal duties on others are properly classifiable as legal claim-rights held by that person. In the passage just quoted, Bowen is raising not that issue but instead the distinct issue of the extent to which—or the conditions under which—the relevant interests (whether of the dead or of the living) should be legally protected. According to the adherents of the justificatory version of the Interest Theory, the interests of dead people should be legally protected insofar as those interests are sufficiently weighty morally to justify the imposition of legal duties on people who are still alive. In taking such a position, the justificatory Interest Theorists are not addressing my question about the status of dead people as potential holders of legal claim-rights; instead, they are addressing the distinct issue that has just been broached. At a very high level of abstraction, they are indicating the extent to which—or the conditions under which—the interests of the dead should be legally protected.

Note that this second rejoinder to Bowen's argument is not simply pointing out that the justificatory version of the Interest Theory differs from my non-justificatory version. After all, any full exposition of right-holding in the former version has to come to grips with the status of dead people and of other beings as potential holders of rights. Raz, the pre-eminent champion of a justificatory version of the Interest Theory, does indeed address that matter at the outset of his explication of right-holding: "'X has a right' … only if X can have rights" (1986: 166). At a very high level of abstraction, that element of Raz's explication focuses on the question whether various beings are included in the class of potential holders of rights. That question, in one of its applications, is what I am pondering in my meditations on dead people. However, in the passage from Bowen which I have quoted most recently above, he prescinds from that opening element in Raz's explication of right-holding. He concentrates instead on the distinct issue about the extent to which—or the conditions under which—certain interests should be protected. That latter issue is of course addressed (at a high level of abstraction) by Raz's justificatory account of right-holding, but it is separate from the matter addressed by the opening element of his account, and it is therefore separate from the matter addressed by my ruminations on the presence of dead people in the outlooks and conduct of the living. Accordingly, Bowen commits a *non sequitur* when he contends that the tenor of my ruminations is somehow inconsistent with the Razians' approach to questions about the extent to which—or the conditions under which—certain interests should be legally protected.

1.2.3.2 A second broadside

A second objection leveled by Bowen against my discussion of dead people is even wider of the mark. As he is aware, my Interest Theory of right-holding is an account of the holding of legal rights. Though most aspects of that account can be extended to the holding of moral rights, not every aspect can be so transferred. I state as much at the outset of "Rights Without Trimmings," and I have likewise highlighted certain important differences between the nature of legal rights and the nature of moral rights in some subsequent writings of mine. My forthcoming book *Rights and Right-Holding* will present a systematic catalogue of such differences.

Picking up on the fact that my non-justificatory version of the Interest Theory has been propounded as an account of the holding of legal rights, Bowen endeavors to parlay that fact into a critique of my theory. He submits: "Now, however plausible we find this [version of the Interest Theory] when it comes to legal rights, it is much less plausible that the Nonjustificatory version of the Interest Theory is the correct theory of *moral* rights" (2022: 62, emphasis in original). One misstep by Bowen should be noted straightaway. As I have emphasized in recent years, the Interest Theory as I expound it is a theory of right-holding rather than of rights. It is only a component in a full theory of the nature of rights. Another crucial component is the Hohfeldian analysis of legal positions.

More serious are some concomitant misrepresentations in Bowen's chapter. Bowen adduces the following example (2022: 62-3, emphasis in original), which is a variant of a situation sketched by me in 2018 when I annotated the file of an earlier paper of his:

> Some innocent victims are kidnapped. The kidnappers make the victims carry out some strenuous labor. They threaten that, if any of the ... victims do not carry out the labor, all of the victims will be killed. It is plausible that, without any reasonable means of escape, each of the victims is under a moral duty to carry out the labor—and it is plausible that they owe this duty to the other victims. However, Kramer's discussion of other cases implies that performing the action required by the duty will also necessarily be typically beneficial for the kidnappers. Since this is sufficient for the duty to be owed to the kidnappers on what would be Kramer's Nonjustificatory

> version of the Interest Theory of *moral* rights, this would mean the victims owe their duty to carry out the labor to the kidnappers (in addition to the other victims), and that the kidnappers have rights against the victims that they carry out the labor (in addition to the other victims). But this is very implausible.

Before I comment on this passage directly, I should also quote a footnote that occurs at its outset: "This example was originally offered to me by Kramer in comments on an earlier version of my 'Beyond Normative Control: Against the Will Theory of Rights' as a counterexample to the claim that, when one violates a duty owed to *X*, one wrongs *X*" (2022: 62 n.38). Strictly speaking, the statement in this footnote is true. However, it is highly misleading, for it is not coupled with any indication by Bowen that I no longer hold the view which he here attributes to me. Bowen knows that I do not any longer hold that view—a view which I never articulated in any of my published writings—because I explicitly told him so in July 2019. As I told him at that time, the informal annotation which I had inserted into the file of his paper during the previous year was doubly mistaken. It failed to distinguish between legal claim-rights and moral claim-rights, and it inappositely affirmed that sometimes a breach of a duty does not wrong the person to whom the duty is owed. When we do distinguish between legal claim-rights and moral claim-rights in order to concentrate on the latter, we can see that my version of the Interest Theory in application to some moral duties is not determinative on its own. Sometimes a moral duty D is not owed to some person P and is therefore not correlated with any moral claim-right held by P, even though my version of the Interest Theory if brought to bear on D without amplification would generate the conclusion that P holds a claim-right which is correlated with D. Whereas my version of the Interest Theory is always determinative for identifying the location of a right in the legal domain, it is sometimes not determinative for that purpose in the moral domain. Because Bowen knows that I now take such a position on this matter, I am dismayed that he writes as if I were still cleaving to the erroneous view expressed in my annotation on his 2018 paper.

Bowen goes on to suggest that the scenario of the kidnappers can be handled properly if my version of the Interest Theory is confined to legal rights. However, his approach to the matter is simplistic, as he presumes that the Justificatory version of the Interest Theory is apt for moral rights (2022: 63, emphasis in original, footnote omitted):

> [W]hile the Nonjustificatory version of the Interest Theory is correct when it comes to legal rights, some form of the Justificatory version of the Interest Theory is correct for moral rights: minimally, a moral duty is owed to someone, and they hold a correlative right to that duty, only if their interests play *some* role in grounding the duty. It is a separate question the extent to which one's interests must play a justificatory role in grounding the duty. Going this way, one need not conclude that the victims' duties are owed to the kidnappers, that the kidnappers hold rights correlative to those duties, nor that the victims would wrong the kidnappers if they infringed the duty.

Bowen errs in thinking that the only way to escape the unpalatable conclusions mentioned in the final sentence of this passage is to embrace the justificatory version of the

Interest Theory. Rather, the scenario of the kidnappers can be satisfactorily handled through the following necessary condition for the holding of a moral claim-right:

> A person P holds a moral claim-right correlative to a moral duty D only if the existence of D is not due to some moral wrong(s) perpetrated by P.

Availing myself of that necessary condition for the holding of a moral claim-right, I can enunciate the following necessary and sufficient condition for the holding of such a claim-right:

> *Extended Interest Theory for the Holding of Moral Claim-Rights*: A person P holds a moral claim-right correlative to a moral duty D if and only if (1) D deontically and inherently protects some aspect of P's situation that on balance is typically beneficial for a being like P, and (2) the existence of D is not due to some moral wrong(s) perpetrated by P, and (3) P belongs to the class of potential holders of claim-rights.

The second conjunct in the Extended Interest Theory for the Holding of Moral Claim-Rights is an encapsulation of one of the significant differences between moral entitlements and legal entitlements. At the same time, the first conjunct preserves the general non-justificatory orientation of any proper criterion for identifying the holders of claim-rights. Such an orientation avoids the formidable problems that afflict the Razian version of the Interest Theory. In response to the differences between the legal domain and the moral domain, the suitable tack is to amplify my version of the Interest Theory rather than to abandon it. (As is evident, the role of the third conjunct in the Extended Interest Theory corresponds to the role of the parenthetical closing portion in my formulation of the Interest Theory for the holding of legal claim-rights.)

1.2.3.3 A third line of attack

Bowen next trains his fire directly on my attentiveness to the presence of the dead in the conduct and outlooks of the living (2022: 64):

> Kramer's methodology is to begin with what he takes to be paradigmatic right-holders, "mentally competent human adults," and then to look at the similarities and differences between such right-holders and the class of putative potential right-holders under examination. We then need to attend to the moral significance of these similarities and differences. And, it looks like Kramer thinks the salient similarities between the dead and the living is that the dead figure prominently in the lives of the living. But that just seems beside the point. Lots of things figure in the lives of the living.

Bowen is assailing a ridiculous straw man in this passage. At no point does my "Getting Rights Right" suggest that the status of dead people as potential holders of claim-rights is grounded on the sheer fact that dead people figure prominently in the lives of people who survive them. Had I been foolish enough to adopt such a position, I would have committed myself to the thesis that earthquakes and volcanic eruptions are potential holders of claim-rights—since those natural calamities, as well as countless other natural events and entities, figure prominently in the lives of people who have been affected by them. Rather, the purpose of my focus on the presence of the dead in the outlooks and conduct of the living is to ascertain the length of time during which each dead person is morally assimilable to the person he or she was while still alive. Any typical dead person was a paradigmatic member of the class of potential right-holders while still alive, and even the exceptional dead people who were not paradigmatic members of that class during their lifetimes were nonetheless of the same species as the paradigmatic members and were therefore also potential holders of rights. That aspect of each dead person's situation is constitutive of a crucial difference between each such person and an earthquake or a volcanic eruption or a river. Whereas the effects of a dead person on the conduct and outlooks of living people are due to what that person did or said or intended while he or she was a potential holder of claim-rights, the effects of an inanimate occurrence or entity on the conduct and outlooks of living people are not similarly analyzable. At no point has a river or an earthquake or a volcanic eruption ever occupied the status of a potential holder of claim-rights. Hence, there is no purchase for any question about the moral assimilability of such a natural entity or event to some previous phase when it possessed that status. By contrast, I am grappling with just such a question about a dead person when I seek to pin down how long he or she remains a potential holder of claim-rights.

Bowen goes on to assert that "it is just not clear why focusing on the various ways in which the dead figure in the lives of the living amounts to a morally relevant similarity to Kramer's paradigm right-holders" (2022: 64). Bowen's bafflement is itself baffling. I have just recounted in a nutshell why I devote so much attention to the influence of the dead on the outlooks and conduct of the living, and I explain that matter at considerably greater length in "Getting Rights Right." What is obvious is that living people have interests in the occurrence or non-occurrence of sundry events that will emerge (if at all) after their deaths. The overall trajectory of the life of such a person would be enhanced by the occurrence of some of those events and by the non-occurrence of others.[10] What is not obvious, and what is therefore addressed by my cogitations on dead people in "Getting Rights Right," is the length of time during which the aforementioned interests of each such person will be protectable through claim-rights held by him or her after his or her death. Bowen apparently thinks that he does not need to wrestle with that question. As we shall see, his neglect of it saddles his own account of posthumous right-holding with some preposterous implications.

1.2.3.4 A fourth assault

Bowen next adverts to something which I myself highlight in "Getting Rights Right": namely, the fact that people figure prominently in the lives of their successors for varying periods. Some people will posthumously remain potential holders of claim-rights longer than will others. Bowen thinks that that corollary of my approach to this matter is problematic (2022: 65):

> [H]ow much one figures in the lives of the living is going to depend on how influential one is. No matter how successful I could hope to be in my philosophical career, for

[10] For one of the many passages in Shakespeare's plays where this point is recognized, see *The Comedy of Errors*, III.i.98–106.

> example, it is very likely that Shakespeare will figure more in the lives of others than I. This means that Shakespeare will be a potential right-holder for far longer than I. But, this might strike one as implausible. Suppose Shakespeare and I were to have been contemporaries—then, our status as potential right-holders should have been morally equal; yet, this equality breaks down after we die.

As we shall discover, the worry expressed by Bowen in this passage is deeply ironic. His own preferred approach to the matter of posthumous right-holding will call for extreme inequalities among the spans of time during which various dead people are included in the class of potential right-holders.

How telling is Bowen's complaint against my account of posthumous right-holding? Two main responses to this question are appropriate here. First is a point made repeatedly in "Getting Rights Right," where my discussion of posthumous right-holding concentrates almost entirely on legal rights rather than on moral rights. We need to distinguish between (1) questions about the span of time during which a dead person remains a potential holder of legal claim-rights and (2) questions about the degree to which and the ways in which the interests of a dead person should be legally protected. With perfect consistency, an expansive position on the matters covered by the former set of questions can be combined with a highly restrictive position on the matters covered by the latter set of questions, and vice versa. Accepting that some person P after death will remain a potential holder of legal claim-rights for quite a lengthy period is entirely compatible with insisting that the interests of P should receive very little protection through the establishment of legal duties. Conversely, accepting that some person P after death will remain a potential holder of legal claim-rights for quite a short span is fully compatible with insisting that certain interests of P should be amply and prolongedly safeguarded through the establishment of legal duties. When we keep in mind the distinction drawn in this paragraph between two sets of questions, we can see that the prospect of inequalities among dead people in the sustainedness of their classifiability as potential holders of legal claim-rights is far less troubling than it might at first appear. Those disparities do not entail any disparities among the degrees to which—or the ways in which—the interests of various dead people are to be furthered through the imposition of legal duties. Disparities of the latter kind might obtain, of course, but they never follow simply by dint of the fact that disparities of the former kind obtain.

Second is a point which is suggested but insufficiently developed in "Getting Rights Right" and which will be elaborated rigorously in my forthcoming book on rights and right-holding. That is, although there will undoubtedly be some inequalities among dead people in regard to the lengths of the periods during which they remain potential holders of legal claim-rights, those inequalities will not be vast. This point relates to my criticism of Bowen for his contention that my account of posthumous right-holding attaches determinative importance to the sheer fact that dead people figure saliently in the outlooks and conduct of people who are still alive. Of crucial significance is not the sheer salience of the influence of the dead, but the mode of that influence. My focus on the presence of dead people in the conduct and outlooks of the living is aimed at ascertaining the assimilability or inassimilability of each dead person to the person who he or she was while alive. Accordingly, the modes of influence investigated by such an enquiry are those which are characteristic of a living person on his or her contemporaries. Memories of a dead person P on the part of his or her contemporaries (including much younger contemporaries, and contemporaries who never met P) are obviously among those modes of influence, as are the inheritance of assets from P and any other direct ways in which P has affected his or her contemporaries. After a few generations have passed, however, any familiarity with the life of P on the part of people in later generations is historical knowledge rather than genuine memories. Somebody can of course feel great admiration for her ancestors or for other people from the past, but after a few generations such attitudes are harbored toward them as historical figures rather than as coevals. Likewise, the bequest of property by P to his or her direct heir(s) is very different from the bequest of that property three or four generations later by a descendant of P to the descendant's own legatees. Whereas the former bequest is a direct connection to P on the part of the heir(s), the latter bequest is a historical connection to P.

Whenever P's presence in the minds and conduct of her successors is sufficient to ground her status as a potential holder of legal claim-rights, that presence consists in the relatively direct connections between P and her coevals (again, including those who are much younger and those who never met her). By contrast, when P's presence consists only in historical connections—because all her contemporaries have ceased to exist—her status as a potential holder of legal claim-rights no longer obtains. Moreover, even when some of her contemporaries are still alive, P may have ceased to be a potential holder of such claim-rights because nobody's conduct or outlook is any longer influenced by what P said or did or intended. Thus, although dead people will remain potential right-holders for varying amounts of time, the disparities among those lengths of time will be quite limited.

This second response to Bowen's complaint is of course in need of some further exposition and justification. I cannot devote any additional discussion to it here, but it will be explored in *Rights and Right-Holding* in the context of a broader set of reflections on the role of time in the holding of rights. Furthermore, although the distinction between temporally proximate connections and historical connections is left largely implicit in "Getting Rights Right," that distinction captures nicely the general drift of my ruminations there on the circumstances under which dead people belong to the class of potential holders of rights. For the moment, then, I will desist from pursuing this matter—which has been introduced in the present context simply to indicate that it defuses the consternation expressed by Bowen (consternation much better directed against his own account of posthumous right-holding, as we shall see).

1.2.3.5 Mistaken impressions

One of the most interesting objections in Bowen's chapter is pressed not by Bowen himself but by Kurki. Bowen writes (2022: 65 n.45): "Visa Kurki has raised some additional complications in private communication. Following Shakespeare's death, the living's picture of him could well have gradually shifted from what he was actually like. At the limiting case, someone could die and the living could have a completely false view of them." As is well known in the literature in the philosophy of language that has developed from the work of Saul Kripke and Hilary Putnam and others, the germane response to Kurki's conundrum will depend on the referential intentions of the contemporaries of Shakespeare who contemplate him after his death. If their referential intentions are *de re*, and if there is not any radical reference failure in their discourses about Shakespeare—a failure that would consist in their talking about someone who has in fact never existed—then their erroneous attributions of sundry accomplishments and characteristics to him do not prevent their utterances from referring to him. In such circumstances, he is present in the outlooks and conduct of his surviving contemporaries (albeit in decidedly peculiar ways), and he therefore continues to possess the status of a potential holder of legal claim-rights. By contrast, if the referential intentions of those contemporaries are *de dicto*, then their sweeping mistakenness about the traits and doings of Shakespeare is such that he is not genuinely exerting any influence on their thoughts and conduct. In these extreme circumstances, that influence is actually exerted by someone else—perhaps Francis Bacon or Edward de Vere—to whom the contemporaries' erroneous descriptions apply. If none of the coevals of Shakespeare is referring to him *de re*, and if none of them has any accurate recollections of what Shakespeare did or said or intended, then he is no longer present among them and is therefore no longer a potential holder of legal claim-rights.

1.2.3.6 Purposes mistook and fall'n on the inventor's head

Bowen complains that my account of posthumous right-holding classifies dead people as potential right-holders for disparate lengths of time. As has been observed, however, the inequalities among dead people in that respect are quite modest under my account. By contrast, the inequalities among them under Bowen's preferred approach to posthumous right-holding are vast—indeed, virtually limitless. Bowen supposes that well-being either is a matter of satisfying one's desires or is a matter of attaining worthwhile objectives, and he argues as follows for the status of dead people as potential holders of rights (2022: 67):

> Now, many of my desires may be satisfied after I die. Many of the potential accomplishments that are relevant for the Objective List can be affected after I die. (In fact, it is plausible that many of my most strongly held desires and most important accomplishments survive my death. For example, how my loved ones fare.) Because of this, both Desire and Objective List Theories can say that things can be good or bad for us (can affect our well-being) after we die. If we endorsed the Well-being View of Interests, this means the dead are bearers of interests, and so potential right-holders on the Interest Theory. This is because our interests can be served or potentially ground duties after we die.

I will here concentrate on only one major difficulty that afflicts Bowen's line of reasoning. Whereas the contents of some people's desires or of their worthwhile objectives extend far into the future, the contents of some other people's desires or of their worthwhile objectives extend little if at all into the future. One person might desire that human beings continue to live and flourish on the planet Earth until it is ultimately engulfed by the sun hundreds of millions of years hence, and she might pursue various projects that will conduce to the fulfillment of her desire. Another person might desire simply that she herself will enjoy a comfortable existence until she eventually dies, and she might give nary a thought to the prospect of human survival and flourishing long after her demise. Under Bowen's approach to the posthumous holding of rights, the first of these people will qualify as a potential right-holder for hundreds of millions of years. In sharp contrast, the second person will qualify as a potential right-holder for only quite a short time after her death. Countless other attitudes and objectives harbored by people are likewise possible, of course, with contents that project into the future even further or at diverse intermediate levels. Hence, anybody who endorses Bowen's analysis of posthumous right-holding is thereby committed to accepting that there can be (and almost certainly will be) gaping inequalities among dead people in regard to the lengths of time during which they are potential holders of rights. Bowen has lumbered himself with such a conclusion precisely because he does not engage in the sorts of enquiries which he derides me for undertaking.

1.3 Rowan Cruft and the Interest Theory of Right-Holding

Having known Cruft for more than two decades, I am delighted that he has moved on from his undergraduate and postgraduate endeavors in Cambridge to become one of the United Kingdom's leading political philosophers at the University of Stirling. He believes that the Interest Theory of right-holding (as I expound it) does not quite succeed in providing a necessary condition or a sufficient condition for the holding of a legal right. Throughout his piquant discussion of the matter, Cruft appears to have in mind two main concerns which he does not sufficiently disentangle. I will maintain that both of those concerns are misguided, and also that Cruft errs in thinking that every moral claim-right is justificatorily grounded on the interests of the individual who possesses the claim-right. Moreover, Cruft's perception of a tension between my Interest Theory of right-holding and my allegiance to legal positivism is baseless.

1.3.1 Unquestioning Deference to Officials' Self-Understandings?

Let us start with the two concerns that run throughout the chapter by Cruft. In the first place, he often seems to think that a philosopher must take at face value the terms that have been employed by the legislators or administrators in a system of governance to frame the laws which they bring into existence—or the terms that have been employed by the system's adjudicators and administrators to characterize those laws in their official pronouncements thereon. Such an assumption appears to underlie an oft-repeated assertion in Cruft's chapter: "[L]awmakers can create rights wherever they want, independently of the location of any interests" (2022: 38). The position epitomized in this quoted statement is central to Cruft's essay, yet it appears to rest on the assumption which I have specified.

Suppose that, in a certain municipality Arborea, the local authorities enact an ordinance that purports to bestow legal claim-rights on leaves that have fallen from trees. Under the terms of the ordinance, each homeowner in Arborea is legally obligated to gather any leaves that have fallen onto an adjoining sidewalk from trees planted on the homeowner's property. The leaves are to be stored in sacks, so that they can be taken away by municipal functionaries for compost heaps or for other useful projects. By the reckoning of the local authorities, the ordinance furthers the interests of leaves.

Instead of rotting as a slippery mush on the sidewalks of Arborea, the leaves end their existence in ways that serve valuable purposes. Consequently, the authorities designate their enactment as the "Upholding of Rights of Fallen Foliage Ordinance," in the sincere belief that a correlate of the legal duty imposed on each homeowner by the ordinance is a legal claim-right held by each leaf (or by the leaves collectively on each relevant portion of the sidewalk). Now, when a legal philosopher seeks to specify the deontic upshot of such a law, must he or she accept at face value the terms in which the ordinance is drafted and the terms in which the legal-governmental officials characterize what they have done? Cruft apparently thinks that the answer to this question is affirmative, such that the Arborean lawmakers have indeed bestowed legal claim-rights on the fallen leaves of their city. By contrast, when I have delimited the class of potential holders of legal claim-rights—in my 2001 essay "Getting Rights Right" and in some subsequent writings—I have excluded fallen leaves from that class.

Important here is clarity concerning what is at issue between Cruft and me. Neither of us doubts that the Arborean authorities have enacted a genuine law in the form of their ordinance, and neither of us doubts that that law imposes a legal duty or a set of legal duties on every homeowner in the city. Nor does either of us doubt that the legal duty incumbent on every homeowner under the ordinance is correlated with a legal claim-right or with an array of legal claim-rights. Rather, we disagree only about the location of the relevant claim-right(s). Cruft believes that a legal claim-right is held by each leaf or by the leaves collectively on each stretch of the sidewalk, whereas I maintain that claim-rights correlated with the legal duties of homeowners are held by the Arborean government and perhaps also by members of the public individually or collectively. Perhaps Cruft would agree with me that legal claim-rights are held by the local government in this scenario, but he will insist that such a claim-right is also held by each leaf or by the leaves collectively on each stretch of a sidewalk. Though I of course accept that the Arborean officials and their ordinance earnestly *purport* to confer a legal claim-right on each leaf or on the leaves collectively, I part ways with Cruft as I deny that the deontic upshot of the ordinance actually includes the holding of any legal claim-rights by the leaves.

Strange though Cruft's position is in relation to the scenario of Arborea, it is even more peculiar in relation to the following scenario. Suppose that the government in another municipality, Superstitia, enacts an ordinance which purports to confer upon the god Apollo a legal claim-right to the sacrifice of a goat annually by every head of a household in the city. Explicitly framed in terms of investing Apollo with the legal claim-right just mentioned, the ordinance imposes a legal obligation on every head of a household in Superstitia. Cruft has committed himself to the conclusion that a legal claim-right held by the non-existent god Apollo is a correlate of the legal obligation incumbent on every head of a Superstitian household. (Note that, unlike dead people and the people in future generations, Apollo never has existed and never will exist.) A more sensible exposition of the deontic upshot of the Superstitian ordinance will conclude that that enactment does not produce the instances of right-holding which its drafters have aspired to produce. Sincere though the drafters are in presuming to bestow legal claim-rights upon Apollo, what they have instead done is to bestow legal claim-rights solely upon their own system of governance. Cruft errs in thinking otherwise.

Let us glance at one further example. In the city of Innumeratia, the local authorities enact an ordinance which purports to impose a legal duty on the number 7 to become smaller than the number 6. Framing their new law in explicitly deontic terms, the legislative officials in Innumeratia pride themselves on having at last given the number 6 its due by endowing it with a legal claim-right to be made greater than the number 7. Cruft has tied himself to the conclusion that the legislators in Innumeratia have indeed conferred a legal claim-right upon the number 6.

Why has Cruft saddled himself with such a preposterous array of verdicts? The answer to this question appears to lie in his conception of legal positivism. He thinks that positivists do contend, and are correct in contending, that "lawmakers can create rights wherever they want, independently of the location of rights-independent interests" (2022: 41). He thus thinks that legal positivists would contend, and would be correct in contending, that the legal-governmental officials in Innumeratia have bestowed a legal claim-right upon the number 6 to be made greater than the number 7—and that the legal-governmental officials in Superstitia have bestowed some legal claim-rights upon Apollo, and that the legal-governmental officials in Arborea have bestowed some legal claim-rights upon the fallen leaves. *Pace* Cruft, however, nothing in legal positivism commits its proponents to such risible conclusions. On the one hand, legal positivists do maintain that the status of any norm N as a law in any particular jurisdiction J is dependent on N's being treated as a law in J by the officials who operate the system of governance that presides there. On the other hand, no legal positivist should accept that every N treated as a law in J by the legal-governmental officials there will necessarily have produced the deontic upshot that is attributed to N by the officials. In particular, the upshot envisaged by the officials will not have occurred if its occurrence is impossible.

This point about impossibility is obvious when the envisaged upshot is a mathematical or scientific matter rather than a deontic matter. Suppose that, instead of enacting an ordinance that purports to impose a legal duty on the number 7 to become smaller than the number 6, the authorities in Insania enact a declaratory law which affirms that the number 6 is greater than the number 7. The authorities pride themselves on having brought about the state of affairs that is proclaimed in their declaratory law. Does Cruft believe that we have to defer to the ways in which the officials understand the upshot of their own legislative endeavors, and that we therefore have to conclude that 6 is greater than 7 in Insania? Since I have no reason to doubt Cruft's sanity, I presume that the answer to this question is negative. However, the absence of deference to the officials' self-understandings here should be paralleled by an absence of deference in response to each of the three scenarios above.

The number 6 as a timeless and invariant abstract entity has no interests. It is not susceptible to being improved, nor is it susceptible to any worsening of its condition. Consequently, the holding of legal claim-rights by the number 6 is a conceptual impossibility. Just as the mathematical impossibility of a state of affairs in which 6 exceeds 7 is a decisive ground for rejecting the Insanian officials' beliefs about the upshot of their declaratory law, so too the conceptual impossibility of the holding of legal claim-rights by the number 6 is a decisive ground for rejecting the Innumeratian officials' beliefs about the deontic upshot of their ordinance which purports to invest the number 6 with a legal claim-right.

Apollo as a being that never has existed and never will exist is likewise devoid of interests. Though his existence is not a mathematical impossibility, it is nomologically impossible and probably also metaphysically impossible. Apollo is thus not susceptible to improvements in his condition, nor is he susceptible to any worsening therein. Hence, the holding of legal claim-rights by Apollo is a conceptual impossibility. Accordingly, there is a decisive ground for declining to acquiesce in the Superstitian officials' understanding of the deontic upshot of their ordinance relating to the sacrifice of goats. Contrary to what those officials presume, the ordinance does not confer any legal claim-rights on the non-existent god Apollo.

Somewhat different is the vignette concerning the efforts of the municipal legislators in Arborea to bestow legal claim-rights upon the leaves that have fallen onto the sidewalks of the city. I will assume here *arguendo* that fallen leaves have some interests. That is, I assume *arguendo* that the condition of such leaves is susceptible to being improved and to being worsened; the leaves can acquire value by being used in certain ways, and they can lose value by being used in other ways or by being left to fester. Still, although fallen leaves are endowed with interests (or so I assume here), they are not included in the class of potential right-holders. Their exclusion from that class does not mark any departure from the standard for inclusion which I have broached in section 1.2.2 above. In other words, the exclusion of fallen leaves from the category of potential holders of rights is straightforwardly consistent with the sway of political and social and economic conditions under which every member of a society can be warranted in feeling a strong sense of self-respect. Indeed, because such leaves are unequivocally not entities endowed with ultimate value, the inclusion of them in the class of potential right-holders is an ethical impossibility.[11] Given the ethical impossibility of the holding of claim-rights by fallen leaves, there is a decisive basis for rejecting what the Arborean officials think about the deontic upshot of the Upholding the Rights of Fallen Foliage Ordinance. Contrary to what the officials presume, they have not succeeded in conferring any legal claim-rights upon fallen leaves.

Now, if (as I believe) my version of the Interest Theory is correct as an account of the necessary and sufficient conditions for the holding of a legal claim-right, then there is a decisive basis for rejecting any ascriptions of legal claim-rights which are inconsistent with that account. The states of affairs envisioned by any such ascriptions are conceptual impossibilities. As a matter of conceptual necessity, there are never genuinely any instances of right-holding that are not identifiable as such by the criterion encapsulated in my version of the Interest Theory. Legislators or other legal-governmental officials in some jurisdiction might believe that they have brought into existence such instances of right-holding, but they are mistaken in so believing—just as the Superstitian officials are mistaken in believing that they have invested the inexistent god Apollo with legal claim-rights to the sacrificing of goats.

Notwithstanding Cruft's apparent view to the contrary, the question whether a law has conferred a legal claim-right on some party is both an interpretive matter and a conceptual matter. As legal positivists emphasize with their attentiveness to the

[11] For an explication of the property of ethical impossibility, see Kramer 2009: 157–61.

variability of the techniques adopted by judges and administrators in endeavors of legal interpretation, the interpretive aspect of any question about the correctness of an ascription of a legal claim-right is largely determined by the courts and administrators. By contrast, the conceptual aspect is governed by my version of the Interest Theory along with ethical considerations that delimit the class of potential holders of rights. If the officials in some jurisdiction profess to have bestowed a claim-right upon some party, and if their attribution of a claim-right to that party is at odds with my version of the Interest Theory, then the holding of the claim-right by that party—in the circumstances contemplated by the officials—is a conceptual impossibility. (Likewise, if that attribution of a claim-right is at variance with the ethical considerations that delimit the range of potential holders of rights, then the deontic upshot affirmed in that attribution is an ethical impossibility.)

1.3.2 Modes of Enforcement

The other main concern that suffuses some portions of Cruft's critique of the Interest Theory is his awareness that the arrangements for giving effect to claim-rights can vary significantly. Though Cruft does not articulate his view on this matter as explicitly and directly as might be wished, it quite clearly underlies his position in much of the latter half of his chapter. Consider, for example, the following passage (2022: 45-6, footnotes deleted, emphases in original):

> Often we have reasons to create some sort of legal duty, and whether it is a party's right makes little difference to our achievement of the ends that justify the creation of the law. For instance, if our aim is to secure efficient traffic management, we can do that by creating a set of legal duties about the rules of the road and parking. Whether these involve *rights* (e.g., that others stop at red lights, or respect spaces one has paid for), and who might hold such rights, are in my view issues that are not central to whether the aims of the system will be achieved. A system that involved the same legal *duties* (to stop on red, to respect paid-for spaces) but without these being anyone's rights, or with all the rights being held by the state as a "sovereign right monopoly," could be just as effective—or nearly as effective—as one that involved individually held rights.

In one of the footnotes which I have omitted, Cruft acknowledges that his reflections in this passage presuppose the falsity of my version of the Interest Theory of right-holding. Instead of identifying the holders of legal claim-rights by reference to the factors that are invoked in the Interest Theory, Cruft is identifying them by reference to the factors that are invoked in the Will Theory. He presumes that the location of a legal claim-right correlative to a specified legal duty is dependent on the location of the legal powers to waive or effectuate that duty. Cruft concludes that, if those powers are not in the hands of any private individual and are instead vested solely in legal-governmental officials *qua* legal-governmental officials, then no private individual holds any legal claim-right correlative to the specified legal duty. Any legal claim-right correlative to that duty is held solely by the prevailing system of governance. In so concluding, Cruft has plighted his allegiance to the Will Theory's criterion for the holding of legal claim-rights. I therefore look forward to his future work in which he will defend the Will Theory against the medley of objections that have been raised against it.[12]

1.3.3 The Justificatory Bases of Moral Rights

Like his erstwhile doctoral student Bowen, Cruft believes that Raz's justificatory version of the Interest Theory is correct as an account of basic moral rights and of many derivative moral rights (2022: 47, emphases in original, footnotes omitted):

> An "Interest Theory" of specifically *pre-legal moral or natural rights* seems to me extremely plausible. If we consider those rights most likely to exist independently of law, as natural rights, we find rights that very plausibly serve their holders' interests: for example, rights against torture and assault, rights to have a say in how one's community is run, rights to minimal freedom or autonomy, rights against discrimination and to equal treatment and concern. For such pre-legal moral or natural rights, an approach based on Raz's version of the "Interest Theory" strikes me as especially attractive: a person A holds a natural moral right that someone B perform some action or inaction (not torture A, give A say in how we should live together, etc.) if and only if A's interests are sufficiently important to constitute a major part of the moral grounds for B's natural moral duty to perform that action or inaction. On this account, to refer to a person's pre-legal moral or natural rights is to refer to those duties borne by others that exist independently of our say-so, and which *owe their existence largely to the importance of that particular person's interests*—rather than, for example, to the importance of the aggregated interests of many, or to the importance of values distinct from human interests.

I encourage Cruft to become acquainted with my 2014 book *Torture and Moral Integrity* and with my 2017 book *Liberalism with Excellence*, because they reveal why his embrace of Raz's justificatory version of the Interest Theory is misguided. As I have there argued at length in ruminations on the wrongness of punitive torture and sadistic torture and interrogational torture (2014: 187–203, 206–12; 2017b: 256–64), the interests of potential victims of those types of torture are not sufficient to ground the absoluteness of the moral principles that forbid the perpetration of such conduct. That is, they are not sufficient to ground the fact that the principles in question are morally binding always and everywhere. I adduce several examples in my 2014 book to illustrate this point, and several further examples in my 2017 book. Here I shall mention only a couple of them.

Suppose that, instead of being sheltered by Argentina and Paraguay and Brazil for three decades after the Second World War, Josef Mengele had been captured and placed on trial. Mengele was directly responsible for hundreds of thousands of murders at Auschwitz and for thousands of acts of grisly torture. Nonetheless, as I have argued in the books just mentioned, he had a moral claim-right not to be subjected to punitive torture. Given that the right not to be subjected to torture is the very first item

[12] For my most recently published critique of the Will Theory of right-holding, see Kramer 2013. That article also recounts some of my earlier objections to the Will Theory. In *Rights and Right-Holding*, I will greatly strengthen and extend my 2013 critique.

in Cruft's list of moral rights, Cruft presumably thinks that the standard articulated in Raz's justificatory version of the Interest Theory is both necessary and sufficient for explaining why Mengele had a moral right not to be subjected to punitive torture. In fact, however, the standard articulated in Raz's theory is neither necessary nor sufficient. It is insufficient, because Mengele's interests in not being subjected to excruciating pain and humiliation were of no positive moral weight. Nor is the standard articulated in Raz's theory necessary, since the pivotal consideration that undergirded Mengele's moral right not to be subjected to punitive torture was the moral integrity of the potential perpetrators of the torture. In the final sentence of the passage quoted most recently above, Cruft appears to think that the lone alternatives to the interests of potential victims of torture—as justificatory bases for a moral principle that prohibits the administering of punitive torture—are aggregative maximands and humanity-independent values. He thereby strikingly disregards the orientation of many a deontological theory of morality. Instead of focusing on any of the justificatory factors which Cruft recounts, we have to focus on the moral integrity of the potential perpetrators of torture if we hope to explain why Mengele in all his vileness was endowed with a moral right not to be subjected to punitive torture. I cannot here go into the relevant explanation, which I have lengthily supplied in the books cited above. Here my point is simply that Cruft's Razian approach to the justification of moral rights will fail to yield any satisfactory explanation of Mengele's right.

Now suppose that a certain entity which very closely resembles a live human being is in fact a computerized automaton. Such an entity is incapable of experiencing pain or humiliation, though it can simulate the outward behavior that would be impelled by such sensations. Not knowing that the automaton is devoid of any genuine sensations, some thugs overpower it and subject it to torture for their sadistic amusement. If we aspire to explain why the thugs' conduct is seriously wrong, we cannot succeed by adverting to the interests of the automaton in being free from agony and humiliation. After all, *ex hypothesi*, the automaton is not capable of undergoing such sensations (or, indeed, any sensations). To account for the wrongfulness of the hoodlums' sadistic abuse, we need to advert not to the interests of the automaton but instead to the moral integrity of the hoodlums which they debase through their infliction of the torture. In this scenario, the moral claim-rights that correlate with the moral duties breached through the infliction of sadistic torture are held not by the automaton but by the louts who have stooped to such savagery—and by the broader community. Degrading themselves through such behavior, the louts have committed wrongs both against themselves and against the community whose system of governance is morally obligated to secure the conditions under which every member of the community can be warranted in harboring an ample sense of self-respect. Cruft's Razian approach to these matters, focused as it would be on the putative interests of the automaton, is bootless for coming to grips with the moral bearings and subtleties of this situation.

1.4 Visa Kurki on the Interest Theory and Legal Positivism

Among the contributors to this volume who were doctoral students under my supervision, Kurki is the youngest. Upon my first encounter with him, I was greatly impressed not only by the acuity of his intellect but also by the steeliness of his determination and self-discipline. For an academic philosopher, the steeliness is as important as the acuity. Kurki combines those properties in abundance.

Covering some of the same matters which Cruft's chapter addresses, Kurki's incisive essay proceeds from a perspective much closer to my own. I will thus be brief in my engagement with Kurki, in keeping with what I have said at the outset of these replies to the contributors. Indeed, given that there are so few points of disagreement between him and me, the brevity of this section is inevitable.

1.4.1 Hollowly Nominal Claim-Rights

My first point of partial disagreement with Kurki arises when he glancingly adverts to my emphasis on the role of immunities in securing the continuation and the very existence of claim-rights and other entitlements. I accept one of his reservations. He notes that I draw a contrast between "hollowly nominal" claim-rights which are unprotected by any immunities and "genuine" claim-rights which are amply protected by immunities, and he observes that in my early writings on rights I drew a contrast between "nominal" claim-rights which are unenforceable and "genuine" claim-rights which are enforceable and quite regularly enforced (2022: 78 n.22). I agree with Kurki that my use of the "nominal"/"genuine" terminology to mark two separate distinctions is potentially confusing. I believe that that terminology is much better suited to the more recent context in which I have employed it, and that I should have eschewed it in my early ruminations on the matter of enforceability—not least because, in one of the early essays containing those ruminations and that terminology, I in fact explore the reality and importance of unenforceable legal claim-rights (2001: 65–73). In *Rights and Right-Holding*, I will remedy my early terminological infelicities.

More dubious or at least misleading, however, is the following passage by Kurki about hollowly nominal claim-rights (2022: 78):

> Kramer must think that hollowly nominal rights are nevertheless rights. Denying that hollowly nominal rights are rights might *ipso facto* mean abandoning the Correlativity Axiom, according to which rights and duties always correlate with each other. If hollowly nominal rights were not rights, Jim would bear the duty not to punch John, but John would not hold any correlative right.

Two things should be said in response to this passage. First, some immunities are partly constitutive of the sheer existence of a claim-right and its correlative duty. For example, if one's claim-right against being punched in the face could be extinguished through an assailant's clenching of his fist or through his thrusting of his arm toward one's face, the claim-right would not really exist as such. It would not exist in a situation where the very movements of an assailant's body that would be involved in contravening the correlative duty are sufficient to extinguish that duty.

Second, the Correlativity Axiom is not rendered problematic by the fact that the existence of any claim-right is dependent on the existence of accompanying immunities. Although a specified claim-right would not exist in the absence of the immunities that are partly constitutive of its existence, the duty correlated with that claim-right would likewise not exist in the absence of those immunities. Just as a hollowly nominal claim-right is always correlated with a hollowly nominal duty, the inexistence of any claim-right entails—and is entailed by—the inexistence of the duty that would be correlated with it. Thus, Kurki's worries about the Correlativity Axiom in the passage above are a red herring. A hollowly nominal claim-right is indeed a claim-right even though it is hollowly nominal; and it is correlated with a hollowly nominal duty. An inexistent claim-right is not a claim-right, of course, and it is correlated not with a duty but with the absence of a duty. These conclusions are exactly what the Correlativity Axiom provides.

1.4.2 An Anarchistic Threat to the Correlativity Axiom?

My only significant disagreement with Kurki arises in the closing pages of his essay, where he discusses the Correlativity Axiom afresh from quite a different angle. He contends that, even if all legal duties are correlated with legal claim-rights (something which he doubts), the unfailingness of their correlativity is a contestable matter that has to be established through substantive argumentation rather than through axiomatic stipulation. As he declares: "That every legal duty would [be correlated with a legal claim-right] is certainly subject to empirical refutation, or at least to conceivable counterexamples" (2022: 89). Yet, as Kurki explicitly acknowledges, I have always maintained that every legal duty is owed to the system of governance that imposes it. Some legal duties are only so owed, whereas countless other such duties are owed also to further parties. Whenever a legal duty is owed to someone, he or she or it is the holder of a legal claim-right correlative to that duty. Consequently, every legal duty is correlated with a legal claim-right vested in the system of governance that has imposed the duty. This thesis about every legal duty, a thesis that is sufficient to sustain the Correlativity Axiom, is a straightforward corollary of my version of the Interest Theory of right-holding. Hence, my endorsement of the Correlativity Axiom is not really a matter of stipulation but is instead a matter of embracing the implications of the best account of right-holding.

Kurki tries to show that my thesis about every legal duty does not follow from the Interest Theory of right-holding (2022: 90). He retorts that "we could think of an anarchist party winning the majority in a parliamentary election and thereby enacting legislation aimed toward dismantling the state. Would the ensuing duties be correlated by the state's right-to-be-dismantled?" Three rejoinders are appropriate here. First, the content of the legal claim-right at issue should be formulated in a way that reveals why every legal duty is correlated with a legal claim-right. Hence, the relevant claim-right is the legal right of a system of governance to compliance (by officials and by ordinary citizens) with each legal requirement which the system has established as a legal requirement. This formulation of the content of the claim-right covers the specific substance of any legal duty *qua* something that is legally required.

Second, such a formulation of the content of the relevant claim-right patently leaves open the possibility that the fulfillment of any particular legal duty will be detrimental to the system of governance that has imposed the duty. That possibility is entirely in keeping with my version of the Interest Theory of right-holding, which deliberately leaves room for anomalous cases in which the fulfillment of some legal duties would harm the parties to whom the duties are owed. If a legal mandate LM is such that the fulfillment of it would be detrimental to the system of governance which has introduced it, LM nonetheless confers legal claim-rights on that system of governance to the conformity of citizens and officials with the requirements of LM—because conformity with legal mandates is typically or generally beneficial for a system of governance, even if conformity with LM is an exception to that general pattern. Accordingly, notwithstanding that compliance with the state-dismantling legislation of the anarchists would be injurious to the system of governance through which the legislation is enacted, the legislation confers rights-to-compliance upon that system of governance. It does so because compliance with the legislative enactments of such a system is typically conducive to the effectiveness of the system's operations, and because typical conduciveness (rather than invariable conduciveness) is all that is needed under the terms of the Interest Theory of right-holding.

Third, Kurki is not really in a position to invoke the example of the anarchists and their daft legislation. After all, he subscribes to H.L.A. Hart's argument about the minimum content of natural law (Kurki 2022: 76), and a central strand of that argument is that no credibly possible society larger than a handful of families can endure for more than the briefest period without a system of governance that will give effect to legal prohibitions on very serious modes of misconduct. From Kurki's own perspective, then, quite chimerical is the prospect of the takeover of a system of governance by anarchists who eliminate without replacement the institutions of law-creation and law-application in a credibly possible (and sizable) society that continues as a functionally cohesive society. I heartily join Kurki in maintaining that the prospect of a sizable and cohesive society with no such institutions is too outlandishly fanciful to be taken seriously in any theory of law or theory of right-holding.

1.4.3 Anencephalic Infants

Kurki adduces one further example in his effort to impugn the Correlativity Axiom (2022: 90, footnote omitted):

> An example that I find particularly problematic is that of anencephalic infants. Such infants lack a brain cortex and can therefore never become sentient. This renders them unable to hold rights, as they are not of ultimate value. Anencephalic infants are, however, treated as natural persons by at least some Western legal systems. Thus, causing bodily harm to such an infant may engender a tort-law duty to compensate. However, toward whom is such a duty borne? The infant cannot hold any rights. Are such rights, then, held by the state? Kramer would likely provide such a response, given that he thinks that all legal duties are also owed to the state.

What Kurki says at the end of this passage is correct, and its correctness is sufficient to shield the Correlativity Axiom against his critique. However, I should note further that what he says about the ultimate value of anencephalic infants is not correct—or, at any rate, it is not in accordance with my own view of the matter.

On the one hand, one of the two properties which I have long fixed upon as jointly sufficient for the ultimate value of a being is inapplicable to an anencephalic infant. That is, I have long held that a being is of ultimate value if (1) it is *un être pour soi* and (2) the furtherance of its interests is intrinsically valuable.[13] Though the second

[13] For the first of the two properties, I use the Sartrean phrasing—rather than the language of "consciousness"—in order to leave open the question whether some future computerized entities will partake of ultimate value despite their lack of consciousness.

of these properties is appositely predicable of an anencephalic infant, the first of them is not. As Kurki observes, an anencephalic infant never has been sentient and never will be sentient. Kurki therefore might appear to be correct in thinking that, on my account of ultimate value, anencephalic infants are devoid of such value.

On the other hand, although the two properties just specified are together sufficient for the ultimate value of a being, only the second of them is necessary. As I state explicitly in "Getting Rights Right" (2001: 36, 45–57), human beings have to be differentiated from other beings in any account of ultimate value. All living human beings are possessed of ultimate value, even if they are permanently insentient (either because they are deeply and irrecoverably comatose or because they are anencephalic). As has been suggested in section 1.2.2 of my replies to Bowen above, the reason for distinguishing between human beings and other beings in this fashion is that questions about the inclusion of various beings in the class of potential right-holders are questions about the extent to which the paradigmatic members of that class are morally obligated to accept that other beings are also members—a matter which in turn hinges on whether the exclusion of certain other beings would be consistent with the social and political and economic conditions under which every paradigmatic member can be warranted in harboring a strong sense of self-respect. As will be argued in my *Rights and Right-Holding*, the inclusion of all living human beings in the class of potential holders of rights is vital on exactly these grounds. For now, I will simply say that the inclusion of anencephalic infants in that class is something that must be recognized by any system of governance if it is to fulfill its paramount moral responsibility to bring about the conditions just mentioned.

1.5 Mark McBride and Hybrid Theories of Right-Holding

McBride is the only contributor to this volume whom I supervised both at an undergraduate level and at a doctoral level. His formidable strengths as a student were immediately apparent to me, and I am proud and very pleased that he has gone on to become a philosopher with excitingly original ideas. Like Kurki, McBride has contributed a characteristically rigorous and perceptive essay to this collection which the two of them have edited.

Pondering an objection posed by me against Gopal Sreenivasan's theory of right-holding, McBride endeavors to show that his own alternative explication of right-holding can handle the objection satisfactorily. McBride and Sreenivasan are alike in that each of them propounds an account of right-holding that is supposed to be a hybrid of the Interest Theory and the Will Theory. However, as is demonstrated by my objection to Sreenivasan's analysis, his approach entails wildly implausible conclusions—wildly implausible attributions of rights—that would be rejected both by the Interest Theory and by the Will Theory. I aim to show here that McBride's ostensibly hybrid theory does not fare any better.

McBride's account of right-holding is largely a more elaborate and refined version of Sreenivasan's account. Like the latter, the former insists that X's holding of a claim-right always involves (1) X's having an interest in either possessing or lacking control over the correlative duty and (2) X's possessing or lacking such control in accordance with X's interest. Again like Sreenivasan's account, McBride's theory further insists that the congruence between X's actually possessing or lacking control and X's interest in possessing or lacking control must be by design rather than fortuitous, if X is to be classifiable as the holder of the relevant claim-right. However, McBride furnishes a much more rigorous exposition of the "by design" requirement than does Sreenivasan, and he takes account of the fact that control is a scalar property rather than a binary all-or-nothing property.

McBride repeatedly declares that the foremost thought-experiment which I have marshaled against Sreenivasan's theory of right-holding is aimed at hybrid theories generally, and he more boldly states that that thought-experiment "is the single, prominent generalizable *no control* counterexample to hybrid theories" (2022: 98, emphasis in original). His assertion about the generality of my target is overstated but not really unfair, for, although I have presented my scenario of Mark and Paul and Liam solely against Sreenivasan, I have proceeded in the concluding section of my "Theories of Rights" article to proclaim: "Instead of searching for a [hybrid] third way, analysts of rights are best advised to develop ever more refined versions of the Interest Theory or the Will Theory" (Kramer and Steiner 2007: 310). However, misleading at best is the suggestion that that scenario is the single prominent generalizable counterexample to hybrid theories. To be sure, it is—as far as I am aware—the only counterexample to hybrid theories that has heretofore appeared in the philosophical literature on right-holding. Still, I have never implied that it is the sole major counterexample or a uniquely pertinent counterexample. Indeed, I will begin my critique of McBride's hybrid Tracking Theory of right-holding with a quite different thought-experiment. (Admittedly, McBride refers to my earlier thought-experiment specifically as a no-control counterexample. By contrast, the scenario contemplated in my next subsection will depict a situation in which certain powers of control are conferred. However, the scenario could easily be redrafted to depict instead a situation in which the powers of control are withheld.)

1.5.1 Changing the Subject

In a key respect, the approach undertaken by McBride to expound rigorously the "by design" condition is surprising. Given that McBride follows Sreenivasan in employing the language of "design," one might presume that his exposition would take its inspiration from the large body of philosophical writings on intentions.[14] However, he turns not to that literature but instead to epistemology as he develops an account of right-holding that quite closely resembles Robert Nozick's famous tracking theory of knowledge. McBride's choice of philosophical inspiration is of far-reaching importance, for it makes his analysis of the "by design" condition significantly different from what it would otherwise have been. On the one hand, the two main counterfactuals which McBride presents as constitutive of the "by design" condition would doubtless

[14] I should make clear that the intentions in question need not be mental states or entities. In legal interpretation, for example, the intentions ascribed to laws or to lawmakers are not mental states or entities. Rather, when a legal interpreter ascribes an intention to some law L, he or she is seeking to make sense of L in its context by concluding that it has been adopted to promote some value(s) or to address some problem(s). See Kramer 2017b: 75–87.

also have been included in his analysis if he had turned to the philosophical literature on intentions. On the other hand, he would almost certainly have included also an aim-attaining element in his analysis. That is, he would have maintained that the congruence between a right-holder's having or lacking control over some duty and a right-holder's interest in having or lacking control over that duty must be an aim ascribable to the law which confers or withholds the control (or ascribable to the lawmakers who are responsible for the existence of that law). In other words, the congruence must be intentional or "by design." Because McBride's explication of the "by design" condition lacks this additional element, it delivers a host of outlandish conclusions.

Consider the following example. In the country of Bigotria, the prevailing system of governance has been ordered by the courts to make legally possible and permissible the ownership of various assets by black people. Officials in Bigotria reluctantly comply with the injunction, and they therefore have to determine the exact array of entitlements that will be encompassed in the ownership of the specified assets. They decide to bestow upon each black person full control over the duties that are owed to him or her through his or her ownership of any of those assets. They do so not out of any solicitude or other favorable attitudes toward black people, but instead out of poisonous prejudice. Because the Bigotrian officials are so firmly convinced that black people are less intelligent than other people, the officials gleefully presume that endowing black people with full control over the duties owed to them will leave them highly vulnerable to being exploited and outmaneuvered. In other words, the officials invest black people with legal powers of full control over others' duties precisely because the officials believe that black people have interests in lacking such control. In fact, of course, the officials' beliefs about the mental prowess of black people are hideously wrong. Given that the black people in Bigotria are no less shrewd than other people, and given that they are best positioned to judge when they will benefit from engaging in sundry transactions, they as owners of assets have clear interests in being endowed with legal powers that enable them to control the legal duties owed to them by others. There is a match between their having interests in such control and their possessing such control.

Is the congruence between the possession of control and the interests in control "by design"? Let us suppose here that the relevant counterfactuals in McBride's exposition of right-holding are satisfied. I do not want to explore that matter in any detail yet, because I will shortly express my worries about McBride's selectivity in his contemplation of counterfactual possibilities. Still, we can easily come up with possibilities that satisfy the counterfactual elements in his account of right-holding. In a nearby possible world, the Bigotrian officials are not in the grip of any serious racist prejudices and are thus clear-sighted in discerning that black people have interests in possessing full control over the duties that are owed to them through their ownership of assets. Free of any serious racist prejudices, the officials straightforwardly assign such control to black people. In another nearby possible world, most of the black people in Bigotria have interests in being deprived of full control over the duties that are owed to them through their ownership of assets—not because their being possessed of such control would leave them vulnerable to being outwitted, of course, but because it would leave them vulnerable to being coerced by the many bigots in their country. In such a possible world, most of the black people in Bigotria will be better off if the officials there (who are free of serious racial prejudices) possess many of the legal powers that provide control over the legal duties owed to the black people through their ownership of assets. Recognizing as much, the Bigotrian officials do indeed vest themselves with those powers. These two counterfactual scenarios indicate that there are nearby possible worlds which together satisfy the two counterfactual elements in McBride's exposition of right-holding. Those two counterfactual elements constitute the "by design" condition in his exposition.

In the actual world, however, the congruence between the interests of black people in possessing control over duties and their possession of control over those duties is against the designs of the Bigotrian officials rather than in accordance with their designs. That congruence is inadvertent rather than intentional. Nonetheless, McBride's explication of the "by design" condition purely in terms of counterfactuals will have classified that congruence as "by design." The stark focus on counterfactuals in his explication is something which McBride proclaims loudly: "[A] selling point of my own hybrid Tracking Theory, is its (near) *value-neutrality*: the justificatory status of right-holding is explained in terms of the holding of certain counterfactuals" (2022: 107 n.33, emphasis in original). Whatever may be the virtues of the counterfactual-focused approach in McBride's estimation, it does not yield a credible account of a "by design" condition. An approach that classifies outright fortuities as achievements "by design" is changing the subject rather than shedding light on the explanandum.

1.5.2 Overconfident Assertions

To introduce his model of right-holding, McBride asks us to contemplate the situation of a promisee under an ordinary contract. In response, we should recall straightaway that such a situation is not a point of contention between the Interest Theory and the Will Theory. Each of those theories will deliver the verdict that a promisee under an ordinary contract is a holder of claim-rights vis-à-vis the promisor. Hence, as we examine how McBride approaches the matter, we should attend to the difficulties that impede him from delivering a similar verdict. We should likewise attend to the strangeness of his theory in its conclusions about contracts that are relevantly atypical.

McBride begins by announcing that "the match condition [requiring congruity between the promisee's interest in possessing control over correlative duties and the promisee's actual possession of such control] is straightforwardly met" (2022: 102). The straightforwardness derives entirely from his stipulation that the contract is ordinary or quotidian. Were the circumstances instead slightly unusual, there could be some other person or people who would reach decisions about the contractual duties that would be better for the promisee than the decisions which the promisee herself would reach, and the superiority of the decisions would exceed any detriment incurred by the promisee through the sheer fact that she would not be in control of the contractual duties. In any familiar system of contract law, the promisee—who, we can assume, is an adult of sound mind—will in these somewhat unusual circumstances still be vested with legal powers of control over the contractual duties that are owed to her. Hence, the Will Theory as well as the Interest Theory will continue to classify the promisee as a holder of claim-rights that correlate with those duties. A very different conclusion follows from McBride's Tracking Theory of right-holding. Since his theory's match condition is not satisfied (in relation to the promisee) under the slightly unusual circumstances just specified, his theory generates the conclusion that the promisee is not a holder of any contractual claim-rights in those circumstances. McBride professes to have crafted a hybrid account of right-holding, yet here his account in application to somewhat unusual circumstances has yielded a verdict that is at odds with both of the theories from which the hybrid is constructed.

McBride ventures to declare, with reference to the situation of a promisee under an ordinary contract, that the "by design" condition is also "straightforwardly met." Again, any straightforwardness derives entirely from his stipulation that the contract is ordinary. He asserts that, "in the closest situations in which ... it *ceases to be* in [the promisee's] interests on balance to have control, [the promisee] *ceases to be* granted control" (2022: 102, emphases in original). He seeks to back up that assertion by contending that "a paradigm case of the foregoing cessation is when Y ceases to be a promisee, on account of there no longer being an operative promise" (2022: 102). However, quite dubious is the notion that such an eventuality exemplifies what it is supposed to exemplify. After all, the standard that has to be satisfied is formulated by McBride as follows: "If it were not in [the promisee's] interests on balance to have control over [the promisor's] duty to ϕ, then [the promisee] would not have control over [the promisor's] duty to ϕ" (2022: 102). So formulated, the relevant standard presupposes the existence of the promisor's duty to φ. Though the presupposition is cancellable, the fact of its being appurtenant to the standard in question is sufficient to throw doubt on the declaration by McBride that the eventuality which he broaches is a paradigmatic instance of the satisfaction of that standard. Let us instead contemplate a counterfactual scenario in which the promisor's duty continues to exist and in which the promisee ceases to have an on-balance interest in possessing control over that duty. The most obvious such scenario is the one envisaged in the last paragraph above, where the promisee would benefit on balance if control over the promisor's duty were to be vested in the party who is better placed to reach wise decisions about that duty. As has been noted, such a state of affairs in any familiar legal system would not result in the promisee's being deprived of control over the promisor's duty. In sum, in a nearby possible world, the "by design" condition in McBride's exposition of right-holding is not satisfied. Consequently, even if the actual circumstances of the contract between the promisor and promisee are not the slightly unusual circumstances pondered in the last paragraph above, McBride will be led to the conclusion that the promisee is not a holder of claim-rights under that contract.

1.5.3 Altruistic Interests versus Purely Vicarious Interests

McBride proceeds to train his attention on the example of Liam and Mark and Paul which I wield against Sreenivasan's hybrid theory of right-holding. His first main line of reasoning on the matter pertains to the fact that the judge who declines to endow Liam with any legal powers of control over Mark's legal duty has based her decision partly on Liam's interest in ensuring that Mark is treated fairly by Paul. McBride retorts (2022: 105, emphases in original):

> A chief problem for Kramer—and this leads us to our second important distinction—is that this moral dimension to the judge's reasoning appears to involve the judge basing [her] attribution of control over a duty, a key element of right-holding for

> hybridity, on "wholly vicarious" interests. But such interests are *not* "interest[s] of the requisite sort" which could form "the bases for attributions of rights", according to Kramer [Kramer and Steiner 2007: 303]. Kramer *precludes* invocation of such interests in determinations of right-holding.

McBride here commits four errors. First, when I disallow purely vicarious interests as bases for the attribution of rights, I am talking about claim-rights. By contrast, McBride in his comments on the scenario of Liam and Paul and Mark is talking about the conferral or withholding of legal powers. Under my Interest Theory of right-holding, legal powers are not integrally connected to legal claim-rights at all. Second, in the scenario just mentioned, the judge decides to withhold legal powers of control from Liam and thus does not bestow any such powers upon him. Hence, even if I were a Will Theorist, I would not ascribe any rights to Liam concerning Mark's duty. Third, McBride is talking about a situation in which a judge invokes certain interests of Liam when deliberating whether legal powers of control over Mark's duty should or should not be conferred upon Liam. By contrast, when I look askance at the invocation of purely vicarious interests as bases for the attribution of rights, I am talking about efforts to identify the holders of claim-rights rather than about a decision whether or not to bestow some legal entitlement (such as a power or a claim-right) upon someone. A factor that is appropriately invoked as a justificatory basis for such a decision can nonetheless be inappropriate as a basis for the identification of holders of claim-rights.

Fourth, and perhaps most important, McBride errs in contending that the interest of Liam in bringing about the fair treatment of Mark is a purely vicarious interest. McBride himself refers to a distinction which I underscore in my 2007 article: "I recognize that Kramer makes clear here that an interest can be benevolently other-directed and nonetheless not wholly vicarious. But, if Kramer is to argue that the moral dimension of Liam's interest in … being assigned the power to waive Mark's legal duty (here, say, for *the sake of justice*) is *not* wholly vicarious, we need to hear more as to why this is so" (McBride 2022: 105, emphases in original). In my 2007 article—Kramer and Steiner 2007: 302–4—I have in fact already said enough to make abundantly clear here why Liam's interest is altruistic rather than purely vicarious. In that earlier article, in response to a thought-experiment by Sreenivasan, I have contemplated a situation in which someone owes a duty to a young woman to pay her £100. I have pondered whether the grandmother of the young woman also has a claim-right that is correlated with that duty. In the envisaged situation, there is no requirement that the grandmother be made aware of the fulfillment of the duty owed to the granddaughter, nor is there any requirement that she be made to benefit financially or in any other material way from the fulfillment of that duty. Hence, the only interest of the grandmother that could be invoked in support of identifying her as the holder of a claim-right—correlated with the duty of someone to pay £100 to her granddaughter—is a purely vicarious interest, which resides wholly in the fact that another person's interests have been furthered.

Had the person who owed the obligation to the granddaughter also owed a duty to make the grandmother aware of the payment of £100 upon its occurrence, then the grandmother would have held a claim-right to be informed of that payment upon its occurrence. Her interest in being so informed is a personal interest rather than a purely vicarious interest, since news of a benefit undergone by a close relative will typically induce at least a modicum of gratification. Nevertheless, although the interest is personal rather than purely vicarious, it can be entirely altruistic. In other words, any gratification elicited in the grandmother might be focused entirely on the fact that someone whom she loves has fared well. The grandmother might neither want nor expect any financial gain or other material gain for herself from the good fortune of her granddaughter. Still, notwithstanding that in such circumstances her interest in being apprised of the matter is thoroughly altruistic rather than selfish, it is a personal interest rather than a purely vicarious interest. It does not reside wholly in the fact that someone else's interests have been furthered. Rather, it resides in being supplied with news that is likely to induce gratification.

In the vignette involving Liam and Mark and Paul, Liam's stake in being granted some powers of control over Mark's duty is likewise personal even though it is altruistic. Endowed with those powers, Liam can play a significant role in ensuring that Mark is treated fairly. They provide him not only with opportunities to know that Mark has been treated fairly, but also with opportunities to know that he himself has helped to bring about such a result (either by exerting his powers or by being ready to exert them if necessary). Thus, although we can suppose that Liam is not seeking any praise or material benefits for himself and is instead concentrating solely on upholding Mark's dignity and basic well-being, his interest in being assigned the powers of control over Mark's duty is personal rather than purely vicarious.

1.5.4 Tendentious Counterfactuals

McBride concludes his defense of his hybrid theory against my Liam/Mark/Paul thought-experiment by declaring that the circumstances which would satisfy the "by design" condition for Liam's holding of a right are so peculiar as to be unproblematic for his theory. He refers to those circumstances as "a situation in which Liam's moral interests in (seeing) justice being done defeat his prudential interest in not being pummeled. Insofar as the judge grants control to Liam in such situations, again, we have an extremely odd situation where Liam's (mixed) interests seem almost *constitutive* of the design of the original contractual set up. It is no bullet for hybridity to bite to grant a right to Liam in such outré circumstances" (2022: 110, emphasis in original). What is extremely odd is that McBride takes for granted that the situation recounted in my thought-experiment is that of a contract. I did not envisage it as a contract, and I did not present it as such. Rather, in the passage which McBride quotes earlier in his chapter, I refer to "the judge or other legal official whose directive has placed Mark under a duty to pay Paul" (Kramer 2013: 259). As that wording suggests, I envisage a situation where a legal-governmental official has issued a compensatory order or a debt-repayment order or some other such directive to Mark. Although the issuance of the directive may have arisen from a breach of contract by Mark, the involvement of a contract is a wholly contingent feature of the thought-experiment. In the scenario as I have presented it rather than as McBride has rewritten it, the legal-governmental official—at the time of issuing the directive in question—takes into consideration both the import of Liam's interest in bringing about the fair treatment of Mark and the import of Liam's interest in not being pummeled by Paul. In a nearby possible world, which is not at all outré, the prospect of a pummeling by Paul no longer looms.

Perhaps Paul in the nearby possible world is not strong enough to constitute a serious threat to Liam, or perhaps he is simply undisposed to resort to such ruffianism. In either event, the legal-governmental official in that nearby possible world who discerns the situation correctly will endow Liam with some legal powers of control over the duty owed by Mark to Paul.

The nearby possible world which I have just delineated is quite mundane. It should scarcely be dismissed as "outré" or "extremely odd." Given the proximity of that possible world and other relevantly similar possible worlds, the "by design" condition in McBride's exposition of right-holding is satisfied for the scenario which I have presented against Sreenivasan. McBride has therefore committed himself and his Tracking Theory to the conclusion that Liam in the scenario is indeed to be classified as the holder of a right correlative to Mark's duty. Because Liam in that scenario does not hold any legal powers of control over Mark's duty, the proponents of the Will Theory will reject McBride's conclusion. And because Liam's situation is not intrinsically and beneficially protected through the imposition of a duty on Mark to pay Paul, the proponents of the Interest Theory will likewise reject McBride's conclusion. Accordingly, two verdicts on the Tracking Theory of right-holding are appropriate here. First, McBride with that theory does have to bite the bullet in response to my Liam/Mark/Paul thought-experiment, regardless of how many times he overconfidently asserts that he is not biting a troublesome bullet. Second, the Tracking Theory is not aptly classified as a hybrid of the Interest Theory and the Will Theory, as it reaches sundry conclusions which no Interest Theorist or Will Theorist would countenance. Instead of being a hybrid of the Interest Theory and the Will Theory, it is an extremely odd alternative to them.

2. Legal Positivism and General Jurisprudence

I now turn to the contributors who concentrate on matters relating to legal positivism or the general nature of law. As has been remarked, the chapters by Cruft and Kurki could have been included under this heading; however, each of them has more aptly been grouped with the other chapters on rights and right-holding. Thus, the present section will comprise my responses to the contributions by Wilfrid J. Waluchow, Brian Bix, Pierluigi Chiassoni, and Gerald Postema.

2.1 Wilfrid J. Waluchow and Inclusive Legal Positivism

In his characteristically gracious and elegant paper, Waluchow endeavors to highlight the import of the debates between Inclusive Legal Positivists and Exclusive Legal Positivists. I should start by proclaiming something emphatically which Waluchow himself is far too modest to say. If anyone deserves to be lauded as the founder of Inclusive Legal Positivism, Waluchow is the man. There were important prefigurations of the Inclusivist position in some of the work of Hart and David Lyons and Philip Soper and Jules Coleman—as Waluchow has always readily acknowledged—but it was Waluchow who first presented a systematic elaboration of that position in his magisterial 1994 book *Inclusive Legal Positivism*. Theorists who have subsequently participated in the multifarious debates between Inclusivists and Exclusivists are the intellectual heirs of that book. It is a landmark by which all of us have been guided.

2.1.1 Razian Foundations

Because there is so little in Waluchow's excellent essay with which I disagree, my remarks here will be swift. First, it is not clear to me whether Waluchow accepts Raz's conception of morally binding practical authority and Raz's thesis that every legal system purports to be endowed with morally binding practical authority. If Waluchow does accept either or both of those Razian positions, then he and I diverge. In Chapter 4 of my 1999 book *In Defense of Legal Positivism*, I argue at length against Raz's insistence that every credibly possible legal system purports to be endowed with morally binding practical authority; and in Chapters 5 and 6 of my 2017 book *Liberalism with Excellence* and especially in Chapter 5 of my 2021 book *Freedom of Expression as Self-Restraint*, I argue against Raz's service conception of practical authority. Of course, the fact that I reject those Razian positions does not for me lessen the importance of oppugning the arguments by philosophers whose advocacy of Exclusive Legal Positivism is grounded on those positions. Like Waluchow, I have devoted considerable effort to showing that Exclusive Legal Positivism is unsustainable even if Raz's conception of practical authority and his claims about the professed authority of every legal system are countenanced *arguendo*. Exposing the errors in the reasoning of Exclusivists is vital as a means of illuminating the nature of law, for those errors typically occur in analyses that distort major aspects of the workings of legal systems. Still, crucial though the task of rebutting the unsound arguments of Exclusivists is, my dissent from Razianism goes well beyond the details of the debates between Exclusivists and Inclusivists over the role of moral principles as conditions for legal validity. The distortions to which the Razian Exclusivists have been driven in their cogitations on legal validity are symptomatic of much deeper weaknesses in the Razian foundations on which the edifice of Exclusivism has been built.[15]

2.1.2 Due Circumspection

Second, I should defend myself to some degree against Waluchow's mild criticism in his remarks on my countering of Raz's analogy between moral principles and foreign laws as norms that can be applied by courts in any particular jurisdiction without being incorporated into the law of that jurisdiction. Waluchow quotes two germane passages from my *Where Law and Morality Meet*, of which the first is the following: "[W]hen [moral principles] receive formal recognition within L as binding legal norms, they are not some borrowings from another system in which they have an authoritatively established status. Until that point of formal recognition, they are free-floating—that is, free of any institutional affiliation which has been authoritatively set. They are

[15] In addition to rejecting Raz's conception of morally binding practical authority and his insistence that every credibly possible legal system purports to be endowed with such authority, I even more sweepingly reject Raz's reasons-fundamentalism (in the second sense of that hyphenated term specified by Scanlon 2014: 2: "Reasons [are] fundamental in the further sense of being the only fundamental elements of the normative domain"). See my account of the domain of morality in Chapter 1 of Kramer 2014. For the foremost presentation of Raz's ruminations on reasons, see Raz 1999.

consequently available for incorporation into L" (Kramer 2004: 40–1). The other passage quoted by Waluchow is in relevant part as follows: "[T]he moral principles drawn upon by mildly Incorporationist judges in hard cases are sometimes laws of the system in which they are invoked and applied" (Kramer 2004: 43).

Waluchow is correct to observe that my wording in the final sentence of the initial passage should have been slightly more circumspect or qualified. Instead of stating unreservedly that moral principles are available for incorporation into the law of any jurisdiction, I should have declared that Razians and other Exclusivists have failed to show any reason why moral principles are not so available. Still, although I accept Waluchow's misgivings on that point, the inordinate boldness of my phraseology is greatly extenuated by the fact that I was writing in the context of my wide-ranging ripostes to Exclusivism. With such ripostes, undertaken by Waluchow and by me and by certain others such as Coleman and Kenneth Himma, we Inclusivists have methodically dismantled the sundry lines of reasoning through which the Razians and other Exclusivists have sought to show that moral principles cannot serve as legal norms or as criteria for legal validity. Thus, the sentence to which Waluchow has taken exception is not to be assessed in isolation. Its expression of confidence is backed up by the volley of ripostes to which I have just referred.

As for the other passage which Waluchow queries, he has somewhat misinterpreted it—though the responsibility for the misinterpretation is chiefly mine, since my wording of the passage is not as clear and precise as it should have been. When Waluchow quotes the passage, he adds italics to "are": "[T]he moral principles drawn upon by mildly Incorporationist judges in hard cases *are* sometimes laws of the system in which they are invoked and applied" (Waluchow 2022: 138, emphasis added by Waluchow). To construe the passage correctly, he should instead have italicized "sometimes." I employed that adverb as a possibility operator. In other words, "sometimes" is to be construed as equivalent to "in some credibly possible legal systems." When the quoted statement is so construed—in accordance with my intentions—it affirms not an actuality but a credible possibility which might or might not be an actuality. It affirms exactly what Waluchow rightly thinks that it should be affirming. Now, as I have said, the responsibility for his misreading of my statement is really mine much more than his. I could and should have formulated the modal operator with greater precision and explicitness. My only defense is that the inclusion of precise formulations of operators in one's sentences can render one's prose quite tediously plodding; consequently, I often opt instead for shorthand formulations. Still, the shorthand gives rise to a risk of misunderstanding—and that risk has obviously materialized in this instance.

2.1.3 An Unexplained Shift

Though I concur with the general drift of nearly everything in Waluchow's essay, there are a few junctures at which the essay overstates its claims. One such juncture occurs in his discussion of the upshot of any judgment wherein a court deems a statute (or some other ostensible law) to be unconstitutional and therefore legally invalid. Waluchow ponders whether the punishment of a defendant who has contravened such a statute in the domain of criminal law will be upheld by the court that has judged the statute to be unconstitutional. In the key paragraph of his meditations on this matter, he begins by talking about what will *typically* happen: "[T]his is not how courts *typically* treat a defendant's actions in this kind of case. *Most* courts will routinely treat [a defendant] A as having done nothing legally wrong at [the time when A acted]. In other words, A will *typically* be exonerated on the ground that the statute under which his actions were deemed illegal both is and was at the time he acted legally invalid, and that A did not, therefore, act contrary to valid law." However, Waluchow finishes the paragraph by recounting what will *invariably* happen: "The consequence is that his conviction will *invariably* be deemed void, as will any subsequent attempt at prosecution under the impugned statute" (2022: 143, emphases added). This shift to a stronger modality is problematic. To be sure, that shift is justified with reference to the invalidation of criminal statutes under American constitutional law (Kay 2014: 53; Traynor 1977: 553 n.54). Nonetheless, philosophical argumentation about the operations of legal systems has to be sustainable with reference to every such system that is credibly possible. There can credibly be legal systems in which the subjection of criminal defendants to punishments is occasionally countenanced even if the statutes violated by the defendants are subsequently judged to be unconstitutional.

Of course, Waluchow can reasonably reply that his rebuttal of the Exclusivist account of invalidation requires him simply to show that some credibly possible legal systems—such as the actual legal systems in Canada and the United States—operate in accordance with his own Inclusivist account of invalidation rather than in accordance with the Exclusivist account. Such a reply would of course be correct, but it would leave mysterious why he has shifted from a relatively mild modality to a much stronger modality in the passage from which I have quoted. After all, to rebut the arguments of Exclusivists, he need only advert to credibly possible legal systems in which the invalidation of criminal-law statutes is *sometimes* or *frequently* or *typically* conducted in ways that are at odds with Exclusivism. Naturally, his case against the arguments of Exclusivists is strengthened by the existence of actual legal systems where the invalidation of criminal-law statutes is *invariably* conducted in ways that are not plausibly reconcilable with those arguments. Nonetheless, he could clinch his case even if there were no such actual legal systems.

2.1.4 Scope Restrictions

In the closing pages of his essay, Waluchow argues in favor of Inclusivism on the ground that it can accommodate the full range of techniques through which the workings of legal systems affect the practical reasoning of the people who are governed by those workings. Throughout that portion of his chapter, Waluchow presumes that Exclusive Legal Positivists are committed to the proposition that the operations of legal systems call for the addressees of duty-imposing laws to exclude all moral considerations as bases for judging whether to comply with those laws. He commends Inclusivism on the ground that, unlike Exclusivism, it recognizes that the issuance of legal mandates does not have to "exclude[e] moral reasons entirely" as bases for responses to those mandates (2022: 146). However, such argumentation overlooks the fact that Raz and his followers have always accepted that the exclusionary force of a legal directive is typically subject to scope restrictions. As Raz declares: "It should be remembered that exclusionary reasons may vary in scope; they may exclude all or only some of the reasons which apply to certain practical problems" (1999: 40). Thus, the discussion by Waluchow in the closing pages of his chapter is largely failing to engage with Exclusivism as it has been espoused by Razians. Like Waluchow himself and other Inclusivists, the Razians agree that legal requirements should not and typically do not exclude all moral factors as bases for people's decisions about satisfying those requirements.

Still, although Waluchow has misdirected his attack by writing as if the Razians are committed to an extreme position which they in fact eschew, my defense of them against his attack does not really redound to their benefit. Without their acknowledgment of scope restrictions on the exclusionary force of legal requirements, their Exclusivism would be outlandish; with their acknowledgment of such restrictions, however, their Exclusivism is not readily distinguishable from Inclusivism. It is not surprising that the role of scope restrictions in Raz's account of exclusionary reasons has been invoked in the past both by Waluchow (2000: 58) and by me (2004: 23–4, 45–9) in our critiques of Exclusivism. When that role is given due salience, we find that the Exclusivists have largely deprived themselves of grounds for balking at the prospect of legal systems in which consistency with certain moral principles is a necessary condition for the status of norms as laws.

2.1.5 Indeterminacy versus Disagreement

Having expressed some friendly reservations about a few aspects of Waluchow's chapter, I will conclude my discussion of his essay by lodging a complaint about one aspect of my own early work on Inclusive Legal Positivism and Incorporationism. As Waluchow correctly reports, I reject extreme Incorporationism and embrace moderate Incorporationism, and I do so because extreme Incorporationism—which envisages the existence of a large-scale system of law in which the sole necessary and sufficient condition for legal validity is the correctness of norms as moral principles—presents a model of law that is inconsistent with the functionality of a legal system in any credibly possible society larger than a handful of families. Though I fully stand by my embrace of moderate Incorporationism and my rejection of extreme Incorporationism for the reason just indicated, my perusal of Waluchow's chapter has led me to worry that my work on these matters in the late 1990s and early 2000s was not always sufficiently attentive to a distinction which I have highlighted in some of my later work: namely, the distinction between indeterminacy and indemonstrability (Kramer 2007: 17–19, 50–3, 202–5; 2009: 56, 88, 90–9; 2018: 112–17, 120, 128–30). A legal question is *determinately* answerable if and only if (1) some answer to it is uniquely correct or (2) the answers to it within a range are different from all other answers in being correct. Hence, if neither of those disjuncts is true in relation to some legal question, there are no determinately correct answers to that question. A legal question is *demonstrably* answerable if and only if the singular correctness of the answer thereto would be perceived by virtually every informed person who competently mulls over the reasons or arguments in favor of it. Now, as should be apparent, determinate correctness does not entail demonstrable correctness. The latter involves more than the former. Precisely because determinate correctness does not entail demonstrable correctness, the absence of the latter property does not entail the absence of the former; there may be some determinately correct answer to a legal question even though the answer is not demonstrably correct.

On the one hand, in any jurisdiction there is a substantial overlap between the class of legal questions that are not determinately answerable and the class of legal questions that are marked by persistent disputes. Intractable disagreements among legal experts are often centered on inquiries that are not determinately answerable even in principle, and inquiries that are not determinately answerable often give rise to intractable disagreements. On the other hand, not all persistent disagreements among legal experts pertain to questions that lack determinate answers, and not all questions that lack determinate answers are foci of persistent disagreements. (All or most legal experts in the relevant jurisdiction might converge in recognizing that a certain question is not determinately answerable, or they might converge in mistakenly perceiving some answer to that question as uniquely correct.) Wide-ranging though the extensional overlap between the class of indeterminate matters and the class of insurmountably contentious matters is, those two categories are not equivalent.

My worry about some of my early work on Incorporationism is that, with my references to hard cases, I occasionally elided the distinction between the indeterminate and the insuperably contentious. The former side of that distinction, rather than the latter, is the point of purchase for moderate Incorporationism. This observation will become clearer through the disambiguation of the notion of hard cases. Some hard cases are hard not only in that they involve entrenched wrangling among experts, but also in that they reveal the limited determinacy of the prevailing matrix of enacted laws.[16] In a hard case of that kind, those laws do not yield any determinate answer to the question that is at issue between the parties to a dispute. Hence, a hard case of that type is quite different from a hard case in which the question at issue is determinately answerable on the basis of the enacted laws of the jurisdiction, and in which the legal experts diverge from one another unremittingly when they address that question. Further categories of hard cases could be distilled, but the two categories delineated here are sufficient for my present purposes.

In one salient respect, the two types of hard cases are alike. A hard case in either category will be marked by significant disagreements among the experts who ponder how the case should be resolved. Still, despite that major affinity between the sets of hard cases under consideration here, the first category is crucially different from the second. Unlike the hard cases in the first category, the hard cases of the second kind involve only indemonstrability and not indeterminacy. In a hard case of that second type, the question that divides the litigants is determinately answerable under the enacted laws of the jurisdiction.

Moderate Incorporationism is the thesis that, in any particular jurisdiction, the correctness of norms as principles of morality can be a sufficient condition for the status of those norms as laws to be invoked and applied in any hard cases where the points of contention are not determinately answerable by reference to the enacted laws of the jurisdiction. Moderate Incorporationism, then, pertains to the hard cases in my

[16] I am using the phrase "enacted laws" broadly to encompass any laws that emanate directly from any of the decision-making organs of a system of governance such as legislatures or administrative agencies or adjudicative bodies. Those laws are differentiated here from correct principles of morality, which can also possess the status of laws in virtue of being treated as such by legal-governmental officials. Even when the correct principles of morality do possess that status in virtue of being so treated, they *qua* correct principles of morality do not originate in any of the decision-making organs of a system of governance.

first category but not to the hard cases in my second category. Within a moderately Incorporationist system of governance, the adjudicative and administrative officials are not authorized to have recourse to the correct principles of morality as the bases for their rulings in hard cases of the second kind. In hard cases of that kind, the officials in such a system of governance are both legally authorized and legally obligated to have recourse to the enacted laws as the bases for their rulings. Of course, the judges and administrators and other legal experts in such a system of governance will frequently be unable to differentiate between hard cases of the first type and hard cases of the second type. They will probably therefore often be inclined to have recourse to principles of morality in hard cases of the latter type as much as in hard cases of the former type. Still, if the Rule of Recognition in their system of legal governance is indeed moderately Incorporationist, they err in so doing. They are not authorized to resort to moral principles in cases where the enacted laws of their system are sufficient to generate determinately correct answers to the questions that have to be resolved. (Naturally, even if the legal-governmental officials all recognize that those laws are sufficient to answer determinately each question that is controverted in a hard case of this second type, they will diverge from one another in identifying the implications of those laws. At least some of the officials, and perhaps all of them, will be identifying those implications incorrectly. However, even the officials who do misidentify the implications of the enacted laws are not committing the error which I have just been discussing. They are not resorting to moral principles as the bases for their decisions under the misapprehension that the enacted laws fail to provide any determinate answer to each legal question that is at issue.)

Obviously, nothing preordains the fact that the Rule of Recognition in some particular jurisdiction is moderately Incorporationist. The legal-governmental officials there might instead have adhered to a Rule of Recognition that would have authorized and obligated them to resort to moral principles in every case where the chief questions at issue are not *demonstrably* answerable by reference to the enacted laws that bear on those questions. In such a system of governance, widespread disagreement among experts—rather than indeterminacy—would be the key factor that warrants the recourse to moral principles. Such a system of governance is possible, but it is not a moderately Incorporationist system. When the Rule of Recognition in a jurisdiction is moderately Incorporationist, the legal-governmental officials there are neither authorized nor obligated to fall back upon moral principles in cases where the enacted laws are sufficient to answer determinately the questions that have to be decided. Unlike the system of governance posited at the outset of this paragraph, a moderately Incorporationist system of governance differentiates clearly between indemonstrability and indeterminacy (even though the cashing out of that distinction will itself be indemonstrable in a number of contexts).

My early work on Incorporationism was not always adequately alert to the contrast between indemonstrability and indeterminacy. It thus sometimes blurred the difference between the two types of systems of governance recounted in the preceding paragraph. In a paper which I have contributed to a festschrift for Waluchow—a paper whose topic I chose in response to Waluchow's essay for this volume—I underline and amplify the distinctions which I have drawn in this subsection (Kramer 2022a). I have consequently brought together my work on legal positivism with my work on legal objectivity.

2.2 Brian Bix on Collective Mistakes

Bix is the contributor whom I have known for the longest period: three full decades. From his first book onward, I have admired the limpidity of his prose and the perspicacity of his analyses. I have also long admired him as a person. His contribution to this volume reinforces my attitudes, as it is characteristically lucid and incisive and gracious. Because there is so little in his essay with which I disagree, my responses will be especially few and laconic.

2.2.1 A Matter of Fashion

In the first half of his chapter, Bix twice broaches the matter of fashionableness in attire. He writes: "If there is a matter defined by the *collective* judgment of some group (think of fashion, which is generally defined by some designated 'elite' group in society), then when the relevant group makes a claim about that matter (e.g., the fashionable length of skirt or width of tie for this year), they will, by definition, be correct" (2022: 114, emphasis in original). He slightly later writes: "We have already mentioned fashion as an area where one might reasonably doubt the possibility of universal error among the group that sets what counts as fashion for its community" (2022: 115). Because Bix does not revisit these statements at any subsequent juncture, I assume that he stands by them and does not regard them as impugned by his cogitations later in his chapter.

In fact, however, the considerations that lead him to acknowledge the possibility of collective mistakes by officials about the contents of laws should also lead him to acknowledge the possibility of collective mistakes by the aficionados of apparel about the fashionableness of sundry designs of clothing. Let us suppose here that certain pronouncements and actions of key people—celebrities, pundits, manufacturers, designers, retailers, magazine editors, models, and some other trend-setting members of the public—are constitutive of the prevailing standards of fashionableness in the society where those people reside or work. The constitutive role of those pronouncements and actions is analogous to the role of the attitudes and decisions and behavior of legal-governmental officials in constituting the laws and operations of a system of legal governance. Yet, just as the officials can collectively be mistaken when they reflect upon the implications and contours of the laws which their attitudes and decisions and behavior collectively constitute, the cynosures of fashionableness can collectively be mistaken when they reflect upon the contours and implications of the standards of trendiness which their pronouncements and actions collectively constitute. Even more than the officials in regard to legal norms, the mavens of fashionableness will be prone to misidentify the standards which they have collectively constituted. They might overestimate or underestimate the popularity of certain modes of apparel, for example. Still more important, those mavens can err in their judgments about the conditions under which some of the prevailing standards of fashionableness are applicable. For example, they might conclude that the requirements imposed by some of those standards are applicable in circumstances where the wearing of certain attire will give rise to adversity or invidiousness. In so concluding, they might be running athwart the purpose for which the wearing of the attire was introduced. Such misconstruals of the prevailing standards of fashionableness are not inevitable, of course, but they are abidingly possible. When such misconstruals do occur, they will usually be incorporated quickly into the prevailing standards which they thereby alter.

To underscore the potential for collective misjudgments in this area of life, an example from a somewhat different area of life will be helpful. A practice of tipping the drivers of taxis after receiving rides from them is constituted in a society by the actions and dispositions of multitudinous people. Let us suppose that such a practice exists in some society S if and only if (1) all or most adults throughout S very commonly do tip such drivers after receiving rides from them, and (2) all or most adults in S are firmly disposed to continue to tip such drivers, and (3) all or most adults in S are disposed to respond censoriously when they become aware that anyone has declined to tip a courteous taxi driver after receiving a ride. Now suppose that all or most people in S incorrectly think that very few other people there share their behavioral patterns and dispositions in this matter. That is, all or most people in S think that the conditions for the existence of a practice of bestowing tips on the drivers of taxis do not obtain there. They consequently think that such a practice does not exist there. Within S, then, a practice of tipping the drivers of taxis is robustly in existence, yet all or most people in S believe that no such practice does exist there. In S, there is a collective misapprehension about the very existence of a practice that is constituted by the actions and dispositions of the people who are under that misapprehension. The existential mind-independence of that practice is only weak, but its observational mind-independence is strong. Much the same is true of the standards of fashionableness in any society.

2.2.2 Longstandingness and Moral Egregiousness

As Bix rightly observes, my affirmation of the possibility of collective mistakes by legal-governmental officials in their pronouncements on the contours or implications or existence of legal norms is coupled with my recognition that the erroneous determinations of the officials will typically become absorbed into the law of their jurisdiction. Very often any subsequent decisions that accord with their missteps are not themselves erroneous, for those subsequent decisions can be reflective of the fact that the law has been modified—perhaps slightly or perhaps more far-reachingly—by the missteps. This point is especially pertinent in relation to common-law systems with their generally strong doctrines of precedent, but it applies in varying degrees to civil-law systems as well.

In some fascinating ruminations on mistaken judgments by the US Supreme Court with regard to matters of American constitutional law, Bix quotes from Antonin Scalia's dissenting opinion in *Obergefell v. Hodges* (2022: 120-1). Scalia's fulminations prompt me to emphasize that the extent to which the mistaken judgments of legal-governmental officials become ensconced in the law of their system of governance is a matter that varies from one jurisdiction to the next. It is a matter that hinges on the content of the Rule of Recognition in each jurisdiction, and that content is of course contingent on the actions and dispositions of the officials therein. *Pace* Scalia, then, there is ample room for a system of governance in which the overruling of hoary decisions and doctrines can be a way of reasserting the law as it has always been.

Is such a Rule of Recognition desirable? In a system of governance like that of the United States, where some constitutional provisions articulate standards for legal validity that are overtly moral, the Rule of Recognition should both authorize and obligate the topmost adjudicative officials to overturn hoary judgments (as well as more recent judgments) that are morally egregious. Insofar as those officials act correctly in accordance with that authorization and that obligation, they are reasserting the law as it has always been. If the Rule of Recognition in the United States is accurately understandable along these lines,[17] then *Obergefell v. Hodges* and *Brown v. Board of Education* are properly classifiable as reassertions of the Equal Protection Clause of the Fourteenth Amendment to the US Constitution. Each of those decisions served to correct decades of misrepresentations of that Clause. Because the overturning of those misrepresentations by the topmost court of the land has always been legally permissible and legally obligatory as well as legally possible (if the Rule of Recognition in the United States is along the lines suggested in this paragraph), the overturning in each case is a restoration. It returns the law to a state of affairs where the full-blown Equal Protection Clause in relation to a certain matter is legally binding not only on the topmost adjudicative officials but also on all other legal-governmental officials in the jurisdiction. Thitherto, since the mistaken decision by the topmost court that has now been undone, the lower-tier adjudicators had been legally bound to effectuate not the full-blown Equal Protection Clause but instead that Clause as it was erroneously construed in the mistaken decision. Henceforth, with the erroneous construal removed, the lower-tier adjudicators will be legally bound to effectuate the full-blown Equal Protection Clause just as the adjudicators on the topmost court have always been so bound.

Probably, the preceding paragraph has accurately recounted the way in which the overruling of morally egregious hoary cases is handled under the Rule of Recognition in the United States. Even if the paragraph is not fully accurate in application to the Rule of Recognition there, it has tersely limned the way in which the reversal of morally egregious longstanding judgments can and should be handled under a credibly possible Rule of Recognition. Despite Scalia's ranting, there is nothing silly or preposterous in the notion that those morally grotesque judgments have always been legally mistaken and have never fully entered into the law of the jurisdiction where they have been rendered. Under the Rule of Recognition that prevails in this or that particular jurisdiction, the notion denounced by Scalia—the notion that some judgments of the topmost court which have gone unreversed for many decades are nonetheless such that the topmost court is both legally permitted and legally obligated to set those judgments aside as null and void—can be true there.

2.2.3 Legally Valid and Not Legally Valid

My discussion in the foregoing subsection leads us into a crux that surfaces repeatedly in Bix's fine chapter. Bix himself encapsulates that crux in a pithy formulation at the end of his chapter, as he declares that "law is not an area of clear bivalence; we can sensibly say that, at a given point, '*Plessy* both is and is not the law'" (2022: 124). His invocation here of the logical Law of Bivalence is inapposite. Were there any

[17] I think that the Rule of Recognition in the United States is indeed along these lines, but the content of the Rule of Recognition in any jurisdiction is partly a complex empirical matter into which I do not wish to sally forth here. Thus, I frame this point as a conditional proposition in order to avoid making anything hinge on that complex empirical matter.

logical difficulty in the situation to which he is adverting, the relevant principle of logic would be either the Law of Excluded Middle—which maintains that it can never be the case that neither a proposition *p* nor the negation of *p* is true—or the Law of Noncontradiction, which maintains that it can never be the case that both *p* and the negation of *p* are true. In any event, there is no logical conundrum in the situation to which Bix is referring. We can recognize as much when we keep in mind what has been said in my foregoing subsection.

To facilitate my engagement with Bix's example of *Plessy v. Ferguson*, I will assume here that the Rule of Recognition in the United States is as I have indicated that it might be in section 2.2.2 above. (If that assumption is inaccurate, then my present discussion pertains to a credibly possible system of legal governance rather than to the actual system of legal governance in the United States.) We have seen in section 2.2.2 the sense in which the 1896 ruling by the US Supreme Court in *Plessy* did enter into the law of the United States, and the sense in which it did not. That ruling never really entered into the law of the United States, because the Justices on the Supreme Court from 1896 onward were legally authorized and legally obligated under the prevailing Rule of Recognition to overturn *Plessy* at any time. Had the decision in *Plessy* gone against racial segregation rather than in favor thereof, it would have entered fully into American law—in which event the Justices on the Supreme Court would thereafter have been neither legally permitted nor legally obligated to overrule that decision. However, since the *Plessy* ruling in fact upheld the practice of racial segregation in public facilities, the Justices were thenceforward both legally obligated and legally permitted to undo that ruling as null and void.

We have likewise seen in section 2.2.2 the sense in which the *Plessy* judgment did enter into the law of the United States. Although that judgment was voidable by the US Supreme Court from the moment it was rendered, and although the voiding of it by the Court was both legally obligatory and legally permissible, it was not voided until it was overruled nearly six decades later.[18] As a consequence, for nearly six decades the administrators and lower-echelon adjudicators in the American system of governance were legally obligated to treat that judgment as an authoritative part of the law in their jurisdiction. They were not legally at liberty to perform their roles in ways that were inconsistent with the terms of the *Plessy* decision (for example, by issuing directives to public bodies requiring those bodies to desegregate their facilities). In precisely this manner, that decision figured alongside the countless other rulings of the Supreme Court as a binding basis for the determinations of administrators and lower-tier adjudicators in their capacities as public officials.

Now, the sense in which the *Plessy* judgment and other morally outrageous judgments of the US Supreme Court entered into the vast matrix of legal norms in the American system of governance is entirely consistent with the sense in which the *Plessy* judgment and the other morally outrageous judgments did not enter into that vast matrix. Whereas the former sense pertains to what was legally binding on administrators and lower-echelon adjudicators in the American system of governance, the latter sense pertains to what was legally binding on the Justices of the US Supreme

[18] Like Bix, I here assume that *Plessy* was overruled outright by *Brown v. Board of Education*—though, disconcertingly, the *Brown* judgment did not state explicitly that it was overruling *Plessy* altogether.

Court. Whereas the Justices were legally bound to orient themselves toward the Equal Protection Clause *simpliciter*, the administrators and lower-tier adjudicators were legally bound to orient themselves toward the Supreme Court's construal of the Equal Protection Clause. Hence, contrary to what Bix suggests at the end of his chapter, we do not encounter any logical mystery with regard to the place of *Plessy* in the law of the United States during the first half of the twentieth century.

Bix quotes a statement by Connie Rosati that might seem to uncover a different crux. Meditating on the possibility of a world in which the *Plessy* decision would never be overruled, Bix writes as follows (2022: 121, footnote omitted, quoting Rosati 2004: 292):

> One can then imagine an alternative version of American legal history, one where *Plessy v. Ferguson* was never overruled by *Brown v. Board of Education*, or any other case. Relating to that alternative legal history, Rosati comments: "It seems decidedly odd to say that people never discovered what the law really is, that they didn't know and never will know that the law is not *Plessy*."

On the one hand, the counterfactual scenario conjured up here by Rosati is indeed odd. On the other hand, it is not imponderable. If the Rule of Recognition in the counterfactual United States is the same as what my present subsection has assumed to be the Rule of Recognition in the actual United States, and if the *Plessy* ruling in the counterfactual history would indefinitely persist without being deemed by the U.S. Supreme Court to be null and void, then the people in the counterfactual United States would indeed never discover what the law on segregation in public education there really is. To be sure, we might conclude that the Rule of Recognition in the counterfactual United States is very likely not the same as the Rule of Recognition which I have tentatively ascribed to the actual American system of governance in this subsection. Still, such a conclusion is not forced upon us as it would be if the proposition broached by Rosati—her proposition about never discovering what the law really is—were thoroughly outlandish.

To see why the proposition which she floats is not ridiculous, we should attend to the distinction between the property of being unknowable and the property of being unknown. In the sentence which Bix quotes from Rosati, her wording can easily incline readers to think that she envisages a situation in which the veritable content of the Equal Protection Clause is not only unknown in the counterfactual United States but also unknowable there. Such a situation would indeed be preposterous. As I have argued elsewhere (2009: 51–6), all basic principles of morality and most derivative principles of morality are always knowable by human beings even if some of the principles are unknown in this or that particular society. Hence, were Rosati contemplating a scenario in which the true content of the Equal Protection Clause is unknowable rather than merely unknown, we would be justified in dismissing that scenario. Instead, however, the counterfactual situation which she ponders is one in which that true content would remain unknown indefinitely but would not be unknowable. Consequently, although that situation is odd (as Rosati says), it is to be taken seriously as a possibility.

2.3 Gerald Postema and the Rule of Law

Having known Postema for somewhat over two decades, and having relished his presence as a colleague when he was the Goodhart Visiting Professor at Cambridge throughout the 2013–14 academic year, I am delighted to have an opportunity to interact with him here. I have engaged with his sundry writings since the mid-1980s, and I have always profited greatly from doing so—even when I disagree with his positions and arguments. His brilliant 1986 book on Bentham is a particularly enviable achievement. Our present exchange is anchored by our shared admiration for the work of Lon Fuller on the principles of legality.

2.3.1 Guidance by Laws as Norms

In the first half of his chapter, Postema has seriously underestimated the extent to which my conception of the guiding function of law diverges from his own conception. Though his prose is occasionally elusive or metaphorical in ways that impede me from pinning down exactly what he is asserting, he clearly believes that duty-imposing laws guide the conduct of their addressees only insofar as those addressees fully accept the laws instead of merely obeying them. My distinction here between full acceptance and mere obedience is the same as Hart's distinction in Chapter 6 of *The Concept of Law*, where one's acceptance of a duty-imposing norm N consists in one's adoption of the internal point of view marked by the critical reflective attitude (that is, a disposition to comply with N insofar as it is applicable to one's conduct, a disposition to reproach other people who contravene N, and a disposition to acknowledge the appropriateness of any criticisms directed against oneself for transgressions of N). Mere obedience consists solely in a disposition to comply with N insofar as it is applicable to one's conduct. Like Hart, and unlike Postema, I have always contended that the duty-imposing norms of a legal system can fulfill their function of guiding people's conduct even if the addressees of the norms are merely obeying them and are not fully accepting them. Perhaps the addressees are Holmesian bad men who obey the benign legal requirements of a liberal-democratic system of governance only in order to avoid the sanctions that will be imposed for noncompliance, or perhaps the addressees are decent citizens who obey the malign legal directives of a repressive system of governance only in order to avoid such sanctions. Whatever may be the specifics of the reasons for the withholding of full acceptance by some citizens, they are being guided by the duty-imposing laws of their system of governance when they merely obey those laws.

Postema will presumably retort that the citizens who merely obey the duty-imposing laws are not being guided by the laws as norms—a rather opaque phrase which he uses repeatedly—but any such retort would be misguided. On the one hand, when Postema proclaims that the citizens with their mere obedience are not being guided by the duty-imposing laws as norms, he might simply be pointing out that they are not fully accepting those laws. If so, then the retort about not being guided by the laws as norms is scarcely a consideration in support of Postema's position. Rather, it is a reiteration of his position. On the other hand, if that claim about not being guided by the laws as norms is suggesting that the citizens who merely obey the duty-imposing laws are not engaging with the laws as norms (where "engaging with the laws as norms" is not equivalent to "fully accepting the laws"), then that claim is misconceived. Citizens who merely obey the duty-imposing laws in their system of governance are engaging with all eight of the aspects of those laws that are distilled in Fuller's principles of legality.

Either through her own efforts or through the efforts of lawyers, each of those citizens has to construe the laws as general standards in order to ascertain how the requirements imposed by those laws bear on her own situation and conduct. To construe the laws and their requirements as general standards, each citizen through her own efforts or through the efforts of lawyers has to avail herself of the fact that the laws are promulgated and are thus knowable. Her obedience to those laws is possible only because they are applicable to her conduct now and in the future rather than in a starkly retroactive manner that would render obedience by her impossible. Similarly, her obedience is possible only because the laws have been formulated in terms that are sufficiently perspicuous to be followable. Likewise, were the laws rampantly riddled with contradictions or with pairs of jointly unfulfillable duties, their followability would be greatly impaired. Even more plainly, a disaffected citizen would not be able to obey the duty-imposing laws if the requirements imposed by them were all or nearly all far beyond her capabilities, or if the laws were changing so rapidly that she and any lawyers could not keep abreast of them. Finally, such a citizen is motivated to obey those laws precisely because she well-foundedly expects a strong correlation between noncompliance and the levying of sanctions and between compliance and the withholding of sanctions. Both motivationally and cognitively, then, the obedience of disaffected citizens is oriented toward all the features of legal norms and legal systems that are encapsulated in Fuller's principles of legality.

Hence, if the notion of being guided by duty-imposing laws as norms is not equivalent to the notion of fully accepting those laws rather than merely obeying them, then I am at a loss to know why disaffected citizens who merely obey the laws are not being guided by them as norms. Such citizens are certainly being guided by those laws in ways that integrally involve the faculties of rational agents. As such agents, the disaffected citizens (perhaps with assistance from lawyers) need to figure out what the laws require and how those requirements bear on their own conduct in any number of circumstances, and they need to adjust their conduct accordingly. The task of figuring out the general terms and the concrete bearings of the laws might be quite straightforward or might instead be very laborious, and much the same is true of the task of conforming one's behavior to those terms and bearings. Whatever the specifics, the faculties of a person that have to be exercised for mere obedience are central to her status as a rational deliberator. Thus, when I emphasize that the directing of people's conduct through the issuance of norms is reliant on their exercising the deliberative and decisional abilities that constitute their rational agency, I am describing a phenomenon that includes the directing of the conduct of disaffected citizens through the issuance of duty-imposing laws which they merely obey.

2.3.2 Lawishness and the Discipline of Law

Postema adverts to the property of lawishness at many junctures in the first half of his chapter, but his discussions of the matter only gradually become explicit and precise enough to enable me to be confident that I have understood correctly what he has in mind when he invokes that property. As he introduces the neologism "lawishness," he explains that it applies to the stance of someone who is "committed in principle to governing according to the discipline of law" (2022: 169). This language, particularly the phrase "in principle," appears to indicate that lawishness is a profoundly moral property. That is, the commitment involved in governing lawishly is apparently a moral commitment undertaken on the basis of moral considerations.[19] Somewhat later in the chapter, Postema declares that officials who govern lawishly have adopted "a sincere, principled and public commitment to submit to law's constraints" (2022: 173). Though the wording here is closely similar to that at the earlier juncture in his chapter, it even more strongly suggests that lawishness is a moral property. My suspicions on this score are borne out when Postema proceeds to contend that "[u]ndertaking to govern lawishly (and thus accepting law's rule on a principled basis) is not only to adopt a technique, but also to establish an environment that has the earmarks of a dignity-respecting relationship, one that individual citizens may experience as dignity-respecting. The effect of establishing this environment, regardless of motivations for doing so, is to put rulers and legal subjects into a morally inflected relationship in which certain reciprocal obligations are embedded" (2022: 175).

Were Postema writing here about the Rule of Law rather than about the rule of law, his claims about governing lawishly would be unexceptionable. In other words, were he writing about the formal characteristics of laws and the procedural aspects of law-application in liberal-democratic systems of governance—rather than about those formal characteristics and procedural aspects in *every* system of legal governance—he would be on a solid footing in his contentions about the nature of lawishness. However, in the first half of his chapter he is supposedly training his focus on the rule of law. He is recounting what he perceives as some attributes of every system of legal governance. Quite bemusing, then, is his ascription to me of premises which entail the conclusion that governing lawishly is intrinsic to the rule of law. Postema asserts that "it follows from Kramer's premises that satisfaction of Fuller's standards alone is not sufficient for the existence of a functioning legal system; also necessary are conditions for uptake on the part of legal subjects and rulers' principled commitment to govern lawishly" (2022: 173). It is not clear to me which premises Postema is invoking here, but he seems to be harking back to something that he had said in an earlier footnote: "[O]n [Kramer's] view, law cannot function as law, cannot effectively operate in its jurisdiction according to its distinctive mode, unless those addressed by law are able and willing to take up the dictates *as norms* (2022: 171 n.11, emphasis in original). In this latest quotation, Postema is imputing to me the proposition that duty-imposing laws do not guide people as norms unless the addressees of those laws fully accept them and do not merely obey them. As I have argued sustainedly in section 2.3.1 above, I reject rather than endorse that proposition. I subscribe neither to that proposition nor to any other proposition that might serve as a premise from which

[19] Postema appears to envisage a commitment that is moral both in the sense of being nonprudential and in the sense of being morally worthy. For the distinction between those two senses of "moral," see Kramer 2018: 151–3.

Postema could validly derive his conclusions about lawishness as a morally laden feature of every system of legal governance. Postema as an opponent of legal positivism is welcome to draw those conclusions in his own theorizing, but he errs in thinking that I as a proponent of legal positivism am aligned with him.

Nevertheless, something can be salvaged from the phrase "the discipline of law"—a phrase which Postema introduces at the same juncture where he coins the neologism "lawishly." As I have indicated in my opening quotation from Postema in this subsection, he equates governing lawishly with being "committed in principle to governing according to the discipline of law" (2022: 169). Though Postema never really elucidates that wording, a legal positivist can agree that governance through the rule of law always involves considerable discipline. In a benign system of governance, the discipline of law—the self-discipline of legal-governmental officials in adhering to the Fullerian principles of legality at the expense of potential short-term gains—is thoroughly or largely moral in character. However, as I have argued in many portions of my *In Defense of Legal Positivism* and in some of my subsequent writings,[20] the officials who run malign systems of governance will often have strong prudential reasons for adhering to those principles of legality at fairly high levels. Insofar as they have such reasons and act in accordance therewith, the officials will frequently be forgoing short-term gains for the sake of pursuing their long-term objectives. Selfishly exploitative though those objectives may be, they will typically be furthered through a regime's retention of its grip on power for a lengthy period. As I have argued in the aforementioned writings, the retention of such a grip for a long period will generally be facilitated (at least in a large-scale society) through conformity with the Fullerian principles at quite high levels. Sundry deviations from those principles in circumscribed geographical regions or in circumscribed areas of life or for circumscribed periods of time can also be serviceable for the retention of a regime's grip on power—as I have likewise observed in the aforementioned writings—but the coordination of the officials' own activities and the effective direction of citizens' conduct will generally require the regularity that is secured through fairly high levels of adherence to Fuller's principles of legality. Thus, provided that the notion of the discipline of law is understood broadly enough to encompass the fulfillment of Fuller's principles by officials who are pursuing long-term selfishly exploitative aims sometimes at the expense of short-term gains, a legal positivist can and should agree that the discipline of law is integral to the operations of every system of legal governance.

Two clarifications or caveats should be added here. First, Postema suggests more than once in his chapter that any substantial degrees of compliance with the Fullerian principles of legality by the officials in a malevolent system of governance will be an effort to simulate a commitment to governing lawishly. Such chicanery is one possibility, of course, but it is not what I am envisaging here. I am talking about officials who have strong reasons for being genuinely concerned to abide by the Fullerian principles at quite high levels, albeit on the basis of selfishly exploitative considerations rather

[20] Especially germane, in addition to *In Defense of Legal Positivism*, are the articles which I wrote in a seven-year debate with Nigel Simmonds. For my final contribution to that debate, see Kramer 2011b. Scattered throughout that final contribution are citations to my previous contributions.

than on the basis of moral considerations. Insofar as the officials act in accordance with those reasons, they exert the discipline that is requisite to keeping their regime in control and to keeping it functionally effective as they strive to realize their nefarious purposes through it.

Second, Postema appears to take for granted that the officials in a malign system of governance will depart from Fuller's principles of legality more frequently or more markedly than will the officials in a benignly liberal-democratic system of governance. The correctness of such an assumption in any comparison between one particular system of governance and another is very much a contingent matter. Of pivotal importance in this context is Fuller's eighth principle, which calls for congruity between the laws of a jurisdiction as they are formulated and the laws of a jurisdiction as they are implemented. On the one hand, the officials in a repressive system of governance will undoubtedly be more inclined than the officials in a benevolent system of governance to deviate malignly from the eighth Fullerian principle. They will typically be more inclined than the benevolent officials to punish or mistreat people who have not contravened any legal duties, in order to cow those people and to flaunt the dominance of their own sway. On the other hand, the officials in a malevolent system of governance will typically be far less inclined than the officials in a liberal-democratic system of governance to deviate benignly from the eighth Fullerian principle, and a malevolent regime will typically monitor people's behavior through heavy-handed techniques of surveillance that can greatly reduce the incidence of undetected and unpunished violations of the law. As was apparent to anyone who visited the Soviet Union during its heyday, the officials in a Communist dictatorship tend to cleave to the terms of legal requirements with infuriating rigidity in circumstances where the officials who run a liberal-democratic system of governance would be complaisantly flexible. In such circumstances, the fulfillment of the eighth principle of legality at a particularly high level is a means of asserting and reinforcing the ascendance of an autocracy. Likewise, as is evident to anyone who has visited any major Chinese city in recent decades, a regime that employs a totalitarian network of surveillance to monitor constantly the comings and goings and doings of its citizens—with the use of pervasive face-recognition technology and other such techniques—can thereby go a long way toward ensuring that very few contraventions of the law will escape detection. Even most minor infractions are espied and registered by such methods of surveillance. When the system of governance in a liberal democracy eschews such dystopian prying into the lives of its citizens and when it opts instead to respect its citizens by subjecting them to much lighter patterns of monitoring, the very likely effect of its position on the matter is to lessen significantly the extent of the system's adherence to the eighth principle of legality.

I am of course not endeavoring here to establish that the pattern of conformity with Fuller's principles of legality is always (or even typically) more attenuated under a liberal-democratic system of governance than under a despotic system. Rather, my point is to emphasize that complicated factors are at work in determining the pattern of such conformity under any given system of governance. We cannot safely take for granted that the levels of compliance in liberal democracies are always higher than the levels in countries ruled by dictatorships. In some credibly possible instances, the latter levels are higher than the former.

2.3.3 Upper-Case Letters versus Lower-Case Letters

In the second chapter of my 2007 book *Objectivity and the Rule of Law*, I sustainedly differentiate between the rule of law and the Rule of Law. Whereas the former is a distillation of the individually necessary and jointly sufficient conditions for the existence and functionality of a system of legal governance, the latter is a moral ideal comprising the formal characteristics of legal norms and the procedural characteristics of law-creation and law-application in a robustly liberal system of governance. What fascinates me about Fuller's principles of legality is that they can be construed in two quite distinct ways, whereby they serve either as an exposition of the rule of law or as an exposition of the Rule of Law. Moreover, although the two interpretations are distinct, they converge on some salient points—most notably, as Postema observes, on the import of the deliberative agency of the human beings to whom laws are addressed. However, the word "import" in the preceding sentence is potentially very misleading, for it needs to be understood in two divergent though overlapping ways. When an exposition of the Rule of Law highlights the import of deliberative agency, it is laying stress on such agency as a property that is morally pregnant. All the principles of the Rule of Law are ways of paying due respect to everyone who is endowed with that property. By contrast, when an exposition of the rule of law highlights the import of deliberative agency, it is laying stress on such agency as a property that is crucial for the functioning of any system of legal governance. Even in a repressive system that shows very little respect for individuals, the addressees of the law are treated as deliberative agents in that they (perhaps with the assistance of lawyers) are expected to become acquainted with the contents of legal norms and to adapt their behavior accordingly. Their agency is the vehicle through which a system of legal governance performs its function of guiding people's conduct.

Hence, although the deliberative agency of individuals is at the heart of Fuller's principles of legality in each of my two elaborations thereof, the ways in which it figures are very different between the two elaborations. Because of that major difference and other major differences between the rule of law and the Rule of Law, I use the upper-case letters to distinguish the latter clearly from the former. Postema does not follow that practice. His disinclination to follow it is not unacceptable, of course, particularly since he does not descry nearly as sharp a distinction between the rule of law and the Rule of Law as I do. Nonetheless, his use of the phrase "rule of law" to cover both the rule of law and the Rule of Law can easily result in confusion and paralogisms. My worry about the second half of his chapter—which is generally excellent in its insightfulness and eloquence—is that it does sometimes commit such missteps and that it attributes them to me. Of course, by Postema's own reckoning, the missteps are not missteps. The lines of thought that constitute those mistakes are ascribed to me by Postema commendatorily rather than condemnatorily. Still, by my reckoning as a legal positivist, those lines of thought are fallacious. Thus, despite my admiration for the subtle and lapidary musings by Postema on matters of political morality, I will briefly take exception to the handful of passages in which he saddles me with positions which I do not in fact espouse.

Early in the second half of his essay, Postema writes as follows (2022: 180, emphases in original):

> Like Fuller, Kramer argues that laws, simply by virtue of what they are, serve or manifest respect for important moral values. Values intrinsic to the rule-of-law ideal are

served by what law distinctively *is*, rather than what this or that set of laws seeks to *do* (or, more precisely, the policies and goals that governments seek to serve through the laws they enact).

Postema is here attributing to me the view that laws simply by dint of their status as laws are possessed of some moral value. Additionally or perhaps alternatively, he is attributing to me the view that a legal system of governance simply by dint of its status as a legal system of governance is possessed of some moral value. Far from embracing either of those views, I have repeatedly oppugned each of them in my defenses of legal positivism. Of course, while assailing those views, I have always readily accepted that the existence of a legal system of governance is essential for the realization of major moral ideals; the rule of law is a necessary condition for the Rule of Law. Unlike the two views which Postema ascribes to me, the proposition about the rule of law as a necessary condition for the Rule of Law is entirely compatible with my legal-positivist insistence that law is not an inherently moral phenomenon.

Another passage that is highly misleading at best is the following statement: "Kramer's account of the ... moral value [of the Rule of Law] is built around the pivotal assumption that the moral conception [of law] shares with the jurisprudential conception, namely, that at the heart of the law is a special regard for the rational, self-directing agency of legal subjects" (2022: 180). As is apparent from what I have already said in the present subsection, Postema in this statement elides the distinction between the two ways in which the deliberative agency of individuals is central to my expositions of the Fullerian principles of legality. Though the phrase "special regard" could be construed as neutral between those two ways, it strongly suggests an attitude of respect or solicitude. So understood, that phrase does not denote an attitude that is necessarily operative in the rule of law. In some credibly possible legal systems, the deliberative agency of individuals is valued by the governing officials solely as a vehicle for the efficient steering of people's conduct.

One further place where Postema foists upon me a view which I do not endorse is slightly later in his chapter, where he asserts that "Kramer concedes that the rule of law does not guarantee that the government otherwise respects dignity, and he recognizes that signal failures of the government to do so may undermine the efforts of the rule of law" (2022: 181). In its context, the quoted statement is quite clearly concerned with the Rule of Law rather than with the rule of law. Thus, I assume that each of Postema's two uses of the phrase "rule of law" is a reference to the Rule of Law. In that event, however, the opening half of the statement is deeply puzzling. In any given society S, the Rule of Law does not obtain as such unless the system of governance which presides over S is generally respectful of the dignity of citizens. To be sure, the fact that the Rule of Law obtains in S at some time *t* does not guarantee that it will continue to obtain there at some subsequent time *t+n*. Moreover, the Rule of Law can obtain in S even if the system of governance there is not perfectly respectful of the dignity of citizens in every context; a system of governance can be robustly liberal-democratic without being perfect. Perhaps the opening half of the quoted sentence is merely making one of these points, about the continuity of the Rule of Law over time or about the likelihood that robustness will fall short of perfection. If so, however, the wording of that portion of the sentence is highly misleading.

Also somewhat puzzling is the second half of the statement just quoted. Given that the phrase "rule of law" is to be construed as denoting the Rule of Law, Postema's use of the weak modal auxiliary "may" is curious. If a system of governance markedly and sustainedly fails to comply with the principles of liberal democracy, then its failures undo or preclude the existence of the Rule of Law in the society over which the system presides. The rule of law does not amount to the Rule of Law in the presence of such failures.

2.3.4 Liberal Democracy and Individualism

My final responses to Postema are focused on the perspicacious concluding pages of his essay. Richly suggestive and incisive though those pages are, Postema there underestimates my own contributions to political philosophy and also the resourcefulness of the liberal-democratic tradition more generally. He worries that the main theories of the Rule of Law in the contemporary English-speaking world are unduly individualistic in their orientation and are thus unable to come to grips adequately with questions about the Rule of Law on an international scale. He contends that present-day Anglophone philosophers, including me, have understood the Rule of Law parochially by taking it to be indisseverably connected to the values of liberal democracy. Though he readily accepts that liberal-democratic conceptions of the Rule of Law are vital, he urges his contemporaries to recognize that the principles of the Rule of Law are also to be found in some ancient and medieval sources. In the settings of ancient and medieval societies, those principles were typically elaborated and justified in non-individualistic terms.

My responses to Postema's reservations are threefold. First, although I am by no means an expert in medieval political thought, I do have quite a wide acquaintance with ancient Greek and Roman political and ethical thought, and I have worked daily on a Biblical commentary for nearly four decades.[21] Moreover, a future book of mine, to be entitled *Shakespeare's Trials*—informed by my annual reading and watching of every one of the Bard's plays—will focus partly on what the trial scenes in Shakespearean drama reveal about aspects of the Rule of Law in the Renaissance. Hence, I am familiar with much of the broader canvas on which Postema sketches his account of the Rule of Law. Still, notwithstanding that the principles of the Rule of Law were partly anticipated in sundry pre-modern bodies of thought, the modern conception of the Rule of Law developed in Western liberal democracies is unparalleled in its systematicity and its moral acuity. Firmly dissociated from the hierarchical outlooks that were prevalent in ancient and medieval times, the liberal-democratic conception of the Rule of Law avoids the errors and ugliness of those outlooks while incorporating their strengths. Furthermore, liberal political philosophy is not indissolubly tied to premises that are individualistic in any problematic sense, and it is amply capable of addressing matters of international or global justice. I will expand upon these points in my next few paragraphs.

[21] See Kramer 2015. In my role as a Biblical commentator, I will note that—like many other modern Biblical commentators—I do not share Postema's assumption that the Letter to the Ephesians in the New Testament was genuinely written by Paul.

Second, even by the time I published my 2007 book *Objectivity and the Rule of Law* (the chief work of mine on which Postema concentrates in his chapter), I had made clear that I do not take the strongly individualistic conclusions of liberalism to be grounded perforce in individualistic premises. For example, my 1997 book *John Locke and the Origins of Private Property* argues that the justification of private property famously propounded by John Locke in his *Second Treatise of Government* was ultimately grounded—by Locke's own reckoning—in the designs of God for humanity as a whole. Even more in several of my subsequent books, *The Ethics of Capital Punishment* and *Torture and Moral Integrity* and *Liberalism with Excellence* and *Freedom of Expression as Self-Restraint*, I have elaborated an array of ideas centered on the paramount moral responsibility of every system of governance to bring about the political and social and economic conditions under which everyone within the jurisdiction of the system can be warranted in harboring a sturdy sense of self-respect. As I maintain in those books, a key aspect of the fulfillment of that paramount responsibility is the adherence of a system of governance to the Rule of Law. Such adherence is of benefit to individuals directly (through enhanced security and respect, for example), but is also of benefit to them indirectly because the levels of self-respect that are warranted for them are partly dependent on the character of the system of governance that presides over their society. With this largely non-individualistic orientation, I derive conclusions that are ringingly individualistic in that they are very much in keeping with civil libertarianism. Moreover, I do so while drawing upon insights in ancient and Renaissance texts[22]—insights which I transmute by secularizing them or by extracting them from the hierarchical settings in which they were articulated. Thus, my philosophizing on these matters in my overall *oeuvre* is far less provincial than Postema surmises. Indeed, if Postema peruses the sixth chapter of *The Ethics of Capital Punishment* and the final three chapters of *Liberalism with Excellence* and the fourth chapter of *Freedom of Expression as Self-Restraint*, I think that he will find them fruitful for the cogitations which he pursues in the final several pages of his essay. Those chapters help to explain why the members of any community (including the global community) are indeed members one of another.

Third, not only is my own work more cosmopolitan than Postema allows, but so is the liberal tradition in political philosophy. I have already suggested as much with regard to Locke, and the same point applies to some of my fellow exponents of liberalism in the present day. For example, much of what Postema says in the closing pages of his essay is strikingly reminiscent of the meditations by Ronald Dworkin in Chapters 6 and 7 of *Law's Empire*. Similarly, much of what Postema says in those pages is quite closely akin to the reflections on dignity in some of Jeremy Waldron's recent writings. Admittedly, Waldron's 2012 book *The Harm in Hate Speech* is disconcertingly illiberal in some salient respects; but overall it remains within the liberal tradition, and Waldron there and elsewhere has been a prominent exegete of liberal political thought. What should also be briefly mentioned here is that many liberal political philosophers

[22] For instance, in Kramer 2011a I draw quite heavily on the Hebrew Scriptures and on some ancient Greek tragedies, and in Kramer 2017b I draw quite heavily on portions of the Hebrew Scriptures and on passages from several of Shakespeare's plays.

during the past few decades have grappled sustainedly with problems of global justice. Martha Nussbaum, Charles Beitz, Thomas Pogge, and Simon Caney are only a few of those who have written at length on such matters from liberal perspectives. Accordingly, although recourse to texts and thinkers outside the liberal tradition can be extremely valuable, excursions through that tradition in all its richness can likewise serve many of Postema's purposes.

2.4 Pierluigi Chiassoni and the Coherence of Legal Positivism

Having known Chiassoni for somewhat over a decade, and having engaged in some pleasantly stimulating conversations with him during that time, I am pleased to have an opportunity to joust with him here in writing. Though I shall make a few remarks about the first half of his paper, I shall concentrate chiefly on the second half. Whereas the first half of the paper is largely expository and is mostly quite accurate, the latter half has left me somewhat nonplused. That latter half is at times decidedly ungenerous; moreover, it continually attributes to me some positions which I have never espoused, and it adopts some positions of its own that are outlandish.

2.4.1 A Problematic Sentence

Chiassoni goes astray near the outset of his chapter, when he writes: "Like every common law theory of positivism of Hartian descent, Kramer's theory understands 'the separation thesis' as a signpost for a set of multiple and heterogeneous claims, encompassing both meta-theoretical and theoretical separation theses" (2022: 149). I never use the phrase "the separation thesis," except to indicate my rejection of it. Such wording is badly misguided, as is the slightly less rebarbative phrase "the separability thesis." As I have repeatedly complained in my books on legal positivism, any such wording erroneously conveys the impression that there is only one main point of contention between legal positivists and their opponents. Of course, Chiassoni himself in the quoted sentence adverts directly to the plurality of the points of contention. However, he thereby highlights the situation that leads me to eschew any phrasing such as "the separability thesis" or "the separation thesis."

Even more surprising in the sentence just quoted is the suggestion that my jurisprudential theorizing is like all other Hartian jurisprudential theorizing in its recognition of the multiplicity of the debates between legal positivists and their opponents. On the contrary, as I have repeatedly observed in my books on legal positivism, far too many contemporary legal philosophers disregard that multiplicity. Hart himself was fully attuned to the multifariousness of those debates, but most of his intellectual descendants have not been. Most of his intellectual heirs write as if there is only one central issue over which the legal positivists and the natural-law theorists have quarreled; they write as if the positivist position on the one issue which they single out can be aptly designated as "the separability thesis." Having striven repeatedly against that narrowness of horizons displayed by so many contemporary legal philosophers, I am puzzled that Chiassoni aligns them with me.

2.4.2 The Conflation of the Meta-Theoretical and the Theoretical

Chiassoni conflates a meta-theoretical matter and some theoretical matters in the following passage, which occurs just after the sentence that I have assailed above (2022: 149, footnote omitted):

> Among the meta-theoretical separation theses, the epistemological separation thesis concerns the philosophically and scientifically proper way of making inquiries on the law as a complex social and political normative phenomenon. It urges avoiding any confusion between "the law as it is," on the one side, and "the law as it ought to be" from some moral standpoint, on the other. It outlaws the smuggling of value-laden, ethically committed ingredients into descriptive accounts of law.

Although Chiassoni professes to be recounting a meta-theoretical thesis here, he is in fact recounting primarily a pair of theoretical theses which he conflates with the meta-theoretical tenet. One of the theoretical matters is the question whether the law as it exists in any given jurisdiction is distinguishable from the law as it ought to be. A second theoretical matter pertains to law as a general phenomenon. Can the nature of law as a general phenomenon be distinguished from what law ought to be?

Each of those theoretical questions is to be contrasted with a meta-theoretical matter which I have discussed in quite a recent essay (2019a: 376–7). I state there the nature of value-independence as follows (2019a: 376):

> If a project of theoretical elaboration is value-independent in the sense specified here, it is not grounded on any ethical values. That is, the justifications for its theses do not consist in invocations of ethical values. Some values do of course underlie any such project, but they are theoretical-explanatory or logical/mathematical or aesthetic rather than ethical.

In the context of a philosophical account of law or of legal systems, a key meta-theoretical matter is whether the account can and should be value-independent. Like quite a few other legal positivists, I have argued for an affirmative answer to that meta-theoretical or methodological question (1999: 233–9; 2018: 12–23). Hart likewise generally answered that question affirmatively, but in some uncharacteristic argumentation at the end of the ninth chapter of *The Concept of Law* he departed from his usual stance by presenting some moral considerations in favor of his position on the status of evil laws as laws. Most other positivists have been wise to look askance at that methodological aberration on his part.

2.4.3 Illusory Limits

Again near the outset of his chapter, Chiassoni declares that "Hart, for instance, defends a variety of limits of the law thesis according to which, at any moment in the life of a legal system, existing law is tantamount to the set of valid explicit and definite legal rules" (2022: 149). This assertion by Chiassoni is strongly reminiscent of Dworkin's complaint that Hart had supposedly overlooked the role of moral principles in the law of the United States and of other jurisdictions. Quite strange is the recurrence of that complaint, for—as I have observed elsewhere (2018: 176–8)—Hart in his Postscript to the second edition of *The Concept of Law* explicitly endorsed Incorporationism and reaffirmed his longstanding acceptance of Inclusivism. Given that those jurisprudential doctrines are inconsistent with the proposition that the law in every credibly possible jurisdiction is limited to explicit legal rules, we can safely conclude that that proposition is something misattributed to Hart by Chiassoni rather than something to which Hart actually subscribed.

Hence, when Chiassoni reproves Hart for ostensibly failing to grasp that "the limits of the law are not something for a general and descriptive legal theory to establish once and for all, being contrariwise an issue that fatally belongs to the realm of legal scholarship, doctrines, ideologies, and values" (2022: 150), he purports to be chiding Hart while he in fact is rehearsing one of Hart's chief contentions. By embracing Incorporationism and Inclusivism, Hart reaffirmed the jurisdiction-specificity of the limits of the law. More broadly, as I have emphasized elsewhere (2018: 11–12), Hart was keenly alert to the sundry aspects of law that are indeed variable across jurisdictions. Chiassoni's reproach is therefore a curious instance of what the Duke describes in his colloquy with Escalus at the outset of Shakespeare's *Measure for Measure*: "Of government the properties to unfold/Would seem in me t' affect speech and discourse,/Since I am put to know that your own science/Exceeds, in that, the lists of all advice/My strength can give you" (I.i.3–7).

2.4.4 Chimerical Difficulties

There are a number of other missteps in the first half of Chiassoni's chapter (including some repetitions of the missteps to which I have already taken exception here). However, those mistakes are largely quite minor. Let us move on, then, to the second half of his chapter—where the dubiousness of his arguments becomes more serious. My perplexity really began when I came upon his treatment of my Inclusive Legal Positivism. Chiassoni conjures up five versions of Inclusivism, most of which are absurd and are patently inconsistent with what I have written about Inclusivism. Rather obscure to me is the point of such an endeavor. Chiassoni himself, at the end of his discussion, acknowledges: "The previous analysis has been a willful exercise in uncharitableness" (2022: 159). Exactly why he has devoted multiple pages to that exercise is not clear.

Although a sustained set of rejoinders to Chiassoni's reflections on Inclusivism would not be worthwhile, a few terse responses here to those reflections are in order. First, the correct version of my Inclusive Legal Positivism is what Chiassoni labels as the "morally objectivist legality thesis" (2022: 159, italics removed). Only one small modification in Chiassoni's encapsulation of that version of Inclusivism is requisite here. Chiassoni formulates the morally objectivist legality thesis as follows: "[T]he *consistency* or *compatibility* of a norm (e.g., N_i) with the *objectively correct principles of morality* M_o (i.e., with the true principles of morality that have always existed and will always exist as strongly human mind-independent entities) *can*, but *need not, be* a *necessary condition* for the status of norm N_i as a *legal* norm" (2022: 159, italics in original). The parenthetical portion of Chiassoni's formulation is somewhat too sweeping. Although all basic principles of morality and most derivative principles of morality are strongly mind-independent existentially, not all derivative principles are. Quite a few derivative principles of morality are variable in their contents across societies. Any credible account of the objectivity of morality has to leave room for some derivative moral principles that are variable, even while it affirms the invariance of all basic moral principles and most derivative moral principles. Given that I have discussed this matter at length elsewhere (2009: 161–72), and given that my amendment here to Chiassoni's formulation is narrowly focused and friendly, I will not dilate further on that amendment.

Second, if anyone purports to be a proponent of Inclusive Legal Positivism while adhering to a thoroughly relativistic conception of morality, then he or she is espousing a theory that is indistinguishable from some or all versions of Exclusive Legal Positivism. Let us leave aside here my doubts about the very coherence of moral relativism (Kramer 2009: 38–40). Of central importance instead in the present context is that a relativistic version of Inclusivism would in effect maintain that the inclusion of moral principles as touchstones for legal validity in any particular jurisdiction is on a par with the inclusion of other customary precepts as such touchstones in that jurisdiction. Exclusivists have always accepted that customary precepts can enter into the law of a jurisdiction as substantive legal norms that serve as bases for decisions by adjudicators and administrators, and they consequently will accept that customary precepts in any jurisdiction can enter into the Rule of Recognition there as criteria that specify necessary conditions for the status of norms as laws. Given that those precepts are the contents of widely shared beliefs and attitudes in a community, the discerning of them by adjudicators and administrators is a complex empirical enquiry rather than a moral enquiry. Hence, when adjudicators and administrators invoke customary precepts as criteria in their Rule of Recognition, they are not doing anything that is inconsistent with an Exclusivist account of law-ascertainment. They are not engaging in moral deliberations. Accordingly, given that moral relativists contend that the correct principles of morality in any society are customary precepts, a relativistic version of Inclusive Legal Positivism will be fully consistent with Exclusive Legal Positivism—which is why any such version would be a wholesale distortion of Inclusivism rather than a genuine elaboration of it. Inclusive Legal Positivists are advancing a theory that proclaims the possibility of the role of objectively correct moral principles as criteria in any society's Rule of Recognition; they are not advancing a theory that proclaims the possibility of such a role for customary precepts (though of course they are likewise not *denying* the possibility of such a role for customary precepts).

Third, the unfoundedness of some of Chiassoni's reservations about my positions is epitomized in the following passage (2022: 159, footnote omitted):

> What about, for instance, a norm of conduct N_j, never previously endowed with any legislative or judicial formulation, that a jurist, in a doctrinal essay, claims to belong to the legal system because of its consistency to some moral principle? Is N_j a legal norm by the inclusivist criterion? If the answer is in the affirmative, morality would be not (only) a necessary, but (also) a sufficient condition of N_j's legality. In such a case, however, inclusivism would seem to slide into incorporationism.

In none of my writings on these matters have I suggested that, under an Inclusivist Rule of Recognition, consistency with this or that moral principle is a *sufficient* condition for the status of any norm as a law. I have instead always maintained that, under an Inclusivist Rule of Recognition, consistency with this or that moral principle is a *necessary* condition for the status of any norm as a law. Chiassoni is inattentive here to what I have actually written. Moreover, he also errs in his remark about Incorporationism at the end of the quoted passage. It is not the case that, under an Incorporationist Rule of Recognition, the *consistency* of a norm with this or that moral principle is sufficient for the status of that norm as a law. Rather, under such a Rule of Recognition, the *correctness* of a norm as a moral principle is sufficient for the status of that norm as a law.

Fourth, Chiassoni poses the following question: "Why should a thesis purporting to account for the possible content of the legality criteria of actual legal systems rule out extreme subjectivist morality conditions? No theoretical reason appears to support that position" (2022: 160). On the contrary, there are powerful theoretical reasons for denying that any Inclusivist Rule of Recognition grounded on an extreme subjectivist understanding of morality could ever genuinely be operative in any jurisdiction. For one thing, just as a purportedly Inclusivist Rule of Recognition informed by moral relativism would be indistinguishable from an Exclusivist Rule of Recognition, so too would any purportedly Inclusivist Rule of Recognition informed by moral subjectivism. According to moral subjectivism, moral principles as the contents of certain beliefs and attitudes of each individual are fundamentally empirical phenomena that can be descried through the introspection of each individual or through testing and surveys by psychologists. Thus, in a system of governance with a putatively Inclusivist Rule of Recognition informed by moral subjectivism, the processes of law-ascertainment would be entirely compatible with the Exclusivists' account of those processes. Law-ascertainment in that jurisdiction would draw solely upon empirically discoverable touchstones for the status of norms as laws. In such a system of governance, the Rule of Recognition would not be genuinely Inclusivist at all. Furthermore, in such a system the putatively Inclusivist touchstones for the status of norms as laws would be radically individualized in that the set of those touchstones correctly invocable by each adjudicative or administrative official would be distinctively personal to him or her. With regard to those supposedly Inclusivist criteria, then, the processes of law-ascertainment in that system would be at odds with what Hart correctly characterized as an essential feature of every credibly possible instance of the rule of law: "[T]he ultimate rule of recognition in terms of which the validity of other rules is assessed . . . , if it is to exist at all, must be regarded from the internal point of view as a public common standard of correct judicial decision . . . . This is not merely a matter of the efficiency or health of the legal system, but is logically a necessary condition of our ability to speak [correctly] of the existence of a single legal system" (Hart 1994: 116). Were some of the fundamental standards for ascertaining the law in a society so fractionated that each official there would be correct in adhering to his or her own discrete set of such standards, the collective activity in which the operations of a legal system consist would *pro tanto* be non-existent.

2.4.5 Relativism Redux

Chiassoni raises the specter of moral relativism not only in connection with Inclusivism but also in connection with Incorporationism. He writes as follows (2022: 160, emphases in original):

> What should count as a correct moral principle is ... something for each legal system (and each legal culture) to determine. It may happen, accordingly, that a legal system endorses a relativistic variety of incorporationism ... or, alternatively an objectivist variety, so that the incorporationist thesis should read, more precisely, as follows: a *norm's objective or relative correctness as a moral principle* can, but need not be, a *sufficient condition* for its status as a legal norm in this or that jurisdiction.

As is manifest from what I have said in the preceding subsection, Incorporationism is no more susceptible to being combined with moral relativism than is Inclusive Legal Positivism. If a supposedly Incorporationist Rule of Recognition were grounded on a relativistic understanding of morality, it would not actually be an Incorporationist Rule of Recognition at all. Instead, it would be a Rule of Recognition under which some customary norms—the principles of morality as understood by relativists—are among the laws of the jurisdiction in which that Rule of Recognition obtains. Like Inclusivism, then, Incorporationism as a jurisprudential theory distinguishable from Exclusivism is integrally connected to an objectivist understanding of morality.

2.4.6 Preposterous Possibilities

Equally puzzling is Chiassoni's response to my arguments against extreme Incorporationism and in favor of moderate Incorporationism. While extreme Incorporationists affirm the possibility of a system of legal governance wherein the sole criterion for the status of any norm as a law is the correctness of a norm as a moral principle, moderate Incorporationists affirm the possibility of a system of legal governance wherein any norms which possess the status of laws by dint of their correctness as moral principles are properly invocable in cases where laws from other sources do not yield determinate answers to the points at issue. In the first few chapters of my 2004 book *Where Law and Morality Meet*, I have argued that extreme Incorporationism highlights a possibility that cannot be realized in any sizable society over a sustained period of time. That possibility is a bare logical possibility rather than a credible possibility. By contrast, moderate Incorporationism highlights a possibility that is credibly realizable in any society.

Chiassoni retorts as follows (2022: 161-2, emphasis in original):

> [W]hat robust incorporationism claims is the *possibility*, for any legal system having, *qua* legal system, a dynamic and coercive character, to be grounded on a robustly incorporationist rule of recognition. Claiming such a possibility fits together with, and does not rule out, the possibility for legal systems to adopt more moderate versions of the rule of recognition, and even strictly exclusivist ones keeping moral principles completely outside of positive law. What robust incorporationism points to, accordingly, is a spectrum of possible forms of legal systems: from the extreme of those adopting a robust incorporationist rule of recognition, to the extreme of those adopting a strictly exclusivist one. This way of proceeding seems perfectly in tune with the requirements of a genuinely general and descriptive jurisprudence.

In my rejection of extreme Incorporationism, I have always been aware that extreme Incorporationists advert to an extreme Incorporationist Rule of Recognition as only one possibility among others in any given society. My complaint has never been that those Incorporationists deny other possibilities. Rather, my complaint has been that they devote nearly all their attention to one possibility—the possibility of an extreme Incorporationist Rule of Recognition—that cannot be realized in any credibly possible society on a sizable scale over a long period. By devoting so much attention to a state of affairs that is logically possible but preposterously improbable, the extreme Incorporationists provide an unhelpfully skewed and unilluminating theory of the workings of national legal systems. I have sought to drive this point home with my example of a Hamletist theory of law (2004: 97–100). I there envisage a system of legal governance in which every official sincerely and unremittingly believes that she is performing the role of Hamlet as she carries out her adjudicative or administrative responsibilities. Such a system of legal governance is outlandishly unlikely but not logically impossible. Now, suppose that some legal philosophers elect to devote nearly all their attention to Hamletist systems of law and to explaining why such systems are logically possible. Perhaps some other legal philosophers will similarly preoccupy themselves with Macbethian systems of law or Othelloan systems of law. These philosophers are not denying that other types of systems of law are possible, but they center their theories on the fanciful possibilities that engross them. Should we conclude that they are thereby making valuable contributions to the philosophy of law, or should we contrariwise conclude that they are largely squandering their time and that they should focus their energies instead on delineating the essential properties of credibly possible legal systems? Chiassoni apparently favors the former conclusion, whereas I straightforwardly favor the latter. Any pertinent insights generated by the theorizing of the Hamletists could also be generated by theorizing that does considerably more to illuminate the nature of law.

Chiassoni alleges that I have adopted a tendentiously narrow conception of the workings of legal systems (2022: 162, footnote omitted):

> Kramer's sponsoring of a narrow notion of "existing legal system" (only normative social orders endowed with an adequate degree of regularity, uniformity, or consistency are existing legal systems) is open to the same form of criticism Hart waged against natural-lawyers' recourse to a narrow concept of law. From the standpoint of dispassionate legal knowledge, there seems to be nothing wrong (and much to commend) in saying something like: "This is a legal system, but the degree of regularity, uniformity, or consistency in the decisions of its officials is so low that it fares pretty badly as a conduct-coordinating device."

In the statement at the end of this passage, the phrase "pretty badly" is mild enough to keep the statement intelligible. By contrast, if that phrase were altered to "barely at all" or "not at all," the statement would become unintelligible. As I have maintained elsewhere during one of my principal discussions of Incorporationism,[23] some considerable degree of efficacy in the guiding of conduct is necessary if an apparent system of law is indeed to be existent as a functional system of law. On the one hand, as I observe

[23] See Kramer 2004: 26–8. See also Kramer 1999: 140–6.

there, the concepts of efficiency and existence in application to legal systems are neither intensionally nor extensionally equivalent—which is why in many contexts we can correctly talk, as Chiassoni does, about inefficient legal systems. On the other hand, as I have argued in the aforementioned discussion, "a legal system must pass a [non-specifiable] threshold of regularity in its workings it is to exist as a [functional] legal system at all. Above that threshold, the system will be functional and efficient to a greater or a lesser extent. Below that threshold, however, it will be nonexistent—that is, nonexistent as a [functional] legal system—rather than merely inefficient" (2004: 28).

Particularly bemusing in the passage from Chiassoni quoted most recently above is his suggestion that, when I insist that every functional system of law possesses some degree of efficacy in the guiding of conduct, my insistence is somehow aligned with the moralized understandings of law propounded by opponents of legal positivism. Immediately after that passage, he continues in broadly the same vein (2022: 162, footnote omitted):

> [F]rom an austere Benthamite perspective [with its distinction between what a legal system is and what a legal system ought to be], Kramer's opposition to robust incorporationism appears to be laden with preoccupations that belong to the criticism of law, even though it is a rational criticism, or from the standpoint of instrumental, means-to-end, reason. Indeed, as Kramer avows, he adjusts the concept of "existing legal system" to the need of limiting "the range of possible law-ascertaining criteria" to what is "necessary to ensure the functionality of a legal system."

Though Chiassoni does not here reiterate his suggestion that I have aligned myself with opponents of legal positivism when I assert that the operations of every system of legal governance are regularized and efficacious in the guiding of conduct at least to a fairly high degree, he does opine that I have transgressed the distinction between what law is and what law ought to be. Yet my critique of extreme Incorporationism does not presume that an ostensible system of law becomes better and better as it guides conduct more and more effectively. Rather, I simply maintain that an ostensible system of law is not a genuine system of law at all if it fails to guide conduct at or above some minimum level of effectiveness. If all the decisions and directives of an ostensible system of law are a higgledy-piggledy welter of discordant signals that leave the addressees of the system thoroughly befuddled about the legal implications of their conduct, the ostensible system does not exist as a functional system of law. In so contending, I am not drawing on assumptions about what makes one legal system better than another—or on assumptions about how legal systems ought to be. I am instead drawing on a theory about the characteristics which the operations of a system of governance must possess if those operations are to constitute a functional system of law.

2.4.7 Non Sequiturs

Chiassoni proceeds to expatiate on my moderate Incorporationism. Near the outset of his cogitations on the matter is the following declaration: "[T]he ascertainment of the uniquely correct solution for a hard case is . . . a matter of moral argument, and this implies that 'the unique correctness' of the solution 'is *indemonstrable*'" (2022: 162, emphasis in original). One misstep in Chiassoni's pronouncement is his supposition that, in every hard case where the question at issue is answerable in a uniquely correct way, the answer is rooted in moral considerations. Though his supposition is correct in relation to quite a few hard cases with points of contention that are determinately resolvable, the points of contention in some hard cases are determinately resolvable on other grounds. For example, as I have remarked elsewhere (2009: 238–9; 2018: 113–14), intractable wrangling quite often arises over various questions of historical fact to which there are determinately correct answers. Some similarly knotty questions about historical or empirical facts can be at issue in some of the cases where jurists disagree persistently with one another.

Also mistaken in the quoted sentence is its suggestion that the moral character of the considerations which constitute uniquely correct answers to the questions at issue in some hard cases is itself what entails the indemonstrability of those answers. On the one hand, every hard case involves indemonstrability; the indemonstrability of the answer(s) to the key disputed question(s) is a hallmark of every hard case. On the other hand, the indemonstrability of the correct answer to the question in dispute in a given case C is not entailed by the sheer fact that that question is a moral matter. The moral tenor of the question does not in itself entail that C is a hard case.

A further non sequitur occurs in the following assertion by Chiassoni: "If there is *no demonstrable way* to tell whether incorporated moral principles do, or do not, provide a uniquely correct solution to a hard case at hand, the distinction between [hard cases centered on questions with uniquely correct but indemonstrable answers and hard cases centered on questions with no determinately correct answers] falls apart. But mild incorporationism stands on that distinction. Therefore, mild incorporationism falls apart too" (2022: 162-3, emphasis in original). Contrary to what Chiassoni avers here, the distinction between the two categories of hard cases which he mentions is not dependent on the demonstrability of the extension of each category. That distinction partly determines what the judges or administrators in hard cases are legally obligated and legally permitted to do, whether or not the judges and administrators perceive correctly what they are legally obligated and legally permitted to do. Germane here are my remarks on observational mind-independence in my book *Objectivity and the Rule of Law* and in some of my subsequent books (Kramer 2007: 5–6, 8–12; 2009: 25–6, 48–69; 2018: 122–30). In those remarks, I explore at length how people such as legal-governmental officials can be mistaken when they reflect on the phenomena or states of affairs which their beliefs and attitudes and behavior collectively sustain in existence. People can be in error about the implications of the contents of their own beliefs, just as they can be in error about the implications of other propositions. Given the abiding possibility of incongruity between (1) the first-order beliefs and attitudes of officials that sustain the existence of legal norms and (2) the higher-order beliefs of the officials about the norms that are constituted by their first-order beliefs and attitudes, my moderate Incorporationism is a theory partly about the determinacy or indeterminacy of the answers to sundry legal questions—rather than about the higher-order beliefs of officials concerning the determinacy or indeterminacy of those answers. Consequently, my moderate Incorporationism is undamaged by Chiassoni's observation about indemonstrability.

Chiassoni disregards the distinction on which I have just insisted, when he declares: "We have just seen ... that there is no way of demonstrating that incorporated moral principles do provide a uniquely correct solution to a hard case at hand, that the distinction between [the two categories of hard cases] is theoretically unviable" (2022: 163). From an epistemic premise about the indemonstrability of the demarcation between the two categories of hard cases, Chiassoni here invalidly moves to an ontological conclusion—or a semantic conclusion—about that demarcation itself. I readily accept his premise, but his conclusion does not follow therefrom.

Chiassoni further errs when he proclaims: "If we cannot know whether incorporated moral principles do, or do not, provide a uniquely correct solution to a hard case at hand, we cannot know, by Kramer's own standard, whether in a hard case there is law to be applied by judges, or, rather, judges must make new law on the basis of acceptable moral principles" (2022: 163). At least in ordinary circumstances, the answer to the question whether incorporated moral principles provide a uniquely correct solution to this or that hard case is in fact knowable. That answer about a uniquely correct solution will in most instances be indemonstrable, and there will thus be intractable disagreement about it among jurists and other experts. Nonetheless, the jurists and other experts in nearly every instance can know the correct answer even though many of them (locked in intractable wrangling with their fellows) do not know it. Relevantly similar here is the knowability of the answer to the question whether William Shakespeare really wrote the plays that are attributed to him. Quite a number of experts have quarreled over that answer for the past couple of centuries, but the answer is knowable. Much the same is true of the answer to the question whether Lee Harvey Oswald's assassination of the American President John Kennedy in 1963 was a product of a large-scale conspiracy or whether instead Oswald acted predominantly on his own. Tens of millions of Americans, many of them redoubtably well informed, disagree fiercely over the answer to that question; but its indemonstrability is consistent with its knowability. Chiassoni goes astray in inferring the reign of unknowability from the reign of indemonstrability.

Toward the end of his chapter, Chiassoni returns to his Dworkinian claim about Hart's supposed adherence to a "limits of the law thesis" which confines the law in any jurisdiction to the "definite explicit law" there (2022: 163). As I have already maintained, the imputation of such a thesis to Hart is baseless. Of new interest here, however, is the non sequitur which Chiassoni draws from his ascription of that thesis to Hart. Chiassoni declares that the propounding of the limits-of-the-law thesis is "likely to have a momentous practical bearing .... It can ... be used to practical purposes in the practice-of-law game, which jurists ... daily play out of professional privilege and duty" (2022: 163). He elaborates:

> Consider the following example. Suppose you are a jurist favoring a "passive" judicial attitude in constitutional interpretation. In such an event, you will find the Hartian limits of the law thesis quite congenial to your (normative and justificatory) view. In fact, it supports you, with all the authoritative weight of a seemingly *theoretical* claim, in arguing that the constitution reaches up to the point of the determinate linguistic or intentional meaning of its provisions, or, in any case, up to the point of their collectively determinate judicial meaning. In so doing, you will be able to criticize as instances of *unconstitutional* judicial "activism" any reading of the constitution that departs, either from the determinate linguistic or intentional meaning

> of its provisions, if any, or from the determinate collective judicial meaning, once it has been established. In so doing, you will be able to claim that every judicial interpretation of a constitutional provision departing from the meanings above is *legally wrong*: it is a piece of contrary-to-law interpretation, or, in the terminology of medieval jurists, an instance of *interpretatio contra legem*, or, more precisely, *contra constitutionem*. (2022: 163-4, footnote omitted, emphases in original)

Chiassoni here neglects the distinction between indemonstrability and indeterminacy and also the distinction between existential mind-independence and observational mind-independence. He writes as though the contours of the determinate law in any jurisdiction are themselves demonstrable matters on which all or nearly all the legal experts in the jurisdiction agree. In fact, the charting of those contours in virtually any jurisdiction is a matter of intractable debate. For example, when faced with demands from constitutional "originalists" for fidelity by American courts to the US Constitution, Dworkin did not respond by accepting their perception of the determinate contours of the Constitution and by arguing that the courts should go beyond those contours. Rather, he retorted that "textual fidelity [to the Constitution] argues so strongly in favor of a broad judicial responsibility to hold legislation to direct moral standards that a great many constitutional scholars, including those who call most loudly for 'originalism,' actually argue *against* [genuine] textual fidelity as a constitutional standard" (Dworkin 2006: 118, emphasis in original). Argumentation of this kind is commonplace among constitutional theorists in the United States and elsewhere. Thus, when Chiassoni announces that the "limits of the law" thesis has a clear-cut practical bearing, he is giving voice to an illusion. There is no such clear-cut practical bearing, because the "limits of the law" thesis can be invoked powerfully *against* Chiassoni's conservative jurist as well as *by* that jurist.

2.4.8 Misconceived Attributions

Chiassoni's chapter goes especially amiss when it begins to refer to the "limits of the law" thesis not only as Hartian but also as Kramerian. Chiassoni twice characterizes that thesis as "the Hartian (or Kramerian) thesis" (2022: 164). He chides Hart and me for our supposedly having failed to grasp that a properly jurisprudential thesis about the limits of law "must avoid taking sides as to the existing law/definite explicit law/implicit law issue. That issue should be regarded—and presented—as one that wholly belongs to the province of legal practice and juristic value-laden controversies" (2022: 164). Throughout my writings on Inclusive Legal Positivism and Incorporationism, I have sought to emphasize that the existence of an Inclusivist or Incorporationist Rule of Recognition in any particular jurisdiction is an abiding possibility but not a necessity. In short, I have underscored the very point which Chiassoni here upbraids me for overlooking. Moreover, the fourth chapter of my 2004 book *Where Law and Morality Meet* sustainedly explores how moral principles can enter the law of a jurisdiction implicitly rather than explicitly and discretely. Thus, I am perplexed to find that Chiassoni is imputing to me the untenable "limits of the law" thesis.

Furthermore, my writings serve as a corrective to an equivocation of which Chiassoni himself appears to be guilty. It is certainly an equivocation of which Hart was guilty. In my 2018 book on Hart, I reproach him at length for running together indemonstrability with indeterminacy (2018: 112–17, 128–30). Chiassoni appears to be guilty of a comparable conflation with his use of the term "definite" in his formulations of the "limits of the law" thesis. He seems sometimes to be using that term to mean "demonstrable," and at other times to be using it to mean "determinate." Such equivocality would be extenuable in a discussion focused solely on Hart, since it would tally with an aspect of his own theorizing. However, in a discussion where the "limits of the law" thesis is characterized as "Kramerian," the ambiguity of the adjective "definite" as employed by Chiassoni is unacceptable. Although I have always submitted that the limits of the law in every particular jurisdiction are set by the determinacy of the prevailing legal norms, I have never suggested that the limits of the law in every jurisdiction are set by the demonstrability of the prevailing legal norms. On the contrary, I have repeatedly agreed with Dworkin—against Hart—that the existence and contents of the laws in any jurisdiction extend beyond what is demonstrable among the officials there (Kramer 2007: 33–6; 2009: 107–8; 2018: 116–17). Accordingly, the equivocality of the adjective "definite" in the formulation of a thesis ascribed by Chiassoni to me is dismaying.

2.4.9 The Nature of Law

Near the end of his chapter, Chiassoni addresses the topic of the nature of law. Specifically, he ponders whether the Razian Exclusive Legal Positivists are correct in purporting to ground their jurisprudential doctrine on the very nature of law (2022: 165):

> Exclusivism claims to derive the no-incorporation thesis and the externality of moral principles thesis ... from "the very nature of law." Such a derivation, unfortunately, looks like a piece of natural-law theory, in its "nature of things" variety. From the standpoint of a genuinely positivist jurisprudence, the issue about whether certain sorts of norms (say, moral principles or customary norms) do, or do not, belong to a legal system is not a matter for legal theory to settle by way of a general thesis, nor by appealing to intrinsic properties of the norms at stake, since it depends, rather, on each legal system's contingent *meta-norms* about membership and applicability.

Now, on the one hand, Chiassoni is correct in holding that the question which he broaches—the question whether any norms of certain sorts (such as moral principles and customary norms) belong to a legal system as some of its laws—is a jurisdiction-specific matter that cannot be resolved on the basis of jurisdiction-transcendent considerations. In addition, he is correct in thinking that Raz's specific appeal to the nature of law is moralized; that appeal relies on the Razian conception of authority, which is a moral conception through and through. On the other hand, Chiassoni should have been more careful to stress that jurisprudential theorists can appeal to the nature of law without relying on Raz's conception of authority or on any other moral thesis. For example, suppose that some officials in a particular legal system bizarrely think that lollipops or bluebirds rather than norms are the main elements of the system. Without relying on any moral principles, a jurisprudential theorist can aptly conclude that those officials are mistaken as a matter of the very nature of law. Indeed, numerous aspects of positivist jurisprudential theorizing pertain to the nature of law.

For instance, as I have argued elsewhere (2007: 183–6), Fuller's principles of legality as an exposition of the rule of law rather than of the Rule of Law are necessary and sufficient conditions for the existence and functioning of a legal system. Those principles, in other words, encapsulate the essence or nature of the rule of law.

2.4.10 A Parting Shot

At the very end of his chapter, Chiassoni accurately states that Hart and I have each ascribed to legal systems the general function of guiding and assessing people's conduct. However, he extracts an odd conclusion from his observation: "The outcome in sum is theories of law that, all-things-considered, have not entirely succeeded in providing purely descriptive, value-neutral, indifferent to practical consequences, accounts of positive legal systems" (2022: 166). This sentence with the phrase "have not entirely succeeded" presupposes that jurisprudential theorists should be striving to do what Chiassoni says that they have not yet done. However, such an implicature is unsustainable. Although I myself use the hyphenated adjective "value-neutral" very differently[24]—in a manner that will be invoked in my response to Lubomira Radoilska's chapter in section 3.2—Chiassoni is clearly employing that adjective, in combination with the phrase "purely descriptive," to mean "not grounded on any evaluative assumptions." Any endeavor to produce a theory that is value-neutral in that sense is badly misguided, as I have emphasized since my earliest publications on legal positivism. In *In Defense of Legal Positivism*, for example, I have written as follows:

> [A]ny theory of legal institutions (or other institutions) must proceed on the basis of certain assumptions about the relative importance of the various facets of those institutions. If a theory were to highlight everything, then it would highlight nothing—since it would give no greater prominence to anything than to anything else. Thus, if a "theory is to be more than a vast rubbish heap of miscellaneous facts described in a multitude of incommensurable terminologies," it must impose order on its field of study by treating some things as more important than others. A fundamental methodological concern at the outset of any investigation of legal institutions, then, lies in determining which characteristics of those institutions are most important. (Kramer 1999: 234, quoting Finnis 1980: 17)

Much more recently, in my 2018 book on Hart, I have similarly declared: "Every theory of law—indeed, every theory of anything—is evaluative. Every such theory rests on judgments concerning what is important and what is unimportant in relation to the topic of the theory. Judgments about importance and unimportance are evaluative judgments, and thus every theory is evaluative" (2018: 15–16). Of course, in each of my writings on legal positivism, I have straightaway gone on to stress that the evaluative judgments appropriate for a philosophical account of the nature of law are theoretical-explanatory rather than moral in character. The values toward which such

[24] As I have stated in an essay on conceptual analysis and distributive justice: "If certain theses are value-neutral, then we can gauge the fulfillment or non-fulfillment of those theses in any number of circumstances without having to undertake any ethical judgments. In other words, the states of affairs recounted by those theses can be ascertained (as present or absent) without any ethical assessments" (2019a: 376).

judgments are oriented are theoretical-explanatory values. As I remark in my book on Hart:

> However, as has been observed, Hart formed his judgments about importance by reference to theoretical-explanatory values rather than by reference to moral values. He picked out certain phenomena as especially important because of their roles in the major institutions on which he was seeking to shed light. Having affirmed that his concentration on those phenomena would best serve his theoretical-explanatory aims, Hart proclaimed: "It is for this reason that they are treated as the central elements in the concept of law and of prime importance in its elucidation." (Kramer 2018: 16, quoting Hart 1994: 17)

Heretofore, I have always assumed that every contemporary legal philosopher concurs that evaluative judgments are indispensable in the construction of a theory of law. One's recognition of the indispensability of such judgments is prerequisite to one's elementary proficiency in the methodology of legal philosophy. I have always assumed that every contemporary philosopher of law displays such proficiency, and that no contemporary philosopher of law is aiming to produce a vast rubbish heap of pointless and miscellaneous observations. I certainly hope that someone of Chiassoni's sophistication does not think that we should be striving to produce such a heap.

3. Ethics at High Levels of Abstraction

I now turn to the chapters by Christine Tiefensee and Lubomira Radoilska, in which they valuably explore some of the most abstract matters of ethics which I have probed in some of my publications.

3.1 Tiefensee on Ethics and Meta-Semantics

Tiefensee arrived in Cambridge about a decade-and-a-half ago to be supervised for her doctorate by Simon Blackburn. I got to know her quite early during her time here, while I was writing *Moral Realism as a Moral Doctrine*; during the subsequent years, she and I have had several piquant conversations about the matters covered in that book. Her prodding has helped to sharpen my thinking about those matters.

I agree with quite a bit of what Tiefensee writes in her contribution to this volume, but I will concentrate here on a few of the main points of disagreement. Those points of divergence are more numerous in the final draft of her essay than in the initial draft. (When I told her in July 2019 that I agreed with nearly everything in her paper, I was talking about the initial draft!) Though she and I converge in some respects, we are quite distant in some other respects—partly because my understanding of the distinction between meta-semantics and semantics is different from hers, and partly because my understanding of the relationship between Moral Realism as a Moral Doctrine and meta-semantics is likewise significantly different from hers. Let us start with some expositions that will serve as points of entry into thinking about these matters.

3.1.1 Moral Realism as a Moral Doctrine

Moral Realism as a Moral Doctrine comprises two principal multifaceted theses. First is the Objectivity Proposition, which proclaims that morality is objective in seven major dimensions: (1) basic moral principles and many derivative moral principles are strongly mind-independent in more than one sense;[25] (2) there are determinately correct answers to countless moral questions; (3) moral principles are uniformly applicable to moral agents, in a number of respects; (4) all basic moral principles and many derivative moral principles are invariant across times and places; (5) individuals can and do converge in their moral views on any number of matters while diverging from one another in their moral views on any number of additional matters; (6) a distinctively moral stance of impartiality can be suitably specified and often achieved; and (7) countless moral judgments are truth-apt in that they are properly evaluable as true or false, and many of them are true. Second is the Reconception of Meta-Ethics Proposition, which declares that the objectivity of morality is itself a moral matter—as the sundry propositions which expound that objectivity are grounded on ethical considerations and are endowed with ethical implications, albeit mainly at very high levels of abstraction. Whereas the Objectivity Proposition with its seven conjuncts is unmistakably a doctrine of moral realism, the Reconception of Meta-Ethics Proposition affirms that such a doctrine—along with every other meta-ethical theory—is a substantive ethical position.

Near the outset of my book *Moral Realism as a Moral Doctrine* (2009: 12–14), I distinguish between two main ways in which the notion of morality or ethics can be understood. On the one hand, that notion can be construed as referring to what I there designate as "morality or ethics *tout court*": namely, "the whole array of correct ethical/moral standards that truly determine the ethical/moral consequences of people's conduct, and ... the diverse categories and properties associated with those standards." On the other hand, the notion of morality or ethics can be construed as referring to "the contents of the ethical/moral convictions that generally prevail among the members of some society (or of some set of societies)" and to "the observable practices of ethical/moral deliberation and judgment that actually give expression to those prevailing convictions" (2009: 12).

This distinction, which partly resembles the familiar distinction between transcendent or objective morality and conventional or positive morality, is what underlies my demarcation of the domain of meta-ethics in the manner briefly suggested in the penultimate paragraph above. As has been stated there, I take the domain of meta-ethics to be concerned with the objectivity of morality and thus to be concerned with morality *tout court* rather than with morality as an observable array of convictions and practices. However, what is not adequately highlighted by my 2009 book—in contrast with the emphasis in two more recent essays of mine (2017d: 199–203, 206 n.18; 2022b: §2.3)—is that such a demarcation of the meta-ethical domain is narrower than the demarcation that has been

[25] The strong mind-independence of basic moral principles is both existential and observational. An entity partakes of strong existential mind-independence if and only if its continued existence is not dependent on the mental functioning of any members of any group individually or collectively. An entity partakes of strong observational mind-independence if and only if the nature of the entity is not dependent on what it is thought to be by any members of any group individually or collectively. See Kramer 2009: 23–6.

taken for granted by some other philosophers. Crucial to my engagement with Tiefensee's chapter is the fact that two chief areas of enquiry are largely omitted from the domain of meta-ethics as I delimit it: the pragmatics of moral discourse and the meta-semantics of moral discourse. To be sure, as will be discussed herein, neither of those areas of enquiry is completely outside the domain of meta-ethics. Each of them has a limited bearing on the objectivity of morality *tout court*, and thus each of them *pro tanto* has a limited place within the meta-ethical domain. Nonetheless, most accounts of the pragmatics of moral discourse and most accounts of the meta-semantics of moral discourse are concerned not with morality *tout court* but instead—at a philosophically high level of abstraction—with morality as an array of observable discourses and practices. They are not about the objectivity of morality. By my reckoning, then, those accounts are not meta-ethical theories. Hence, the Reconception of Meta-Ethics Proposition in Moral Realism as a Moral Doctrine does not apply to those accounts.

3.1.2 Meta-Semantic Imperialism

As far as I can tell, Tiefensee concurs with the gist of what I have said about the relationship between Moral Realism as a Moral Doctrine and theories of the pragmatics or meta-semantics of moral discourse. In particular, the second paragraph of the fourth main section of her essay is very much in accordance with what I have just said about that relationship. To be sure, Tiefensee might not agree with my claim that most accounts of the pragmatics or meta-semantics of moral discourse are not meta-ethical theories at all. Still, that claim is grounded on the crucial distinction between morality *tout court* and morality as an array of observable discourses and practices; provided that that distinction is heeded and is recognized as central to the scope of the Reconception of Meta-Ethics Proposition, I am not interested in issuing taxonomical or terminological ukases to other philosophers about the ways in which they delimit the domain of meta-ethics. Thus, Tiefensee and I are in agreement about a key aspect of the relationship between Moral Realism as a Moral Doctrine and theories that are focused on matters of meta-semantics or pragmatics.

Nevertheless, we are in disagreement about many aspects of meta-semantics. For one thing, Tiefensee in her preoccupation with meta-semantics often overstates the range of matters and arguments which belong to that area of philosophy. Let us begin here with a relatively minor instance. At one juncture (Tiefensee 2022: 202 n.14), Tiefensee suggests that David Enoch's argument about deliberative indispensability is a meta-semantic theory.[26] Earlier in her chapter (2022: 192), she declares that Enoch's argument is inconsistent with Moral Realism as a Moral Doctrine. She is wrong on each of these counts. Enoch's ruminations on deliberative indispensability have nothing to do with meta-semantics, and they are perfectly consistent with Moral Realism as a Moral Doctrine—for they constitute a partly moral argument in favor of the objectivity of morality.

A more significant instance of the meta-semantic imperialism of Tiefensee is her contention that Blackburn's expressivism is best understood as a meta-semantic

[26] For Enoch's argument, see Enoch 2011: 50–84. Worth noting here is that Enoch says very little about meta-semantics at any juncture in his book.

theory. As she is aware, I have argued at some length that Blackburn's expressivism in his later work is best construed as an account of the pragmatics of moral discourse (Kramer 2017d: 199–203). As she is also aware, I have remarked upon an intimate connection between Blackburn's expressivist pragmatics and his account of the meta-semantics or meta-syntax of moral discourse (Kramer 2017d: 204 n. 16). Rather mystifyingly, Tiefensee attaches great importance to designating that intimate connection as explanatory. She even places the noun "explanation" in italics, as she announces that Blackburn's distillation of the pragmatics of moral discourse "provide[s] a metasemantic *explanation* of [the] descriptive, assertoric character of moral sentences" (2022: 193 n.6, emphasis in original). On the one hand, I am wary of the language of "explanation" in this context, because it inappositely tends to convey the impression that Blackburn has been engaged in an aetiological enquiry. On the other hand, I am content to use that language—without italics—and to say that Blackburn has provided a philosophical explanation of the apparently assertoric character of much of moral discourse. My ready acceptance of that proposition does not detract one whit from my view that Blackburn's expressivism in his later work is best construed as a theory of the pragmatics of moral discourse. That theory yields a meta-semantic or meta-syntactic explanation of the apparent assertoricity of much of moral discourse. My chief concern in elaborating my interpretation of Blackburn's later work has not been centered on any matters of meta-semantics, but has instead been to deny that his expressivism is an explication of the semantics of moral discourse.

In another instance of Tiefensee's meta-semantic overreaching, her readers are confronted with another instance of italics (2022: 194, emphasis in original):

> [Moral Realism as a Moral Doctrine] is only *partly* a moral doctrine. More precisely, whilst its [Objectivity Proposition] about moral metaphysics and epistemology is indeed moral, its [Reconception of Meta-Ethics Proposition] concerning the moral interpretation of moral objectivity, is not. Rather, since the [Reconception of Meta-Ethics Proposition] is based on minimalism about semantic notions, and since minimalism is not a moral position but one that is to be defended within metasemantics and philosophical logic, [the Reconception of Meta-Ethics Proposition in Moral Realism as a Moral Doctrine] crucially depends on non-moral considerations that are to be put forward and settled outside of moral discourse.

On the one hand, any adequate defense of minimalism about truth and facts and reality does indeed have to venture into philosophical logic and the philosophy of language. In my discussions of the topic, I have saliently drawn attention to the fact that the sustainability of minimalism is dependent on rebuttals of quite technical objections that have been lodged against it (and I have cited some such rebuttals). On the other hand, Tiefensee errs in declaring that the Reconception of Meta-Ethics Proposition is not moral in character. Its tenability is dependent on the rebuttals just mentioned, but is also dependent on moral considerations—most notably on the moral considerations involved in establishing that sundry statements within moral discourse are truth-apt. Unless statements within moral discourse are truth-apt, a minimalist account of truth will have no purchase on such discourse. Yet, as is proclaimed in the Objectivity

Proposition, and as I have argued at some length in *Moral Realism as a Moral Doctrine* (2009: 273–87), the truth-aptitude of statements within moral discourse is fundamentally a matter of the objectivity of morality. Consequently, the sustainability of the Reconception of Meta-Ethics Proposition is itself unavoidably a moral matter.

Tiefensee disagrees with me about truth-aptitude. In her overweening preoccupation with meta-semantics, she insists that "the truth-aptitude of moral statements—together with their assertoric, representational, descriptive character—is to be explained by metasemantics, not by moral theorizing" (2022: 193 n.6). Remarkably, however, she altogether ignores my arguments on this matter in *Moral Realism as a Moral Doctrine*, and she refers instead only to a fleeting comment about truth-aptitude in my 2017 article "There's Nothing Quasi about Quasi-Realism." Having ignored my arguments on the matter, she provides none of her own. Rather, she simply adverts to the fact that Blackburn's expressivism yields a meta-syntactic explanation of the apparently propositional structure of moral discourse. In so doing, she is peddling an *ignoratio elenchi*. Valuable though Blackburn's expressivist account of the pragmatics of moral discourse is, it does not *per se* serve to vindicate the truth-aptitude of moral discourse. I have sought to signal as much in my last few paragraphs with phrases such as "apparently assertoric" and "apparent assertoricity" and "apparently propositional." As these phrases indicate, Blackburn's expressivism does not and cannot suffice to establish that the *apparently* assertoric character of much of moral discourse is *genuinely* assertoric. Only substantive moral argumentation, of the kind which I supply and which Tiefensee disregards, can suffice to establish the genuineness of the assertoricity.

What is puzzling is that Tiefensee herself in the early portions of her chapter seems to grasp the point which I have made in the preceding paragraph. There she writes, for example, that "if all that is required for a statement purportedly to represent some moral fact is for it to have assertoric form and ascribe a moral predicate to some object, moral statements are clearly representational" (2022: 193). Here the adverb "purportedly" appears to play the same role which I have assigned to the adverb "apparently" in the phrasing which I have quoted just above. Moreover, Tiefensee twice speaks of the "purportedly representational character" of moral sentences (2022: 193, 195 n.7). Again the adverb "purportedly" appears to signal her awareness that Blackburn's meta-syntactic explanation accounts for the superficial grammar of moral discourse rather than for its genuine truth-aptitude. What can establish the genuine truth-aptitude of such discourse are moral considerations. Having appeared to intimate as much, Tiefensee in her keenness to absorb the matter of truth-aptitude into her meta-semantic empire then proceeds as if she had never employed the adverb "purportedly." In the proclamation by her which I have quoted at the outset of my preceding paragraph, that adverb nowhere appears. She thus presumes that Blackburn's expressivism is itself sufficient to clinch the truth-aptitude of statements in moral discourse. By so presuming, she misunderstands both the limits of Blackburnian expressivism and the vital reach of Moral Realism as a Moral Doctrine.

Similar misunderstandings surface when Tiefensee tells her readers that she and her fellow meta-semanticists are able to supply a justification that underpins a minimalist approach to truth and facts and reality in the domain of morality (2022: 196, emphasis in original):

> Minimalism ... should be accepted exactly because we cannot understand the meaning of notions such as "true" and "refers" on the basis of representationalist considerations about the property of truth or some metaphysically robust reference relation, but rather by considering what these concepts allow us to *do* within our language and practices.

She thinks that her meta-semantic doctrine "provides the golden thread linking expressivism, minimalism, and [the Reconception of Meta-Ethics Proposition] by embedding these positions within the wider metasemantic framework it provides" (2022: 196).

The principal snag for such a justificatory foundation is that it would open the floodgates to all sorts of weird discourses. Having invoked her rationale as a foundation for a minimalist approach to moral truth, Tiefensee has committed herself to accepting that nonsensical statements such as James Dreier's "Peter is hello" and Lewis Carroll's "All mimsy were the borogoves" are truth-apt and that a minimalist approach to truth is applicable to discourses composed of such statements. After all, anyone with a penchant for nonsensical utterances can dwell on what the ascription of truth-aptitude to them "allow[s] us to *do* within our language and practices." In other words, Tiefensee's proffered basis for the applicability of the minimalist approach does not enable us to distinguish between "Lynching black people for sadistic pleasure is morally wrong" and "Peter is hello." If we want to explain why the former is truth-apt and the latter is not—and thus if we want to explain why the minimalist approach to truth encompasses the former and not the latter—we have to go beyond Tiefensee's justification by engaging in substantive moral argumentation of the kind which I undertake in *Moral Realism as a Moral Doctrine*.

3.1.3 A Matter of Semantics

Although there are a number of other junctures in Tiefensee's chapter where her devotion to meta-semantics is distortively excessive, I will move on here to a matter of semantics. It arises at one of the many points where Tiefensee seeks to curtail any significant role for Moral Realism as a Moral Doctrine. Impugning the Objectivity Proposition, she asserts that "it ... appears implausible to hold all components of semantics [in the moral domain] to be moral." She elaborates (2022: 194 n.6, emphases in original):

> To use a particularly clear example, take a quick look at the semantics of "ought." Here, we can see that spelling out the general truth-conditions of ought-claims along the lines of Kratzer-style ... deontic semantics is not a moral exercise. Quite the opposite: it is widely regarded to be a boon of this semantics that it provides the *same* general semantic formula for moral *and non*-moral uses of deontic operators alike .... Determining the general semantic schema for deontic operators ... remains a non-moral exercise.

Tiefensee goes awry in thinking that a general semantic scheme for deontic auxiliaries as applied to the domain of morality is a non-moral endeavor. The moral aspect of such an endeavor is in fact especially clear with regard to the scheme expounded by

Angelika Kratzer (which relies heavily on possible-world semantics), but it is likewise clear with regard to the approach taken by Raz in *Practical Reason and Norms* and with regard to the approach derivable from the Hohfeldian analysis. Any explication of the semantics of deontic auxiliaries in the moral domain will have to address a host of matters such as the question whether "morally ought" implies "can" and the question whether "morally must" entails "morally may." *Pace* Tiefensee, those questions are moral rather than non-moral—as are a number of other questions that have to be addressed by any explication of the semantics of deontic auxiliaries in the domain of morality.

Note that I am not here making a point which Tiefensee readily concedes. In a portion of her text which I have omitted from the lengthy quotation just above, she writes: "Importantly, this does not mean that moral considerations are irrelevant for this semantic project. However, they enter the scene only when determining the truth-value of specific moral ought-sentences, namely by examining which moral ordering source is to be plugged into the general Kratzer-style semantic formula" (2022: 194 n.6). I am not talking here about specific applications of a semantic framework like that devised by Kratzer. Rather, I am talking about foundational questions to which the answers significantly determine the very nature or tenor of such a framework. *Pace* Tiefensee, those questions to which I am referring are moral questions.

3.1.4 A Heavy-Handed Correction

In section 3 of her chapter, Tiefensee takes me to task for my reply to a challenge by Dreier (Tiefensee 2022: 198-9). She construes his challenge as meta-semantic, and she accurately observes that my reply is semantic. She rather heavy-handedly chides me for missing Dreier's point. As should be obvious, my reply to Dreier in my 2017 article "There's Nothing Quasi about Quasi-Realism" is based on my interpretation of his challenge as semantic rather than as meta-semantic. He presents the following two formulations (2004: 35):

(E) Edith said that abortion is wrong.

(G) Its being the case that (E) consists of nothing more than ____.

He maintains that the proponents of Moral Realism as a Moral Doctrine have to fill in the blank in his second formulation, and he upbraids any "lazy theorists [who] might just try [to fill in the blank by] more or less repeating (E)." I still think that this wording from him which I quote in my article, especially his reproach to the lazy theorists, is most naturally construable as I construed it. However, I agree that his challenge can alternatively be interpreted as meta-semantic, and Tiefensee's chapter has convinced me that it should be interpreted in that way.

Still, there remains the question of how the proponents of Moral Realism as a Moral Doctrine should respond to Dreier's challenge. Tiefensee predictably contends that they should join her and her fellow meta-semanticists by developing suitable meta-semantic theories. Such a response would be perfectly fine, of course, but an even more pertinent response lies in invoking the distinction between morality *tout court* and morality as an array of observable discourses and beliefs and practices. Whereas the two main theses of Moral Realism as a Moral Doctrine are concerned with morality in the former sense, the meta-semantic theorizing demanded by Dreier is concerned with morality in the latter sense. On the one hand, he is correct in thinking that Moral Realism as a Moral Doctrine does not include any meta-semantic account of the meaningfulness of moral discourse. On the other hand, he errs in thinking that the absence of such an account is a shortcoming of Moral Realism as a Moral Doctrine, and he likewise errs in thinking that the proponents of Moral Realism as a Moral Doctrine impute brute unanalyzability to the meta-semantic basis for the patterns of meanings that are operative in moral discourse. As has just been reaffirmed, Moral Realism as a Moral Doctrine is a theory of morality *tout court*. Neither at a social-scientific level nor at a philosophical level is it a theory of morality as an array of deliberative and evaluative practices. Consequently, its omission of any meta-semantic theorizing is not a display of laziness at all. That omission is not an oversight, and it does not bespeak any assumption that such theorizing will be futile. Instead, it stems from the fact that the questions addressed by the proponents of Moral Realism as a Moral Doctrine—questions about the objectivity of morality *tout court* in its several dimensions—are not the same as the questions addressed by Dreier when he is engaging in meta-semantic ruminations. His ruminations are distinct from the lines of reasoning involved in upholding or assailing the Objectivity Proposition and the Reconception of Meta-Ethics Proposition.

Two caveats should be attached here. First, although advocates of Moral Realism as a Moral Doctrine are not guilty of any oversights or laziness when they decline to engage in the meta-semantic theorizing for which Dreier calls, they will not be deviating at all from Moral Realism as a Moral Doctrine if they do engage in such theorizing—provided, of course, that they make clear that their meta-semantic cogitations are an adjunct to their main doctrine rather than an integral component of it. Second, there are some limited points of intersection between Moral Realism as a Moral Doctrine and meta-semantics. Notwithstanding the fundamental differences between morality *tout court* and morality as an array of discourses and beliefs and practices, some issues pertaining to the latter do also have a bearing on the former. To conclude my replies to Tiefensee, I turn now to two of those issues.

3.1.5 Points of Intersection

As has just been stated, the champions of Moral Realism as a Moral Doctrine do have to grapple with a few issues of pragmatics and meta-semantics in order to sustain the Objectivity Proposition. In so grappling, of course, they will be rebutting certain arguments of their opponents.

3.1.5.1 The main issue for moral realists in pragmatics: judgment-internalism

In expositions of the pragmatics of moral discourse, the main issue that has to be addressed by supporters of Moral Realism as a Moral Doctrine is something which I have indeed addressed in my previous work on these matters (2009: 275–85; 2019b). That is, when non-cognitivists strive to cast doubt upon the truth-aptitude of moral assertions, they often contend that everyone who sincerely affirms a moral judgment is inclined to act in accordance with the tenor of the judgment. Philosophers who endorse such a view about sincere moral judgments are frequently known as "motivational internalists" or "judgment-internalists"; I shall use the latter label here. What these philosophers maintain is that, whenever anyone genuinely harbors some moral conviction, he or she is disposed to conform his or her conduct to that conviction. If somebody is of the conviction that every act of torturing a baby for pleasure is morally wrong, she is disposed to refrain from performing any such act. Likewise, if she is of the conviction that keeping one's promises made to one's friends is morally obligatory, she is disposed to keep promises which she has made to her friends. Of course, the strength of her disposition to refrain from torturing any babies for pleasure is almost certainly much greater than the strength of her promise-keeping disposition. That latter disposition is susceptible to being overtopped by some of her other ethical dispositions in certain credibly possible circumstances. Nonetheless, if she is not endowed with any inclination at all to keep her promises made to her friends—in other words, if she fails to fulfill her promises to her friends even when there are no significant ethical or prudential considerations that militate against her fulfillment of them—then she does not genuinely harbor the conviction that keeping one's promises made to one's friends is morally obligatory. So these philosophers declare.[27]

Having postulated this conceptual link between moral convictions and motivations, non-cognitivists parlay that link into an attack on the semantic objectivity of moral discourse by trading upon a widely accepted view about beliefs (a view usually traced to David Hume). That is, they submit that no belief is ever in itself possessed of any motivational force. Only when a belief is combined with some desire(s) concerning the event or the state of affairs to which the belief pertains, will a person be motivated to act on the basis of its content. There is never a conceptual connection between someone's harboring of a belief and her being motivated to behave in some way. Given as much, however, moral convictions cannot be beliefs. No belief is ever linked conceptually to any behavioral dispositions in the way in which every moral conviction is. Accordingly, moral convictions must be non-cognitive. Given that the only real alternative to their being cognitive is their being conative, such convictions are desires or emotional attitudes rather than beliefs; the utterances that express those convictions are not genuinely declarative and truth-apt, even if they appear to be so. Such is the gist of the line of reasoning propounded, in various forms, by many non-cognitivists over the years.

In the past writings of mine which I have cited above, I have rebutted the non-cognitivists' line of reasoning by adducing some counterexamples that tell cogently against the conceptual claim of judgment-internalism. I have maintained that the links between certain conative attitudes and sincere moral assertions are quasi-conceptual rather than conceptual, in a sense which I have sought to specify rigorously. I have also contested the Humean dogma about beliefs. I shall not recapitulate my arguments here, because I would simply be repeating what I have written elsewhere and because I would be moving quite far afield from my engagement with the chapter by Tiefensee (who is scarcely a devotee of the non-cognitivist position). Rather, the point to note here is that judgment-internalism is an account—an untenable account—of the pragmatics of moral discourse. Non-cognitivists marshal that thesis about the

[27] For a throng of citations to many important discussions of judgment-internalism (from sundry perspectives), see Kramer 2009: 276 n. 8. For a helpful overview of judgment-internalism as well as reasons-internalism, see Finlay and Schroeder 2017.

pragmatics in order to support their anti-realist claims concerning the semantics of moral discourse. Because judgment-internalism does lend itself to being marshaled in that manner, it has to be impugned directly by anyone who aspires to uphold the semantic conjunct (the seventh conjunct) in the Objectivity Proposition. Accordingly, my critiques of non-cognitivism in my past work have been trained largely on the judgment-internalist thesis about the pragmatics of moral discourse. That focus has been essential in spite of the fundamental differences between morality *tout court* and morality as an array of discourses and beliefs and practices.

3.1.5.2 *The main issue for moral realists in meta-semantics: naturalistic dogmas*

Although I have here emphasized that meta-semantic theorizing is separate from Moral Realism as a Moral Doctrine because the former is concerned with morality as an array of discourses and practices rather than with morality *tout court*, there is one strand of meta-semantic theorizing which the proponents of Moral Realism as a Moral Doctrine do have to oppugn. In my earlier work I have indeed sustainedly contested that strand, albeit mainly in its epistemological guise rather than in its meta-semantic guise (2009: 190–207, 247–9). Tiefensee toward the end of her chapter declares that the defenders of Moral Realism as a Moral Doctrine "simply have nothing to contribute to … metasemantic debate" (2022: 203). She makes this assertion partly because she glimpses that meta-semantic theorizing is indeed separate from Moral Realism as a Moral Doctrine, but also partly because she is inclined to disparage Moral Realism as a Moral Doctrine. At any rate, her pronouncement is considerably overstated. There is in fact a crucial role in meta-semantic debate for the supporters of Moral Realism as a Moral Doctrine.

The dubious strand of meta-semantic theorizing to which I have referred in the preceding paragraph is the claim by some naturalistic meta-semanticists that, for all discourses (rather than only for certain discourses), meaning and reference are fixed through causal relationships between sentences or sub-sentential units and their referents. I will here designate that claim as the "Causal Fixing Tenet." Given that the defenders of Moral Realism as a Moral Doctrine along with other non-naturalistic moral realists hold that moral properties and entities are not causally efficacious, the Causal Fixing Tenet is obviously something which they must reject—since their acceptance of it would commit them to the conclusion that all or most utterances in moral discourse are meaningless. Tiefensee of course recognizes as much, and indeed she repeatedly underlines this point in the second half of her chapter. However, what she altogether omits to notice is that the proponents of Moral Realism as a Moral Doctrine can aptly participate in debates over the merits of the Causal Fixing Tenet by assailing it on moral grounds.

Although I obviously cannot reproduce here the lengthy arguments which I have presented in *Moral Realism as a Moral Doctrine* against an epistemological version of the Causal Fixing Tenet—and although any attempt to reproduce those arguments would be out of place in replies to Tiefensee, who is obviously not espousing that tenet—the pith of my approach consists in denying that moral properties and entities are causally efficacious, and in then deploring the implications that follow from the Causal Fixing Tenet. Given that moral properties and entities are not causally efficacious, the Causal Fixing Tenet entails that all ascriptions of such properties and affirmations of such entities are either meaningless or false. Thus, for example, the proposition "Lynchings of black people by sadistic racists are morally worse than feats of rescue that save children from drowning" is either meaningless or false by the reckoning of the proponents of the Causal Fixing Tenet. Because the Causal Fixing Tenet lumbers its advocates with such a verdict and with countless other morally preposterous verdicts, the truth of that tenet is at odds with basic principles of morality. The truth of that tenet is therefore morally impossible.[28] Consequently, there are overwhelming grounds for rejecting the Causal Fixing Tenet.

In sum, there is a vital role for the supporters of Moral Realism as a Moral Doctrine in the debates over meta-semantics, even though many of the issues in those debates are fundamentally separate from the topics addressed by the Objectivity Proposition and the Reconception of Meta-Ethics Proposition. I am not sure why Tiefensee disregards that role, but my sense from reading her chapter is that she cleaves to some doubts about the objectivity of morality. She appears to think that the objectivity of morality is not sufficiently solid to serve as a basis for impugning the positions taken in the meta-semantic disputation with which she is engrossed. On the one hand, any serviceable moral argumentation obviously has to be presented less laconically and summarily than has been done in the preceding paragraph. Were I actually taking part here in the aforementioned disputation—rather than simply indicating how I would take part in it—I would naturally have to advance some much more ample lines of reasoning. On the other hand, I have elaborated just such lines of reasoning in *Moral Realism as a Moral Doctrine*. Moreover my subsequent books, which in the field of political philosophy have sought to show rigorously how some basic principles of morality generate far-reaching conclusions on matters of public policy, have joined the works of sundry other contemporary analytic philosophers in supplying some grounds for dispelling Tiefensee's reservations about the solidity of moral argumentation.

3.2 Lubomira Radoilska and the Problem of Value

I became acquainted with Radoilska at approximately the same time that I became acquainted with Tiefensee, around the middle of the first decade of the twenty-first century. Having encountered Radoilska in a myriad of seminars and conferences since then, I have greatly valued her contributions to the philosophical life of Cambridge (where she still resides, even though her principal faculty position for a number of years has been at the University of Kent in Canterbury). I am very pleased that she is a contributor to this volume. Given the prolongedness of my replies to some of the other contributors, I am especially delighted by her illuminating essay because I have very little to say in response to it—since I concur with virtually everything in it! She elegantly brings together some of my ideas from the methodology of political philosophy and some of the chief contemporary concerns in moral epistemology.

My only misgiving is on a point that is clearly remediable within the general drift of her essay. In a footnote to her discussion of the Equal Protection Clause in the

[28] The notion of moral impossibility is to be understood by reference to my explication of the notion of moral necessity in Kramer 2009: 157–61.

Fourteenth Amendment of the US Constitution, Radoilska writes that "the content of such choices [made by jurists in their interpretations of the Equal Protection Clause] tends to appear as independent from ethical values" (2022: 214 n.32). If Radoilska is suggesting that American jurists and other Americans have tended to believe that the interpretive choices of judges in implementing the Equal Protection Clause are value-independent, I think that she is clearly incorrect. I am not aware of any knowledgeable observer in the United States who has seriously supposed that the choices made by judges in construing the Equal Protection Clause are ungrounded on any ethical values; rather, many such choices are often criticized for being grounded on badly misguided ethical values. If Radoilska (despite her use of the word "independent") is instead suggesting that American jurists and other Americans have tended to believe that the interpretive choices of judges in implementing the Equal Protection Clause are value-neutral—or should be value-neutral—then she might be correct about some so-called constitutional originalists but not about anyone else who is competent to discuss such matters. Even most originalists recognize that the endeavor of assessing whether a situation complies with the Equal Protection Clause is not a value-neutral enterprise, and everyone else or just about everyone else recognizes as much. Thus, richly thoughtful though Radoilska's discussion of the Equal Protection Clause is, her example is not well suited for her purposes. To make plausible her worry that legal interpretation in a liberal democracy is perceived inappositely as value-neutral, she needs to come up with a better example.

4. Matters of Freedom

I now come to the two chapters that are mainly on the topic of freedom. I will deal relatively briefly with the chapter by Michael Garnett and then move on to a lengthier encounter with the chapter by Ian Carter and Hillel Steiner.

4.1 Michael Garnett on Freedom as Uncoercedness

I have known Garnett for nearly a decade-and-a-half, since I read one of his early papers on freedom. He has become a regular participant in the UK Analytic Legal and Political Philosophy Conference which I organize annually, and we have encountered each other in several other contexts as well. I have always found him to be a genial and stimulating interlocutor, and I am glad that he has contributed a perceptively challenging essay to this collection.

4.1.1 The First Half of the Chapter

I was rather perplexed while I was reading the first half of Garnett's chapter, because it reinvents some wheels that have long been familiar to negative-liberty philosophers: the distinction between being free to perform some action and performing that action freely, the distinction between freedom as sets of opportunities and freedom as achievements, the distinction between particular freedoms and overall freedom. Moreover, I was further perplexed because Garnett imputes to negative-liberty philosophers some tenets that are in fact squarely rejected by me. He writes, for example, that "it's common for nonprevention views of freedom to restrict the scope of freedom-limiting preventions to those *brought about by other people*, on the grounds that freedom (in the politically-relevant sense) is an inherently social concept" (2022: 223, emphasis in original). By my reckoning, the view ascribed here by Garnett to negative-liberty theorists is a conflation of freedom-limiting preventions and unfreedom-engendering preventions. Whereas the latter are always due to the actions or dispositions of other people, the former can be wholly nonhuman in their origins. All unfreedom-engendering preventions are freedom-limiting preventions, but not all freedom-limiting preventions are unfreedom-engendering preventions. As will be seen in my next main section, my insistence on this point is what chiefly pits me against Carter and Steiner.

Immediately after the sentence that has just been quoted, Garnett asserts that "accounts of coercion often take coercion necessarily to involve at least some physical restriction of the victim's available options .... [I]t's natural to think that both prevention (in the freedom-relevant sense) and coercion essentially involve being stopped from doing things by other people, and that the differences between them in this context are therefore negligible" (2022: 223–4). Not only do I reject this view which Garnett here recounts, but so do Carter and Steiner and G.A. Cohen and Serena Olsaretti and various other negative-liberty theorists. We all distinguish between being unfree to φ and feeling unfree to φ, and we definitely do not presume that every instance of the latter is an instance of the former. Precisely because feeling unfree to φ does not entail being unfree to φ, Cohen developed a sophisticated account of the conditions under which someone's actions are performed involuntarily. He developed that account not as an element of his conception of freedom but as a separate theory. Olsaretti has embraced Cohen's account with some important modifications and refinements. She too is well aware that, in so doing, she is presenting an explication of the conditions under which someone who chooses to φ has made that choice involuntarily—rather than an explication of the conditions under which someone is unfree to φ.[29]

One caveat should be attached to the preceding paragraph. Despite the nonequivalence of being unfree to φ and feeling unfree to φ, most instances of coercion do involve the imposition of unfreedom. Carter and I in particular have striven to capture the subtle and intricate ways in which many exertions of coercion diminish the levels of overall freedom of the people who are subjected to those exertions (Carter 1999: 224–32; Kramer 2003: 194–209). Indeed, Garnett himself approvingly sketches the efforts by Carter and me to explain those freedom-reducing effects. Still, those explanations are entirely consistent with our recognition that some instances of coercion do not produce any such effects—as the people subjected to those instances of coercion are made to *feel* unfree without actually *being* unfree.

Slightly later in his chapter, Garnett announces: "Sometimes we ascribe freedom and unfreedom to persons, or to groups of persons. We say that someone is or isn't a free person" (2022: 224). In the second sentence of this quotation, Garnett's use

[29] For Cohen's conception of voluntariness, see especially Chapter 12 of Cohen 1988. For Olsaretti's conception of voluntariness, see especially Chapters 5 and 6 of Olsaretti 2004.

of the first-person plural pronoun excludes not only me but also nearly all other negative-liberty philosophers. Such philosophers eschew the phrase "free person" — which almost always appeared as "free man" before the final quarter of the twentieth century—since they regard that phrasing as the hallmark of a positive-liberty theory. Within the framework of a negative-liberty theory, the concept of a free person as such is unintelligible. Negative-liberty theorists instead characterize someone as free to this or that extent, or as free in these or those ways. Garnett himself is of course attuned to these latter modes of speaking, and he explicitly makes mention of them and endorses them. Nonetheless, throughout his chapter he continues to appeal to the notion of a free person—which is something that sets him against the negative-liberty philosophers to whose camp he purports to belong. I will say a bit more on this matter presently.

Somewhat later, Garnett asserts that "to be coerced is to *act* unfreely, whereas to be prevented is not to act at all, but to *be* unfree" (2022: 226, emphases in original). Quite unexceptionable is the main distinction broached here by Garnett, the distinction between being unfree to perform some action and performing that action unfreely—a dichotomy to which I have already adverted as something standardly invoked by negative-liberty theorists. Still, one's being unfree to perform some action seldom results in one's not acting at all. To be sure, there are some situations in which a person is altogether prevented from acting for a certain span of time. For example, in *The Quality of Freedom* I adduce the situation of Dorothy who is carried along for a while by a tornado (2003: 26, 161–2, 245–7, 250–4). Dorothy during the period of her ride through the skies is prevented from acting at all as an agent, since the movements and positioning of her body are controlled entirely by the impetus of the winds through which she is carried along. However, most instances of being made unfree to φ are not of this kind. For example, if the path ahead of me is insurmountably obstructed by some humanly erected barrier, I have been made unfree to walk further on the path but have not been made unfree to act at all. In any ordinary circumstances, I am able to stand still or to turn around or to veer to the left or right of the path.

The final sentence from the first half of Garnett's chapter on which I shall concentrate here is his assertion that negative-liberty philosophers adhere to "the basic Hobbesian analysis of freedom as the absence of physical obstacles to possible bodily movements" (2022: 228). In application to me, this quoted wording is doubly inapposite. In *The Quality of Freedom* I include quite a long discussion of psychological incapacities, and I criticize Carter robustly for maintaining that all contents of freedoms and unfreedoms—all instantiations of the "φ" variable in ascriptions of freedoms and unfreedoms—are bodily movements (2003: 255–71, 163–9).

Although the present subsection might strike some readers as an exercise in captiousness, it has exposed some fairly substantial misrepresentations of my theory of freedom. Some of those misrepresentations are also distortive of the theories propounded by all or most other negative-liberty philosophers. Still, heretofore my remarks on Garnett's chapter have been entirely defensive. As I turn now to the second half of his chapter, I shall be going on the offensive to advance some deeper objections to the positions which Garnett espouses. A few of the points made in this subsection will surface again in what follows.

4.1.2 The Second Half of the Chapter

One of my main worries about the second half of Garnett's chapter is that it tries to cram too much into a theory of freedom. Garnett correctly observes that some instances of coercion do not circumscribe the opportunities or the combinations of conjunctively exercisable opportunities available to any person who is subjected to the coercion, and he concludes that such instances of coercion are nonetheless freedom-reducing and that the concept of negative liberty should be expanded to take account of their freedom-reducing effects. He makes a parallel observation about certain situations involving the manipulation of people's preferences, and he draws a parallel conclusion about those situations. In each case, negative-liberty philosophers will readily agree with Garnett's observation while dissenting from his conclusion.

4.1.2.1 Coercion with no loss of freedom

As Garnett contends, it is possible for somebody to undergo severe coercion without being deprived of any freedoms or of any combinations of conjunctively exercisable freedoms. His scenario of coercion exerted through the implantation of a heart chip usefully illustrates this point. I shall not be demurring at that scenario itself, which is structurally similar to some of my own examples. In particular, I happily concur with Garnett's assessment that the coerced person *B* in his scenario "doesn't *act* any more freely as a result of the chip's malfunction; *B* continues to act under coercion" (2022: 230, emphasis in original). Far more problematic, however, is Garnett's assertion that "it would seem perverse to insist, as the prevention-only theorist seemingly must, that a person so pervasively subject to coercion can nevertheless be perfectly free" (2022: 230). As has been indicated in section 4.1.1 above, no negative-liberty theorist would ever frame the matter in the way posited here by Garnett—because the notion of perfect liberty is unintelligible within the framework of a negative-liberty theory. The property of perfect liberty certainly cannot be cashed out as the property of being free in every possible respect, since not all types or instances of freedom for any person are compatible with one another (Kramer 2003: 222–4). Nor is there any other way of meaningfully cashing out the idea of perfect freedom. Within the contours of any of the main negative-liberty theories, the characterization of anyone as free *tout court* or as a free person or as perfectly free is nonsensical.

Presumably, what Garnett means to do in the most recently quoted sentence is to condemn as perverse the insistence by negative-liberty theorists that the coercion in his scenario does not deprive the coerced person of any freedoms (or of any combinations of conjunctively exercisable freedoms) in the period after the heart chip has ceased to function. He is correct in thinking that negative-liberty theorists will press such an insistence, but his denunciation of their stance as perverse is much more puzzling. After all, any negative-liberty philosopher will recognize that the coercive treatment of *B* by *A* in Garnett's scenario is seriously wrong even after that treatment has ceased to be freedom-reducing. However, instead of explaining the wrongfulness of the coercion in the second half of the scenario by reference to the effects of the coercion on *B*'s freedom (effects that are non-existent in that second half), a negative-liberty philosopher will explain the wrongfulness by reference to the effects on *B*'s autonomy or self-direction—and on *B*'s general well-being—and also by reference to the malignity of *A*'s outlook in exercising the interpersonal subjection that is occurrent throughout the scenario. Garnett wants to classify those aspects of the situation as curtailments of *B*'s freedom, but there is no reason for subsuming those aspects under the same rubric as the opportunity-curtailing effects that have ceased to be operative in the second half of the scenario. Garnett proclaims that "there are … distinct kinds of disvalue at work in the case—blocked opportunities and interpersonal subjection—and … both are relevant to judgements regarding *B*'s degree of socio-political freedom" (2022: 232). I of course agree that there are distinct kinds of disvalue involved, and indeed my concurrence with Garnett on that point is precisely what leads me to resist his inclination to hold that all of those kinds of disvalue constitute reductions in *B*'s socio-political freedom. Diminutions in *B*'s autonomy and well-being can occur and can be seriously wrong even when they are not accompanied by any diminutions in *B*'s freedom. Likewise, the outlook of *A* in his mistreatment of *B* is seriously wrong even during the period when that mistreatment does not genuinely lessen *B*'s freedom.

My other chief worry about Garnett's ruminations on coercion is elicited not least by the sentence which I have quoted most recently above. In my quotation of that sentence, the first set of ellipses has been inserted because I have omitted the word "two." Garnett throughout his meditations on coercion writes as if there are only two ethically significant sets of effects that are taking place in the scenario of the heart chip: the circumscription of *B*'s opportunities and of her combinations of conjunctively exercisable opportunities, and the sustainment of the relationship of interpersonal subjection between *A* and *B*. Garnett ignores the effects on *B*'s autonomy and well-being. Consequently, he is not in a position to come to grips adequately with a variant of his scenario where those last-mentioned effects are occurring in the absence of any relationship of interpersonal subjection. Suppose that Gladys during her nightly slumber has dreamt about wolves and, upon awakening, has become firmly convinced that there are many packs of dangerous wolves in the vicinity of her residence. As a result, for several weeks she is terrified to venture outside her residence. She relies on her stocks of food and on deliveries of groceries as her means of staying alive. Yet, throughout this period, her belief about the presence of wolves is entirely baseless. There are neither any wolves nor any other dangerous predators in the region during the weeks when her fear of such creatures keeps her confined to her home. Now, in these circumstances there is no relationship of interpersonal subjection nor any genuine reduction in Gladys's opportunities and combinations of conjunctively exercisable opportunities. All the same, her false belief about the presence of wolves severely impairs her autonomy during this period—as Gladys involuntarily forgoes most of her usual activities. A negative-liberty theorist like me, attuned to the severe impairment of *B*'s autonomy in Garnett's scenario of the heart chip, can readily discern that a broadly similar impairment is occurring in Gladys's situation. By contrast, Garnett with his focus exclusively on reductions in opportunities and on interpersonal subjection has not left himself adroitly positioned to explain the badness of Gladys's ordeal.

4.1.2.2 The manipulation of preferences

One relatively minor query about Garnett's discussion of the manipulation of preferences is his classification of such manipulation as a type of coercion. In the broader philosophical literature on these matters, the manipulation of preferences is normally treated as an autonomy-vitiating factor that is distinct from the autonomy-vitiating factor of coercion. I see no reason to join Garnett in regarding the former as a species of the latter.

My more important queries about his discussion of manipulation are twofold. First, Garnett somewhat misunderstands my previous reflections on mind-control (Kramer 2003: 23–4, 250, 255–60). In the thought-experiments which I have devised, the control over the intentions or preferences of some hapless person is thoroughgoing inasmuch as the victim is prevented from forming any intentions or preferences contrary to those which the controller has instilled into him or her. That prevention can be effected in either of two ways. An intention to φ might be instilled into the victim V just before the point at which V will seek to act in accordance with that intention by φ-ing, so that there is not enough time for the formation of any contrary intention. Alternatively, the controller of V's mind might monitor the flow of V's mental states and processes closely in order to stymie any deviation by V from the intentions which the controller has induced. (As must be obvious, my thought-experiments are in the domain of science fiction. They do not imply that what they depict is technologically feasible at present.) Note that I am not presuming that there is anything special about the intentions themselves which the controller has implanted into V's mind. Rather, the timing of the implantation or the surveillance that follows the implantation is what prevents V from acting in any ways that are not to the liking of the controller.

Garnett points out that the manipulation of preferences or intentions is not guaranteed to succeed. He is of course correct, but his observation on that point is entirely consistent with the negative-liberty theories propounded by contemporary philosophers. Carter and I in particular have separately emphasized that every ascription of freedom or unfreedom is probabilistic. Whether the probabilistic qualification attached to some such ascription is implicit or explicit, a probabilistic qualification is indeed borne by every such ascription. In the thought-experiment involving V and the controller of V's mind, there is a small probability that the means through which the controller exerts dominion over V's mind will cease to function, and there is likewise a small probability that the controller will abandon his inclination to exert that dominion. Thus, when I claim in the preceding paragraph that V is prevented from acting in any ways that are not to the liking of the controller, my claim carries an implicit probabilistic qualification. In that respect, my ascription to V of the unfreedom to act in those ways is like any other ascription of unfreedom.

My other important objection to Garnett's account of the manipulation of preferences is similar to one of my foremost reservations about his account of coercion. Having classified the autonomy-impairing effects of coercion as freedom-reducing even when those effects do not involve any curtailment of someone's opportunities or of her combinations of conjunctively exercisable opportunities, Garnett classifies the autonomy-impairing effects of the manipulation of preferences in a cognate fashion. However, he again offers no adequate rationale for accepting that the autonomy-impairing effects of manipulation are freedom-diminishing even when they do not consist in any circumscription of someone's opportunities or of her combinations of conjunctively exercisable opportunities. Garnett adverts afresh to a relationship of interpersonal subjection, which exists here between (1) the person into whom some intention has been implanted and (2) the person who has implanted that intention.

Garnett is of course correct in fixing upon that feature of the manipulation as a key wrong-making property, but he errs in contending that the freedom of the former person has been diminished by the manipulation even when no opportunities or combinations of opportunities have been removed from her. He declares that "to be a free person in the negative sense one must *both* be unprevented from performing a wide range of actions *and* uncoerced insofar as one performs any of those actions" (2022: 236, emphases in original). Here we can see the import of my earlier remarks on the phrase "a free person." Within the terms of any contemporary negative-liberty theory, that phrase—so redolent of positive-liberty theorizing—is meaningless. Of course, that phrase might be construed in ordinary terms simply as an indication that some person is not legally a slave. Such an indication would leave open any questions about the level of the person's overall freedom as gauged by a contemporary negative-liberty theory. Or the phrase "a free person" might be construed in ordinary terms to denote someone who enjoys a high level of overall freedom as gauged by a contemporary negative-liberty theory. An interpretation of the phrase along those lines can be countenanced, but it scarcely warrants Garnett's insistence that no one can be a free person except in the absence of coercion or manipulation. If a person is subjected to an instance of wide-ranging coercion or manipulation that does not reduce her opportunities or combinations of conjunctively exercisable opportunities at all, then she can still be a free person in the sense just specified; wrongful though the occurrence of that instance of coercion or manipulation is, it does not detract even slightly from her status as a free person in the specified sense. What it does instead is to undermine her autonomy.

At the end of his chapter, Garnett quotes a passage from Friedrich Hayek to reinforce his contention that every instance of socio-political freedom is inconsistent not only with prevention but also with coercion and manipulation (even where the coercion or manipulation is not itself productive of any prevention). Hayek wrote:

> The question of how many courses of action are open to a person is, of course, very important. But it is a different question from that of how far in acting he can follow his own plans and intentions, to what extent the pattern of his conduct is of his own design, directed toward ends for which he has been persistently striving rather than toward necessities created by others in order to make him do what they want. (Hayek 2011: 60–1, quoted in Garnett 2022: 237).

Far from supporting Garnett's position, this passage from Hayek militates against it. By distinguishing carefully between the matter of unpreventedness and the matter of uncoercedness or unmanipulatedness, Hayek aptly recognized that a person can sometimes be coerced or manipulated into not φ-ing even though the coercion or manipulation leaves her unprevented from φ-ing—and even though it leaves her unprevented from *both* φ-ing *and* availing herself of any opportunities that she could exercise in conjunction with φ-ing in the absence of the coercion or manipulation. When Hayek sought to encapsulate the significance of uncoercedness or unmanipulatedness, he framed the matter not in terms of freedom but instead in terms of self-direction or self-determination or autonomy. His phraseology strikingly prefigures Raz's preoccupation with the conditions under which individuals can be authors of their own lives.

As Raz has proclaimed near the outset of his influential exposition of autonomy: "The ruling idea behind the ideal of personal autonomy is that people should make their own lives. The autonomous person is a (part) author of his own life" (1986: 369). As Raz further remarks: "Autonomy is an ideal of self-creation .... An autonomous person's well-being consists in the successful pursuits of self-chosen goals and relationships" (1986: 370).

Of course, the emphasis of Hayek on the ideal of self-determination stemmed from a capaciously liberal outlook that also lies behind the emphasis of negative-liberty theorists on the vitality of individual freedom. Still, although the championing of autonomy and the championing of individual freedom are both broadly liberal in their orientation, and although the conditions for the realization of high levels of autonomy and the conditions for the realization of high levels of individual freedom obviously overlap, autonomy is a distinct ideal rather than a mere dimension or constituent of freedom. Just as Raz should really have entitled his 1986 book *The Morality of Autonomy* rather than *The Morality of Freedom*, so too Garnett should accept that his attractive account of non-prevention and his attractive account of uncoercedness and unmanipulatedness are explications of different though imbricated values.

4.2 Carter and Steiner on Bivalence versus Trivalence

Having known Steiner for nearly three decades and Carter for more than two decades, I regard each of them with great admiration and friendship. They have mounted a robust critique of my theory of freedom, and I will respond here with commensurate robustness. From the outset, then, I should stress that the altercation between us is a family quarrel. I can accentuate that point by quoting my tribute to them that appears at the end of the Preface in my book *The Quality of Freedom*: "In the absence of Ian's work as a stimulus, my book on freedom would have been very different from what it is—and it would have been markedly inferior. In the absence of Hillel's work, I very likely would not have written a book on freedom at all" (2003: ix).

4.2.1 Armchair Conjectures

Carter and Steiner proceed quite curiously in the first several pages of their chapter, as they offer conjectures from their respective armchairs about common suppositions and common ways of speaking. Indeed, their manner of proceeding is curious in multiple respects. For example, near the outset of their discussion of bivalence, they include one terse paragraph on the fact that certain non-Germanic languages each lack a single word that corresponds to "unfree" or "unfreedom." Quite remarkably, a few pages later, that one observation gets puffed up into the claim that "[w]e have already seen how the bivalent understanding of *specific* freedoms and unfreedoms is reflected in much of ordinary discourse about freedom" (2022: 243, emphasis in original). Unless Carter and Steiner are alluding here to a portion of their chapter which they have subsequently elected to omit, they must be referring back to the one short paragraph which I have mentioned above. They thereby exhibit a flair for hyperbole on a scale that I associate with Donald Trump. The linguistic fact which they highlight in the aforementioned paragraph is interesting but is not readily interpretable.

Perhaps it indicates that freedom is widely understood as a bivalent property in the countries where certain languages are spoken, or perhaps it indicates that widespread understandings of freedom as a trivalent property are not fully reflected in some of the ordinary adjectival repertoires of those countries. Carter and Steiner proceed as if the truth of the former hypothesis and the falsity of the latter were too obvious to be in need of any substantiation, and they thus treat a complex matter of sociolinguistics as something that can be settled through armchair surmises. Such speculations are especially inadvisable in light of the frequency with which deontic freedoms (freedoms as permissions) and modal freedoms (freedoms as abilities) are run together in ordinary discourse. Carter and Steiner and I agree that deontic freedom is a bivalent property; our disagreement over bivalence versus trivalence pertains only to modal freedom. Hence, the frequent conflation of deontic freedoms and modal freedoms in the contexts of everyday discourse makes especially hazardous the endeavor of interpreting the linguistic fact on which Carter and Steiner place so much weight.

Furthermore, even if Carter and Steiner are correct in the hypothesis which they infer from that linguistic fact, I am mystified by their apparent assumption that their inference has a bearing on the dispute between them and me. Our dispute is a somewhat arcane matter of philosophy; it is not a matter of sociolinguistics and is certainly not an effort to track everyday understandings of freedom as closely as possible. Unlike Carter and Steiner, I do not pretend to descry the contours of the prevalent everyday understandings from my desk chair with any great confidence. Insofar as I can discern those understandings, they are multiple and quite often inconsistent and imprecise. In that respect, they resemble the pre-theoretical understandings of many other phenomena which philosophers seek to explicate rigorously and precisely. Consequently, although I believe that the terminology in my theory of freedom is in keeping with many of the patterns of quotidian discourse on the topic, the extent of the conformity with such patterns is not a consideration that has perceptibly influenced my terminological and conceptual choices. Philosophical theorizing very frequently involves some neologisms and terminological regimentation to capture the conceptual distinctions and nuances that are crucial within the theorizing. If those distinctions and nuances are not adequately reflected in some of the pathways of mundane discourse, then a philosopher is entirely justified in amplifying those pathways for the sake of philosophical precision and comprehensiveness. Hence, even if Carter and Steiner were correct in their overconfident and unsubstantiated inference from the one linguistic fact to which they point, no conclusion in favor of a bivalent conception of freedom would follow.

Why do Carter and Steiner place so much emphasis on ordinary discourse (that is, on ordinary discourse as they perceive it to be from their armchairs)? Their only gesture toward a justification for that emphasis is their quotation of a remark by J.L. Austin. On the one hand, they themselves acknowledge that "[o]rdinary language is of course not the last word in conceptual analysis" (2022: 240 n.3)—a concession fully in accord with Austin's own avowal that ordinary language "can everywhere [in philosophical theorizing] be supplemented and improved upon and superseded" (1956: 11). On the other hand, Carter and Steiner quote Austin's partly countervailing pronouncement that ordinary usage "*is* the *first* word" (Austin 1956: 11, emphases in original, quoted in Carter and Steiner 2022: 240 n.3). However, to the extent that

Austin's aphorism is true, it is far too loosely constraining to be serviceable for Carter's and Steiner's purposes. That aphorism is true because a philosophical theory that jarringly clashes with widely accepted ways of thinking and speaking will of course stand in need of an especially powerful justification. Nonetheless, even if the sociolinguistic inference which Carter and Steiner overconfidently derive from their one linguistic fact is correct, they have not come close to showing that my trivalent conception of freedom is jarringly in conflict with widely accepted ways of thinking and speaking. Instead, the very most they have shown is that the presentation of my theory in certain non-Germanic languages will require a modicum of terminological innovation.

Carter and Steiner continue with unsubstantiated empirical assertions propounded from their armchairs, when they declare that their own bivalent conception of freedom "reflects much of ordinary discourse both about degrees of freedom and about its value: it is common to suppose that when a person or group or society has become more unfree, it has become less free, and vice versa; and to suppose that, if freedom is valuable to a certain extent, then unfreedom is disvaluable to that same extent, and vice versa" (2022: 243). Carter and Steiner furnish nary a shred of evidence in support of their large empirical claims about what "it is common to suppose." Each of those claims is an *ipse dixit*. In any event, I am happy to grant that "it is common to suppose that when a person or group or society has become more unfree, it has become less free." Under the terms of my own theory of freedom, every increase in unfreedom entails a decrease in overall freedom. Much more dubious is the contention by Carter and Steiner in the quoted passage—encapsulated in the first instance of the phrase "and vice versa"—that it is also common to suppose that the relationship of entailment between increases in unfreedom and decreases in overall freedom is matched by a relationship of entailment in the other direction. No more than Carter and Steiner have I carried out any empirical research into the matter of social psychology on which they confidently pronounce here. Thus, I am not inclined to retort robustly that their contention about widespread perceptions of a matching relationship of entailment is false. Nevertheless, three things can aptly be said about their contention. First, their confidence in their empirical claim is not founded on any empirical research. That claim is an airy surmise. Second, their confidence is especially misbegotten in light of the frequency with which deontic freedom and modal freedom are conflated in ordinary discourse. Carter and Steiner are talking about modal freedom when they engage with my theory, but the putatively common supposition which they invoke might (if it exists) be a product of the running together of modal freedom and deontic freedom. Third, even if Carter and Steiner are correct in their ungrounded empirical conjecture, the truth of that conjecture has virtually no bearing on the dispute between them and me about bivalence versus trivalence—as I have explained in the penultimate paragraph above.

Even more dubious, and indeed laughable, is the suggestion in the passage quoted above that "it is common ... to suppose that, if freedom is valuable to a certain extent, then unfreedom is disvaluable to that same extent, and vice versa." Positions on the value of freedom and disvalue of unfreedom are somewhat recondite philosophical doctrines. Even among political philosophers, propositions about the value of freedom and disvalue of unfreedom have often been poorly understood—which is why Carter had to carry out so much important pioneering work on the topic in the

1990s. I cannot see any basis for thinking that those propositions are sufficiently well understood in the settings of everyday life to form the contents of common suppositions. To say the least, Carter and Steiner have not provided any such basis.

Yet another wholly unsubstantiated empirical claim is smuggled in at a somewhat later juncture, where Carter and Steiner tell their readers that "it is normally assumed that, because social freedom is a relation *between* agents, increases and decreases in one's freedom must depend directly on the actions and motivations of others, and not directly on one's own actions" (2022: 246, emphasis in original). This evidence-free assertion commends the Carter/Steiner bivalent conception of freedom as what is normally assumed. We are not told who normally assumes that conception. Political philosophers? Ordinary members of the public? Carter and Steiner and their students? Nor, of course, are we furnished with any empirical grounding for this bit of rodomontade. Far from enhancing the persuasiveness of Carter's and Steiner's argumentation, this lamely unsupported posturing detracts seriously therefrom.

4.2.2 Missing Dispositions

Though there are several other features of the opening pages of the chapter by Carter and Steiner to which I take exception, I will concentrate on only one of those further features before moving to the later sections of the chapter. Carter and Steiner exhibit a peculiar reluctance to take account of the role of dispositions in giving rise to freedoms and unfreedoms. Now, that reluctance on the part of Steiner is unsurprising. Particularly in his early work on freedom, but even in his later work to quite a considerable degree, Steiner has never fully grasped the extent to which the existence of sundry freedoms and unfreedoms is due to dispositions rather than to any actually occurrent actions. I have criticized him on this score at length in *The Quality of Freedom* (2003: 185–240). What is far more puzzling, however, is that Carter has signed on to the formulations at which I will look askance here. Hitherto, Carter and I have been aligned in tracing the dispositional provenances of countless freedoms and unfreedoms, and in reproaching Steiner for neglecting the import of dispositions. In the chapter which he has co-authored with Steiner for this volume, however, Carter appears to have succumbed to Steiner's superstitious wariness of dispositions.

Carter and Steiner supply this statement of their understanding of unfreedoms: "[A] person is socially unfree to do x if, and only if, there is some other action or set of actions, y, of another person or set of persons, where the occurrence of y implies the impossibility of the occurrence of x, and y either (i) does occur or (ii) would occur if x were attempted" (2022: 241). Though this formulation is somewhat wordy, it is otherwise unexceptionable. It encapsulates the property of being unfree to φ, both as that property is understood by Carter and Steiner and as it is understood by me. However, what is objectionable is that the formulation just quoted is presented as a more precise rendering of the sentence that immediately precedes it. The relevant portion of that preceding sentence is as follows: "[A] person is unfree to do x if x is prevented, actually or hypothetically, by the behavior of others" (2022: 241). Unlike the formulation which I have applauded above, this initial statement of the nature of unfreedoms by Carter and Steiner is a buzzing hive of confusion. Quite confounding is their reference to being prevented hypothetically. They presumably mean that the prevention occurs in a counterfactual world where the triggering circumstances for the performance of a preventative action are present. Yet Carter and Steiner and I live in the actual world, and the unfreedoms which we have to ascertain are in the actual world. Thus, one of the questions to be addressed whenever we are inquiring about a person's unfreedom to φ is whether the person has been prevented in the actual world from φ-ing. In particular, that question must be addressed in application to any circumstances where a preventative action has not occurred in the actual world (because the triggering conditions for the performance of that action have not arisen in the actual world). On the basis of their original statement of the nature of unfreedoms, Carter and Steiner seem to be committed to answering that question with reference to such circumstances in either of two untenable ways. First, they might contend that the person is not prevented from φ-ing in the actual world but is prevented from φ-ing in the germane counterfactual world and is thereby rendered unfree-to-φ in the actual world. Such an answer would imply that someone can be unfree-to-φ in the actual world without being prevented in the actual world from φ-ing. Any implication along those lines is clearly unacceptable to Carter and Steiner, who—like me—take unfreedoms in the actual world to be instances of prevention in the actual world. Second, then, Carter and Steiner might contend that a person who is unfree-to-φ in the actual world is prevented in the actual world from φ-ing and that the prevention is due to the preventative behavior by other people which occurs in the counterfactual world. (That behavior does not occur in the actual world, because the conditions that would have triggered it are not present.) Such a position would be outlandish, however. Prevention in the actual world is not caused by some course of behavior that never occurs in the actual world.

Carter and Steiner with their initial statement of the nature of unfreedoms have landed themselves in this quandary because that initial statement presumes that behavior is the only source of unfreedoms. They have thus blinded themselves to the origins of unfreedoms in the actual world whenever any unfreedoms exist in the absence of relevant instances of preventative behavior in the actual world. As Carter has heretofore always recognized, unfreedoms of that kind are caused not by preventative behavior (which never occurs) but instead by the dispositions of people to engage in preventative behavior. If certain people are firmly disposed to perform certain actions in the event that P attempts to φ, and if the occurrence of those actions would prevent P from φ-ing, and if the specified people are able to perform the specified actions, and if P does not ever attempt to φ, then P has been made unfree-to-φ not by any preventative actions (which never occur) but instead by the dispositions of certain people to engage in such actions if P does ever attempt to φ. Those dispositions, rather than the non-occurrent actions, are the source of P's unfreedom to φ. Another way of phrasing the matter is that P has been rendered unfree-to-φ by the fact that certain other people will perform preventative actions—actions that will prevent P from φ-ing—if he ever tries to φ. If P does try to φ, he will be prevented from φ-ing by the behavior of those other people; if P does not ever try to φ, he is prevented from φ-ing by the dispositions of those other people to engage in such behavior in the event of his trying to φ.

An even worse misstep in the same vein is committed by Carter and Steiner at a slightly later juncture in their chapter. There they announce that, under their bivalent conception of freedom, "unfreedom is defined as the presence of … preventive actions on the part of others, and freedom is then defined simply as the *absence of unfreedom*."[30] By proclaiming that preventative actions are the sole sources of unfreedoms, Carter and Steiner have altogether neglected the role of dispositions-to-perform-preventative-actions as sources of unfreedoms, and they have thereby plunged themselves into the absurdities of Steiner's very early conception of freedom. Steiner supposedly abandoned that very early conception quite a few years ago, but apparently he still clings to it. As for Carter, his embrace of such a model is utterly baffling—because, until now, he has been one of the most trenchant opponents of it.

4.2.3 Self-Liberation

Carter and Steiner strangely blunder by declaring that self-liberation—the liberation of a person by himself or herself from some constraint—is not possible under their bivalent conception of freedom. They write: "[O]ne's freedom must depend directly on the actions and motivations of others, and not directly on one's own actions.... On [the Carter/Steiner bivalent] conception of freedom, the term 'self-liberation' should not be taken literally, as if one could liberate oneself unilaterally, but can at most refer to a course of action, violent or otherwise, that somehow motivates others to cease preventing one from doing certain things" (2022: 246). Contrary to what Carter and Steiner suggest here, their account of freedom leaves ample room for people to liberate themselves. Suppose for example that Jessica is being held hostage by Leonard, who has tied her up with a rope. She manages to undo the knots, and she grabs his gun and kills him instantly by shooting him. She takes the keys from his pocket and releases herself from the room in which he had immured her. Under the Carter/Steiner conception of freedom, as much as under my conception, Jessica has liberated herself from her captivity and has done so not by depending on the actions and motivations of others but by directly relying upon her own actions. She has not sought to motivate Leonard to alter his behavior and dispositions. Rather, she has rendered his behavior and dispositions otiose by killing him. Admittedly, she was free at time t to escape from the room at time $t+n$ even though she was not free at t to escape from the room at t; but she has become free at $t+n$ to escape from the room at $t+n$ only because she has pursued the course of self-liberatory conduct which I have sketched.

This simple scenario of Jessica and Leonard is merely one of a plethora of examples that could be adduced to rebut the assertions in the latest quotation from Carter and Steiner. Despite what is stated in those assertions, the hyphenated noun "self-liberation" is applicable literally to numerous instances of unfreedom-removing conduct by people—even when the conduct in question is being assessed from the perspective of Carter's and Steiner's understanding of freedom. Let us ponder a variant of the scenario of Jessica and Leonard. Sven has abducted Bianca and has bound her securely with some ropes in a sealed room. Left alone in the room for an extended period, Bianca persistently struggles to untie the knots in the ropes with which she has been restrained. She notices that a couple of rats are scurrying around in a corner of

[30] 2022: 241, emphasis in original. Still further in their chapter, Carter and Steiner persist with their utter disregard of the role of dispositions in giving rise to unfreedoms: "I am free at time t to do x at t+1 if I am not unfree at t to do x at t+1. And I am *un*free at t to do x at t+1 if there is an action or set of actions of another person or group that is a sufficient condition for my non-performance of x at t+1" (2022: 251, emphasis in original). Although the second sentence in this quotation is formulated on its surface as a conditional, it is quite clearly functioning as a biconditional in the context created by the first of the quoted sentences.

the room, and she manages to slide toward them in the hope of inducing them to gnaw at the ropes. Succeeding in that effort, and continuing to strive mightily to undo the knots that are being gradually loosened by the rats' gnawing, she finally extricates herself from her fetters. Whether or not she proceeds to escape from the room, she has already liberated herself from many of the unfreedoms that had been imposed on her by Sven. Through her own strenuous exertions and through her deft manipulation of the rats, Bianca has liberated herself to stand up and to walk around the room and to jump up from the floor and so forth. Her freeing of herself to perform those various actions has occurred without any dependence on the motivations and actions of other people.

4.2.4 The Example of the Deluded Prisoner

Carter and Steiner marshal their "Deluded Prisoner 2" vignette to try to expose some preposterous conclusions that ostensibly follow from my account of freedoms and unfreedoms (2022: 246):

> White is in the same prison as Red and is subject to a similar set of preventions. A friend of White brings him a copy of Kramer's *The Quality of Freedom*, together with a special poison. Whoever drinks this poison will become paralyzed for life, save for the minimal bodily functions necessary for survival. Having read the first chapter of *The Quality of Freedom*, White laughs at Red for thinking he has made himself more free simply by desiring to do less. Convinced that he has discovered the true path to liberation, White then drinks the poison, as a result of which he spends the rest of his life staring into space and being spoon-fed by one of the guards.

Carter and Steiner think that, under my account of freedoms and unfreedoms, White has not only eliminated virtually all of his remaining freedoms but has also eliminated all of his unfreedoms. However, as I pointed out to them in July 2019, no such conclusion about unfreedoms genuinely follows from my account. Every loss of freedom that White has undergone in the Deluded Prisoner 2 vignette is an instance of unfreedom, since the actions of other people are causally involved under the criterion for causation which I expound at great length in Chapter 4 of *The Quality of Freedom*. Most notable is the fact that the special poison has been supplied to White by a friend, without whose action White would not have been able to ingest the poison. Likewise, if the noxious substance has been manufactured by other people, their roles in producing it are further ways in which the actions of other people are causally involved in every loss of freedom that White incurs. Moreover, as Carter and Steiner themselves point out, even my having written *The Quality of Freedom* is a causal factor if White would not have ingested the poison in the absence of his having read (and grossly misconstrued) that book. Hence, under the criterion for causation expounded rigorously in my 2003 volume, White has greatly increased his array of unfreedoms and has not removed any of them.

Carter and Steiner have responded to my July 2019 comment neither by altering their thought-experiment at all nor by presenting a philosophical criterion for causation that competes with mine, but instead by inserting a footnote in which they fall back upon their own causal intuitions. The insolidity of such an approach in this context is evident from their declaration that "any inability of agent A that has one of

A's own actions [such as White's consumption of the poison] as its proximate cause counts as a *self-inflicted* inability of A and therefore cannot qualify as a case of social unfreedom of A" (2022: 246 n.23, emphasis in original). In the phrase "its proximate cause," the pronoun "its" is functioning both as an indexical and as the definite article—such that the phrase as a whole is presumed by Carter and Steiner to be a definite description. They are thus supposing that there is exactly one proximate cause of an event such as the incapacitating of White or exactly one proximate cause of a state of affairs such as White's incapacitation. Their supposition along those lines is charmingly naïve, for any event or state of affairs is attributable to a vast array of causes among which quite a few can aptly be singled out as proximately causative of that event or state of affairs. When Carter and Steiner single out White's act of ingesting the poison as the proximate cause of White's incapacitation, they are not applying any rigorous criterion for the proximity of causes; rather, they are bringing to bear their unprincipled intuitions. Exactly because I wanted to get away from such intuition-mongering in my discussion of the sources of inabilities in Chapter 4 of *The Quality of Freedom*, I expounded a rigorous criterion for causal attributability and then applied that criterion to differentiate between unfreedoms and mere inabilities.

To get a sense of how flabby Carter's and Steiner's intuitions about proximate causes are, we should contemplate an example in which Sam the Sniper takes aim at Vincent the Victim who is walking along the street below Sam. Sam from his rooftop perch calculates that, if he pulls his trigger at some time *t*, the bullet will reach the location where Vincent will step at *t*+2. When Vincent steps onto that location at *t*+2, the bullet pierces his leg and cripples him. Are the resultant losses of freedoms to be classified as self-inflicted and thus not as unfreedoms at all by Carter's and Steiner's reckoning, or are they to be classified as unfreedoms? The peddling of intuitions by Carter and Steiner is of no avail for coming to grips with such questions appositely.

Five postscripts are needed here. First, nothing just said should be construed as casting doubt generally upon the importance of the distinction between remote and diffuse causation on the one hand and proximate and focused causation on the other hand. In my 2021 book *Freedom of Expression as Self-Restraint*, which I will discuss later in my replies to Christopher Kutz, I invoke that distinction repeatedly to explain why certain utterances are constitutive of communication-independent misconduct. Nevertheless, in the present context of differentiating between unfreedoms and mere inabilities, that distinction is largely beside the point. It affects the probabilistic qualifications that are attached to ascriptions of unfreedoms and to ascriptions of mere inabilities, but it does not otherwise bear on the division between the two. I say more on this matter in *The Quality of Freedom* (2003: 335–42).

Second, Carter and Steiner go astray in their footnote when they aver that my way of distinguishing between unfreedoms and self-caused inabilities should be rejected because it "reduces that category [of self-caused inabilities] almost to nothing" (2022: 247 n.23). My approach obviously narrows that category, but it falls far short of reducing the category almost to nothing. For example, I am currently neither free nor unfree to converse in Hungarian. I am not currently free to do so, because I am unable to do so; but my inability is self-caused as a product of my disinclination to learn Hungarian and is not a product of any preventative actions or dispositions on the part of other people. Likewise, if I foolishly go out of my residence during a fierce electrical storm to enjoy a view of the tempestuous sky, and if I am struck by a bolt of lightning, any incapacities incurred by me as a result of the mishap are either self-caused or naturally caused and are not ascribable to the actions or dispositions of other people. Similarly, if Joe visits a waterfall and throws his university yearbook into the cascade so that the book is irretrievably carried away and destroyed, Joe's inability to look at his yearbook any more is self-caused and is not something that can be traced to the actions or dispositions of other people. Countless other examples could be adduced here to show that the category of self-caused inabilities is scarcely hollowed out by my delimitation of it.

Third, unlike Carter, who believes that potential actions are the only contents of freedoms and unfreedoms (Kramer 2003: 157–69), I have always maintained that those contents also include any processes which a person might undergo. Among the chief processes for White in the Deluded Prisoner 2 vignette are those through which his body would be moved into areas that lie beyond the walls of his cell. He is not able to undergo any such relocation of his body, because the people responsible for his incarceration are resolutely disposed to keep him immured in his cell. They stand ready to thwart any efforts by anyone else to carry him out of the cell. Thus, contrary to what Carter and Steiner assume, their vignette does not depict a situation in which White has removed all of his previous unfreedoms. Many of those unfreedoms remain, as the actions and dispositions of the jailers prevent White from being carried beyond his dungeon.

Fourth, Carter and Steiner at the end of their inserted footnote belatedly and fleetingly respond to my July 2019 comments, in the manner which I there recommended to them. In other words, they laconically indicate how their scenario of Deluded Prisoner 2 could be modified to eliminate the roles of other people's actions in bringing about the new inabilities of White. I have always recognized that such modifications are possible, and indeed I advised that they should be undertaken. Those modifications do not make the scenario of White troublesome at all for my theory of freedom (as will be seen hereafter), but they do eliminate the baselessness of Carter's and Steiner's claims about the character of White's new inabilities as purely self-caused.

Fifth, when the Deluded Prisoner 2 scenario is refashioned along the lines just suggested, Carter and Steiner are clearly committed to the proposition that White has not undergone any diminution whatsoever in his level of overall freedom. By their reckoning, his particular freedoms and unfreedoms have not been affected at all by his act of consuming the incapacitative poison. Their conclusion on this point is only one among the myriads of hollow ascriptions of freedoms to which their bivalentist theory commits them. Under their theory, White's freedom to jump around his prison cell has not been impaired one whit by his thoroughgoing paralysis, and an unimprisoned person who has become thoroughly paralyzed in a similar manner is still entirely free to run a marathon in three hours. Such ascriptions of freedoms would be apt in theories focused on deontic liberty, but in a theory focused on modal liberty such ascriptions come across as parodic rather than as enlightening.

4.2.5 No Arbitrary Stipulations

Keeping their focus on the scenario of White in the prison, Carter and Steiner proceed to consider how the implications of the scenario are affected by a major feature in my account of the overall freedom of each person. That feature is what they decry as my "stipulation that a person's overall freedom is not represented by the basic fraction we have been working with up to now, but by the basic fraction with the numerator squared" (2022: 247). Their wording here is objectionably tendentious, for the noun "stipulation" will almost inevitably be construed by many readers as denoting an arbitrary fiat that lacks any principled rationale. Of course, if that noun were to be construed as a neutral term that denotes a precise specification of a certain aspect of a theory, it would be unexceptionable. Nonetheless, as I pointed out to Carter and Steiner in July 2019, their use of "stipulation" will very likely be perceived by most readers as pejorative. Given that they have retained that term in their chapter, I infer that they are content to mislead their readers.

Let me state emphatically, then, that the squaring of the numerator in the complicated fraction that encapsulates my approach to the measurement of freedom is not at all arbitrary. On the contrary, that aspect of my theory epitomizes the central inspirations behind the theory. I have developed an account of negative liberty in a context where Carter and Steiner and Cohen had propounded their competing accounts. We have been united as negative-liberty theorists, but there have been many points of contention among us as well. On the one hand, I concur with Steiner and Carter in holding that the measurement of any person's overall freedom has to involve a proportion between (1) the person's overall array of combinations of conjunctively exercisable freedoms and (2) the overall array just mentioned plus her overall array of combinations of consistent unfreedoms.[31] Such a proportion enables a theorist to take into account the moral significance of the distinction between unfreedoms and mere inabilities—where unfreedoms as inabilities caused by the actions or dispositions of other people are of particular concern in the domain of political morality. Though Carter and Steiner disagree with me over the question whether mere inabilities are instances of freedom or not, the three of us have always been aligned against Cohen as we insist on distinguishing between mere inabilities and unfreedoms so that the latter as products of social relationships are given special weight in our calculations of people's levels of freedom. On the other hand, I have always been aligned with Cohen against Carter and Steiner as I maintain that the proportion outlined above is not the only key parameter in the aforementioned calculations. Also pivotal in any measurements of each person's overall freedom is the sheer quantity of the person's array of combinations of conjunctively exercisable freedoms. That quantity, which is the sole parameter in the numerator of Carter's and Steiner's freedom-measuring fraction, has to be squared in the numerator of my fraction. The squaring of the specified quantity in the numerator, where the product is divided by the denominator, is of course equivalent to multiplying that quantity by the proportion to which Carter and Steiner and I assign special importance. Hence, far from being an arbitrary stipulation, the squaring of the numerator is essential as my way of combining the two insights which I bring together within my theory of freedom: Carter's and Steiner's insight into the

[31] I am here omitting any mention of probabilistic qualifications and evaluative multipliers. (I shall touch upon those matters at subsequent junctures in my replies to Carter and Steiner.) Furthermore, as I go on to state in the text, I am prescinding in this subsection from the fact that Carter and Steiner classify mere inabilities as freedoms.

peculiar importance of unfreedoms in one's measurements of social and political liberty; and Cohen's insight which ascribes centrality to the sheer range of the combinations of conjunctively exercisable opportunities available to any person whose liberty is being measured.

Carter and Steiner unfoundedly assert that "Kramer makes the move of squaring the numerator exactly in order to avoid various crazy measurements that would inevitably result from conjoining his ability-based trivalence with the measurement of overall freedom in terms of the basic fraction" (2022: 247). I told Carter and Steiner in July 2019 that this assertion by them is groundless and that the genuine rationale for the squaring of the numerator is as I have limned it in the preceding paragraph. I therefore take umbrage at their not having removed or modified their false assertion. Even more egregious is the following passage at a somewhat later juncture in their chapter:

> [T]he numerator-squaring move is of an ad hoc nature, and its limited efficacy is symptomatic of this fact. It is not unlike the ploy of an accountant who, in auditing a company whose financial health he would rather not question, decides to square the figure representing its assets, claiming that this gives "paramount emphasis" to assets vis à vis liabilities. Fortunately, squaring the numerator of our freedom-measuring fraction is unlikely to land us in jail, but it is similarly ad hoc inasmuch as it has no basis in an analysis of the concept of freedom, deriving instead from a disappointing degree of fit between the results of one such an analysis, on the one hand, and certain commonsense comparisons of degrees of freedom, on the other. (2022: 249)

Carter and Steiner here attribute to me a ploy worthy of a devious accountant, but in fact the only ploy is their reiteration of their utterly baseless insistence that my reason for squaring the numerator in the freedom-measuring fraction is that I can thereby circumvent some problematic implications of my trivalentist account of freedom.

What is true, as I explained to Carter and Steiner in July 2019, is that I quite rapidly realized in the early 2000s that the squaring of the numerator—which I have undertaken for the reason outlined in the penultimate paragraph above—will indeed avert some disconcerting conclusions that would otherwise have followed from my theory of freedom. Although the fending off of those conclusions is not the basis for the squaring of the numerator, it is a fortunate consequence thereof, and I am happy to avail myself of it. Still, were the avoidance of those conclusions the motivating factor that has impelled my squaring of the numerator, there would be some merit to Carter's and Steiner's complaints about an ad hoc maneuver. However, since the warding off of any troublesome implications is not the motivating factor and is instead only a byproduct, Carter's and Steiner's complaints are wholly without foundation.

4.2.6 One Role of the Evaluative Multipliers

Continuing with their penchant for intuition-mongering, Carter and Steiner endeavor to demonstrate that my squaring of the numerator in the freedom-measuring fraction will generate a host of implausible corollaries (2022: 248):

> As a result of [the] squaring [of] the numerator, the addition of particular freedoms will make marginally increasing contributions to a person's overall degree of freedom. This is strongly counterintuitive. It entails, for example, that redistributing resources from the poor to the rich will generally increase the overall level of societal freedom. It is debatable whether specific freedoms make marginally diminishing contributions to overall freedom, but few would agree that they make marginally increasing contributions. Indeed, as we shall see in section 3, Kramer himself holds that the marginal contributions of qualitatively similar freedoms are *decreasing* ones. The intuition motivating this view is in tension with the more general assertion of marginally increasing contributions entailed by the numerator-squaring move.

To show why the ostensible problem deplored by this passage is not genuinely perturbing, I should briefly review how evaluative multipliers figure in my approach to the measurement of freedom (Kramer 2003: 402–4, 425–71).

On the one hand, statements which impute freedoms or unfreedoms to people are not themselves evaluative. An ascription of a freedom-to-φ to some person P leaves open whether the freedom-to-φ is good for P and whether φ-ing itself would be good for P. On the other hand, the property of overall freedom is a partly evaluative property. In one's measurements of the overall freedom of P, an evaluative multiplier is attached to each item in every combination of conjunctively exercisable freedoms and to each combination of consistent unfreedoms. An evaluative multiplier attached to one of P's particular freedoms reflects the extent to which that freedom is promotive of certain values that are internal to the property of overall liberty, and an evaluative multiplier attached to any of P's combinations of consistent unfreedoms reflects the extent to which that combination will have set back those values for P. Now, typically (perhaps almost invariably) the furtherance of the specified values by the addition of some particular freedom to the situation of P will be greater if P's current level of overall freedom is meager than if that current level for P is instead ample. Generally, perhaps almost invariably, a new freedom of some type will matter more favorably to P's situation when P's existing level of overall freedom is low. Accordingly, the sizableness of the evaluative multipliers attached to additional freedoms for P will typically be in inverse relation to the highness of P's level of overall freedom. As a result, the putative problem deplored by Carter and Steiner will be systematically offset by the role of the evaluative multipliers in my calculations of each person's level of overall freedom. Of course, Carter and Steiner do not include any evaluative multipliers in their own approaches to the measurement of overall freedom. Almost alone among philosophers of freedom, they each take overall liberty to be a value-neutral property. However, they purport to be mounting a critique of my account of overall freedom, rather than a critique of their own accounts. Given that evaluative multipliers do figure saliently in my account, the observations in this paragraph defuse the difficulty on which Carter and Steiner seize in the passage quoted above.

I have not denied, and do not need to deny, that there could arise exceptional circumstances in which the relationship between the evaluative multipliers and a person's level of overall freedom will not be as I have recounted in the preceding paragraph. Although I cannot readily fathom what such circumstances would be, I can allow that they might obtain. In such a situation where the values of particular freedoms are so out of line with normal patterns, however, the difficulty delineated by Carter and Steiner will be unproblematic. When Carter and Steiner (in the passage above) submit that that difficulty "entails ... that redistributing resources from the poor to the rich will generally increase the overall level of societal freedom," they appear to be insinuating that I am somehow committed to a principle of distribution under which resources should be reassigned from the poor to the rich. However, even if I leave aside the fact that the freedom-potentiating effects envisaged by Carter and Steiner will hardly ever be present, I am scarcely committed to any principle of the sort just mentioned. As *The Quality of Freedom* points out at many junctures, my theory of the nature of liberty does not commit me to any specific principle for the distribution of freedom. Furthermore, as is evident from my tomes of political philosophy over the past decade, any principle that calls for the reassignment of resources from the poor to the rich in the service of an aggregate maximand is thoroughly alien to my conception of justice.

4.2.7 No Bullet to be Bitten

Persisting with their focus on the scenario of White in the prison cell, Carter and Steiner declare that my squaring of the numerator in the freedom-measuring fraction "only mitigates the absurdity of the outcome of *Deluded Prisoner 2* without eliminating it, for it leaves in place the judgment that White makes himself *freer* by drinking the poison." They condescendingly muse that "[p]erhaps Kramer will be tempted at this point to bite the bullet and accept that White increases his own freedom, emphasizing the isolated nature of the case and the smallness of the increase when considered in *inter*personally relative terms" (2022: 248, emphases in original). They somewhat disingenuously quote the phrase "mildly odd" from *The Quality of Freedom* as if I had been using that phrase there in response to their objection—when I was actually using that phrase in response to a very different crux broached by Martin van Hees.

There is in fact no bullet whatsoever to be bitten, even if I leave aside the fact that the scenario of White as Carter and Steiner present it does not involve the elimination of any unfreedoms at all. Let us suppose that they modify their thought-experiment to do away with the roles of the actions of other people in the incapacitation of White. Even so, as I have explained in the third postscript in section 4.2.4 above, the thought-experiment does not depict a situation in which the unfreedoms of White are entirely extinguished. On the contrary, while eliminating nearly all of his remaining freedoms, and while changing many of his unfreedoms into mere inabilities, White has left a huge number of his unfreedoms in place. He is still unfree to undergo the relocation of his body anywhere outside the confines of his dungeon, just as he was unfree to undergo such a relocation at the time of his ingestion of the poison. An attempt on the part of anyone to relocate White's body by carrying it beyond those confines would be stymied by the people responsible for keeping White immured in his cell. Hence, having removed virtually all of his remaining freedoms while leaving a vast array of his unfreedoms in place, White has not produced the upshot which Carter and Steiner proclaim. He has not made himself freer. Given the continuation of that vast array of unfreedoms, and given the roles of evaluative multipliers and the squaring of the numerator in my measurements of the level of White's overall liberty, his act of self-incapacitation will not have increased his overall freedom under any circumstances that are even minimally credible.

Note that the features of Carter's and Steiner's thought-experiment which enable this retort are not modifiable in any significant ways that would parry the retort. That is, to try to make the point which the scenario of White is designed to illustrate, Carter and Steiner need to portray a situation in which White's freedoms before the ingestion of the poison have already been quite sharply limited by the actions and dispositions of other people—and in which his unfreedoms are commensurately wide-ranging. My rejoinder to Carter and Steiner trades on the fact that the wide-rangingness of the unfreedoms removed by White's action of ingestion (through the transformation of those unfreedoms into mere inabilities) is paralleled by the wide-rangingness of his unfreedoms that are left in place by his action.

4.2.8 On the Units of Measurement

Turning their attention for a moment to the units of measurement that are involved in calculations of people's levels of overall liberty, Carter and Steiner contend that "the smaller the [units] we are working with in describing any given scenario, the larger the number of people in that scenario who will fall into the category of individuals who are in a position to increase their own freedom through self-disablement" (2022: 249). A first point to be noted here is that the size of the units of measurement in any calculations is not an arbitrary matter. As I have maintained elsewhere (2003: 381–2), the appropriate size for any such units is determined by the purposes that are being pursued through the calculations. On this point, so far as I am aware, Carter and I are in agreement.

Even more important, the complaint here by Carter and Steiner is completely misdirected. Given that the denominator in the freedom-measuring fraction includes the vast array of combinations of consistent unfreedoms which White continues to bear even after his other unfreedoms have been converted into mere inabilities through his incapacitation, and given that the combinations of conjunctively exercisable freedoms available to White are quite sharply limited before his incapacitation and are severely limited thereafter, the upshot of employing small units of measurement in a squared numerator will be dominated by the upshot of employing those small units of measurement to calculate the vast array of combinations of consistent unfreedoms in the denominator. Consequently, the effect envisaged by Carter and Steiner will not be operative. Because Carter and Steiner incorrectly presume that the only thing in the denominator of my freedom-measuring fraction in application to White's situation is the range of his combinations of conjunctively exercisable freedoms, they likewise incorrectly presume that the use of smaller and smaller units in my freedom-measuring fraction will eventually make its squared numerator large enough to offset the severe reduction in White's combinations of conjunctively exercisable freedoms. What Carter and Steiner have failed to recognize is that the use of those smaller and smaller units will increase the magnitude of the denominator far more than the magnitude of the numerator—since the denominator includes not only the range of White's combinations of conjunctively exercisable freedoms but also his enormously larger range of combinations of consistent unfreedoms. Their failure to glimpse this point is due to their having forgotten that the contents of freedoms and unfreedoms in my theory of negative liberty include not only actions and omissions but also processes that might be undergone.

4.2.9 Tweaking and Self-Congratulation

In the chapter by Carter and Steiner, Carter lauds himself for having presented a theory of freedom that "does not suggest . . . a tweaking of the formula so as to accommodate as many as possible of the remaining counterexamples, where such surface manipulation has no grounding in the analysis of freedom he has provided" (2022: 250). He is of course contrasting his own theory with mine as he perceives it. In other words, he is persisting with the accusations about arbitrariness and ad hoc adjustments to which I have retorted in section 4.2.5 above. Carter and Steiner continue: "The ad hoc nature of Kramer's formula-tweaking is illustrated by the fact that he might just as well have favored cubing the numerator, or raising it to some yet greater power, or simply multiplying it by a constant" (2022: 250). Once again, Carter and Steiner have not managed to grasp the rationale for the squaring of the numerator in my freedom-measuring fraction—even though that rationale is presented in my 2003 book, and even though I expounded it afresh for them in July 2019. As I have indicated in the second paragraph of section 4.2.5 above, the squaring of the numerator enables me to bring together (1) the Carter/Steiner insight into the character of overall freedom as a proportion and (2) Cohen's insight into the character of overall freedom as the gamut of the combinations of conjunctively exercisable freedoms with which this or that person is endowed. My aspiration to combine those two insights is what has led me to discern that the numerator in the freedom-measuring fraction should be squared. Combining those insights in that fashion is not a matter of tweaking or arbitrariness or ad hoc stipulations.

As is manifest, the reason why the numerator should be squared rather than cubed is that the squaring of it delivers the parameter which combines the two aforementioned insights. If we let "F" stand for a person's range of combinations of conjunctively exercisable freedoms, and if we let "U" stand for a person's range of combinations of consistent unfreedoms, and if we prescind here from evaluative multipliers and probabilistic qualifications, the freedom-measuring fraction with the numerator squared is obviously equivalent to $F \times F/(F + U)$. The product of that multiplication is exactly the parameter to which I have just referred. By contrast, the cubing of the numerator would of course be equivalent to $F^2 \times F/(F + U)$. Far from delivering the parameter that combines the Carter/Steiner insight with Cohen's insight, this latter multiplication delivers a very different quantity.

Suppose that the height of Joseph to the tops of his shoulders is 5/6 of his height to the top of his head, and suppose that his height to the top of his head is six feet. If we let "S" stand for the height of a person to the tops of his or her shoulders, and if we let "H" stand for a person's height from the tops of the shoulders to the top of the head, the fraction S/(S+H) represents the proportion of a person's overall height that consists in S. Now, because in application to Joseph we know that S/(S+H) = 5/6, and because we know that S+H = 6 feet, we can easily calculate that S = 5 feet. Suppose that we have some reason to ascertain the product of S and S/(S+H). Perhaps, for example, that product is quite strongly predictive of a person's aptitude in some sport. In application to Joseph, we can easily calculate that 5 x 5/6 = 4.167 feet, and we can therefore easily see that $S^2/(S+H) = 4.167$ feet. Predictions about Joseph's likely aptitude as a participant in the specified sport can henceforth be made on the basis of that calculated parameter. Carter and Steiner now come along and dismissively proclaim that the squaring of the numerator in the aptitude-predictive fraction could just as well have been replaced by the cubing of the numerator—which would have yielded a figure of 20.8 for Joseph. As should be immediately apparent, the squaring of the numerator in the aptitude-predictive fraction is not arbitrary, and the replacement of it with a cubed numerator is distortive and obfuscatory. Given that those points about non-arbitrariness and distortiveness are immediately apparent with regard to the aptitude-predictive fraction, I am at a loss to know why Carter and Steiner are unable to grasp the truth of the parallel points that pertain to the freedom-measuring fraction.

4.2.10 A Botched Example

Having futilely endeavored to impugn my trivalentist theory of freedom, Carter and Steiner turn to the task of defending their own bivalentist account. Let us begin here with an example which I presented in *The Quality of Freedom* against Steiner (2003: 218–22). Carter is apparently content to join Steiner in trying to deflect my example and to vindicate Steiner's conception of freedom—including his blindness toward the dispositional dimension of freedoms and unfreedoms. Although the original presentation of the example makes numerous telling points against Steiner's conception, I will here abridge it quite sharply for the purpose of responding to Carter and Steiner in their chapter.

My scenario involves Emily and Elmer, who are the only two inhabitants of an island that contains a steep crag. Neither of them is able to ascend the upper reaches of the cliff at all, and therefore neither of them is able to walk on a ridge of rock at the top of the cliff. Because these inabilities of each of them are due not to the actions or dispositions of other people but solely to the terrain and to the natural limitations of Emily and Elmer as human beings, Carter's and Steiner's theory generates the conclusion that Elmer and Emily are each entirely free to ascend the upper reaches of the cliff and to walk along its ridge at the top. Elmer eventually invents some contraption that enables any user of it to scale the topmost portions of the crag and thus to walk on the strip of rock at the top. Because the resources on the island are exiguous, only one such device can be constructed. Consequently, only one person at a time can ascend the upper slope of the bluff, and only one person at a time can walk on the strip of rock at the peak. Still, Elmer usually lets Emily avail herself of the device when she requests it and when he himself does not wish to make use of it. Thus, each of them is frequently free to clamber up the summit of the bluff and to walk on the summit's ledge. Now, if Elmer stops Emily from employing his invention at a given time—either because he is then using the invention for his own purposes or because he simply obstructs her from gaining access to it—he will have made her unfree to scale the crag's pinnacle and to walk on its ledge during that time. Similarly, if Elmer would have stopped Emily from using his device at a certain time had she attempted to use it then, she was unfree to ascend the pinnacle and to walk on the ledge at that time. Conversely, on each occasion when Emily makes use of the contraption, she will have rendered Elmer unfree to walk on the ridge of rock at that time. Her availing herself of the device prevents him from availing himself of it.

Accordingly, under Carter's and Steiner's conception of liberty, there has been a straightforward reduction in each person's overall freedom as a result of Elmer's invention of the facilitative contraption. Before his innovation, Elmer and Emily were each free at all times to climb the topmost portion of the cliff and to walk along its ledge. Though neither of them could in fact perform such feats at that stage (or, rather, largely *because* neither of them could perform such feats at that stage), each of them was unprevented by the other from doing so. Each of them was therefore always free to do so, according to Carter's and Steiner's conception of liberty. Elmer's innovation transforms this situation of unalloyed freedom into a situation of freedom-cum-unfreedom. Elmer is still often free to scale the crag's summit and to walk on the strip of rock at the very top, but is no longer always so. Whenever he lets Emily use his device or is otherwise obstructed by her from using it himself, he is unfree to ascend the summit and to walk thereon. Even more substantially changed is the posture of Emily. Before the invention of the facilitative contraption, she was free at all times to climb the zenith of the cliff and to walk at the very top. Afterward, however, she is unfree-to-do-those-things whenever Elmer prevents her from using his device (either because he wishes to use it himself or because he simply does not want her to have it at some particular time). In sum, under Carter's and Steiner's conception of liberty, neither Elmer nor Emily has gained any new freedoms in regard to clambering up the top reaches of the crag and walking on the ridge of rock. Any freedoms of those sorts currently enjoyed by either of them are freedoms that pre-existed the advent of Elmer's device. At the same time, as has just been described, Emily and Elmer have each acquired some new unfreedoms in regard to ascending the apex of the cliff and walking on the ridge. Hence, by the reckoning of Carter and Steiner, technological progress in the form of Elmer's innovation has brought about a straightforward decrease in the overall liberty of Elmer and Emily.

Carter and Steiner respond in their chapter by declaring that my critique neglects the distinction between highly general act-types and more specific act-types. They write: "Emily is free (albeit unable) to clamber up the shuddersomely steep slope with the sole aid of her own limbs both before *and after* Elmer's invention and withholding of his contraption, as long as no one else is preventing her from doing so. After Elmer's invention and withholding of the contraption, Emily becomes unfree to ascend the hill *using Elmer's contraption*" (2022: 252 n.35, emphases in original). Their response is bizarrely inapposite, since my scenario does not involve any claim about the relatively specific act-type of clambering up the slope with the sole aid of one's own limbs. Instead, it involves a claim about the more general act-type of clambering up the slope as well as about the act-type of walking on the ridge at the top. Those two latter act-types are things which Emily and Elmer are each now unfree to perform at certain times, whereas prior to the invention of Elmer's device those latter act-types were things which Emily and Elmer were each always free to perform—by the reckoning of Carter's and Steiner's account of freedom. Thus, Carter and Steiner are committed to holding that my thought-experiment depicts a situation in which some benign technological progress has impaired the overall freedom of both Elmer and Emily. Carter and Steiner are committed to holding that that impairment of the overall freedom of the island's two inhabitants has occurred even though each of those inhabitants has acquired new abilities and has not incurred any new inabilities. The fact that Elmer and Emily have remained free throughout to scale the cliff with their own limbs is completely beside the point.

4.2.11 The Problem of Infinity

Carter and Steiner devote much of the second half of their chapter to trying to defend their theory against a set of objections which I have raised in connection with the limitlessness of the category of mere inabilities. I will start my ripostes to them by pondering the craftiness of their initial presentation of the problem which they are seeking to defuse. They write: "It is important to remember that the measurement of bivalent freedom does not take account of magical actions that defy the laws of physics (such as Mary's simply making her body zoom up into the air and into outer space all on its own), and should therefore include only actions involving the use of the relevant technological resources—in Mary's case, longevity-increasing resources as well as space-travel resources—access to which might be currently withheld by others" (2022: 253-4).

When Carter and Steiner affirm that the laws of physics serve to delimit the range of modes of conduct that are to be taken into account within their theory, they are resorting to an ad hoc stipulation that is in tension with their conception of freedom. Let us recall that they formulate their conception as follows: "On a *bivalent* approach to social freedom, ... unfreedom is defined as the presence of ... preventive actions [or dispositions] on the part of others, and freedom is then defined simply as the *absence of unfreedom*" (2022: 241, emphases in original). If some action is impossible for a person solely because it would contravene the laws of physics, its impossibility is not due at all to the preventative actions or dispositions of other people. Consequently, under the "free if and only if not unfree" conception of liberty to which Carter and Steiner adhere, they should conclude that a person is free to perform every action that is impossible for her solely because it would contravene the laws of physics. Given the infinite expansiveness of the category of actions that are impossible for any person solely because they would contravene the laws of physics, Carter and Steiner are committed to the proposition that the range of everyone's combinations of conjunctively exercisable freedoms is infinitely expansive. They now try to wriggle out of that commitment through an ad hoc stipulation. I will acquiesce in their unprincipled and arbitrary subterfuge, because my critique of their theory can proceed here without contesting the stipulation which they introduce as a *deus ex machina*. However, it should be noted again that that stipulation is at best in tension—if not in outright conflict—with their own formulation of their understanding of freedom. Their effort to disown some clear implications of their conception of freedom is a display of theoretical gerrymandering.

Equally damaging is a second assumption made by Carter and Steiner. In addition to presuming that they have to take into account only the courses of conduct for each person that are consistent with the laws of physics, they are presuming that they have to take into account only the courses of conduct for each person that are consistent with the constraints imposed by the actual faculties of human beings and by the limitedness of the people and things available in the actual world. My critique of their theory will take aim at that latter assumption. That is, I will here contest the notion that the actual faculties of human beings and the limitedness of the medley of things in the actual world play any role in delimiting the domain of the courses of conduct that have to be taken into account by Carter and Steiner.

4.2.11.1 Counterfactual possibilities

In consistency with the laws of physics, human beings could have been endowed with sundry faculties markedly different from those with which they are endowed. To take one obvious example that connects directly with the passage which I have just quoted from Carter and Steiner, human beings could have been like many other past and present creatures in possessing the ability to soar through the air without any mechanical devices. They are obviously not actually endowed with the faculties to fly in that manner, but in full consistency with the laws of physics they could have been so endowed if the antecedent conditions from which the present world unfolded had been different. Those conditions were of course not different from what they were, but that fact is scarcely attributable to the actions or dispositions of human beings. Hence, the inability of each person to soar through the air without the aid of any machinery is classifiable by Carter and Steiner as one of the freedoms of each person. And, naturally, that conclusion about that specific inability is paralleled by similar conclusions about the multitudinous other inabilities of human beings—physical inabilities and mental inabilities—which flow from the fact that the antecedent conditions of the universe were not different from what they were. All of those countless inabilities are freedoms by the reckoning of Carter and Steiner.

Furthermore, the resources of the world available to human beings could have differed markedly from what they are, if the early conditions of the universe had been different. Had human beings been endowed with much greater physical and mental abilities than they are, and had the resources available to them been far more abundant or far more versatile, they could have furnished themselves with capabilities and devices that currently lie beyond their reach in the actual world. Among those capabilities and devices would be many that pertain to traveling through outer space, but myriads of other capabilities and devices could additionally or alternatively have materialized if the early conditions of the universe had been different. All of the actual inabilities of human beings that stem from the absence of the envisaged capabilities and devices are classifiable by Carter and Steiner as freedoms, for those inabilities obtain because the early conditions of the world were not different from what they were—and the fact that those conditions were as they actually were is not ascribable to the actions or dispositions of human beings.

Moreover, in full conformity with the laws of physics, countless actually inexistent objects and people would have existed if the early conditions of the universe had differed from what they were. Each person's inabilities in the actual world to see and enter any of the innumerable houses that would have been built, and each person's inabilities in the actual world to see and greet any of the innumerable people who would have been born, are classifiable as freedoms under Carter's and Steiner's conception of liberty. Any of those actually inexistent objects and people would have existed if the early conditions of the universe had differed from what they were in certain ways. The fact that those early conditions did not differ from what they were in any of those innumerable ways is hardly due to actions or dispositions of human beings. Thus, all the inabilities just mentioned are freedoms by the reckoning of Carter and Steiner.

Because the counterfactual worlds are limitless in number, the freedoms envisaged here are limitless in number.

4.2.11.2 The non-identity problem

In the minds of readers familiar with the work of Derek Parfit, there may have arisen some worries at this stage about the non-identity problem. In his immensely influential meditations wherein he pondered some cruxes in the philosophy of population ethics (1984: Pt. IV), Parfit highlighted the ways in which changes at certain junctures in the world would lead to significant changes at later junctures. After presenting a certain thesis about the sameness of a person across possible worlds, Parfit concluded that major alterations in behavior during a certain period of time would bring about major alterations in the world at subsequent periods to such an extent that none of the individuals in those considerably later periods would be the same as the individuals who would have existed then if the alterations in the earlier period had not occurred. Parfit's reflections have engrossed population ethicists and environmental ethicists for the past four decades, but here my concern with those reflections is naturally focused instead on the points at issue in my confrontation with Carter and Steiner.

In section 4.2.11.1, I have repeatedly ascribed sundry inabilities to individuals in the actual world by invoking the things which those individuals could have done or experienced if the early conditions of the actual world had been different. A reader of Parfit may be inclined to object that the inabilities in question are not assignable to individuals in the actual world, because those individuals would not have existed if the early conditions of the actual world had been different. Consequently, although we can meaningfully invoke far-reaching counterfactuals to ascribe multitudinous inabilities that exist in the actual world at the level of a society or a species, we cannot meaningfully invoke such counterfactuals to ascribe multitudinous inabilities in the actual world to individuals. Such is the query that will very likely have occurred to readers of Parfit.

My response lies in contemplating each individual in the actual world one by one. For each such individual P, any counterfactual world invoked in section 4.2.11.1 could have existed even while the counterfactual-world people in the ancestral line of P were sufficiently close to their actual-world counterparts (genetically and circumstantially) to ensure the sameness of P as a person across the counterfactual/actual divide. This point is especially evident in relation to any of the counterfactual worlds envisaged in the final paragraph of section 4.2.11.1, where each such world contains objects or people that do not exist in the actual world. Differences of those kinds between the actual world and any counterfactual world are patently consistent with the sameness of P between the two worlds. Moreover, even the other counterfactual worlds adduced in section 4.2.11.1 can be consistent with the sameness of P across the counterfactual/actual division. To be sure, P in some of those latter counterfactual worlds will not be genetically identical to P in the actual world. For example, in a world where P and other human beings are capable of flying without any gliders or mechanical devices, or in a world where P and other human beings are considerably more intelligent and considerably stronger than in the actual world, the genetic make-up of P will be slightly different from the genetic make-up of P in the actual world. However, thorough genetic equivalence is neither a necessary condition nor a sufficient condition for the sameness of a person across the actual/counterfactual divide, under Parfit's thesis about such sameness. Provided that there is a nearly complete genetic identity, and provided that the circumstances of P's conception and birth in a counterfactual world are essentially the same as those in the actual world, P is the same person in each world. Thus, with regard to any given individual P in the actual world, my invoking of counterfactual worlds for the purpose of attributing countless inabilities to P is apposite. Since we measure the freedom of each individual in the actual world one by one, my pondering of each individual in the actual world one by one for the purpose of gauging the sameness of each person across the actual/counterfactual division is apt.

4.2.12 Companions in Guilt?

Carter and Steiner adopt a "*tu quoque*" tack in their main rejoinder to my critique of their inclusion of mere inabilities in the category of freedoms. Accepting that mere inabilities are indeed limitless, they contend that much the same is true of abilities and that the category of freedoms as I understand it is in this respect on a par with the category of freedoms as they understand it. Here they draw upon a fact which I have myself accentuated in my book on freedom: namely, the fact that the present abilities of human beings include abilities to acquire further abilities in the future. For example, Carter has the ability to learn how to speak in Hebrew. If he exercises that ability, he will thereby equip himself with further abilities to participate in forms of social and academic interaction with Israelis in which he is not currently able to participate. Unless he does avail himself of his ability to learn to speak in Hebrew, however, he will not possess those further abilities. Any number of other examples could be offered here, of course.

Carter and Steiner seek to parlay this fact about the ability-acquiring abilities of human beings into a critique of my trivalentist account of liberty. In the first paragraph of their "*tu quoque*" riposte, they present the gist of their reasoning (2022: 254-5):

> Kramer thinks that the set of his actual abilities is finite. On closer examination, however, this understandably intuitive claim is false. As we have already seen, Kramer's actual abilities include the ability to acquire further abilities. And we cannot rule out that these further abilities might include the ability to fly to Alpha Centauri. Kramer might answer this somewhat surprising claim by observing that, by the time humanity has developed the ability to fly to Alpha Centauri, he will certainly be dead. But the ability to extend our lifespans to that future time and beyond—more precisely, the ability to acquire that ability—is also among our current abilities.

Although the opening portion of the final sentence in this passage is worded untenably, the portion of the sentence between the dashes is apt. To see why, we should attend to my cogitations on freedom and time in *The Quality of Freedom* (2003: 76–91). There I indicate that the present abilities of any person include abilities to do things in the future. Every ascription of freedom to anybody explicitly or implicitly includes two temporal elements: one is focused on the time at which the ascribed freedom exists, and the other is focused on the time of the conduct or occurrence to which the ascribed freedom pertains. For example, I am free in January 2022 to fly to New York in July 2022, because at least one course of conduct available to me in January 2022 will result in my flying to New York in July 2022. That freedom is one of my present freedoms, even though the action to which it pertains is six months away.

Now, although human beings are not currently able to fly in spaceships to a planet orbiting one of the Alpha Centauri stars, they might currently possess the ability to do so in the very distant future. That is, there might be some course of conduct currently open to them that would eventuate over some centuries in the occurrence of flights by human beings with spaceships to the aforementioned planet. Likewise, although human beings are not currently able to extend human lifespans to the period in the remote future (if such a period ever arrives) when human beings will be capable of flying in spaceships to an Alpha Centauri planet, there might currently be available to them some course of conduct that would ultimately lead in the distant future to the specified extension of lifespans. In other words, human beings might be free now to extend human lifespans considerably at some distant point in the future. When we take account of the twofold temporal indices in any ascription of freedom, we can see how the abilities mentioned by Carter and Steiner could be classified by them as "also among our current abilities."

Carter and Steiner submit that I might currently be free to undergo eventually the augmentation of my lifespan to an indefinite length, and they conclude that the freedoms currently possessed by me are unlimitedly expansive. (I here of course construe "indefinite" as "infinite" or "unlimited" rather than merely as "unspecifiable." Were Carter and Steiner using the term in the latter sense, their assertions about the augmentation of my lifespan would be wholly unsupportive of their contention that the range of my present abilities is infinitely expansive.) Carter and Steiner of course allow that the probability of my ever achieving an infinitely long lifespan is shuddersomely low, but they maintain that the lowness of the probability will be reflected in the qualification that is implicitly or explicitly attached to the ascription of the relevant freedom. After all, as I have already remarked, every ascription of freedom to anyone implicitly or explicitly carries a probabilistic qualification. Thus, Carter and Steiner argue, the freedom to become endowed with an infinitely long lifespan at some point in the distant future can properly be attributed to me—with a very heavy probabilistic qualification—as one of the freedoms which I currently possess.

Fatally undermining any such line of thought is the fact that there is no course of conduct available to me that will result at some future point in my achieving an infinitely long lifespan. There are of course researchers who are working to extend the human lifespan, and some of them are serious scientists. However, no researchers who are serious scientists—rather than absurd fantasists—are under the delusion that their efforts might ultimately result in immortality for human beings. Much less are they under the delusion that their efforts might ultimately result in immortality for any human beings who are alive at present. Every serious scientist knows that, although the augmentation of human lifespans by decades or perhaps by centuries might be possible, the prospect of infinitely long lifespans is a chimera. People who hope for a situation in which "death shall be no more" (Revelation 21:4) are suited for religious musings on the hereafter but not for scientific research. Hence, were I to donate some of my money to any researchers who hold out the possibility of eventual immortality through successive extensions of my lifespan, I would be squandering my funds on charlatanry rather than devoting them to a course of conduct that might ultimately eventuate in the swallowing up of death. Accordingly, although a philosopher of freedom can correctly ascribe to me various current freedoms to undergo hereafter some extensions of my lifespan by decades—provided that the ascriptions of those freedoms to me are accompanied by heavy probabilistic qualifications—no philosopher of freedom can correctly ascribe to me any current freedoms to undergo eventually the protraction of my lifespan to infinity. Any ascriptions of the latter freedoms are illusory, for there are no courses of conduct available to me that could culminate in the upshot to which those freedoms pertain.

Thus, when Carter and Steiner go on to point out that "the sum of an infinitely large set of freedoms, each weighted by a very low probability, is still infinity" (2022: 255), their observation is correct but irrelevant. It is an *ignoratio elenchi*. Extremely low probability weightings are apposite for ascriptions to me of present freedoms to undergo eventual extensions of my lifespan by centuries, but zero is the only apt weighting for any ascription to me of a present freedom to undergo eventual extensions of my lifespan to infinity. Ergo, although Carter and Steiner are correct in thinking that the temporal indexing of freedoms is such that it makes my present array of freedoms much more expansive than many philosophers and ordinary people might assume, they err in trying to show that that present array is infinite.

Note that my critique of Carter's and Steiner's bivalentist theory of freedom in section 4.2.11 does not rely at all on any illusions about the possibility of immortality. My critique is fully consistent with the proposition that there is no probability (not even a tiny probability) that human beings will someday be able to live forever. I invoke not the prospect of endless actions for each person in the future, but instead the innumerable possibilities that are closed off to each person by the fact that the early states of the universe did not differ from what they were in any of the innumerable ways in which they could have been different. My invocation of those countless closed-off possibilities does not rest on any assumptions about extensions of the lifespans of human beings. Thus, whereas the effort by Carter and Steiner to expose a problem of infinite expansiveness in my category of freedoms is vitiated by the dependence of that effort on the possibility of endowing human beings with immortality, my endeavor to expose a problem of infinite expansiveness in their category of freedoms is unmarred by any such dependence.

Note also that my exposure of that problem of infinite expansiveness is unaffected by the spatial and temporal limits which Carter and Steiner impose on their measurements of each person's overall freedom, in section 2.4 of their chapter. All the closed-off possibilities conjured up by me in section 4.2.11 above are such that, if they had been actualized, they would have occurred in what Carter and Steiner designate as "the set of all jurisdictions" (2022: 256). Hence, all the countless inabilities that ensue from the closing off of those possibilities are within the ambit of Carter's and Steiner's measurements. Because those inabilities are limitless in number, and because none of them is attributable to the actions or dispositions of human beings, the category of freedoms as Carter and Steiner understand it is limitlessly expansive. (I endorse spatial and temporal limits largely akin to those which Carter and Steiner place on their measurements of each person's overall freedom. However, I do so not in order to try to dodge a problem of infinite expansiveness; after all, *pace* Carter and Steiner, my theory is not plagued by such a problem. Instead, my endorsement of those limits is grounded on the moral reasons for the status of freedom as a fundamental desideratum—reasons that are touched upon by Carter and Steiner in their discussion of the limits which they advocate.)

4.2.13 Multiple Missteps

My incorporation of evaluative multipliers into my measurements of each person's overall liberty is badly misunderstood and misrepresented by Carter and Steiner. Indeed, this portion of their chapter imbues me with a wearisome sense of *déjà vu*, since the errors that abound in it are repetitions of some of the errors which I sought in *The Quality of Freedom* to correct in their earlier work (2003: 241–5, 443–6). I have heretofore been under the impression that Carter and Steiner accepted my corrections of their earlier mistakes. However, given that those fallacious lines of argument are rehashed by Carter and Steiner in their chapter for this volume, I have to infer with a sigh that my impression was unduly sanguine.

In the first place, Carter and Steiner several times suggest that "a freedom's [value] is a function of the value of the action that it is the freedom to do" (2022: 260). Although they might be correct in imputing such a view to Charles Taylor, any imputation of it to me is wholly unfounded. What is true is that the high value of φ-ing entails the high value of being free to φ. However, the low value of φ-ing does not entail the low value of being free to φ. I have made this point repeatedly—with examples—in my 2003 book.

Second, even when Carter and Steiner finally get around to acknowledging that the view (about each freedom's value) which they appear to be attributing to me is in fact rejected by me, they blunder further by invoking Carter's distinction between the content-independent value and the content-dependent value of any freedom (2022: 256-7). Although I of course accept that distinction as far as it goes, it is simplistic because Carter presumes that the content-dependent value of a freedom-to-φ is a simple function of the value of φ-ing. Given that Carter is incorrect on that point, his dichotomy should be amplified into a trichotomy: the content-independent value of the freedom to φ, the content-dependent value of the freedom to φ, and the value of φ-ing. Again, this point is made emphatically in *The Quality of Freedom*.

Third, Carter and Steiner wrongly suppose that the content-dependent value of any particular freedom is to be gauged by reference to the interests of people other than the person whose freedoms are under consideration. Carter's and Steiner's examples of life-saving acts as highly valuable and life-taking acts as highly detrimental are clearly founded on such a supposition. In fact, however, the content-dependent value of any particular freedom is to be gauged by reference to the objectively defined interests of the person who possesses that freedom. Very few freedoms indeed are of no value or of negative value to a typical human being who is endowed with them; the freedom-to-take-someone-else's-life would hardly ever be of no value or of negative value to the possessor of such a freedom, even though she would very likely blench at the thought of exercising it.

Fourth, Carter and Steiner go astray in the other direction when they declare that I insist that "the value of the *freedom* to do any action, including negatively and neutrally valued ones, must be positive" (2022: 262, emphasis in original). Extremely uncommon though freedoms of negative value are, we need not think that absolutely every particular freedom is of positive value on balance to any typical human being who possesses it. As I have observed in *The Quality of Freedom* (2003: 444–5), there can be some particular freedoms that would on balance probably be of negative value for a typical human being. For example, suppose that a narrow path with a steep bank on each side is not fenced at all to prevent people from plunging down either of the stony banks. The presence of a suitably high barrier on one side or the other of the path would remove the freedom of a typical person to topple down the inclination on that side, but would probably not thereby deprive her of anything valuable. (If someone derives gratification from the risk of tumbling over onto rocks and mud, she still has the opportunity to hazard such a risk on the other side of the path.) At any rate, although there doubtless can be some particular freedoms that are each of negative value or of no value on balance to any typical person who is possessed of them, they are rare—far rarer than the particular freedoms of a person that are each of negative value or of no value on balance for other people. We can easily recognize as much when we keep in mind the distinction between the value of φ-ing and the value of being free to φ.

Fifth, Carter and Steiner write too sweepingly when they assert that any freedom with an evaluative multiplier of 1 will contribute "only slightly" to a person's overall freedom (2022: 262). Whether such a freedom contributes slightly or significantly to a person's level of overall liberty will depend entirely on the physical dimensions of that freedom. As I have time and again emphasized in my ruminations on the evaluative component of the endeavor of measuring each person's overall freedom, the reason for attaching an evaluative multiplier of 1 to any of the few genuinely disvaluable freedoms possessed by a person P is that each such freedom contributes no more and no less than its physical dimensions to P's level of overall liberty. If those dimensions of any disvaluable freedom are sizable, then the contribution of that freedom is sizable.

Sixth, Carter and Steiner commit some especially weird missteps in the following passage (2022: 264, emphases in original):

> [Negative content-dependent values of freedoms are] exactly what is involved in those many common cases where persons choose to enter into *enforceable* agreements or contracts not to do certain actions which they would otherwise be unprevented from doing. In so choosing, they are clearly assigning negative values, not only to those actions themselves, but also to the *freedoms* to do those actions.

Pace Carter and Steiner, just about everyone who enters into a contractual commitment to refrain from performing some action A has done so not because she perceives the freedom-to-perform-A as negative in its content-dependent value, but instead because the terms of the contract provide her with some inducement that is sufficient to render her willing to enter into the contractual commitment. Moreover, except in extremely unusual circumstances, she does not in fact relinquish her modal freedom-to-perform-A. Instead, she relinquishes her deontic freedom-to-perform-A. Of course, if contractual requirements are generally well enforced in the jurisdiction, her taking on the contractual commitment-not-to-perform-A will eliminate the conjunctive exercisability of some of her modal freedoms. Specifically, she will no longer be able to combine her exercising of her modal freedom-to-perform-A with her exercising of any of her modal freedoms that will be removed from her as a penalty for her performance of A. In that respect, her modal freedom is affected by her having entered into the contract. However, in any ordinary situation, the effect on her modal freedom does not consist in the elimination of her modal freedom to perform A.

4.2.14 The Rationale for an Evaluative Multiplier of 1

Continuing to ascribe to me erroneously the view that every freedom is of positive value on balance for the person who possesses that freedom, Carter and Steiner proclaim that my putative position on that matter "evidently stands in need of justification" (2022: 263). They then purport to recount my justification—for a position which I do not espouse—by quoting a passage where, in accordance with Carter's pioneering work on the topic, I am explaining the content-independent constitutive value of every freedom. What makes their discussion so mystifying is that the passage which they quote is immediately preceded in my book by a paragraph where I explicitly state that the content-independent value of any freedom can be more than offset by its content-dependent disvalue (Kramer 2003: 431). Of course, since very few freedoms are of content-dependent disvalue for the person who possesses them, the offsetting effect which I describe will be extremely rare. Still, given that I explicitly allow for it as a possibility, I am nonplused to find that Carter and Steiner take me to be denying that any such effect can ever occur.

Carter and Steiner labor under their misconception about my position on the content-dependent value of every freedom because, within my theory of liberty, no evaluative multiplier attached to any particular freedom is ever lower than 1. Carter and Steiner mistakenly presume that the evaluative multipliers are simple functions of the content-dependent values of freedoms, and they further mistakenly presume that the content-dependent values are simple functions of the values of the actions or occurrences to which the freedoms pertain. Hence, despite the many statements by me to the contrary in my 2003 book, they are under the misapprehension that I do not accept that any freedom can ever be devoid of positive content-dependent value. That misapprehension derives from a concatenation of missteps on their part.

Nevertheless, even someone who does not share Carter's and Steiner's misconceptions might wonder why the evaluative multipliers in my measurements of each person's overall freedom can never be lower than 1. That question about the multipliers is what Carter and Steiner are really seeking to address, even though they formulate it ineptly as a question about the content-dependent values of freedoms. Of course, those two questions would be equivalent if the multipliers were designed to track the content-dependent values unremittingly. They are so designed in relation to any freedom whose content-dependent value is positive, but not in relation to any freedom (an anomalous freedom) whose content-dependent value is zero or negative. Hence, the two questions are not equivalent; nonetheless, the question about the evaluative multipliers is of course interesting in its own right.

Carter and Steiner proceed as if the answer to the question about evaluative multipliers were mysterious, but what is really mysterious is their sense of perplexity. I present the rationale for my position on this matter straightforwardly in *The Quality of Freedom* (2003: 445–6). As I suggest there, the role of the evaluative multipliers does not consist in tracking comprehensively the content-dependent values of each person's freedoms. Although the multipliers do track the positive content-dependent values, they do not track the negative content-dependent values. The reason for this asymmetry is that the role of the evaluative multipliers is to enable one's measurements of the magnitude of anybody's overall liberty to take account of the augmentative contributions made by certain freedoms to that magnitude—augmentative contributions stemming from the fact that the freedoms in question are especially promotive of some of the values associated with overall liberty as a desideratum.

By taking for granted that my partly evaluative approach to the measurement of liberty has to assign negative multipliers to the extremely uncommon freedoms that are each on balance of negative content-dependent value for someone who possesses them, Carter and Steiner are presupposing that my approach must decline to assign primacy to the purely physical dimensions of each person's overall freedom. Their whole attack therefore fails to land any blows at all against my approach, which does indeed assign primacy to the physical dimensions of everyone's overall liberty by insisting that the level of any evaluative multiplier can never be lower than 1. If a multiplier were to be given a lower numerical value, the freedom associated therewith would not be counted to the full extent of its physical proportions and would perhaps be counted negatively. Such an upshot would be untenable, as Steiner has elsewhere correctly proclaimed with regard to unfreedoms: "[I]t makes no sense to say that my being prevented from doing [something] is an instance of unfreedom but, because it lacks significance, that prevention cannot be counted in estimating the extent to which I'm unfree. Instances, as was suggested, necessarily count in the computation of whatever they instantiate" (Steiner 1994: 46). Correct though this pronouncement is, Steiner draws from it an erroneous conclusion. He asserts that, because "an action's significance or eligibility [i.e., attractiveness] has no bearing on *whether* a person is free to do it . . . it cannot have any bearing on *how much* freedom he has if he is free to do it."[32] Steiner's premise in this compressed argument is solid, but his conclusion is a non sequitur. Instead of inferring that the significance or attractiveness of any particular freedom has no bearing whatsoever on the extent of that freedom's contribution to a person's overall liberty, we should infer that it never has any *diminutional* bearing on that contribution. As has been stated, every freedom or unfreedom must count at least to the full extent of its physical proportions. A qualitatively-oriented multiplier can increase the weight of a freedom or an unfreedom beyond its purely physical dimensions, but can never reduce that weight. To assume that such a multiplier can play a diminutional role is to assume that the unimportance or disvalue of a particular freedom affects the very existence of that freedom as such. Steiner is right to denounce any assumption along those lines—but he errs in thinking that his denunciation is inconsistent with a partly evaluative conception of the freedom-measuring enterprise. One should wholeheartedly endorse his insistence that "[w]e must and do distinguish between whether we have a freedom and what that freedom is worth" (1994: 48), while realizing that that insistence requires no more than the disallowance of any diminutional role for each qualitatively-oriented multiplier.

[32] Steiner 1994: 46, emphases in original. Although Steiner refers here to the attractiveness of φ-ing, I will treat his remark as if it refers instead to the content-dependent attractiveness of being free to φ.

4.2.15 Qualitative Diversity and Similarity

In the final main section of their chapter, Carter and Steiner turn their attention to my reflections on the importance of qualitative diversity among the freedoms which anyone possesses. Like nearly all other philosophers of freedom, I have maintained that—*ceteris paribus*—new liberties which enhance the diversity of a person's existing array of liberties will be greater contributors to the person's overall freedom than will new liberties that do not enhance the diversity of the existing array (2003: 463–71). Carter and Steiner do not make clear in their chapter whether they endorse that widely held position on the freedom-potentiating effect of diversity. Indeed, as I shall recount imminently, they appear quite wary of it. Nonetheless, Carter in the past has endorsed that position, for he sought to accommodate it in his account of overall freedom without using any evaluative multipliers (Carter 1999: 191–204). As I have demonstrated in the pages from my 2003 book which I have cited just above, Carter's endeavor was unsuccessful.

Carter and Steiner sound what they take to be a cautionary note about the prevailing view on the import of diversity. They write (2022: 264, emphases in original):

> Whether a set of objects, which might be used in exercising certain freedoms, *is* qualitatively more diverse than another such set, seems very much to depend upon functional judgments about those objects themselves: that is, judgments about what those objects are *for*.... Any judgment that the former set represents more diversity than the latter in any objective sense—that is, in a sense that is not relative to the purposes of a user—would appear to embrace an implausibly teleological view of inanimate objects.

To these observations the appropriate response is "So what?!" Carter and Steiner appear to think that they are proffering a deep insight here, but in fact their observations are both banal and largely misguided. In the context of measuring each person's level of overall liberty in some society, most judgments about the diversity of particular freedoms will indeed have to be reached by reference to the typical purposes of human beings in that society or by reference to the peculiar purposes of individuals therein. Nobody has ever suggested otherwise. (Whether our efforts to gauge the diversity of freedoms should be oriented toward the typical purposes of human beings in a society or instead toward the distinctive purposes of individuals therein is a question to which the answer will depend on the reasons for undertaking one's project of measuring the overall levels of freedom in that society. As Carter is well aware, the suitability of coarse-grainedness or fine-grainedness in one's measurements of those levels will hinge on such reasons.) What is misguided in this passage from Carter's and Steiner's chapter is their suggestion that their rather jejune observations about the import of purposes somehow warrant the conclusion that the diversity of freedoms is not a property "in any objective sense." Admittedly, Carter and Steiner go on to indicate that those quoted words are simply a way of reiterating their emphasis on the import of purposes. However, those words are extremely misleading—since they might be taken to imply that there are no determinate standards of correctness for judgments about diversity, or that there is no distinction between what seems to be a diverse set of freedoms and what is actually a diverse set of freedoms. Carter and Steiner encourage their readers to detect such implications, when they write that "diversity, like beauty, is often in the eye of the beholder" (2022: 264). Insofar as Carter and Steiner are intending to deny that there are any objective standards of correctness for judgments about diversity, they are going astray. They will do well to acquaint themselves with my expositions of two key distinctions in Chapter 1 of my 2007 book *Objectivity and the Rule of Law* and Chapters 2 and 3 of my 2009 book *Moral Realism as a Moral Doctrine*: the distinction between existential mind-independence and observational mind-independence, and the distinction between mind-independence and determinate correctness.

At any rate, the principal aim of Carter's and Steiner's discussion does not reside in their largely misconceived efforts to cast doubt upon the objectivity of judgments about the diversity of freedoms. Rather, their principal aim is to show that my partly evaluative approach to the measurement of the overall freedom of each person cannot adequately handle the matter of diversity. To that end, they conjure up an example in which someone—whom I shall designate as "Henry"—has received multiple copies of a book. They presume that the evaluative multiplier attached to the freedom conferred through the arrival of the first copy is 4, and that the evaluative multipliers attached to the freedoms conferred through the arrivals of the second and third copies are 3 and 2 respectively. They then confront me with an ostensible crux (2022: 266, emphases in original, footnote omitted):

> Kramer's ... conception of evaluative multipliers stipulates that any valuable freedom [that is, any freedom vested with positive content-dependent value] must have an [evaluative multiplier] greater than 1. It must be greater than 1 because, otherwise, its contribution to overall freedom would reflect only that freedom's bare physical dimensions. So the [evaluative multiplier] of that fourth copy must lie between 2 and 1. But the same is also true of the [evaluative multipliers] of the fifth, sixth, seventh, and ... *n*th acquired copies: the freedom afforded by each successively acquired copy must be of less value than its predecessor, but none can have an [evaluative multiplier] as low as 1. Hence the amount by which each would be lower would itself continuously *diminish*: the difference in value between the fifth and sixth copies would be *less* than the difference in value between the fourth and fifth copies. Each successive valuable freedom is indeed less valuable than its similar predecessor but, due to Kramer's stipulation that its value must be greater than 1, the rate at which its value diminishes must itself diminish. Paradoxically, then, the *more* similar freedoms [Henry] acquires, the *less* dissimilar their values are: the diminution of their marginal value, we might say, is itself diminishing.

Carter and Steiner here misunderstand how the effects of diversity or homogeneity are to be registered in the evaluative multipliers. Although the evaluative multiplier that is attached to the freedom conferred through the receipt of the first book will indeed be higher than the evaluative multiplier that is attached to the freedom conferred through the receipt of any subsequent copy of the book,[33] the former multiplier

[33] As I will make clear presently, I am here proceeding on the basis of a certain assumption that manifestly also underlies Carter's and Steiner's presentation of their scenario. That is, I am assuming that considerations about diversity are not dominated by any countervailing evaluative considerations.

does not remain unchanged by the arrival of the subsequent copies. When freedoms are indistinguishable both in their sizableness and in their qualitative properties, the evaluative multipliers attached to them should be the same. Thus, if each copy of the book is in the same condition as every other copy, the evaluative multiplier that is attached to the freedom conferred by the possession of each copy should be the same. Accordingly, if the considerations relating to diversity are not dominated by any countervailing evaluative considerations, the evaluative multiplier that is attached to the freedom conferred by the possession of the first book will be lowered to match the evaluative multiplier that is attached to the freedom conferred by the possession of any subsequent copy of the book. Because the latter multiplier will be lower than the initial figure for the former multiplier, that initial figure itself has to be adjusted downward to reflect the fact that the possession of the first book does not any longer play as important a role in the diversity of Henry's freedoms as it did when no other copy of the volume had been obtained. Mutual adjustments of this kind will occur at every stage of the Carter/Steiner scenario.

Of course, the effect described by Carter and Steiner can still occur, even though it will be less common and more complicated than they suppose. However, their professed sense of puzzlement about that effect is misplaced. Far from constituting a difficulty or paradox for my approach to the measurement of freedom, the occurrence of that effect in some circumstances is exactly what would be expected under my approach. By the time Henry receives (say) his fiftieth copy of the same book, the diminution in the impact of each additional copy on his overall freedom will be significantly slighter than the diminution in the impact of each additional copy after he has received only two or three printings of the book. In other words, the reason for the diminution in the rate of decline of the marginal contribution made by each copy of the book to Henry's overall freedom is that the diversity-related difference between forty-nine copies and fifty copies is considerably less significant than the diversity-related difference between two copies and three. Hence, when the effect described by Carter and Steiner is registered in my measurements of someone's overall liberty, those measurements are capturing accurately the subtlety of the ways in which the acquisition of new freedoms can affect someone's overall liberty through diversity-related considerations.

Note, by the way, that my discussion of the thought-experiment of Henry and the books has been premised on an assumption that also underlies Carter's and Steiner's meditations on the matter. That is, I have assumed that considerations pertaining to diversity are the dominant factor in determining the highness or lowness of the evaluative multipliers that are attached to the freedoms which Henry gains through the arrivals of the successive copies of the book. Though that assumption is not at all fanciful, there are many credible circumstances in which it will not be true. For example, if Henry intends to provide the copies of the book to sundry individuals and libraries as gifts, or if he is a retailer who intends to sell the copies of the volume to his customers, the diversity-related considerations that bear on the highness or lowness of the evaluative multipliers might be subordinate to other qualitative considerations that bear thereon. Typically, the content-dependent values of the freedoms gained by a retailer through his obtention of multiple copies of a best-selling book will be greater than the content-dependent values of the freedoms gained by such a person through the arrival of lone copies of multiple different books that are each only moderately popular. For a bookseller, the diversity of his or her wares is an important consideration but is often not the dominant evaluative factor.

When I introduced the import of diversity at the outset of this subsection, I included a "*ceteris paribus*" clause. My point in the preceding paragraph has simply been to indicate that that clause is often not satisfied. Carter and Steiner would of course agree with me on that point—and so I can end my lengthy replies to their lengthy chapter on a rare note of harmony!

5. On Liberal Democracy

I turn now to the chapters by Mark Reiff and Collis Tahzib, who most sustainedly focus on my 2017 book *Liberalism with Excellence.* Although I could easily also include the chapters by Christopher Kutz and Antony Duff in this section, I will classify them separately in recognition of the fact that they address more specific matters within the philosophy of liberal institutions and values. By contrast, Reiff and Tahzib concern themselves with the general character of liberal democracy.

5.1 Mark Reiff and Liberal Neutrality

I have known Reiff since he was a student in the LLM program at Cambridge during the 1998–99 academic year. Having practiced law for a decade-and-a-half before returning to academia, he initially stood out because he was quite a bit older than most of his fellow students. However, he quickly stood out additionally because of the acuity of his questions in the lectures and because of his outstanding results on the examinations. He went on to become an equally impressive PhD student, as he completed a top-notch dissertation comfortably within three years while playing a major role in the philosophical life of Cambridge. He then embarked on a career of distinguished scholarship which continues to this day. I am grateful to him for contributing a chapter to this collection.

Near the outset of his chapter, Reiff suggests that the aspirational perfectionism which I expound in *Liberalism with Excellence* "does not make a perfectionist exception to the usual liberal requirement of government neutrality; it simply relies on a more nuanced and precise conception of how the principle of neutrality should be understood by liberals" (2022: 272-3). There is a clear sense in which Reiff is correct on this point. As I have sought to emphasize in Chapter 3 of *Liberalism with Excellence*, my critique of liberal neutralism arrives at the conclusion that certain positions in debates over foundational questions of justice are "neutral after all" (2017b: 145–6). That is, after maintaining at length that the efforts of liberal neutralists to abide by the constraints of public reason will have left them wholly unable to come to grips with the debates which I have just mentioned, I then contend that the neutralists can nonetheless fulfill the requirement of neutrality by providing arguments for the correct answers to the questions at issue in those debates. In other words, once the requirement of neutrality is clearly differentiated from the unsatisfiable constraints of public reason, that requirement is itself satisfiable. Furthermore, because the pursuit of societal excellence is connected within aspirational perfectionism to the promotion of a primary natural good—the good of warranted self-respect—the deliberations necessary for the adoption and implementation of that pursuit can themselves be in keeping with the requirement of neutrality. Thus, despite all the critiques of Rawls and of other liberal neutralists in the first few chapters of *Liberalism with Excellence*, the book is Rawlsian in some key respects. In its opening chapter, I remark saliently on the dividedness of the volume as both Rawlsian and anti-Rawlsian (2017b: 30–3). By separating the best aspects of Rawlsianism from the constraints of public reason and more broadly from contractualism, *Liberalism with Excellence* does indeed endeavor to uphold the aims of neutralists through the purification or refinement of those aims. On that point, Reiff and I are in agreement. As will become apparent in these brief replies, he and I also concur on some other matters; but I will concentrate here on some significant points of disagreement.

5.1.1 Political Classifications and Popularity

I begin with a couple of minor points that surface quite early in Reiff's chapter. While Reiff is contemplating a medley of mostly repellent theories which he designates as "hard perfectionism," he writes: "Other labels, such as populism, nationalism, fascism, totalitarianism, authoritarianism, and so on, are often used to describe these views, but each of these labels is misleading in important ways and in any event none of them (with the possible exception of populism) can be used to describe a family of views that ranges from far left to far right" (2022: 275). Though Reiff may be correct about the potential misleadingness of the various designations which he broaches, he is decidedly incorrect in submitting that none of those designations apart from "populism" is commonly employed to cover a family of views ranging from the hard left to the hard right. With the partial exception of "fascism," each of the specified labels is in fact applicable both to regimes of the hard left and to regimes of the far right. "Fascism" is of course applied mainly to far-right regimes and parties, but it is sometimes affixed—in scholarly contexts, rather than simply as a term of abuse—to regimes that are on the left of the political spectrum (Seton-Watson 1966). It has been applied to Hugo Chavez's period of rule in Venezuela and to Fidel Castro's reign in Cuba, and even more often it is applied to Juan Peron's regime in Argentina.[34] In any event, each of the other labels listed by Reiff is applicable routinely to the hard left and the hard right alike. For example, sentiments accurately describable as "nationalism" are exploited by numerous hard-left regimes, ranging from Castro's Cuba to the Khmer Rouge in Cambodia to the contemporary Chinese dictatorship under Xi Jinping.

Similarly mistaken is the next sentence in Reiff's chapter: "['Populism'], in turn, is misleading because populists are rarely popular (especially on the right) outside a particular hard perfectionist segment of the polity" (2022: 275). Were Reiff's pronouncement here true, it would render inexplicable the fact that populist governments have managed to come to power through elections in quite a number of European and South American countries during recent decades. Admittedly, the populist candidate

[34] Lewis 1980; Payne 1980: 172–5. Though Peron's ideology is not easily locatable on the political spectrum, it is overall more readily identifiable as hard-left than as hard-right.

Donald Trump won his single term as President of the United States in 2016 on the basis of a minority of the popular vote. However, the very fact that Trump received more than 74 million votes when he unsuccessfully ran for re-election in 2020 is indicative of the falsity of Reiff's pronouncement.

5.1.2 Inveighing Against Inexistent Opponents

Perhaps the most disconcerting feature of Reiff's chapter, especially in the first half thereof, is that it frequently rails against positions which have never been espoused by anyone. For example, while purporting to grapple with liberal neutralism, Reiff feels a need to rebut the notion that the principle of neutrality among reasonable conceptions of the good is the basis for civil rights such as the right not to be denied service in a restaurant because of one's race or religion or ethnicity. He asserts that "the fact that the principle of neutrality is not available as a defense to a claim of right does not mean it provides a basis for the recognition of the right itself. So I think that this way of thinking about the role of the principle of neutrality is a mistake" (2022: 277). Reiff is correct in contending that such an understanding of the principle of neutrality would be mistaken—but its palpable mistakenness is presumably why nobody adheres to such an understanding of that principle. Rawlsians and other neutralists do not endeavor to ground civil rights on the principle of neutrality; rather, they ground such rights on the deeper premise of the free and equal status of persons or on the deeper premise that every person is to be treated with equal concern and respect. By the reckoning of Rawlsians and Dworkinians and other liberal neutralists, either of those deeper premises is the foundation of the principle of neutrality as well as of civil rights like the one which Reiff discusses. Far from correcting the liberal neutralists on this point, I am here reporting how they perceive the matter. They are not in need of Reiff's scolding.

Equally surprising is Reiff's suggestion that liberal neutralists will be inclined to countenance a legal prohibition on murder because "the prohibition ... is not a violation of the principle of neutrality even though it expresses disfavor for the conception of the good the murderer embraces, for the pursuit of that conception also interferes with the pursuit of a wide variety of other conceptions of the good, a neutral reason" (2022: 277-8). The only things which Reiff cites at this juncture are some irrelevant pages from Rawls and some pages from Nigel Simmonds, who rightly indicates that any conception of liberal neutrality along the lines broached in the quotation here from Reiff is definitely not what liberal neutralists have propounded (Simmonds 2008: 14–15). Simmonds is quite correct, for no liberal neutralist has ever sought to justify a prohibition on murder in the weird manner which Reiff posits and criticizes. Instead, every liberal neutralist would endorse such a prohibition because it is directed against a mode of conduct that is grossly in violation of the status of persons as free and equal. Although the prohibition obviously disfavors the conception of the good pursued by a murderer, its non-neutrality in that respect is entirely unproblematic by the reckoning of any liberal neutralist—since the conception of the good pursued by a murderer is egregiously unreasonable and is therefore not within the ambit of the principle of neutrality. Thus, once again Reiff is tilting at windmills.

Some of Reiff's harshest strictures are reserved for yet another position that has never been embraced by anyone. Noting that some liberal neutralists such as Rawls have limited the requirement of neutrality to constitutional essentials and basic matters of justice, Reiff ponders a version of liberalism that would invert such a limitation by excluding constitutional essentials and basic matters of justice from a requirement of neutrality that would apply only to ordinary matters of public policy. He avows that "I do not think anyone expressly admits to taking this view" (2022: 289), but even that avowal is inadequate—for the inversion of Rawls's limitation on the scope of his neutralism would be discountenanced by every liberal neutralist as bizarre and perverse. Nevertheless, Reiff inveighs against it at some length (2022: 289-90). I do not fathom how such animadversions are supposed to contribute to the debates over liberalism and neutrality.

5.1.3 Misunderstandings of Liberal Neutralism

Closely related to the erecting and toppling of straw men in the first half of Reiff's chapter is his tendency to misconstrue the ideas of liberal neutralists. On the one hand, Reiff argues in favor of dissevering the constraints of public reason from the requirement of neutrality; near the outset of section 5.1 above, I have reaffirmed my insistence on just such a distinction. On the other hand, I reject Reiff's approach to drawing that distinction—because his approach rests on a number of misstatements about the Rawlsian doctrine of public reason. He writes (2022: 287):

> But embracing the idea of public reason is a long way from saying that the government cannot assist in the pursuit of forms of excellence the good of which some people can reasonably deny. This is not what the requirement of public reason could possibly mean, whether it is seen as part of the principle of neutrality or free-standing. In a liberal society, which by definition is characterized by reasonable pluralism about the good, anything that has a reasonable justification will almost always also be subject to reasonable objections. If neutrality precluded government from acting in these cases, then government could do nothing, or hardly anything. The principle of neutrality would be paralytic.

Reiff in this passage swerves from talking about the doctrine of public reason to talking about the requirement of neutrality, and it is indeed that latter requirement on which he is really concentrating. Because he wants to maintain that his own position on the promotion of excellence by a system of governance is in accordance with the requirement of neutrality, he feels impelled to reject that requirement as it is understood by virtually all liberal neutralists. Although the opening sentence in the quoted passage does not encapsulate the constraint of public reason, it does accurately encapsulate the requirement of neutrality (provided that "cannot" is construed as "cannot legitimately"). Reiff insists that the thesis articulated in that sentence could not possibly be what liberal neutralists have in mind, but it is indeed what they have in mind. He errs in contending that the principle of neutrality so understood would be inconsistent with everything or virtually everything that might be done by a system of governance, for that principle does not debar such a system from acting in furtherance of the demands of justice.

Rawlsians and other neutralists hold that every system of governance is morally obligated to remain neutral among all reasonable conceptions of the good, where the phrase "conceptions of the good" refers to visions of what is worthwhile in life beyond the fulfillment of any demands of justice. In effect, the principle of neutrality disallows any actions by a system of governance that are not undertaken for the purpose of satisfying the demands of justice or for the purpose of securing the provision of public goods. Since many actions that can be performed by a system of governance will be for either of the purposes just mentioned, many governmental actions can be fully in keeping with the requirement of neutrality even if people reasonably contest them. Neutralists standardly distinguish between disagreements among proponents of reasonable conceptions of the good and disagreements among proponents of reasonable conceptions of justice. Whereas a system of governance should strive to refrain from entering into the former disagreements, it will have to enter into the latter disagreements in order to address matters of justice at all. So the liberal neutralists affirm (Quong 2011: 192–220). Of course, Reiff might be inclined to impugn such a distinction, but he does not do so in his chapter. Instead, he writes as if the absence of any such distinction can be taken for granted or as if liberal neutralists have never sought to draw it. His objurgation of liberal neutralists for championing a requirement that supposedly excludes nearly all governmental endeavors is therefore unsustainable.

That mistake by Reiff crops up again slightly later in his chapter, when he asks his readers to "consider whether the claim that affording everyone a veto over how their tax dollars can be used is a reasonable position. For it seems clear that government could not possibly function if it gave each individual taxpayer a veto over how their tax money is spent across innumerable permissible activities" (2022: 288). He goes on to declare: "The principle of neutrality is designed to regulate what liberal government can do within the set of reasonable options it could feasibly pursue, not to be a tool for making it so government cannot do anything to which anyone reasonably objects, for this would make it impossible for government to function in a pluralistic society" (2022: 288). All of these assertions by Reiff about the paralyzing impact of liberal neutralism are rooted in his inattentiveness to the distinction between debates over matters of justice and debates over policies that are not matters of justice. That distinction is central to liberal neutralism—as I have remarked in the last paragraph above—yet Reiff pays no heed to it as he insists that the principle of neutrality, understood as neutralists themselves understand it, would disallow all governmental measures on matters of justice as well as on policies that are not matters of justice.

Reiff's failure to come to grips with the actualities of liberal neutralism is evident also in the following passage: "Public reason is meant to require that unreasonable arguments not be offered in favor of a position in public discourse and debate—not that there be no reasonable arguments *against* that position. Not being able to reasonably reject an argument does not mean that one has to accept it or be unreasonable, for then reasonable pluralism could not exist" (2022: 287, emphasis in original). Excluded by the constraint of public reason are not only arguments with premises and conclusions that are unreasonable, but also arguments with reasonable premises and conclusions that would nonetheless be unreasonable if marshaled in public-policy debates where other disputants reasonably object to those premises and conclusions. Such arguments would be proffered in support of policies that favor some reasonable conception(s) of the good over others, where no requirements of justice are at stake. In such contexts, the fact that other disputants reasonably reject the premises and conclusions of one's arguments is sufficient—in the eyes of liberal neutralists—to render morally illegitimate the basing of any governmental policies on those arguments. By the reckoning of Rawlsian neutralists, any deviations from this constraint of public reason on the part of citizens or on the part of a system of governance would show disrespect for the people whose reasonable objections would thereby be flouted.

5.1.4 Consequentialism versus Deontology

When Reiff unveils his own conception of the principle of neutrality, it turns out to be a strongly consequentialist prescription for the distribution of largesse to activities such as sports, culture, and the arts. That largesse is to be distributed to the sundry activities in proportion to the levels of support for them in the community at large. Although numerous questions could be raised about the implementation of such a proposal, I shall concentrate here instead on its consequentialist tenor.

Reiff's first disconcerting comment on the topic occurs halfway through his chapter, when his emphasis on balancing comes to the fore: "[B]alancing does indeed seem to occur in not only interest versus interest contests but in right versus interest contests and right versus right contests as well, where it takes place in the context of defining more precisely the scope of the right or rights involved" (2022: 284). The balancing of competing interests is of course the hallmark of consequentialism, but Reiff goes astray in submitting that the task of defining more precisely the contours of certain rights is itself an exercise in balancing. Such a task consists in specifying more precisely when the wrong-making features of some mode of conduct are present and when they are absent. It does not consist in weighing the gravity of those features in order to ascertain whether the avoidance of them is overridden by competing considerations that are weightier. When someone thinks that the endeavor of defining more precisely the contours of deontological rights is a matter of balancing, he or she has embraced a consequentialist understanding—a distortive understanding—of rights.

Considerably worse is a somewhat later passage, which should be quoted here in full (2022: 285-6, emphasis in original, footnote omitted):

> But even when claims of right are presented, balancing occurs. While balancing is the main event for those employing some form of consequentialist moral reasoning, those employing some form of deontological moral reasoning have to do this too. They just do it in the context of more precisely defining the scope of the right or rights at issue, for only if what appears to be a conflict between one right and another or a right and a competing interest is an actual conflict, and not one that can be resolved by coming to a better understanding of the scope of the rights involved, would winner-take-all apply. Indeed, if some sort of balancing was not part of the process of resolving borderline disputes about the scope of rights, it is unclear how these disputes could possibly be resolved. It is simply part of the process by which people think. So the kind of balancing or weighing up process that I am referring to here is always required. The distinction between consequentialist and deontological moral reasoning only matters with regard to where this occurs, not whether. The form of moral reasoning employed determines whether balancing *is* the decision procedure, or merely part of the process of determining what the precise conflict at issue is and therefore what is to be decided, after which the conflict is then resolved according to

> a much more straightforward decision procedure than balancing (rights are absolute and therefore cannot conflict and rights always prevail over competing interests).

While this passage is marred by the consequentialist misconception at which I have bridled in my preceding paragraph—the misconception about the delimitation or precisification of the contours of rights—it adds some further errors. On the one hand, Reiff is correct in contending that the contours of rights are sometimes in need of precisification by legal-governmental officials who have to reach decisions in concrete cases. For example, a court or some other decision-maker may have to judge whether a certain instance of communicative conduct is open to being legally proscribed as an act of inciting some serious wrongdoing or whether it instead is an act of advocating some repugnant ideas and is thus exempt from legal proscription. (Because the distinction between incitement and advocacy is vague in the philosophically technical sense, a decision-maker might be warranted in concluding that there is no determinately correct answer to the question just broached—in which event the case should be decided in favor of the party whose communicative liberties are at stake.) On the other hand, Reiff goes amiss in the passage above when he asserts that "if some sort of balancing was not part of the process of resolving borderline disputes about the scope of rights, it is unclear how these disputes could possibly be resolved." As I have already sought to stress, the precisification of the contours of a deontological right is not an exercise in balancing. It is not an effort to curtail or adjust the contours of the right in order to accommodate other desiderata. Rather, it is an effort to specify more precisely the sorts of circumstances in which the factors that account for the all-or-nothing operativeness of the right are present, and the sorts of circumstances in which those factors are absent. Whenever the relevant factors are present, the right is fully operative; if the right is a claim-right, any contravention of it will give rise to remedial obligations.

Even more important, an endeavor to resolve disputes about the contours of claim-rights may lead to the conclusion that the claim-rights under scrutiny are in conflict because their correlative duties are in conflict. When someone is under a duty to φ and is simultaneously under a duty not to φ, the claim-rights correlative to those duties are obviously in conflict as well. Given the existence of that conflict in which the contents of the claim-rights are contradictories, one and only one of those claim-rights will be fulfilled in any given context. Hence, an endeavor to resolve a dispute about those claim-rights will have to prescribe a suitable remedy for the breaching of whichever claim-right has gone unfulfilled.

At the end of the passage above, Reiff asserts that "rights are absolute and therefore cannot conflict." On the contrary, deontological claim-rights can and sometimes do conflict with other claim-rights partly because they are absolute. As I have explained elsewhere (2014: 8–9; 2016; 2017b: 255–6; 2019c; 2021: 2–3), deontological moral prohibitions on various modes of conduct are absolute in that they are binding always and everywhere. There are no exceptions to their bindingness. Far from precluding the possibility of conflicts with other claim-rights, the exceptionlessness of the claim-rights that correlate with the duties imposed by deontological prohibitions is promotive of the occurrence of such conflicts. Precisely because a deontological claim-right CR is insusceptible to being canceled or suspended when there simultaneously exists a claim-right with a contradictory or contrary content, conflicts between CR and other claim-rights can occur and persist. When a conflict of that kind does occur, at least one of the conflicting claim-rights will have been transgressed.[35] Consequently, remedial obligations will have been engendered by any such situation.

Now, some readers might think that I am being unfair to Reiff by taking exception to his misrepresentations of deontological phenomena in consequentialist terms. After all, in his cogitations on the fostering of various forms of excellence, he is clearly envisioning a situation in which the decisions to be made are not about the effectuation of deontological claim-rights and duties. He is talking instead about the determinations that are to be reached by a system of governance which has allotted some funding for subventions that will support activities and undertakings in which excellence can be achieved. He believes that, so long as the subventions are apportioned in line with the popularity of those activities and undertakings, the distribution of such funding will be in accordance with the principle of liberal neutrality. He construes the principle of neutrality as a consequentialist tenet that calls for a patterned distribution of resources. Hence, some readers might suppose, I am being unfair to Reiff when I criticize him for proceeding from a consequentialist perspective as he mulls over the matters which he is addressing. Those readers could draw upon some remarks by Reiff himself near the midpoint of his chapter (2022: 283-4):

> [S]upport of excellence in sport, culture, and the arts does not typically raise questions of commutative justice. Absent unusual circumstances, no one has an individual right to support from the government for their favored form of excellence, and it violates no one's individual right to provide it. The questions such support raises are accordingly purely distributive—that is, these questions are simply about how government should allocate the burdens and benefits of the collection and application of the various resources at its command within the scope of what commutative justice allows.

Any such worry about unfairness to Reiff is baseless, however, for the gravamen of my complaint about his chapter is exactly that he transmogrifies the deontological principle of neutrality into a consequentialist principle. By the reckoning of liberal neutralists, the principle of neutrality among reasonable conceptions of the good—a principle that is a corollary of the fundamental premise about the status of persons as free and equal—is generative of deontological restrictions on the ends and means that can permissibly be chosen by any system of governance in its operations. For reasons which I have impugned in sections 5.1.2 and 5.1.3 above, Reiff dismisses the principle of neutrality as it is understood by liberal neutralists. He then replaces it with a consequentialist principle of neutrality that prescribes the patterned distribution of resources which he commends. He thus inclines himself, in the passage just quoted, to affirm a proposition which the liberal neutralists would deny: namely, the proposition that the bestowal of governmental largesse which he envisages is such that "it violates no one's individual right to provide it." Instead of trying to show that the bestowal of the governmental subventions is needed for satisfying some requirements of justice,

[35] For some much more ample discussions of moral conflicts, see Kramer 2014: 1–19; 2016; 2019c: 10–12; 2021: 4–5.

he presumes that those subventions can permissibly be conferred without being necessary for the satisfaction of such requirements—since no one's individual rights are at stake. With his transmutation of a deontological principle into a consequentialist guideline in this fashion, Reiff is endeavoring to direct liberalism down a profoundly unsatisfactory path.

5.2 Collis Tahzib and Edificatory Perfectionism

Having known Tahzib for the past few years, I admire his philosophical acuity and agility, and I am pleased that he has contributed such a stimulating essay to this collection. Striving to defend edificatory perfectionism against some of the objections to it which I advance in the middle chapters of my *Liberalism with Excellence*, he raises several challenging points to which I will respond here. I should begin, however, by mentioning that my critique of the quidnunc mentality is extended and elucidated in Chapter 4 of my 2021 book *Freedom of Expression as Self-Restraint*. I will here occasionally draw on my ruminations in that chapter. Tahzib did not have access to my 2021 book while he was writing his chapter—though he has had access, and has availed himself of his access, to my 2017 article "On Political Morality and Warranted Self-Respect"—but I am not being unfair to him, because my recent reflections on the dynamic of overweeningness and demeaningness are elaborations of the ideas presented in *Liberalism with Excellence*.

5.2.1 A Public/Private Distinction

Let us start with quite a small point. After a careful exposition of one main strand in my critique of edificatory perfectionism, Tahzib queries whether the outlook most plausibly attributable to the officials in an edificatory-perfectionist system of governance—the outlook which I designate as the "quidnunc mentality"—is really self-abasing. He does so with the following rhetorical question (2022: 303, emphasis in original): "[D]oes an individual who feels more successful when he manages to persuade his neighbor or his colleague to adopt a healthier, less calorific diet really thereby *abase* himself?" As is to be expected with a rhetorical question, the answer thereto is negative in application to any ordinary circumstances. However, that negative answer is not damaging at all for my critique of edificatory perfectionism.

As I have always readily allowed (2017b: 288), some attitudes or courses of conduct that would not be officiously intrusive among close friends or neighbors or colleagues are nonetheless both presumptuous and degrading when they are adopted by the functionaries in a system of governance. My critique of the quidnunc mentality is very much a contribution to political philosophy—with a focus on principles of political morality—rather than a contribution to the philosophy of interpersonal relationships among intimates. To be sure, as my example of the meddlesome village busybody suggests, my analysis of the overweeningness and demeaningness of the quidnunc mentality does carry over to some extent into the ethics of the relationships among individuals. However, its implications for the ethics of interactions among *intimates* are very limited. Though some degree of opacity for each person in ties of friendship or kinship is essential, modes of interaction that involve high degrees of mutual identification can be entirely unexceptionable in the presence of such ties even though those modes of interaction would be starkly improper when pursued by governmental functionaries in their dealings with the citizenry. Hence, the negative answer to Tahzib's rhetorical question (in application to ordinary circumstances) does not cast doubt upon the correctness of my strictures against the sway of a quidnunc mentality among governmental officials.

5.2.2 The Matter of Permissibility

Tahzib next comments warily on my claims that the quidnunc mentality which suffuses any edificatory-perfectionist policies of a system of governance is such that it undermines the moral permissibility of those policies. "[O]ne might wonder how the attitudes of self-aggrandizement and self-abasement are relevant to permissibility as opposed to character evaluation" (2022: 303). The full answer to this question is given by my overall account of the ways in which the moral bearings of a system of governance affect the levels of self-respect that are warranted for the citizens over whom the system presides. I discuss those ways at some length in Chapter 8 of *Liberalism with Excellence*, and they are explored at even greater length in Chapter 4 of my recent book on freedom of expression (2017b: 368–73; 2021: 139–59). I obviously cannot here fully recapitulate my expositions of the connections between the character of a system of governance and the warranted self-respect of citizens, but a few brief remarks are in order.

The paramount moral responsibility of every system of governance is to bring about the political and economic and social conditions under which everyone within the jurisdiction of the system can be warranted in feeling a strong level of self-respect. Of key importance in the fulfillment of that responsibility is the tenor of the system of governance itself. When such a system adheres to the constraints imposed upon it by the principles of liberal democracy (including the principle of freedom of expression), and when it sustains a robust ethos of liberal-democratic values among the members of the public, every such member who is generally law-abiding can warrantedly take pride in the tenor of the system and the robustness of the ethos as sterling collective accomplishments. As a source of pride in this fashion, a system of governance bolsters the levels of self-respect that are warranted for the generally law-abiding people within the society ruled by the system. For some of the people in that society, this bolstering of those levels is crucial as one of the conditions under which each of them can be warranted in harboring a sturdy sense of self-esteem. Consequently, the compliance of a system of governance with the modes of self-restraint required of it by the principles of liberal democracy is partly but indispensably constitutive of its fulfillment of the paramount moral responsibility that is incumbent upon it. Deviations from those modes of self-restraint detract from the fulfillment of that responsibility, and are thus morally impermissible rather than merely undesirable or suboptimal.

Obviously, the skimpy synopsis presented here is only the barest sketch of my critique of the quidnunc mentality that permeates edificatory perfectionism. This synopsis consists of assertions rather than of any full-blown arguments. However, I have supplied the argumentation in *Liberalism with Excellence* and *Freedom of Expression as Self-Restraint* and "On Political Morality and Warranted Self-Respect" (and I shall supply further argumentation in some of my future books, especially *A Stoical Theory of Justice*). I have not been endeavoring in this subsection to dispel Tahzib's wariness through the provision of a thorough justification of my claims about the moral impermissibility of edificatory-perfectionist policies. Rather, I have merely been pointing out that such a justification would encompass my whole critique of those policies and of the outlook that impels them.

5.2.3 The Matter of Absoluteness Differentiated from the Matter of Stringency

Tahzib introduces some outright confusion when he writes as follows: "[E]ven if self-aggrandizement and self-abasement are relevant to permissibility, it is unclear why these vices are *so* great—and why manifesting them is *so* wrong—that they could form the basis of a deontological prohibition of the particularly stringent kind Kramer seeks. Even if it is *ordinarily* impermissible to be self-aggrandizing and self-abasing, that is, these traits are presumably all-things-considered permissible when something more important is at stake" (2022: 303, emphasis in original). As I have already observed in section 5.1.4 of my rejoinders to Reiff above—and in the books of mine which I cite there—the absoluteness of a deontological moral principle consists in its exceptionlessness. Such a principle is morally binding always and everywhere. Tahzib errs when he conflates the matter of absoluteness or exceptionlessness with the matter of stringency.

Indeed, in the books which I have cited in my ripostes to Reiff, I have differentiated between weak absoluteness and strong absoluteness precisely in order to separate the matter of exceptionlessness from the matter of stringency. Whereas a weakly absolute moral principle is always and everywhere binding, a strongly absolute moral principle is not only binding always and everywhere but is also more stringent than any moral requirements that might come into conflict with it. As I have also emphasized in the cited books, including *Liberalism with Excellence* (2017b: 255–6) on which Tahzib concentrates, my ascriptions of absoluteness to the moral principles which I invoke against the quidnunc mentality of edificatory perfectionism are ascriptions of weak absoluteness rather than of strong absoluteness. I am therefore perplexed by Tahzib's running together of the distinct properties of exceptionlessness and stringency.

Tahzib stumbles further in the latest passage from his chapter by presuming that a conflict between moral duties will result in the cancellation or suspension of one of those duties. As I have already underscored in section 5.1.4 of my replies to Reiff and in the previous writings of mine which I cite at note 35 above, the upshot of a moral conflict is not the cancellation or suspension of one of the clashing duties. Rather, one of those duties is fulfilled while the other one is transgressed; the transgression gives rise to remedial obligations. Although the duty that is contravened may well be less stringent than the duty that is fulfilled, its lower degree of stringency does not result in its being canceled or suspended. Instead, the lower degree of stringency bears on the onerousness or lightness of the remedial obligations that are generated by the violation of the duty.

Of course, I am not denying that some situations which appear on first inspection to comprise certain moral duties are such that they turn out not to comprise those moral duties when all things have been considered. Such ostensible moral duties are merely *prima facie* and are thus not genuine moral duties (Kramer 2014: 2–4). However, Tahzib in the quoted passage is not talking about states of affairs in which the initial appearances of moral duties turn out to be unfounded. Rather, he is talking about states of affairs in which certain moral duties come into conflict with some more stringent moral duties and are supposedly thereby negated or suspended. As I have sought to emphasize in my sundry writings on moral conflicts, any such depiction of the upshot of a moral conflict is mistaken. A moral duty is never deprived of its reality or continued existence by the sheer fact that it is in conflict with some other moral requirement(s).

5.2.4 Collective Intentions and Outlooks

Tahzib next expresses some unease about my ascribing of intentions or outlooks to legislative bodies and other collectivities. He backs up his unease by quoting a characteristically overconfident pronouncement from Jeremy Waldron on the matter. I am rather puzzled by this short portion of Tahzib's chapter, since in *Liberalism with Excellence* I quite lengthily explain why intentions or purposes or outlooks can aptly be attributed to collectivities and to the products of collective processes of decision-making (2017b: 75–87, 269–70). I there cite some of the many other writings by philosophers and legal scholars on the ascription of intentions to laws and legislatures. Furthermore, as Tahzib is very likely aware, there have been numerous additional germane publications by philosophers on the existence of group agency and intentions.[36]

Thus, I am unmoved by the statement from Waldron, whose meditations on the topic are concerned to establish that there is no legislative or collective intention that is a simple function of the intentions of individuals. Since I have always accepted and indeed stressed that the intentions or purposes correctly imputable to laws are not aggregates or other functions of the intentions of individuals, Waldron's arguments are entirely undamaging to my account of the purposes of laws and to my account of the quidnunc mentality that imbues the policies of edificatory perfectionism. As I have proclaimed in *Liberalism with Excellence* and elsewhere, my ascribing of purposes to laws and policies is not an exercise in mind-reading. It is instead an exercise in pinning down the values which the laws or policies are designed to realize or the perceived problems which the laws or policies are designed to address.

5.2.5 Self-Abasement and Self-Aggrandizement

Tahzib's final preliminary challenge is presented as follows (2022: 304, footnote omitted): "[I]t is unclear that self-aggrandizement and self-abasement have the same moral status when understood as generalized supervenient properties imputed to a collective 'self' as they do when understood as actual psychological character flaws of a village busybody. Given that state attitudes are not at all like individual attitudes, is it really plausible to suppose that they are deeply morally significant in the way that individual attitudes and intentions are sometimes thought to be?" It is not clear to me what work is being done by the adverb "deeply" in the closing sentence of this quotation, but the answer to the question in that sentence is straightforwardly affirmative. Self-abasingness and self-aggrandizement are especially problematic when evinced by a system of governance, because those properties affect far more people than are

[36] For a few of the contributions to the philosophical literature on these matters, see Bacharach 2006; Gilbert 1989; 2000; 2014; List and Pettit 2011; Tuomela 1995; 2002; 2007; 2013.

affected by self-abasingness and self-aggrandizement on the part of any individual(s). In section 5.2.2 above, I have indicated one of the foremost ways in which the self-abasingness and self-aggrandizement of such a system detrimentally affect the citizenry as a whole. By deviating from the ethical strength of a country where the constraints imposed by the principles of liberal democracy are robustly upheld, an edificatory-perfectionist system of governance lowers the level of self-respect that is warranted for each person within its jurisdiction.

In short, like the other preliminary queries which Tahzib broaches, this latest query is baseless. Since the unfoundedness of each of those preliminary challenges is evident from *Liberalism with Excellence* and from some of my other books, the inclusion of those challenges in Tahzib's chapter is rather irksome. Still, with his preliminary misgivings out of the way, I can move on to his main defense of edificatory perfectionism.

5.2.6 The Charge of Begging the Question

Having put aside his opening worries, Tahzib proceeds to the accusation that I beg the question against edificatory perfectionists in my critique of the officiousness of the justifications which they provide for the policies that are commended by them. Now, even if the charge of begging the question were correct, it would not necessarily be damaging. Most arguments beg the question against sundry opposing arguments in one way or another, and thus the pivotal point to be ascertained is whether a specific way of begging the question is vicious or not. For example, suppose that someone endorses the view—often associated with Thales of Miletus—that everything in the world derives ultimately from water. An opponent of such a view would do well to contest it by adverting to any number of things in the universe that do not derive from water, and by explaining why countless components of the universe cannot possibly have originated from water. Arguments along these lines would of course be question-begging, in that they would presuppose the falsity of the Thalesian or quasi-Thalesian doctrine which they are oppugning. Nonetheless, their begging of the question is not a vice; rather, the vice of dogmatic circularity is properly ascribable to the quasi-Thalesian doctrine and its proponents.

Thus, even if Tahzib were correct in asserting that I beg the question against edificatory perfectionists, he would have to show that the vice of dogmatic circularity is properly imputable to me rather than to himself and his fellow quidnuncs. He has shown no such thing, or so I shall argue here. Moreover, I shall maintain that there is a clear-cut sense in which my critique of edificatory perfectionism does not beg the question against those quidnuncs. Before I launch into these arguments, however, I should clarify what is at issue by accentuating what is not at issue.

5.2.6.1 Points of convergence

As I have stated at several junctures in *Liberalism with Excellence*, the deep division between edificatory perfectionism and aspirational perfectionism is accompanied by some notable points of convergence. Some of those points pertain to the sorts of policies that are advocated by perfectionists of both kinds (Kramer 2017b: 34). Although the aims and justifications of those policies are markedly different between the two types of perfectionism, the policies themselves—involving subsidies for the arts and sports and academia, for example—are quite often broadly similar.

An even more important point of convergence is that perfectionists of all stripes, edificatory and aspirational alike, reject the insistence by Rawlsians on the constraints of public reason and on the whole apparatus of contractualism. In the opening portion of my rejoinders to Reiff in section 5.1, I have already referred to my strictures in *Liberalism with Excellence* against the limitations envisaged by Rawlsians in their cleaving to the notion of public reason. My strictures are focused partly on the impossibility of abiding by those limitations in debates over foundational matters of justice such as abortion, and partly on the inconsistency between those limitations and the deliberations that are essential for implementing the prescriptions of aspirational perfectionism. As for the apparatus of contractualism from which the Rawlsians derive their doctrine of public reason, I have concentrated in *Moral Realism as a Moral Doctrine* on the redundancy of that apparatus and on its inconsistency with moral realism (2009: 67–9).

When I reject contractualism and the constraints of public reason, I can obviously join forces with edificatory perfectionists who similarly reject those aspects of Rawlsian neutralism. Although my challenges to neutralism are far from the same as the challenges pressed by edificatory perfectionists, there are clear overlaps between them, and there is room for collaboration. Some of the most sophisticated edificatory perfectionists, such as Steven Wall, have much to say that is valuable in response to liberal neutralism.

What is more, aspirational perfectionists and edificatory perfectionists can readily agree that there are determinately correct answers to sundry questions about the goodness of various pursuits and modes of life. Such matters of ethics are predominantly objective rather than predominantly subjective. Of course, while agreeing that these matters of ethical evaluation are predominantly objective, perfectionists of various stripes will differ considerably in their answers to ethical questions. As I have remarked in *Liberalism with Excellence* (2017b: 36), most though not all edificatory perfectionists are consequentialists in their ethical outlooks. By contrast, aspirational perfectionism is a strongly deontological moral doctrine. Notwithstanding, the objectivity of ethics is something on which the perfectionists in the two rival camps converge. To be sure, that point of convergence does not in itself sharply distinguish the perfectionists from most of the liberal neutralists. Although some neutralists embrace skepticism about the existence or knowability of determinately correct answers to questions concerning the goodness of multifarious ways of life, most do not (Kramer 2017b: 11–12). Still, although most liberal neutralists do not subscribe to any skepticism of that kind, an affirmation of the objectivity of the answers to those questions about the goodness of ways of life is not integral to their neutralism in the way in which such an affirmation is integral to most versions of perfectionism. (Worth acknowledging here also is that not all liberal neutralists are contractualists. Central though contractualism is to Rawlsianism, it has not won the favor of some other neutralists such as Dworkin. Hence, even the repudiation of contractualism does not differentiate the perfectionists from the neutralists in any blanket fashion. What bears the principal load in differentiating between them is the fact that perfectionists reject the limitations imposed by the Rawlsian doctrine of public reason and by any comparable neutralist restriction on the terms of public disputation.)

One further point of convergence between edificatory perfectionism and aspirational perfectionism is that most contemporary proponents of the former and all contemporary proponents of the latter are pluralists in two senses which I have recounted elsewhere (2017b: 35). Ethical pluralism is the thesis that multiple inconsistent ways of life are incommensurably or equally good, while political pluralism is the thesis that governmental institutions should permit and encourage the pursuit of heterogeneous ways of life by citizens. Most edificatory perfectionists and all aspirational perfectionists in the present day embrace both of these types of pluralism. Of course, in so doing, they are not endorsing an anything-goes doctrine that would reek of skepticism. The equal or incommensurable goodness of myriad incompatible ways of life is an objective fact, and the range of those estimable ways of life is hardly all-encompassing. Still, notwithstanding that perfectionists rightly oppose ethical skepticism by maintaining that some modes of life are objectively inferior to others, most edificatory perfectionists and all aspirational perfectionists are sufficiently broad-minded to accept that human beings can thrive along numerous paths.

5.2.6.2 Viciously dogmatic circularity?

Tahzib points out that Raz and Wall have furnished some arguments in support of their assertions about the moral duties that are incumbent on systems of governance to edify the citizens over whom those systems preside. He remarks upon my manifest awareness of those arguments, but he proceeds as if I have never grappled with them sustainedly. He writes as follows (2022: 307, emphases in original, footnote omitted):

> [T]he edificatory perfectionist is not *assuming* the existence of edificatory-perfectionist duties (which would indeed beg the question in the opposite direction). Rather, the edificatory perfectionist [has presented] arguments as a way of *supporting* the existence of edificatory-perfectionist duties. The edificatory perfectionist accepts, of course, that these elaborate and extensive arguments in support of the existence of edificatory-perfectionist duties might ultimately fail. But he simply maintains that the proponent of the quidnunc mentality objection must *demonstrate* how they fail. To demonstrate such failure, the proponent of the quidnunc mentality objection would need either to provide some specific reason to reject the arguments of Raz and Wall, or to provide some general reason to think that duties of edification do not exist, or ideally both.

By conveying the impression that I have cavalierly omitted to contest the arguments advanced by the likes of Raz and Wall, Tahzib ignores the fifth chapter of *Liberalism with Excellence*. My animadversions on edificatory perfectionism are not confined to the sixth chapter of that book, where I present my critique of the quidnunc mentality. Rather, most of the second half of Chapter 5 in the book is a vigorous confrontation with Raz's autonomy-centered perfectionism (Kramer 2017: 227–49). Furthermore, quite a bit of the rest of that chapter is devoted to impugning the version of edificatory perfectionism propounded by Peter de Marneffe (Kramer 2017: 207–27). In each case, I have striven to undermine the arguments and positions of edificatory perfectionists by exposing the profound illiberality of their doctrines. As I have essayed to show, the tenor of edificatory perfectionism is such that it inclines its proponents to neglect systematically the ways in which the drive for edification stifles freedom. Near the end of the fifth chapter of *Liberalism with Excellence*, I have offered a partial summary of my efforts in that chapter (2017b: 249):

> This chapter has endeavored to highlight the illiberality of edificatory perfectionism. I have of course engaged here with only a few of the many sophisticated proponents of edificatory-perfectionist doctrines, but the queries raised are generalizable *mutatis mutandis* to other versions of such doctrines. What has been at issue is not the illiberality of anyone's temperament, but the illiberality of edificatory perfectionism as an alternative to neutralism. Perfectionism of that kind strongly disposes its devotees to scant the importance or value of freedoms that are unserviceable for the fruition of the devotees' edificatory objectives.

Hence, when Tahzib upbraidingly alleges that I beg the question against edificatory perfectionists by failing to come to grips with the arguments which they provide in favor of their contentions about edificatory duties that are incumbent on systems of governance, he is disregarding the lengthy chapter of *Liberalism with Excellence* that precedes the chapter on which he concentrates. Moreover, the charge of begging the question (in any damaging way) is baseless for an independent reason. That reason emerges more clearly in *Freedom of Expression as Self-Restraint* than in *Liberalism with Excellence*, but the argumentation on this point in the 2021 book is a development of a line of thought in the 2017 book. It begins from my fundamental premise that the paramount moral responsibility incumbent on any system of governance is a duty to bring about the political and economic and social conditions under which everyone within the jurisdiction of the system can be warranted in sustaining a high level of self-respect. That premise does not beg any questions against edificatory perfectionism. Of course, I am not implying that all edificatory perfectionists endorse the specified premise or that all edificatory perfectionists would endorse it if they were to ponder it carefully. Still, edificatory perfectionists can embrace my conception of the paramount moral responsibility borne by every system of governance, and can venture to argue that the edification of the citizenry in any society is necessary for the fulfillment of that responsibility there.

Crucial for parlaying my fundamental premise into a critique of edificatory perfectionism is an affinity between laws for the edification of the citizenry and laws which forbid odious modes of discourse. In *Freedom of Expression as Self-Restraint* I argue against legal prohibitions on pornography and hateful utterances, except when those modes of discourse are constitutive of serious communication-independent wrongdoing. (Communication-independent wrongdoing is not distinctively communicative, in that it can be perpetrated either through communicative conduct or through non-communicative conduct.) Although my arguments against such legal prohibitions are multiple, a key point is that the imposition of those legal restrictions presupposes the failure of a system of governance to fulfill its paramount responsibility. Central to the fulfillment of that responsibility is the cultivation of a robust liberal-democratic ethos in the society over which a system of governance presides. In the presence of such an ethos, and in the presence of diverse other measures that are obligatory for any system of governance in response to its paramount responsibility, the odious modes of discourse that must be legally tolerated under the principle of freedom of expression (insofar as they are not constitutive of serious communication-independent wrongdoing) are rendered innocuous. Instead of serving to discredit the people who are reviled or disparaged in those modes of discourse, such fulminations will have served to discredit the bigots who engage in the reviling or disparagement. When a system of governance complies with its paramount moral responsibility by carrying out the sorts of measures that have been mentioned here, it enables itself to continue to comply comfortably with that paramount responsibility by satisfying the constraints that are imposed on every system of governance under the principle of freedom of expression. Hence, when some such system legally proscribes the marketing of pornographic materials or the utterance of hateful sentiments in circumstances where the marketing of those materials or the utterance of those sentiments is not constitutive of serious communication-independent wrongdoing, the ban presupposes the failure of the system to live up to its paramount responsibility. Such a ban also presupposes the depravity of the populace over whom the system presides, for it presupposes that substantial numbers of citizens are susceptible to being persuaded by the messages conveyed in the outlawed filth. Those presuppositions are of course degrading both for the system and for the society, but they also accentuate the overweeningness of the legal ban—since they underscore the fact that the ban would be wholly superfluous if the system were abiding by its paramount responsibility. (A point worth noting here is that the paramount responsibility incumbent on every system of governance is not fancifully utopian. As I emphasize at quite a few junctures in *Liberalism with Excellence* and in *Freedom of Expression as Self-Restraint*, the fulfillment of that responsibility is realistically achievable. Its achievability should become further apparent in my next few paragraphs.)

I naturally say far more in *Freedom of Expression as Self-Restraint* about the justification and content of the principle of freedom of expression, but the skeletal outline in the foregoing paragraph is sufficient for my highlighting of an affinity between the laws which contravene that principle and the laws which prescribe the policies of edificatory perfectionism. Those latter laws are not aimed at averting the infliction of harm by some people upon others; if they were so aimed, the policies prescribed by them would not be edificatory-perfectionist. Instead, they are aimed at steering people toward lives with more valuable or wholesome or uplifting pursuits. Such laws, like the laws which forbid odious modes of discourse that are not constitutive of any serious communication-independent wrongdoing, presuppose the failure of a system of governance to satisfy its paramount responsibility.

As is stressed at several junctures in *Liberalism with Excellence* and in some of my subsequent writings (including *Freedom of Expression as Self-Restraint*), the fulfillment of that paramount moral responsibility hardly ever amounts to a situation in which each member of a society is actually endowed with a strong sense of self-respect and is actually warranted in being so endowed. If a situation along those lines were required under the paramount responsibility that is incumbent on every system of governance, then that responsibility would be fancifully utopian in what it demands. However, although that responsibility does require sedulous efforts from every system of governance to abide by the principles of liberal democracy, it does not require the realization of a utopia. What is demanded instead is that, within the jurisdiction of a system of governance, the political and economic and social conditions are such that everyone can be warranted in harboring a strong sense of self-respect. Within that state of affairs, the level of self-respect that is actually warranted for any particular person P is also vitally dependent on other factors such as the conduct and achievements of P. Similarly, the level of self-respect that is actually harbored by P is partly and crucially dependent on other factors such as the temperament of P. Those additional factors are not within the control of any liberal-democratic system of governance—which is why warranted self-respect is a primary natural good rather than a primary social good. It is never directly a distribuendum under any principles of justice. It is something which every system of governance is morally obligated to promote for each person over whom the system presides, but it is not something which any such system can ever guarantee or directly distribute. What a system of governance can do, and what it is morally obligated to do, is to bring about the political and economic and social conditions under which the prospect of being warranted in enjoying a hearty sense of self-respect is meaningfully available to everyone within its jurisdiction.

A system of governance that embraces edificatory perfectionism is thereby moving away from the satisfaction of its paramount responsibility. Insofar as such a system has complied with that responsibility, it has rendered superfluous the pursuit of any distinctively edificatory-perfectionist objectives. After all, its compliance with that paramount responsibility consists in securing the political and economic and social conditions that have just been mentioned. Almost inevitably, some people living in those conditions will choose to busy themselves with pastimes or undertakings or activities that are not edifying, even while they neglect any number of pastimes or undertakings or activities that would enrich their lives far more. Such a state of affairs is perfectly consistent with the fact that the prevailing system of governance has fulfilled its paramount responsibility, since that responsibility does not involve any obligation on the part of such a system to induce people to occupy themselves with high-minded pastimes. Far from being integral to the system's paramount responsibility, an illiberal obligation with that content would be antithetical thereto. It would morally require the system to intrude into the activities of adult individuals even though those activities are not inflicting any harm on others, and even though the intrusions would thus be superfluous for the system's compliance with its paramount responsibility.

Hence, laws that prescribe the adoption of edificatory-perfectionist policies are superfluous intrusions and are therefore overweeningly presumptuous on the part of any system of governance that enacts them. At the same time, those laws are demeaning for that system because they presuppose its failure to discharge its paramount responsibility. Had that responsibility been fulfilled (with, for example, adequate arrangements in place to attend to the calamities of people who undergo destitution or serious injury or illness or addiction), the enactment of edificatory-perfectionist laws would have been without any rationale. Accordingly, the enactment of such laws bespeaks some major lapses in the discharge of that responsibility.

5.2.6.3 *The harm principle*

Tahzib poses the following challenge (2022: 308): "[T]he burning question that edificatory perfectionists will have at this point is this: why is it that citizens' failures to realize edification and flourishing can be safely ignored by the state, whereas citizens' failures to realize other values such as freedom and equality cannot be safely ignored by the state?" At least at first glance, the answer to Tahzib's question is obvious. When Dorothy regularly watches professional wrestling and soap operas while declining to listen at all to classical music, her pattern of behavior does not harm anyone else even though it deprives her own life of the betterment that could be gained through the alteration of that pattern. By contrast, when Betty kidnaps somebody else or robs money from somebody else, she has inflicted serious harm and indignity on another person. Of course, the fact that Betty's conduct would inflict harm on another person is not in itself a sufficient basis for the outlawing of that conduct. As I have emphasized in *Liberalism with Excellence* (2017b: 46), the harm principle formulated by John Stuart Mill lays down a necessary condition rather than a sufficient condition for the permissibility of legal restrictions on any mode of conduct. Still, the fact that that necessary condition covers Betty's conduct and not Dorothy's conduct is a difference of considerable moral significance between their respective situations.

Tahzib contends that any recourse to the harm principle here will be unavailing. The first oddity in his discussion of this point is his assertion that I do "not provide a specification or defense of Mill's harm principle" (2022: 309). In *Liberalism with Excellence*, I in fact quote Mill's harm principle and defend it against Raz's revision of it (2017b: 46–9). I likewise invoke Mill's harm principle at quite a few other junctures in that book—as can be ascertained from a glance at its Index. Admittedly, Tahzib does fleetingly mention some of those other invocations of the harm principle. Nevertheless, I am taken aback to be told by him that I have not provided any specification or defense of a principle which I have in fact expounded and championed.

To try to bolster his contention that I cannot successfully resort to the harm principle as an element in my critique of the quidnunc mentality of edificatory perfectionism, Tahzib adverts to the distinction between moralized and non-moralized conceptions of harm. Although he appears unaware of the fact, I have explored that very distinction in my ruminations on the harm principle in *Liberalism with Excellence* (2017b: 52–3). As I indicate there, questions about the conformity of edificatory-perfectionist policies with the harm principle are to be addressed on the basis of a moralized conception of harm. Tahzib evinces no acquaintance with my stance on that matter, but he concurs with the stance itself. However, he thinks that he can draw upon such a position to shield edificatory perfectionism against the accusation that it contravenes the harm principle. He writes as follows (2022: 310, emphases in original, footnote omitted):

> This [moralized approach to the harm principle] means that if edificatory-perfectionist duties exist, then a state that fails to promote the edification of the citizenry *harms* the citizenry and a citizen who fails to contribute (through paying taxes) towards programs aimed at the edification of her fellow citizens *harms* those other citizens. Edificatory-perfectionist state action would then be compatible with the moralized harm principle.... Kramer would of course deny that any such edificatory-perfectionist duties exist, and so he would deny that edificatory-perfectionist policies are consistent with the harm principle. But, as the foregoing discussion illustrates, if we adopt a moralized account of harm, inconsistency with the harm principle is not an independent argument against edificatory-perfectionist duties.

Tahzib is quite wrong in presuming that he has managed to protect edificatory perfectionism against the charge that it runs afoul of the harm principle. He is correct in stating that, if edificatory-perfectionist duties are incumbent on systems of governance, the noncompliance of any such system with those duties will harm the citizens over whom the system presides. Likewise, if the citizens in each society are under moral duties to contribute through taxation to the implementation of edificatory-perfectionist programs, the noncompliance of any citizen with those duties will harm other citizens. All the same, the very point at issue in this context is whether the existence of those duties would be consistent with the harm principle. Although Tahzib is correct in declaring that I deny the existence of any edificatory-perfectionist duties, a key reason for my denying their existence is that the harm principle rules them out. After all, the edificatory-perfectionist duties envisaged by Tahzib would morally require a system of governance to intervene significantly in individuals' lives in ways that would not involve the averting of harm inflicted by some people on others. Instead, the interventions would be designed to steer people away from modes of living that are insufficiently lofty. Likewise, the edificatory-perfectionist duties envisaged by Tahzib would morally require each citizen to contribute payments for governmental programs that intervene significantly in individuals' lives in ways that would not involve the averting of harm inflicted by some people on others. In sum, those duties would morally require systems of governance to impose certain legal obligations on citizens that are at odds with the Millian harm principle. Now, although moral conflicts can occur in some contexts—whereby people are under moral duties to φ and are simultaneously under moral duties not to φ—there are no moral conflicts in the contexts envisioned by Tahzib. Rather, the fact that edificatory-perfectionist duties would morally require governmental measures that squarely violate the harm principle is one strong reason for concluding that there are no such duties.

Tahzib thinks that an argument like the one in the preceding paragraph is begging the question, in a damaging fashion, against edificatory perfectionism. He retorts (2022: 311, emphasis in original):

> [I]nconsistency with the harm principle is not an independent argument against edificatory-perfectionist duties. To say that edificatory-perfectionist policies are inconsistent with the harm principle, one must first have established that there are no edificatory-perfectionist duties. So, like the quidnunc mentality objection itself, the claim that citizens' failures to live edified lives could be safely ignored by the state without thereby harming others *already presupposes* the non-existence of edificatory-perfectionist duties—again, at least if we are working with a moralized account of harm. Hitching the quidnunc mentality objection to the wagon of the moralized harm principle thus does not help here because it fails to give us what we are looking for: an independently persuasive, morally substantive argument against edificatory-perfectionist duties.

Tahzib goes astray here, for he is presenting edificatory perfectionism as a creed marked by outlandishly dogmatic circularity. He is suggesting that edificatory-perfectionist duties would lift themselves up by their own bootstraps into conformity with the harm principle simply through their own existence. Although the implementation of those duties would not avert or remedy the infliction of any non-moralized harm by anyone upon anyone else, and although the contravening of those very duties would be the only ostensible moralized harm averted or remedied by the implementation of them, Tahzib believes that that one element of ostensible moralized harm is sufficient to vindicate the consistency of edificatory-perfectionist duties with the Millian harm principle. Such a position is untenable, however. When I maintain that any edificatory-perfectionist moral duties would be at odds with the harm principle and would therefore not be veritable moral duties, I have in mind precisely the fact that the implementation of such duties would not avert or remedy the infliction of any non-moralized harm by anyone upon anyone else and would not avert or remedy any moralized harm apart from contraventions of those very duties. The fact that the implementation of such duties would avert or remedy contraventions of those very duties is no basis at all for deeming them to be consistent with the Millian harm principle, since duties cannot bootstrap themselves into consistency with that principle simply by existing as such. Instead, the genuine consistency of a duty D with the harm principle consists in the fact that the implementation of D will avert or remedy the infliction of some non-moralized harm by somebody on somebody else, or in the fact that the implementation of D will avert or remedy a transgression of some moral obligation(s) beyond D itself. Since neither of those bases for the consistency of a duty with the harm principle is applicable to edificatory-perfectionist duties, those duties would be inconsistent with that principle and are thus non-existent as moral obligations. Tahzib's bootstrapping defense of those duties is otiose. (Note that I am not here begging the question by assuming that edificatory-perfectionist moral duties do not exist. Rather, I am explaining why they do not exist.)

5.2.6.4 Fruitless arguments

Tahzib seeks to assure his readers that edificatory perfectionists are not guilty of begging the question when they take as given that edificatory-perfectionist moral duties exist. He explains that "arguments [in favor of the existence of such duties] are developed, extensively and elaborately, elsewhere in the work of edificatory perfectionists such as Raz and Wall" (2022: 311). As I have already observed in section 5.2.6.2 above, the fifth chapter of *Liberalism with Excellence* does in fact sustainedly oppugn the arguments propounded by edificatory perfectionists; it does so by exposing the profound illiberality of those arguments and their conclusions. Let me go further here by contemplating briefly whether any of the arguments extolled by Tahzib can plausibly be thought to establish the existence of edificatory-perfectionist moral duties. Tahzib does not recount the lines of reasoning to which he admiringly adverts, but this subsection will laconically survey the main lines of reasoning which I have encountered in the writings of edificatory perfectionists.

Especially prominent and lengthy are the arguments by edificatory perfectionists against the constraints of Rawlsian public reason and against any similar neutralist limitations on the range of considerations that can properly be invoked in justification of governmental programs. As I have already remarked in section 5.2.6.1 above, aspirational perfectionists can and do join with edificatory perfectionists in railing against such limitations. Of course, some of the details of the positions espoused by certain edificatory perfectionists on this matter might be tied to the quidnunc mentality that pervades their broader argumentation. Nevertheless, the posing of objections to the doctrine of public reason is certainly not inherently linked to the quidnunc mentality as a general matter, and is not supportive of the proposition that any system of governance bears some edificatory-perfectionist moral duties. Aspirational perfectionists, who deny the existence of such moral duties, are allies of the edificatory perfectionists in pushing back against the restrictions on public deliberation that are favored by Rawlsians and other neutralists.

A second main category of lines of reasoning by edificatory perfectionists is centered on the nature and value of autonomy. Though I obviously do not concur with the aspects of those lines of reasoning which I assail in the fifth chapter of *Liberalism with Excellence*, many of the reflections by the likes of Raz and Wall on the nature and import of autonomy are valuably illuminating. As I have remarked in *Liberalism with Excellence*, nearly all liberal neutralists and aspirational perfectionists agree that autonomy is an ideal for which individuals should strive. Moreover, such philosophers can readily welcome the fact that the political arrangements which they respectively prescribe are in general highly promotive of autonomy even though the fostering of autonomy is not one of the purposes of those arrangements (Kramer 2017b: 294–5). Accordingly, the opponents of edificatory perfectionism can and do endorse much of what is said about autonomy by the leading advocates of such perfectionism. Esteem for the value of autonomy is scarcely unique to edificatory perfectionists, and does not in itself commit anybody to the proposition that edificatory-perfectionist moral duties are incumbent on systems of governance.

Closely related to the ruminations by edificatory perfectionists on the nature and conditions of autonomy are their arguments that highlight the ways in which certain governmental programs can designedly steer people toward the attainment of high levels of autonomy. Concomitant to such arguments are passages in which the edificatory perfectionists underscore the improvements in the lives of individuals that can occur through the realization of the edificatory objectives of the policies which those perfectionists commend. Now, although liberal neutralists and aspirational perfectionists may dissent from some of the specifics of the claims advanced by edificatory perfectionists on these points, they can perfectly well accept the gist of those claims. That is, at least *arguendo* they can accept that certain governmental programs designed to increase the incidence of high levels of autonomy among the individuals in a society would be likely to succeed pretty well in that design, and they can wholeheartedly accept that the lives of individuals who do attain high levels of autonomy are thereby enhanced. What the neutralists and the aspirational perfectionists resist is not the truth of those general theses but is instead the notion that those theses can be parlayed into a defense of edificatory-perfectionist policies. The resistance of these philosophers to the end-justifies-the-means consequentialism of edificatory perfectionists is mounted on firmly deontological grounds. In the eyes of liberal neutralists, the adoption of edificatory-perfectionist policies for the cultivation of the autonomy of individuals is morally illegitimate because it disrespects the rational agency of people whose conceptions of the good do not assess autonomy favorably. (I present the neutralists' objections in much greater detail in *Liberalism with Excellence*.) In the eyes of aspirational perfectionists, the moral illegitimacy of the adoption of edificatory-perfectionist policies is due principally to the quidnunc mentality in which those policies are grounded. Of course, I am currently defending my critique of edificatory perfectionism against Tahzib's onslaughts, and I am thus not taking for granted the soundness of that critique. My point here is simply to indicate that the soundness of that critique is consistent with the truth of assertions about the benefits undergone by individuals through the heightening of their autonomy. Such assertions do not ever suffice to establish the existence of edificatory-perfectionist moral duties, for they fail to overcome the ends-do-not-justify-the-means objections that are lodged against edificatory perfectionism by its opponents.

One other approach by edificatory perfectionists is instantiated in Tahzib's own chapter. That is, those perfectionists tend to dwell on the virtuousness of solicitude shown by a person toward her kith and kin, and they affirm that there are relevant affinities between such solicitude and the outlook that is aptly ascribable to the governmental officials who introduce and implement the policies of edificatory perfectionism. Yet, as I have already maintained in section 5.2.1, there are no pertinent analogies across the divide between the attitudes appropriate for intimates toward one another and the attitudes appropriate for legal-governmental functionaries toward citizens. Indeed, one way of presenting my critique of the quidnunc mentality associated with edificatory perfectionism is that that critique reaffirms the divide just mentioned. It insists that the relative transparency aptly characteristic of relationships among intimates is overbearingly and degradingly officious when it is reproduced—or seemingly reproduced, in an ersatz form—in the dealings of governmental functionaries with citizens.

In short, no arguments of the types propounded by Tahzib and his fellow theorists can establish that any system of governance is under some edificatory-perfectionist moral duties. Several of those arguments are unexceptionable in themselves, but they are consistent with the proposition that no edificatory-perfectionist moral duties exist. They are consistent with my critique of the quidnunc mentality that would imbue any edificatory-perfectionist system of governance. By contrast, the "bootstrapping" lines of reasoning advanced by Tahzib and Raz are inconsistent with that critique; but, through the viciousness of their circularity, those "bootstrapping" lines of reasoning inadvertently reveal that the existence of edificatory-perfectionist moral duties would be inconsistent with the Millian harm principle, and they therefore inadvertently reveal that no such duties exist. Hence, none of the edificatory-perfectionist argumentation lauded by Tahzib goes any way toward supporting the proposition that edificatory-perfectionist moral obligations are incumbent on systems of governance. My conclusion about their argumentation, combined with my previous investigations of the far-reaching illiberality of edificatory perfectionism, greatly reinforces my condemnation of the meddlesomeness and degradingness of the programs championed by edificatory perfectionists.

5.2.7 Edificatory Perfectionism as a Theory of Justice?

Near the end of my chapter on the quidnunc mentality of edificatory perfectionism in *Liberalism with Excellence*, I broach the possibility of repackaging edificatory perfectionism as a theory of justice (2017b: 289–96). Such a tack might conceivably be attempted by some edificatory perfectionists as a way of shielding their doctrine against my critique thereof. I have floated this possibility not because I believe that it would be successful, but instead precisely because I have wanted to explain why it would be unsuccessful. I ponder whether some edificatory perfectionists might try to present autonomy as a primary natural good in Rawls's sense and whether they might expound principles of justice that would cover opportunities to attain autonomy. Those opportunities would be understood as primary social goods that are thus distribuenda to be allotted in accordance with the specified principles of justice.

In *Liberalism with Excellence*, I adduce two main problems that would fatally afflict any such effort to repackage edificatory perfectionism as an account of what justice requires. First is the manifest fact that edificatory perfectionists have not heretofore presented their theories along those lines at all. As I declare (2017b: 293):

> To say the least, autonomy-centered perfectionists such as Raz and Wall do not perceive or present their theorizing as non-perfectionist. They do not take themselves to be peddling some slightly amended versions of Rawls's theory of justice. Quite the contrary .... Hence, were any defenders of autonomy-centered perfectionism disposed to shield their creed against my critique by re-elaborating it as a variant of Rawls's theory of justice with a slightly altered index of primary goods, they would be radically transforming their creed and would therefore in effect be abandoning it.

A second difficulty is that the revamping of edificatory perfectionism would render it indistinguishable or virtually indistinguishable from Rawlsian liberalism. After all, the items in Rawls's index of primary social goods can very plausibly be characterized as the vital desiderata that constitute opportunities for the attainment of autonomy. Hence, instead of adding to the Rawlsian index of distribuenda that are to be allotted in accordance with suitable principles of justice, the revamped edificatory-perfectionist theory would simply be recapitulating that index under the heading of "opportunities for the attainment of autonomy." As I write: "The primary social goods apportioned by [Rawls's] principles—basic legal rights and powers and liberties, opportunities to gain offices and positions of influence, and entitlements to wealth and income—are all themselves opportunities open to anyone with sufficient mental and physical capacities, and are integrally connected to the conditions for the attainment of autonomy" (2017b: 295, footnote omitted).

Although I fully stand by those two objections to any transformation of edificatory perfectionism into a theory of justice, I now think that *Liberalism with Excellence* should also have pressed a third objection which I there inaptly put aside as surmountable. However, before I recount that third criticism and explain why it is insurmountable, I should explore briefly Tahzib's curious responses to my meditations on these matters. His first main response consists in observing that edificatory perfectionists such as Raz and Wall do not elaborate their theories along Rawlsian lines at all (Tahzib 2022: 314-15)—as if I have not made that very point emphatically in *Liberalism with Excellence* when entertaining the proposal about the repackaging of edificatory perfectionism as a theory of justice. One of the chief grounds adduced by me for looking askance at that proposal is perplexingly treated by Tahzib as if it is something to which I am unattuned.

Even more bemusing is the second response by Tahzib, which is an intensification of his first response. He feels a need to draw my attention to the fact that many edificatory perfectionists have submitted that systems of governance are morally permitted to steer people toward the attainment of desiderata other than autonomy. Although most contemporary edificatory perfectionists do attach particular importance to autonomy as an ideal toward which the members of any society should be prodded by the prevailing system of governance, most of them also attach great importance to other ideals—such as aesthetic refinedness—toward which the members of a society should likewise be prodded. I make this point in my initial overview of edificatory perfectionism in Chapter 1 of *Liberalism with Excellence* (2017b: 34–6), and at many junctures thereafter. Thus, I am nonplused by Tahzib's second response. Tahzib seems to have misread my thought-experiment about the repackaging of edificatory perfectionism, for he seems to construe it as an effort of mine to summarize the ideas that have actually been propounded by the exponents of such perfectionism. On the contrary, one of the main purposes of the thought-experiment—as I have already indicated—is to emphasize that any conversion of edificatory perfectionism into a theory of justice would constitute a major departure from the actualities of such perfectionism.

Having sought in *Liberalism with Excellence* to show the unsustainability of any such transformation of edificatory perfectionism, I now think that I have there understated the case against that transformation. In particular, I conflate two distinct questions in the final sentence of this passage: "[E]ven though the attainment of autonomy is especially important in the socioeconomic and political settings of modern Western societies, it is essential as a constituent of a fully good life for anyone in every society. If the socioeconomic arrangements of a society systematically thwart the attainment of autonomy by the society's members, they systematically preclude those members from leading fully good lives. Autonomy can thus fittingly be classified as a primary natural good" (2017b: 291). The first two sentences in this quotation are fully apt, but the concluding sentence is a non sequitur. Whereas the question addressed by the first two sentences is whether the attainment of autonomy is partly constitutive of a fully good life for everyone in any society, the question addressed by the closing sentence in the quotation is whether the attainment of autonomy is serviceable for the realization of everyone's ends regardless of what those ends might be. Although the answer to the question addressed by the first two sentences is affirmative, the answer to the question addressed by the closing sentence is negative. Given Rawls's understanding of primary goods—an understanding which I have defended and refined in *Liberalism with Excellence* (2017b: 325–8)—the attainment of autonomy is not correctly classifiable as a primary natural good. People can quite credibly pursue certain ends to which the attainment of autonomy is not conducive. Hence, although I am correct in *Liberalism with Excellence* when I affirm that autonomy is a constituent of a fully good life for everyone, I go astray there in inferring that autonomy is accurately classifiable as a Rawlsian primary natural good.

Having here firmly disentangled the two questions addressed by the sentences which I have just quoted, I can now strengthen my rejection of the possibility of repackaging edificatory perfectionism as a theory of justice. To be so repackaged, edificatory perfectionism would have to be centered on a desideratum that can be included in the Rawlsian roster of primary goods. None of the desiderata commended by edificatory perfectionists—not even that of autonomy, which is universally a constituent of a fully good life—can correctly be included in that roster. Accordingly, the aim of re-elaborating edificatory perfectionism as a theory of justice is a non-starter.

6. Philosophy and Public Affairs

I shall conclude these lengthy replies by turning to the chapters from Antony Duff and Christopher Kutz. Capital punishment and freedom of expression are not the only areas of applied philosophy on which I have written, but they are two of the foremost areas. My reflections on those issues are very much in keeping with the deontological tenor of the aspirational-perfectionist liberalism which I have developed in *Liberalism with Excellence*. Thus, this final main section dovetails nicely with the preceding main section.

6.1 R.A. Duff and the Purgative Rationale for Capital Punishment

I have known Duff for nearly a quarter of a century, and I have esteemed him for an even longer period as the leading philosopher of criminal law in the world. With his geniality as a person and his acuity as a thinker, he has enhanced the philosophical life of the United Kingdom admirably for nearly half a century. Cruft and Reiff and I were delighted to put together a festschrift for Duff just over a decade ago, and I am similarly delighted to welcome Duff aboard as a contributor to the present volume.

6.1.1 A Reframing of the Purgative Rationale

Because of the profuseness and grotesqueness of the atrocities perpetrated by a defilingly evil malefactor, the continuation of his life is at odds with the political and economic and social conditions under which every member of a society can be warranted in harboring a high level of self-respect. Formulations that approximate this way of framing the matter, with an orientation toward the paramount moral responsibility of every system of governance as I have articulated that responsibility in *Liberalism with Excellence* and in subsequent writings, do appear occasionally in *The Ethics of Capital Punishment* (2011: 249, 252). Nevertheless, those formulations are only approximations of the way in which I now frame the matter of capital punishment along with sundry other matters. Not until my article "On Political Morality and the Conditions for Warranted Self-Respect" (2017c: 340–2)—an article written shortly after the publication of *Liberalism with Excellence*, and under the direct inspiration of that book—did I sustainedly focus the justification of capital punishment on the conditions for the warrantedness of ample levels of self-respect among the members of the societies in which any morally justifiable executions would take place. Duff has not consulted the writings in which I have reframed the purgative rationale for the death penalty along those lines. Nonetheless, I am not being unfair by cleaving here to my current way of formulating that rationale, since it extrapolates from the ideas that are presented in *The Ethics of Capital Punishment* and especially in my 2015 article "The Purgative Rationale for the Death Penalty" which Duff has perused.

Certain features of the purgative rationale that would otherwise be somewhat puzzling are quite readily understandable when that rationale is elaborated in the manner in which I now elaborate it. Duff touches upon a few of these features. I will broach one example here and mull over a further example later. In a footnote about halfway through his chapter, Duff adverts to one aspect of my cogitations on the abduction and trial and execution of Adolf Eichmann by Israel: "From Kramer's comments on Eichmann, … it also seems that the members of all polities are 'tainted' by the evildoer's continued existence, even when they could have done nothing to bring him to justice, or did all that could have reasonably been expected of them" (2022: 334 n.28 of typescript). Though I stand by the substance of what is accurately attributed to me here by Duff, I am now less strongly inclined to use the secularized religious language which I have employed so frequently in *The Ethics of Capital Punishment*. Because the purgative rationale for the death penalty in that book is inspired by many passages in the Hebrew Scriptures, I chose there to secularize some of the religious notions and terminology from those Scriptures. Without abandoning that approach entirely, I now think that a more illuminating approach lies in concentrating directly on how the continuation of Eichmann's life—past the time required for a fair trial with appellate procedures—would have detracted from the conditions under which everyone in any society can be warranted in sustaining a hearty sense of self-respect. My arguments in *The Ethics of Capital Punishment* about the appropriateness of classifying Eichmann's atrocities as crimes against humanity, and about the ways in which the continuation of Eichmann's life would have constituted an affront to humanity, provide much of the crucial support for my claims about the impairment of the conditions just mentioned. However, as I have maintained in "On Political Morality and the Conditions for Warranted Self-Respect (cited above), the upshot of the arguments about Eichmann's atrocities should be presented straightforwardly with reference to the conditions for warranted self-respect rather than in the somewhat quaint religious terms that are so prominent in *The Ethics of Capital Punishment*. When the upshot of the arguments is reframed in that fashion, the explanation for the universality of Eichmann's defilingness and for the differing degrees of his defilingness across sundry societies is much more apparent. Because Eichmann's multitudinous outrages were crimes against humanity, every member of humanity would have been diminished to some degree by the continuation of his life. That is, the conditions under which every such member can be warranted in harboring a high level of self-respect would have been sapped to some degree by the devotion of resources to the continuation of a life that constituted a repudiation of humanity. In societies with direct links to Eichmann, the adverse effects on those conditions would have been especially pronounced; but the adverse effects would have occurred to lesser extents even in societies with no such direct links, and the occurrence of those effects would have been independent of anyone's awareness of them.

6.1.2 Suicide versus Execution

Among the many interesting points raised in Duff's excellent and densely argued chapter, the first with which I will engage here is the matter of suicide versus execution for defilingly evil offenders. Duff suggests that the significance of the distinction between suicide and execution for such offenders will depend on whether the turpitude of their wrongdoing leaves any room for their reintegration into their communities. His pondering of this question is fascinating, as he first delineates a situation in which the outlook of an offender is such that either suicide or execution will be fully suitable (2022: 325-6):

> First, the seeking or acceptance of death might be an expression of a kind of despair. I realize that my crimes make my continued life morally impossible: I cannot live with myself (which is a moral rather than a psychological remark), because I can see no way in which my life can, given the extravagantly evil deeds that it now contains, make acceptable sense; I cannot live with other people, since those crimes irretrievably sundered the moral bonds (of humanity) between us, so that there is no way back. If that is my attitude, then the choice between suicide and execution is a contingent one: there is nothing inherently preferable about either mode of death.

Duff then contrasts that situation with one in which an offender strives for some degree of reintegration into the prevailing community through submission to death as a course of conduct that betokens atonement. In such circumstances, Duff contends, the aspiration of the offender is best realized through a trial and a resultant execution (2022: 326, footnote omitted):

> [S]econd, I might seek or accept death as an act not of despair, but of atonement: as the only way in which I can adequately express my recognition of what I have done, and communicate that recognition to others. Seeking death is now a positive act, belonging in the same moral category as other acts of atonement for lesser wrongs. It might also, perhaps paradoxically, be a means of reconciling myself with other people, by showing my repentant recognition of the horror of my deeds, and my earnest desire to atone for them as best I can: I can make my peace with others through my death, which thus restores a kind of community with them even as I leave them—in and by my leaving them in this way (one manifestation of such reconciliation might be the way in which others think and talk of me after my death). Now if that is how and why I seek death, I might see execution (if my polity practices capital punishment) as the more appropriate mode of death: in pleading "Guilty" at my trial, and accepting the judicial execution that follows, I subject myself to the polity's (my polity's) law (to my law); I show that I am ready to answer for my crimes in the appropriate public forum, and subject myself to what the polity prescribes as the appropriate kind of atonement.

Although Duff's ruminations on this matter are powerfully thought-provoking, and although they are consistent with my account of the purgative rationale for capital punishment, I do not entirely agree with them. On the one hand, I agree that the abject submission of a defilingly iniquitous malefactor to an execution can effect a minimal reconciliation between the malefactor and his community. As is famously said of the Thane of Cawdor in *Macbeth*: "[V]ery frankly he confess'd his treasons,/ Implored your highness' pardon and set forth/A deep repentance. Nothing in his life/ Became him like the leaving it" (I.iv.5–8). On the other hand, I believe that such a minimal reconciliation can also occur through an abject act of suicide and that the key distinction is therefore not between suicide and execution but instead between the different aims that can be pursued through suicide. A defilingly heinous wrongdoer who remains utterly impenitent might commit suicide as an act of defiance in advance of a scheduled execution, as Heinrich Himmler did at Nuremberg. Here, of course, we are concentrating on defilingly heinous wrongdoers who have finally come to recognize the enormity of their misdeeds and who are seeking to atone for their crimes through submission to death. Such a wrongdoer discerns that the termination of his life is morally imperative. An execution on the basis of the purgative rationale can be wholly appropriate as a means of bringing about that termination, but an act of suicide by the wrongdoer can likewise be wholly appropriate. Everything depends on the motivation.

Consider for example the suicide of Othello at the end of the play that bears his name. Let us suppose here that the crimes perpetrated by Othello are viler and more numerous than those portrayed in the play, so that he can correctly be classified as a defilingly flagitious evildoer. With the scales finally fallen from his eyes in the closing scene of the drama, Othello is overcome by remorse and anguish, and he recognizes that the continuation of his life would be morally obscene. One way of construing his act of stabbing himself to death is that it amounts to his taking ultimate control over his life by ending it. As he once summarily executed a Turk at Aleppo for traducing the republic of Venice, so he now summarily executes himself for having wronged the republic of Venice even more grievously. If this interpretation of his action is correct, then his suicide is inapposite as the means of terminating his life even though it has produced a morally vital result. Though the purgative rationale for capital punishment does call for his death in circumstances where his outrages (beyond those depicted in Shakespeare's play) have been so numerous and grotesque as to be extravagantly evil, the basis for that moral requirement is that the continuation of his life would be inimical to the conditions under which every member of his society can be warranted in sustaining a high level of self-respect. Given as much, his commission of suicide as a vehicle for his own self-assertion is a deviation from the proper orientation for the ending of his life. It is an orientation focused on himself rather than on the other members of his society. (Worth noting here is that an execution can likewise serve inappositely as a vehicle for the self-assertion of the person who is put to death. This point is of course especially applicable to convicts who remain staunchly unrepentant. For example, Timothy McVeigh—who murdered 168 people in his bombing of a federal office building in Oklahoma City in 1995—provided a written copy of the poem "Invictus" as his final words before his execution.)

However, the decision by Othello to slay himself can also be interpreted quite differently. Instead of using his suicide to reconsolidate his mastery over his own life and his status as the commander in charge of Cyprus, he might be undertaking it simply in order to ensure that the demands of morality will be fulfilled. Having observed that "I have done the state some service, and they know't—No more of that" (*Othello*, V.ii.339–40), he may worry that the judiciary in Venice will misguidedly treat him with leniency if he is brought to trial there. Accordingly, with his clear-sighted descrial of what morality requires, he ensures that there will be no opportunities for misguided clemency. In so doing, he ensures that the republic of Venice is purged of the defilement with which it would be tainted if his life were to be spared. His focus lies on his fellow Venetians rather than on himself. Hence, when his suicide is impelled by this motivation, it effects the minimal reconciliation between Othello and Venice which Duff and I have envisaged as a possibility. Stemming from such a motivation, the suicide is no less suitable than an execution grounded on the purgative rationale.

Obviously, Shakespeare's play in its bottomless greatness leaves itself open to these two readings and to other possible readings. There is no need here for me to choose between them. Rather, my purpose is simply to indicate that either interpretation of Othello's behavior could plausibly be correct and that his suicide arising from the outlook encapsulated in the second interpretation would meet the concerns of the purgative rationale for the death penalty as effectively as would an execution after a fair trial. Of course, a system of governance morally obligated to give effect to that rationale is *ipso facto* morally obligated to provide for fair trials that will lead (perhaps after some appellate proceedings) to executions of defilingly evil offenders. Governmental functionaries should patently not rely upon such offenders to commit suicide with appropriate outlooks. Nonetheless, in some circumstances that are not utterly preposterous, the suicide of such an offender could be an alternative to a properly conducted execution as a means of attaining the minimal reconciliation to which I have referred.

6.1.3 The Matter of Insanity Redux

In *The Ethics of Capital Punishment*, I readily accept that a defilingly evil offender cannot permissibly be executed on the basis of the purgative rationale if he has become insane by the scheduled time of the execution. However, I there provide an inapposite explanation of the impermissibility: "In the circumstances envisaged here, where [a defilingly evil offender] has become thoroughly insane, he has permanently or temporarily ceased to exist as the person who carried out extravagantly evil atrocities" (2011: 247). In my 2015 article "The Purgative Rationale for the Death Penalty," in response to some insightful comments by John Danaher, I have renounced the statement which I have just quoted. Writing as follows in that article, I correct my explanation of the impermissibility of a purgative execution in circumstances where a heinous offender has become insane (2015: 392):

> I erred in suggesting that the impropriety of a purgative execution in the envisaged situation is due to the inapplicability of the purgative rationale. That rationale, focused as it is on the defilingness of the life of any malefactor who has perpetrated an array of atrocities, is in fact applicable to such a malefactor even if he has become insane before the scheduled date of his execution. Hence, the moral impermissibility of a purgative execution in those circumstances is not due to any limit on the scope of the purgative rationale. Instead, it is due to the absence of a necessary condition for the legitimacy of any process of implementing that rationale. Like retributivism, the purgative justification for the death penalty is deontological. It lays emphasis on the responsibility of a heinous miscreant for the iniquities which he has committed and which bring him within the ambit of the purgative rationale. His responsibility as a reflective agent on the occasions when he perpetrated those iniquities is a necessary condition for the applicability of the purgative rationale to his life. What should be added, however, is that his responsibility as a reflective agent at the time of his trial and at the time of his execution is a necessary condition for the legitimacy of

> any implementation of that rationale. If such a miscreant becomes thoroughly insane before his execution has been conducted, then—although the purgative rationale is indeed applicable to him—a necessary condition for the propriety of proceeding with the execution is unfulfilled.

Duff takes issue with my corrected explanation. He retorts: "On the one hand, there is a widely shared sense, or intuition, even among supporters of the death penalty that it would be grotesquely wrong to execute someone who is now insane, even if he was fully sane at the time when he committed his horrendous crimes, and indeed at the time of his trial; and that sense reflects, I think, not some constraint on the administration of capital punishment external to the rationale for that punishment, but an understanding of the meaning of (capital) punishment—so that the execution of an insane person is a grotesque travesty of punishment. On the other hand, however, the familiar rationales for (capital) punishment—including Kramer's, as we have just seen—do not seem capable of explaining that sense" (2022: 338). In one sense, Duff is correct in averring that the specifics of the purgative justification for the death penalty do not explain the impermissibility of the administering of that penalty to a monstrously evil offender who has become thoroughly insane. With a focus on the moral imperative of terminating the life of such an offender—a life that constitutes an affront to humanity—the specifics of the purgative justification leave open the question whether the fulfillment of that moral imperative can permissibly proceed in a situation where the offender has lost his sanity.

In a more important sense, however, Duff is incorrect. Both in *The Ethics of Capital Punishment* and in my subsequent writings on the purgative rationale, I have made clear that that rationale is not in itself constitutive of a basic principle of morality. Rather, it is grounded in deeper principles and values of political morality. Most notably, it is grounded on the paramount responsibility of every system of governance to bring about the political and economic and social conditions under which an ample sense of self-respect can be warranted on the part of every member of the society over which the system presides. Derivable from that paramount responsibility is the purgative justification for executions, but also derivable therefrom are the constraints that delimit the circumstances in which the implementation of purgative executions can permissibly take place. In the final chapter of *The Ethics of Capital Punishment* I explore many of those constraints at length, and in the penultimate chapter I discuss more generally why the implementation of such executions is permissible only within liberal-democratic systems of governance (2011: 260–5). I there endeavor to underscore the fact that the same basic principles and values which underlie the purgative rationale for capital punishment are what underlie the restrictions on the range of situations in which the effectuation of that rationale can be morally legitimate.

Specifically in connection with the matter of insanity on which Duff has homed in, the paramount responsibility incumbent on every system of governance is generative not only of the purgative rationale but also of sundry restraints on how that rationale can permissibly be put into effect. In Chapter 6 of my 2017 book *Liberalism with Excellence* and in Chapter 4 of my 2021 book *Freedom of Expression as Self-Restraint*, I have probed some of the requirements of self-restraint imposed on every system of governance by that paramount responsibility, and I have recounted how contraventions of those requirements by any such system are both self-aggrandizing and self-abasing. (These points have surfaced, of course, in my ripostes to Tahzib above.) Like the retributivist account of punishment, the purgative rationale for the death penalty is deontological and is thus centered on holding certain people accountable for the extravagant evil which they have done. Accordingly, while the purgative rationale affirms that the discontinuation of the lives of those people is morally imperative, the requirements of self-restraint which accompany that rationale are such as to disallow any executions of those people in circumstances where they are not thereby being held accountable. Given that someone who has become thoroughly insane by the scheduled date of his execution is not being held accountable by the execution if it goes ahead—since his mental miasma precludes him from being held accountable—the administering of capital punishment to him is morally impermissible even though it is morally obligatory under the purgative rationale. His life continues to constitute an affront to humanity, and the purgative rationale continues to call for the termination of that life. Nevertheless, because he has lost his mind, the circumstances under which he can legitimately be subjected to an execution are not present.

In other words, to a greater extent than Duff allows, there are resemblances between the institutions through which the purgative rationale for the death penalty is given effect and the institutions through which his own alternative conception of punishment is given effect. Though the purgative rationale itself is unlike anything in Duff's conception of punishment, the procedural constraints imposed by the same basic principles of morality that impose purgative obligations are considerably closer to his conception in some salient respects. Among those respects is that purgative executions—like any non-capital punishments in institutions of criminal justice informed by Duff's conception—are morally legitimate only insofar as they are undertaken to hold malefactors accountable for wrongdoing. Because that necessary condition for the legitimacy of any punishment is not met in a situation where an offender has become insane, a purgative execution of such an offender in a situation of this kind would be morally impermissible. When we take account of the full matrix of moral duties that are incumbent on every system of governance, and when we therefore do not train our scrutiny on the purgative duties of such a system in isolation from its other obligations, we can discern quite a large degree of convergence between Duff and me (at least at the level of bottom-line conclusions) on the matter of convicts who have become insane.

6.1.4 The Overabundance of Invocations of Dignity

One reason for my reformulation of the purgative rationale in some of my recent writings is that *The Ethics of Capital Punishment* invokes the notion of dignity too abundantly. To be sure, as is evident in that book's first main set of reflections on the matter (2011: 61–5), nearly all my invocations of the property of dignity construe it as a set of moral constraints on the ways in which human beings can permissibly be treated. With particular reference to the limits on the ways in which miscreants can permissibly be treated by the institutions of criminal justice through which they are tried and convicted and sentenced and punished, my invocations of the dignity of human beings advert to the moral significance of certain elementary features possessed by such beings: their susceptibility to pain and humiliation and fear; their capacity to undergo positive experiences; and (for most human adults) their faculties of rational contemplation and deliberation and decision-making and action.[37] Beings endowed with those characteristics are morally protected, both procedurally and substantively, against many forms of mistreatment.

One point suggested but insufficiently highlighted in *The Ethics of Capital Punishment* has been much more prominently emphasized in some of my subsequent books: namely, the fact that a person's endowment with the basic features outlined above is not always the justificatory basis for the limitations on how the person can permissibly be treated. In *Torture and Moral Integrity* and in *Liberalism with Excellence*, for example, I have advanced a number of arguments in support of the proposition that the absolute wrongness of several types of torture cannot be fully explained solely on the basis of the interests or autonomy of the potential victims of torture. Any focus on the interests or autonomy of the victims has to be combined with a focus on the moral integrity of the potential perpetrators of torture. (One strand of the relevant argumentation has surfaced in my replies to Cruft in section 1.3.3 above.) Although I do likewise make this point in *The Ethics of Capital Punishment*—Kramer 2011: 62—it applies not only to moral protections against the use of punitive torture but also to moral protections against the various other ways in which criminal defendants or convicts might be mistreated by a system of governance. Notwithstanding that any defilingly evil defendant or convict partakes of dignity by dint of being endowed with the elementary characteristics of human adults that have been listed in the preceding paragraph, the justificatory basis for the impermissibility of mistreating him procedurally or substantively is typically not centered on his interests. Instead, the justificatory basis is typically centered on the moral integrity of the prevailing system of governance which would demean itself by stooping to mistreat him in accordance with his deserts.

Even more important here is that the property of dignity occasionally gets invoked in *The Ethics of Capital Punishment* in contexts where I would now refer instead to the political and social and economic conditions under which everyone in a society can be warranted in feeling a sturdy sense of self-respect. Consider, for example, the following passage from Chapter 6 of that book (2011: 236):

> With the sheer extravagance of his array of iniquities, [a defilingly evil offender] has established that his life is antithetical to the dignity of humankind. He has set himself firmly against such dignity rather than in support of it, as he has committed atrocities which in their overweeningness are determinative of the ethical character of his whole life. Those atrocities vest his life with its horrible significance, for they ethically dominate the sundry other things that he has done. Having dedicated himself to the murderous destruction and perverse exploitation of features of people that are fundamentally characteristic of them as human beings, he has pitted his life against the nature of humanity generally. His life therefore stands as an affront to the dignity of

[37] As I indicate in Kramer 2011: 61 n.22, non-human animals are also possessed of dignity. However, because their faculties of rational agency are far less sophisticated than those of most adult human beings, the moral constraints in which their dignity consists are not as extensive. Broadly the same is true of human babies and infants, and of human adults who are mentally incapacitated.

> humankind and as a blot on the relationship between humankind and his community, especially if his community is assigning large quantities of resources to the sustainment of his existence.

Though the notion of dignity as I invoke it in this passage is obviously related very closely to that notion as I invoke it in passages where I am probing the moral limitations on the procedures and substantive measures that can permissibly be undertaken against convicts, the clarity and precision of this passage can be greatly enhanced through the refocusing of it on the conditions under which high levels of self-respect can be warranted for the sundry members of a society. It is those conditions to which the life of a defilingly iniquitous malefactor is inimical, for the extravagant evildoing in his life constitutes his contemptuous repudiation of those conditions and his determined assault upon them.

I have tersely contemplated the property of human dignity in this subsection because Duff broaches that property at several junctures in his chapter. He does so, of course, in order to resist my conclusions about the purgative rationale for capital punishment. He writes, for example (2022: 340): "In ordinary punishments there is always room to hope that the offender will come in the end to accept his punishment as a justified response to his wrongdoing, even after his sentence is completed; but carrying out an execution removes any such hope. Is this something that we can properly do to a human being who retains his 'dignity'?" One thing to be noted here is that what Duff says about capital punishment is also true of a term of lifelong imprisonment. There is no opportunity for a convict to become repentant after such a term of incarceration has been completed. I have devoted several pages in *The Ethics of Capital Punishment* to mulling over such affinities between the death penalty and lifelong imprisonment (2011: 286–90). Even more important in the present context is that I likewise devote many pages in *The Ethics of Capital Punishment* and in *Torture and Moral Integrity* to maintaining that executions conducted on the basis of the purgative rationale are consistent with the constraints imposed by the property of human dignity. I am particularly concerned there to differentiate between the moral bearings of capital punishment and the moral bearings of torture (2011: 61–5, 110–15, 259–60; 2014: 188–9, 197–9). Moreover, as I have observed in *Liberalism with Excellence* (2017: 259–60), the distinction which I draw between the morality of capital punishment and the morality of torture is directly connected to the requirements of self-restraint which I have expounded in my critique of edificatory perfectionism and in my justification for the principle of freedom of expression. That distinction can therefore be articulated straightforwardly with reference to the political and social and economic conditions under which every member of a society can be warranted in sustaining an ample sense of self-respect. Of course, I do not expect Duff to embrace my arguments on these matters. Nonetheless, they constitute my reply to the question which he reasonably poses in the quotation just above. I have not left that question unaddressed.

6.1.5 Alternatives to Death

In the closing portion of his chapter, Duff eloquently mounts an argument for an alternative to the death penalty that would suitably reflect the appallingness of the crimes perpetrated by a defilingly evil offender. A substantial portion of his advocacy of such an alternative should be quoted here (2022: 341):

> Suppose instead that the alternative consisted in a protracted, even endless, attempt to bring the wrongdoer to recognize the evil he perpetrated: an attempt that might include life imprisonment, perhaps even periods of solitary confinement, but not simply as ways of isolating him or making him suffer; they would instead be integral parts of a communicative endeavor to convey to him, to persuade him to grasp, the terrible implications of his crimes—an endeavor that of its very nature seeks a response from him. He would still exist in the world: but perhaps what affronts the world is not his existence as such, but an existence in which his wrongdoing is not addressed with adequate seriousness, in which he is allowed not to confront it; and that is not the existence he would have on this account. The point is not that such a communicative endeavor is likely to succeed—we might be empirically fairly confident that it will not: it is, rather, that we can in this way do justice to the seriousness of the offender's wrongdoing without thinking that we must end his life; and in doing so we treat him as someone who retains his dignity as a responsible, reflective human being.

In response to this splendid passage, I will first intensify the stance taken in *The Ethics of Capital Punishment*, but I will then proceed to an accommodating remark that goes quite a long way toward bridging the gulf between Duff and me.

On the one hand, although in *The Ethics of Capital Punishment* I repeatedly reject lifelong imprisonment-without-parole as a punishment for any defilingly evil criminal that could serve adequately as an alternative to a purgative execution, I make a curious partial concession at one juncture in Chapter 6 of that book. I there accept that a defilingly evil offender's "grievous wrongs against his community and against his particular victims can be handled satisfactorily through lifelong imprisonment-without-parole in conditions of solitary confinement." To be sure, I immediately add that the offender's "besmirching of the relationship between his community and humanity cannot similarly be rectified through the intensification of the drabness of his confinement or through any other punitive measure short of the death penalty" (2011: 236). Nevertheless, I do not now fathom why I made even a partial concession on this point. After all, the outrages committed by the offender against his victims and his community are comprised within the outrages committed by him against humanity. This point can be framed most perspicuously in the terms which I now favor. If the expenditure of resources on the continuation of the life of a defilingly evil criminal (past the time needed for a fair trial and for appellate procedures) is damaging to the full conditions under which every member of humankind can be warranted in harboring an ample sense of self-respect, then *a fortiori* that expenditure of resources is damaging to the full conditions under which every member of the evildoer's community can be warranted in harboring such a sense of self-respect.

On the other hand, I shall close my replies to Duff in a spirit of compromise. His proposed alternative to purgative executions does take very seriously the concerns that undergird the purgative rationale. A system of governance that handles defilingly evil offenders in the manner envisaged by Duff would be responding to those concerns earnestly. I am not here abandoning the purgative rationale for the death penalty. I remain of the view that, by declining to operate in accordance with that rationale, a Duffian system of governance would be failing to fulfill some of the obligations imposed upon it by its paramount moral responsibility to bring about the political and social and economic conditions under which everyone within its jurisdiction can be warranted in feeling a hearty sense of self-respect. I stand by the arguments in *The Ethics of Capital Punishment* which substantiate that view. Still, even though a Duffian system of governance would be falling short of full compliance with the obligations incumbent upon it, its pursuit of its approach to extreme evil would be admirably dogged. As I have observed in the fourth and seventh chapters of *Freedom of Expression as Self-Restraint* (2021: 152–3, 296–301), the character of any system of governance as a liberal democracy is a scalar property. Such a system can fall short of perfect compliance with some of the principles of liberal democracy while nonetheless satisfying the requirements of those principles to high degrees. In that event, as I remark in *Freedom of Expression as Self-Restraint*, "the minor deviations from [a few of the principles of liberal democracy] will not appreciably lower the level of self-respect that is warranted for any member of the society [in which those deviations occur]" (2021: 152–3). Though a Duffian system of governance would indeed be deviating from what is required of it under the purgative justification for capital punishment, its attentiveness to the concerns which inform that justification would mitigate the impact of the deviations. The overall conformity of that system to the principles of liberal democracy might well be high enough to enable it to discharge its paramount moral responsibility. Thus, although the divergence between Duff and me is in one sense far-reaching indeed, it is in another sense largely inconsiderable.

6.2 Christopher Kutz and Freedom of Expression

Having known Kutz for nearly two decades, and having admired his scholarly work for an even longer period, I am gratified to have an essay by him in this collection. Given that he concentrates on my most recently published book, his chapter is especially fitting as the final port of call in my long journey through this volume.

6.2.1 Communication-Independence

Kutz's chapter mischaracterizes a number of the ideas presented in *Freedom of Expression as Self-Restraint*. Let us begin here with the notion of communication-independence—a notion that is central to virtually every chapter in my book. To delineate the property of communication-independence as tersely as possible here, I will present an excerpt from a paragraph in one of the many portions of my book where I expound the nature of that property. In this excerpt, I am contemplating Oliver Wendell Holmes's famous scenario of a man who maliciously shouts "Fire" in a crowded theater (2021: 67):

> [I]f the adjective "communication-independent" were supposed to indicate that the wrongfulness of the act of shouting "Fire" is not due to the communicative import of such an utterance, then that adjective would be inapposite. However, when I characterize the wrongfulness of the utterance as communication-independent,

> or when I contend that the utterance can properly be subjected to sanctions as a communication-independent mode of misconduct, there is no suggestion that the wrongfulness is unattributable to the content and context of the message which the shout of "Fire" has expressed. Rather, the point is that that shout belongs to a category of misconduct—the category of inducement (or attempted inducement) of a perilous public disturbance—that is not inherently communicative. Any number of potential or actual instances of such misconduct are communicative, and any number of potential or actual instances of such misconduct are non-communicative. These heterogeneous instances are categorized together on the basis of the wrong-making properties which they have in common. Those properties are instantiated by any endeavor to initiate or exacerbate a situation of dangerous public disorder, whether the endeavor is communicative or non-communicative in its character. Precisely because the actions that instantiate those wrong-making properties can be either communicative or non-communicative, the instantiation of those properties is communication-independent. And because the wrongness of any such action does not hinge on whether the action is one of the communicative instances or one of the non-communicative instances in the category of misconduct to which it belongs, its wrongness is likewise communication-independent.

I say far more about communication-independence in my book with further examples, but this passage should suffice for the moment to reveal the untenability of some of the ways in which Kutz characterizes that property. For example, he asserts that I point "to the wrong-making features of a situation or course of conduct, and whether they inhere in the speech itself, as it were, or in some set of (presumably physical) causes and effects that can be cleaved off from the speech" (2022: 344). This confusing description by Kutz does not correctly encapsulate the relevant distinction. To know whether some type of communicative conduct can be proscribed in consistency with the principle of freedom of expression, we have to ask whether the conduct of that type is constitutive of serious wrongdoing that can be perpetrated both through communicative actions and through non-communicative actions. If the answer to such a question is affirmative, then a legal prohibition on the conduct can be consistent with the principle of freedom of expression—though, of course, consistency with that principle is only one necessary condition for the moral permissibility of proscribing the type of communicative conduct.

Also mistaken is a comment by Kutz on my example—borrowed from John Stuart Mill—involving a fiery orator who delivers a harangue about the iniquity of corn-dealers to an irate mob gathered outside the home of a corn-dealer. Kutz declares that "what makes that speech wrong is that it has a tendency to cause others to commit physical acts of violence upon the corn dealer" (2022: 345). Had I specified the communication-independent wrongness of the orator's tirade in this fashion, I would have thereby undermined much of the argumentation in the rest of my book. Fortunately, I have not made such an error. Instead I have maintained that, because of the proximity of the speaker's utterances to the mob's rampages and because of the role of those utterances in deliberately and directly impelling the rampages, the declamation of the speaker is subsumed into the mob's violence as one of the opening stages thereof. That declamation constitutes the speaker's direct participation in a lynching.

This type of serious wrongdoing, the direct participation of a person in a lynching, can occur either through communicative actions or through non-communicative actions. An inflammatory diatribe that stirs up a mob into a frenzy is one way in which somebody can directly contribute to the perpetration of a lynching, and the placing of a rope around the victim's neck is another such way. Those two modes of direct participation, along with countless other possible modes of such participation, are grouped together in a category of evildoing—on the basis of the wrong-making properties which all of them share. Because the incendiary tirade belongs to that category of evildoing, it is aptly classifiable as communication-independent misconduct.

Kutz proceeds to adduce an example of a highwayman who accosts and threatens a victim (2022: 345). Two aspects of his discussion of the example, very closely related to each other, should be remarked upon here. First, while correctly stating that the issuance of a threat by the highwayman and the perpetration of incitement by the inflammatory orator belong to distinct categories of misconduct, Kutz appears to think that I am unaware of their distinctness. Yet, throughout my book, my ruminations on incitement are in fact separate from my ruminations on threats or assaults. (As is presumably evident, I am here using the term "assaults" in its relatively narrow and technical sense to denote any course of conduct that culpably places someone in apprehension of an imminent attack.) Second, Kutz contends that the category of wrongdoing to which threats and assaults belong is not communication-independent. Yet in my principal treatment of threats and assaults in my book—in Kramer 2021: 99–101—I argue that that category of wrongdoing is indeed communication-independent. Its wrong-making features can be instantiated both by communicative courses of conduct and by non-communicative courses of conduct. Kutz naturally is entitled to impugn my arguments if he wishes to do so, but he does not do so.

6.2.2 Vagueness and Communication-Independence

Near the outset of his chapter, Kutz suggests that my efforts to elucidate the main concepts pertaining to the principle of freedom of expression are aimed at showing that those concepts have sharp boundaries. He admonishes that "some unclarity is needed, to unsettle the authorities and reclaim the space of rebellious possibility for the individuals. Put otherwise, the logical clarity of Kramer's principle is what renders it unfit for liberal democratic service. I will focus in this contribution on the case of incitement, as a way of showing why Kramer might want to dull his [analytical] razor if he wants to protect freedom" (2022: 343-4). This picture of my theoretical enterprise in *Freedom of Expression as Self-Restraint* is misdirected. It is true that I strive to elucidate the relevant concepts in that book as in my other books, but what the elucidation reveals—in this area of political philosophy as in other areas—is that those concepts do not have sharp boundaries. They are vague in the technical sense. I state as much explicitly at more than one juncture in *Freedom of Expression as Self-Restraint*, as in the following passage from the book's third chapter: "Of course, like the other limits and distinctions established by the principle of freedom of expression, the boundaries just mentioned will be flanked by a gray area of borderline cases in which the applicability or inapplicability of the relevant concepts is not fully determinate. Every distinction drawn in the domain of political philosophy is accompanied by such a gray area." Admittedly, I straightaway add: "Nonetheless, although the potential for borderline cases is ineliminable, most cases do not fall within the gray area. In countless situations, ... the implications of the principle of freedom of expression are fully determinate" (2021: 107). Still, that observation is fully consistent with the proposition that all or most of the key concepts in the philosophy of freedom of expression do not have sharp boundaries. As I aver in a later chapter of the book: "Any vague property is such that, alongside the numerous cases in which it is determinately present or determinately absent, there are borderline cases in which it is neither determinately present nor determinately absent" (2021: 301).

In my reflections on the prohibitability of acts of solicitation to commit crimes, I contend that such acts are subsumed into the crimes which they designedly instigate (2021: 69–72). Mulling over my approach to the matter, Kutz retorts that "what is needed [for Kramer's purposes] is a sharp distinction between utterances that are 'subsumed' into an ensuing crime and utterances that are not" (2022: 346). As is apparent from what I have just been saying, this retort by Kutz is inapposite. At several junctures in *Freedom of Expression as Self-Restraint*, I forthrightly acknowledge that the major concepts which I invoke are embeddable in sorites paradoxes and are therefore neither determinately applicable nor determinately inapplicable to various borderline cases. My account of the principle of freedom of expression does not need concepts with sharp boundaries that would avert the occurrence of any borderline cases. The chimera of such boundaries is denied, rather than affirmed or presupposed, in my book. Whenever some instance of communicative conduct is neither determinately protected by the principle of freedom of expression nor determinately unprotected by it, the indeterminacy is to be resolved in favor of the protectedness of the conduct.

6.2.3 Solicitation to Commit a Crime

When pondering the crime of solicitation to commit a crime, Kutz declares: "So the difference between protected advocacy and unprotected incitement or solicitation cannot be specificity of intent, for (in every jurisdiction) a crime of solicitation can be found even when the specific addressee is unknown, or the specific acts unforeseen" (2022: 346). I am a philosopher rather than a legal scholar, and my book on freedom of expression recounts what the law of any jurisdiction should be rather than what the law of any jurisdiction is. Nonetheless, Kutz's assertion is at variance with my understanding of the crime of solicitation as it is defined in the jurisdictions of the United States and England. Specificity of intention or orientation is not the only key factor, but it is a key factor. On the one hand, as is indicated in a classic American study of the crime of solicitation from which I quote in my book, "[i]t is, of course, unnecessary for the actor to go into great detail as to the manner in which the crime solicited is to be committed." On the other hand, as the authors of that study immediately add: "But it is necessary ... that, in the context of the knowledge and position of the intended recipient, the solicitation carry meaning in terms of some concrete course of conduct that it is the actor's object to [induce]" (Wechsler, Jones, and Korn 1961: 627, quoted in Kramer 2021: 72).

Of course, as is signaled by the second of these quoted sentences with its reference to the position of the intended recipient, the specificity of the intention or orientation in an act of solicitation is only one chief consideration. Also of great importance in many a context is the relationship between the addressor and the addressee(s) of an act of solicitation. Often there is a pre-existing relationship between the parties—such as the relationship between the ringleader of a criminal gang and the subordinates within that gang—but, even when there is no such pre-existing relationship, the status of a communication as an act of solicitation is frequently determined partly by the ability and inclination of an addressor to benefit the addressee(s) for compliance with the solicitation or to harm the addressee(s) for noncompliance. Although that aspect of a situation might not be stated explicitly in the communication through which a crime is solicited, its perceptibility by the parties is ofttimes crucial for the status of a communication as an act of solicitation.

Kutz submits that "we might wonder whether there is a difference to be found between the militant agitator who writes a pamphlet saying, 'Will someone do justice to these greedy banks?' and the crime boss who lets the word go out, that he would be pleased to see some banks knocked off" (2022: 346). One point to be noted afresh here is that I do not insist on the sharpness of the edges of the relevant concepts. I readily allow that there can be borderline instances in regard to either of the two types of communications which Kutz envisages. Everything will depend on the details of the instances. Nevertheless, what can be said with considerable confidence is that most credible instances of the first type of communication which he delineates will be properly classifiable as advocacy rather than as incitement, and that many credible instances of the second type of communication which he delineates will be properly classifiable as solicitation. Typical instances of exhortations by radical agitators in pamphlets are not subsumed into any misdeeds that might ultimately be inspired by them, because the connections between them and the misdeeds are not sufficiently focused and proximate to warrant the classification of the exhortations as some opening stages of the misdeeds. Very different in those respects are many credible instances of communications through which a criminal kingpin expresses his wishes for bank heists to his subordinates and associates (with clear suggestions of rewards for compliance with those wishes, attached to the communications as implicatures thereof). Many such communications from a kingpin are properly classifiable as the opening stages of the criminality which they designedly instigate.

Kutz demurs as follows: "The trouble, of course, is that Kramer's distinction between communication that is 'subsumed' by the following crime and those independent is a conclusory distinction, not a logical or semantic one" (2022: 347). In *Freedom of Expression as Self-Restraint*, I do not suggest that the distinction to which he refers is a matter of logic or semantics. It is manifestly an ethical distinction, drawn in a book that is a work of political and moral philosophy. Of course, that distinction is partly focused on empirically observable features of the situations to which it is applied, but the ethical significance of those features is patently an ethical matter rather than a logical or semantic matter. I am therefore surprised when Kutz further reprovingly declares: "The distinction, in other words, is a substantive political judgment.... No work is done by a formal criterion" (2022: 347). Precisely because the substance of his pronouncement here is wholly unexceptionable, I have always concurred with it. At no point in my book do I presume that the distinction between advocacy and incitement or between advocacy and solicitation is somehow formal rather than substantively ethical.

Kutz later comments on the example of the leader of a criminal gang (2022: 347): "A prosecutor will charge, and a jury convict the crime boss on his utterance, not because it is somehow linked to a communicatively-independent crime, but because we understand the crime boss to be operating within a structure that gives his utterances the force of commands therein: it will (likely) be acted upon once uttered (or so presents a danger), because of the broader set of norms and roles inhabited by boss and underling." The dichotomy posed here is a false dichotomy. In significant part because the utterance by the boss of the criminal gang is located in relationships which endue it with the force of a behest and which implicitly or explicitly attach to it the prospect of a reward for compliance, that utterance is subsumed into the communication-independent misdeeds which it designedly sets into motion. It constitutes the boss's direct participation in those misdeeds through his performance of the opening stage in each of them. Hence, Kutz's own explanation of the proscribability of the gangster's utterance does not exclude or supersede my explanation. Rather, as is apparent from my antepenultimate paragraph above, the factor highlighted in his explanation is one major consideration that enters into my own explanation.

6.2.4 Another False Dichotomy

Kutz introduces another false dichotomy when he seeks to account for the moral protectedness of exhortations by anarchists in pamphlets: "We excuse—in a liberal society—the anarchist's pamphlet, not because resulting crimes are communicatively-dependent, nor because the anarchist's words are, or might be, suitably general. Rather, we protect the utterance because we understand it to be a general message conveyed not as command but potential persuasion, in a community of rational equals; and protecting their status (as audience members) entails protecting the speaker as well, even at some risk of incidental crime" (2022: 347). Kutz's terminology here is redolent of the Meiklejohnian tradition of thinking about freedom of expression, in which the moral protectedness of political communications is held to be grounded on the requirements for deliberation and self-governance in a democratic polity. I discuss that addressee-focused tradition at a couple of junctures in *Freedom of Expression as Self-Restraint* (2021: 29–30, 118–22), and I there pithily present a few of the reasons for my general discountenancing of that tradition. In particular, I laconically explain why such an approach cannot vindicate any absolute principle of freedom of expression. There is no need for me to elaborate on that matter at this juncture – since, notwithstanding what I have just said, the substance of the second sentence in this latest remark by Kutz can be extricated from the vocabulary in which he phrases it. When that sentence is reconstrued in the manner which I shall outline, it exposes the untenability of the sentence which precedes it.

That is, we should take the second sentence in the quotation to be adverting to the two chief considerations which I have broached here and in my book when I have explained why acts of solicitation are subsumed into the communication-independent wrongdoing which they intentionally bring about. Kutz's statement touches both upon the open-endedness of the audience to whom the remonstrations in any typical pamphlet by an anarchist are addressed, and upon the absence of any credible prospect of rewards from the anarchist for compliance with those remonstrations. Such considerations, pondered in light of the principle of freedom of expression, lead to the conclusion that the anarchist's expostulations are morally protected by that principle because they are not subsumed into any criminality that might be prompted by them. Because of the diffuseness of the links between the expostulations and any instances of such criminality, none of those instances is a later stage of a unified wrongful enterprise in which the expostulations are the opening stage. In other words, the very factors invoked by Kutz in the second sentence of the quotation above are rightly adducible against the first sentence therein.

6.2.5 Incitement in Rwanda

Kutz next turns his attention to the horrific radio broadcasts that occurred in Rwanda during the spring of 1994, through which the members of the Tutsi minority were repeatedly vilified in repugnantly incendiary terms and through which they were time and again accused of actively conspiring against the Hutu majority and against the Rwandan government. As the genocide of Tutsis got under way in April 1994, the radio broadcasts issued instructions on the best means of locating and slaughtering the Tutsis. Until the broadcasts were forcibly shut down by the main rebel group that was fighting against the government, they fervently encouraged and congratulated the perpetrators of the genocide.

Kutz proclaims that, if the people responsible for the hideous broadcasts were to be legitimately punished, "it [would] have to be because the risk posed by the speech (viewed *ex post*) to the civil liberties of Tutsis was too great, weighed against the low value of its content, and not because it is somehow itself 'part of' the genocide." He seeks to justify his statement as follows: "Otherwise there will be no way to protect those instances and types of speech that must be protected, for the freedom of expression principle to have any content at all. For example, pro-Hutu speech in a political campaign might have had a similarly predictable causal long-term effect on Tutsi civil liberties, but restricting such speech would be tantamount to shutting down the political arena altogether" (2022: 347). Several rejoinders are apposite here.

First, as I contend in *Freedom of Expression as Self-Restraint* (2021: 282–3), many of the rebarbative radio broadcasts in the spring of 1994 were straightforwardly instances of incitement under the *Brandenburg v. Ohio* standard. Many of them vigorously encouraged and assisted the genocidal onslaughts of the Hutus against the Tutsis. Contrary to Kutz's suggestion that those broadcasts were not a part of the genocide in Rwanda, the people responsible for the broadcasts were direct participants in the genocide through their poisonous urging on of the butchery and through their dispensing of information.

Second, the two radio stations that disseminated the hate-filled propaganda were both very closely connected to the Rwandan government. One of them, Radio Rwanda, was owned and operated by the government as its official station; and the other, Radio Télévision des Milles Collines (RTLM), was set up by the government as a nominally private station that nonetheless had intimate and extensive ties to the Hutu-dominated regime. Hence, even before the spring of 1994—when many of the broadcasts by the two stations were unequivocally incitements to genocide—the obsessive denunciation of Tutsis by RTLM was grossly in contravention of the moral duties incumbent on every system of governance to uphold the fundamental equality of the members of its society. Transgressions of those duties are communication-independent modes of misconduct even when they are perpetrated through communications. Every system of governance is both morally obligated and morally permitted to avert such transgressions and to impose sanctions on the officials who are responsible for them.

Third, as I remark at more than one juncture in *Freedom of Expression as Self-Restraint*, there can be societies in which the attitudes and institutions that prevail among the general public are egregiously illiberal and in which the enactment of hate-speech prohibitions might be the lesser of two wrongs. Rwanda in the 1990s was a powder-keg country of this sort. Let us suppose counterfactually that RTLM had been genuinely independent of the government in Rwanda, and let us concentrate solely on the broadcasts by RTLM in 1993 and very early 1994 before the station moved into outright incitement of acts of genocide. Although those broadcasts during that period were suffused with vile bigotry and conspiracy theories against Tutsis, most and perhaps all of them were classifiable as advocacy rather than as incitement. If undertaken by a genuinely non-governmental radio station, then, those broadcasts would have been protected by the principle of freedom of expression. Outlawing them would have been morally impermissible. Nevertheless, in a society where the attitudes of the general public were so drenched with the toxicant of ethnic hatred, the outlawing of RTLM's promotion of such hatred might have been less gravely wrong than the toleration of that promotion. As I write in my book (2021: 288):

> At the very best, [hate-speech] laws in some extreme circumstances might be less gravely wrong than would the non-enactment of them. In a situation where a system of governance has miserably fallen short of promoting a robust ethos of liberal-democratic values in the society over which the system presides, the dissemination of malicious falsehoods about some vulnerable minority group might very seriously jeopardize the basic dignity of the members of that group—even where the *Brandenburg* standard for incitement is not satisfied. In such a quandary, the enactment of some legal restrictions on the dissemination of those falsehoods might be less gravely wrong for a certain period than would the continuation of a policy of legally permitting the dissemination. As [the opening chapter of *Freedom of Expression as Self-Restraint*] has explained, conflicts of this type can arise between the principle of freedom of expression and some other moral requirements in extreme circumstances. When such a moral conflict does occur, a system of governance is under a moral obligation to abide by the principle of freedom of expression and is simultaneously under a moral obligation to deviate from that principle. Moreover, notwithstanding that the former obligation is always dauntingly stringent, it can be less stringent in some conceivable situations than the latter obligation. Although the moral constraints imposed by the principle of freedom of expression on any system of governance are absolute in that they are always and everywhere binding, their absoluteness—as Chapter 1 has recounted—is weak rather than strong. Formidably stringent though the principle of freedom of expression is, there can be extreme circumstances in which a conflicting moral requirement is even more so. Nonetheless, as Chapter 1 has emphasized, a moral obligation that has been overtopped in stringency by a conflicting moral obligation is still binding. Hence, even in the truly exceptional situations where the principle of freedom of expression has been so overtopped, it remains fully binding. Contraventions of it are morally wrong even when they are morally optimal.

6.2.6 Incitement by an Egomaniacal Fantasist

In the next example of incitement which Kutz contemplates, the real source of his dissatisfaction with my approach to freedom of expression becomes evident. As I will emphasize, however, his dissatisfaction is due to his misunderstanding of the tenor of my book. He adverts to the harangue delivered at length by the American President Donald Trump to a furious mob in Washington, DC on January 6, 2021:

> [A]n American President who urges a crowd of supporters to march on the legislature in order to be "strong," "show strength," and "fight like hell" to "stop" the certification of the election of his opponent, *might* be thought to be merely engaging in the usual political tropes of a rally, and so to be engaged in protected, "hot" speech. But when it is clear that the President knows the crowd includes many who are armed, whose prior communications have evinced a desire for violent action, who then engage in violent action while the President himself watches on television and refrains from coming to the aid of the legislature, then potential criminal liability for such speech would seem to be necessary to the survival of the state of law itself. An ambiguous message, with no evidence of violent intent, might have led to the same destruction; as might a more specific speech, delivered in prior, calmer times. If we decide to protect these latter forms of speech (as the *Brandenburg* test does), but not the actual speech delivered to the hot crowd, that is because we judge that the dangers posed by immediate exhortation outweigh the dangers of reduced scope for political rhetoric. Nothing metaphysical here. (2022: 347-8, emphasis in original)

Although the final two sentences in this passage are my main concern, I will first comment on the disgraceful declamation by Trump.

I join Kutz in believing that Trump could properly be subjected to legal sanctions for his diatribe, and I also join Kutz in being carefully attentive to the context and tone of that diatribe. I will briefly add a few observations to the details which Kutz has aptly mentioned. First, the audience of irate supporters consisted of people who revere Trump and who wholeheartedly endorse his persistent falsehoods about his having won the November 2020 election which had then been stolen from him by the chicanery of the Democrats. Second, having uttered those falsehoods on numerous occasions in the weeks leading up to his January 2021 tirade, he voiced them again and again in that tirade itself. He vehemently urged his supporters not to let the election be stolen from them. Third, as Trump well knew, some of the heavily armed people at the rally were from far-right militias that are violently hostile to the present system of governance in the United States. Fourth, the tone of Trump's oration was as important as its substance and context. Somebody reading the transcript of the oration might credibly conclude that—even when its explosive context is taken into account—it is not determinately classifiable as incitement. However, when the outpouring of Trump's bile is heard in its entirety, its determinate classifiability as an instance of incitement is quite plain. Portions of the speech that can seem moderate on the page of a transcript are revealed to be angrily sarcastic when they are heard. Together, then, the tone and the substance and the context of the diatribe were sufficient to render it properly susceptible to legal sanctions.

Kutz and I concur, therefore, on how Trump's vituperation should have been treated. However, as is made clear by the penultimate sentence in my latest quotation from Kutz, he and I diverge over the justification for our shared verdict. Kutz believes that the justification must reside in consequentialist balancing. I of course maintain instead that, because Trump's vituperation was an instance of incitement, it was an instance of communication-independent misconduct. It was one of the initial stages of the violence and other criminality which it designedly instigated. Determinately classifiable as Trump's participation in such misconduct, his ranting was unprotected by the principle of freedom of expression. I reach this conclusion without having to engage in the hand-waving charade of balancing.

Even more bemusing is the final sentence in the quotation above. Far from purporting to be undertaking any metaphysical enquiries that are prior to my ethical enquiries in *Freedom of Expression as Self-Restraint*, my contentions about the classifiability of any communications as incitement or as advocacy are ethical contentions. To be sure, as I have already stated in section 6.2.3, those ethical contentions are grounded partly on observations of the empirical features of any communication in question (such as the features of Trump's diatribe which I have outlined in the preceding paragraph and which Kutz outlines in his own discussion of the matter). Even so, any claims by me about the subsumption of this or that communication into the criminality which it provokes are ethical claims.

In his next sentence, Kutz again misapprehends the nature of my argumentation: "So the first move, of distinguishing communications that are 'part of' the prohibited conduct from those that are not part of it, but merely advocate it, fails for lack of a non-conclusory basis with which to make the mereological judgment" (2022: 348). Throughout my cogitations on the distinction between incitement and advocacy or between solicitation and advocacy in *Freedom of Expression as Self-Restraint*, my mereological judgments are ethical judgments through and through. I do indeed reach mereological judgments, but they are not prior to my ethical judgments. They are neither value-independent nor value-neutral.

Also mistaken is Kutz's assumption that my so-called first move described in the sentence just quoted is separate from my so-called second move described in the following sentence: "Kramer's second move, deployed in the case of perjury and elsewhere, is to distinguish between cases where the wrong can itself be committed in a way free of communication, and cases where it cannot" (2022: 348). Although the wording by Kutz here is somewhat rough, it is largely correct as a summation of the property of communication-independence. What is incorrect is any suggestion that this so-called second move is not also my so-called first move. Both when I am distinguishing incitement or solicitation from advocacy and when I am ruminating on perjury or defamation, the aim of the enterprise is to ascertain whether the specified communicative conduct is constitutive of communication-independent wrongdoing. In other words, my enterprise is thoroughly ethical. A theorist pursuing such an endeavor has to pin down the nature of the wrongdoing that is constituted by some type or instance of communicative conduct; any determination of that kind is patently an ethical judgment.

6.2.7 Perjury and Defamation

Let us proceed, then, to examine Kutz's remarks on my analyses of perjury and defamation. Kutz submits that my account of the communication-independent wrongdoing constituted by some defamatory statements is along the following lines: "[T]hough libels are routinely committed through verbal expression, they can be committed in other ways, such as by displaying embarrassing photographs" (2022: 348). However, the main point of my reflections on the communication-independence of the wrongdoing constituted by some defamatory statements is that some such statements belong to a wider category of wrongdoing—the category of actions which culpably and baselessly tarnish someone's reputation in the eyes of upright members of his or her community. Unless the laws in a system of governance are such that the communicative actions and the non-communicative actions in that category are treated broadly on a par with regard to the legal sanctions in which they can result, the legal proscription of the defamatory statements in that category is not communication-neutral and is therefore violative of the principle of freedom of expression. (Any defamatory statements which fall outside that category of communication-independent wrongdoing are not legitimately proscribable at all.)

More problematic are the comments by Kutz on the outlawing of perjury. He begins those comments by noting that perjurious statements are inherently communicative. Such an observation is correct but beside the point, since the outlawing of perjurious statements is morally permissible under the principle of freedom of expression only if such statements are proscribed not *qua* statements but *qua* culpable efforts to prejudice legal proceedings. The category of culpable efforts to prejudice legal proceedings is a communication-independent type of misconduct, even though the perjurious statements in that category are of course communicative. How do we know, in any particular jurisdiction, whether perjurious statements are proscribed there as members of that communication-independent category of wrongdoing rather than as statements? We have to scrutinize the laws of the jurisdiction to ascertain whether non-communicative efforts to prejudice legal proceedings are treated broadly on a par with communicative efforts. If and only if the answer to that question is affirmative, the laws of the jurisdiction which prohibit perjury are in keeping with the principle of freedom of expression.

Kutz adverts to acts of fabricating evidence and tampering with evidence, but there are also quite a few other ways in which the integrity of legal proceedings can be deliberately subverted. Evidence can be deliberately withheld or destroyed; judges or jurors can be bribed; judges or jurors can be intimidated. To ascertain the answer to the question broached in my preceding paragraph, we have to examine how the laws of a jurisdiction deal with the sundry ways in which the integrity of legal proceedings can be culpably undermined. Kutz declares that "it is notable that perjury is punished substantially more severely" in some jurisdictions than is tampering with evidence. He surmises that "[t]he extra severity of perjury's punishment … reflects its explicitly communicative character and the special harm done by willfully false expression in the juridical context. If that isn't punishment of expression *qua* expression, I'm not sure what is" (2022: 349). Though Kutz thinks that he is posing an objection to my analysis of the permissibility or impermissibility of legal constraints on perjury, he is not really doing any such thing. If he is correct when he declares that in certain jurisdictions the sanctions attached to the perpetration of perjury are significantly more severe than the sanctions attached in those jurisdictions to other ways of corrupting the integrity of legal proceedings, and if the disparities among the sanctions imposed are not explicable by reference to disparities in the gravity of the different ways through which the integrity of such proceedings can be corrupted,[38] then his observation constitutes an objection to the laws that proscribe perjury in the specified jurisdictions. If constitutional guarantees of communicative liberty in those jurisdictions correspond in their contents to the moral principle of freedom of expression—as they morally should—then the laws which proscribe perjury there ought to be invalidated as unconstitutional enactments.

When Kutz incorrectly supposes that he has raised a point which tells against my analysis of the proscribability of perjury rather than against the proscriptions imposed on that mode of conduct in some jurisdictions, he appears to be under the impression that *Freedom of Expression as Self-Restraint* is an endeavor to explain or justify the legal prohibitions on communicative conduct that exist in some particular jurisdiction(s). I warn against any such impression in the opening pages of my book and at quite a number of other junctures thereafter. As I have already affirmed herein, I am a philosopher rather than a legal scholar. My book on freedom of expression is a work of political and moral philosophy rather than a work of legal scholarship. It does not seek to explain or justify the laws that actually exist in this or that jurisdiction. Instead, it expounds a moral principle with which the laws of any jurisdiction must be consistent if those laws are to be morally legitimate. Hence, insofar as the laws of some particular jurisdiction are at variance with that principle, the laws there are morally wrongful.

Also to be queried here is Kutz's assertion that "Kramer leaves largely uninspected what it means to target expression *qua* expression" (2022: 349). In fact, the test which I have outlined in the antepenultimate and penultimate paragraphs above is presented at considerably greater length more than once in *Freedom of Expression as Self-Restraint*, especially in the third chapter of the book. As I have sought to underscore in that chapter, the key to the legitimacy of any prohibition of perjury in a given jurisdiction is whether the system of governance there treats broadly on a par the communicative instances and non-communicative instances in the communication-independent category of misconduct to which perjury belongs.

6.2.8 Back to the Advocacy/Incitement Distinction

Kutz returns to the distinction between advocacy and incitement as, from his consequentialist perspective, he launches a challenge to the import of the property of communication-independence (2022: 349-50):

> At fear of pointing out the obvious, expression is always targeted, for either support or punishment, because of non-expressive circumstances. Returning to the advocacy/incitement distinction, I cannot discern any difference in that respect between the (rightful) punishment of perjurious speech and the wrongful punishment

[38] Of course, the gravity of the different ways of prejudicing various legal proceedings has to be gauged in a communication-neutral fashion. It cannot permissibly be gauged in the manner envisaged by Kutz in my latest quotation from him.

> of seditious or inflammatory speech. Any of those consequences can presumably be achieved through non-expressive means, and so it would seem appropriate, on Kramer's argument, that all could be sanctioned. Troops could be stirred to insubordination by military defeats or debacles, resistance to police could be encouraged by provocateurs, and so forth. The fact that the object or likely effect of the communication could be and is separately targeted by law, or that the act can be subsumed into a joint communicative and non-communicative category, seems entirely irrelevant to the question whether the expressive side of the grouping should be free from sanction. It is virtually always possible to show that the governmental objective is unrelated to speech, and therefore all the work has to be done on balancing the burden on speech against that interest.

As I have explained throughout my 2021 book, the question whether any course of communicative activity can be prohibited in accordance with the principle of freedom of expression is settled by asking whether the course of activity is constitutive of serious communication-independent wrongdoing. Some type or instance of communicative conduct can be constitutive of such wrongdoing in either of two main ways. It can itself amount to such wrongdoing—as perjurious statements (for example) do—or it can be so closely and designedly connected to such wrongdoing that it is one of the initial stages thereof, as tirades of incitement (for example) are. Kutz in the passage above, with his consequentialist inclination to turn issues of communicative freedom into matters of balancing, sweeps aside my analyses of communication-independent wrongdoing as he presses upon me the consequentialist thesis that communications can be properly subjected to legal proscription if they are associated with harmful consequences as their "likely effect[s]." For consequentialists, the regulation of communicative activities is at one with the regulation of any other activities in that the moral permissibility or impermissibility of any regulation hinges entirely on the consequences of imposing some legal restrictions versus the consequences of abstaining from such restrictions. From a consequentialist perspective, my deontological approach to the regulation of communicative activities is incomprehensible.

6.2.9 Standing Laws and Law-Application

At many junctures in *Freedom of Expression as Self-Restraint*, I emphasize that the principle of freedom of expression requires communication-neutrality not only in the standing laws of a jurisdiction but also in the acts of administration and adjudication through which those laws are implemented. Kutz unhelpfully groups together two situations that are markedly different: a situation in which a standing law of a jurisdiction was lacking in communication-neutrality, and a situation in which an instance of enforcement of a communication-neutral law may have been lacking in communication-neutrality. As I maintain in my book (2021: 51), the statute that was enacted by the US Congress in the 1960s to prohibit the destruction of draft cards was not communication-neutral. By contrast, an Arkansas ordinance in the 1970s that banned the unenclosed storage of ruined cars and trucks was communication-neutral as a standing law. Nonetheless, as I argue (2021: 27–9, 40–1, 52–3), the local police may have contravened the requirement of communication-neutrality when they enforced that ordinance against a man who had left his son's demolished truck on his lawn as a protest against the role of the police in causing his son to crash. Kutz groups these two situations together as if both of them involved failings only at the level of law-administration and not also at the level of legislation.

Kutz correctly maintains that multiple purposes were being pursued through the statute that forbade the destruction of draft cards and through the municipal ordinance that forbade the open-air storage of wrecked automobiles, but he is thereby making a point which I myself make. In my remarks on the draft-card enactment in *Freedom of Expression as Self-Restraint* I explicitly state that multiple purposes were ascribable to that enactment, and I likewise submit that the aim of squelching anti-war protests was the dominant purpose and was itself sufficient to impel the Congress to pass the statute. In my book's ruminations on the Arkansas ordinance, I not only impute multiple communication-unrelated purposes to that ordinance; in addition, I contend that the ordinance itself was communication-neutral. As for the enforcement of that law against the aggrieved father, I leave open the question whether the police were transgressing the principle of freedom of expression or not, and I outline the sorts of evidence that could have been gathered at the time to ascertain the answer to that question.

Also to be noted here is that Kutz does not specify any communication-unrelated purposes. He proclaims that "[i]n the draft case, the state concern was the encouragement of non-compliance with the draft," and that "in the [Arkansas] case, it was presumably concern that leaving the display would engender further disrespect for law enforcement in mind" (2022: 350). Neither of those purposes is communication-neutral. Each of them is directed against the distinctively communicative effects of the legally proscribed mode of conduct.

Curious as well is Kutz's diagnosis of the wrongness of the challenged law, or of the challenged action of law-enforcement: "State action in these cases was wrong, not because they targeted an inherently communicative object, but because they targeted a communicative means to a non-communicative object forbidden to state authorities. That forbidden object is discussion of the grounds of state legitimacy itself" (2022: 350-1). In these sentences, Kutz's prose is quite opaque. Though the words "object forbidden to state authorities" would normally denote some objective which any system of governance is morally disallowed from pursuing, Kutz is apparently using that phrase instead to denote an activity with which any system of governance is morally disallowed from interfering. Still, even if the opacity of his prose is lessened through such an interpretation, his pronouncement remains untenable. After all, the activity of discussing the grounds of state legitimacy is scarcely non-communicative.

6.2.10 Advertising of Illegalities

When Kutz turns his attention to my cogitations on the advertising of illegalities, he correctly notes that my analysis of such advertising resembles my analysis of solicitation to commit crimes. However, that correct perception is clouded by some missteps in his summaries of those analyses. Kutz attributes to me the view that "the communicative act somehow merges metaphysically into the resulting crime, and so the legitimacy of punishing the crime extends to the legitimacy of punishing the advertisement" (2022: 351). As I have stated already, I do not proceed in my book by first engaging in a metaphysical investigation which can then serve as the basis for my ethical investigation. Instead, the metaphysics and the ethics are inseparable in my claims about the subsumption of certain communications into the criminality which those communications designedly and directly instigate. Although my analyses of solicitation and of incitement and of advertisements about illegalities do pronounce upon the metaphysics of those types of communicative activities, my metaphysical theses are grounded on ethical considerations as much as on premises about certain empirical properties of each activity.

Kutz next alleges that the activity of advertising the availability of children for the sexual gratification of paedophiles is not subsumed into the activity of paedophiliacally abusing children (2022: 351). He adduces three reasons in support of his allegation, each of which is misconceived. First, he notes that in American law the elements of proof required to convict someone of the crime of sexually molesting a child are different from the elements of proof required to convict someone of the crime of sexually trafficking a child. Such an observation does not vindicate Kutz's conclusion, since there are obviously different ways in which people can participate in the same type of communication-independent misconduct. As I several times emphasize in Chapter 3 of *Freedom of Expression as Self-Restraint*, we need to take a synoptic view of the laws in a jurisdiction when we ponder whether those laws are in accordance with the principle of freedom of expression. In the United States there may well be separate laws with distinctive elements of proof that cover the different ways in which people can participate in the communication-independent misconduct of paedophiliac abuse, but that feature of American law is entirely consistent with the possibility that those different ways are treated broadly on a par with regard to the severity of the sanctions imposed. Unless there are disparities among the sanctions that do not reflect disparities in the gravity of the different modes of participation, the possibility just mentioned is an actuality—in which event the overall matrix of laws can be consistent with the principle of freedom of expression. (I obviously am not taking any position here on whether the possibility mentioned is an actuality in the United States. I am simply indicating, at an abstract level, how the answer to that question would be ascertained.)

Second, Kutz remarks that the advertising of the availability of children for paedophiliac abuse is not a necessary condition for the occurrence of such abuse. An observation along those lines, correct though it is, is immaterial – because the status of that advertising as a way of participating in such abuse does not hinge on the indispensability of the advertising for the occurrence of the abuse. Consider here an analogy. If one of the men in a gang of bank robbers is assigned the task of watching out for law-enforcement officials and alerting his fellow gangsters to the arrival of any such officials, his communicative conduct constitutes his participation in a bank robbery even though the use of a lookout is not essential for the occurrence of such a robbery. Much the same is true of advertisements that publicize the availability of children for the sexual gratification of paedophiles; an advertisement of that kind is one of the opening stages in paedophiliac abuse even though some instances of such abuse occur in the absence of any advertisements.

Third, Kutz points out that the advertising of the availability of children for paedophiles is not a sufficient condition for the molesting of the children by such people. Again, his contention is unavailing. He is of course right when he declares that advertisements do not always lead to the results which they are designed to bring about, but hardly any crime is such that its opening stage inevitably leads to its consummation. Though *Freedom of Expression as Self-Restraint* does not probe in detail the topic of unsuccessful attempts to commit crimes, I do touch upon it at a few junctures. For example, when pondering the subsumption of instances of incitement into the serious communication-independent wrongdoing which they are intended to instigate, I write as follows (2021: 261, emphasis in original): "Such an utterance by somebody is an opening stage of the wrongdoing which the inciter is endeavoring to provoke; it constitutes his participation in that wrongdoing. (Of course, if the provocation is unsuccessful, the utterance of incitement constitutes an *attempt* to participate in such wrongdoing rather than an instance of actual participation therein.)" Although the topic of attempts to commit crimes is a large matter that can rewardingly be examined in depth,[39] many such attempts are properly susceptible to legal restrictions and sanctions. And since the category of those attempts is communication-independent, the principle of freedom of expression allows the imposition of legal sanctions for acts of communication that are rightly classifiable as such attempts.

6.2.11 Categories of Communication-Independent Wrongdoing

Kutz launches into a broader attack against my appeals to categories of communication-independent wrongdoing. Drawing upon a line of thought prompted by some comments from McBride, he writes as follows (2022: 351-2):

> Put more abstractly, the question is how to sort and individuate wrongs. At a certain level of description, all wrongs might be thought to blend together—for example, crimes against the state, or crimes against persons, or attacks on the public trust. And within each broad grouping, communicative and non-communicative instances might be found—in which case Kramer's principle will restrict no occasions of liability, since all might be deemed cases of communicative independence. Alternatively each instance of wrongdoing might be individuated by its specific characteristics—so verbal encouragement to another to hire a child prostitute would be a different type of act from tacit encouragement by way of presenting the child directly, in which case there could be liability only for the latter. The test itself can do nothing, since it rests on a necessarily under-specified theory of act-individuation—necessarily because the categories we sort various instances into will reflect a variety of heterogeneous substantive concerns about maximizing freedom, preventing risky behaviors, and responding symbolically to harm.

Although the problem noticed by Kutz and McBride is genuinely a matter that has to be addressed by my account of freedom of expression and by many other such accounts, it is far from an insurmountable difficulty.

One point to be noted at the outset is that Kutz errs in saying that, if all types of wrongdoing were to be lumped together within some staggeringly abstract category, the result would be to eviscerate the principle of freedom of expression by rendering morally permissible all legal restrictions on wrongful types of communications.

[39] There are of course numerous treatments of the topic by philosophers and legal theorists. Still the best treatment, in my estimation, is Duff 1996.

Rather, given that communications of sundry types are wrongful solely because their contents are odious and because they are intended to alter people's outlooks malignly (while not being likely to induce any other wrongdoing in a direct and focused manner), they are not legitimately proscribable irrespective of how the categories of communication-independent wrongdoing are individuated. Moreover, if all types of wrongdoing were to be lumped together, the most probable upshot would consist in the undermining of the moral permissibility of nearly all legal limitations on communications. After all, under the principle of freedom of expression, the severity of the sanctions imposed for the perpetration of wrongdoing through communications has to be broadly on a par with the severity of the sanctions imposed for the perpetration of the same type of wrongdoing through non-communicative conduct. However, if every variety of wrongdoing were in the same category as every other variety, we would almost certainly find a myriad of disparities among the levels of punitive severity in any particular legal system. Most of those disparities would probably not be explicable by reference to disparities among the levels of gravity of the wrongs committed. Hence, the most probable upshot of the lumping-together approach would be nearly the opposite of what Kutz suggests.

In any event, the matter of individuating the categories of communication-independent wrongdoing is not nearly as formidable as Kutz supposes. Let us start here with communications (such as acts of incitement or advertisements of illegalities) that are subsumed into the communication-independent misdeeds which they are aimed at sparking, and let us then contemplate the communications (such as defamatory statements or perjurious statements) that are free-standingly constitutive of communication-independent wrongdoing. With regard to communications of the former kind, the individuation of the categories of communication-independent wrongdoing is not really a problem at all. Each such communication takes its wrong-making properties from any misdeeds which it impels or which it aims to impel. For example, inciting a mob to perpetrate a lynching is seriously wrongful because participating in a lynching is seriously wrongful. Likewise, advertising the availability of children for the sexual pleasure of paedophiles is seriously wrongful because participating in paedophiliac abuse is seriously wrongful. No conundrum about the individuation of categories of communication-independent wrongdoing has to be solved here.

When Kutz poses that conundrum, then, he presumably has in mind the other set of communications to which I have referred: communications, such as perjurious or defamatory statements, that are free-standingly constitutive of communication-independent wrongdoing. At what level of abstraction should we specify the relevant communication-independent wrongdoing for each such communication? The answer to this question lies in what I say throughout my ruminations on communication-independence. That is, I repeatedly state that we have to ascertain whether the legal restrictions directed against some mode of wrongful communicative activity are broadly on a par with the legal restrictions directed against any non-communicative conduct that partakes of the same wrong-making properties—where the wrong-making properties in question are sufficient to render morally legitimate the proscription of the non-communicative mode of conduct. The extreme abstractions invoked by Kutz are not wrong-making features. Rather, they are conclusory designations at very high levels of abstraction. Nor could Kutz resort instead to highly abstract features such as harmfulness. Many harmful modes of conduct are not morally wrong. To pin down why a mode of communicative conduct such as perjury is seriously wrong, we need to specify the properties that differentiate it from otherwise similar modes of conduct that are not seriously wrong. With regard to perjurious testimony, the key wrong-making property resides in the fact that the testimony is a deliberate or reckless effort to divert the outcome of a legal proceeding from being based on what has happened in the situation to which the proceeding pertains. With regard to a defamatory allegation that is proscribable in consistency with the principle of freedom of expression,[40] the key wrong-making consideration is that the allegation unfoundedly and culpably (maliciously, recklessly, or negligently) tarnishes the reputation of someone about whom the allegation is made. The level of concreteness adopted here in specifying the relevant wrong-making features of perjury or defamation has not been chosen arbitrarily. Had I moved to a much higher level of abstraction, I would have failed to indicate why each of those modes of communication is wrongful; and had I omitted any of the elements in either of my specifications of wrong-making properties, I would have failed to indicate why each of the aforementioned modes of communication is wrongful or why the gravity of each of them is sufficient to render morally permissible the imposition of legal restrictions.

Admittedly, what has just been said is compatible with the existence of some leeway when one fixes upon the capaciousness or narrowness of the relevant category of wrongdoing. For example, perjury could be placed in a broader category of wrongdoing by grouping it together with other deliberate or reckless efforts to divert the operations of a system of governance from the functions respectively assigned to those operations. Such leeway does indeed exist, but three things should be said in response. First, although the selection of a broader category of wrongdoing might (or might not) alter some of the specifics of the conclusions about the legitimacy or illegitimacy of the restrictions imposed on certain types of communications within a particular jurisdiction, it would not affect the basic tenor and soundness of my approach to these matters. The general enquiry to be carried out would remain the same, even though some of its specific findings within a particular jurisdiction might (or might not) be altered.

Second, because the enquiry just mentioned will always involve comparisons of the levels of severity in the sanctions imposed for communicative instances and non-communicative instances of a type of wrongdoing, and because such comparisons have to take into account the relative gravity of the wrongs committed, an enquiry which begins with a quite capacious category of wrongdoing and which aims to keep the comparisons of gravity from becoming imponderable will very likely have to resort to degrees of concreteness approximating the degrees which I generally favor. In other words, the classifications invoked by me (or classifications nearly the same) will very likely resurface in any endeavor to gauge the permissibility or impermissibility of legal restrictions on communications. Those classifications have been designed to capture the distinctively wrong-making properties of the communications to which they pertain, without prejudging whether the wrongfulness of the communications is communication-independent or not. Hence, any significant departures from those

[40] As I make clear in my book, not every defamatory statement classified as a tort in English law is proscribable in consistency with the principle of freedom of expression.

classifications will very likely have to be reined in for the purpose of ascertaining meaningfully whether disparities in the heaviness of sanctions correspond to disparities in the gravity of wrongs.

Third, and most important, the appropriateness of a level of abstraction or concreteness for a category of wrongdoing is a partly ethical and partly empirical matter. One's investigation of the laws in any system of governance should be designed to ferret out the extent to which that system abides by the principle of freedom of expression. Though one's investigation should often go beyond the ways in which the laws and legal principles and legal doctrines of a system are arranged, one needs to pay some attention to those ways when one is selecting a level of abstraction or concreteness in one's delimitations of categories of communication-independent wrongdoing. If a system of governance categorizes capaciously the crimes and torts which it prohibits, that feature of the system weighs in favor of adopting a relatively high level of abstraction when one delimits the categories of communication-independent wrongdoing for that jurisdiction. Conversely, if a system of governance categorizes narrowly the crimes and torts which it prohibits, that feature weighs in favor of a relatively high level of concreteness when one delimits the categories of communication-independent wrongdoing there. Such factors will not always be conclusive, of course, but they militate in favor of thinking that some degree of variability in one's categorizations across jurisdictions can be salutary.

Even in application to a single jurisdiction, there remains some latitude in selecting the appropriate level of abstraction or concreteness for the categories of communication-independent wrongdoing. Theorists or jurists can reasonably disagree with one another about how those categories should be specified in any particular jurisdiction, and some of their conclusions about certain legal restrictions in that jurisdiction might (or might not) diverge as a result. The possibility of such divergences would be troublesome if I were questing for algorithmic univocality in my theory of freedom of expression, as Kutz intermittently contends. However, as I have already emphasized in my rejoinders to Kutz, *Freedom of Expression as Self-Restraint* does not pursue such a quest. When we ponder how we should assess the specific curbs on communications in this or that jurisdiction, we should be guided by Aristotle's dictum in the *Nicomachean Ethics* that "it is a mark of the trained mind never to expect more precision in the treatment of any subject than the nature of that subject permits" (Aristotle 1976: 65 [1094b]).

6.2.12 The Irrelevance of Motives

Kutz seeks to deliver one further blow to my reflections on the advertising of illegalities (2022: 352):

> *Contra* Kramer, the advertiser may not be seeking to bring about the imminent occurrence of the heinous crime (though the person who pays the advertiser may be doing so). The advertiser can be fully pleased with the communicative performance itself, independent of any criminal outcome therefrom. Perhaps the advertiser views the advertisement as artwork, or commentary on a corrupt society, or hopes that anyone responding to the advertisement will in fact be arrested. It is a distinct wrong from the pedophiliac crime itself. An unstinting commitment to freedom of expression would

> demand the freedom to express oneself thus. But such an unstinting commitment would have to accept the moral cost of supporting, even non-deliberately, a market for sexual abuse, and a form of moral complicity (if not quite criminal complicity) in the resulting acts.

Participation in the perpetration of paedophiliac abuse, through the advertising of the availability of children for such abuse, is wrongful regardless of the motives that have prompted someone to participate. Those motives can have a bearing on the gravity of the wrong committed, but not on the question whether it is a wrong.

Of course, sometimes a party involved in the advertising of illegalities will not have committed a wrong—because that party has neither known nor had any grounds for knowing about the tenor of the advertisement in question. Suppose for example that a paedophile places an advertisement with a newspaper, and that the advertisement is written in a code known to the members of a circle of paedophiles but not to the press or to the public. If the people who manage the newspaper have no reasonable grounds for suspecting the propriety of the advertisement or the uprightness of the person who has placed the advertisement, then they themselves have not participated in the perpetration of paedophiliac abuse. They have been duped unknowingly into facilitating the occurrence of such abuse, but the intentions requisite for participation are not ascribable to them. However, a situation of this kind is not what Kutz envisions in the passage quoted above. He is talking instead about people who knowingly produce or place advertisements that publicize the availability of children for the sexual gratification of paedophiles. Although someone responsible for one of those advertisements might be acting on the basis of the strange motives which Kutz hypothesizes, he or she has knowingly undertaken an opening stage in a course of terrible abuse.

The one possible exception is the person who hopes that any paedophiles responding to the advertisement will be arrested. As it stands, the example is underdescribed. If the specified person not only hopes for the apprehension of some paedophiles but also has taken steps to ensure that they will be apprehended—and especially if the person is acting in liaison with the police on the matter—then he is not engaging in an opening stage of wicked abuse. Rather, he is carrying out a ploy to combat such abuse. By contrast, if the person merely hopes for some arrests without having taken any significant steps to ensure that they will occur, his conduct can rightly be subjected to sanctions in accordance with the principle of freedom of expression. His hopes may have a bearing on the gravity of his misdeed, but they do not alter its status as a misdeed.

Also to be noted here is that the passage from Kutz above might give rise to a misconception. He there proclaims that "an unstinting commitment to freedom of expression would demand the freedom to express oneself thus [by producing or placing an advertisement that publicizes the availability of children]." One's unstinting commitment to freedom of expression is entirely consistent with one's countenancing of governmentally imposed restrictions that are directed against communications *qua* serious communication-independent misconduct. Since a person's advertising of the availability of children is constitutive of the person's participation in the serious communication-independent misconduct of paedophilia, that act of advertising can be subjected to legal sanctions in full consistency with the principle of freedom of expression. Of course, Kutz has tried to argue that that act of advertising is not constitutive of any communication-independent misconduct. His arguments to that effect are unsuccessful, and he has therefore misapplied the principle of freedom of expression; however, he has not here mischaracterized that principle. Nonetheless, his statement about an unstinting commitment is likely to be misconstrued by other consequentialists who read his chapter. They will be inclined to view that statement approvingly as a dismissal of the preposterous notion that no utterances in speech or writing can ever permissibly be subjected to legal restrictions. When consequentialists heap contumely upon absolutist accounts of freedom of expression, they usually presume that such accounts espouse the preposterous notion just mentioned. What should be stressed here anew, then, is that the absolute moral principle of freedom of expression does not disallow legal prohibitions (or other governmental measures) that are directed against communications *qua* serious communication-independent misdeeds. Absolutely disallowed by that principle instead are legal prohibitions—or other measures by a system of governance—that are directed against communications which are not constitutive of any serious communication-independent misconduct.

6.2.13 Advertisements of Cigarettes

Kutz again tries to steer me in a consequentialist direction when he mulls over my comments about the banning of advertisements for cigarettes in the United States (2022: 352-3). His remarks begin too broadly when he attributes to me the proposition that the regulating of cigarette advertisements is morally illegitimate. Cigarette advertisements, like other advertisements, can quite properly be regulated to guard against fraud. Moreover, such advertisements can properly be barred from magazines or television programs that are addressed exclusively or predominantly to children. However, a scheme of regulation cannot legitimately be extended into any general bans on the advertising of cigarettes—like the bans that have existed in the United States for half a century. At any rate, such bans are morally impermissible in any country where the vending and smoking of cigarettes themselves have not been outlawed. As I summarize the matter in *Freedom of Expression as Self-Restraint* (2021: 91–2):

> Notwithstanding that the banned advertisements would be the initial stages of transactions through which cigarettes are sold to adults, those transactions are legally permissible and should be legally permissible; hence, the fact that the advertisements would initiate those transactions is not a proper ground for any legal prohibitions. Nor is there any other communication-independent ground for such prohibitions. However effective the legal restrictions on advertisements of cigarettes may have been in helping to reduce the popularity of smoking, they have been directed against the advertisements qua acts of communication. Those restrictions have not been directed against the advertisements qua instances of communication-independent wrongdoing, since the advertisements are not constitutive of any such wrongdoing. Instead, the purpose of the legal bans is to avert the [distinctively] communicative effects—the conveyance of messages about the glamor and pleasurability of smoking—that would have been produced by the advertisements.

As is stated fleetingly in this passage, a legal prohibition on the purchasing and smoking of cigarettes by adults would itself be morally illegitimate. Such a prohibition would not contravene the principle of freedom of expression, of course, but it would run athwart other principles of liberalism. Smoking can rightly be excluded from certain places to protect non-smokers and especially children against the hazards and stench of cigarette fumes, but any general proscription of the purchasing and consumption of cigarettes by adults would be illiberally paternalistic. Thus, Kutz stumbles when he writes that "per Kramer's logic, a government intent on reducing the physical incidence of smoking could justify restricting cigarette advertising on that same basis—just as it can ... ban smoking altogether" (2022: 352). The auxiliary verb "can" in the final clause of this quotation is patently intended to be deontic and is thus equivalent to "can permissibly." Given as much, the assertion contained in that clause is false. Precisely because of the falsity of that assertion, the claim advanced in the rest of the quotation is also false. (Perhaps Kutz disagrees with me about the illiberality of outlawing the smoking of cigarettes altogether, but he does not clearly indicate as much—and he does not provide any arguments in support of such dissent. In any event, with his reference to "Kramer's logic," he purports to be recounting a position to which I am committed.)

Let us now suppose *arguendo* that a ban on the purchasing and consumption of cigarettes by adults would be morally permissible, and let us suppose—in line with the actual world—that the purchasing and consumption of cigarettes by adults have not been outlawed in the United States. In such circumstances, would a blanket ban on the advertising of cigarettes be morally permissible? Even though the advertising of cigarettes in the posited circumstances would amount to participation in prohibitable communication-independent misconduct, the answer to this question is negative. In the circumstances envisaged, a communicative mode of participation in that misconduct would be singled out for disadvantageous treatment in comparison with the treatment accorded to non-communicative modes of participation. Hence, the imposition of a legal prohibition on advertisements for products that are not themselves legally prohibited is violative of the principle of freedom of expression. Such a prohibition would transgress the constraint of communication-neutrality.

Kutz commends his consequentialist approach as an alternative to my own approach: "The relevant criticism to apply to the state is that unless and until it has had the gumption to render smoking illegal, it should not be intruding on its subjects' capacities to weigh for themselves the pros and cons of smoking. That position, whether or not ultimately defensible, is, boringly, a matter of weighing the value of citizen autonomy against the public health and paternalistic concerns underlying the restriction, and in consideration of whether less speech-restrictive means might accomplish the same result" (2022: 353). Albeit for different reasons, each of the sentences in this quotation—especially the second sentence—is dubious.

Notwithstanding that the problem with the first sentence might arise simply from infelicitous wording, that sentence currently implies that a system of governance would be acting impermissibly by dispensing ample information to the public about the dangers of smoking. In fact, however, the dissemination of an abundance of information on that topic is both morally permissible and morally obligatory for any system of governance. Likewise morally permissible are laws that require the inclusion of a health warning on every package of cigarettes. Measures such as these are some of the means through which a system of governance discharges its public-health responsibilities without contravening any of its responsibilities under the principle of freedom of expression.

More deeply problematic is the second of the quoted sentences. Kutz again is inclined to turn the protection of communicative liberties into a matter of consequentialist cost/benefit calculations, but here his keenness to adopt such a tack is especially disconcerting because he assumes that paternalistic concerns are to be weighed favorably in those calculations. Of course, such an assumption is readily understandable from a consequentialist perspective, since the pursuit of paternalistic concerns is oriented toward the bringing about of good consequences. By the reckoning of someone who writes from such a perspective, those good consequences are to be balanced against the desideratum of individual autonomy with which any paternalistic policies interfere. Instead of recognizing that the autonomy of any typical human adult is morally shielded by deontological constraints on what can legitimately be done to him or her, consequentialists perceive it as a factor which contributes to the goodness of states of affairs and which has to be balanced against other goodness-conducive considerations. Such philosophers wishfully think that the ersatz rigor of consequentialism is the acme of sophistication for one's grappling with questions about the legitimacy of restrictions placed by a system of governance on the communicative activities of citizens. In their eyes, deontological absolutes are either unintelligible or superstitious. As Jed Rubenfeld has observed in the context of debates over freedom of expression: "The cost-benefit thinker cannot understand deontological commitments" (2002: 760).

Having argued against consequentialism in *Freedom of Expression as Self-Restraint* and at even greater length in *The Ethics of Capital Punishment* and *Torture and Moral Integrity*, I will not here rehearse all my objections to it. Most of those objections center on two main vices of consequentialism: the imponderability of the calculations which it requires (Kramer 2021: 182 n. 13, 231–2), and its denial of any moral absolutes (Kramer 2021: 6–7). Each of those vices can be avoided straightforwardly in the present context as in other contexts, for a proponent of the deontological principle of freedom of expression is able to handle the matter of advertisements of illegal activities perfectly well—not least by explaining why the status of activities as illegal can make a decisive difference.

6.2.14 The Distinctiveness of Aspirational-Perfectionist Liberalism

Kutz and I are not quite as far apart in the final third of his chapter as in the earlier portions thereof. Still, he misleadingly synopsizes my aspirational-perfectionist liberalism by partly assimilating it to edificatory perfectionism. He imputes to me the view that "the state's function is enabling individuals to live their best lives" and that "a decent system of governance is obliged to … create the material conditions that enable citizens to live their best lives" (2022: 353, 354). Though accurate in one respect, these statements stray from accuracy by encapsulating a key part of the doctrine which edificatory perfectionists have championed. On the one hand, Kutz wisely uses the words "enabling" and "enable" rather than "steering" and "steer" or "impelling" and "impel" or "prodding" and "prod." *Pro tanto*, he eschews the terminology and the aims of edificatory perfectionism and adopts the vocabulary and the aims of aspirational perfectionism. Nonetheless, he goes amiss when he suggests that the pursuit of the best lives attainable by citizens is an element of the role which aspirational perfectionists assign to every system of governance. Rather, my focus is on the levels of self-respect which individuals are warranted in feeling; that focus is not suffused with the maximizing outlook that is characteristic of consequentialism.

As I have already declared, the paramount moral responsibility of any system of governance resides in bringing about the political and social and economic conditions that enable everyone in the relevant jurisdiction to be warranted in harboring a strong sense of self-respect. Even though those conditions might also have the effect of enabling everyone to lead the best life attainable by him or her—within the constraints imposed by the fact that everyone else will have been similarly enabled—such an effect is not integral to aspirational perfectionism as an ideal. As has been discerned by Paul Billingham and Anthony Taylor (2018: 74–5), the paramount responsibility of every system of governance comprises a sufficientarian element rather than a maximizing element. What the fulfillment of that responsibility makes realistically achievable for each individual is not the maximizing of his or her warranted level of self-respect but is instead a warrantedly strong level of self-respect for him or her.

As I have noted already in section 5.2.6.2 above and frequently in *Freedom of Expression as Self-Restraint* and *Liberalism with Excellence*, the satisfaction of that paramount responsibility is fully consistent with a state of affairs in which not everyone is actually warranted in feeling a hearty sense of self-respect. Instead of being aimed at ensuring that such a state of affairs does not arise, the paramount responsibility is aimed at ensuring that the occurrence of any such state of affairs is not due to the political or economic or social conditions over which a system of governance can legitimately exercise control. Thus, although sufficientarianism is itself a consequentialist doctrine, the sufficientarian element in the responsibility at the heart of aspirational perfectionism does not imbue that responsibility or aspirational perfectionism with a consequentialist hue. The political conditions which go toward fulfilling that responsibility consist in a government's compliance with an array of deontological constraints, including those imposed by the principle of freedom of expression.

In the two aspects just sketched, as well as in some other aspects, aspirational perfectionism differs markedly from edificatory perfectionism. Whereas aspirational perfectionism is concerned with the levels of self-respect that are warranted for individuals, edificatory perfectionism is concerned with the worthiness of the pursuits in which individuals engage. And whereas aspirational perfectionism is concerned first and foremost with the discharging of certain deontological obligations by a system of governance as crucial for enabling individuals to be warranted in sustaining high levels of self-respect, edificatory perfectionism in a fundamentally consequentialist vein is concerned with the sticks or carrots that can induce people to opt for wholesome ways of life. Insofar as those ways of life are disfavored by citizens, a system of governance that follows the prescriptions of edificatory perfectionism has failed in its objectives. By contrast, a system of governance that follows the prescriptions of aspirational perfectionism may very well have conformed impeccably therewith even though quite a few individuals within the jurisdiction of the system are not warranted in feeling any high levels of self-respect.

Aspirational perfectionism and edificatory perfectionism are not to be conflated, then. Nor should aspirational perfectionism be mistaken for the addressee-centered Meiklejohnian approach to freedom of expression. Kutz approvingly attributes to me the view that "[a] policy of state censorship or distorted communication is one that degrades the capacity of individuals to judge for themselves among conflicting ethical claims" (2022: 354). Although I concur with what Kutz says here, I believe that his approval of it stems not from his agreement with the Stoical aspirational perfectionism which I have elaborated in *Freedom of Expression as Self-Restraint*, but instead from his adherence to the Meiklejohnian school of thought. Among the diverse theorists who work within that school of thought, there is generally an emphasis on the addressees of utterances—with the idea that those addressees are the members of a democratic polity whose deliberations on matters of public affairs will not truly constitute a situation of self-governance unless those deliberations are uncurtailed by censorship. I naturally endorse that concern, but it differs from (or is only one strand in) the main focus of Stoical aspirational perfectionism. In my elaboration of that latter doctrine, I concentrate principally on the ways in which a system of governance simultaneously aggrandizes itself and demeans itself through the clamping of restrictions upon communications that are not constitutive of any communication-independent misconduct.

6.2.15 Communication-Independence Redux

My mention of communication-independence at the end of the preceding subsection returns us to a topic that resurfaces in the closing third of Kutz's chapter. Kutz unexceptionably observes that the circumstances in every actual society are non-ideal and that decisions about the proscribability of communications are therefore always being reached by judges and other legal-governmental officials in non-ideal circumstances. That point is something on which I meditate in the final chapter of *Freedom of Expression as Self-Restraint* and more briefly in a few of the other chapters. However, Kutz proceeds to draw an inapt conclusion from his correct observation about the pervasiveness of non-ideal circumstances. He submits that "the state is always in a credible position to assert that, regrettably, restrictions on certain expression must be enacted, because the communications present too great a danger to legitimate non-communicative objects of state concern. And if this is so, then defining the principle of freedom of expression as applying only to the realm of the exclusively communicative is, effectively, to rule out its application to almost any significant cases of real or contemplated censorship" (2022: 354).

Kutz here misconstrues the notion of communication-independence. When he contends that certain modes of expression pose dangers to non-communicative objects of state concern, he is talking about the distinctively communicative effects of those modes of expression. That is, he is talking about the tendencies of those modes of expression to influence the outlooks and propensities of people through the messages or sentiments which the modes of expression convey; the changes in those outlooks and propensities may ultimately lead to non-communicative misconduct by the people in whom the changes occur. Yet unless the relationship between some communication and any non-communicative misconduct is so focused and direct that the communication is subsumed into the misconduct as one of its opening stages (as is the case with incitement or solicitation), any communication covered by Kutz's remarks here is morally protected by the principle of freedom of expression against censorship. Legal-governmental officials might credibly affirm that there are diffuse and remote causal connections between certain types of communications and serious non-communicative harms—like the connections posited by Catharine MacKinnon between the marketing of pornography and the occurrence of sexual violence, or like the connections posited by Waldron between the dissemination of hateful sentiments through leaflets or orations and the erosion of the dignity of people in vulnerable minority groups—but the officials will not thereby be adverting to anything that removes the specified types of communications from the protection conferred upon them by the principle of freedom of expression. Though the harms to which the officials refer are communication-independent misdeeds, the specified modes of communication are not themselves constitutive of such misdeeds. Those modes of communication do not amount to communication-independent misdeeds on their own, and they are not subsumed into any such misdeeds. Hence, governmental restrictions imposed on those modes of communication will contravene the requirement of communication-neutrality. Thus, far from countenancing all or nearly all of the instances of censorship which Kutz contemplates in the quoted sentences, the principle of freedom of expression disallows all or nearly all of those instances.

A misunderstanding of communication-independence also enters into Kutz's reflections on the Black Lives Matter protests that erupted in the United States and in other countries during the summer of 2020. Though I of course agree with Kutz that the "Fuck the Police" and "All Cops are Bastards" signs which he describes are morally protected by the principle of freedom of expression and legally protected in the United States by the First Amendment, two aspects of his reflections are antithetical to my own positions on these matters. First, in keeping with his allegiance to the Meiklejohnian tradition, he thinks that the signs of the demonstrators are morally protected at least partly because of the contents of their communications. On the one hand, despite initial appearances to the contrary, he does not deviate from viewpoint-neutrality. He seems to deviate therefrom when he writes that "it would of course be wrong to prohibit such expression, because the capacity to form and articulate arguments about the proper limits on policing, and on the remediation of racism in American society, is a core attribute of warranted self-respect *for citizens alert to the historical and current injustices of their society*" (2022: 355, emphasis added). In the portion of the quoted sentence which I have italicized, Kutz seems to be suggesting that people at certain points of the political spectrum are to be shown special solicitude in the extent to which they are legally allowed to communicate their views. Any such suggestion by Kutz would of course be starkly at odds with the requirement of viewpoint-neutrality that is imposed by the principle of freedom of expression. However, he subsequently adds—albeit somewhat grudgingly—that "[s]adly, the same is true with respect to the speech rights of legally but obtrusively armed zealots protesting 'fascist' public health measures" (2022: 355). Kutz is here talking about people quite far to the right of the political spectrum. Granting that the principle of freedom of expression morally protects them just as much as it protects people who strive for racial justice, Kutz articulates a point of principle which I ungrudgingly proclaim throughout *Freedom of Expression as Self-Restraint*. As I declare at the end of Chapter 2 of that book: "In the manner of the rain that falls on the just and the unjust, the neutrality-requiring principle of freedom of expression extends its protection to the enlightened and the benighted alike" (2021: 64). On the other hand, notwithstanding that Kutz abides by the constraint of viewpoint-neutrality, he transgresses the constraint of subject-neutrality. For him as for others who work in the Meiklejohnian tradition, utterances on matters of public affairs receive preferential treatment in comparison with utterances on matters of private or commercial affairs. By contrast, the principle of freedom of expression—with its requirement of subject-neutrality as well as viewpoint-neutrality—serves as a censorship-delegitimizing shield for all of these utterances alike. (Admittedly, Kutz later in his chapter salutarily puts a bit of distance between himself and the Meiklejohnian tradition by maintaining that art and literature and music and scientific discourse are protected by the principle of freedom of expression independently of their conduciveness to enhancing the deliberations of a democratic polity.[41] Nonetheless, even in that brief paragraph he does not dissent from the Meiklejohnian thesis that commercial communications are largely or wholly beyond the scope of the principle of freedom of expression.)

Second, Kutz misrepresents the property of communication-independence as he insists anew on the need for cost/benefit balancing. Asserting that "we cannot avoid [a] tradeoff [between] a bedrock commitment to a principle of respecting political agency [and] the risks of how that agency might manifest [itself]," Kutz alleges that "Kramer's conceptual razor cannot save the speech [of the Black Lives Matter protesters] categorically from the state's legitimate objectives of protecting lives and property. The fact that the effects of the speech cannot be precisely known and predicted specifically in advance doesn't loosen, as a metaphysical matter, the connection between the expression and its effects" (2022: 355). Given that Kutz refers here afresh to metaphysics, I should repeat that any metaphysical questions about the subsumption of an act of communication into misdeeds inspired by it are thoroughly ethical questions. Throughout my book on freedom of expression, I underscore the ethical import of a distinction that is obscured in this latest quotation: namely, the distinction between (i) an act of communication that is connected in a direct and focused manner to some communication-independent wrongdoing which it designedly brings about, and (ii) an act of communication that is connected diffusely and remotely to some communication-independent wrongdoing that might ultimately be inspired by it. Although the sentiments or ideas conveyed by an act of communication of the former kind might not be any more nefarious than the sentiments or ideas conveyed by an act of communication of the latter kind, an act of communication of the latter kind is not legitimately proscribable by any system of governance. It is not subsumed into any misdeeds that might be inspired by it, for it is not properly classifiable as one of the opening stages in any of those misdeeds. Thus, for example, although the New Testament has inspired countless instances of violent persecution against Jews over the centuries in most countries where Christianity is the dominant religion, the publishing or marketing of the New Testament in such a country has not been properly classifiable as one of the opening stages in any of the atrocities ultimately provoked by it.

[41] Kutz 2022: 356. For Meiklejohn's own position on this matter, see Meiklejohn 1961: 257.

Chapters 4, 5, and 6 of *Freedom of Expression as Self-Restraint* develop at length the ethical reasons for attaching great significance to the distinction highlighted here, though those reasons are also outlined in some of the book's other chapters. I obviously cannot in these replies recapitulate the whole of the Stoical aspirational-perfectionist justification for the principle of freedom of expression which I present in Chapter 4 of that book, but I should summarily say here that that justification lays stress on the ways in which any legal restrictions neglectful of the aforementioned distinction are both overweening and degrading for a system of governance that adopts those restrictions. Among the moral obligations incumbent on any system of governance under its paramount moral responsibility—all of which are realistically satisfiable—is an obligation to cultivate and sustain a robust ethos of liberal-democratic values among the people in the jurisdiction over which the system presides. Because overweening legal restrictions on communications are obviated by the fulfillment of that obligation along with the fulfillment of other obligations incumbent on the prevailing system of governance, the system effectively condemns itself when it enacts such restrictions.

Although I cannot here flesh out the extremely sketchy remarks in the preceding paragraph, the requisite amplification of those remarks is in Chapter 4 (and Chapters 5 and 6) of my book on freedom of expression. What is to be emphasized here is that the justification for the principle of freedom of expression which I provide in that chapter—a justification that is a deontological defense of the absoluteness of that principle—is my riposte to any insistence on the indispensability of balancing. Notwithstanding that Kutz in this portion of his chapter concurs with most of my concrete conclusions about the impermissibility of any legal restrictions on the placards of the left-wing or right-wing protesters, his consequentialist route to those conclusions is regrettable. Consequentialist approaches to matters of freedom of expression are generally both vaporous and precarious. They are vaporous because, as Rubenfeld contends, "in First Amendment controversies, the language of balancing betrays a strange unreality .... The rhetoric of balancing is a disguise in such contexts. It serves as a conclusory, obfuscatory language masking more fundamental, although frequently very poorly thought-through instincts about the freedom of speech" (2001: 789). And consequentialism is precarious as a basis for the protection of communicative liberties, because it is squarely opposed to moral absolutes. Hardly coincidental is the fact that nearly all of the philosophers whose illiberality I assail in *Freedom of Expression as Self-Restraint*—such as Waldron and Frederick Schauer—are consequentialists.

6.2.16 Further Missed Targets

Seeking to dissociate himself from my deontological absolutism on matters of freedom of expression, Kutz supposes that a deontologist "must either defend an indefensible absolutism that countenances no communicative restrictions whatsoever, or rely on a conceptual division that nominally preserves the absolutism [of] the principle, but at the cost of ad hocery" (2022: 357). I believe that Kutz recognizes that I do not opt for the outlandishness of the first disjunct in his dichotomy. However, he apparently presumes that I opt for his second disjunct. It is not clear to me what the phrase "conceptual division" denotes in his formulation, but it probably refers to the distinction between governmental measures that are directed against communications *qua* communications and governmental measures that are directed against communications *qua* communication-independent misconduct. Kutz is contending that I resort to ad hoc maneuvers in my efforts to sustain that distinction. Yet his condemnation of my arguments as marred by ad hoc maneuvers is unsustainable when the property of communication-independence is accurately understood and when the key distinctions in my arguments—such as the distinction on which I have concentrated in section 6.2.15 above – are heeded. Though my discussions of various types of proscribable communications are themselves diverse, they collectively make clear that (as I have already stated in these replies) there are two main ways in which communications can be constitutive of communication-independent misconduct. Any communication that does constitute communication-independent wrongdoing either itself amounts to such wrongdoing or else is subsumed into such wrongdoing as one of the opening stages thereof. Hence, notwithstanding the diversity of my cogitations on prohibitable communications, there are no ad hoc stratagems in any of them.

Kutz submits that the primary error in my theorizing about freedom of expression "lies in thinking that the line separating protected from unprotected speech can be defined by the formal characterization of some set of effects, as communicatively-dependent or independent" (2022: 358). I presume that the adjective "formal" is meant to imply that I take the contrast between distinctively communicative wrongdoing and communication-independent wrongdoing to be a matter of logical analysis rather than a matter of substantive ethics. Having sought already to dispel that misconception, I will here state again that the contrast just mentioned is ethical through and through. Harking back to the notions of value-independence and value-neutrality which I have invoked above in my replies to Chiassoni in section 2.4.2 and to Radoilska in section 3.2, I should reaffirm here that the division between distinctively communicative wrongdoing and communication-independent wrongdoing is neither value-independent nor value-neutral. Its justificatory basis is entirely a matter of political morality, and the judgments required for applying it are likewise judgments of political morality. That division cannot be drawn through any purely logical analysis, nor do I ever suggest otherwise in my book.

Kutz moves on to assail the import of communication-independence: "The state's object, whether in protection or restriction, is the same. And since protecting the conditions of self-respect is fundamentally a matter of protecting the conditions of free and reasoned communication, Kramer steps in exactly the wrong direction by defending such restrictions as applying only to the non-communicative genre" (2022: 358). Albeit the wording in the first of these two quoted sentences is somewhat unclear, Kutz appears to be assuming that a legal restriction on communicative activities is communication-neutral if the ultimate purpose behind the imposition of it resides in preventing some communication-independent type of wrongdoing. Such an assumption neglects most of the key distinctions in my account of freedom of expression, and it is not at all in keeping with my conception of communication-independence. When we need to ascertain whether a legal restriction on some communicative activity is directed against that activity *qua* communication-independent misconduct, we have to proceed in two steps. We first need to ask whether the communicative activity is constitutive of serious communication-independent misconduct—either because the activity is itself the communication-independent misconduct or because it is subsumed into such misconduct as an opening stage thereof. If and only if the answer to that first step of the inquiry is affirmative, we move to the next step by asking whether communicative instances and non-communicative instances of the relevant type of communication-independent misconduct are treated broadly on a par by the system of governance in the jurisdiction where the misconduct takes place. If and only if the answer at each of these stages of the inquiry is affirmative, the legal restriction in question is consistent with the principle of freedom of expression.

In the second of the two sentences which I have quoted from Kutz at the outset of the preceding paragraph, he appears to be worrying that my account of freedom of expression is not adequately protective of communications that should be secure against governmental trammels. Any such suggestion, if it is what he is suggesting in his rather cryptic prose, is unfounded. Not only does the principle of freedom of expression morally safeguard every instance of communication which Kutz wishes to see safeguarded, but it also morally safeguards many other instances and types of communications. It shields not only reasoned communications but also all unreasoned communications that are not constitutive of any serious communication-independent wrongdoing. It shields not only political communications but also all private and commercial communications that are not constitutive of any serious communication-independent wrongdoing. As a moral absolute, the principle of freedom of expression is far more expansively protective than is any consequentialist approach.

Toward the end of Kutz's chapter, we encounter an instance of the illiberality of the Meiklejohnian school of thought. There we are told that " 'glamour ads' that do nothing other than juxtaposing an objectively risky product [such as fattening foods or cigarettes] with attractive models do not contribute in any significant way to reasoned decision-making; if anything, they deform it. And so, it seems not an unreasonable accommodation, within the same value field, to permit individuals to consume a product while restricting uninformative forms of their promotion" (2022: 358). According to Kutz, these restrictions imposed by a system of governance on certain communications would be morally legitimate and commendable even though the communications are not constitutive of any communication-independent wrongdoing such as fraud. He thinks that the communications are legitimately prohibitable because they are insufficiently edifying. He thus exhibits the edificatory outlook against which I have inveighed in Chapter 6 of *Liberalism with Excellence* and Chapter 4 of *Freedom of Expression as Self-Restraint* (and in my replies to Tahzib in section 5.2 above).

6.2.17 Advocacy and Advertising

Kutz queries whether my stance on the *advertising* of illegalities is compatible with my stance on the *advocacy* of illegalities. He declares (2022: 358): "[I]t is hard to see a principled, non-pragmatic reason that coheres with the rest of Kramer's view for why the state cannot prohibit advertisements for legal goods. After all, Kramer's account of the incitement/advocacy line resists such consistency, since the interesting (and protected) cases of advocacy have as their object illegal activities (strikes, draft resistance, revolution)." I in fact directly address the distinction between advocacy and advertising in my discussion of the latter activity. As I stress there, the key to the matter is that the connections between the advertising of illegalities and the illegalities themselves are direct and focused whereas the connections between the advocating of illegalities and any illegalities themselves are diffuse and remote. A quotation here from the main portion of my remarks on the matter is apposite (2021: 90):

> By contrast [namely, by contrast with a situation in which the availability of children for exploitation by paedophiles is advertised], if someone were to publish a newspaper article calling for the legalization of child prostitution and paedophilia (while rhapsodizing about the pleasures that could be derived from those activities), or if someone were to distribute copies of a leaflet with such a message, there would be no comparable basis for subjecting him or her to any legal sanctions. Though the ideas articulated in the article or leaflet might be just as reprehensible as the messages expressed in the forbidden advertisements, the propagation of those ideas through the article or leaflet does not constitute any direct participation in some communication-independent misconduct. As an instance of advocacy, the dissemination of those ideas is not subsumed into any acts of paedophilia or child prostitution as some of the initial stages thereof. Any causal connections between the advocacy and such acts are diffuse and remote, rather than highly focused and direct. In precisely that regard, the distribution of the article or leaflet differs crucially from the placing of an advertisement. Whereas an advertisement that notifies potential customers about the availability of slaves or child prostitutes is intended to initiate transactions that ensue directly from the notification, there is no such proximity between the publication of the aforementioned article or leaflet and any nefarious misdeeds that might ultimately be inspired by it. Consequently, the publication of the article or leaflet is not correctly classifiable as one of the initial stages in the perpetration of any of those misdeeds.

I should append a few comments at this juncture, to accentuate some points made already in these replies. First, here as elsewhere in *Freedom of Expression as Self-Restraint*, my distinction between an unprotected mode of communication and a protected mode of communication is an ethical distinction. It is neither value-independent nor value-neutral. Of course, in drawing and applying that distinction, I am attentive to empirical features of the communicative activities which I am contemplating. Nevertheless, the judgments which I reach about those activities as protected or unprotected—judgments reached through my attention to the empirical features of the activities—are thoroughly ethical.

Second, like the other major distinctions which I draw in my book on freedom of expression, the demarcation between advocacy and advertising is marked by vagueness in the technical sense and is thus marked by the potential for borderline cases in which the concepts pertaining to that demarcation are neither determinately applicable nor determinately inapplicable. Because properties such as directness and diffuseness are embeddable in sorites paradoxes, the possibility of borderline cases is ineliminable. As I have already indicated in these replies, my book states explicitly that the key concepts on which it relies are vague in this technical sense.

Third, although the possibility of borderline cases is ineradicable, countless potential cases are not in the borderline area of indeterminacy. In myriads of circumstances, the protectedness or unprotectedness of specified types of communications will be fully determinate. Moreover, in any circumstances where a type of communication is not determinately classifiable under the relevant concepts as protected or unprotected, the indeterminacy is to be resolved in favor of protection. Hence, both in borderline cases of indeterminacy and in the innumerable cases where types of communications are determinately classifiable, the outcomes to be reached are determinately prescribed. (I am of course not suggesting that the outcomes which should be reached are always clearly discernible. As I have stressed in several of my books—Kramer 2007: 17–21; 2009: 88–101; 2018: 112–20—the distinction between determinacy and indeterminacy is not equivalent to the distinction between demonstrability and indemonstrability nor to the distinction between confidence and uncertainty. Also worthy of mention here is that the division between determinacy and indeterminacy is itself marked by higher-order vagueness. Higher-order indeterminacy, like lower-order indeterminacy, should be resolved in favor of protecting a mode of communication against governmental restrictions.)

Fourth, when engaged in the endeavor of differentiating between advocacy and advertising, we often need to look past some of the superficial aspects of communications in order to concentrate on their properties that are chiefly relevant to such an endeavor. For example, we should often not attach decisive importance to the question whether the people responsible for some communication have paid to have it appear somewhere. Some organization might pay to place a full-page statement in a newspaper, wherein the organization extols the pleasurableness of paedophilia or the benefits derivable from the enslavement of illegal migrants. Odious though such a communication would be, it is very likely classifiable as protected advocacy rather than as proscribable advertising (unless, of course, it specifically indicates that children or migrants are available somewhere to be purchased or rented for exploitation). The sheer fact that the organization has paid to have the statement appear in the newspaper—or the sheer fact that the statement is labeled as a "paid advertisement"—does not affect the correctness of classifying the statement as an instance of advocacy. In this context, as in any number of other contexts, judgments about the implications of the principle of freedom of expression should be oriented toward the deep ethical issues at stake rather than toward superficialities.

6.2.18 Deviations from Content-Neutrality

I will move toward concluding these lengthy replies to Kutz's chapter by scrutinizing his comments on a scenario that surfaces at multiple junctures in *Freedom of Expression as Self-Restraint*: a scenario involving a municipal government that operates a network of buses throughout its territory. The officials who manage the network have to decide whether the backs and sides of the buses should be rented out to organizations and individuals for the placing of advertisements. On the one hand, for reasons which I expound (2021: 154), the officials can permissibly decline to make the sides and backs of the buses available for advertisements at all. On the other hand, if they do decide to rent out those areas of the buses for advertisements, they have to abide by constraints of neutrality that are integral to the principle of freedom of expression. Of course, if the number of would-be advertisers exceeds the number that can be accommodated on the sides and backs of the buses, the local officials can permissibly have recourse to an aleatory selection procedure or to a first-come-first-served policy or to some other neutral device for prioritizing certain would-be advertisers over others.

However, they cannot permissibly choose among advertisements in ways that are at odds with any of the requirements of subject-neutrality and viewpoint-neutrality and speaker-neutrality. That is, they cannot permissibly exclude certain topics or perspectives as such, nor can they permissibly exclude certain organizations or individuals from the same opportunities that are open to other organizations and individuals for the placing of advertisements. In this context of a municipal bus service, then, the blanket exclusion of advertisements can be morally legitimate whereas much narrower restrictions that contravene any of the aforementioned requirements of neutrality are morally illegitimate.

Albeit on Meiklejohnian grounds rather than on my Stoical aspirational-perfectionist grounds, Kutz largely endorses my assessments of the moral bearings of the decisions that might be reached by the local government about advertisements on the buses. However, he initially responds to my scenario as follows (2022: 359):

> I should say that I am unpersuaded of the merits of this concern, for it seems to me reasonable for a city to restrict advertisements to those, for example, issued by public health authorities about the danger of smoking, and not permit advertisements encouraging smoking (even if such advertisements are otherwise permitted). Moreover, it is certainly possible to imagine cases where a blanket restriction of a category of speech is far worse than a selective restriction, since a blanket restriction may effectively prevent an entire subject of concern from alighting in the public mind, while a selective presentation might at least spark a citizenry to inquire elsewhere about the subject.

In the first of these two sentences, Kutz purports to be taking issue with my analysis of the moral intricacies of the decisions which the municipal government has to reach. However, that first sentence is an assertion rather than a line of reasoning in support of its verdict on the matter. By contrast, I present arguments in *Freedom of Expression as Self-Restraint* to support my own verdicts on the situation of the municipal government (2021: 153–9).

What is more, a version of the situation envisaged by Kutz in the first of the quoted sentences could be consistent with the principle of freedom of expression. While declining to make the sides and backs of the local buses available for advertisements, the officials who manage the bus service might elect to use them instead—and, indeed, would be well advised to use them instead—partly for the posting of "No Smoking on the Bus" signs. Alongside those signs could be posted some information about the dangers of cigarettes, in the form of warnings or similar statements issued by a local or national public-health agency. That dispensation of information, in furtherance of the no-smoking policy for the buses, would scarcely turn the sides and backs of the buses into public fora. Unlike a situation in which the officials accept advertisements from anti-smoking organizations while declining to accept advertisements from pro-smoking organizations, a situation where public-health warnings are concomitants to the "No Smoking on the Bus" signs would be consistent with the requirements of neutrality established by the principle of freedom of expression.

As for the second of the quoted sentences, it is presented by Kutz as an objection to my position; yet its main point about the wrongfulness and gravity of any blanket exclusions of communications in various contexts is a point which I make explicitly at the juncture in *Freedom of Expression as Self-Restraint* where I first broach the scenario of the buses and advertisements (2021: 38–9). Admittedly, my Stoical aspirational-perfectionist rationale for adopting such a position is different from Kutz's addressee-centered Meiklejohnian rationale. Nonetheless, Kutz and I agree that wholesale exclusions of communications would be very seriously wrongful in numerous contexts. What makes the scenario of the municipal bus service so interesting is that it recounts a context in which a wholesale exclusion of communications could be morally legitimate even though any selective exclusions athwart the constraint of content-neutrality or speaker-neutrality would be morally illegitimate. As I argue (2021: 41–2, 153–9), a context of this latter kind cannot be handled adequately by any of the standard justifications for versions of the principle of freedom of expression—whereas it can be handled perfectly well by my Stoical aspirational-perfectionist justification. I argue for that conclusion while also expressly allowing that in many other contexts an across-the-board prohibition on communications would be gravely wrongful.

6.2.19 Concluding Remarks on Kutz's Chapter

I will close my ripostes to Kutz's chapter with two brief further comments. First, in the final paragraph of his chapter, Kutz castigates me for what he regards as my "attempt to render as absolute a principle whose exceptions he rightly acknowledges" (2022: 359). I defend the principle of freedom of expression as a moral absolute because there are no exceptions to it. I repeatedly state as much in *Freedom of Expression as Self-Restraint*, and I definitely do not accept that there are any exceptions to that principle. I do of course readily affirm that certain types and instances of communication can permissibly be prohibited by any system of governance, but those types and instances are not exceptions to the principle of freedom of expression. On the contrary, their susceptibility to properly targeted legal prohibitions is a corollary of that principle—a principle which holds that governmental restrictions on communicative activities are morally illegitimate unless the restrictions are directed against such activities *qua* serious communication-independent wrongdoing. When Kutz alleges that my acceptance of the legitimacy of such restrictions is tantamount to my acknowledging that there are exceptions to the principle of freedom of expression, he is assuming that that principle indefensibly provides that no governmental restrictions on communicative activities are ever morally legitimate. As I have already noted in these replies, I firmly warn against any such misunderstanding on the opening page of *Freedom of Expression as Self-Restraint* and on quite a few pages thereafter.

My second closing remark follows quite smoothly from the first. These retorts to Kutz's chapter have been predominantly critical in their substance and in their tone. I do not apologize for the critical tenor of my retorts, because Kutz's chapter itself partakes of such a tenor. At the same time, I am grateful to Kutz (and likewise to McBride) for prompting me to dilate upon a few of the ideas developed in my book on freedom of expression. Although our perspectives on issues of freedom of expression are markedly divergent, and although the room for fruitful engagement is therefore often quite limited, I hope that my replies to Kutz have helped to clarify a few of the chief matters that are at stake in any such engagement. I encourage readers to peruse *Freedom of Expression as Self-Restraint* for much more ample expositions of those matters and for discussions of numerous other topics that are vital to the philosophy of freedom of expression.

7. A Pithy Coda

When I began to write these replies to the contributors in October 2020, I had not yet read most of their chapters. I told Kurki and McBride that I expected the overall length of my replies to be approximately 10,000 words. As time went on, my predictions of the overall length rose steadily. Not until the final couple of weeks in April 2021, however, did I fully realize that the length would extend to somewhat more than 110,000 words—just over eleven times my original estimate! As these replies proved to be much longer than I had originally anticipated, the span of time devoted to writing them increased commensurately. Thus, having begun by warmly thanking Kurki and McBride for their labors in putting this volume together and contributing two fine essays to it, I must finish by thanking them also for their patience. I must likewise express my hearty appreciation to the other contributors and to the Oxford University Press for putting up with an endeavor of writing that occupied me for nearly six months rather than for the originally envisaged four weeks. In extenuation, I shall simply note that the amount of time devoted to that endeavor is reflective of my determination to engage closely with every chapter. Though I apologize to the editors and the contributors and the publisher for the protracted delay, its protractedness has been due predominantly to the many challenges posed by the contributors in their scrutinizing of my work.

Bibliography

Chapter 1

Bamforth, Nicholas. "Hohfeldian Rights and Public Law," in *Rights, Wrongs and Responsibilities*, ed. Matthew H. Kramer, 1–27. Basingstoke, UK: Palgrave, 2001.

Blackstone, William. *Commentaries on the Laws of England in Four Books*, 192–211. Philadelphia: Robert Bell, 1771.

Brown, Stuart M. Jr., "Inalienable Rights." *Philosophical Review* 64, no. 2 (April 1955).

Coke, Edward. *The Second Part of the Institutes of the Laws of England*. London: Printed for E. and R. Brooke, Bell-Yard, near Temple-Bar, 1797.

Corbin, Arthur L. "Rights and Duties." *Yale Law Journal* 33, no. 5, 501–527 (March 1924).

Donohue, Laura K. "Bulk Metadata Collection: Statutory and Constitutional Considerations." *Harvard Journal of Law and Public Policy* 38, no. 3, 757–900 (Summer 2014).

Donohue, Laura K. "Section 702 and the Collection of International Telephone and Internet Content." *Harvard Journal of Law and Public Policy* 39, no. 1, 117–265 (Winter 2015).

Donohue, Laura K. *The Future of Foreign Intelligence: Privacy and Surveillance in a Digital Age*. New York: Oxford University Press, 2016.

Dworkin, Ronald. "Law as Interpretation," *Critical Inquiry* 9, no. 1, 179–200 (September 1982).

Finnis, John. *Natural Law and Natural Rights*. Oxford: Clarendon Press, 1980.

Halpin, Andrew. "The Concept of a Legal Power," *Oxford Journal of Legal Studies* 16, no. 1, 129–152 (Spring 1996).

Halpin, Andrew. "'Concept of a Legal Power,' to Visa A.J. Kurki, 'Legal Competence and Legal Power,'" in *New Essays on the Nature of Rights*, ed. Mark McBride, 31–47. Oxford: Hart Publishing, 2017.

Hardyns, Wim and Rummens, Anneleen. "Predictive Policing as a New Tool for Law Enforcement? Recent Developments and Challenges," *European Journal on Criminal Policy and Research* 24, no. 3, 201–218 (September 2018).

Hart, H.L.A. "Are There Any Natural Rights?" *Philosophical Review* 64, no. 2, 175–191 (April 1955).

Hart, H.L.A. *The Concept of Law*. Oxford: Clarendon Press, 1961.

Hart, H.L.A. *Essays on Bentham: Studies in Jurisprudence and Political Theory*. Oxford: Clarendon Press, 1982.

Hart, H.L.A. *Punishment and Responsibility: Essays in the Philosophy of Law*, 2nd ed. Oxford: Oxford University Press, 2008.

Hohfeld, Wesley Newcomb. "Some Fundamental Legal Conceptions as Applied in Judicial Reasoning," *Yale Law Journal* 23, no. 1, 16–59 (November 1913).

Hohfeld, Wesley Newcomb. "Fundamental Legal Conceptions as Applied in Judicial Reasoning," *Yale Law Journal* 26, no. 8, 710–770 (June 1917).

Howard, Dick A.E. *Magna Carta: Text and Commentary*, rev. ed. Charlottesville, VA: University Press of Virginia, 1998.

Hurd, Heidi M. and Moore, Michael S. "Hohfeldian Analysis of Rights," *American Journal of Jurisprudence* 63, no. 2, 295–354 (December 2018).

Kleinig, John. "Human Rights, Legal Rights, and Social Change," in *Human Rights*, eds. Eugene Kamenka and Alice Erh-Soon Tay, 36–47. New York: St Martin's Press, 1978.

Kramer, Matthew H. *In the Realm of Legal and Moral Philosophy: Critical Encounters*. Basingstoke, UK: Macmillan Press, 1999.

Kramer, Matthew H. "Rights Without Trimmings," in *A Debate over Rights: Philosophical Enquiries*, eds. Matthew H. Kramer, N.E. Simmonds, and Hillel Steiner , 7–111. Oxford: Oxford University Press, 2000.

Kramer, Matthew J. "Getting Rights Right," in *Rights, Wrongs and Responsibilities*, ed. Matthew H. Kramer, 28–95. Basingstoke, UK: Palgrave, 2001.

Kramer, Matthew H. *Where Law and Morality Meet*. Oxford: Oxford University Press, 2004.

Kramer, Matthew H. "Of Final Things: Morality as One of the Ultimate Determinants of Legal Validity," *Law and Philosophy* 24, no. 1, 47–97 (January 2005).

Kramer, Matthew H. "Moral Rights and the Limits of the Ought-Implies-Can Principle: Why Impeccable Precautions Are No Excuse," *Inquiry* 48, no. 4, 307–355 (August 2005).

Kramer, Matthew H. *Objectivity and the Rule of Law*. Cambridge: Cambridge University Press, 2007.

Kramer, Matthew H. "Rights in Legal and Political Philosophy," in *The Oxford Handbook of Law and Politics*, eds. Keith E. Whittington, R. Daniel Kelemen, and Gregory A. Caldera, 414–427. Oxford: Oxford University Press, 2008.

Kramer, Matthew H. *The Ethics of Capital Punishment: A Philosophical Investigation of Evil and Its* Consequences. Oxford: Oxford University Press, 2011.

Kramer, Matthew H. "There's Nothing Quasi about Quasi-Realism: Moral Realism as a Moral Doctrine," *Journal of Ethics* 21, no. 2, 185–212 (June 2017).

Kramer, Matthew H. "On No-Rights and No Rights." *The American Journal of Jurisprudence,*" 64, no. 2, 213–223 (December 2019).

Kurki, Visa A.J. "Hohfeldian Infinities: Why Not to Worry," *Res Publica*, 23, no. 1, 137–146 (February 2017).

Locke, John. *Second Treatise of Civil Government and a Letter Concerning Toleration*, ed. J. W. Gough. Oxford: Basil Blackwell, 1948.

Luban, David. "Time-Mindedness and Jurisprudence," 101 *Virginia Law Review* 903 (2015).

MacCormick, D.N. "Rights in Legislation," in *Law, Morality, and Society: Essays in Honour of H.L.A. Hart*, eds. P.M.S. Hacker and Joseph Raz, 188–209. Oxford: Clarendon Press, 1977.

MacCormick, Neil. *H.L.A. Hart*. Stanford: Stanford University Press, 1981.

Moore, Michael S. "A Natural Law Theory of Interpretation," *Southern California Law Review*, 58, no. 1 & 2, 277–398 (January 1985).

Oliver, Dawn. *Common Values and the Public-Private Divide*. London: Butterworths, 1999.

Postema, Gerald J. "Analytic Jurisprudence Confronted," in *Legal Philosophy in the Twentieth Century: The Common Law World*, 547–576. New York: Springer, 2011.

Postema, Gerald J. "Jurisprudence, the Sociable Science," *Virginia Law Review* 101, 869 (2015).

Raz, Joseph. "Legal Principles and the Limits of Law," *Yale Law Journal* 81, no. 5, 823–854 (April 1972).

Schiller, Marvin. "Are There Any Inalienable Rights?" *Ethics* 79, no. 4, 309–315 (July 1969).

Simmonds, N.E. "Rights at the Cutting Edge," in Matthew H. Kramer, N.E. Simmonds, and Hillel Steiner, *A Debate over Rights: Philosophical Enquiries*, 113–232. Oxford: Oxford University Press, 2000.

Sinnott-Armstrong, Walter. "Moral Dilemmas and Rights," in *Moral Dilemmas and Moral Theory*, ed. H.E. Mason, 48–65. New York: Oxford University Press, 1996.

Stevenson, Megan. "Assessing Risk Assessment in Action," *Minnesota Law Review* 103, no. 1, 303–384 (November 2018).

Meijer, Albert and Wessels, Martin. "Predictive Policing: Review of Benefits and Drawbacks," *International Journal of Public Administration* 42, no. 12, 1031–1039 (2019).

Sumner, L.W. *The Moral Foundations of Rights*. Oxford: Clarendon Press, 1987.

Thompson, Judith Jarvis. *The Realm of Rights*. Cambridge, MA: Harvard University Press, 1990.
Von Savigny, Friedrich Karl. *Jural Relations, or, The Roman Law of Persons as Subjects of Jural Relations: Being a Translation of the Second Book of Friedrich Karl von Savigny's System of Modern Roman Law*, trans. W.H. Rattigan. London: Wildy and Sons, 1884.
Waldron, Jeremy. *The Right to Private Property*. Oxford: Clarendon Press, 1988.
Waldron, Jeremy. *Law and Disagreement*. Oxford: Oxford University Press, 1999.
Weinrib, Ernest J. "Why Legal Formalism," in *Natural Law Theory: Contemporary Essays*, ed. Robert P. George, 341–364. Oxford: Oxford University Press, 1992.
Wellman, Carl. *Real Rights*. New York: Oxford University Press, 1995.
Westen, Peter. "Poor Wesley Hohfeld," *San Diego Law Review* 55, no. 2, 449–468 (May–June 2018).
White, Alan R. *Rights*. Oxford: Clarendon Press, 1984.

Chapter 2

Bowen, Joseph. "Beyond Normative Control: Against the Will Theory of Rights," *Canadian Journal of Philosophy* 40 (2020): 427–43.
Brownlee, Kimberley. *Being Sure of Each Other*. Oxford: Oxford University Press, 2020.
Cruft, Rowan. *Human Rights, Ownership, and the Individual*. Oxford: Oxford University Press, 2019.
Darwall, Stephen. "Bipolar Obligation," in *Oxford Studies in Metaethics*, vol. 7, ed. R. Shafer-Landau, 333–58. Oxford: Oxford University Press, 2012.
Fabre, Cécile. *Whose Body is it Anyway?* Oxford: Oxford University Press, 2006.
Feinberg, Joel. "The Nature and Value of Rights," in *Rights, Justice, and the Bounds of Liberty*, 143–58. Princeton: Princeton University Press, 1980.
Gilbert, Margaret. *Rights and Demands*. Oxford: Oxford University Press, 2019.
Hart, H.L.A. *Punishment and Responsibility*. Oxford: Oxford University Press, 1968.
Ihara, Craig K. "Are Individual Rights Necessary? A Confucian Perspective," in *Confucian Ethics: A Comparative Study of Self, Autonomy, and Community*, eds. K.-L. Shun and D.B. Wong, 11–30. Cambridge: Cambridge University Press, 2004.
Kramer, Matthew H. "Rights without Trimmings," in *A Debate Over Rights: Philosophical Enquiries*, eds. M.H. Kramer, N.E. Simmonds and H. Steiner, 7–112. Oxford: Oxford University Press, 1998.
Kramer, Matthew H. "Refining the Interest Theory of Rights," *American Journal of Jurisprudence* 55 (2010): *31–9*.
Kramer, Matthew H. "In Defence of the Interest Theory of Right-Holding: Rejoinders to Leif Wenar," in *New Essays on the Nature of Rights*, ed. M. McBride, 49–84. Oxford: Hart Publishing, 2017.
Kramer, Matthew H. and Hillel Steiner. "Theories of Rights: Is there a Third Way?" *Oxford Journal of Legal Studies* 27 (2007): 281–320.
Kramer, Matthew H., N.E. Simmonds, and H. Steiner, eds. *A Debate Over Rights: Philosophical Enquiries*. Oxford: Oxford University Press, 1998.
Kurki, Visa A.J. "Rights, Harming and Wronging: A Restatement of the Interest Theory," *Oxford Journal of Legal Studies* 38 (2018): 430–50.
MacCormick, Neil. *Legal Right and Social Democracy: Essays in Legal and Political Philosophy*. Oxford: Clarendon 1982.
Rawls, John. *A Theory of Justice*. Oxford: Blackwell, 1971.
Raz, Joseph. *The Morality of Freedom*. Oxford: Clarendon, 1986.
Raz, Joseph. "Rights and Individual Well-Being," in *Ethics in the Public Domain*, 44–59. Oxford: Oxford University Press, 1994.

Schaab, Janis. "Why it is Disrespectful to Violate Rights: Contractualism and the Kind-Desire Theory." *Philosophical Studies, 175 (2018): 97–116.*
Thompson, Michael. "What is it to Wrong Someone? A Puzzle about Justice," in *Reason and Value: Themes from the Moral Philosophy of Joseph Raz*, eds. R.J. Wallace, P. Pettit, S. Scheffler, and M. Smith, 231–48. Oxford: Oxford University Press, 2004.
Wenar, Leif. "The Nature of Claim-Rights." *Ethics* 123 (2013): 202–29.

Chapter 3

Basl, John. *The Death of the Ethic of Life*. Oxford, New York: Oxford University Press, 2019.
Basl, John and Joseph Bowen. "The Rights of Artificial Intelligences," in *The Oxford Handbook of the Ethics of AI*, eds. Mark Dubber, Frank Pasquale, and Sunit Das, 289–306. Oxford: Oxford University Press, 2020.
Bowen, Joseph. "Beyond Normative Control: Against the Will Theory of Rights," *Canadian Journal of Philosophy* 50, no. 4 (2020): 427–43.
Bowen, Joseph. "Robust Rights and Harmless Wronging," in *Oxford Studies in Normative Ethics Volume 12*, ed. Mark Timmonds. New York: Oxford University Press, 2022.
Bradley, Ben. *Well-Being and Death*. Oxford: Oxford University Press, 2009.
Cruft, Rowan. *Human Rights, Ownership, and the Individual*. Oxford: Oxford University Press, 2019.
Cruft, Rowan. "Rights: Beyond Interest Theory and Will Theory?" *Law and Philosophy* 23, no. 4 (2004): 347–97.
Cruft, Rowan. "The Circularity of the Interest and Will Theories of Rights," in *New Essays on the Nature of Rights*, ed. Mark McBride, 169–186. London: Hart Publishing, 2017.
Fabre, Cécile. "Posthumous Rights," in *The Legacy of H.L.A. Hart: Legal, Political, and Moral Philosophy*, eds. Matthew H. Kramer, Claire Grant, Ben Colburn, and Antony Hatzistavrou, 225–38. Oxford: Oxford University Press, 2008.
Fabre, Cécile. *Social Rights Under the Constitution: Government and the Decent Life*. Oxford: Oxford University Press, 2000.
Feinberg, Joel. *Moral Limits of the Criminal Law, Vol. 1, Harm to Others*. Oxford: Oxford University Press, 1984.
Feldman, Fred. "Some Puzzles About the Evil of Death," *The Philosophical Review* 100, no. 2 (1991): 205–27.
Heathwood, Chris. "Desire Satisfactionism and Hedonism," *Philosophical Studies* 128, no. 3 (2006): 539–63.
Johansson, Jens. "The Timing Problem," in *The Oxford Handbook of Philosophy of Death*, eds. Ben Bradley, Fred Feldman, and Jens Johansson, 255–73. Oxford: Oxford University Press, 2012.
Kramer, Matthew H. "Getting Rights Right," in *Rights, Wrongs and Responsibilities*, ed. Matthew H. Kramer, 28–95. Basingstoke: Palgrave, 2001.
Kramer, Matthew H. "In Defence of the Interest Theory of Right-Holding: Rejoinders to Leif Wenar on Rights," in *New Essays on the Nature of Rights*, ed. Mark McBride, 49–83. London: Hart Publishing, 2017.
Kramer, Matthew H. *Liberalism with Excellence*. Oxford: Oxford University Press, 2017.
Kramer, Matthew H. "Refining the Interest Theory of Rights," *The American Journal of Jurisprudence* 55, no. 1 (2010): 31–39.
Kramer, Matthew H. "Rights Without Trimmings," in *A Debate Over Rights: Philosophical Enquiries*, eds. Matthew H. Kramer, N.E. Simmonds, and Hillel Steiner, 7–112. Oxford: Oxford University Press, 2000.

Kurki, Visa A.J. "Rights, Harming and Wronging: A Restatement of the Interest Theory," *Oxford Journal of Legal Studies* 38, no. 3 (2018): 430–50.

Luper, Steven. "Posthumous Harm," *American Philosophical Quarterly* 41, no. 1 (2004): 63–72.

MacCormick, Neil. "Children's Rights: A Test-Case for Legal Rights," in *Legal Right and Social Democracy: Essays in Legal and Political Philosophy*, ed. Neil MacCormick, 154–66. Oxford: Clarendon Press, 1982.

MacCormick, Neil. "Rights in Legislation," in *Law, Morality, and Society: Essays in Honour of H. L. A. Hart*, eds. P.M.S. Hacker and Joseph Raz, 189–209. Oxford: Clarendon Press, 1977.

May, Simon Căbulea. "Desires, Interests and Claim-Rights," in *New Essays on the Nature of Rights*, ed. Mark McBride, 85–98. London: Hart Publishing, 2017.

McMahan, Jeff. "Death and the Value of Life," *Ethics* 99, no. 1 (1988): 32–61.

Nozick, Robert. *Anarchy, State and Utopia*. Oxford: Basil Blackwell, 1974.

Owens, David. *Shaping the Normative Landscape*. Oxford: Oxford University Press, 2012.

Parfit, Derek. *Reasons and Persons*. Oxford: Oxford University Press, 1984.

Pitcher, George. "The Misfortunes of the Dead," *American Philosophical Quarterly* 21, no. 2 (1984): 183–8.

Raz, Joseph. "Rights and Individual Well-Being," *Ratio Juris* 5, no. 2 (1992): 127–42.

Raz, Joseph. *The Morality of Freedom*. Oxford: Oxford University Press, 1986.

Sumner, L.W. *Welfare, Happiness, and Ethics*. Oxford: Clarendon, 1996.

Tadros, Victor. *Wrongs and Crimes*. Oxford: Oxford University Press, 2016.

Taylor, Charles. "The Concept of a Person," in *Human Agency and Language: Philosophical Papers Volume 1, ed. Charles Taylor, 97–114.* Cambridge: Cambridge University Press, 1985.

Van Duffel, Siegfried. "Adequacy Constraints for a Theory of Rights," in *New Essays on the Nature of Rights*, ed. Mark McBride, 187–202. London: Hart Publishing, 2017.

Chapter 4

Baltrimienė, Milda. "The Problem of the Nature of Individual Rights in Contemporary Theories of Legal Positivism," *Problemos* 92 (2017): 50–62.

Barker, Kit. "Private Law, Analytical Philosophy and the Modern Value of Wesley Newcomb Hohfeld: A Centennial Appraisal," *Oxford Journal of Legal Studies* 38, nob . 3 (2018): 585–612.

Berg, Jessica. "Of Elephants and Embryos: A Proposed Framework for Legal Personhood," *Hastings Law Journal* 59, no. 369 (2007): 369–406.

Calverley, David J. "Imagining a Non-Biological Machine as a Legal Person," *AI & Society* 22, no. 22 (2008): 523–37.

Charlie, Webb. "Three Concepts of Rights, Two of Property," *Oxford Journal of Legal Studies* 38, no. 2 (2018): 246–69, doi:10.1093/ojls/gqy006 (abstract).

Cruft, Rowan. *Human Rights, Ownership and the Individual*. Oxford: Oxford University Press, 2019.

Dworkin, Ronald. "Taking Rights Seriously," in *Taking Rights Seriously*, 223–48. Harvard University Press, 1977.

Eleftheriadis, Pavlos. *Legal Rights*. Oxford: Oxford University Press, 2008.

Enoch, David. "Reason-Giving and the Law," in *Oxford Studies in Philosophy of Law: Volume 1*, eds, 1–38. Leslie Green and Brian Leiter. Oxford: Oxford University Press, 2011.

Frydrych, David. "Kramer's Delimiting Test for Legal Rights," *American Journal of Jurisprudence* 62, no. 2 (2017): 197–207, doi:10.1093/ajj/aux019.

Frydrych, David. "The Theories of Rights Debate," *Jurisprudence* 9, no. 3 (2018): 566–88.

Fuller, Lon. *The Morality of Law*. New Haven: Yale University Press, 1965.

Gardner, John. “Legal Positivism: 5 ½ Myths,” *American Journal of Jurisprudence* 46, no. 1 (2001): 199–227.

Hart, H.L.A. “Definition and Theory in Jurisprudence,” in H.L.A Hart, *Essays in Jurisprudence and Philosophy*, 21–48. Oxford: Oxford University Press, 1984.

Hart, H.L.A. *The Concept of Law*. Oxford: Clarendon Press, 1994.

Hartney, Michael. “Some Confusions Concerning Collective Rights,” *Canadian Journal of Law & Jurisprudence* 4, no. 2 (1991): 293–314.

Hohfeld, Wesley Newcomb. “Some Fundamental Legal Conceptions as Applied in Legal Reasoning,” *Yale Law Journal* 23, no. 1 (1913): 16–59.

Jörg Neuner, “Zur Rechtsfähigkeit Des Anencephalus,” *Medizinrecht* 31, no. 10 (2013): 647–51, doi:10.1007/s00350-013-3527-9.

Jovanović, Miograd. A. *Collective Rights. A Legal Theory*. Cambridge: Cambridge University Press, 2014.

Kramer, Matthew H. “Rights Without Trimmings,” in *A Debate over Rights. Philosophical Enquiries*, eds. Matthew H. Kramer, N.E. Simmonds, and Hillel Steiner, 7–112. Oxford: Oxford University Press, 1998.

Kramer, Matthew H. “Do Animals and Dead People Have Legal Rights?,” *Canadian Journal of Law & Jurisprudence* 14, no. 1 (2001): 29–54.

Kramer, Matthew H. “Legal and Moral Obligation,” in *The Blackwell Guide to the Philosophy of Law and Legal Theory*, eds. Martin P. Golding and William A. Edmundson, 179–190. Blackwell Publishing Ltd, 2005.

Kramer, Matthew H. *Objectivity and the Rule of Law*. Cambridge: Cambridge University Press, 2007.

Kramer, Matthew H. *Where Law and Morality Meet*. Oxford: Oxford University Press, 2008.

Kramer, Matthew H. “Rights in Legal and Political Philosophy,” in *The Oxford Handbook of Law and Politics*, eds. Gregory A. Caldeira, R. Daniel Kelemen, and Keith E. Whittington. Oxford: Oxford University Press, 2008, doi:10.1093/oxfordhb/9780199208425.003.0023 417.

Kramer, Matthew H. *In Defense of Legal Positivism: Law Without Trimmings*. Oxford: Oxford University Press, 2010.

Kramer, Matthew H. *Liberalism with Excellence*. Oxford: Oxford University Press, 2017.

Kramer, Matthew H. “In Defence of the Interest Theory of Right-Holding: Rejoinders to Leif Wenar on Rights,” in *New Essays on the Nature of Rights*, ed. Mark McBride, 49–83. Oxford: Hart Publishing, 2017.

Kramer, Matthew H. “Conceptual Analysis and Distributive Justice,” in *The Oxford Handbook of Distributive Justice*, ed. Serena Olsaretti, 367–386. Oxford: Oxford University Press, 2018.

Kurki, Visa A.J. “Rights, Harming and Wronging: A Restatement of the Interest Theory,” *Oxford Journal of Legal Studies* 38, no. 3 (2018): 430–50.

Kurki, Visa A.J. *A Theory of Legal Personhood*. Oxford: Oxford University Press, 2019.

MacCormick, Neil. “Rights in Legislation,” in *Law, Morality and Society*, ed. P.M.S. Hacker and Joseph Raz, 189–209. Oxford: Clarendon Press, 1977.

McBride, Mark. “Preserving the Interest Theory of Rights,” *Legal Theory* 26, no. 1 (2020): 3–39.

Perry, Ronen. “Correlativity,” *Law and Philosophy* 28, no. 6 (2009): 537–84.

Rainbolt, George W. *The Concept of Rights*. Dordrecht: Springer, 2006.

Raz, Joseph. *The Authority of Law*. Oxford: Oxford University Press, 1979.

Raz, Joseph. “On the Nature of Rights,” *Mind* 93, no. 370 (1984): 194–214.

Simmonds, N.E. “The Analytical Foundations of Justice,” *The Cambridge Law Journal* 54, no. 02 (1995): 306–41.

Simmonds, N.E. “Rights at the Cutting Edge,” in *A Debate over Rights. Philosophical Enquiries*, eds. Matthew H. Kramer, N.E. Simmonds, and Hillel Steiner, 113–232. Oxford: Oxford University Press, 1998.

Tierney, Brian. *The Idea of Natural Rights: Studies on Natural Rights, Natural Law and Church Law 1150–1625*. Atlanta: Scholars Press, 1997.
Van Duffel, Siegfried. "Adequacy Constraints for a Theory of Rights," in *New Essays on the Nature of Rights*, ed. Mark McBride, 187–202. Oxford: Hart Publishing, 2017.

Chapter 5

Hart, H. *Essays on Bentham*. Oxford: Oxford University Press, 1982.
Kramer, M. "Rights without Trimmings," in *A Debate over Rights*, eds. Matthew H. Kramer, N.E. Simmonds, and Hillel Steiner, 7–111. Oxford: Oxford University Press, 1998.
Kramer, M. "Refining the Interest Theory of Rights," *American Journal of Jurisprudence* 55 (2010): 31–9.
Kramer, M. "Some Doubts about Alternatives to the Interest Theory of Rights," *Ethics* 123 (2013): 245–63.
Kramer, M. "In Defense of the Interest Theory of Right-Holding: Rejoinders to Leif Wenar on Rights," in *New Essays on the Nature of Rights*, ed. M. McBride, 49–83. Oxford: Hart Publishing, 2017.
Kramer, M. and Steiner, H. "Theories of Rights: Is There a Third Way?," *Oxford Journal of Legal Studies* 27 (2007): 281–310.
McBride, M. "The Tracking Theory of Rights," in *New Essays on the Nature of Rights*, ed. M. McBride, 149–168. Oxford: Hart Publishing, 2017.
McBride, M. "Preserving the Interest Theory of Rights," *Legal Theory* 26 (1) (2020): 3–39.
McBride, M. "The Unavoidability of Evaluation for Interest Theories of Rights," *Canadian Journal of Law & Jurisprudence* 33 (2) (2020): 293–315.
McBride, M. "The Tracking Theory of Claim-Rights." *Analytic Philosophy*.
McBride, M. (ms) *The Tracking Theory of Rights*. Oxford: Hart Publishing, forthcoming.
Nozick, R. *Philosophical Explanations*. Harvard: Belknap Press, 1981.
Raz, J. *The Morality of Freedom*. Oxford: OUP, 1986.
Sreenivasan, G. "A Hybrid Theory of Claim-Rights," *Oxford Journal of Legal Studies* 25 (2005): 257.
Sreenivasan, G. "Duties and their Direction," *Ethics* (2010) 120, no. 3, pp. 465–94.
Sreenivasan, G. "Public Goods, Individual Rights, and Third Party Benefits," in *New Essays on the Nature of Rights*, ed. M. McBride, 127–148. Oxford: Hart Publishing, 2017.
Steiner, H. "Working Rights," in *A Debate over Rights*, eds. Matthew H. Kramer, N.E. Simmonds, and Hillel Steiner, 233–301. Oxford: Oxford University Press, 1998.
Wenar, L. "The Nature of Rights," *Philosophy and Public Affairs* 33 (2005) 223–52.
Wenar, L. "The Analysis of Rights," in *The Legacy of H.L.A. Hart*, eds. Matthew H. Kramer et al., 251–73. Oxford: Oxford University Press, 2008.
Wenar, L. "The Nature of Claim-Rights," *Ethics* 123 (2013): 202–29.

Chapter 6

Alexy, Robert. *The Argument from Injustice: A Reply to Legal Positivism* (Stanley L. Paulson & Bonnie Litschewski Paulson, trans.). Oxford: Clarendon Press, 2002.
Alexy, Robert. "An Answer to Joseph Raz," in *Law, Rights and Discourse*, ed. George Pavlakos, 37–55. Oxford: Hart Publishing, 2007.
Barnett, Randy E. and Bernick, Evan. "The Privileges or Immunities Clause Abridged: A Critique of Kurt Lash on the Fourteenth Amendment," *Notre Dame Law Review* 95 (2019): 499–589.

Beltrán, Jordi Ferrer and Ratti, Giovanni Battista, eds. *The Logic of Legal Requirements: Essays on Defeasibility*. Oxford: Oxford University Press, 2012.

Bird, Alexander and Tobin, Emma. "Natural Kinds," in *The Stanford Encyclopedia of Philosophy*, https://plato.stanford.edu/entries/natural-kinds/, ed. Edward N. Zalta. 2017.

Bix, Brian H. "Global Error and Legal Truth," *Oxford Journal of Legal Studies* 29 (2009): 535–47.

Bix, Brian H. "Defeasibility and Open Texture," in *The Logic of Legal Requirements: Essays on Defeasibility*, eds. Jordi Ferrer Beltrán and Giovanni Battista Ratti, 193–201. Oxford: Oxford University Press, 2012.

Brink, David O. "Legal Interpretation, Objectivity, and Morality," in *Objectivity in Law and Morals*, ed. Brian Leiter, 12–65. Cambridge: Cambridge University Press, 2001.

Chemerinsky, Erwin. *Constitutional Law: Principles and Policies*. 4th ed. New York: Wolters Kluwer, 2011.

Coleman, Jules L. "Incorporationism, Conventionality, and the Practical Difference Thesis," *Legal Theory* 4 (1998): 381–425.

Coleman, Jules L. and Leiter, Brian. "Determinacy, Objectivity, and Authority," *University of Pennsylvania Law Review* 124 (1993): 549–637.

Dworkin, Ronald. *Taking Rights Seriously*. Rev. ed. Cambridge, Mass.: Harvard University Press, 1978.

Dworkin, Ronald. *Law's Empire*. Cambridge, Mass.: Harvard University Press, 1986.

Finnis, John. "On the Incoherence of Legal Positivism," *Notre Dame Law Review* 75 (2000): 1597–1611.

Fuller, Lon L. *The Morality of Law*. Rev. ed. New Haven: Yale University Press, 1969.

Hart, H.L.A. "The Ascription of Responsibility and Rights," *Proceedings of the Aristotelian Society* 49 (1948–49): 171–94.

Hart, H.L.A. *The Concept of Law*. 3rd ed. Oxford: Oxford University Press, 2012.

Holmes, Oliver Wendell. "The Path of the Law," *Harvard Law Review* 10 (1987): 457–78.

Kramer, Matthew H. *In Defense of Legal Positivism*. Oxford: Oxford University Press, 1999.

Kramer, Matthew H. *Where Law and Morality Meet*. Oxford: Oxford University Press, 2004.

Kramer, Matthew H. *Objectivity and the Rule of Law*. Cambridge: Cambridge University Press, 2007.

Kramer, Matthew H. "Is Law's Conventionality Consistent with Law's Objectivity?," *Res Publica* 14 (2008): 241–52.

Leiter, Brian. "Objectivity and the Problems of Jurisprudence," *Texas Law Review* 72 (1993): 187–209.

Leiter, Brian. "Legal Indeterminacy," *Legal Theory* 1 (1995): 481–92.

Leiter, Brian, ed. *Objectivity in Law and Morals*. Cambridge: Cambridge University Press, 2001. (2001a)

Leiter, Brian. "Objectivity, Morality, and Adjudication," in *Objectivity in Law and Morals*, ed. Brian Leiter, 66–98. Cambridge: Cambridge University Press, 2001. (2001b)

Levinson, Sanford. "Law as Literature," *Texas Law Review* 60 (1982): 373–403.

Lewis, David K. *Convention: A Philosophical Study*. Cambridge, Mass.: Harvard University Press, 1969.

Lorde, Audre. *The Master's Tools Will Never Dismantle the Master's House*. London: Penguin, 2018.

Marmor, Andrei. *Positive Law and Objective Values*. Oxford: Oxford University Press, 2001.

Marmor, Andrei. *Interpretation and Legal Theory*. Rev. 2nd ed. Oxford: Hart Publishing, 2005.

Marmor, Andrei. "The Conventional Foundations of Law," in *New Essays on the Normativity of Law*, eds. Stefano Bertea and George Pavlakos, 143–57. Oxford: Hart Publishing, 2011.

Murphy, Mark. "Theological Voluntarism," in *The Stanford Encyclopedia of Philosophy*, ed. Edward N. Zalta, https://plato.stanford.edu/entries/moral-cognitivism. 2012.

Patterson, Dennis. "Theoretical Disagreement, Legal Positivism, and Legal Interpretation," *Ratio Juris* 31 (2018): 260–75.
Postema, Gerald J. "Coordination and Convention at the Foundations of Law," *Journal of Legal Studies* 11 (1982): 165–203.
Putnam, Hilary. "The Meaning of 'Meaning,'" in *Mind, Language and Reality*, 215–71. Cambridge: Cambridge University Press, 1975.
Putnam, Hilary. "Comments on Russell Goodman," in *Reading Putnam*, ed. Maria Baghramian, 219–24. New York: Routledge, 2013.
Raz, Joseph. *Engaging Reason*. Oxford: Oxford University Press, 1999.
Rescorla, Michael. "Convention," in *The Stanford Encyclopedia of Philosophy*, ed. Edward N. Zalta, https://plato.stanford.edu/entries/moral-cognitivism/. 2015.
van Roojen, Mark. "Moral Cognitivism vs. Non-Cognitivism," in *The Stanford Encyclopedia of Philosophy*, ed. Edward N. Zalta, https://plato.stanford.edu/entries/moral-cognitivism/ . 2018.
Rosati, Connie S. "Some Puzzles About the Objectivity of Law," *Law and Philosophy* 23 (2004): 273–323.
Schauer, Frederick. "Necessity, Importance, and the Nature of Law," in *Neutrality and Theory of Law*, eds. Jordi Ferrer Beltrán, José Juan Moreso, and Diego M. Papayannis, 17–31. Dordrecht: Springer, 2013.
Shapiro, Scott J. "On Hart's Way Out," *Legal Theory* 4 (1998): 469–507.
Stavrapolous, Nicos. *Objectivity in Law*. Oxford: Oxford University Press, 1996.
Tiefensee, Christine. "Metasemantics, Moral Realism and Moral Doctrines," ch. 10, this volume. 189–204. 2021.
Waluchow, W.J. "Matthew Kramer and Inclusive Legal Positivism: Dancing on the Head of a Pin," ch. 7, this volume. 2021, 189–204.

Chapter 7

Bix, Brian. "Patrolling the Boundaries: Inclusive Legal Positivism and the Nature of Jurisprudential Debate," *Canadian Journal of Law and Jurisprudence* XII, no. 1 (1999): 17–33.
Coleman, Jules L. "Incorporationism, Conventionality, and the Practical Difference Thesis," *Legal Theory* 4, 381 (1998): 381–425.
Coleman, Jules L. *The Practice of Principle: In Defence of a Pragmatist Approach to Legal Theory*. Oxford: Oxford University Press, 2001.
Hart, H.L.A. and Green L. *Concept of Law*. Oxford: Oxford University Press, 2012.
Himma, Ken. "Law's Claim of Legitimate Authority," in *Hart's Postscript*, ed. Jules Coleman. Oxford: Oxford University Press, 2001: 271–309.
Himma, Ken. "Substance and Method in Conceptual Jurisprudence and Theory," *Virginia Law Review* 88 (2002): 1119–228.
Kramer, Matthew. *Where Law and Morality Meet*. Oxford: Oxford University Press, 2004.
Kramer, Matthew. *H.L.A. Hart*. Cambridge: Polity Press, 2018.
Lyons, David. "Principles, Positivism and Legal Theory," *Yale Law Journal* 87 (1977): 415–35.
Marmor, Andrei. *Positive Law and Objective* Values. Oxford: Oxford University Press, 2001.
McBride, Mark. "The Inner Logic of Exclusivism (and Inclusivism): Raz's Foreshadowing," *Australian Journal of Legal Philosophy* 4 (2017): 81–120.
McBride, Mark. "The Inner Logic of Exclusivism (and Inclusivism): Shapiro's Shadowing," *Ratio Juris* 32, no. 3 (2019): 363–89.

Perry, Stephen "Judicial Obligation, Precedent and the Common Law," *Oxford Journal of Legal Studies* 7 (1987): 215–57.

Postema, Gerald J. "Coordination and Convention at the Foundations of Law," *Journal of Legal Studies* 11 (1982): 165–203.

Postema, Gerald. *Legal Philosophy in the Twentieth Century: The Common Law World*. The Netherlands: Springer, 2011.

Raz, Joseph. *The Authority of* Law. Oxford: Oxford University Press, 1979.

Raz, Joseph. "Authority and Justification," *Philosophy and Public Affairs* 14 (1985): 3–29.

Raz, Joseph. "Authority, Law and Morality," *The Monist* 3 (1985): 295–324.

Raz, Joseph. *The Morality of Freedom*. Oxford: Oxford University Press, 1986.

Raz, Joseph. *Ethics In the Public Domain*. Oxford: Oxford University Press, 1995.

Raz, Joseph. *Practical Reason and Norms*. Oxford: Oxford University Press, 2002.

Raz, Joseph. "The Problem of Authority: Revisiting the Service Conception," *Minnesota Law Review* 90 (2006): 1003–44.

Raz, Joseph. *Between Authority and* Interpretation. Oxford: Oxford University Press, 2009.

Schauer, Fred. "Positivism Through Thick and Thin," in *Analyzing Law: New Essays in Legal Theory*, ed. Brian Bix, 65–78. Oxford: Clarendon Press, 1988.

Soper, E. Philip. "Legal Theory and the Obligation of a Judge: The Hart/Dworkin Dispute," *Michigan Law Review* 75 (1977): 473–519.

Waluchow, Wilfrid J. "Herculean Positivism," *Oxford Journal of Legal Studies* 5, no. 2 (Summer, 1985): 187–210.

Waluchow, Wilfrid J. *Inclusive Legal Positivism*. Oxford: Oxford University Press, 1994.

Waluchow, Wilfrid J. "Authority and the Practical Difference Thesis: A Defense of Inclusive Legal Positivism," *Legal Theory* 6, no. 45 (2000): 45–80.

Chapter 8

Bayón, J.C. *El contenido mínimo del positivismo jurídico*. 2002. http://www.enj.org.

Bulygin, E. *Il positivismo giuridico*. Milano: Giuffrè, 2007.

Coleman, J. *Negative and Positive Positivism. 1982*. In Cohen, M. (ed.), *Ronald Dworkin and Contemporary Jurisprudence*, Totowa, N.J.: Rowland & Allanheld, 28–48. 1983.

Coleman, J.L. *Incorporationism, Conventionality, and the Practical Difference Thesis*. In Coleman, J. ed. *Hart's Postscript. Essays on the Postscript to The Concept of Law*. Oxford: Oxford University Press, 99–147, 2001.

Coleman, J., ed. *Hart's Postscript. Essays on the Postscript to The Concept of Law*. Oxford: Oxford University Press, 2001.

Coleman, J.L. "Legal Positivism: Anglo-American Legal Positivism since H.L.A. Hart," in *The Encyclopedia of Philosophy*, ed. D.M. Borchert. 2nd ed, vol. 5, 239–45. Farmington Hill, Mich.: Thomson Gale, 2006.

Coleman, J. Shapiro S., ed. *The Oxford Handbook of Jurisprudence and Philosophy of Law*. Oxford: Oxford University Press, 2002.

Hart, H.L.A. (1958a). "*Legal and Moral Obligation*," in A.I. Melden (ed.), *Essays in Moral Philosophy*. University of Washington Press, 82–107 (1958).

Hart, H.L.A. (1958b). "Positivism and the Separation of Law and Morals," in Hart, 49–87 (1983b) 1983.

Hart, H.L.A. "*Immorality and Treason*," 1959 In The Philosophy of Law, Dworkin, R. ed., Oxford: Oxford University Press, 83–8. 1977.

Hart, H.L.A. *The Concept of Law*. Oxford: Clarendon Press, 1961.

Hart, H.L.A. *Law, Liberty and Morality*. London: Oxford University Press, 1963.

Hart, H.L.A. *The Morality of Criminal Law. Two Lectures*. London: Oxford University Press, 1964.
Hart, H.L.A. (1966). "*Legal Duty and Obligation*," in H.L.A. *Hart, Essays on Bentham. Jurisprudence and Political Theory*. Oxford: Clarendon Press, 1982.
Hart, H.L.A. (1967a). "Legal Positivism," in *The Encyclopedia of Philosophy*, ed. D.M. Borchert. 2nd ed, vol. 5, 239–45. Farmington Hill, Mich.: Thomson Gale, 2006.
Hart, H.L.A. (1967b). "*Problems of the Philosophy of Law*," in H.L.A. Hart, *Essays in Jurisprudence and Philosophy*. Oxford: Clarendon Press, 88–119, 1983.
Hart, H.L.A. *Punishment and Responsibility. Essays in the Philosophy of Law*. Oxford: Clarendon Press, 1968.
Hart, H.L.A. "*El nuevo desafío al positivismo jurídico*," *Sistema* 36 (1980): 3–18.
Hart, H.L.A. (1982a). *Commands and Authoritative Legal Reasons*. In H.L.A. *Hart, Essays on Bentham. Jurisprudence and Political Theory*. Oxford: Clarendon Press, 1982.
Hart, H.L.A. (1982b). *Essays on Bentham. Jurisprudence and Political Theory*. Oxford: Clarendon Press, 1982.
Hart, H.L.A. (1983a). *Introduction*. In Hart, 1–18. (1983b) 1983.
Hart, H.L.A. (1983b). *Essays in Jurisprudence and Philosophy*. Oxford: Clarendon Press, 1983.
Hart, H.L.A. *Comment*. In R. Gavison (ed.), *Issues in Contemporary Legal Philosophy. The Influence of H. L .A. Hart*, 35–42. Oxford: Clarendon Press, 1987.
Hart, H.L.A. "Answers to Eight Questions," 1988. In *Reading H L A Hart's The Concept of Law*, eds. L. Duarte d'Almeida, J. Edwards, and A. Dolcetti, 279–97. Oxford: Hart, 2013.
Hart. H.L.A. "Postscript," in *The Concept of Law*, 3rd ed. With a Postscript edited by P. Bulloch and J. Raz. And with an Introduction and Notes by L. Green, 238–76. Oxford: Oxford University Press, 2012.
Himma, K.E. "*Inclusive Legal Positivism*,' in Coleman J., Shapiro S. (eds.) *The Oxford Handbook of Jurisprudence and Philosophy of Law*, 125–65. Oxford: Oxford University Press, 2002.
Kelsen, H. *General Theory of Law and State*. Cambridge. Mass.: Harvard University Press, 1945.
Kramer, M.H. *In Defense of Legal Positivism. Law Without Trimmings*. Oxford: Oxford University Press, 1999.
Kramer, M.H. *Where Law and Morality Meet*. Oxford: Oxford University Press, 2004.
Kramer, M.H. "There's Nothing Quasi about Quasi-Realism: Moral Realism as a Moral Doctrine," *Journal of Ethics* 21, no. 2, 185–212 (June 2017).
Kramer, M.H. *H. L. A. Hart. The Nature of Law*. Cambridge: Polity Press, 2018.
Kramer, M.H. *The Legal Positivism of H.L.A. Hart*. Cambridge University, Faculty of Law, Legal Studies Research Paper Series. Paper No. 11/2019. March 2019.
Lyons, D. "On Formal Justice," *Cornell Law Review* 58, no. 5 (1973): 833–61.
Moreso, J.J. "In Defense of Inclusive Legal Positivism," in *The Legal Ought*, ed. P. Chiassoni, 37–63. Turin: Giappichelli, 2001.
Raz, J. "The Institutional Nature of Law," 1975, in The Authority of Law, ed. J. *Raz*. Oxford: Clarendon Press, 103–21. 1979.
Raz, J. "Legal Reasons, Sources, and Gaps," in Raz, 53–77. 1979.
Raz, J. "Legal Positivism and the Sources of Law," in J. Raz, The Authority of Law, 37–52. Oxford: Clarendon Press, 1979.
Raz, J. "A Postscript to Legal Principles and the Limits of the Law," in ed. M. Cohen, *Ronald Dworkin and Contemporary Jurisprudence*, Totowa, N.J.: Rowland & Allanheld, 81–6. 1983.
Raz, J. *Authority, Law and Morality*, in Raz, J. (1992), Ethics in the Public Domain, Oxford: Oxford University Press, 1985.
Raz, J. *Ethics in the Public Domain. Essays in the Morality of Law and Politics*. Oxford: Clarendon Press, 1994.
Raz, J. *The Authority of Law. Essays on Law and Morality*. Oxford: Clarendon Press, 1979. 2nd ed. 2009.

Raz, J. "The Problem of Authority: Revisiting the Service Conception," in J. Raz, *Between Authority and Interpretation. On the Theory of Law and Practical Reason*, 126–65. Oxford: Oxford University Press. 2009 [2006].

Shapiro, S. *The "Hart-Dworkin" Debate: A Short Guide for the Perplexed*. University of Michigan Law School. Public Law and Legal Theory Working Paper Series. Working Paper No. 77. March 2007.

Chapter 9

Althusius, Johannes. *Politica*. Frederick S. Carney, ed. and tr. Indianapolis: Liberty Fund, 1964.

Anderson, Elizabeth. "What is the Point of Equality?," *Ethics* 109 (1999): 287–337.

Bentham, Jeremy. *Securities against Misrule and Other Constitutional Writings for Tripoli and Greece*. Ed. Philip Schofield. Oxford: Clarendon Press, 1990.

Bracton, *On the Laws and Customs of England*. S. E. Thorne, tr. Cambridge, Mass.: Belknap Press, 1968.

Cheesman, Simon. *Opposing the Rule of Law*. Cambridge: Cambridge University Press, 2015.

Crawford, James. "International Law and the Rule of Law," *Adelaide Law Review* 24 (2003): 3–12.

Ferguson, Adam. *An Essay on the History of Civil Society*, ed. F. Oz-Salzberger. Cambridge: Cambridge University Press, 1995 (first published 1767).

Fraenkel, Ernest. *The Dual State: A Contribution to the Theory of Dictatorship* (first published 1941). Oxford: Oxford University Press, 2017.

Fuller, Lon. *The Morality of Law*. Revised ed. New Haven: Yale University Press, 1969.

Hart, *The Concept of Law*. 2nd ed. Oxford: Oxford University Press, 1994.

Hobbes, Thomas. *Leviathan*, ed. Richard Tuck. Cambridge: Cambridge University Press, 1996.

Holmes, Stephen. "Lineages of the Rule of Law," in *Democracy and the Rule of Law*, eds. José María Maravall and Adam Prezworski. Cambridge: Cambridge University Press, 2003: 19–61.

Hume, David. *Enquiry Concerning the Principles of Morals*, ed. Tom L. Beauchamp. Oxford: Oxford University Press, 1998.

Kramer, Matthew. *Objectivity and the Rule of Law*. Cambridge: Cambridge University Press, 2007.

Krygier, Martin. "Tempering Power," in *Constitutionalism and the Rule of Law*, eds. Maurice Adams, Ernst Hirsch Ballin, and Anne Meuwese, 34–59. Cambridge: Cambridge University Press, 2017.

Locke, John. *Second Treatise of Government*, ed. C.B. Macpherson. Indianapolis: Hackett Publishing Co., 1980.

Lyons, David. *The Moral Aspects of Legal Theory*. Cambridge: Cambridge University Press, 1993.

Marmor, Andrei. "The Rule of Law and Its Limits," *Law and Philosophy* 23 (2004): 1–43.

Pettit, Philip. *Republicanism: A Theory of Freedom and Government*. Oxford: Oxford University Press, 1997.

Pettit, Philip. *On the People's Terms*. Cambridge: Cambridge University Press, 2012.

Postema, Gerald J. "Jurisprudence as Practical Philosophy," *Legal Theory* 4 (1998): 329–57.

Postema, Gerald J. "Conformity, Custom, and Congruence: Rethinking the Efficacy of Law," in *The Legacy of Hart*, ed. Matthew Kramer, 45–65. Oxford: Oxford University Press, 2008.

Postema Gerald J. "Law's Ethos: Reflections on a Public Practice of Illegality," *Boston University Law Review* 90 (2010): 1847–68.

Postema, Gerald J. *Legal Philosophy in the Twentieth Century: The Common Law World*. Dordrecht: Springer, 2011.

Postema, Gerald J. "Law's Rule: Reflexivity, Mutual Accountability, and the Rule of Law," in *Bentham's Theory of Law and Public Opinion*, eds. Xiaobo Zhai and Michael Quinn. Cambridge: Cambridge University Press, 2014: 7–39.

Postema Gerald J. "Fidelity in Law's Commonwealth," in *Private Law and the Rule of Law*, ed. Dennis Klimchuk, 20–4. Oxford: Oxford University Press, 2014.
Postema, Gerald J. "Covenant Membership as a Community of Equals," in *Encyclopedia of the Philosophy of Law and Social Philosophy*, eds. M.N.S. Sellers and Stephan Kirste. Dordrecht: Springer, 2020.
Raz, Joseph. "The Rule of Law and its Virtue," in *The Authority of Law*, 210–29. Oxford: Oxford University Press, 1979.
Rubin, Edward L. "Law and Legislation in the Administrative State," *Columbia Law Review* 89 (1989): 397–403.
Rundle, Kristen. *Forms Liberate: Reclaiming the Jurisprudence of Lon Fuller*. Oxford: Hart Publishing Co., 2013.
Scheffler, Samuel. "What is Egalitarianism?," *Philosophy and Public Affairs* 31 (2003): 5–39.
Tamanaha, Brian. "The Functions of the Rule of Law." (2018). Available at:https://ssrn.com/abstract=3113820.
Tushnet, Mark. "Authoritarian Constitutionalism," *Cornell Law* Review 100 (2105): 422–31.
Twining, William. *Globalization and Legal Theory*. Evanston: Northwestern University Press, 2000.
Waldron, Jeremy. "The Concept and the Rule of Law," *Georgia Law Review* 43 (2008): 1–61.
Waldron, Jeremy. "How Law Protects Dignity," *Cambridge Law Journal* 71 (2012): 200–22.
Wallace, R. Jay. *The View from Here*. Oxford: Oxford University Press, 2013.
Weifang, He. *In the Name of Justice*. Washington, DC: Brookings Institution Press, 2012.

Chapter 10

Blackburn, S. *Ruling Passions. A Theory of Practical Reasoning*. Oxford: Clarendon Press, 1998.
Boyd, R. "How to be a Moral Realist," in *Essays on Moral Realism*, ed. G. Sayre-McCord, 181–228. Cornell: Cornell University Press, 1988.
Boyd, R. "What Realism Implies and What it Does Not," *Dialectica* 43 (1989): 5–29.
Brandom, B. *Making it Explicit. Reasoning, Representing, and Discursive Commitment*. Cambridge, Mass.: Harvard University Press, 1994.
Brink, D. *Moral Realism and the Foundations of Ethics*. Cambridge: Cambridge University Press, 1989.
Chrisman, M. *The Meaning of "Ought": Beyond Descriptivism and Expressivism in Metaethics*. New York: Oxford University Press, 2016.
Chrisman, M. "Conceptual Role Accounts of Meaning in Metaethics," in *The Routledge Handbook of Metaethics*, eds. T. McPherson and David Plunkett, 260–74. London: Routledge, 2017.
Dreier, J. "Metaethics and the Problem of Creeping Minimalism," *Philosophical Perspectives* 18 (2004): 23–44.
Dreier, J. "The Real and the Quasi-Real: Problems of Distinction," *Canadian Journal of Philosophy* 48 (2018): 532–47.
Dworkin, R. "Objectivity and Truth: You'd Better Believe it," *Philosophy and Public Affairs* 25 (1996): 87–139.
Dworkin, R. *Justice for Hedgehogs*. Cambridge, Mass.: Belknap Press, 2011.
Enoch, D. *Taking Morality Seriously*. Oxford: Oxford University Press, 2011.
Gibbard, A. *Thinking How to Live*. Cambridge, MA: Harvard University Press, 2003.
Köhler, S. "Expressivism, Meaning, and All *That*," *Canadian Journal of Philosophy* 48 (2018): 337–56.
Kramer, M. *Moral Realism as a Moral Doctrine*. Chichester: Wiley-Blackwell, 2009.
Kramer, M. "There's Nothing Quasi About Quasi-Realism: Moral Realism as a Moral Doctrine," *The Journal of Ethics* 21 (2017): 185–212.

Kratzer, A. "The Notional Category of Modality," In *Words, Worlds, and Contexts*, eds. H.J. Eikmeyer and H. Rieser, 38–74. Berlin and New York: de Gruyter, 1981.
Nagel, T. *The View from Nowhere*. Oxford: Oxford University Press, 1986.
Parfit, D. *On What Matters: Volume Two*. Oxford: Oxford University Press, 2011.
Ridge, M. *Impassioned Belief*. Oxford: Oxford University Press, 2014.
Rosen, G. "Blackburn's Essays in Quasi-Realism," *Noûs* 32 (1998): 386–405.
Scanlon, T. *Being Realistic about Reasons*. Oxford: Oxford University Press, 2014.
Schroeder, M. *Being For: Evaluating the Semantic Program of Expressivism*. Oxford: Oxford University Press, 2008.
Schroeter, L. and Schroeter, F. "The Generalized Integration Challenge in Metaethics," *Noûs* 53 (2019): 192–223.
Shafer-Landau, R. *Moral Realism. A Defence*. Oxford: Oxford University Press, 2003.
Simpson, M. "Solving the Problem of Creeping Minimalism," *Canadian Journal of Philosophy* 48 (2018): 510–31.
Sinclair, N. "The Moral Belief Problem," *Ratio* 19 (2006): 249–60.
Tiefensee, C. *Expressivism, Minimalism and Moral Doctrines*. Doctoral Thesis, catalogued by the Cambridge University Library, 2011.
Tiefensee, C. "Inferentialism, Bifurcations and Ontological Commitment," *Philosophical Studies* 173 (2016): 2437–59.
Tiefensee, C. "Relaxing about Moral Truths," *Ergo* 6 (2019): 869–90.
Tiefensee, C. "'Saving which Differences?' Creeping Minimalism and Disagreement", *Philosophical Studies* 176 (2019): 1905–21.
Tiefensee, C. "Metasemantics for the Relaxed," in *Oxford Studies in Metaethics*, ed. R. Shafer-Landau, Vol. 16, 108–33. Oxford: Oxford University Press, 2021.
Wedgwood, R. *The Nature of Normativity*. Oxford: Oxford University Press, 2007.

Chapter 11

Blackburn, S. "Disentangling Disentangling," in *Thick Concepts*, ed. S. Kirchin, 122–35. Oxford: Oxford University Press, 2013.
Carter, I. *A Measure of Freedom*. Oxford: Oxford University Press, 1999.
Carter, I. "Value-freeness and Value-neutrality in the Analysis of Political Concepts," *Oxford Studies in Political Philosophy* 1 (2015): 280–6.
Christensen, D. and Lackey, J., eds. *The Epistemology of Disagreement: New Essays*. Oxford: Oxford University Press, 2013.
Dworkin, R. *Law's Empire*. London: Fontana Press, 1986.
Dworkin, R. *Justice for Hedgehogs*. Cambridge, Mass.: Harvard University Press, 2011.
Fricker, M. *Epistemic Injustice: Power and the Ethics of Knowing*. Oxford: Oxford University Press, 2007.
Heal, J. "The Disinterested Search for Truth," *Proceedings of the Aristotelian Society* 88 (1987): 97–108.
Jones, K. "Second-Hand Moral Knowledge," *The Journal of Philosophy* 96, no. 2 (1999): 55–78.
Kramer, M. *Moral Realism as a Moral Doctrine*. Oxford: Wiley-Blackwell, 2009.
Kramer, M. "Conceptual Analysis and Distributive Justice," in *The Oxford Handbook of Distributive Justice*, ed. S. Olsaretti, 368–86. Oxford: Oxford University Press, 2018.
Long, R.T. Review of Putnam, H. *The Collapse of the Fact/Value Dichotomy and Other Essays*. Cambridge, MA: Harvard University Press, 2002. *Reason Papers* 28 (2006): 125–31.
Mackie, J. *Ethics: Inventing Right and Wrong*. London: Penguin, 1977.
McDowell, J. "Non-Cognitivism and Rule-Following," in *Mind, Value, and Reality*, ed. J. McDowell, 198–219. Cambridge, Mass.: Harvard University Press, 1998.

McGrath, S. "Moral Disagreement and Moral Expertise," in *Oxford Studies in Metaethics*, ed. Russ Shafer-Landau, Vol. 4, 87–108. Oxford: Oxford University Press, 2008.
Medina, J. *The Epistemology of Resistance: Gender and Racial Oppression, Epistemic Injustice and Resistant Imaginations*. New York: Oxford University Press, 2013.
Medina, J. "Epistemic Injustice and Epistemologies of Ignorance," in *The Routledge Companion to the Philosophy of Race*, eds. L. Alcoff, P. Taylor, and L. Anderson, 247–60. New York and Abingdon, Oxon: Routledge, 2017.
Pohlhaus, G. "Varieties of Epistemic Injustice," in *The Routledge Handbook of Epistemic Injustice*, eds. I..J. Kidd, G. Pohlhaus, and J. Medina, 13–26. New York: Routledge, 2017.
Radoilska, L. "Aiming at the Truth and Aiming at Success," *Philosophical Explorations* 20 (2017): 111–26.
Rawls, J. *A Theory of Justice*. Cambridge, Mass.: Harvard University Press, 1971.
Schwitzgebel, E. and Ellis, J. "Rationalization in Moral and Philosophical Thought," in *Moral Inferences*, eds. J.F. Bonnefon and B. Trémolière, 170–90. New York: Routledge, 2017.
Setiya, K. "Does Moral Theory Corrupt Youth?," *Philosophical Topics* 38, no. 1 (2010): 205–22.
Streumer, B. *Unbelievable Errors: An Error Theory about All Normative Judgements*. Oxford: Oxford University Press, 2017.
Williams, B. *Ethics and the Limits of Philosophy*. Cambridge, Mass.: Harvard University Press, 1985.

Chapter 12

Benn, Stanley I. *A Theory of Freedom*. Cambridge: Cambridge University Press, 1988.
Berlin, Isaiah. "Two Concepts of Liberty," in *Four Essays on Liberty*, 118–172. London: Oxford University Press, 1969.
Berofsky, Bernard. "Global Control and Freedom," *Philosophical Studies* 131, no. 2 (2006): 419–45.
Carter, Ian. *A Measure of Freedom*. Oxford: Oxford University Press, 1999.
Cooper, John M. "Stoic Autonomy," in *Autonomy*, eds. E.F. Paul, F. Miller Jr., and J. Paul, 1–29. Cambridge: Cambridge University Press, 2003.
Day, J.P. "Threats, Offers, Law, Opinion and Liberty," *American Philosophical Quarterly* 14, no. 4 (1977): 257–72.
Double, Richard. *The Non-Reality of Free Will*. Oxford: Oxford University Press, 1991.
Frankfurt, Harry G. "Freedom of Will and the Concept of the Person," *Journal of Philosophy* 68, no. 1 (1971): 5–20.
Frankfurt, Harry G. "Three Concepts of Free Action," in *The Importance of What We Care About*, 47–57. Cambridge: Cambridge University Press, 1988.
Garnett, Michael. "Freedom and Indoctrination," *Proceedings of the Aristotelian Society* CXV, no. 2 (2014): 93–108.
Garnett, Michael. "Agency and Inner Freedom," *Nous* 51, no. 1 (2017): 3–23.
Garnett, Michael. "Coercion: The Wrong and the Bad," *Ethics* 128, no. 3 (2018).
Gingerich, Jonathan. *Freedom's Spontaneity*. PhD thesis (UCLA) University of California, 2018.
Haji, Ishtivaque and Cuypers, Stefaan E. *Moral Responsibility, Authenticity, and Education*. New York: Routledge, 2008.
Hayek, Friedrich A. *The Constitution of Liberty*, ed. Ronald Hamowy. Chicago: University of Chicago Press, 2011.
Hobbes, Thomas. *Leviathan*, ed. Richard Tuck. Cambridge: Cambridge University Press, 1991.
Kisner, Michael J. *Spinoza on Human Freedom: Reason, Autonomy and the Good Life*. Cambridge: Cambridge University Press, 2011.

Kramer, Matthew K. *The Quality of Freedom*. Oxford: Oxford University Press, 2003.
Kristjánsson, Kristjan. *Social Freedom: The Responsibility View*. Cambridge: Cambridge University Press, 1996.
Lind, John. *Three Letters to Dr Price*. London: T. Payne, 1776.
Mele, Alfred R. *Autonomous Agents: From Self-Control to Autonomy*. Oxford: Oxford University Press, 1995.
Miller, David. "Constraints on Freedom," *Ethics* 94, no. 1 (1983): 66–86.
Oppenheim, Felix. *Dimensions of Freedom: An Analysis*. New York: St. Martin's Press, 1961.
Pettit, Philip. *Republicanism: A Theory of Freedom and Government*. Oxford: Clarendon Press, 1997.
Rosen, Frederick. *Classical Utilitarianism from Hume to Mill*. London: Routledge, 2003.
Skinner, Quentin. "The Third Concept of Liberty," *Proceedings of the British Academy* 117 (2002).
Steiner, Hillel. "Individual Liberty," in *Proceedings of the Aristotelian Society*, vol. 75: 33–50. Aristotelian Society, Wiley, 1974.
Swanton, Christine. "Robert Stevens on Offers," *Australasian Journal of Philosophy* 67, no. 4 (1989): 472–75.
Taylor, Charles. "What's Wrong with Negative Liberty," in *The Idea of Freedom*, ed. A. Ryan, 175–93 (Oxford: Oxford University Press, 1979).
Watson, Gary. "Free Agency," *Journal of Philosophy* 72 (1975): 205–20.
Wertheimer, Alan and Miller, Franklin G. "Payment for Research Participation: A Coercive Offer?," *Journal of Medical Ethics* 34 (2008): 389–92.
Wood, Allen W. *Karl Marx*. Henley-on-Thames: Routledge, 1981.
Yaffe, Gideon. "Indoctrination, Coercion and Freedom of Will," *Philosophy and Phenomenological Research* 67, no. 2 (2003): 335–56.
Zimmerman, David. "Coercive Wage Offers," *Philosophy and Public Affairs* 10, no. 2 (1981): 121–45.

Chapter 13

Austin, J.L. "A Plea for Excuses," in J.L. Austin, *Philosophical Papers*, 3rd ed, 175–204. Oxford: Clarendon Press, 1979.
Berlin, Isaiah. *Two Concepts of Liberty*. Oxford: Oxford University Press, 1958.
Berlin, Isaiah. *Four Essays on Liberty*. Oxford: Oxford University Press, 1969.
Carter, Ian. *A Measure of Freedom*. Oxford: Oxford University Press, 1999.
Carter, Ian. "Social Power and Negative Freedom," in *Power, Voting and Voting Power: 30 Years After*, eds. M.J. Holler and H. Nurmi, 27–62. Berlin: Springer, 2013.
Carter, Ian. "Equality of Opportunity, Responsibility, and Personal Identity," *Ethical Theory and Moral Practice* 21 (2018): 825–39.
Carter, Ian and Kramer, Matthew H. "How Changes in One's Preferences can Affect One's Freedom (and How They Cannot). A Reply to Dowding and van Hees," *Economics and Philosophy* 24 no. 1 (2008): 81–96.
Cohen, G.A. *Self-Ownership, Freedom and Equality*. Cambridge: Cambridge University Press, 1995.
Day, J.P. *Liberty and Justice*. London: Croom Helm, 1987.
Feinberg, Joel. *Social Philosophy*. Englewood Cliffs: Prentice Hall, 1978.
Kramer, Matthew H. *The Quality of Freedom*. Oxford: Oxford University Press, 2003.
Kristjánsson, Kristján. *Social Freedom. The Responsibility View*. Cambridge: Cambridge University Press, 1996.

Lancaster, Kevin J. "A New Approach to Consumer Theory," *Journal of Political Economy* 74 (1966): 132–57.
Miller, David. "Constraints on Freedom," *Ethics* 94 (1983): 66–75.
Oppenheim, Felix E. *Dimensions of Freedom. An Analysis*. New York: St. Martin's Press, 1961.
Oppenheim, Felix E. *Political Concepts. A Reconstruction*. Oxford: Blackwell, 1981.
Pettit, Philip. "Keeping Republican Freedom Simple: On a Difference with Quentin Skinner," *Political Theory* 30 (2002): 339–56.
Sen, Amartya. *Inequality Reexamined*. Oxford: Oxford University Press, 1992.
Steiner, Hillel. "Individual Liberty," *Proceedings of the Aristotelian Society* 75 (1974–75): 33–50.
Steiner, Hillel. "How Free: Computing Personal Liberty," in *Of Liberty*, ed. A. Phillips Griffiths. London: Cambridge University Press, 1983: 73–89.
Steiner, Hillel. *An Essay on Rights*. Oxford: Blackwell, 1994.
Steiner, Hillel. "Freedom and Bivalence," in *Freedom, Power and Political Morality. Essays for Felix Oppenheim*, eds. I. Carter and M. Ricciardi. Basingstoke: Palgrave, 2001: 57–68.
Taylor, Charles. "What's Wrong with Negative Liberty," in *The Idea of Freedom*, ed. Alan Ryan. Oxford: Oxford University Press, 1979: 175–93.
Van Parijs, Philippe. *Real Freedom for All. What, If Anything, Can Justify Capitalism?* Oxford: Oxford University Press, 1995.

Chapter 14

Arneson, Richard. "Liberal Neutrality on the Good: An Autopsy," in *Perfectionism and Neutrality: Essays in Liberal Theory*, eds. Steven Wall and George Klosko, 191–218. Oxford: Rowan and Littlefield, 2003.
Berlin, Isaiah. "The Originality of Machiavelli," in *Against the Current*. Princeton University Press, 2001, 25–79.
Dworkin, Ronald. "What Rights Do We Have?," in Dworkin, *Taking Rights Seriously*, 266–78. Cambridge: Harvard University Press, 1977.
Dworkin, Ronald. *Law's Empire*. Cambridge: Harvard University Press, 1986.
Janus v. AFSCME. 585 U.S. ___. 2018.
Kramer, Matthew H. "Rights without Trimmings," in *A Debate over Rights*, ed. Matthew H. Kramer, N.E. Simmonds, and Hillel Steiner, 7–111. Oxford: Oxford University Press, 1998.
Kramer, Matthew H. *The Quality of Freedom*. Oxford: Oxford University Press, 2003.
Kramer, Matthew H. *Liberalism with Excellence*. Oxford: Oxford University Press, 2017.
Kymlicka, Will. "Liberal Individualism and Liberal Neutrality," *Ethics* 99 (1989): 883–905.
Masterpiece Cakeshop v. Colorado Civil Rights Commission. 584 U.S. ___. 2018.
Quong, Jonathan. *Liberalism without Perfection*. Oxford: Oxford University Press, 2011.
Rawls, John. "The Priority of the Right and Ideas of the Good," in Rawls, *Collected Papers*, 449–72. Cambridge, Mass.: Harvard University Press, 1999.
Rawls, John. "The Idea of Public Reason Revisited," in Rawls, *Collected Papers*, 573–615. Cambridge, Mass.: Harvard University Press, 1999.
Rawls, John. *A Theory of Justice*, rev. ed. Cambridge, Mass.: Harvard University Press, 1971, 1999.
Rawls, John. *Justice as Fairness: A Restatement*. Cambridge, Mass.: Harvard University Press, 2001.
Rawls, John. *Political Liberalism*, exp. ed. New York: Columbia University Press, 2005.
Rawls, John. "The Idea of Public Reason," in Rawls, *Political Liberalism*, 212–54. New York: Columbia University Press, exp. ed., 2005.
Raz, Joseph. *The Morality of Freedom*. Oxford: Oxford University Press, 1986.
Reiff, Mark R. "The Attack on Liberalism," in *Law and Philosophy*, eds. Michael Freeman and Ross Harrison. Oxford: Oxford University Press, 2007.

Reiff, Mark R. "Proportionality, Winner-Take-All, and Distributive Justice," *Politics, Philosophy, and Economics* 8 (2009): 5–42.

Reiff, Mark R. "Trump and the End of Liberalism," *The Critique* (January 15) 2017. (http://www.thecritique.com/articles/trumpandliberalism/).

Reiff, Mark R. "A Philosopher Argues Why No One Has the Right to Refuse Services to LGBT People," *The Conversation* (July 25) 2017.

Reiff, Mark R. *In the Name of Liberty*. Cambridge: Cambridge University Press, 2020.

Reiff, Mark R. *The Unbearable Resilience of Illiberalism*. Forthcoming.

Sher, George. *Beyond Neutrality: Perfectionism and Politics*. Cambridge: Cambridge University Press, 1997.

Simmonds, Nigel E. *Central Issues in Jurisprudence*. 4th ed. London: Sweet & Maxwell, 2013.

Stolberg, Sheryl Gay. "The Faces of Intermarriage, 50 Years After Loving v. Virginia," *The New York Times* (July 6) 2017.

Swenson, Kyle. "Company's Ban Against Gay Weddings Is Akin to 'White Applicants Only' Sign, Judge Says," *The Washington Post* (September 22) 2017.

Chapter 15

Billingham, P. and Taylor, A. "Liberal Perfectionism, Moral Integrity, and Self-Respect," *The American Journal of Jurisprudence* 63 (2018): 63–79.

Boonin, D. *The Non-Identity Problem and the Ethics of Future People*. Oxford: Oxford University Press, 2014.

Bradley, B. "Doing Away with Harm," *Philosophy and Phenomenological Research* 85 (2012): 390–412.

Brinkmann, M. "Political Anti-Intentionalism," *Res Publica* 24 (2018): 159–79.

Caney, S. "Consequentialist Defences of Liberal Neutrality," *The Philosophical Quarterly* 41 (1991): 457–77.

Chan, J. "Legitimacy, Unanimity, and Perfectionism," *Philosophy & Public Affairs* 29 (2000): 5–42.

Carlson, E. "More Problems for the Counterfactual Comparative Account of Harm and Benefit," *Ethical Theory and Moral Practice* 22 (2019): 795–807.

Dworkin, R. "Can a Liberal State Support Art?," in Dworkin, *A Matter of Principle*, 221–33. Oxford: Clarendon Press, 1985.

Dworkin, R. "Foundations of Liberal Equality," in *Equal Freedom: Selected Tanner Lectures on Human Values*, ed. S. Darwall, 190–306. Ann Arbor: University of Michigan Press, 1995.

Enoch, D. "Intending, Foreseeing and the State," *Legal Theory* 13 (2007): 69–99.

Feinberg, J. *Harm to Others: The Moral Limits of the Criminal Law, Vol. 1*. Oxford: Oxford University Press, 1984.

Feinberg, J. *Harmless Wrongdoing: The Moral Limits of the Criminal Law, Vol. 4*. Oxford: Oxford University Press, 1990.

Gardner, J. and Shute, S. "The Wrongness of Rape," in *Oxford Essays in Jurisprudence: Fourth Series*, ed. J. Horder, 193–218. Oxford: Oxford University Press, 2000.

Gaus, G. "On the Difficult Virtue of Minding One's Own Business: Towards the Political Rehabilitation of Ebenezer Scrooge," *The Philosopher* 5 (1997): 24–8.

Holtug, N. "The Harm Principle," *Ethical Theory and Moral Practice* 5 (2002): 357–89.

Johansson, J. and Risberg, O. "The Preemption Problem," *Philosophical Studies* 176 (2019): 351–65.

Johansson, J. and Risberg, O. "Harming and Failing to Benefit: A Reply to Purves," *Philosophical Studies* 177 (2020): 1539–48.

King Jr. Martin Luther. "Remaining Awake Through a Great Revolution," in *A Testament of Hope: The Essential Writings and Speeches of Martin Luther King, Jr.*, ed. J. Washington, 268–78. New York: Harper Collins, 1986.
Kramer, M. *Torture and Moral Integrity: A Philosophical Enquiry*. Oxford: Oxford University Press, 2014.
Kramer, M. "Legal Responses to Consensual Sexuality between Adults: Through and Beyond the Harm Principle," in *Hart on Responsibility*, ed. C. Pulman, 109–28. Basingstoke: Palgrave Macmillan, 2014.
Kramer, M. "One Cheer for Autonomy-centered Perfectionism: An Arm's-length Defense of Joseph Raz's Perfectionism Against an Allegation of Internal Inconsistency," *Argumenta* 1 (2015): 79–95.
Kramer, M. *Liberalism with Excellence*. Oxford: Oxford University Press, 2017.
Kramer, M. "On Political Morality and the Conditions for Warranted Self-Respect," *Journal of Ethics* 21 (2017): 335–49.
Larmore, C. *Patterns of Moral Complexity*. Cambridge: Cambridge University Press, 1987.
Mill, J.S. *On Liberty*. London: Penguin, 1985.
Pallikkathayil, J. "Neither Perfectionism nor Political Liberalism," *Philosophy & Public Affairs* 44 (2016): 171–96.
Parfit, D. *Reasons and Persons*. Oxford: Oxford University Press, 1984.
Patten, A. "Liberal Neutrality: A Reinterpretation and Defense," *The Journal of Political Philosophy* 20 (2012): 249–72.
Purves, D. "Harming as Making Worse Off," *Philosophical Studies* 176 (2019): 2629–56.
Quong, J. *Liberalism Without Perfection*. Oxford: Oxford University Press, 2011.
Rawls, J. *Political Liberalism*. New York: Columbia University Press, 1996.
Raz, J. *The Morality of Freedom*. Oxford: Oxford University Press, 1986.
Raz, J. "Liberalism, Skepticism, and Democracy," *Iowa Law Review* 74 (1989): 761–86.
Ripstein, A. "Beyond the Harm Principle," *Philosophy & Public Affairs* 24 (2006): 215–45.
Scanlon, T. *Moral Dimensions: Permissibility, Meaning, Blame*. Cambridge, Mass.: Harvard University Press, 2008.
Schouten, G. *Liberalism, Neutrality, and the Gendered Division of Labor*. Oxford: Oxford University Press, 2019.
Sher, G. *Beyond Neutrality: Perfectionism and Politics*. Cambridge: Cambridge University Press, 1997.
Stephen, J.F. *Liberty, Equality, and Fraternity*. Cambridge: Cambridge University Press, 1967.
Stewart, H. "Harms, Wrongs, and Set-Backs in Feinberg's *Moral Limits of the Criminal Law*," *Buffalo Criminal Law Review* 5 (2001): 47–67.
Tadros, V. *Wrongs and Crimes*. Oxford: Oxford University Press, 2016.
Tahzib, C. "Perfectionism: Political not Metaphysical," *Philosophy & Public Affairs* 47 (2019): 144–78.
Tahzib, C. "Perfectionist Duties," in *Oxford Studies in Political Philosophy, Vol. 7*, eds. D. Sobel, P. Vallentyne, and S. Wall, 124–60. Oxford: Oxford University Press, 2021.
Tahzib, C. *A Perfectionist Theory of Justice*. Oxford: Oxford University Press, forthcoming.
Thomson, J.J. "Feinberg on Harm, Offense, and the Criminal Law: A Review Essay," *Philosophy & Public Affairs* 15 (1986): 381–95.
Thomson, J.J. "Self-Defense," *Philosophy & Public Affairs* 20 (1991): 283–310.
Waldron, J. *Law and Disagreement*. Oxford: Oxford University Press, 1999.
Wall, S. *Liberalism, Perfectionism and Restraint*. Cambridge: Cambridge University Press, 1998.
Wall, S. "Enforcing Morality." *Criminal Law and Philosophy* 7 (2013): 455–71.
Wall, S. "Moral Environmentalism," in Paternalism: Theory and Practice, edited by C. Coons and M. Weber, 93–114. Cambridge: Cambridge University Press, 2013.
Woodward, J. "The Non-Identity Problem." *Ethics* 96 (1986): 804–31.

Chapter 16

Bassiouni, M.C. and Wise, E.M. *Aut Dedere Aut Judicare: The Duty to Extradite or Prosecute in International Law*. Leiden: Nijhoff, 1995.

Danaher, J. "Kramer's Purgative Rationale for Capital Punishment: A Critique," *Criminal Law & Philosophy* 9 (2015): 225–44.

Duff, R.A. *Trials and Punishments*. Cambridge: Cambridge University Press, 1986.

Duff, R.A. *Criminal Attempts*. Oxford: Oxford University Press, 1996.

Duff, R.A. *Punishment, Communication, and Community*. Oxford: Oxford University Press, 2001.

Duff, R.A. "Can We Punish the Perpetrators of Atrocities?," in *The Religious in Responses to Mass Atrocities*, eds. T. Brudholm and T. Cushman, 79–104. Cambridge: Cambridge University Press, 2009.

Duff, R.A. "Psychopathy and Answerability," in *Responsibility and Psychopathy*, eds. L. Malatesti and J. McMillan, 198–212. Oxford: Oxford University Press, 2010.

Duff, R.A. *The Realm of Criminal Law*. Oxford: Oxford University Press, 2018.

Gaita, R. *Good and Evil: An Absolute Conception*. 2nd ed. London: Routledge, 2004.

Hoskins Z. and Duff, R.A. "Legal Punishment," in the *Stanford Encyclopedia of Philosophy (Winter 2021 edition)*, ed. E. Zalta. https://plato.stanford.edu/archives/win2021/entries/legal-punishment/.

Kramer, M. *The Ethics of Capital Punishment: A Philosophical Investigation of Evil and its Consequences*. Oxford: Oxford University Press, 2011.

Kramer, M. "The Purgative Rationale for the Death Penalty: Replies to Steiker and Danaher," *Criminal Law and Philosophy 9* (2015): 379–94.

Moore, M.S. "Four Reflections on Law and Morality," *William & Mary Law Review* 48 (2007) : 1523–69.

Murphy, J.G. "Marxism and Retribution," *Philosophy & Public Affairs* 2 (1973): 217–43.

Murphy, J.G. *Getting Even: Forgiveness and its Limits*. Oxford: Oxford University Press, 2003.

Nagel, T. "War and Massacre," *Philosophy and Public Affairs* 1 (1972): 123–44.

R (on the application of Wells) v. Parole Board for England and Wales [2010] 1 AC 553.

Renzo, M. "Responsibility and Answerability in the Criminal Law," in *The Constitution of the Criminal Law*, ed. R.A. Duff et al., 209–36. Oxford: Oxford University Press, 2013.

Reydams, L. *Universal Jurisdiction: International and Municipal Legal Perspectives*. Oxford: Oxford University Press, 2004.

Ryngaert, C. *Jurisdiction in International Law*, 2nd ed. Oxford: Oxford University Press, 2015.

Winch, P. "Eine Einstellung zur Seele," *Proceedings of the Aristotelian Society* 81, no. 1 (1980).

Chapter 17

Kramer, M.H. *Freedom of Expression as Self-Restraint*. Oxford: Oxford University Press, 2021.

Meiklejohn, A. "The First Amendment as an Absolute," *The Supreme Court Review*, 1961 *(1961)*: 245–66.

Post, R. *Democracy, Expertise and Academic Freedom*. New Haven: Yale University Press, 2012.

Rousseau, J.-J., *Du contrat social*. Amsterdam: Michel Rey, 1762.

Scanlon, T.M. "A Framework for Thinking About Free Speech." Unpublished essay, Harvard University, 2018.

Scanlon, T.M. "A Theory of Freedom of Expression," *Philosophy & Public Affairs 1* (1972): 204–26.

Chapter 18

Aristotle. *Ethics*. J.A.K. Thomson and Hugh Tredennick, trs. Harmondsworth: Penguin Books, 1976.

Austin, J.L. "A Plea for Excuses," *Proceedings of the Aristotelian Society, New Series* 57 (1956): 1–30.

Bacharach, Michael. *Beyond Individual Choice*, eds. Natalie Gold and Robert Sugden. Princeton, NJ: Princeton University Press, 2006.

Billingham, Paul and Taylor, Anthony. "Liberal Perfectionism, Moral Integrity, and Self-Respect," *American Journal of Jurisprudence* 63 (2018): 63–79.

Bix, Brian. "Objectivity, Conventions, and the Possibility of Universal Error," in *Without Trimmings: The Legal, Political, and Moral Philosophy of Matthew Kramer*, eds. Visa Kurki and Mark McBride, 113–24. Oxford: Oxford University Press, 2022.

Bowen, Joseph. "The Interest Theory of Rights at the Margins: Posthumous Rights," in *Without Trimmings: The Legal, Political, and Moral Philosophy of Matthew Kramer*, eds. Visa Kurki and Mark McBride, 51–71. Oxford: Oxford University Press, 2022.

Carter, Ian. *A Measure of Freedom*. Oxford: Oxford University Press, 1999.

Carter, Ian and Steiner, Hillel. "Freedom without Trimmings: The Perils of Trivalence," in Visa Kurki and Mark McBride (eds), *Without Trimmings: The Legal, Political, and Moral Philosophy of Matthew Kramer*, eds. Visa Kurki and Mark McBride, 239–67. Oxford: Oxford University Press, 2022.

Chiassoni, Pierluigi. "Kramer's Theory of Legal Positivism: Merits and Demerits," in *Without Trimmings: The Legal, Political, and Moral Philosophy of Matthew Kramer*, eds. Visa Kurki and Mark McBride, 149–66. Oxford: Oxford University Press, 2022.

Cohen, G.A. *History, Labour, Freedom*. Oxford: Oxford University Press, 1988.

Cruft, Rowan. "Rights, Positivism, and the Vice of Self-Puffery: Why Kramer's Interest Theory is Nearly Right," in *Without Trimmings: The Legal, Political, and Moral Philosophy of Matthew Kramer*, eds. Visa Kurki and Mark McBride, 37–49. Oxford: Oxford University Press, 2022.

Donohue, Laura. "Correlation and Constitutional Rights," in *Without Trimmings: The Legal, Political, and Moral Philosophy of Matthew Kramer*, eds. Visa Kurki and Mark McBride, 3–36. Oxford: Oxford University Press, 2022.

Dreier, James. "Meta-Ethics and the Problem of Creeping Minimalism," *Philosophical Perspectives* 18 (2004): 23–44.

Duff, R.A. *Criminal Attempts*. Oxford: Oxford University Press, 1996.

Duff, R.A. "Purgative Punishment and the Importance of Perspective," in *Without Trimmings: The Legal, Political, and Moral Philosophy of Matthew Kramer*, eds. Visa Kurki and Mark McBride, 321–42. Oxford: Oxford University Press, 2022.

Dworkin, Ronald. *Justice in Robes*. Cambridge, MA: Harvard University Press, 2006.

Enoch, David. *Taking Morality Seriously*. Oxford: Oxford University Press, 2011.

Finlay, Steve and Schroeder, Mark. "Reasons for Action: Internal versus External," in *Stanford Encyclopedia of Philosophy (Fall 2017 Edition)*, ed. Edward Zalta. http://plato.stanford.edu/archives/fall2017/entries/reasons-internal-external/ 2018. (access date: July 4, 2018).

Finnis, John. *Natural Law and Natural Rights*. Oxford: Oxford University Press, 1980.

Garnett, Michael. "Prevention, Coercion, and Two Concepts of Negative Liberty," in *Without Trimmings: The Legal, Political, and Moral Philosophy of Matthew Kramer*, eds. Visa Kurki and Mark McBride, 223–37. Oxford: Oxford University Press, 2022.

Gilbert, Margaret. *On Social Facts*. London: Routledge, 1989.

Gilbert, Margaret. *Sociality and Responsibility*. Lanham, MD: Rowman & Littlefield, 2000.

Gilbert, Margaret. *Joint Commitment*. Oxford: Oxford University Press, 2014.

Hayek, Friedrich. *The Constitution of Liberty*. Chicago, IL: University of Chicago Press, 2011.
Kay, Richard. "Retroactivity and Prospectivity of Judgments in American Law," *American Journal of Comparative Law Supplement* 62 (2014): 37–67.
Kramer, Matthew. "Rights without Trimmings," in Matthew Kramer, N.E. Simmonds, and Hillel Steiner, *A Debate over Rights*, 7–111. Oxford: Oxford University Press, 1998.
Kramer, Matthew. *In Defense of Legal Positivism*. Oxford: Oxford University Press, 1999.
Kramer, Matthew. "Getting Rights Right," in *Rights, Wrongs, and Responsibilities*, ed. Matthew Kramer, 28–95. Basingstoke: Palgrave Macmillan, 2001.
Kramer, Matthew. *The Quality of Freedom*. Oxford: Oxford University Press, 2003.
Kramer, Matthew. *Where Law and Morality Meet*. Oxford: Oxford University Press, 2004.
Kramer, Matthew. *Objectivity and the Rule of Law*. Cambridge: Cambridge University Press, 2007.
Kramer, Matthew. *Moral Realism as a Moral Doctrine*. Oxford: Wiley-Blackwell, 2009.
Kramer, Matthew. "Refining the Interest Theory of Rights," *American Journal of Jurisprudence* 55 (2010): 31–9.
Kramer, Matthew. *The Ethics of Capital Punishment*. Oxford: Oxford University Press, 2001a.
Kramer, Matthew. "For the Record: A Final Reply to N.E. Simmonds," *American Journal of Jurisprudence* 56 (2011b): 115–33.
Kramer, Matthew. "Some Doubts about Alternatives to the Interest Theory of Rights," *Ethics* 123 (2013): 245–63.
Kramer, Matthew. *Torture and Moral Integrity*. Oxford: Oxford University Press, 2014.
Kramer, Matthew. "Why Would an Atheist Write a Commentary on the Bible?," *The Philosophers' Magazine* 70, no. 3 (2015): 55–59.
Kramer, Matthew. "Moral Conflicts, the 'Ought Implies Can' Principle, and Moral Demandingness," in *The Limits of Moral Obligation*, eds. Marcel van Ackeren and Michael Kühler, 163–84. London: Routledge, 2016.
Kramer, Matthew. "In Defense of the Interest Theory of Right-Holding: Rejoinders to Leif Wenar on Rights," in *New Essays on the Nature of Rights*, ed. Mark McBride, 49–83. Oxford: Hart Publishing, 2017a.
Kramer, Matthew. *Liberalism with Excellence*. Oxford: Oxford University Press, 2017b.
Kramer, Matthew. "On Political Morality and the Conditions for Warranted Self-Respect," *Journal of Ethics* 21 (2017c): 335–49.
Kramer, Matthew. "There's Nothing Quasi about Quasi-Realism: Moral Realism as a Moral Doctrine," *Journal of Ethics* 21 (2017d): 185–212.
Kramer, Matthew. *H.L.A. Hart: The Nature of Law*. Cambridge: Polity Press, 2018.
Kramer, Matthew. "Conceptual Analysis and Distributive Justice," in *Oxford Handbook of Distributive Justice*, ed. Serena Olsaretti, 367–85. Oxford: Oxford University Press, 2019a.
Kramer, Matthew. "Shakespeare, Moral Judgments, and Moral Realism," in *Routledge Companion to Shakespeare and Philosophy*, eds. Craig Bourne and Emily Bourne, 234–45. London: Routledge, 2019b.
Kramer, Matthew. "The Demandingness of Deontological Duties: Is the Absolute Impermissibility of Placatory Torture Irrational?," *Moral Philosophy and Politics* 6 (2019c): 9–40.
Kramer, Matthew. *Freedom of Expression as Self-Restraint*. Oxford: Oxford University Press, 2021.
Kramer, Matthew. "Incorporationism, Inclusivism, and Indeterminacy," in *Law, Morality, and Judicial Reasoning: Essays on W.J. Waluchow's Jurisprudence and Constitutional Theory*, eds. Thomas Bustamante, Saulo De Matos, and André Coelho, 2022a.
Kramer, Matthew. "On the Properties of Quietism and Robustness," in *Oxford Handbook of Moral Realism*, eds. Paul Bloomfield and David Copp. Oxford: Oxford University Press, 2022b.

Kramer, Matthew and Steiner, Hillel. "Theories of Rights: Is There a Third Way?," *Oxford Journal of Legal Studies* 27 (2007) 281–310.
Kurki, Visa. "Are Legal Positivism and the Interest Theory of Rights Compatible?," in *Without Trimmings: The Legal, Political, and Moral Philosophy of Matthew Kramer*, eds. Visa Kurki and Mark McBride, 73–91. Oxford: Oxford University Press, 2022.
Kutz, Christopher. "Kramer's Razor and the Freedom of Expression," in *Without Trimmings: The Legal, Political, and Moral Philosophy of Matthew Kramer*, eds. Visa Kurki and Mark McBride, 343–59. Oxford: Oxford University Press, 2022.
Lewis, Paul. "Was Peron a Fascist? An Inquiry into the Nature of Fascism," *Journal of Politics* 42 (1980): 242–56.
List, Christian and Pettit, Philip. *Group Agency*. Oxford: Oxford University Press, 2011.
McBride, Mark. "Tracking the Resilience of Hybridity," in *Without Trimmings: The Legal, Political, and Moral Philosophy of Matthew Kramer*, eds. Visa Kurki and Mark McBride, 93–110. Oxford: Oxford University Press, 2022.
Meiklejohn, Alexander. "The First Amendment is an Absolute," 1961 *Supreme Court Review* 245–66.
Olsaretti, Serena. *Liberty, Desert, and the Market*. Cambridge: Cambridge University Press, 2004.
Parfit, Derek. *Reasons and Persons*. Oxford: Oxford University Press, 1984.
Payne, Stanley. *Fascism*. Madison, WI: University of Wisconsin Press, 1980.
Postema, Gerald. "From Law's Existence to Law's Rule: Reflections on Kramer's Understanding of the Rule of Law," in *Without Trimmings: The Legal, Political, and Moral Philosophy of Matthew Kramer*, eds. Visa Kurki and Mark McBride, 167–85. Oxford: Oxford University Press, 2022.
Radoilska, Lubomira. "Distinguishing Value-Neutrality from Value-Independence: Toward a New Disentangling Strategy for Moral Epistemology," in *Without Trimmings: The Legal, Political, and Moral Philosophy of Matthew Kramer*, eds. Visa Kurki and Mark McBride, 205–19. Oxford: Oxford University Press, 2022.
Raz, Joseph. *The Morality of Freedom*. Oxford: Oxford University Press, 1986.
Raz, Joseph. *Practical Reason and Norms*. 3rd ed. Oxford: Oxford University Press, 1999.
Reiff, Mark. "Neutrality and Excellence," in *Without Trimmings: The Legal, Political, and Moral Philosophy of Matthew Kramer*, eds. Visa Kurki and Mark McBride, 271–96. Oxford: Oxford University Press, 2022.
Rosati, Connie. "Some Puzzles About the Objectivity of Law," *Law and Philosophy* 23 (2004): 273–323.
Rubenfeld, Jed. "The First Amendment's Purpose," *Stanford Law Review* 53 (2001) 767–832.
Rubenfeld, Jed. "A Reply to Posner." *Stanford Law Review* 54 (2002): 753–67.
Scanlon, Thomas. *Being Realistic about Reasons*. Oxford: Oxford University Press, 2014.
Seton-Watson, Hugh. "Fascism, Right and Left," *Journal of Contemporary History* 1 (1966) 183–97.
Shakespeare, William. *The Riverside Shakespeare*. Ed. G. Blakemore Evans. Boston, MA: Houghton Mifflin Company, 1974.
Simmonds, Nigel. *Central Issues in Jurisprudence*. 3rd ed. London: Sweet & Maxwell, 2008.
Tahzib, Collis. "Does Edificatory Perfectionism Express a Quidnunc Mentality?," in *Without Trimmings: The Legal, Political, and Moral Philosophy of Matthew Kramer*, eds. Visa Kurki and Mark McBride, 297–317. Oxford: Oxford University Press, 2021.
Tiefensee, Christine. "Metasemantics, Moral Realism and Moral Doctrines," in *Without Trimmings: The Legal, Political, and Moral Philosophy of Matthew Kramer*, eds. Visa Kurki and Mark McBride, 189–204. Oxford: Oxford University Press, 2022.
Traynor, Roger. "Quo Vadis, Prospective Overruling: A Question of Judicial Responsibility," *Hastings Law Journal* 28 (1977): 533–68.

Tuomela, Raimo. *The Importance of Us*. Stanford, CA: Stanford University Press, 1995.

Tuomela, Raimo. *The Philosophy of Social Practices*. Cambridge: Cambridge University Press, 2002.

Tuomela, Raimo. *The Philosophy of Sociality*. Oxford: Oxford University Press, 2007.

Tuomela, Raimo. *Social Ontology: Collective Intentionality and Group Agents*. Oxford: Oxford University Press, 2013.

Waluchow, W.J. "Authority and the Practical Difference Thesis: A Defense of Inclusive Legal Positivism," *Legal Theory* 6 (2000): 45–81.

Waluchow, W.J. "Matthew Kramer and Inclusive Legal Positivism: Dancing on the Head of a Pin," in *Without Trimmings: The Legal, Political, and Moral Philosophy of Matthew Kramer*, eds. Visa Kurki and Mark McBride, 125–48. Oxford: Oxford University Press, 2022.

Wechsler, Herbert, Jones, William, and Korn, Harold. "The Treatment of Inchoate Crimes in the Model Penal Code of the American Law Institute: Attempt, Solicitation, and Conspiracy (Part One)," *Columbia Law Review* 61 (1961): 571–628.

Index

For the benefit of digital users, indexed terms that span two pages (e.g., 52–53) may, on occasion, appear on only one of those pages.